REVIEW OF

Child Development Research

VOLUME SEVEN

Advisory Board

REVIEW OF
Child Development
Research

Volume Seven

The Family

Editor
ROSS D. PARKE

Associate Editors
ROBERT N. EMDE
HARRIETTE P. McADOO
GENE P. SACKETT

Prepared under the auspices of the
Society for Research in Child Development

THE UNIVERSITY OF CHICAGO PRESS
Chicago and London

Volume 1 (1964) and Volume 2 (1966) were published by
Russell Sage Foundation, New York
Volume 3 (1973), Volume 4 (1975), Volume 5 (1975), and Volume 6 (1982)
were published by The University of Chicago Press, Chicago

The University of Chicago Press, Chicago 60637
The University of Chicago Press, Ltd., London

International Standard Book Number: 0-226-64666-1
Library of Congress Catalog Card Number: 64-20472

Contents

Preface

AT A TIME when the family as an institution is undergoing a variety of rapid changes, it is particularly appropriate that the Society for Research in Child Development devote a volume to studies of the family. This volume underscores the growing recognition among child development researchers that children's development can be fully explored only in the context of serious study of the family unit.

The study of the family has had a long history in the social sciences. For many years the family as an institution was studied mainly by members of a few disciplines, notably sociology and anthropology. These researchers were concerned more with the description and analysis of the structure and function of families and only minimally with the impact of families on children's development. Psychologists have traditionally studied the effect of child-rearing practices on children, but investigation typically was restricted to the mother-child dyad.

Interest in families has burgeoned in recent years. Current empirical and theoretical approaches to families are characteristically interdisciplinary, which reflects the assumption that families can best be understood by combining the insights of a variety of disciplinary perspectives. Both psychology and sociology have modified their approaches to the study of the family, bringing investigators from the two disciplines closer to one another. Psychology has moved beyond the mother-child relationship to a recognition of other actors such as fathers, siblings, and extended family members, and to the multiple set of relationships which exist among family members. Sociologists have retained their commitment to the study of the family unit but at the same time increased their concern with the effect of families on children's development.

In addition to psychology's increased commitment to studies of the family and sociology's growing awareness of children, there have been other trends. Most noteworthy is the currently popular biological-ethological approach to the family. Implicit in this approach is the recognition that the study of families can often be informed by evolutionary considerations and recent advances in sociobiological theorizing. Historians over the last decade have rediscovered the family as well and have made significant progess in demonstrating the value of historical analyses for current theorizing about family functioning and organization.

vii

One aim of *SRCD 7: The Family* is to highlight these multidisciplinary approaches to the study of the family, reflecting the interdisciplinary nature of the SRCD. Thus the volume includes a sampling of recent theoretical perspectives on the family—sociological, historical, and ethological theoretical viewpoints as well as the psychological.

A variety of other conceptual and methodological trends are represented in this volume. First, a social systems perspective recognizes the interdependence of family members and emphasizes that change in one member or relationship within the family system will have an effect on the other members. Second, in an ecological viewpoint, the embeddedness of families in a variety of informal and formal social networks is given explicit recognition. Third, families are viewed from a developmental perspective. Researchers are aware of the necessity of taking into account the child's developmental status in terms of understanding both the child's role in the family and the family's impact on the child. Nor is the consideration of development restricted to children. Under the influence of a life-span developmental perspective, the changes which ensue in adults as individuals and as family members are also of interest. Finally, researchers are considering the family as a unit, with its own unique traditions and history and its own developmental course, which is not captured by analysis of either child or adult developmental trajectories alone. Of particular interest is the interplay among these various developmental courses.

Another aspect of this developmental focus is the recognition that the family as an institution shifts over time. Monitoring and describing these changes in family structure, in fact, has been a focus of demographers for many decades. Only recently has the influence of these family structural changes on children become a concern. Moreover, families come in diverse forms, and the multiplicity of family forms both within and across cultures is being recognized.

Families do not exist in a historical and cultural vacuum. Not only does the concept of a family change, but individual families encounter a variety of normative and nonnormative life events which require adjustment and reorganization on the part of family members. The way in which families cope with these transitions can often yield important insights into family functioning.

Organization of the Volume

The volume can be roughly divided into three sets of chapters. The first set represents a sampling of current approaches to the study of the family, including ethological, comparative, psychological, sociological, and historical viewpoints. In the second section of the volume the families' relationships with outside institutions such as the school, the workplace, and the community are considered. The last group of chapters is concerned with the diversity of families, as illustrated by a discussion of ethnic families and the impact of divorce on family organization. Finally, the chapters on the transition to parenthood and divorce provide examples of how families manage normative and nonnormative life transitions.

Acknowledgments

A number of individuals merit thanks for their assistance in the development of this volume. Thanks to the Advisory Committee for Volume 7 for their guidance in conceptualizing this volume. Under the chairmanship of Gerald Siegel of the University of Minnesota, this group consisted of Gerald Patterson, of the Oregon Social Learning Center, Beatrice Whiting of Harvard University, and the associate editors of the volume, Robert Emde, Harriette McAdoo, and Gene Sackett. Thanks are also due to a variety of individuals who generously commented on various chapters. Their insightful suggestions led to significant improvements in these chapters, and the quality of the volume owes much to their efforts. These include Brenda Bryant, Andrew Cherlin, David Dooley, Judith Dunn, Frank Furstenberg, Paul Glick, Robert Henderson, E. Mavis Hetherington, Ellen Hock, Luis Laosa, Chaya Piotrkowski, John Santrock, Graham Spanier, and Sheldon White. My personal appreciation is extended to the associate editors of this volume, Robert N. Emde, Harriette P. McAdoo, and Gene P. Sackett for their counsel, their editorial assistance, and their patience. Finally, thanks are due to the authors who contributed their time, effort, and expertise. Their willingness to entertain suggestions and undergo revisions made this a better volume.

Finally, some of the editing for this volume was undertaken during my tenure as a Belding Scholar at the Foundation for Child Development, and I am grateful to Dr. Orville Brim, Jr., and the foundation staff for their support and hospitality during this visit. Thanks to JoAnn Townsley and Sally Parsons for their assistance with the numerous clerical tasks involved in editing this volume.

It is hoped that this volume, in the tradition of earlier volumes in this series, will stimulate dialogue between scientists and practitioners. To the extent that the essays presented here lead to improved understanding of families and how to assist them, the aims of this volume will be achieved.

Ross D. Parke
Champaign, Illinois

1 Biological Approaches to the Study of the Family

F. F. STRAYER

Laboratoire d'Ethologie Humaine,
Université du Québec à Montréal

I. Introduction

> The family shows the laws operative within the household that, transferred to outside life, keep the state and the world in order. . . . The family is society in embryo; it is the native soil on which performance of moral duty is made easy through natural affection, so that within a small circle a basis of moral practice is created, and this is later widened to include human relationships in general. [Wilhelm, 1950, p. 143]

During the past 20 years, the increasing emphasis on interdisciplinary research within the social sciences has favored a plurality of conceptual and methodological approaches to the analysis of traditional questions about social development. Those diversified analytic frameworks offer a variety of new and often competing visions about the basic principles of human behavior. Within the field of child psychology, the initial reception of Piaget's use of biological adaptation in the analysis of intellectual growth serves as a classic example of the heated, and in retrospect often fruitless, controversy resulting from the introduction of an interdisciplinary approach to the study of human functioning.

During the past 10 years, efforts to examine the biological bases of human social activity have produced even more acrimonious reactions within the behavioral and biological sciences (Allen, 1976; Griffin, 1978;

I thank Teresa Blicharski, Michell Dumont, and Roger Gauthier for their enthusiastic and sustained support; Gene Sackett for an exceptional blend of tolerance and moral support; and Jarek, Jacob, and Elene who kept the human aspects of it all clearly in the forefront. Thanks are also due to Louise Champagne, Pierrette Precourt, and Marcel Trudel for help with the final version of this manuscript and to Dick Holm for his scenic connection in Seattle. This work was completed with financial assistance from *les Fonds* Formation des chercheurs et d'action concertée (FCAC) for research in human ethology and social ecology.

Harris, 1980; Lande, 1978; Mahern, 1978; Wilson, 1976, 1978). Perhaps
this recent intellectual controversy can be justified as the legitimate defense of opposing scientific and political views. However, it also often
reflects a rudimentary appreciation of the respective claims and limits for
the traditional disciplinary and the newer interdisciplinary approaches to
the analysis of human behavior. (See Caplan, 1978, for a review of the
historical roots and current status of this debate.) Such obstacles to effective scientific collaboration can be overcome only if more attention is given
to the realistic articulation of basic analytic concepts and primary research
objectives within different fields of interdisciplinary study.

II. Analytic Approaches in Behavioral Biology

In his classic discussion of nonhuman primate societies, Hans Kummer
(1971) provided a very thorough and concise summary of the conceptual
framework underlying a biological approach to the study of social behavior.
Initially, biologists attempt to distinguish carefully among analytic problems concerning the structure, causation, and immediate function of behavior. Each of these three perspectives involves a specific set of questions
that taken together constitute a comprehensive but static treatment of
behavioral activity. To account for the more dynamic aspects of behavioral
development and evolution, the original three questions must be reexamined within the historically meaningful time frames of ontogeny and
phylogeny. (See Reigel, 1976, for a parallel treatment of these same
problems within the field of developmental psychology.) Three interrelated concepts of adaptation are necessary in this second phase of analysis.
Phylogenetic adaptation refers to changes in behavioral potential that are
linked to particular selective pressures that shaped the species' evolutionary history. In contrast, changes in behavior during ontogeny are attributable to (1) ecological adaptation, which encompasses traditional concepts of
learning as well as other immediate behavioral adjustments by the individual to pressures in the physical habitat, or (2) social adaptation, which
includes modifications in an individual's behavior that can be linked to
specific pressures from the social environment.

Discussing the limits of human social biology, Kummer (1971) argued
cogently that even the most comprehensive treatment of behavioral phenomena is not identical with an exhaustive scientific analysis of human
adaptation. A conceptual framework in science is useful only within certain
limits and usually provides overly simplified representations of phenomena that are outside the focus of study. With respect to human evolution, the "phenomenon of culture, for example, can readily be recognized

as a social modification. However, this biological definition ignores some of culture's most important aspects" (Kummer, 1971, p. 11). The heuristic advantage of discussing culture as a set of behavioral modifications induced by the social environment is that it forces clearer distinctions among qualitatively different sources of information that operate to shape individual development (Alexander & Borgia, 1978; Barkow, 1980, Campbell, 1975; Lorenz, 1965). However, having adopted this heuristic approach, behavioral biologists can claim to offer no more than partial insights into the nature of human functioning. Furthermore, the ultimate value of this approach must be judged not only in terms of its construction of logically sound evolutionary models and its presentation of convincing comparative data, but, more important, in terms of its elaboration of basic analytic concepts that will contribute to a more comprehensive interdisciplinary study of human behavior.

In spite of the general accord concerning basic analytic perspectives and the necessity of a heuristic approach to the study of behavior, two quite distinct traditions in human behavioral biology, accompanied by two almost independent literatures, have emerged during the past 10 years. Research in sociobiology has focused selectively on the process of phylogenetic adaptation in order to examine genetically influenced social dispositions. The primary objective in this tradition has been the formulation of mathematical models of social selection that predict the emergence of stable interactive styles as traits characterizing individual members of a given species. In contrast, research in social ethology has attempted to provide a detailed descriptive analysis of behavioral activity and its transformations during development. This latter tradition places considerably more emphasis on the inductive derivation of social dispositions, through the direct observation of naturally occuring behavioral activity. Following an extensive comparative analysis, the identification of recurrent patterns of behavioral organization may provide evidence for evolved, species-specific styles of social adaptation in both of these traditions.

III. SOCIOBIOLOGY AND THE FAMILY

From an evolutionary perspective, the principal question about the family concerns its potential impact on individual fitness. In this context, fitness refers to the transmission of genetic information to members of succeeding generations. The definition of fitness in terms of reproductive success, rather than individual survival, provides the key conceptual distinction in modern accounts of how natural selection favors particular modes of social adaptation. Reproductive success is a functional concept that involves

more than simply maximizing the absolute number of immediate descendants. Postnatal caregiving activities that promote the welfare and development of offspring and indirectly ensure the parents own subsequent reproductive viability, become critical factors in the evolution of species-specific
social activity. The importance attributed to the parent-child relationship
provides just an initial indication of the central role of family systems in
sociobiological theories of behavior. A much more comprehensive treatment of the evolutionary significance of the family is presented in Hamilton's (1964a, 1964b) analysis of kinship selection and its corresponding
principle of inclusive fitness (see also (Carlisle, 1981; Emlen and Oring,
1977; Farber, 1973; Michod and Anderson, 1979; West-Eberhard, 1975).

Hamilton's (1964a, 1964b) seminal work demonstrated that individual
reproductive success is optimized not only by maximizing personal reproductive efforts, but also by extending caregiving activities to closely related
kin. In this latter case, individuals promote the transmission of their own
genetic information by contributing to the reproductive efforts of other
family members. Thus, inclusive fitness represents reproductive success as
well as the indirect increases in individual fitness which are attributable to
cooperation among family members who share at least some common
genetic information. The theoretical importance of kinship selection was
most apparent in its application to the classic problem of explaining the
evolution of self-sacrificial or altruistic behavior (Allee, 1943/1978; Darwin,
1859/1978; Kropotkin, 1903/1978). Hamilton's account of kinship altruism,
expressed in terms of evolutionary costs and benefits weighted by the
coefficient of genetic relatedness between individuals, provided a catalyst
for the elaboration of a number of similar biological models which attempt
to explain how social dynamics within the family differentially influence
both individual and inclusive fitness (Breden & Wade, 1981; Charlesworth, 1978; Wade, 1979, 1980; Wade & Breden, 1980; Weigel, 1981).

Trivers's (1971) equally important theoretical analysis of altruistic
activity seemed, on the surface, less directly concerned with the sociobiology of family systems. The principal contribution of this second model was
the demonstration of an evolutionary basis for the emergence of altruism
between individuals from different kinship systems, and even from completely different species. Trivers's formulation of the evolution of reciprocal altruism relied on a more precise contrast between the evolutionary
costs and benefits associated with altruistic intervention. When the potential benefit for a victim greatly exceeds the potential cost for a benefactor,
and when individuals frequently encounter such situations with roles
possibly reversed, then evolved dispositions toward reciprocal altruism
would increase the reproductive fitness of each participant. This reciprocal
benefit would exist even if the coefficient of genetic relatedness were

negligible, and thus Trivers's model extends the evolutionary basis for altruism beyond the immediate kinship system. However, the emergence of such reciprocity clearly would be reinforced by kinship selection. Reciprocal altruism within the family context would always ensure a minimal benefit in terms of inclusive fitness but would offer maximum benefit when the other family members also shared the disposition toward reciprocating.

Like Hamilton's earlier formulation of kinship selection, Trivers's evolutionary account of reciprocal altruism has had far-reaching effects on sociobiological views of the family. The emergence of a disposition toward reciprocal altruism could also provide a social context that facilitates the evolution of altruistic cheating. Individuals might mimic the style of altruists, but actually enhance their own inclusive fitness by failing to accept the marginal risks associated with reciprocation. To avoid this form of exploitation, reciprocal altruists would need additional information that might permit the detection of cheaters, so that aid would be deployed selectively only toward others who were likely to reciprocate. Such a process provides an interesting occasion for other dimensions of social functioning, as well as ontogenetic social adaptation to assume vital roles in the stabilization of presumed phylogenetically selected social dispositions (Strayer, Wareing, & Rushton, 1979). If such discriminative deployment of reciprocal altruism were possible among nonkin, a potential conflict could also emerge within the family system. Family members operating only in terms of inclusive fitness would distribute altruism among kin in terms of their respective coefficients of genetic relatedness. In contrast, reciprocal altruists could distribute their gestures in terms of both relatedness and likelihood of future reciprocation. Such selective use of altruistic gestures within the family context could concentrate a disproportionate frequency of aid among reciprocating individuals and eventually lead to greater selective pressure against family members who are less disposed to forming reciprocal altruistic bonds.

The potential of such conflict between phylogenetically adapted social dispositions has led to a more careful examination of the evolutionary stability of presumed species-specific interactive styles. Maynard-Smith (1974) introduced the concept of "evolutionarily stable strategy" to describe the emergence of a particular adaptive response disposition as a general characteristic of a given breeding population. Such adaptive styles are stable strategies only if they "cannot be invaded by an initially rare mutant adopting an alternative strategy" (Maynard-Smith & Parker, 1976, p. 159). Most of the theoretical research on such strategies has employed computer simulation to analyze survivorship in hypothetical parent populations containing individuals disposed toward the use of different predetermined interactive styles (Maynard-Smith & Parker, 1976;

Maynard-Smith & Price, 1973). Two general types of adaptive strategies
are usually considered. Pure strategies represent dispositions to react in a
specified fashion to a particular social situation (e.g., cooperation, aggressive conflict, mate selection, etc.), while mixed strategies reflect the ability
to select among two or more possible alternative responses in similar social
contexts. According to this analytic perspective, neither pure kinship
altruism nor pure reciprocal altruism can be considered as evolutionarily
stable strategies, since both social dispositions could be replaced by the
mixed strategy of a discriminating reciprocal altruist.

These sociobiological analyses suggest that the family system, because
of its essential reproductive functions and the higher levels of genetic
relatedness between its members, provides the optimal social context for
the evolution of stable mutual aid and reciprocal caregiving strategies.
However, such an idealized view of family life is considerably restrained by
the realization that incipient conflict between family members can differentially strengthen certain family ties and ultimately can reorganize
altruistic behavior among kin. The analysis of the complicated patterns of
social organization resulting from such different but coexisting adaptive
strategies among family members has been the principal theoretical problem in more recent sociobiological treatments of the sources of family
conflict.

According to sociobiology, the original basis of family conflict is found
in the differential reproductive strategies that characterize adult males and
females. These strategies are shaped by selective pressures that begin
operating well before the birth of common offspring and continue to
influence family life throughout the reproductive period. Individual reproductive decisions structure not only the parental relationship (or lack of it),
but also the nature of the family system itself. As early as 1871, Darwin
attempted to explain the evolution of diverse family systems in animals and
man with the single principle of *sexual selection* (see Campbell, 1972).
Actually, sexual selection entailed two basic processes—male competition
and female choice. Intermale competition for access to reproductively
active females and female selection of preferred breeding partners should
differentially influence the reproductive success of the two sexes.

Bateman (1948) first provided empirical evidence supporting the predictions derived from these views of sexual selection in his precise estimate
of variation in male and female reproductive fitness within small, ex-
perimentally established breeding groups with balanced sex ratios (*Drosophila melanogaster*). Sexual competition among males leads to greater
diversity in the total number of offspring per individual. Because some
males produce considerably more than an average number of young, other
males are forced to limit their reproductive potential when the number of

sexually active females is held constant. Moreover, because female choice differentially favors some males, a basic conflict arises between the sexes. Females are attracted to more vigorous males, while their mates jealously guard exclusive access to the female as a vitally important reproductive resource.

Fundamentally, males depend on female cooperation to attain even average reproductive fitness. In contrast, owing to their lower variability in total number of offspring, females are much more likely to attain near-average numbers of total offspring. Despite their relatively secure reproductive status, however, in certain cases females can, by selectively choosing more vigorous mates, maximize the chances that their own male offspring will be more attractive and thus also more successful reproductively. In this sense, strategic infidelity can directly enhance the female's individual fitness measured in terms of grandchildren and great-grandchildren (Weatherhead & Robertson, 1979). Unfortunately, such an optimizing strategy engenders family conflict since it simultaneously reduces the fitness of her current mate. In sharp contrast, given his substantially greater reproductive potential, the male's infidelity implies little risk for the female's reproductive output. The direct costs of male infidelity are absorbed by other reproductively active males. However, indirect costs of male infidelity may accrue if such activities lead to a reduction in his availability for postnatal caregiving (see below).

The far-reaching effects of sexual selection on the nature of family life have been elucidated most clearly by Trivers (1972). Trivers reformulated the Darwinian view of sexual selection in terms of a single concept—*parental investment*—which elegantly integrates both pre- and postconception components of reproductive success. At a formal level, Trivers defined parental investment as "any investment by the parent in such individual offspring that increases the offspring's chance of surviving (and hence reproductive success) at the cost of the parent's ability to invest in other offspring" (p. 139). Fundamentally, parental investment refers simply to the relative allocation of resources and care among different offspring. More importantly, parental investment clearly implies potential conflict between parents and their offspring in allocation of resources within the family. To maximize personal fitness, parents attempt to strategically balance the number of offspring and levels of pre- and postnatal care. In contrast, offspring attempt to maximize their own immediate receipt of parental care, with less concern for their parents' future reproduction (Brockelman, 1975; Kleiman, 1979; Macnair & Parker, 1979; Smith & Fretwell, 1974).

According to Trivers (1972), relative parental investment not only governs the operation of sexual selection but also determines the nature of family dynamics. Since males usually invest less at a metabolic level in the production of gametes, there should be strong general tendency toward the classical situation of male competition and female choice that Darwin (1871) described. In the absence of other factors, these two parental investment strategies would lead to the establishment of matrilineal, monoparental family systems (Barash, 1980; Fox, 1972). However, as postnatal caregiving needs increase, and as females gain control over the fertilization process (by either metabolic or behavioral means), female choice can be used effectively to maximize paternal investment in offspring. As male investment increases, both male competition and female choice become less important determinants of variability in reproductive success. Finally, when males invest equally with their mates to assure postnatal survival of offspring, the variability in reproductive success reaches virtually the same level for the two sexes. In this latter case, selection favors reproductive bonding between parents and the emergence of nuclear or extended biparental systems (Caspari, 1972; van den Berghe, 1979a, 1979b, 1980; van den Berghe & Barash, 1977; Wittenberger & Tilson, 1980).

As in the preceding analysis of social altruism, neither of these two extremes in parental investment strategies represents necessarily stable evolutionary strategies. Trivers (1972) suggested that especially in species in which natural selection has already favored strong paternal investment, a mixed strategy of parental investment would be optimal for males. This mixed strategy would entail bonding with a single female and investing in postnatal care for common young, but remaining open to mating with other females when subsequent parental investment could be minimized or completely withdrawn. However, such a mixed investment strategy among males could marginally reduce male parental investment in the original pair-bonded context and thus reintroduce male competition and female choice into the social dynamics of the monogamous family unit.

An important consequence of such differential investment by bonded parents involves differential costs and benefits association with desertion at any given moment by either parent. Trivers (1972) suggested that desertion would be regulated by cumulative differences in past offspring investment, with lower investment (usually among males) leading to a greater tendency to desert. However, Dawkins and Carlisle (1976) criticized this formulation as being imprecise and emphasized that benefits from future reproductive opportunities, not the costs from past expenditure, should control decisions by either parent to withdraw postnatal caregiving activities (see also Maynard-Smith, 1977; Robertson & Biermann, 1979).

A second form of potential family conflict arises because of paternal uncertainty concerning the genetic relatedness between males and their presumed offspring. Owing to internal fertilization, genetic relatedness of mothers and offspring is always certain, but the situation is less clear for males and perhaps even more uncertain for human males because of hidden ovulation (Strassmann, 1981). Pair-bonded fathers pay a potentially much higher cost for female infidelity. Not only do such males lose reproductive access to their mates, but they also risk investing their own parental caregiving activities to increase the viability of another male's offspring. Such high costs of parental investment in offspring suggest that selective pressures should favor the emergence of more sophisticated reproductive strategies that would sensitize pair-bonding males to infidelity of their mates and thus reduce their vulnerability to misplaced parental investment.

Aside from its central role in the sociobiological analysis of parental conflict, parental investment theory also provides the conceptual basis for linking reproductive success and social conflict across generations in stable family systems. Trivers (1974) provided the initial extension of parental investment to considerations of parent-child conflict and sibling rivalry. The key to understanding how parental investment regulates parent-child and child-child conflict lies in assessing the relative costs and benefits of parental resource allocation from both the parent's and the child's perspective.

Thus when the cost of further investment in a given offspring exceeded the potential benefit to its reproductive success, the parent would be inclined to limit caregiving, while the child would be inclined to solicit additional support. Similarly, when the cost of a given action to a sib exceeded the benefit to the child, the parent would tend to intervene in order to reestablish a cost-benefit ratio of unity. A child would be inclined to behave altruistically toward sibs and parents when the benefit to the other exceeded twice the cost to himself. In contrast, if personal benefit to the child exceeded half the cost to another family member, he should tend to act selfishly. From the parent's point of view, the critical value for these two cost-benefit ratios would be unity.

In order to maximize their personal reproductive fitness, parents should encourage offspring to act altruistically when the benefit to another family member (full sib or the parent itself) marginally exceeds the cost to the offspring. Similarly, only when one offspring's benefit surpassed another's cost would selfishness be encouraged by the parent. It is important to note that such strategic regulation of offspring altruism and selfishness is not necessarily extended by the parent to its mate (Craig, 1979). Given the lower level of genetic relatedness between parents, each would be more tolerant when offspring attempted to exploit the other parent. Trivers's (1974) model of parent-child conflict has been criticized by Alexander (1974) on the basis that such calculated selfishness among offspring would ultimately lead to the reduction of their own reproductive fitness when as adults they were forced to relive such strategic conflict with their own offspring. In addition, Alexander suggested that given the nature of social power in the parent-child dyad, parents could always force offspring to cooperate in a manner that would maximize parental reproductive fitness. Subsequent analyses employing mathematical models to explore parent-offspring conflict tend to confirm the position as Trivers developed it. These more recent studies indicate that at least under certain conditions, parent-child conflict can emerge as an evolutionarily stable strategy (Feldman & Eshel, 1982; Metcalf, Stamps, & Krishnan, 1979; Parker & Mcnair, 1978a, 1978b; Stamps, Metcalf, & Krishnan, 1978).

A third application of parental investment theory relates to the differential contribution of paternal and maternal grandparents in caregiving activities directed toward grandchildren. Following from the principle of reduced parental investment under conditions of paternal uncertainty, Barash (1976) suggested that grandparental investment should be regulated by matrilineal kinship, with maternal grandmothers most certain of genetic relatedness and thus most likely to allocate resources to their daughters' children. Following the same logic, maternal grandfathers should allocate more resources than either paternal grandparent, and paternal grandfathers should invest the least resources in their sons' offspring. Once again, these general ideas have been formalized in a mathematical model of three-generation family conflict (Fagen, 1976; see also Oberdieck, Cheney, & Johnson, 1978; and Partridge & Nunney, 1977). Preliminary support for some of the predictions from the grandparental investment model has been provided by survey data on frequency and duration of visits between children and their grandparents (Smith, 1981). These sociobiological views of grandparental roles in the family system complement existing theoretical views on transgenerational effects that have been elaborated in the family therapy literature (Cohler, Grunebaum, & Robbins, 1981).

The basic theoretical principles that form the conceptual core of sociobiological views on altruism and conflict have already generated an impressive variety of new empirical studies that directly increase our knowledge about animal adaptation (e.g., Kurland, 1980). In contrast, human research has focused primarily on the use of existing data banks within the social sciences to examine predictions derived from particular theoretical models included in the evolutionary view of social behavior (Daly & Wilson, 1978; Lennington, 1981; Morgan, 1979; Thiessen & Gregg, 1980; van den Berghe, 1979a, 1979b, 1980).

The majority of such studies support the selected sociobiological predictions. However, relatively few investigators have seriously considered how alternative and more traditional disciplinary models might account for their findings. Thus, although sociobiological research on human behavior demonstrates the heuristic value of the evolutionary perspective, virtually all recent studies are vulnerable to Wilson's (1975) criticism that investigators in the social sciences all too often support their theories through advocacy rather than strong inference. One of the rare exceptions to this general trend is Lennington's (1981) sociobiological analysis of child abuse. Lennington admits that although her results support an evolutionary model, many of her findings are equally consistent with alternative, especially economic, models for child abuse. In discussing these results, Lennington elaborated critical hypotheses that could provide important evidence for a meaningful choice between these different explanatory models. It is certain that if sociobiological concepts are to contribute to our general understanding of the family as a principal organizing influence on individual development, then considerably more attention must be given to the design and implementation of critical empirical studies using both direct and indirect measures of individual adaptation (Essock-Vitale & McGuire, 1980).

IV. SOCIAL ETHOLOGY AND THE FAMILY

Although questions about the nature of social selection have dominated theoretical interests in behavioral biology during the past decade, more tangible problems of ecological and ontogenetic adaptation have remained the central preoccupation in ethological research. Crook (1970) argued that there are two quite distinct conceptual approaches in modern ethology. The better-known approach, classical ethology, focuses directly on the detailed analysis of behavioral patterns, their immediate causation, and their subsequent course of development. In contrast, social ethology deals more directly with functional questions about the coordination of dyadic exchange patterns, the organization of social relations between individuals, and ecological variations in the nature of group structure.

Social ethology emerged as a separate branch of behavioral biology owing to a marked increase in field information about social behavior among nonhuman primates. Given the complexity and diversity of primate societies and their impact on individual development, the classic ethological approach to the analysis of individual differences proved inadequate. Social exchange, dyadic relations, and group social structure among primates could not be reduced to a simple calculus of individual differences in behavior. The immediate social environment—consisting of participants and ongoing activities—appeared to be the critical determinant of individual functioning. To provide a more adequate account of the contextual influences on social behavior, primatologists were forced to develop more elaborate methods for the analysis of group organization.

According to Crook (1970), the concern in primatology with the social context of individual adaptation directly parallels the more traditional emphasis in classical ethology on the physical environment as the context for both species and individual development. However, social ethologists assume that environmental influences on the individual are most often mediated by the social ecology of their stable group. In this sense, social ethologists reformulate the traditional organism-environment dichotomy in terms of three continually interacting systems: the physical habitat, the social ecology of the group, and the organism itself. An adequate understanding of individual adaptation to the physical environment requires at least a preliminary analysis of the organization of the social system in which the individual develops.

Although it was apparent even to the earliest primatologists (e.g., Yerkes, 1928; Zuckerman, 1932) that the integration of individuals into a stable social unit placed important limitations on their activities, it was less clear how to analyze the patterns of social exchange that constitute the social organization of the primate group. Today, researchers consider that the stability and organization of any social unit depend on a delicate balance struck between social activities promoting group cohesion and those leading to social dispersion (Wilson, 1975). In this view, group dominance hierarchy formalizes dyadic roles during periods of aggressive conflict and thus serves as a regulatory system that minimizes dispersive agonistic exchanges between group members. In contrast, activities that promote group cohesion attract individuals to one another and maintain them in a coordinated social unit. Dominance relations have undoubtedly received the most research attention in both human and primate social ethology. Comprehensive studies of cohesive activities have been both fewer in number and more limited in scope, largely because interest in different forms of cohesive activity has been fragmented. By using only certain behaviors in studies of social attraction, many theorists have provided arguments that alone are not sufficient to account for observed patterns of social cohesion. The theoretical difficulties involve determining the relative utility of general descriptive concepts such as leadership, control roles, attention structures, attachment bonds, and kinship patterns as necessary and/or sufficient dimensions for the analysis of primate social organization (Chance & Jolly, 1970; DeVore, 1965; Jay, 1968; Jolly, 1972; Kummer, 1971).

In addition to this theoretical confusion, corresponding methodological problems entailed the development of appropriate empirical techniques for the derivation of these proposed descriptive dimensions of social organization. With the increasing awareness that standardized procedures for assessing primate social relations provided reliable information but failed to predict social behavior within the group setting (Bernstein, 1970; Strayer, Bovenberk, & Koopman, 1975), researchers began to emphasize the descriptive analysis of spontaneously occurring behavior as the most appropriate means of identifying basic dimensions of social ecology for stable groups. This trend toward the use of direct observation culminated in a more systematic approach for the inductive analysis of social relations and group structures (Hinde & Stevenson-Hinde, 1976; Strayer, 1980a, 1981).

The current approach in social ethology stresses clear distinctions among four levels of social description. The first level entails identification of the diversity of behavioral action patterns that characterize the activities of the various members of the social group. Second, the examination of recurrent sequential combinations of these action patterns during the course of social exchange between individuals permits the isolation of characteristic forms of social interaction for members of a stable group. Third, the regularity and diversity of such forms of interaction for different dyads suggests larger categories of qualitatively different forms of social participation that can be used as converging measures of specific dimensions in social relations. Finally, analysis of general principles that summarize the organization of obtained relationships provides an empirical basis for the derivation of the social structures that constitute the organization of the stable group.

Currently, one of the best illustrations of the application of this ethological framework in the analysis of human social behavior is my own research on the social ecology of the preschool peer group (Strayer et al., 1979; Strayer, 1980a, 1980b, 1981). In these studies, I and my colleagues distinguish between the behavioral ecology and the social organization of the stable social unit. Behavioral ecology refers to the quality of behavioral activity observed within a group. Pertinent measures of behavioral ecology include rates of specific actions or classes of actions, relative time allocated to different forms of social participation, and relative frequencies of different forms of dyadic social exchange. All of these measures are similar to indices that have been used in psychological research on individual differences in behavior.

In my analyses of social organization, at the levels of social relations and group structure, primary attention is given to the dyadic context of observed social exchanges. For example, it sometimes happens that the most aggressive or domineering child in a group never directs aggression to, or dominates, a particular group member. If, however, he always responds to aggression from that other child by withdrawing or submitting, the established dyadic dominance relation is clearly not in his favor. Such relationships, in which a less aggressive child dominates a more aggressive peer, are often observed among young children and reflect the fact that having the highest frequency of aggressive or dominance exchanges is not identical to having the highest dominance status within the social unit. (Perhaps an apt analogy is to the difference between the number of scientific publications and the level of scientific impact.) Generally, an examination of the complete set of such relations in a stable group permits the derivation of a linear status structure where, in this case, the aggressive child has a group dominance role inferior to that of the other group member in question.

Similar empirical findings concerning the organization of social activities have been obtained in observational research on other forms of preschool social behavior—affiliative or attachment activities, prosocial or altruistic behaviors, and influence or control activities. In each case, distinctions can be made between the behavioral ecology analyses, which stress frequency and rate measures, and the organizational analyses, which emphasize dyadic asymmetries or reciprocities in social relationships and specific roles within the stable group. At the end of the preschool period, control and influence seem to be hierarchically structured, with group control roles highly correlated with agonistic dominance roles (Strayer, 1981). In contrast, preschool altruism seems structured according to a network of reciprocity with central and peripheral group roles. This latter network maps almost perfectly onto the network of stable friendship relations that emerge from the analysis of dyadic affiliation (Strayer et al., 1979).

V. Current Limits of Human Behavioral Biology

Although the conceptual framework for the analysis of social organization elaborated within social ethology has been applied profitably to the study of children's peer groups, ethological researchers have not yet examined the family as a principal social unit influencing individual adaptation. Instead, the vast majority of empirical and theoretical interest has focused on the mother-child relationship as the principal building block of subsequent social competence (Ainsworth, 1969; Bowlby, 1969, 1973; Sroufe, 1978). Recent interest in the father-child relationship (Lamb, 1976; Lamb & Goldberg, 1982; Radin, 1981). although providing a necessary complement to previous attachment research, offers only partial answers to the important question how the family as a system influences child adaptation. The empirical approach of social ethology together with the theoretical models of sociobiology suggest analytic perspectives that should furnish unique insights into the family system as a critical context for child and adult social development. At the moment, unfortunately, ethological and sociobiological views of the human family remain a collection of provocative models, heuristic concepts, and potentially useful methods. The current value of these views for our understanding of human adaptation is severely limited by a dearth of empirical facts.

These two analytic traditions in modern behavioral biology reflect to a large extent the well-known dialectic between theoretical and empirical approaches in scientific enquiry. Ultimately the mathematical models in human sociobiology will be tested and revised to accommodate the empirical findings of social ethology. Similarly, ethological research will be guided increasingly by the theoretical formulations of potential phylogenetic pressures that may have influenced species-specific social adaptation. The present lack of a dynamic collaboration between these areas places severe constraints on their immediate contribution to scientific knowledge about human social behavior. However, such constraints represent only short-term obstacles, which can be removed systematically in the coming years. Even in its present embryonic form, behavioral biology offers a number of potentially important concepts for the analysis of human social systems, as well as a variety of evolutionary speculations about the nature and origins of certain interactive strategies that may characterize our species-specific or modal patterns of social development. A complete analysis of the human family cannot ignore these biological relevant questions. More important, the conceptual approach developed in behavioral biology, although speculative at the moment, will continue to attract the energies of researchers interested in an integrated view of the life sciences.

REFERENCES

Ainsworth, M. D. S. Object relations, dependency and attachment: A theoretical review of the infant-mother relationship. *Child Development*, 1969, **40**, 969–1025.

Alexander, R. D. The evolution of social behavior. *Annual Reviews of Ecological Systems*, 1974, **5**, 325–383.

Alexander, R. D., & Borgia, G. Group selection, altruism, and the levels of organization of life. *Annual Reviews of Ecological Systems*, 1978, **9**, 449–474.

Allée, W. C. Where angels fear to tread: A contribution from general sociology to human ethics. In A. L. Caplan (Ed.), *The sociobiology debate: Readings on the ethical and scientific issues concerning sociobiology*. New York: Harper & Row, 1978. (Originally published, 1943.)

Allen, L. Sociobiology—another biological determinism: Sociobiology study group of science for the people. Dialogue: The critique. *Bioscience*, 1976, **26**, 182.

Barash, D. P. Some evolutionary aspects of parental behavior in animals and man. *American Journal of Psychology*, 1976, **89**, 195–217.

Barash, D. P. Human reproductive strategies: A sociobiologic review. In J. S. Lockard (Ed.), *The evolution of human social behavior*. New York: Elsevier, 1980.

Barkow, J. H. Biological evolution of culturally patterned behavior. In J. S. Lockard (Ed.), *The evolution of human social behavior*. New York: Elsevier, 1980.

Bateman, A. J. Intrasexual selection in drosophila. *Heredity*, 1948, **2**, 349–368.

Bernstein, I. S. Primate status hierarchies. *In* L. Rosenblum (Ed.), *Primate behavior: Developments in field and laboratory research*. New York: Academic Press, 1970.

Bowlby, J. *Attachment and loss*. (Vol. 1): *Attachment*. New York: Basic Books, 1969.

Bowlby, J. *Attachment and loss*. (Vol. 2): *Separation*. New York: Basic Books, 1973.

Breden, F., & Wade, M. J. Inbreeding and evolution by kin selection. *Ethology and Sociobiology*, 1981, **2**, 3–16.

Brockelman, W. Y. Competition, the fitness of offspring, and optimal clutch size. *American Naturalist*, 1975, **109**, 677–699.

Campbell, D. T. *Sexual selection and the descent of man, 1871–1971*. Chicago: Aldine, 1972.

Campbell, D. T. On the conflicts between biological and social evolution and between psychology and moral tradition. *American Psychologist*, 1975, pp. 1103–1126.

Caplan, A. L. Ethics, evolution, and the milk of human kindness. In A. L. Caplan (Ed.), *The sociobiology debate: Readings on the ethical and scientific issues concerning sociobiology*. New York: Harper and Row, 1978.

Carlisle, T. R. Altruism between in-laws: Some predictions from kin-selection theory. *Behavioral Ecology and Sociobiology*, 1981, **8**, 157–159.

Caspari, E. Sexual selection in human evolution. In B. Campbell (Ed.), *Sexual selection and the descent of man, 1871–1971*. Chicago: Aldine, 1972.

Chance, M. R., & Jolly, C. J. *Social groups of monkeys and men*. London: Cape, 1970.

Charlesworth, B. Some models of the evolution of altruistic behaviour between siblings. *Journal of Theoretical Biology*, 1978, **72**, 297–319.

Cohler, B. J., Grunebaum, H. U., & Robbins, D. M. *Mothers, grandmothers, and daughters: Personality and childcare in three-generation families*. New York: Wiley, 1981.

Craig, R. Parental manipulation, kin selection, and the evolution of altruism. *Evolution*, 1979, **33**, 319–334.

Crook, J. H. Social organization and the environment: Aspects of contemporary social ethology. *Animal Behaviour*, 1970, **18**, 197–209.

Daly, M., & Wilson, M. *Sex, Evolution and Behavior: Adaptations for reproduction*. North Scituate, Mass.: Duxbury, 1978.

Darwin, C. Neuter insects. In A. L. Caplan (Ed.), *Sociobiology debate: Readings on the ethical and scientific issues concerning sociobiology*. New York: Harper and Row, 1978. (Originally published, 1859.)

Darwin, C. *The descent of man, and selection in relation to sex*. New York: Appleton, 1871.

Dawkins, R., & Carlisle, T. R. Parental investment: A fallacy. *Nature*, 1976, **262**, 131–133.

DeVore, I. *Primate behavior: Field studies of monkeys and apes*. New York: Holt, Rinehart & Winston, 1965.

Emlen, S. T., & Oring, L. W. Ecology, sexual selection, and the evolution of mating systems. *Science*, 1977, **197**, 215–223.

Essock-Vitale, S. M. & McGuire, M. T. Predictions derived from the theories of kin selection and reciprocation assessed by anthropological data. *Ethology and Sociobiology*, 1980, 1, 233–245.

Fagen, R. M. Three-generation family conflict. *Animal Behavior*, 1976, 24, 874–879.

Farber, B. *Family and kinship in modern society*. Glenview, Ill: Scott Foresman, 1973.

Feldman, M. W., & Eshel, I. On the theory of parent-offspring conflict: A two-locus genetic model. *American Naturalist*, 1982, 119, 285–292.

Fox, R. Alliance and constraint: Sexual selection in the evolution of human kinship systems. In B. Campbell (Ed.), *Sexual selection and the descent of man, 1871–1971*. Chicago: Aldine, 1972.

Gaulin, S. J. C., & Schlegel, A. Paternal confidence and paternal investment: A cross-cultural test of a sociobiological hypothesis. *Ethology and Sociobiology*, 1980, 1, 301–311.

Griffin, D. R. Humanistic aspects of ethology. In M. S. Gregory, A. Silvers, and D. Sutch (Eds.), *Sociobiology and human nature: An interdisciplinary critique and defense*. San Francisco: Jossey-Bass, 1978.

Hamilton, W. D. The genetical evolution of social behaviour. I. *Journal of Theoretical Biology*, 1964, 7, 1–16. (a)

Hamilton, W. D. The genetical evolution of social behaviour. II. *Journal of Theoretical Biology*, 1964, 7, 17–52. (b)

Harris, M. Sociobiology and biological reductionism. In A. Montagu (Ed.), *Sociobiology examined*. London: Oxford University Press, 1980.

Hinde, R. A., & Stevenson-Hinde, J. Towards understanding relationships: Dynamic stability. In P. Bateson and R. Hinde (Eds.), *Growing points in ethology*. Cambridge: Cambridge University Press, 1976.

Jay, P. C. *Primates: Studies in adaptation and variability*. New York: Holt, Rinehart & Winston, 1968.

Jolly, A. *The evolution of primate behavior*. New York: Macmillan, 1972.

Kleiman, D. G. Parent-offspring conflict and sibling competition in monogamous primates. *American Naturalist*, 1979, 114, 753–760.

Kropotkin, P. Mutual aid: A factor of evolution. In A. L. Caplan (Ed.), *The Sociobiology debate: Readings on the ethical and scientific issues concerning sociobiology*. New York: Harper & Row, 1978. (Originally published, 1903.)

Kummer, H. *Primate societies: Group techniques of ecological adaptation* Chicago: Aldine, 1971.

Kurland, J. A. Kin selection theory: A review and selective bibliography. *Ethology and Sociobiology*, 1980, 1, 255–275.

Lamb, M. E. The role of the fathers: An overview. In M. E. Lamb (Ed.), *The role of the father in child development*. New York: Wiley, 1976.

Lamb, M. E., & Goldberg, W. A. The father-child relationship: A system of biological, evolutionary and social perspectives. In L. W. Hoffman, R. Gandelman, & H. R. Schiffman (Eds.), *Parenting: Its causes and consequences*. Hillsdale, N.J.: Erlbaum, 1982.

Lande, R. Are humans maximizing reproductive success? *Behavioral Ecology and Sociobiology*, 1978, 3, 95–98.

Lennington, S. Child abuse: The limits of sociobiology. *Ethology and Sociobiology*, 1981, 2, 17–31.

Lorenz, K. *Evolution and modification of behavior*. Chicago: University of Chicago Press, 1965.

Macnair, M. R., & Parker, G. A. Models of parent-offspring conflict. (3): Intra-brood conflict. *Animal Behaviour*, 1979, 27, 1202–1209.

Mahern, R. Altruism, ethics, and sociobiology. In A. L. Caplan (Ed.), *The sociobiology debate: Readings on the ethical and scientific issues concerning sociobiology.* New York: Harper & Row, 1978.

Maynard-Smith, J. The theory of games and the evolution of animal conflict. *Journal of Theoretical Biology,* 1974, **47,** 209–221.

Maynard-Smith, J. Parental investment: A prospective analysis. *Animal Behaviour,* 1977, **25,** 1–19.

Maynard-Smith, J., & Parker, G. The logic of asymmetric contests. *Animal Behaviour,* 1976, **24,** 159–175.

Maynard-Smith, J. & Price, G. R. The logic of animal conflict. *Nature,* 1973, **246,** 15–18.

Metcalf, R. A., Stamps, J. A., & Krishnan, V. V. Parent-offspring conflict that is not limited by degree of kinship. *Journal of Theoretical Biology,* 1979, **76,** 99–107.

Michod, R. E., & Anderson, W. W. Measures of genetic relationship and the concept of inclusive fitness. *American Naturalist,* 1979, **114,** 637–647.

Morgan, C. J. Eskimo hunting groups, social kinship, and the possibility of kin selection in humans. *Ethology and Sociobiology,* 1979, **1,** 83–87.

Oberdieck, F., Cheney, C. D., & Johnson, C. A critique of Fagen's conflict model. *Animal Behaviour,* 1978, **26,** 309–310.

Parker, G. A., & Macnair, M. R. Models of parent-offspring conflict. (1): Monogamy. *Animal Behaviour,* 1978, **26, 97–110.** (a)

Parker, G. A., & Macnair, M. R. Models of parent-offspring conflict. (2): Promiscuity. *Animal Behaviour,* 1978, **26** 111–122. (b)

Parker, G. A., & Macnair, M. R. Models of parent-offspring conflict. (4): Suppression: Evolutionary retaliation by the parent. *Animal Behaviour,* 1979, **27,** 1210–1235.

Partridge, L., & Nunney, L. Three-generation family conflict. *Animal Behaviour,* 1977, **25,** 785–786.

Radin, I. Parent-child relations: Childbearing fathers in intact families. *Merrill-Palmer Quarterly of Behavior and Development,* 1981, **27,** 489–514.

Reigel, K. F. *Psychology of development and history.* New York: Plenum, 1976.

Robertson, R., & Biermann, G. C. Parental investment strategies determined by expected benefits. *Journal of Comparative Ethology,* 1979, **50,** 124–128.

Smith, C. C., & Fretwell, S. D. The optimal balance between size and number of offspring. *American Naturalist,* 1974, **108,** 499–506.

Smith, M. *Grandparental investment: A sociobiological analysis.* Unpublished dissertation, York University, 1981.

Sroufe, L. A. Attachment and the roots of competence. *Human Nature,* 1978, **1,** 50–59.

Stamps, J. A., Metcalf, F. A., & Krishnan, V. V. A genetic analysis of parent-offspring conflict. *Behavioral Ecology and Sociobiology,* 1978, **3,** 369–392.

Strassmann, B. I. Sexual selection, parental care, and concealed ovulation in humans. *Ethology and Sociobiology,* 1981, **2,** 31–41.

Strayer, F. F. Child ethology and study of preschool social relations. In H. C. Foot, A. J. Chapman, & J. R. Smith (Eds.), *Friendship and social relation in children.* Toronto: Wiley, 1980. (a)

Strayer, F. F. Social ecology of the preschool peer group. In W. A. Collins (Ed.), *Minnesota symposia on child psychology.* (Vol. **13**): Development of cognition, affect, and social relations. Minneapolis: University of Minnesota, 1980. (b)

Strayer, F. F. The organization and coordination of asymmetrical relations among young children: A biological view of social power. *New Directions and Methodologies for the Social and Behavioral Sciences,* 1981, **7,** 33–49.

Strayer, F. F., Bovenberk, A., & Koopman, R. F. Social affiliation and dominance in captive squirrel monkeys (*Saimiri sciureus*). *Journal of Physiological Psychology,* 1975, **89,** 308–318.

Strayer, F. F., Wareing, S., & Rushton, J. P. Social constraints on naturally occurring preschool altruism. *Ethology and Sociobiology*, 1979, **1**, 3–11.

Thiessen, D., & Gregg, B. Human assortative mating and genetic equilibrium: An evolutionary perspective. *Ethology and Sociobiology*, 1980, **1**, 111–140.

Trivers, R. L. The evolution of reciprocal altruism. *Quarterly Review of Biology*, 1971, **46**, 35–57.

Trivers, R. L. Parental investment and sexual selection. In B. Campbell (Ed.), *Sexual selection and the descent of man, 1871–1971*. Chicago: Aldine, 1972.

Trivers, R. L. Parent-offspring conflicts. *American Zoologist*, 1974, **14**, 249–264.

van den Berghe, P. L. Mating and reproductive systems in nonhumans. In *Human family systems: An evolutionary view*. New York: Elsevier, 1979. (a)

van den Berghe, P. L. The sociobiology of human mating and reproduction. In *Human family systems: An evolutionary view*. New York: Elsevier, 1979. (b)

van den Berghe, P. L. The human family: A sociobiological look. In J. Lockard (Ed.), *The evolution of human social behavior*. New York: Elsevier, 1980.

van den Berghe, P. L., & Barash, D. Inclusive fitness and human family structure. *American Anthropologist*, 1977, **79**, 809–823.

Wade, M. J. The evolution of social interactions by family selection. *American Naturalist*, 1979, **113**, 399–417.

Wade, M. J. Kin selection: Its components. *Science*, 1980, **210**, 665–667.

Wade, M. J., & Breden, F. The evolution of cheating and selfish behavior. *Behavioral Ecology and Sociobiology*, 1980, **7**, 167–172.

Weatherhead, P. J., & Robertson, R. J. Offspring quality and the polygyny threshold: The sexy son hypothesis. *American Naturalist*, 1979, **113**, 201–208.

Weigel, R. M. The distribution of altruism among kin: A mathematical model. *American Naturalist*, 1981, **118**, 191–201.

West-Eberhard, M. J. The evolution of social behavior by kin selection. *Quarterly Review of Biology*, 1975, **50**, 1–33.

Wilhelm, H. *The I ching: Or book of changes*. Princeton, N.J.: Princeton University Press, 1950.

Wilson, E. O. *Sociobiology*. Cambridge, Mass.: Harvard University Press, 1975.

Wilson, E. O. Academic vigilantism and the political significance of sociobiology. *Bioscience*, 1976, **26**, 183–190.

Wilson, E. O. *On human nature*. Cambridge, Mass.: Harvard University Press, 1978.

Wittenberger, J. F., & Tilson, R. L. The evolution of monogamy: Hypotheses and evidence. *Annual Review of Ecological Systems*, 1980, **11**, 197–232.

Yerkes, R. M. *The great apes*. New Haven, Conn.: Yale University Press, 1928.

Zuckerman, S. *The social life of monkeys and apes*. London: Routledge, 1932.

2 Naturalistic and Experimental Studies of Nonhuman Primate and Other Animal Families

G. MITCHELL and C. SHIVELY
University of California, Davis

I. INTRODUCTION

What is an animal family? Knowing how difficult it has been for us to define family for humans, we should be even more hesitant to apply this term to nonhumans. There are several distinct types of social groups that might be called families. The monogamous unit, consisting of one male and one female and their offspring, is one type. Another is the polygamous family, of which there are two subtypes: polygynous and polyandrous. Polygynous families include one male, several females, and their offspring, while polyandrous families are composed of one female, several males, and their offspring. Any of these family types may be extended to include one more generation. These types apply to human as well as nonhuman families (see Leibowitz, 1978). In this chapter we will review family styles of many different animals in naturalistic environments and then discuss the numerous experimental studies of family structure in nonhuman primates.

II. NATURALISTIC STUDIES OF ANIMAL FAMILIES

A. MONOGAMY

Most behavioral biologists would probably agree with the basic assumptions of Wittenberger and Tilson (1980), who suggested that monogamy is primarily the absence of polygamy, the logical product of selection when conditions favoring polygyny, polyandry, or even promiscuity are not met. Wittenberger and Tilson define monogamy as a pro-

We gratefully acknowledge Christie Atkinson-Myers for her assistance in compiling the bibliography.

longed association (for at least 20%–25% of the breeding season) and an essentially exclusive mating relation between one male and one female. Monogamy cannot evolve unless (1) females obtain benefits that they would not obtain without monogamous pair bonding, (2) females are able to ascertain the true mated status of potential mates, and (3) males do not desert.

In addition, Wittenberger and Tilson suggested that monogamy should evolve under several circumstances, such as when (1) male parental care is indispensable to female reproductive success and is not shared with other females; (2) in territorial species, pairing with an immediately unavailable unmated male is always better than pairing with an already mated male; (3) in nonterritorial species, the majority of males can reproduce most successfully by defending exclusive access to a single female; (4) aggression by mated females prevents males from acquiring additional mates; or (5) males are less successful with two mates than with one.

The following taxonomic review of monogamous species in naturalistic environments is based on the review by Wittenberger and Tilson (1980) except where indicated.

1. Arthropods

Some crustacean males sequester females and mate with several each season. Others (e.g., the starfish-eating shrimp) live in monogamous pairs, which the males maintain by fighting off rivals. Wood roaches, soil-burrowing roaches, and wood-boring beetles are monogamous because males cannot defend more than one female. Desert woodlice live in pairs that defend a territory (their burrow). Burying beetles show intrasexual aggression that has led to monogamy. In horned beetles, monogamy occurs because males defend access to individual females. Monogamy is much rarer in invertebrates than in vertebrates. Wilson (1975) estimates that less than one invertebrate species in 10,000 is monogamous. Polyandry is common in invertebrates.

2. Fish

Fish are sometimes monogamous in that mated pairs defend territories and reproduce exclusively with one mate. Others are not monogamous in a reproductive sense but do behave monogamously in defending an exclusive territory. Fish show several family patterns. For example, when parental care is absent or provided by only one parent, promiscuity prevails, as in mouthbreeding by either sex. (Of several hundred species of mouthbreeders, only three show monogamy; in these three cases, both parents carry the fry in their mouths.) Sometimes the male guards the eggs and the female deserts him to lay more eggs elsewhere. When both parents tend the eggs and guard the fry, reproductive monogamy results. Fish are quite variable in their forms of sexual adaptation, and polyandry is common (Leibowitz, 1978).

3. Frogs and Toads

In frogs and toads, prolonged clasping of the female by the male (amplexus) predisposes many species to monogamy. In common frogs, for example, amplexus lasts 1–12 days, while the breeding season itself lasts only 12–14 days. In neotropical frogs, amplexus lasts several months! Monogamy results from male guarding, indeed clasping, of one female. In general, however, amphibians are only slightly less variable than fish in their reproductive strategies (Leibowitz, 1978).

4. Reptiles

Female side-blotched lizards may be courted by more than one male yet mate with only one. Although the pair does not stay together in a single territory for a prolonged period, neither male nor female obtains more than one mate. Both sexes defend against like-sex intruders. The Nile crocodile is also monogamous, as males defend individual females and both parents tend and defend their young. Overall, however, reptilian mating systems are extremely variable. It is commonplace, for example, for male lizards to tolerate multiple females within their territories (Wilson, 1975). Some species (e.g., *Sauromalus obesus*) have true polygynous harems.

5. Altricial Birds

When broods of altricial birds are so large that one parent cannot rear them alone, both parents feed the young and monogamy results. Male assistance in feeding may be necessary even when only one chick is reared at a time. Often parents must forage for food over long distances (e.g., king penguins). Moreover, the large size of some chicks greatly increases food requirements (e.g., vultures). In other species, difficult-to-capture prey limits the feeding potential of a single parent, making two feeding parents necessary (e.g., eagles). Continuous nest attention is imperative in some altricial birds (e.g., storks and pelicans). Male parental aid substantially increases female reproductive success in most altricial forms. Noncolonial passerines are usually monogamous, but may be polygynous when there is a difference in food availability between territories. Sometimes monogamous males defend individual females rather than territories (e.g., black rosy finches).

6. Brood-parasitic Altricial Birds

Cowbirds and cuckoos lay their eggs in the nests of other species, and the host species provides the parental care. Nonetheless, some cowbirds are reproductively monogamous, with males defending either the host's nest or the female herself. Other cowbirds, however, are apparently promiscuous. Less is known about the parasitic cuckoo, but males do apparently defend access to females first and territories second. They may even form temporary pair bonds during such defense.

7. Precocial Birds

Male parental aid or protection is necessary for the precocial flamingos, cranes, gulls, doves, terns, puffins, geese, quail, rails, and sun bitterns. Monogamy prevails in many of these species because differences in territorial quality are not great. In ducks, bustards, and grouse, male parental care is minimal but monogamy results because males defend individual females rather than territories. Guarding behavior by male ducks protects females from harassment by unmated males. Some nonmigratory ducks defend territories rather than females, but they are still monogamous. Bustard males are monogamous *and* defend territories. The grouse male defends food resources and provides vigilance over the female. Once pair bonds form, males guard females. "An estimated 91% of *all* bird species are monogamous during at least the breeding season" (Wilson, 1975, p. 330).

8. Mammals

According to Kleiman (1977), there are two forms of mammalian monogamy, facultative and obligate. Facultative monogamy results at low densities when there are so few members of the other sex available that only a single mate is found. Obligate monogamy occurs when a female needs help in rearing the young and when the carrying capacity of the habitat allows only one female at a time to breed on the same home range. Regardless of the type, monogamous adults show little sexual dimorphism (even behaviorally) and they display infrequent sexual behavior except during bond formation. In obligate monogamy the young show delayed sexual maturity in the presence of parents, older juveniles help in parenting, and the adult male may carry, feed, defend, and socialize the young

(Kleiman, 1977). Monogamous bonding is relatively rare among mammals, however, as adult females are committed to an expenditure of time and energy furnishing milk to their young. Hence, polygyny is usually the rule. Mammals do not show a reversal of sex roles in which females court and then leave the parental duties to the males (Wilson, 1975).

Kleiman (1977) lists about 105 mammalian species that show various kinds of monogamy, including home range overlap, proximity, family groups, breeding pairs, cohabitation, mating preferences, and unisexual aggression. Among marsupials, the honey possum lives in pairs in close proximity. Monogamous insectivores include solenodons, microgales, and various shrews. Several species of bat display monogamy, including the false vampire, hollow-faced, pouched, tomb, leaf-nosed, horse-shoe, yel-low-winged, and trumpet-eared varieties. Among rodents, monogamy has been reported for muskrats, mice, beaver, African porcupine, and azonti, among others. Among the carnivores, wolves, coyotes, jackals, foxes, some dogs, badgers, otters, and some kinds of mongooses are monogamous. Seals that breed on ice floes are bound in pairs in close proximity and in family groups, as are bowhead whales. Of the African antelopes, duikers, dik-diks, klipspringers, steinboks, and reedbucks are all classified as dis-playing facultative monogamy.

9. Nonhuman Primates

Several nonhuman primates display monogamy, including indris, marmosets, tamarins, night monkeys, titis, sakis, Mentawai leaf monkeys, gibbons, siamangs, and possibly pygmy chimpanzees (Patterson, 1979). Primate monogamy is probably obligate, as the solitary female cannot rear her young without aid from the male, and the carrying capacity of her habitat does not permit the presence of another breeding female (Kleiman, 1977).

Of the 105 monogamous mammalian species listed by Kleiman (1977), 22 are primates. There are 57 primate genera, but 17 of these (almost 30%) are monogamous. Like most mammals, the majority of primates are polygynous; none are polyandrous. Monogamy in New World marmosets and tamarins is evidently not a primitive condition, but is derived from polygyny through phyletic dwarfism (Leutenegger, 1980).

10. Humans

There is disagreement in the biological literature about which bond-ing type is most applicable to humans. Most researchers and scholars agree that polyandry, nonexistent among nonhuman primates, is least applicable to humans. However, whether it is more accurate to classify humans as monogamous or polygynous is debatable. Lovejoy (1981) and Morris (1967), for example, stand firmly on the side of monogamy, while Campbell (1979) and Symons (1979) do not.

B. FAMILY STRUCTURE IN ANIMAL AND HUMAN SOCIETIES

There is, in general, an inverse relation between the amount of sexual dimorphism and the extent of monogamous behavior: monogamous species typically display little sexual dimorphism (Alexander, Hoogland, Howard, Noonan, & Sherman, 1979). Because most mammals are polygynous, one might expect most male mammals to be larger than females. However, as Ralls (1976) has noted, "females are larger than males in more species of mammals than is generally supposed" (p. 245). The phenomenon does not appear to be correlated with a large degree of male parental investment, polyandry, matriarchy, or sexual selection acting on the female sex; Ralls believes that "sexual selection may still often be operating upon the male sex even when it is the smaller" (p. 245). But among nonhuman primates, certain marmosets and tamarins are the only species in which females are larger than males, and in these cases the female-to-male mean ratio is only 1.02 (Ralls, 1976, p. 253). Moreover, in primates, this phenomenon is correlated with male parental investment.

In polygynous species, reproductive success varies more among males than among females. In polyandrous species the reverse is true. Differential reproductive success is the result of competition, and intrasexual competition promotes sexual dimorphism. According to Alexander et al. (1979), polygyny is also correlated with larger number of males conceived and born, higher mortality rates among male embryos, more parental care for some male infants, longer juvenile periods in males, higher mortality rates among young adult males, more rapid senescence of males, and shorter life spans of males. Alexander et al. (1979) based their conclusions on a survey of pinnipeds, ungulates, primates, and humans, and they noted that all seven of the above attributes appear in the human species, suggesting an evolutionary history of polygyny for *Homo sapiens*.

Campbell (1979) also pointed out that the human mating system is basically closer to that of the polygynous common chimpanzee than to that of the monogamous gibbon. (Symons, 1979, too, sees the gibbon as being an unlikely model for humanity.) According to Campbell, 84% of human societies permit polygyny. People, he says, display facultative monogamy only under cultural sanctions. Even in societies that ban polygyny, people often practice serial monogamy and temporary extramarital bonds. When polygyny is permitted, it is practiced by the wealthier men. Campbell views monogamy as a limiting instance of polygyny.

One possible scenario for the evolution of different polygynous mating systems was suggested by Eisenberg, Muckenhirn, and Rudran, (1972), who proposed three classes of primate mating systems (unimale, age-graded male, and multimale) and noted that the unimale system occurs in a wide variety of primate species. They suggested that many so-called multi-male systems are really age-graded-male systems; that is, there is usually only one true adult male in these systems, the other males being younger or beyond the prime of life. These three systems are on a continuum of increasing complexity that moves toward the multimale group in which there is increased tolerance among adult males. The specialized complex multimale system is seen in terrestrial foraging forms of intermediate size and evolves from the age-graded-male system. The unimale system or the age-graded system is seen more in arboreal species and is more predictable for leaf eaters than for frugivores. Howler monkeys *(Alouatta)*, colobus *(Colobus)*, and langurs *(Presbytis)* have unimale systems.

But what of the relation between monogamy and polygyny? Eisenberg et al. (1972) suggest that the so-called solitary species are actually "mother families" in which an adult female and her dependent offspring live together without a male but within a male's territory. A given pair of adults (male and female) so arranged, and their descendants, may share a home range. The same adult pair may reproduce again, and a relatively closed family structure and breeding unit would thus be maintained. This system is seen in many nocturnal prosimians (e.g., bush babies, mouse lemurs) and perhaps in the orangutan.

The home ranges of adult females may overlap and a male's home range may contain one to six females and their offspring. This arrangement constitutes a polygynous breeding system, a spatial harem in which spacing is maintained primarily by indirect olfactory and auditory modalities.

At the lower limits of the mating system is the situation in which a male has only one female in his home range, thus creating a monogamy in which there is little proximity. If the female needs aid in rearing the young or if the habitat will not carry more than one breeding female, increasing proximity and a stronger pair bond often result, as in marmosets, titis, gibbons, and siamangs. It requires only the retention of offspring over a generation or two to produce a unimale group from a basic monogamous family group. The unimale group is more complex than the parental group because there is an increased representation of sex and age classes. Thus, in this scenario, monogamy is a more primitive form than the unimale group, and the multimale troop is the most advanced form. The age-graded-male troop represents an intermediate phylogenetic step (Eisenberg et al., 1972). The multimale troop is seen in baboons *(Papio)* and in common chimpanzees *(Pan troglodytes)*, which are the two genera most often used as models for early man—*Pan* on the groups of close phylogenetic ties and *Papio* on the basis of presumed similar ecology. It is noteworthy, however, that both chimpanzees and baboons are extremely labile in regard to social structure (as are many if not most of the other primates). There is not only genetic but also ecological and even protocultural and experiential variability in these species (see McGrew, 1982; Mitchell, 1979; Nagel, 1970; Patersen, 1973).

Eisenberg (1979) tested some of his ideas regarding the evolution of mating systems in the field on neotropical primates and found, as expected, that monogamy seemed to be a phylogenetically ancient trait among New World monkeys. (However, Leutenegger, 1980, shows that at least for the Callitrichids monogamy is a derived characteristic and a consequence of phyletic dwarfism.) Eisenberg called for long-term studies of individual groups to see whether, over generations, the social structure of the primate troop passes through a unimale and an intervening age-graded-male to a mature multimale phase. In those New World monkeys showing the most primitive systems, olfaction predominates. In the more advanced genera, olfactory communication has declined. Vocal duetting is seen in the primitive monogamous forms of the New World, but not in genera showing the most advanced morphological features. Duetting is also seen in the monogamous lesser apes, but olfaction is not prominent in these genera *(Hylobates* and *Symphalangus)* (see Chivers, 1979).

Territoriality is seen in the so-called solitary prosimians (those with spatial harems) and in monogamous nonhuman primates. But most unimale groups are not territorial (there are exceptions), nor are age-graded-males or multimale troops (Goss-Custard, Dunbar, & Aldrich-Blake, 1972). Thus, strict territoriality appears to be a primitive system in primates. Intrasexual tolerance is well developed in the more advanced systems, in which dominance seems to replace territoriality: "It seems apparent that territoriality is but one end of a social continuum. At the other end is the hierarchy, in which individuals are recognized and related to according to their rank. The relationship between the systems is suggested because some behavioral patterns seem to fall into either category, and because in some cases, territories and hierarchies achieve the same adaptive end. For example, once established, they both decrease the likelihood of hostile interaction" (Wallace, 1979, p. 344).

Given this point of view, the most sophisticated social troops are those with dominance hierarchies and many adult males (e.g., savannah baboons). However, large polyspecific groups of arboreal primates can also be exceedingly complex. The continua from monogamy to multimale and from territoriality to dominance certainly do not account for all complex grouping tendencies in primates (Hladik, 1979). In addition, "in those species in which intraspecific variability between troops is dependent on acquired and traditional behaviours we need to be aware that processes of sociocultural change may obscure the ecological base" (Crook, Ellis, & Goss-Custard, 1976, p. 272).

Brace (1979), reviewing 3 million years of human evolution via fossil evidence (and admitting substantial speculation), concluded that human males were always larger than human females and more competitive within their sex. Human groups, he said, included more females than males, but humans were once near-pongid, bipedal, stick-wielding primates with a multimale social organization. Originally, humans existed in a state of "primitive promiscuity" or "group marriage." The long-term pair bonding often seen in contemporary societies had yet to develop. These humans were of the genus *Australopithecus*, not *Homo*, and "we would not recognize them as being truly human" (p. 273).

The australopithecines showed more sexual dimorphism than contemporary humans, but they did not attain the degree of dimorphism seen in baboons (Swindler, 1980). The modern genus *Homo* is intermediate between baboons and gibbons in physical dimorphism. It may be that they are also intermediate in some other basic ways (e.g., territoriality, male care of infants, dominance hierarchy gradient, differential mortality rates). As noted earlier, our contemporary human societies display both monogamy and polygyny (Campbell, 1979). How is it that we have "reverted" somewhat to a more "primitive" monogamous system?

According to Alexander et al. (1979), the answer is that we have not reverted at all. The monogamy displayed by humans is very different from that of the titi monkey or gibbon. As we have noted in regard to sexual dimorphism, humans fall in the region of mildly polygynous species (slightly less dimorphic than common chimpanzees). Harem polygyny does in fact occur in many human societies. But unlike other species of primates, human families come in many forms: monogamous, promiscuous, polygynous, harem-polygynous, and even polyandrous.

Do human populations that show minimal sexual dimorphism also show the most monogamy? The answer is no. In fact, inhabitants of Africa and New Guinea show the least dimorphism but also the least monogamy. Alexander et al. (1979), however, distinguished between two kinds of human monogamy: "ecologically imposed" monogamy (owing to ecological conditions, a man cannot support more than one wife) and "socially imposed" monogamy (cultural phenomena act to impose monogamy as a law or rule for society). The former is more like the monogamy seen in other species. There is, in fact, minimal sexual dimorphism in the monogamy seen in societies that have these kinds of marginal habitats. There is no relation between minimal dimorphism and socially imposed monogamy; sexual dimorphism may even be exaggerated under socially imposed monogamy. People in large nations such as the United States tend to display socially imposed monogamy and, according to Alexander et al. (1979), intergroup aggression between large nations has produced differential male reproductive success similar to that seen in polygynous societies.

Tanner and Zihlman (1976) stressed the importance of the female's choices in mating and suggested that the adult female role was critical in the origins of the hominid line itself. Females, in their perspective, were important because the mother played an innovative role in economics, gathering with tools, sharing food with her offspring, and being socially central (she was the primary socializer of infants). According to Tanner and Zihlman, women very early became innovators in the technology and techniques of gathering and central in passing these skills to the next generation. Males were selected for smaller canines, less aggression toward infants, and most suitable sexual interaction. But monogamy, according to these authors, was not present. Males, whose behavior was less vital to infant care and culture, foraged by themselves on most occasions. This system is, in many respects, much like that seen today in orangutans.

A somewhat different point of view has been expressed by those who assume that contemporary humans are by nature basically monogamous (see Morris, 1967; Benshoof & Thornhill, 1979). According to this camp, humans are unique among primates in that the female does not reveal her ovulation by estrus. Concealed ovulation requires males to stay near the female throughout her cycle. As we know, the relative amount of parental investment by males is a correlate of the type of mating system. In human history, increased hunting ability, bipedality, increasing and prolonged infant dependency, and the dependency of the two sexes on each other for food favored the evolution of monogamy. As the male's investment in infant care increases, it becomes even more important to ensure that the child he rears is his own (Benshoof & Thornhill, 1979). The only way for a male to avoid cuckoldry when ovulation is concealed is to stay near the female throughout her cycle.

As we have seen, *Australopithecus* might have been polygynous, while increases in hunting and in brain size might have led to a more monogamous pattern in *Homo erectus*. Some scholars suggest that there was a reappearance of polygynous tendencies in *Homo sapiens* (Benshoof & Thornhill, 1979). The loss of estrus made knowledge of paternity less likely unless sexual reproduction took place in a social setting of monogamous pairs living in close proximity for prolonged periods. Cooperation among males became important, and male-male bonds were facilitated. Extended female receptivity and the concealment of ovulation could have been responsible for the cementing of male-female bonds. According to Burley (1979), the fact that females themselves could not sense ovulation countered their tendency to avoid conception. However, American women at least do report being conscious of a desire for intercourse and are more receptive at ovulation. The peak of copulatory activity takes place at ovulation (Burley, 1979). Thus, the extent to which ovulation is concealed in humans is debatable. Further, many nonhuman primates engage in sexual behavior "out of season" and even during pregnancy, so humans are not unique in their lack of cyclicity (Mitchell, 1979).

Lovejoy (1981), another proponent of the basic monogamous nature of humans, listed five characteristics that separate man from other hominids: a large neocortex, bipedality, reduced anterior dentition with molar dominance, material culture, and unique sexual and reproductive behavior. Lovejoy used fossils, primate behavior, and demographics to argue that unique sexual and reproductive behavior is the characteristic most responsible for the origin of humans. He based his arguments on the following observations: there is no behavioral contradiction in having both canines and tools; extant pongids use primitive tools; the earliest tools were not used for hunting; there is no evidence that early hominids hunted; bipedality is a mode of locomotion least adapted to hunting; hominids evolved in patchy, diversified mosaic, and variable habitats, not on the savannah; humans developed and retained shorter interbirth intervals but prolonged infant dependency relative to the apes; these additional dependent offspring required that the male help with infant care; the female was not mobile for forage, and the male had to forage for her and their infant; and bipedality was accelerated by the need to carry food. All of these factors, says Lovejoy, primed these hominids for a monogamous mating structure.

Continued female sexual receptivity with concealed ovulation and the development of epigamic characteristics (intersexual selection) pushed humanity further toward monogamy. Lovejoy (1981) noted that man displays a greater elaboration of epigamic adornments than any other primate (e.g., body and facial hair, distinctive somatotypes, conspicuous penis, prominent breasts, etc.), and because these epigamic characteristics are marked in both sexes, their value is cross-sexual, not intrasexual. These adornments show such variability that they are of value in individual recognition, particularly between mates. Lovejoy proposed that such uniqueness plays a major role in the maintenance of pair bonds.

Lovejoy selected intense social behavior as the most likely single cause of the origin of human intelligence. Pair bonding led to direct involvement of males with their offspring, replacing the typical primate matrifocal unit with a bifocal one. The short interbirth intervals made this change necessary. In brief, Lovejoy concluded that the nuclear family can be viewed as an extraordinary adaptation central to the success of early man. Not only does he believe that we are inherently monogamous, but he also believes we are who we are *because* we are monogamous.

The little available data from behavioral primatology on the pygmy chimpanzee *(Pan paniscus)* suggest this species is sometimes monogamous. It is interesting that the polygynous common chimpanzee shows bipedalism only when socially excited, while the pygmy chimpanzee uses bipedalism to view something or to carry food, nest material, or other objects. Food and even water sharing have been seen in this species; and, in other ways (e.g., vestro-ventral copulation) they appear to be more humanlike than the common chimpanzee. The male pygmy chimpanzee is also more active in infant care than is the male common chimpanzee (Patterson, 1979).

In explaining the origins of human monogamy, anthropology and other disciplines have often failed to combine different causative variables. Hunting and gathering, the evolution of the brain, sexual division of labor, sexual dimorphism, concealed ovulation, and other factors are often considered by themselves. Shepher (1978) recommended that we move away from monolithic solutions and linear causality, toward more coordination between primatology and paleoanthropology. We must begin to tie loose ends together in multifactorial analysis.

Whether contemporary people are primarily monogamous or polygynous, they are certainly flexible enough to live in either condition. In fact, humans have extremely wide "tolerance limits" (Kummer, 1971) when it comes to basic changes in mating systems and social structure. As we will see in the next section, dealing primarily with experimental studies of primate family factors, other primates are also quite flexible.

III. EXPERIMENTAL STUDIES OF PRIMATE FAMILIES

As we know, nonhuman primates display a great variety of mating systems: solitary, spatial-harems, monogamous, one-male groups, one-male harem groups, age-graded male groups, and multimale groups. What we have not emphasized is the variety within each of these types. For example, the multimale group of the squirrel monkey is very different from the multimale group of the rhesus macaque. Squirrel monkeys show extreme sexual segregation in adulthood, whereas rhesus macaques do not (Mitchell, 1979). Wrangham (1980), concentrating on multifemale groups, suggested that they fall into two main classes, female-bonded (e.g., langurs) and non-female-bonded (e.g., hamadryas baboons). According to Wrangham, female-bonded groups evolved as a result of female competition for high-quality food patches. Extant primate females in such groups display more female-female alliances, more involvement in the initiation and leading of group movements, and more intergroup interaction than do females in non-female-bonded groups. Female-bonded groups that are nonterritorial contain many males, whereas those that are territorial include only one male. Competition among females is stronger in female-bonded than in non-female-bonded groups. This competition, according to Wrangham, is over feeding. Thus, there is variability within larger groups, and individual selection as well as sexual selection may cause these differences.

Mitchell (1976) and others have emphasized the great variability in infant care shown by nonhuman primate males. Every primate, regardless of gender, has an extremely wide range of behavioral potential (Kuo, 1967), only a small part of which is actually used. Kummer (1971) has also made a plea for increased experimental research to test the tolerance limits of primate behavior. Attempts to classify entire species into monogamous, polygynous, polyandrous, or what have you, can be useful in a heuristic sense but really tell us little about the ontogenetic development (the process) of the pattern in question (see Mason, 1976) or about individual and cultural variability. Primates are remarkably plastic creatures, capable of much more behavior than they may display in one environment, in one troop, in one season. When placed in foreign, novel, or even bizarre environments they often display extraordinary resilience. They have enormous latent behavioral potential (Mitchell, 1976; Mitchell, Arling, & Møller, 1979). It should not surprise us, therefore, that human primates have also been difficult to pigeonhole.

Most of the experimental work on parental behavior in primates has been done on the polygynous rhesus macaque *(Macaca mulatta)*, an Old World, primarily terrestrial monkey that lives in complex multimale groups. However, when free-ranging on an island off Puerto Rico (Cayo Santiago), when in seminatural groups in large outdoor cages, when indoors in "nuclear family" groups, in special playpens and playrooms, or in laboratory dyads, the rhesus macaque has been shown to be capable of a great range of adaptive behavior. The remainder of this chapter will review research showing not only the potential of the rhesus macaque but also the limits to which we can go in dichotomizing or otherwise categorizing *any* primate species into one of two or more mating or family systems.

A. BEHAVIOR OF PARENTS AT BIRTH

On the whole, adult females are more interested in birth than are adult males; however, as might be expected, males of monogamous species exhibit more interest in the birth process than do males of polygynous species because they have greater parental investment. In fact, some male marmosets have been seen assisting the female during her delivery of their infant. The polygynous male squirrel monkey, on the other hand, "retreats" from the birth site and polygynous patas males seem indifferent to birth. Another common finding is that males (even polygynous males) sometimes become sexually excited when a female delivers. This behavior is seen even in those species that do not display rigid postpartum estrus or marked seasonality (Caine & Mitchell, 1979). Rarely is a newborn infant killed or hurt by male or female if the group is stable and the parents have been reared normally (Caine & Mitchell, 1979). Despite their indifference to birth, however, even so-called polygynous males occasionally show warm affection toward infants.

B. PARENTAL EXPERIENCE

Inexperienced monkey mothers are often anxious and awkward. The treatment of firstborn infants varies much more from infant to infant than does treatment of infants born subsequently. Experienced mothers are more relaxed and are more alike in their parenting (Mitchell & Schroers, 1973). Both mothering and fathering are therefore strongly dependent on learning.

C. PEER DEPRIVATION

Infants raised with mothers but with no peers are deprived primarily of play. Later in life, when interacting with strangers and friends, they tend to show more hostility than do peer-raised animals. Dominance relations are not well learned (Alexander, 1966). However, even with this degree of "family" destruction, the animals are capable of reproducing and parenting.

D. MATERNAL DEPRIVATION

Infants reared with peers but with no mother are deprived primarily of nurturance, ventral contact, and huddling. They compensate for this missing ingredient by constantly clinging to one another. As a consequence they, too, end up displaying little play. They are less confident and assertive as they grow older (Chamove, 1966), but they do survive and reproduce.

E. MOTHER-INFANT ATTACHMENT AND SEPARATION

Hansen (1966) described the changing mother-infant affectional system in rhesus macaques. Mother-reared rhesus infants are much more active and outgoing than are infants reared without mothers (Chamove, 1966). Female infants receive more sustained contact from the mother than do male infants and are restrained and retrieved more frequently than males. Males, however, are played with, withdrawn from, and punished more than females. Ventral contact, nipple contact, and sustained embracing decrease and threats and punishment increase with the infant's age (Mitchell, 1979).

A monkey separated from its mother initially protests vigorously and then after 48–72 hours lapses into a behavioral depression in which it displays little activity and sits in a crouched position. Repeated mother-infant separations can have long-term effects on the infant's assertiveness and vocalizations. The direction of these effects is increased vocalization and decreased dominance (see Mitchell, 1979). The effects of separation vary with age. What is surprising is that the infants can survive these repeated separations and sojourns of loneliness and still be capable of reproducing and rearing offspring of their own.

F. PEER-PEER ATTACHMENT AND SEPARATION

In normal peer-peer relations, the frequency of protection, retrieval, and embracing is greatly reduced relative to mother-infant relations. Play is the most prominent activity. The longer two young individuals know each other, the greater the rapport and the more play and affection one sees. Peer-peer separations can also produce protest and depression.

In a study of like-sexed adolescent rhesus macaques, it was found that bonds are specific for an individual friend and persist after a 2-year separation. Female-female bonds were particularly strong after a long separation. Cross-sexed early peer-peer bonds also persist after long separations (Erwin, Maple, Willott, & Mitchell, 1974; Mitchell, Maple, & Erwin, 1979). Monkeys remember their family bonds and friendships over long periods of time.

G. ISOLATION REARING

Raising a primate like the rhesus macaque in social isolation from an early age produces abnormal behavior such as crouching, rocking, fear of novelty, fear of conspecifics, self-directed orality, and self-clasping. Postpubescent abnormalities include abnormal social aggression, self-biting, and bizarre movements (see Mitchell, 1968). As adults, these animals are poor sex partners and even poorer parents (Arling & Harlow, 1967). This is hardly conducive to a normal family situation, but even in these animals therapy has been possible and family life can exist (see Mitchell et al., 1979; Suomi, Harlow, & Novak, 1974).

H. BRUTAL OR INDIFFERENT MOTHERING

Female rhesus macaques raised in social isolation are brutal or indifferent to their firstborn infants and are more inclined toward brutality with male than with female infants. Their behavior toward their infants is usually arbitrary, and they do not protect their infants adequately from external danger. As a result, their offspring, and most notably the males, grow up to be hyperaggressive themselves (Mitchell et al., 1967). These females usually improve with the second infant, and may also improve with age (Arling, Ruppenthal, & Mitchell, 1969).

I. COMMUNICATION IN PARENTING

As rhesus macaques grow older, they vocalize less and use facial expressions more frequently. Young infants rarely show facial expressions, but their mothers frequently do. Females vocalize more frequently than males into adulthood, except in the aggressive vocal categories for which the reverse is true (see Mitchell, 1979). Inexperienced mothers (not isolates) vocalize more than experienced mothers, and so do their infants (Mitchell & Schroers, 1973; Stevens & Mitchell, 1972).

J. ALLOPARENTAL BEHAVIOR IN PREADOLESCENTS

Male rhesus preadolescents are more aggressive toward infants than are their female counterparts, who are quite gentle. Male preparental affection is awkward and rough, though it may be quite playful. Male infants elicit more play and aggression from preadolescents than do female infants. Isolate infants do not elicit as many positive social behaviors (Mitchell et al., 1979). However, both male and female preadolescents do display caregiving behavior.

When preadolescent infant pairs are separated from one another after a bond is established, their response is much like that of the mother-infant dyad. Cross-sexed pairings produce the most noticeable protests at separation (Mitchell et al., 1979).

K. MALE CARE OF INFANTS

Redican, Gomber, and Mitchell (1974) showed that it is possible for polygynous males from a terrestrial species that lives in multimale troops to raise young infants successfully in the absence of their mothers or other troop members. The infants so reared do not show behavioral pathology. Male-to-infant and infant-to-male attachment increases with time and the males become quite protective and extremely playful with their infants. The form of play developed in these dyads is of high intensity and very high frequency. Nothing like it is seen in mother-infant dyads (Redican & Mitchell, 1974). Remarkably, even isolation-reared adult males of this supposedly nonpaternal species can develop strong parental care, play, and protection. They too successfully rear normal infants up to the late juvenile and early preadolescent stage (Redican et al., 1974). Such findings indicate that regardless of how male primates are classified—monogamous or polygynous, paternal or nonpaternal—they are extremely flexible and will do what has to be done when faced with new and even bizarre circumstances.

By way of demonstrating the degree of affection and protection these males display for their infants, we performed separation experiments. We found an increasingly intense attachment over time on the part of the adult males. One adult male bit himself severely moments after he was forcefully separated from his infant. The normal mother's response to a separation from her infant is geared toward retrieval of her offspring. Our males' responses were more likely to be aggression directed toward the experimenter who caused the separation (Mitchell et al., 1979).

L. INTERTAXA ATTACHMENTS AND SEPARATIONS

Primates of different taxa are quite capable of forming attachments for one another. When raised together, a dyad composed of members of different taxa forms strong bonds. Even in adulthood, intertaxa attachment can occur, although it takes longer. The bonds formed between baboons and rhesus macaques in our laboratory are quite like those seen within each species (Maple & Mitchell, 1974). While baboons and macaques are both polygynous, it would be interesting to see what kinds of bonds would occur between so-called polygynous males and monogamous females or monogamous males and polygynous females within the primate order. I would hazard a guess that they would form successful bonds if they lived together in captivity and would even display preferences for their alien friend or mate over their own species (if raised apart from their own). Mason and Kenney (1974) have also shown that attachment can occur late in life and that rhesus macaques can even build up strong bonds for dogs if raised with them. Thus primate affectional systems can withstand enormous malformations in attachment object.

M. PREFERENCE TESTS

Choice tests run on baboon-rhesus dyads have shown that bonds between aliens hold up even when conspecifics are provided as choice objects (Maple & Mitchell, 1974; Mitchell et al., 1979).

Preference tests have also indicated that rhesus macaques like some facial expressions better than others. They avoid the threat face as early as 2 months of age (Sackett, 1965, 1966), and prefer the lip smack in the juvenile period (Redican, Kellicut, & Mitchell, 1971).

Two of the most intriguing preference tests published in the primate literature in recent years are the demonstrations by Sackett and collaborators that likes prefer likes (that is, isolates prefer isolates, normals prefer normals) (Pratt & Sackett, 1967) and kin prefer kin (Wu, Holmes, Medina, & Sackett, 1980). This last preference was shown even when those related did not know each other! We all know that recognition depends on previous experience between individuals but, Wu et al. argue, that does not preclude the possibility that recognition can occur in the absence of experience: ". . . juveniles who disperse before littermate siblings are born or adult males who do not participate in rearing their young might benefit from recognition abilities that are independent of prior association between individuals" (p. 225). Young pigtailed macaques are apparently capable of doing just that. Kin recognition (ostensibly) can and does occur in the absence of prior association with relatives. This, it would appear, makes some of the theoretical differences between monogamy and polygyny less sharp, and the implications for sociobiological theory are enormous. The family means something more than who lives together and who rears whom. If any research area should be followed up, this one surely should be. One burning question in particular springs to mind: If these animals recognize their half-siblings, should they not also be able to recognize themselves? There is no evidence that they do (see Gallup, 1977).

N. SEX DIFFERENCES IN PARENTING

As stated above, male care differs from female care in the polygynous rhesus macaque, in that it contains more play and less ventral contact. This is not necessarily true of other species, particularly monogamous ones. It is certainly true, however, that in most monkeys, if not apes, males are more likely to play than are females, even with younger animals. Rhesus males also have an unfemale protection pattern—they will show aggression towards a threatening source rather than retrieving the infant. In general, males of most primate species are more aggressive than females, but this does not preclude their having potential for gentle paternal care.

O. RHESUS MACAQUES IN "NUCLEAR FAMILIES"

A "nuclear family" apparatus was designed for rhesus macaques at the University of Wisconsin Primate Research Center. As we know, the monogamous nuclear family is not the system typically seen in rhesus macaques in the wild. However, in the laboratory they adapted to this system with little problem. In fact, "persons experienced in raising laboratory rhesus monkeys did not anticipate the peaceful adjustment of the animals to the nuclear family arrangement" (Harlow, 1971, p. 304). Rhesus fathers provided infants with contact comfort when mothers rejected infants, they reciprocated play, and they defended their infants (Suomi, 1972). In short, rhesus macaques reared in such controlled family situations developed strong family bonds (Suomi, Eisele, Grady, & Tripp, 1973)—all of this in a species noted for its aggressive, dominance-oriented, polygynous behavior in a "natural" state (also see Suomi et al., 1974).

IV. EPILOGUE

The laboratory of the primate psychologist and one single species of "polygnous" primate have taught us that there is a surprising potential for behavioral change in male and female primates and in primate families (see Mitchell, 1977, 1979). People should be no easier to categorize and no less flexible than their closest "cousins." From this perspective, it matters little how humans evolved, polygynously or monogamously; they are obviously quite capable of surviving, even thriving, in either family system or, indeed, in both of them.

REFERENCES

Alexander, B. K. *The effects of early peer-deprivation on juvenile behavior of rhesus monkeys.* Unpublished doctoral dissertation, University of Wisconsin—Madison, 1966.
Alexander, R. D., Hoogland, J. L., Howard, R. D., Noonan, K. M., & Sherman, P. W. Sexual dimorphisms and breeding systems in pinnipeds, ungulates, primates and humans. In N. A. Chagnon & W. Irons (Eds.) *Evolutionary biology and human social behavior; an anthropological perspective.* North Scituate, Mass.: Duxbury, 1979.

Arling, G. L., & Harlow, H. F. Effects of social deprivation on maternal behavior of rhesus monkeys. *Journal of Comparative and Physiological Psychology*, 1967, **64**, 371–378.

Arling, G. L., Ruppenthal, G. C., & Mitchell, G. Aggressive behavior of the eight-year-old nulliparous isolate female monkey. *Animal Behaviour*, 1969, **17**, 190–213.

Benshoof, L., & Thornhill, R. The evolution of monogamy and concealed ovulation in humans. *Journal of Social and Biological Structures*, 1979, **2**, 95–106.

Brace, C. L. Biological parameters and pleistocene hominid life-ways. In I. S. Bernstein & E. O. Smith (Eds.), *Primate ecology and human origins*. New York: Garland, 1979.

Burley, N. The evolution of concealed ovulation. *American Naturalist*, 1979, **114**, 835–856.

Caine, N., & Mitchell, G. Behavior of primates present during parturition. In J. Erwin, T. L. Maple, & G. Mitchell (Eds.), *Captivity and behavior: Primates in breeding colonies, laboratories, and zoos*. New York: Van Nostrand Reinhold, 1979.

Campbell, B. Ecological factors and social organization in human evolution. In I. S. Bernstein & E. O. Smith (Eds.), *Primate ecology and human origins*. New York: Garland, 1979.

Chamove, A. S. *The effects of varying infant peer experience on social behavior in the rhesus monkey*. Unpublished masters thesis, University of Wisconsin—Madison, 1966.

Chivers, D. J. The siamang and the gibbon in the Malay peninsula. In R. W. Sussman (Ed.), *Primate ecology: Problem-oriented field studies*. New York: Wiley, 1979.

Crook, J. H., Ellis, J. E., & Goss-Custard, J. D. Mammalian social systems: Structure and function. *Animal Behaviour*, 1976, **24**, 261–274.

Eisenberg, J. F. Habitat, economy, and society: Some correlations and hypotheses for the neotropical primates. In I. S. Bernstein & E. O. Smith (Eds.), *Primate ecology and human origins*. New York: Garland, 1979.

Eisenberg, J. F., Muckenhirn, N. A., & Rudran, R. The relation between ecology and social structure in primates. *Science*, 1972, **176**, 863–874.

Erwin, J., Maple, T. L., Willott, J. F., & Mitchell, G. Persistent peer attachments in rhesus monkeys: Responses to reunion after two years of separation. *Psychological Reports*, 1974, **34**, 1179–1183.

Gallup, G. G. Self-recognition in primates: A comparative approach to the bi-directional properties of consciousness. *American Psychologist*, 1977, **32**, 329–338.

Goss-Custard, J. D., Dunbar, R. I. M., and Aldrich-Blake, F. P. G. Survival, mating and rearing strategies in the evolution of primate social structure. *Folia Primatologica*, 1972, **17**, 1–19.

Hansen, E. W. The development of maternal and infant behavior in the rhesus monkey. *Behaviour*, 1966, **27**, 107–149.

Harlow, M. K. Nuclear family apparatus. *Behavior Research Methods and Instrumentation*, 1971, **3**, 301–304.

Hladik, C. M. Ecology, diet, and social patterning in old and new world primates. In R. W. Sussman (Ed.), *Primate ecology: Problem-oriented field studies*. New York: Wiley, 1979.

Kleiman, D. G. Monogamy in mammals. *Quarterly Review of Biology*, 1977, **52**, 39–69.

Kummer, H. *Primate societies: Group techniques of ecological adaptation*. Chicago: Aldine, 1971.

Kuo, Z. Y. *The dynamics of behavior development: An epigenetic view*. New York: Random House, 1967.

Leibowitz, L. *Females, males, families: A biosocial approach*. North Scituate, Mass.: Duxbury, 1978.

Leutenegger, W. Monogamy in Callitrichids: A consequence of phyletic dwarfism? *International Journal of Primatology*, 1980, **1**, 95–98.

Lovejoy, C. O. The origin of man. *Science*, 1981, **211**, 341–350.

McGrew. Personal communication, 1982.

Maple, T. L., & Mitchell, G. Behavioral responses to separation in interspecific pairs of baboons and macaques. *American Zoologist*, 1974, **14**, 224.

Mason, W. A. Primate social behavior: Pattern and process. In R. B. Masterson et al. (Eds.), *Evolution of brain and behavior in vertebrates*. Hillsdale, N.J.: Erlbaum, 1976.

Mason, W. A., & Kenney, M. D. Redirection of filial attachments in rhesus monkeys: Dogs as mother surrogates. *Science*, 1974, **183**, 1209–1211.

Mitchell, G. Persistent behavior pathology in rhesus monkeys following early social isolation. *Folia Primatologica*, 1968, **8**, 132–147.

Mitchell G. Attachment potential in rhesus macaque dyads *(Macaca mulatta)*: A sabbatical report. *JSAS Catalog of Selected Documents in Psychology*, 1976, **6** (Ms. No. 1177).

Mitchell, G. Parental behavior in nonhuman primates. In J. Money & H. Musaph (Eds.), *Handbook of sexology*. New York: Excerpta Medica, 1977.

Mitchell, G. *Behavioral sex differences in nonhuman primates*. New York: Van Nostrand Reinhold, 1979.

Mitchell, G., Arling, G. L., & Møller, G. W. Long-term effects of maternal punishment on the behavior of monkeys. *Psychonomic Science*, 1967, **8**, 109–210.

Mitchell, G., Maple, T. L., & Erwin, J. Development of social attachment potential in captive rhesus monkeys. In J. Erwin, T. L. Maple, & G. Mitchell (Eds.), *Captivity and behavior*. New York: Van Nostrand Reinhold, 1979.

Mitchell, G., & Schroers, L. Birth order and parental experience in monkeys and man. In H. W. Reese (Ed.), *Advances in child development and behavior*. (Vol. 8). New York: Academic Press, 1973.

Morris, D. *The naked ape*. New York: Dell, 1967.

Nagel, U. Social organization in a baboon hybrid zone. *Proceedings of the Third International Congress of Primatology*, 1970, **3**, 48–57.

Paterson, J. D. Ecologically differentiated patterns of aggressive and sexual behavior in two troops of Ugandan baboons, *Papio anubis*. *American Journal of Physical Anthropology*, **38**, 641–647.

Patterson, T. The behavior of a group of captive pygmy chimpanzees *(Pan paniscus)*. *Primates*, 1979, **20**, 341–354.

Pratt, C. L., & Sackett, G. P. Selection of social partners as a function of peer contact during rearing. *Science*, 1967, **155**, 1133–1135.

Ralls, K. Mammals in which females are larger than males. *Quarterly Review of Biology*, 1976, **51**, 245–276.

Redican, W. K., Gomber, J., & Mitchell, G. Adult male parental behavior in feral and isolation-reared rhesus monkeys *(Macaca mulatta)*. In J. H. Cullen, (Ed.), *Experimental behaviour: A basis for the study of mental disturbance*. Dublin: Irish University Press, 1974.

Redican, W. K., Kellicutt, M. H., & Mitchell, G. Preference for facial expressions in rhesus monkeys. *Developmental Psychology*, 1971, **5**, 539.

Redican, W. K., & Mitchell, G. Play between adult male and infant rhesus monkeys. *American Zoologist*, 1974, **14**, 295–302.

Sackett, G. P. Effects of rearing conditions upon the behavior of rhesus monkeys *(Macaca mulatta)*. *Child Development*, 1965, **36**, 855–868.

Sackett, G. P. Monkeys reared in isolation with pictures as visual input: Evidence for an innate releasing mechanism. *Science*, 1966, **154**, 1468–1472.

Shepher, J. Reflections on the origin of the human pair-bond. *Journal of Social and Biological Structures*, 1978, **1**, 253–264.

Stevens, C. W., & Mitchell, G. Birth-order effects, sex differences and sex preferences in the peer-directed behavior of rhesus infants. *International Journal of Psychobiology*, 1972, **2**, 117–128.

Suomi, S. J. Social development of rhesus monkeys reared in an enriched laboratory environment. *Abstracts of the Twentieth International Congress of Psychology*. Tokyo: Japan Science Press, 1972.

Suomi, S. J., Eisele, C. D., Grady, S. A., & Tripp, R. L. Social preferences of monkeys reared in an enriched laboratory social environment. *Child Development*, 1973, **44**, 451–460.

Suomi, S. J., Harlow, H. F., & Novak, M. R. Reversal of social deficits produced by isolation rearing in monkeys. *Journal of Human Evolution*, 1974, **3**, 527–534.

Swindler, D. R. A synopsis of primate phylology. In J. S. Lockard (Ed.), *The evolution of human social behavior*. New York: Elsevier, 1980.

Symons, D. *The evolution of human sexuality*. New York: Oxford University Press, 1979.

Tanner, N., & Zihlman, A. Women in evolution, I: Innovation and selection in human origins. *Signs: Journal of Women in Culture and Society*, 1976, **1**, 585–608.

Wallace, R. A. *Animal behavior: Its development, ecology, and evolution*. Santa Monica, Calif.: Goodyear, 1979.

Wilson, E. O. *Sociobiology: The new synthesis*. Cambridge, Mass.: Harvard University Press, Belknap Press, 1975.

Wittenberger, J. F., & Tilson, R. L. The evolution of monogamy: Hypothesis and evidence. *Annual Review of Ecological Systems*, 1980, **11**, 197–323.

Wrangham, R. W. An ecological model of female-bonded primate groups. *Behaviour*, 1980, **75**, 262–300.

Wu, H. M. H., Holmes, W. G., Medina, S. R., & Sackett, G. P. Kin preference in infant *Macaca nemestrina*. *Nature*, 1980, **285**, 225–227.

3 Psychological Perspectives of the Family

IRVING E. SIGEL
Educational Testing Service
ALBERT S. DREYER
University of Connecticut
ANN V. McGILLICUDDY-DeLISI
Educational Testing Service

OVERVIEW

The notion that the family functions as a critical socialization agent for the child has been widely endorsed, yet only recently has there been perceptible movement in psychological research toward viewing the family as a complex unit. Much contemporary psychological research on the significance of the family for child development has its conceptual roots in psychoanalytic and behavioral theory. Given theoretical assumptions about the mother's paramount influence on the child, it is not surprising that the mother-child dyad has been the most frequent unit of study. This is dramatically evident in Martin's (1975) review of the psychological literature on parent-child relations. Martin presented a comprehensive description of parent behaviors found to be related to children's attachment, independence, achievement, and aggression. Studies cited generally focus on mother's warmth, sensitivity, and patterns of acceptance or rejection, reported to be related to children's positive adjustment. Such an emphasis has contributed greatly to understanding one important segment of the child's family history—the child's relationship with his or her mother.

More recently, some researchers have shifted their investigations to another relationship within the family unit—namely, the father-child dyad (Lamb, 1976b; Parke, 1979; Pedersen, Yarrow, Anderson, & Cain, 1979).

This review covers literature published and in press as of June 1981. We wish to acknowledge with heartfelt thanks the valuable assistance of the following colleagues: Dr. Candice Feiring for her valuable comments, Ann Jungeblut for her editorial contributions, Sheila Kraft for her bibliographical research, and Linda Kozelski and Betty Clausen for help in typing. The current affiliation of Ann V. McGillicuddy-DeLisi is William Paterson College, Wayne, New Jersey.

The research paradigm employed has been essentially the same as that used in exploring mother-child relations but, as we shall see, some comparisons between mother-child and father-child interactions have been reported (Lamb, 1977a; Lewis & Weinraub, 1974). Relatively few psychological studies, however, have extended investigation to triadic relationships among both parents and the child or to the family unit as a whole, including siblings (Lewis & Feiring, in press; McGillicuddy-DeLisi, 1982b; Sigel, 1982).

Three factors may account for the apparent reluctance of researchers to investigate family processes. First, the primary interest of developmental psychologists has been to understand antecedent experiences in the light of particular child outcomes—that is, the dependent variables of interest are child characteristics such as IQ and prosocial behavior. The most widely used research methodologies and analyses are appropriate for dyadic (and possible triadic) data and the research paradigm focuses on linear predictions. The inclusion of additional participants in a study generates data sets that increase the difficulty of analysis and interpretation, and many researchers are not prepared to cope with this complexity. However, the difficulty is compounded by the sorts of questions psychologists typically ask. We are used to asking questions that deal with causal linkages between parent variables and child outcomes—and this points to the second reason for the state of psychological research on the family. While most studies eschew direct statements of causality, they are obviously directed toward establishing causal linkages between familial agents of socialization and child outcomes—the literature is replete with words like "impact" and "influence" when, strictly speaking, "associated with" and "related to" would be more accurate.

A third reason why the influence of the family context has been minimized can be traced, we contend, to heavy emphasis on the study of individual differences and, specifically, the ways in which the family environment and behaviors of individual family members affect the child. The individual difference approach requires specification of the relationships among variables to help account for variability among children. Such an individual difference emphasis differs markedly from the methodologies of other disciplines, such as sociology, that seek to study the family as a developed or developing system. Therefore, the research questions concern the processes that maintain the family as a dynamic organization (Hill & Mattessich, 1979; Kantor & Lehr, 1975).

Nevertheless, during the past few years new perspectives on the study of the family have appeared in the psychological literature. The focus continues to be on individual differences in child outcomes resulting from experiences within the family context, but changes in the conceptual framework of family processes and functions are noted, as well as changes in the family members selected for study, the methodology used to study family influences on individual members, and the content or domain of development that is subject to study.

One example of these changes, mentioned earlier, is the concerted effort to examine the father-child dyad. Focus on the social network within which the child develops—a social reality for all children—has only recently been incorporated into developmental psychological research (Cochran & Brassard, 1979; Feiring & Lewis, 1978; Lewis & Feiring, 1982; Powell, 1983). The role of siblings in child development has also received more attention. Investigators have studied family size, child spacing, and birth order in an attempt to describe the ways in which child outcomes vary with differences in the sibling structure of the family (Dunn & Kendrick, 1980; Sutton-Smith & Rosenberg, 1970). Moreover, research has been undertaken to examine how siblings interact and how sibling interactions are related to the mother's interaction with the targeted child (Cicirelli, 1977). Work is now available that encourgages better understanding of family processes and the manner in which individual family members affect relationships between other family members (Kantor & Lehr, 1975; McGillicuddy-DeLisi, 1982a; Reiss, 1981; Sameroff & Feil, 1981; Sigel, 1982; Sigel, McGillicuddy-DeLisi, & Johnson, 1980).

As we have noted, the earlier unidirectional perspectives on parent-child relationships are readily explained by the importance given to the role of the mother as the major source of influence on the child and of individual differences in child outcomes. Psychological research literature is beginning, however, to reflect an awareness of the oversimplification in such unidimensional models and the limitations of fragmenting the family into artificial units to simplify analyses for research purposes (Bell & Harper, 1977; Lerner & Spanier, 1978). Many researchers now agree that children and parents influence each other, and to further this perspective new models of reciprocal or mutual influences operating among family members are being proposed (Clark-Stewart & Hevey, 1981; Martin, Maccoby, Baran, & Jacklin, 1981; Sigel, McGillicuddy-Delisi, Flaugher, & Rock, 1983).

In addition, data analysis techniques are being adopted and adapted from other fields, such as economics and sociology, as alternative means of testing the new models. As psychological researchers face the challenges of new methodologies and become aware of the importance of context in social interactions, attention is shifting from the laboratory to the home (Carew, 1980; Clarke-Stewart, 1978; Lewis & Feiring, 1982). While not a new issue (Bronfenbrenner, 1977), comparison of laboratory and home environments is currently being reinterpreted in terms of ecosystem analyses or situational effects. This approach avoids the artificiality of the laboratory and demonstrates the role of context as an additional influence on behavior (Borduin & Henggeler, 1981). New procedures such as remote control television (Lewis & Feiring, 1982) and new observational procedures are being developed (Carew, 1980).

The broadening perspective on the family unit not only refocuses attention on family processes in the home environment but also has sparked interest in the management of the daily lives of families (Patterson, 1980). Although researchers tend to work with young parents and their children, there has been some interest in studying parent-child relationships at later ages in an attempt to determine the effect of family life on parents' own development (Troll, 1971; Troll & Smith, 1976). The family unit is viewed as an important source of influence for social, emotional, cognitive, and language development. This may indicate that interest in the family has broadened across the various domains of developmental psychology; certainly there is an increase in *shared* interest in the family (Belsky, 1981). Nevertheless, widening the domains of interest in developmental study has not conclusively shifted the family as a unit to a more central position. Much current research, as we shall see, is still directed to dyadic interactions and ignores the influence of the family unit.

Admittedly, we lack an overall theoretical psychological framework within which to view family processes; but we nevertheless have a rich body of knowledge about certain aspects of the child's development—in particular, socioemotional, cognitive, and language development—and the effects on development of certain family processes.

THE CHILD'S SOCIOEMOTIONAL DEVELOPMENT

Over the past 5 years, the emotional bond that develops between parent and child—referred to as *attachment*—has formed a major theme for much of the psychological research into family interaction and children's socioemotional development. A related theme that pervades the attachment literature is that of *mutual responsiveness*—sensitive responsiveness on the part of both the parent and the child (Bakeman & Brown, 1980; Field, Widmayer, Stringer, & Ignatoff, 1980; Hunt & Paraskevopoulos, 1980; Rutter, 1979). Finally, a number of studies focus on variables that mediate parental sensitivity to respond in dyadic interactions, for example, parental attitudes, perceptions, beliefs, and attributions (Brazelton, Koslowski, & Main, 1974). Other complex arrays of child and family variables, such as the child's temperament (Thomas & Chess, 1977); sex (Parke & O'Leary, 1975); birth order (Lewis & Kreitzberg, 1979); state (Korner,

1974); and responsiveness to tactile, visual, and auditory stimuli (Osofsky, 1976), have also been reported as influencing parent-child relationships.

The attachment construct provides the critical link between parental responsiveness and children's socioemotional development. Attachment—defined as a relatively enduring emotional bond to a specific other person (Maccoby, 1980; Sroufe, 1979)—is a key construct integrating the affective and cognitive aspects of development within the social domain. The attachment relationship seems to have important consequences for later adaptation and development (Matas, Arend, & Sroufe, 1978). Ainsworth, Blehar, Waters, and Wall (1978) have identified three major patterns of attachment during the child's second year. Sroufe and Waters (1977) have demonstrated stable individual differences in quality of attachment in these patterns of behavioral organization. These major patterns are: securely attached, insecurely attached avoidant, and attachment resistant. A *securely attached* child can separate readily from a caregiver to explore when stress is minimal. During the caregiver's or mother's absence, play is considerably reduced and the child is clearly distressed. With the mother's return, the child seeks and maintains contact until comforted and then resumes play. The *insecurely attached* infant may *avoid* the mother when she returns after a brief separation and can be comforted as easily by a stranger as by the mother. The *resistant* type of child is one who is insecurely attached and has difficulty using the mother as a secure base for exploration. The child tends to be fussy and wary in novel situations. On reunion, resistant children simultaneously seek contact with the mother while resisting interaction with her.

The research literature on parent-child attachment deals primarily with infants, but there have been recent efforts (Arend, Gove, & Sroufe, 1979; Waters, Wippman, & Sroufe, 1979) to link early parent-child attachment to later developmental outcomes in the child. While studies of parent-infant interactions have emphasized the attachment phenomenon, studies of the influence of family interaction on the social development of older, school-aged children have typically focused on the development of prosocial behavior—moral thinking, altruism, friendship, and the like. In contrast to investigations of parent-child affect through face-to-face interaction, there have been several recent efforts to examine children's socioemotional development in relation to processes among various family members—the effects of siblings on children's development, the effects of siblings on the parent-child relationship, and, the effects of one parent or the marital relationship on the other parent's relationship with the child. Thus, the current psychological research literature will be examined under the main categories of parent-child relationships (dyadic, triadic, and dyad comparisons), prosocial behaviors, and more complex family processes.

PARENT-CHILD RELATIONSHIPS

Because attachment is no doubt related to early caregiver-infant interaction and because the mother is most frequently the early caregiver, studies of mother-child relationships continue to dominate the literature. Osofsky and Connors (1979) speak of the "synchrony" or "match" of maternal characteristics and infant characteristics necessary to foster an adaptive relationship, and they hold that the sensitive responsiveness between mother and child is mediated, either directly or indirectly, by such synchrony. Growing awareness that the infant's own early responsiveness may influence the parent's behavior led Maccoby (1980) to ask, "Would a given mother have developed a more responsive pattern with a more responsive infant? Perhaps some infants invite and others resist the maternal behavior that leads to attachment" (p. 91). Indeed, there are data suggesting that the infant's own behaviors are important determinants of the type of attachment relationships that will develop with the mother. For example, Ainsworth et al. (1978) report that during the first quarter of life, those infants later classified as resistant cried for longer periods than did other infants. They also showed fewer positive responses and more negative responses to being picked up and put down. Infants later classified as resistant were less active in early interactions with others. It is likely that caregivers' behaviors vary in reaction to differences in infant behavior and that patterns of interaction affecting the development of the attachment relationship are therefore affected by the infant's own early behaviors.

Moreover, the sensitive responsiveness of the caregiver also appears to play a major role in the *nature* of the attachment. Mothers of securely attached babies have been reported to be more responsive to infant signals than mothers of insecurely attached infants (Ainsworth et al., 1978; Clarke-Stewart, 1973). Ainsworth et al. (1978) found that mothers of avoidant babies show a deep-seated aversion to close bodily contact and were more rejecting, angry, and restricted in their expression of affect than were other mothers. A report by Waters, Vaughn, and Egeland (1980) alerts us to the knotty problem of the interaction between "built-in" differences in temperament and maternal behaviors. Children classified as resistant at year 1 appear to have been constitutionally "difficult" newborns as indicated by scores on the Brazelton Neonatal Assessment Scale. Waters and his colleagues suggest that Ainsworth et al.'s (1978) characterization of mothers with resistant, insecurely attached infants as unskilled in holding, face-to-face interaction, and feeding is consistent with the notion that their infants were difficult—more difficult to teach interactive behaviors to and, perhaps, more difficult to learn from as well. If the mother's own personality characteristics or life situations make it difficult for her to be sensitively responsive to infant cues, such a baby is highly likely to form an insecure attachment.

The quality of these early attachment relationships appears to lay the foundation for subsequent personal-social development. Matas et al. (1978), for example, found evidence that infants classified as securely attached as toddlers were more enthusiastic, persistent, and affectively positive at 2 years of age. They were more responsive to mothers' suggestions and less oppositional than children who had been classified as insecurely attached infants. Children in the insecurely attached group either ignored or rejected adult direction, became frustrated easily, and did not seek help on problems when it was clearly needed. Subsequently, these patterns of infant adaptation have been shown to have developmental consequences beyond the mother's sphere. Waters et al. (1979) found that children who were rated as securely attached at 15 months scored higher on scales measuring peer competence and ego strength/effectance at 3½ years of age than children classified as insecurely attached. Arend et al. (1979) found that children classified as securely attached at 18 months were higher on ego resiliency (Block & Block, 1980) on both laboratory and teacher rating composites at 4–5 years. They were also described as moderate in ego control—neither rigid nor impulsive in degree of control. In contrast, children who earlier had been classified as avoidant and as resistant were significantly lower in ego resiliency, with avoidant types tending to be overcontrolled at the preschool age and resistant types undercontrolled. Thus, an effective mother-child relationship seems to be associated with flexible resourcefulness at 4 and 5 years of age. Similarly, at the preschool level Emmerich (1977) found that, among low-income families, children of highly controlling mothers—especially boys—became less well adapted to preschool settings over time.

Ainsworth summarizes the attachment research presented in this section as follows:

> It is clear that the nature of an infant's attachment to his or her mother as a 1-year-old is related both to earlier interaction with the mother and to various aspects of later development. The implication is that the way in which the infant organizes his or her behavior toward the mother affects the way in which he or she organizes behavior toward other aspects of the environment, both animate and inanimate. This organization provides a core of continuity in development. . . . This is not to insist that the organization of attachment is fixed in the first year of life and is insensitive to marked changes in maternal behavior to relevant life events occurring later on. Nor is it implied that attachment to figures other than the mother are unimportant as sup-

plementing or compensating for anxieties in infant-mother attachment—although too little is yet known about how various attachments related together to influence the way in which infants organize their perception and approach the world. [Ainsworth, 1979, p. 936]

Father-Child Relationship

The previous section dealt solely with research concerning the mother-child relationship during the first few years of the child's life. In 1977, Lamb asserted that studies of the father's role in the socioemotional life of his child no longer simply address the issue whether the father-infant relationship exists, but rather, attempt to explore what type of relationship it is (Lamb, 1977b). Most studies of fathers are derived from the same theoretical assumptions that guided investigations of the mother-child relationship. That is, evaluations of the attachment that develops between fathers and children have been conducted in much the same manner as with the mother-child dyad. However, comparisons of the two sets of dyads are now possible, and this has led a number of investigators to describe factors present or absent in each parent's behaviors that appear to influence the relationship and patterns, which appear to vary between the two dyads.

Studies completed in the early 1970s focused on the extent to which infants become attached to fathers as well as mothers. As Lamb's statement indicates, children aged 21–24 months were consistently found to prefer *either* mothers or fathers to strangers (Kotelchuck, 1976; Kotelchuck, Zelazo, Kagan, & Spelke, 1975; Ross, Kagan, Zelazo, & Kotelchuck, 1975; Spelke, Zelazo, Kagan, & Kotelchuck, 1973). In her naturalistic observations of children 12–30 months of age, Clarke-Stewart (1978) found that children's proximal attachment with mothers and with fathers were very similar when the time each parent was available was controlled.

Investigations of infants' preferences for one parent over another have not yielded such consistent findings, however. A variety of factors, such as social context, age and sex of the child, and the choice of dependent variables assessed, apparently influence the findings of such studies. For example, infants over 12 months of age have evidenced preferences for mothers over fathers in proximity-seeking behavior in laboratory situations (Cohen & Campos, 1974; Feldman & Ingham, 1975; Kotelchuck, 1976). On the other hand, Lamb's (1977a) home observations of 7–8-month and 12–13-month infants indicated no preferences for either parent in attachment behaviors, including proximity seeking. The infants did, however, evidence more *affiliative* behaviors (e.g., smile, look, vocalization) towards fathers than towards mothers. In a follow-up study, when the children were 15–24 months old, Lamb (1977b) reports that not only more affiliative but also more attachment behaviors were directed toward fathers than toward mothers. Apparently, the sex of the child was an important factor, however. Nearly all of the boys came to show preferences for fathers over the course of the year on the attachment measure. The findings for girls were less consistent—some preferred their mothers, some their fathers. Thus, in the nonstressful environment of the home, the development of patterns of attachment appear to be contingent upon the age and sex of the child.

If the laboratory is considered a more stressful and unfamiliar setting than the home, some discrepancies in preferences for mothers versus fathers can be interpreted in the light of the social context of the interaction. For example, Lamb (1976a, 1976c) found that 12- and 18-month-olds did show a preference for mothers over fathers under moderately stressful circumstances in the laboratory. However, in stress-free episodes in the laboratory, Lamb's sample either showed no preference for either parent or a slight preference for fathers. This finding is discrepant with those of the three laboratory studies cited earlier (Cohen & Campos, 1974; Feldman & Ingham, 1975; Kotelchuck, 1976), in that children over 12 months evidenced a preference for mothers over fathers in laboratory assessments.

To summarize, infants respond similarly to mothers and to fathers in preference to strangers. The degree of preference for mothers versus fathers appears to vary with several factors, including the stressfulness of the situation, the social context, and the age and sex of the infant. There have been many reports of differences in the ways mothers and fathers interact with their children. Father-infant interactions tend to be more physical, less vocal, and less involved with toys than mothers' play behaviors (Clarke-Stewart, 1978, 1980; Lamb, 1976b, 1977c, 1980; Lynn & Cross, 1974; Parke, 1979; Parke & O'Leary, 1975). The robust findings of differences between fathers' and mothers' behaviors with their infants has led investigators to look at the ways in which the determinants of infant attachment to the father are different from those in the development of the mother-child attachment.

First, mothers are apparently much more involved in caretaking functions than fathers, but extensive involvement in physical care does not seem necessary to the development of the attachment relationship (Kotelchuck, 1976; Lamb, 1977a, Parke & Sawin, 1980). Second, mothers and fathers differ in the amount of time spent with the infant, but sheer quantity of time is a poor predictor of whether or not a relationship will be formed (Clarke-Stewart, 1978; Lamb, 1978b). It is generally agreed that it is the quality of the interaction when the parent and infant are together that is vital. Whether a mother or a father, the parent who responds contingently and appropriately to the infant's signals and who initiates interaction that is appropriate to the baby's current state is most likely to facilitate the development of secure parent-infant attachments (Parke & Sawin, 1980).

The Development of Prosocial Behavior

The rubric "prosocial" includes the cluster of behaviors involved with positive social behavior. Conceptually, prosocial behavior is usually defined as any activity undertaken for the well-being of others (Bryant & Crockenberg, 1980; Staub, 1979). Prosocial behaviors can take many and varied forms such as comforting, sharing, helping, defending, rescuing, cooperating, and the like. In addition, the amount of sacrifice demanded from the actor and the motives for such behavior also vary. For example, the motive may be selfish, as when a person helps or shares with another in the hope of being rewarded for acting prosocially. Cooperation, as Bryant and Crockenberg (1980) point out, by definition involves the expectation either of reciprocity or of direct benefit to self. Or the motive may be altruistic, if the only purpose of the actor is to benefit someone else (Hoffman, 1975; Staub, 1979). Prosocial behavior, it should be noted, even when it has a selfish purpose, still may have social value since the person is indeed acting prosocially rather than by antisocial means such as instrumental aggression. We will consider the relation between prosocial and antisocial behavior in some of the work that follows.

Research on moral development initially involved concerns for the internalization of societal norms and, therefore, the role of parents was the primary focus of the research (Hoffman, 1970). Research in this area has recently expanded to include peers and the mass media. It now also includes cognitive elements as well as the arousal of affects such as empathy and guilt. Because of the complexity of the area, the directions the research has taken, and the constraints we have placed on the literature review, the number of studies concerned with prosocial behavior and psychological aspects of the family are limited. After summarizing briefly the role of parents in the development of prosocial behavior, we will present, in rough chronological order by age of the target child, the research done since 1974 on prosocial behavior as it develops in the family context.

Several parenting dimensions are held to be related to the development of prosocial behavior. First, a nurturant parent-child relationship seems basic (Hoffman, 1970, 1977, 1978; Staub, 1975, 1979; Yarrow, Scott, & Waxler, 1973). Presumably, parental affection and nurturance contribute to prosocial behavior because when the child's signals of need are met responsively, the child feels secure, self-concern is minimized, a positive affective orientation toward people is created, and the child identifies with and imitates the prosocial parent. Next, inductive discipline techniques that point up the relationship between the child's behavior and the feelings of others have been considered important in stimulating prosocial behavior (Hoffman, 1970; Hoffman & Saltzstein, 1967; Staub, 1979). Hoffman (1963) also found that affective (empathic) sensitivities to the feelings of others are related to prosocial behaviors. Children who feel what others are feeling are presumably better able to judge when help or comfort is needed. Presumably, also, parental behaviors that relate to the expression and awareness of feelings would relate also to manifestation of empathy (Feshbach, 1975) and thereby be associated with prosocial behavior. Finally, modeling and reinforcement of prosocial behavior (Staub, 1971; Yarrow et al., 1973) have been suggested as factors likely to facilitate children's prosocial behaviors.

The research up until the mid-1970s suggests, then, that parenting behaviors that facilitate prosocial behaviors in children are nurturance, maternal responsiveness, inductive control techniques, discussion and acceptance of feelings, and reinforcement and modeling of prosocial behavior.

Let us turn now to the research that has been done in the last 5 years or so on prosocial behavior as it develops in the family context. As Hay (1979) indicates, long before they are faced with deliberate moral training, young children act in ways resembling the prosocial behavior of older persons. Children in the first 3 years of life, for example, have been found to share with (Rheingold, Hay, & West, 1976), and minister to the distress of (Hoffman, 1975), their companions. Sharing most often has been investigated in experimental studies of school-aged children (reviewed by Bryan, 1975; Rushton, 1976), with some observational reports of sharing in the preschool classroom (Yarrow & Waxler, 1976). Rheingold et al. (1976) demonstrated that 18-month-old children characteristically shared and gave objects to their mothers and fathers as well as to unfamiliar persons. Infants have also been reported to share with siblings (Lamb, 1978a) and peers (Eckerman, Whatley, & Kutz, 1975; Ross & Goldman, 1977).

The study by Hay (1979) was designed to document the early manifestations of cooperation and sharing displayed by 12-, 18-, and 24-month-old children in interaction with their parents in a play setting. Early forms of sharing were present by 12 months of age but were displayed increasingly more often by 18- and 24-month-old children. The relation of these activities to later sharing and cooperation is, as yet, unclear but is seen by Hay as providing opportunities for prosocial learning.

Zahn-Waxler, Radke-Yarrow, and King (1979) studied children 1½–2½ years old to study behaviors directed toward victims of distress in relation to maternal rearing behavior. Their measurement procedure involved training the mothers of these children to act as observers. Their results indicated that the mothers' explanations of the distress their children had caused to others was related to their children's altruistic behavior (e.g., physical and verbal sympathy). These explanations were associated with the children's altruism even when they were bystanders to another's distress. In addition, empathic caregiving by the mothers was positively associated with children's altruistic behavior.

The prototype that emerges from Zahn-Waxler et al. (1979) of the mother whose child is reparative and altruistic, is of a mother whose communications are of high intensity and clarity both cognitively and emotionally when her child transgresses. They present a picture of an array of maternal influences converging on the child with messages concerning what is expected in socially responsible behavior. The emotional stimulus is highlighted, for example: "Look what you did!" Her demands are strongly stated in a close one-to-one disciplinary encounter. She is also a model of altruism in the caregiving of her child. The effective induction techniques are not calmly dispersed but, rather, are emotionally imposed. These techniques exist side by side with empathic caregiving, and the nurturance is considered to be an important condition of the disciplinary techniques. In summary, Zahn-Waxler et al. (1979) hypothesize that what is being taught by the mothers is a basic orientation to others.

After these studies of very young children and their mothers, other relevant studies omit intervening ages and involve much older children and their families. Bryant and Crockenberg (1980), for example, investigated the maternal, sibling, and situational correlates of prosocial behavior between older siblings. Fifty mothers were videotaped with their first- and later-born daughters in a seminaturalistic game-playing setting. The firstborn daughters were in the fourth or fifth grades (mean age was 10-5) and their sisters were 2 or 3 years younger (mean age 7-11). Of particular importance was their finding of a positive relationship between a mother's responsiveness to her child's expressed needs and infrequent anitsocial and frequent prosocial interaction among her children. This is congruent with the Hoffman (1976) position that having one's own self-concerns taken care of increases the ability to express concern for others.

Several other studies with older children and adolescents provide support for some or all of the elements in the proposition that altruistic behavior is positively related to having mothers who themselves are altruistic, who use victim-centered discipline techniques, and who are affectionate and nurturant (Bar-Tal, Nadler, & Blechman, 1980; Eisenberg-Berg & Mussen, 1978; Gutkin, 1975; Hoffman, 1975; Hower & Edwards, 1979; Parikh, 1980).

What seems to be characteristic of the current work on prosocial behavior are attempts to integrate the complex processes involved (Hoffman, 1979; Hogan, Johnson, & Emler, 1978). Hogan et al. (1978), for example, see rule attunement (through secure attachment), social sensitivity (empathy), and, in addition, self-awareness (autonomy) as central processes involved in moral development. Hoffman (1979) has also been much concerned with a developmental theory of empathy that involves affective arousal and cognitive elements. He presumes that the socialization antecedents of the elements he proposes differ and asserts that close observations of children's behavioral, cognitive, and affective responses to a socialization agent are necessary. Hoffman also suggests the need for designs to assess causal relations with respect to moral development. The Zahn-Waxler et al. (1979) study is identified as a feasible procedure for studying the complex interactions of affect and cognition in moral development.

PROCESSES BETWEEN FAMILY MEMBERS AFFECTING CHILDREN'S
SOCIOEMOTIONAL DEVELOPMENT

The importance of relationships other than the parent-child dyad in the child's development has been largely neglected in psychological studies to date. There is, however, increased attention to other family members and to ways in which a relationship between two family members might affect a third member.

Both the birth order and sex of the children appear to affect the nature of interactions between siblings. For example, Dunn and Kendrick (1979) report that interactions between same-sex siblings are more positive than interactions between brother and sister. Their observations of siblings do suggest that siblings have a significant impact on children's social knowledge. Through the teaching, cooperation, helping, and affection that occurs during interactions with siblings, children apparently develop such skills as role taking. Sutton-Smith and Rosenberg (1970) have reported that with regard to interests, brothers have greater affect on sisters and vice versa than is the case with the same-sex siblings. Siblings also appear to affect children's sex role development, in that second-born children tend to be similar to their older siblings, either male or female, in sex role attributes (Sutton-Smith & Rosenberg, 1970).

Some inferences about effects of siblings have been based on a contrast between only children and those with siblings. Falbo (1979) has warned that such inferences must be guarded as it may be that, in addition to the presence or absence of siblings, the parents of an only child differ from parents with more than one child. Parents of an only child have been found to hold different beliefs about children than parents of more than one child (McGillicuddy-DeLisi & Sigel, 1982) and parental behaviors have also been shown to vary with number, spacing, and birth order of the child. These differences in parent behavior that occur with family constellation are not simply due to the addition of a new dyad. Rather, previously established dyadic relationships appear to be altered. For example, Dunn and Kendrick (1980) found that not only does amount of maternal attention toward the firstborn decrease with the birth of a sibling, but negative confrontations and the child's role in initiating interactions with the mother increase. In additon, the decrease in attention to the firstborn child did not occur during periods when the mother was occupied with the new baby, but during periods when she was not involved in infant caregiving functions (Dunn & Kendrick, 1980). Thus, the introduction of a new member into the family apparently affects the established relationship between other family members.

In addition to siblings' direct effects on the parent–other sibling relationship, other dyadic and triadic relationships in the family unit may affect the child indirectly. For example, Parke (1979) has represented the forms that parents' effects on children may take (Fig. 1). Direct effects are those influences that occur through face-to-face interaction with the child as indicated under A. Note, however, that the father may affect the child by changing the mother-child interaction pattern, or vice versa (see Bi). Provision of economic, emotional, and physical support for the mother may alter the quantity and quality of her interaction with the child. The father's attitudes, beliefs or behaviors toward the child may affect, positively or negatively, the mother's own attitudes and behaviors (see Bii). The marital relationship itself may also affect the infant (see Biv). Husband-wife conflict has been related to higher levels of parental expressions of negative affect to their infant and the degree of discrepancy between mothers' and fathers' perceptions of the child's temperament have been related to differential parental behaviors toward the infant (Pederson, Anderson, & Cain, 1980). The relationship, furthermore, is not unidirectional, since a number of studies have demonstrated that the birth of a child alters the husband-wife relationship (Cowan, Cowan, Coie, & Coie, 1978; Hoffman & Manis, 1978; Lamb, 1978b) as represented in Bv of Figure 1.

Finally, Clarke-Stewart's (1978) study of dyadic and triadic situations revealed that when fathers were present, mothers were less engaging, reinforcing, and responsive in their interactions with the child. Because mothers generally have primary responsibility for child care and because fathers apparently affect the quality of maternal behavior and not just its quantity, the influence of fathers may be paramount. Clarke-Stewart notes that this would fit with the suggestions of Lamb (1975) and Lewis and Weinraub (1976) that the father's influence on child development is pri-

(A) DYAD

Direct-Effect Model

$$F \longleftrightarrow I$$

$$M \longleftrightarrow I$$

(B) TRIAD

Direct and Indirect Models

(i) Impact of father modification of mother's behavior on infant

$$F \rightarrow \quad M \rightarrow I$$

(ii) Impact of father-infant relationship on the mother-infant interaction

$$F - I \rightarrow \quad M - I$$

(iii) Impact of father modification of the infant's behavior on mother-infant
interaction

$$F \rightarrow \quad I \rightarrow \quad M - I$$

(iv) Impact of the father-mother relationship on the infant

$$F - M \rightarrow I$$

(v) Impact of the father-infant relationship on the father-mother relationship

$$F - I \rightarrow F - M$$

FIG. 1—Direct and indirect models of parental influence (Parke, 1979)

marily indirect (mediated by the mother) while the mother's effect is direct.

THE FAMILY AND COGNITIVE DEVELOPMENT

Familial factors have long been considered critical determinants of intellectual development. Since the family unit provides both genetic and environmental factors, it has become of focal interest. The research emphasis over the years has shifted from the genetic (heritable) versus the environmental contribution to the contribution of the psychosocial environment. The rationale offered for this shift is that it represents an expression of the social and political orientation of the investigators

(Kamin, 1974; Taylor, 1980). Although it is beyond the scope of this review to detail the political aspects of the genetic-environmental controversy, it is important to be aware that much of the heat generated by this controversy from the 1930s (Skodak & Skeels, 1949) still persists (Jensen, 1979).

The research literature reviewed in this section ranges from avowed tests of the genetic hypothesis to studies of causal linkages between parental interactions and relationships to children's intellectual competence.

Before embarking on our review, a word of clarification of the term *cognitive development*: the earlier research examining the genetics-environment issue used intelligence tests as the criterion measure of intelligence. Hence the array of studies of heritability of IQ. Actually, these studies concern the heritability of *general intelligence* as assessed by a particular test, typically the Stanford-Binet or WISC.

More recently, however, the definition of "intelligence" has come to include specific abilities, such as concepts of space and verbal competence, and a broad class of cognitive ability functions such as judgment, reasoning, and problem solving.

As will become evident in our literature review, the implication is that generalizations about the importance of family influences on intellectual growth *must* be restricted to the type of cognitive-outcome variable under discussion. We shall highlight this issue more specifically in the context of subsequent discussions.

As many data have been reported during the past 5 years as in all the previous 50 years regarding the genetic-environmental analysis of mental ability (Plomin & DeFries, 1980). The historical continuity and the magnitude of resources devoted to this issue reflect an abiding interest in the nature-nurture question (Eysenck & Kamin, 1981). The genetics research in the cognitive area has not involved family-process variables but has been limited to IQ scores of the parents, treating family environments only in a global undifferentiated way. However, psychological research has gone beyond the genetic-environmental controversy and IQ. A body of research has been developing that evaluates the role of family-process variables (e.g., parent-child interactions, parental values and expectations) and family configuration (e.g., number of children, birth order, and spacing) relative not only to IQ but to other specific intellectual abilities as well. To date, controversy still abounds as to causal linkages between genetic determination and IQ (Taylor, 1980). There is no theoretical or empirical consensus about the role of family-process variables in affecting intellectual outcomes. This may be in part because of the diverse questions posed, in part because of the variety of theoretical perspectives and methods used. In spite of these problems, or perhaps because of them, psychological research continues the search for relevant background factors to enhance our understanding of antecedents for cognitive functioning. Thus, we focus on the current state of knowledge regarding the relationships among an assortment of familial variables and children's intellectual functioning. We begin with an examination of research literature dealing with what is clearly a set of psychological variables.

PARENTAL BEHAVIOR AND ORGANIZATION OF THE HOME

A number of studies have been conducted which report significant relationships between various indices of the home environment and young children's IQ scores. For example, Elardo, Bradley, and Caldwell (1975) reported positive relationships between the physical and temporal organization of the home that provide opportunities for a variety of stimulation and infants' IQ scores. Moreover, the mother's involvement with the child and provision of appropriate play materials were related to IQ performance for children in the age range from 1 to 3 years. These same aspects of the home environment were found to be related to mental test performance and language abilities in later studies, indicating relative stability of the relationships uncovered (see Bradley & Caldwell, 1976; Bradley, Caldwell, & Elardo, 1979; Elardo, Bradley & Caldwell, 1977). Bradley and Caldwell (1976) suggest that by their organization of the physical and temporal environment of the home parents facilitate their children's early transition from sensorimotor to preoperational thinking. Parke (1979) notes that "caretakers and other socializing figures influence the child more indirectly by serving as an organizer of the child's environment. This is manifest in a variety of ways. In fact, this secondary role may be even more important than the role as stimulator since the amount of time that infants spend interacting with the inanimate environment far exceeds their social interaction time" (pp. 41–42). In addition, siblings and peers also serve to mediate the physical environment through organization of physical space, through selection of physical objects, and through the use of toys as mediators in social interaction.

Many studies have reported relationships between parent-child interaction behaviors and children's IQ, although the types of parent behaviors assessed vary dramatically from study to study. For example, Bing (1963) found that children's verbal and nonverbal mental ability scores were related to verbal stimulation, criticism, less permissiveness in object experimentation, and restrictiveness of mothers. Hanson's (1975) work revealed relationships between parental involvement with the child, emphasis on school achievement, teaching of language behavior, parental models of intellectual interests and activities, and children's IQ. Maternal teaching, playing, talking, and social stimulation have been found to relate to children's test scores (Clarke-Stewart, 1973). Carew (1980) reports that for children younger than 2½, mothers' direct role, either unilateral or reciprocal, in creating language-mastery experiences predicts IQ. On the other hand, when the child is between 30 and 33 months of age, reciprocal interactions between mother and child in spatial-mastery activities are related to IQ. Laosa (1983) has found that lower-SES mothers' use of modeling or demonstration techniques is predictive of preschooler's IQ scores. Although it appears to be difficult to isolate one particular aspect of parental behavior that enhances children's IQ performance, it is nevertheless clear that parental behaviors are related to children's IQ. In fact, it has been reported that mothers' behaviors and attitudes can account for more than half the variability in 3-year-olds' IQ scores (Ramey, Farran, & Campbell, 1979).

The relationships that have been found between IQ and home environment or parent's behavior do not necessarily indicate that certain types of experiences with parents *cause* children to develop greater or lesser intellectual skills or IQ. Parents are likely to react differently to brighter children and it is likely that parent and child affect each other's behaviors (Sigel et al., 1983). Bradley et al. (1979), for example, analyzed parent-child data in an effort to determine whether parents were affecting outcomes in their child or whether parents were reacting to ability levels already evidenced. Their results indicated that during the first year, children affect parents who respond to their infant's ability level, while later, parent behavior appears to affect the child's ability level. In addition, the roles of mothers and fathers in this reciprocal relationship may differ. Recent data suggests that mothers' behaviors promote the child's intellectual development, while fathers' behaviors are more likely to be responsive to the child's established ability level (Clarke-Stewart, 1978).

Although most studies of family effects on children's cognitive development have focused on children's IQ as outcomes, several studies of problem-solving abilities in a variety of domains have been conducted. Sigel (1982) has reported that parents who use distancing teaching strategies (an inquiry approach that places a demand on the child to represent objects, events, or people) have children who perform at higher levels on tasks involving memory, object categorization, and transformations. Hatano, Miyake, and Tajima (1980) report that mothers who evidence directive (nondistancing) styles have children who receive lower scores on a Piagetian number conservation task. These findings are consistent with distancing theory (Sigel, 1971, 1972, 1979), which proposes that teaching strategies that encourage the child to reconstruct, anticipate, and attend to transformations serve to enhance the development of children's representational abilities.

The variety of findings reported in the studies above leaves one with the impression that research in this area is largely exploratory rather than confirmatory and is based on theoretical predictions. Indeed, the basic assumption undergirding most of this research is that the family provides primary experiences for developing intellectual competence.

STATUS OR SITUATIONAL CHARACTERISTICS OF THE FAMILY

While family-process variables refer to within-family interactions, status or situational characteristics are descriptive of the family's social position. Interestingly enough, some of the most robust findings regarding the relationship of family characteristics to children's intellectual development consider this class of variables—parental social status, especially the mother's educational level, has repeatedly been demonstrated to be positively related to children's intelligence test scores (e.g., Laosa, 1983). Family constellation is another descriptive characteristic that has consistently been shown to be related to intelligence. However, valuable as these demographic and situational findings are, they are not explanatory. Just what is there about social status or family configuration variables that might account for the effects reported? How do middle-class parents interact with their children differently from lower social status parents?

Both SES and education level of mothers were found to be related to use of inquiry strategies (Laosa, 1978; Sigel, 1982), social transactions (Cohen & Beckwith, 1979), and sensitivity to their child's abilities (Bradley & Caldwell, 1976). Middle-class mothers were also found to vocalize more and give verbal praise more often than lower-class mothers (Streissguth & Bee, 1972, Tulkin & Kagan, 1970, 1972). Several investigations indicated that the variability in children's cognitive functioning with social class is due in large part to different family environments or child-rearing practices (Hunt, 1969; Jones, 1972; Marjoribanks, 1979; McGillicuddy-DeLisi, 1982a; Schoggen & Schoggen, 1971).

In a number of articles, Zajonc (1976) and his colleagues (Berbaum, Marcus, & Zajonc, 1982; Marcus & Zajonc, 1977; Zajonc & Bargh, 1980; Zajonc & Marcus, 1975; Zajonc, Marcus, & Marcus, 1979) have discussed, revised, and defended a confluence model positing that birth order, together with spacing, has a predictable though relatively weak effect on cognitive ability. Specifically, the birth of each child effectively reduces the cognitive functional level of the family and, in general, of each of the later-born siblings. Replication studies have been attempted with greater (Berbaum & Moreland, 1980) and lesser success (Grotevant, Scarr, & Weinberg, 1977) and, as they have evolved, the various mathematical models have been criticized (Galbraith, 1982a, 1982b; Grotevant, Scarr, & Weinberg, 1977). In the most recent exchange, Galbraith (1982a, 1982b) raises questions about details of the confluence calculations and about the logical bases of the model, while Berbaum et al. (1982) refute the criticisms and question the appropriateness of Galbraith's study population.

As in the recent literature concerning family effects on children's socioemotional development, psychological conceptualizations of effects on children's cognitive development are becoming more complex, directing attention to interrelationships among family members rather than almost exclusively to unilateral parent-to-child effects. For example, in addition to simply exploring the effects of parents on children, Bradley and his colleagues (1979) and Lerner and Spanier (1978) have investigated the effects of children on parents. In early work, Cicirelli (1972, 1973, 1974) found evidence that a child's concept learning and conceptual style are affected by interactions with older siblings. Pursuing this line of study further, Cicirelli (1975, 1976, 1977) reported that having an older sister in the family seems to affect mothers' teaching styles with younger siblings. He found that, under these circumstances, mothers tended to use fewer explanations, provided less feedback, and verbalized less when teaching the younger child, regardless of whether the older sister was present during the interaction. This suggests that a portion of the mother's helping or teaching role may be delegated to older sisters and that this role delegation affects mother/child interaction patterns that in turn are related to the problem-solving skills of the younger child.

While much of the research on cognition reflects a developmental perspective, research on the heritability of intelligence does not. Rather, IQ scores for parents and children (both biological and adopted) have been obtained at a single point in time. Such an approach assumes that correlations obtained at one point in time are sufficient to describe the relative contributions of heredity and environment. However, Plomin and DeFries (1980) report that genetic as well as environmental correlations are larger in predictions from age 7 to adulthood than from age 2 to adulthood. In other words, the so-called heritability index decreases with age. This suggests that environmental factors begin to impinge upon the child's functional cognitive level and thus contribute to individual differences in IQ test performance. Psychologists have traditionally sought to disentangle the nature-nurture issue and this line of inquiry has continued in recent years (Plomin & DeFries, 1980; Scarr & Weinberg, 1978; Taylor, 1980).

As summarized in a literature review by DeFries and Plomin (1978), behavior geneticists have studied heritability of cognitive abilities by studying various family arrangements: children reared with their biological parents, children reared by adoptive parents, and identical twins reared apart. Differences in research design and in measures used to assess intelligence (although virtually all are standardized IQ tests such as the WISC and the Stanford-Binet) suggest robustness of findings across studies, leading DeFries and Plomin (1978) to conclude: "Nine of the ten adoption studies which facilitate a strong test of genetic and environmental influences, provided evidence for heritable variance in mental ability. Therefore a prudent person has no alternative but to reject the hypothesis of zero heritability: $\chi^2 = 4.9$ corrected for continuity, $p < .05$" (p. 501).

However, DeFries and Plomin point to flaws in each of the research studies on which the above conclusions are based, in particular, inadequate assessment of home environmental factors and inadequate assessment of the types of family interactions that affect intellectual growth. Although stimulation in the home has been associated with superior cognitive development, children's brightness has been shown to be affected by both genetics and environment, and the determination of parental influence in psychological research poses the classic "chicken-and-egg" problem: Do bright children profit from the home environment because the parents are *responding* to them in a stimulating way, or are the parents the essential "shapers" of the child's intellectual competence? To return momentarily to our historical bias of questioning, it seems doubtful that the causal direction can be determined. But there seems to be sufficient evidence that the family environment should be viewed not simply as one contributor to individual differences, but as a means of enabling the development of children's abilities.

There is no doubt that the family contributes in two ways to the child's developing mental abilities. Children derive genetic material from their parents. Thus, to the degree that genes determine intellectual ability, parents are directly responsible. From the environmental perspective, the family is the primary and probably the most powerful influence on the young child's intellectual functioning; with increasing age, the child becomes subject to a wider array of influences. Unfortunately, details comparing the relative effects of family and other environmental settings are not yet available. Nevertheless, there is evidence that children's attendance at preschool can in fact enhance IQ test performance. Levenstein (1979) reports that intervention programs for preschool children from impoverished homes contribute to higher IQ scores for children than for their mothers. Since no data are available from fathers, it is not possible to address the genetics-environment controversy adequately. Yet, over and above the genetic contribution to intellective abilities, there is cumulating evidence for the effects of family factors on individual differences in intellectual performance.

Language Development and the Family

In 1973, Lewis and Freedle used the metaphor the "cradle of meaning" to describe the significance of mother-infant vocalizations. By 12 weeks of age, they found that infants vocalized in response to maternal vocalizations. Shortly after, Sachs (1977) proposed that the degree to which the mother adapts to the babblings of the prelinguistic infant may influence the initial linguistic communications between mother and child. He further concluded, as did Clarke-Stewart (1973, 1978), that it is the quantity of maternal speech directed toward the child that is significant in relation to children's linguistic competence. In addition, Clarke-Stewart reported that the quantity of maternal speech directed toward others, *not* toward the child, was unrelated to children's linguistic development. On the other hand, Nelson (1973) found that the quality of the mother's speech directed toward the child has particular significance for language development and competence.

Because of the complex nature of language acquisition, psychological investigators have variously focused on the salience of syntactic, semantic, and communication aspects of the problem. A cogent historical perspective of psychological research on the development of language is provided by Gleason and Weintraub (1978). They view the body of language development research from four major theoretical positions: the behaviorist perspective of Skinner (1957); the social learning perspective (Bandura & Harris, 1966; Whitehurst & Vasta, 1975); the psycholinguistic perspective (Chomsky, 1957); and the developmental sociolinguistic perspective (Hymes, 1971; Sinclair-deZwart, 1973).

The role of the parent in the behaviorist model is to provide reinforcement of the child's utterances, while in social learning theory the parent is seen as a model for the child's speech (Gleason & Weintraub, 1978). Grammar has not been stressed in the investigations influenced by social learning theory; rather, such studies have emphasized inputs into the child's communication competence. These researchers have not been interested in parents qua parents, but as representatives of a class of input variables that would lead to increased understanding of the way children acquire communicative competence. Again, the mother was typically selected as the "significant other" in these social learning theory studies of communication, because mothers continue to be viewed not only as the initial but as the primary adult providing language input to the infant and young child. Observational studies of mothers and young children in both experimental and naturalistic settings have provided most of the data used to define how children acquire and develop linguistic and communicative competencies.

Nevertheless, neither the behaviorist model nor the social learning approach has provided sufficient explanatory power over the complexities of language acquisition. A number of psychological researchers have examined the broader linguistic environment that influences the child. Much of this work, which heavily emphasized the language mothers use to address children, was completed prior to 1975 (Brown, 1973; Hess & Shipman, 1965; Phillips, 1973; Snow, 1972). As summarized by Gleason and Weintraub (1978), these studies consistently "supported the existence of a language spoken to children that was different from language addressed to adults and was characterized by its syntactic and semantic simplicity, its redundancy, and the presence of features designed to enhance interaction" (p. 179).

As Bandura (1977) points out, it is the total communicative experience that provides young children with opportunities to elaborate their own competencies. In spite of such pleas to broaden investigations of language acquisition and development, most recent studies have continued to employ the mother-child dyad. Although mothers employ special speech styles with their children (Farwell, 1975), these styles have been found to vary with social class (Hall & Dore, 1980), age of the child (Bellinger, 1979; Reichle, Longhurst, & Stepanich, 1976), sex of the child (Cherry & Lewis, 1976), and ethnic background (Laosa, 1980). For example, working-class mothers tend to use more imperatives and requests in their verbal interactions with their preschool children than middle-class mothers (Hall & Dore, 1980). As another instance, mothers generally tend to use more complex explanations with older children than with younger children (Reichle et al., 1976); that is, they seem to attempt to adapt to the child's level of comprehension.

Similarly, mothers tend to adopt different strategies to stimulate development that are appropriate to different age and comprehension levels. Mothers interacting with infants stimulate vocalization from the child by vocalizing to the child (Lewis & Freedle, 1973). Moerk (1975) reported that with somewhat older children, mothers stimulate children to verbalize by engaging them in conversation. Questions are an important activator and mothers increase their use of questions until the child reaches the age of 5. Open-ended questions are especially important in expanding children's language competencies and in language development (Buium, 1976; Endsley, Hutcherson, Garner, & Martin, 1979; Longhurst & Stepanich, 1975). Questions involve not only descriptions of objects and events, but also past and future events (Moerk, 1975). The open-ended questions can lead to a dialogue wherein the adult not only influences the child but is also influenced by the child (Harris, 1975). Moreover, the use of question strategies has also been found to influence children's problem-solving strategies (Sigel & Saunders, 1979; Sigel et al., 1980).

As with the area of socioemotional development, most research has been done using mother-child dyads but a few studies have focused on the father. Studies of frequency of father-child interactions have shown that little difference exists between fathers' and mothers' verbal interactions with their children (Golinkoff & Ames, 1979). When differences are found, they generally involve the use of controlling statements (Gleason, 1975): fathers use more direct controlling statements while mothers were more indirect (McLaughlin, Schultz, & White, 1980). Fathers use more complex language with girls than with boys, while mothers use more complex language with boys as observed in a game situation with 5-year-olds. This pattern is consistent with Cherry and Lewis's (1976) report that mothers talked more to their daughters than to their sons. Golinkoff and Ames (1979) found that when both parents were present with their infant, the father spoke less frequently to the child and took fewer conversational turns than the mother.

Dickson (1980), in his review of the literature on parental communication style, concludes that communication accuracy has been understudied, in contrast to communication style. Parents' accuracy provides models for their children's communication skills, including word meanings. According to Dickson, " . . . children who early in life develop good communication skills are able to create their own rich verbal environment by engaging others in sustained interaction" (Dickson, 1980, p. 127). The accuracy of communication skills can be considered in the context of both language development and cognitive development. We include it under the rubric of language, because communication does require language.

The role of familial variables in reference to language and concept attainment has been virtually ignored. The exception is the work of Nelson and Bonvillian (1978) who report their results from a longitudinal study demonstrating that by age 4½, birth order and spacing do make a difference in children's length of utterance and concept attainment. After a detailed presentation of their well-designed research effort, they conclude that "the clearest advantage of being a laterborn close spaced (<2 years) after a sibling was in terms of syntax; these children tended to produce and imitate complex sentences. Laterborns more widely spaced after a sibling were likely to show less complex sentences and much slower concept mastery, relative either to firstborns or short-lag laterborns" (p. 540). Even though the number of children involved in this study is small, the experimental controls employed enable us to accept these generalizations.

In sum, while psychologists interested in language acquisition still direct most of their research at the mother-child dyad, there is increasing interest in fathers also. Essentially, these studies show that language acquisition is influenced by the accuracy, quality, and quantity of verbal interaction with either parent. Evidence is available that birth order is also relevant. However, little is known about how factors such as number of siblings, types of discourse the family employs, etc., influence language development. In spite of these omissions, it seems clear that the child's language acquisition is not only the flowering of innate capabilities but also is subject to environmental influences in the context of family.

PROMISING PERSPECTIVES AND NEW DIRECTIONS

To summarize briefly, we have shown, in historical context, the salience of psychoanalytic and behavioral theory in psychologists' perspectives on the family and its role in the socioemotional, cognitive, and language development of the child. Given historical assumptions about the mother's paramount influence on the child, the early preoccupation in psychological research with the mother-child dyad is not surprising. In seeking an understanding of why the family as a complex unit has only recently become a focus in psychological investigations, we found three factors to be of particular importance: (1) the basic concern in developmental psychology with understanding antecedent experiences relative to specific child outcomes, taken with methodological and data-analysis constraints developing from research paradigms that focus on linear predictions; (2) the effort to establish causal links between family agents of socialization and child outcomes; and (3) psychologists' concern with individual differences, culminating in the specification of the interrelationships that help to explain variability among children.

Breaking with such traditions is difficult and, as our review has shown, psychological research on the family over the past 5 years has continued to emphasize investigation of dyadic relationships. However, in recent years the range has been broadened to include not only father-child dyads but also comparisons between mother-child and father-child interactions. Moreover, the recent literature includes investigations of the role of siblings in child development (as seen in, e.g., the effects of family size, spacing, and birth order) undertaken to further our understanding of the ways in which child outcomes vary with the sibling structure of the family. Studies of sibling interactions and their relation to mothers' interactions with the target child have been reported. Such evidence of increased sensitivity on the part of psychological researchers to reciprocal influences of family members on one another, as well as increased sensitivity to the effects of extrafamilial focus on family functioning, is encouraging and exciting.

Reflecting the current cognitive revolution generally in psychology, developmental researchers are reconceptualizing family-relevant variables and constructs in cognitive terms as, for example, in investigations of belief or construct systems (McGillicuddy-DeLisi, 1982a), expectancies (Goodnow, 1981), developmental conceptualizations (Sameroff & Feil, 1981), and attributions (Hess, King, & Holloway, 1981). This approach is already well established in guiding research on cognition, personality, and social psychology and the effects are readily apparent in the shifting perspectives in developmental research on the family—McGillicuddy-DeLisi's work is influenced by Kelly (1955), the work of Sameroff and Feil by Piaget (1981), and Hess and his colleagues by Kelley (1972). Thus, principles and constructs developed in the context of other areas of psychology have come to be viewed by developmental psychologists as relevant and promising in extending understanding of family interactions and child development. In addition, these new orientations and perspectives may well strengthen the explanatory power of internal forces that influence the family as a unit. Space does not permit a detailed summary of research results following such new perspectives, exemplified by the work of McGillicuddy-DeLisi (1982a) or Sigel et al. (1980), which show that parental belief systems concerning child-rearing practices and child development vary with demographic characteristics—family constellation and SES appear to be the most salient factors. Different belief systems also appear to be related to parental teaching strategies, which are modified, especially by mothers, by the context and demands of the task to be taught (Sigel et al., 1983).

While many psychological researchers have overtly endorsed the notion that family members affect each other, that birth order and family size influence child development, and that ecological factors are important in child development, little systematic or grand-scale research has been initiated within conceptual frameworks incorporating these variables. Nevertheless, increased attention has been given to the complexities of family life, as witness the studies reviewed in this chapter. While continuing to focus on the child, recent studies have examined the roles played by other family members in child development. Thus, the target child is more and more frequently seen in the literature as actively influencing and being influenced by the entire set of family members and as subject to such family factors as number of siblings and family status.

One of the key questions for developmental psychologists concerns the long-term effects of early experience. With the family viewed as a system of mutual influences, it is no longer reasonable to expect one-to-one correspondence between early experience and later outcome as in the simplistic view that has characterized much of parent-child research to date. Within the mutual or reciprocal influence model, it becomes apparent that changes observed after some period of time are outcomes not only of the parents' influence on the child but of the child's influence on the parents. From this perspective, the original parental act is no longer the *only* variable influencing the child. Thus, conceptualizations and data analyses of the relationships between early experience and later outcomes in terms of unidirectional, linear, continuous change is no longer appropriate. One way, for example, to reconceptualize the experience-outcome relationship is to consider the ways in which early experiences provide the child with the prerequisite competencies to cope with new experiences. From this perspective, early experience may serve to set the stage for subsequent actions, thereby serving as a facilitation variable enabling the child to deal with the new and the unexpected. As an instance, parents working with their children to plan and organize their activities may set the stage for the children subsequently to regulate their behaviors effectively. In this way, experience in planning may relate to later self-regulation. This is not to suggest a one-to-one correspondence between planning experience early or later, but rather that planning experiences may be transformed into self-regulation, which is considered to be an ingredient of planning. We thus concur with Rutter (1979) who concludes that "the evidence is unequivocal that experiences at all ages have an impact. However, it may be that the first few years do have a special importance for bond formation and social development" (p. 298).

Limiting the perspective to the family as a system of mutual influences, however, gives only a part of the total picture. The family is in constant change, with each member passing through developmental stages at different points in time. Rarely do we find two siblings at the same developmental level. If we view the family as a dynamic, organic, developing system, each member of the system has to cope with changes in competencies, interests, and actions among its members. For example, a new sibling enters a family with a 4-year-old child already present. While the age difference between the children may be to the parents' advantage in the early days because of the social and intellectual competence of the 4-year-old, by the time the children are 8 and 12, new relationships have evolved and sibling rivalries and competitions may surface that wear heavily on the parents' nerves and patience. What was a peaceful era in the life of the family may now become a conflict-ridden situation. Psychological researchers have tended to examine these issues from a cross-sectional static-time perspective that ignores changes in family dynamics. The point is that *each* member of the family is changing and that these changes influence both the quality and quantity of interactions. To focus on the changing nature of the target child or the children without considering the developing adult is to overlook potentially critical dimensions in family dynamics. Family therapists working within a systems approach do tend to take such a perspective (see Kantor & Lehr, 1975), but as yet it has not been evident in psychological research. According to Kantor and Lehr (1975), the task before us, accepting the concept of the family as a complex system of mutual influences, is to evolve a conceptual framework that shows precisely how the parts interrelate.

The studies of parent-child relationships reviewed in this chapter tended to focus on samples of healthy, functioning individuals. As a consequence, the dependent variables selected for study have generally involved such psychological variables as social understanding, IQ, problem-solving skills, and the like. There is no denying that these are important outcome variables that are presumed to be related to familial experience. However, families often have to accommodate to traumatic events such as chronic illness of a child, divorce, a retarded newborn, and so forth. As we come to learn how family systems deal with the "normal" course of development, we also learn how families cope with intrafamilial trauma. Studies examining family styles of coping with typical as well as atypical events can teach us much about the family as a socializing institution. As an instance, Sigel, McGillicuddy-DeLisi, and Flaugher (1982), in a study of families with a speech-handicapped child find that the handicapped child is treated by the other family members as the latest-born regardless of actual position in birth order.

There is general consensus that the nuclear family is a primary socializing agent and that observations of family functioning will reveal that nuclear families are embedded in extended family networks, including, for example, grandparents, uncles, and aunts. Whether these contacts involve direct interactions with relatives or not, there is reason to believe that these relatives may play a role in influencing parents' behaviors with their children. Yet we know very little about the contributions of the extended family network to the socialization of the parents qua parents or their children, and thus the area seems ripe for investigation (see Tinsley & Parke, 1984).

In addition to the extended family network, every family is a participant in a social environment subject to various changes—political, economical, social, and ideological. These secular changes can affect families in a variety of ways, as well as differentially, depending on the stage of the family and its members. For example, many families with teenagers were faced during the 1960s with teenage drug cultures—a new and profound threat not generally faced by families whose teenagers were growing up in the 1950s. Research on the effects of secular changes on family functioning is sorely needed. Parents, then, have to cope with unanticipated issues—unanticipated because these new issues originate external to the particular family. The family, in other words, must be conceptualized from a social-historical perspective as well as a psychological one. It is in this context that the study of the family joins the life-span approach that advocates incorporating of the historical context as relevant to the understanding of human development.

One can ask whether psychology by its current paradigm method is the appropriate discipline to answer the important questions about the family raised in this chapter and by other investigators. As it now stands, the answer is no: psychology will provide fragmented bits and pieces of information, which even if integrated into a system will still be of limited value. On the other hand, if psychology as a science of human behavior will alter its paradigms, enlarge its conceptualization, and strive for methodologies that can encompass a broader array of interactive variables, it may well contribute significantly to an understanding of human behavior in the context of the family.

In sum, families are embedded in an extended familial network as well as a broader social context. The degree to which we can understand the family as an agent of socialization is the degree to which we can delineate these various sources of influence. Fortunately, our increasing methodological sophistication will be of considerable help in this process. How far we can go only time will tell.

FINAL WORD

That this paper did not cover every psychological aspect of the family is obvious—we chose to be selective. We further tried to keep the focus on a psychological perspective of the family. A large body of research was omitted which tended to allude to the family primarily through social status, not by studying parents directly.

In sum, parents are beginning to be viewed as family members. We may be at the beginning of a new era of research whose implications for science and for public policy will be considerable.

REFERENCES

Ainsworth, M. D. S. Infant-mother attachment. *American Psychologist*, 1979, **34**, 932–937.
Ainsworth, M. D. S., Blehar, M. C., Waters, E., & Wall, S. *Patterns of attachment: A psychological study of the strange situation*. Hillsdale, N.J.: Erlbaum, 1978.
Arend, R., Gove, F. L., & Sroufe, L. A. Continuity of individual adaptation from infancy to kindergarten: A predictive study of ego-resiliency and curiosity in preschoolers. *Child Development*, 1979, **50**, 950–959.

Bakeman, R., & Brown, J. V. Early interaction: Consequences for social and mental development at three years. *Child Development*, 1980, 51, 437–447.

Bandura, A. Self-efficacy: Toward a unifying theory of behavioral change. *Psychological Review*, 1977, 84, 191–215.

Bandura, A., & Harris, M. B. Modification of syntactic style. *Journal of Experimental Child Psychology*, 1966, 4, 341–352.

Bar-Tal, D., Nadler, A., & Blechman, N. The relationship between Israeli children's helping behavior and their perception of parents' socialization practices. *Journal of Social Psychology*, 1980, 111, 159–167.

Bell, R. Q., & Harper, L. V. *Child effects on adults*. Hillsdale, N.J.: Erlbaum, 1977.

Bellinger, D. Changes in the explicitness of mothers' directives as children age. *Journal of Child Language*, 1979, 6, 443–458.

Belsky, J. Early human experience: A family perspective. *Developmental Psychology*, 1981, 17, 3–23.

Berbaum, M. L., Markus, G. B., & Zajonc, R. B. A closer look at Galbraith's "Closer Look." *Developmental Psychology*, 1982, 18, 174–180.

Berbaum, M. L., & Moreland, R. L. Intellectual development within the family: A new application of the confluence model. *Development Psychology*, 1980, 16, 506–515.

Bing, E. Effect of child rearing practices on development of differential cognitive abilities. *Child Development*, 1963, 34, 631–648.

Block, J. H., & Block, J. The role of ego-control and ego-resiliency in the organization of behavior. In W. A. Collins (Ed.), *Minnesota symposia on child psychology* (vol. 13). Hillsdale, N.J.: Erlbaum, 1980.

Borduin, C. M., & Henggeler, S. W. Social class, experimental setting, and task characteristics as determinants of mother-child interaction. *Developmental Psychology*, 1981, 17, 209–214.

Bradley, R. H., & Caldwell, B. M. Early home environment and changes in mental test performance in children from 6 to 36 months. *Developmental Psychology*, 1976, 12, 93–97.

Bradley, R. H., Caldwell, B. M., & Elardo, R. Home environment and cognitive development in the first two years: A cross-lagged panel analysis. *Developmental Psychology*, 1979, 15, 246–250.

Brazelton, T. B., Koslowski, B., & Main, M. The origins of reciprocity: The early mother-infant interaction. In M. Lewis & L. Rosenblum (Eds.), *The effect of the infant on its caregiver: The origins of behavior* (Vol. 1). New York: Wiley, 1974.

Bronfenbrenner, U. Toward an experimental ecology of human development. *American Psychologist*, 1977, 32, 513–531.

Brown, R. *A first language: The early stages*. Cambridge, Mass.: Harvard University Press, 1973.

Bryan, J. H. Children's cooperation and helping behaviors. In E. M. Hetherington (Ed.), *Review of child development research* (Vol. 5). Chicago: University of Chicago Press, 1975.

Bryant, B. K., & Crockenberg, S. B. Correlates and dimensions of prosocial behavior: A study of female siblings with their mothers. *Child Development*, 1980, 51, 529–544.

Buium, N. Interrogative types in parental speech to language-learning children: A linguistic universal? *Journal of Psycholinguistic Research*, 1976, 5, 135–142.

Carew, J. Experience and the development of intelligence in young children at home and in day care. *Monographs of the Society for Research in Child Development*, 1980, 45 (6–7, Serial No. 187).

Cherry, L. & Lewis, M. Mothers and two-year-olds: A study of sex-differentiated aspects of verbal interactions. *Developmental Psychology*, 1976, 12, 278–282.

Chomsky, N. *Syntactic structures.* The Hague: Mouton, 1957.

Cicirelli, V. G. The effect of sibling relationships on concept learning of young children taught by child teachers. *Child Development,* 1972, **43**, 282–287.

Cicirelli, V. G. Effects of sibling structure and interaction on children's categorization style. *Developmental Psychology,* 1973, **9**, 132–139.

Cicirelli, V. G. Relationship of sibling structure and interaction to younger sib's conceptual style. *Journal of Genetic Psychology,* 1974, **125**, 37–49.

Cicirelli, V. G. Effects of mother and older sibling on the problem solving behavior of the younger child. *Develomental Psychology,* 1975, **11**, 749–756.

Cicirelli, V. G. Mother-child and sibling-sibling interactions on a problem-solving task. *Child Development,* 1976, **47**, 588–596.

Cicirelli, V. G. Effects of mother and older sibling on child's conceptual style. *Journal of Genetic Psychology,* 1977, **131**, 309–318.

Clarke-Stewart, K. A. Interactions between mothers and their young children: Characteristics and consequences. *Monographs of the Society for Research in Child Development,* 1973, **38** (6–7, Serial No. 153).

Clarke-Stewart, K. A. And daddy makes three: The father's impact on mother and young child. *Child Development,* 1978, **49**, 466–478.

Clarke-Stewart, K. A. The father's contribution to children's cognitive and social development in early childhood. In F. A. Pedersen (Ed.), *The father-infant relationship: Observational studies in the family setting.* New York: Praeger, 1980.

Clarke-Stewart, K. A., & Hevey, C. M. Longitudinal relations in repeated observations of mother-child interaction from 1 to 2½ years. *Developmental Psychology,* 1981, **17**, 127–145.

Cochran, M. M., & Brassard, J. A. Child development and personal social networks. *Child Development,* 1979, **50**, 601–616.

Cohen, L. J., & Campos, J. J. Father, mother and stranger as elicitors of attachent behaviors in infancy. *Developmental Psychology,* 1974, **10**, 146–154.

Cohen, S. E. & Beckwith, L. Preterm infant interaction with the caregiver in the first year of life and competence at age two. *Child Development,* 1979, **50**, 767–776.

Cowan, C. P., Cowan, P. A., Coie, L., & Coie, J. D. Becoming a family: The impact of a first child's birth on the couple's relationship. In W. B. Miller & L. F. Newman (Eds.), *The first child and family formation.* Chapel Hill, N.C.: Carolina Population Center, 1978.

DeFries, J. C., & Plomin, R. Behavior genetics. *Annual Review of Psychology,* 1978, **29**, 473–515.

Dickson, W. P. Accuracy versus style of communication in parent-child interaction. *International Journal of Psycholinguistics,* 1980, **7**, 119–130.

Dunn, J., & Kendrick, C. Interaction between young siblings in the context of family relationships. In M. Lewis & L. A. Rosenblum (Eds.), *The child and its family.* New York: Plenum, 1979.

Dunn, J., & Kendrick, C. The arrival of a sibling: Changes in interaction between mother and first-born child. *Journal of Child Pschology and Psychiatry,* 1980, **21**, 119–131.

Eckerman, C. O., Whatley, J. L., & Kutz, S. L. Growth of social play with peers during the second year of life. *Developmental Psychology,* 1975, **11**, 42–49.

Eisenberg-Berg, N., & Mussen, P. Empathy and moral development in adolescence. *Developmental Psychology,* 1978, **14**, 185–186.

Elardo, R., Bradley, R., & Caldwell, B. M. The relation of infants' home environments to mental test performance from six to thirty-six months.: A longitudinal analysis. *Child Development,* 1975, **46**, 71–76.

Elardo, R., Bradley, R., & Caldwell, B. M. A longitudinal study of the relation of infants' home environments to language development at age three. *Child Development*, 1977, **48**, 595–603.

Emmerich, W. Structure and development of personal-social behaviors in economically disadvantaged preschool children. *Genetic Psychology Monographs*, 1977, **95**, 191–245.

Endsley, R. C., Hutcherson, M. A., Garner, A. P., & Martin, M. J. Interrelationships among selected maternal behaviors, authoritarianism, and preschool children's verbal and nonverbal curiosity. *Child Development*, 1979, **50**, 331–339.

Eysenck, H. J., & Kamin, L. *The intelligence controversy*. New York: Wiley, 1981.

Falbo, T. Only children, stereotypes, and research. In M. Lewis & L. A. Rosenblum (Eds.), *The child and its family: The genesis of behavior* (Vol. 2). New York: Plenum, 1979.

Farwell, C. B. The language spoken to children. *Human Development*. 1975, **18**, 288–309.

Feiring, C., & Lewis, M. The child as a member of the family system. *Behavioral Science*, 1978, **23**, 225–233.

Feldman, S. S., & Ingham, M. E. Attachment behavior: A validation study in two age groups. *Child Development*, 1975, **46**, 319–330.

Feshbach, N. D. The relationship of childrearing factors to children's aggression, empathy and related positive and negative behaviors. In J. de Wit & W. W. Hartup (Eds.), *Determinants and origins of aggressive behavior*. The Hague: Mouton, 1975.

Field, T. M., Widmayer, S. M., Stringer, S., & Ignatoff, E. Teenage, lower-class, black mothers and their preterm infants: An intervention and developmental follow-up. *Child Development*, 1980, **51**, 426–436.

Galbraith, R. C. Just one look was all it took: Reply to Berbaum, Markus, and Zajonc. *Development Psychology*, 1982, **18**, 181–191. (a)

Galbraith, R. C. Sibling spacing and intellectual development: A closer look at the confluence models. *Development Psychology*, 1982, **18**, 151–173. (b)

Gleason, J. B. Fathers and other strangers: Men's speech to young children. In D. P. Dato (Ed.), *Developmental psycholinguisitics, theory and applications: Georgetown University Round Table*. Washington, D.C.: Georgetown University Press, 1975.

Gleason, J. B., & Weintraub, S. Input language and the acquisition of communicative competence. In K. E. Nelson (Ed.), *Children's language*. New York: Gardner, 1978.

Golinkoff, R. M., & Ames, G. J. A comparison of fathers' and mothers' speech with their young children. *Child Development*, 1979, **50**, 28–32.

Goodnow, J. C. *Issues and problems in studies of parental models of development*. Paper presented at the meeting of the Society for Research in Child Development, Boston, March 1981.

Grotevant, H. D., Scarr, S., & Weinberg, R. A. Intellectual development in family constellations with adopted and natural children: A test of the Zajonc and Markus model. *Child Development*, 1977, **48**, 1699–1703.

Gutkin, D. C. Maternal discipline and children's judgments of moral intentionality. *Journal of Genetic Pscyhology*, 1975, **127**, 55–61.

Hall, W. S., & Dore, J. *Lexical sharing in mother-child interaction* (Tech. Rep. 161). Cambridge, Mass.: Bolt, Beranek, & Newman, 1980.

Hanson, R. A. Consistency and stability of home environmental measures related to IQ. *Child Development*, 1975, **46**, 470–480.

Harris, A. E. Social dialectics and language: Mother and child construct the discourse. *Human Development*, 1975, **18**, 80–96.

Hatano, G., Miyake, K., & Tajima, N. Mother behavior in an unstructured situation and child's acquisition of number conservation. *Child Development*, 1980, **51**, 379–385.

Hay, D. F. Cooperative interactions and sharing between very young children and their parents. *Developmental Psychology*, 1979, **15**, 647–653.

Hess, R. D., King, D. R., & Holloway, S. D. *Causal explanations for high and low performance in school: Some contrasts between parents and children.* Paper presented at the meeting of the Society for Research in Child Development, Boston, March 1981.

Hess, R. D., & Shipman, V. C. Early experience and the socialization of cognitive modes in children. *Child Development*, 1965, **36**, 869–886.

Hill, R., & Mattessich, P. Family development theory and life-span development. In P. B. Baltes & O. B. Brim (Eds.), *Life-span development and behavior* (Vol. **2**). New York: Academic Press, 1979.

Hoffman, L. W., & Manis, J. D. Influence of children on marital interactions and parental satisfactions and dissatisfactions. In R. M. Lerner & G. B. Spanier (Eds.), *Child influences on marital and family interaction: A life span perspective.* New York: Academic Press, 1978.

Hoffman, M. L. Parent discipline and the child's consideration for others. *Child Development*, 1963, **34**, 573–588.

Hoffman, M. L. Moral development. In P. H. Mussen (Ed.), *Carmichael's manual of child psychology* (Vol. **2**). New York: Wiley, 1970.

Hoffman, M. L. Developmental synthesis of affect and cognition and its implications for altruistic motivation. *Developmental Psychology*, 1975, **11**, 607–622.

Hoffman, M. L. Empathy, role taking, guilt, and development of altruistic motives. In T. Lickona (Ed.), *Moral development and behavior: Theory, research and social issues.* New York: Holt, Rinehart & Winston, 1976.

Hoffman, M. L. Moral internalization: Current theory and research. In L. Berkowitz (Ed.), *Advances in experimental social psychology* (Vol. **10**). New York: Academic Press, 1977.

Hoffman, M. L. Empathy, its development and prosocial implications. In C. B. Keasey (Ed.), *Nebraska Symposium on Motivation, 1977.* Lincoln: University of Nebraska Press, 1978.

Hoffman, M. L. Development of moral thought, feeling, and behavior. *American Psychologist*, 1979, **34**, 958–966.

Hoffman, M. L., & Saltzstein, H. D. Parent discipline and the child's moral development. *Journal of Personality and Social Psychology*, 1967, **5**, 45–47.

Hogan, R., Johnson, J. A., & Emler, N. P. A socioanalytic theory of moral development. In W. Damon (Ed.), *Moral development* (Vol. **2**). San Francisco: Jossey-Bass, 1978.

Hower, J. T., & Edwards, K. J. The relationship between moral character and adolescents' perception of parental behavior. *Journal of Genetic Psychology*, 1979, **135**, 23–32.

Hunt, J. McV. *The challenge of incompetence and poverty.* Chicago: University of Chicago Press, 1969.

Hunt, J. McV., & Paraskevopoulos, O. Children's psychological development as a function of the inaccuracy of their mothers' knowledge of their abilities. *Journal of Genetic Psychology*, 1980, **136**, 285–298.

Hymes, D. Competence and performance in linguistic theory. In R. Huxley & E. Ingram (Eds.), *Language acquisition: Models and methods.* London: Academic Press, 1971.

Jensen, A. R. *Bias in mental testing.* New York: Free Press, 1979.

Jones, P. Home environment and the development of verbal ability. *Child Development*, 1972, **43**, 1081–1087.

Kamin, L. J. *The science and politics of IQ.* Potomac, Md.: Erlbaum, 1974.

Kantor, D., & Lehr, W. *Inside the family.* San Francisco: Jossey Bass, 1975.

Kelley, H. H. Causal schemata and the attribution process. In E. E. Jones, D. E. Kanouse, H. H. Kelley, R. E. Nisbett, S. Valins, & B. Weiner (Eds.), *Attribution: Perceiving the causes of behavior.* Morristown, N.J.: General Learning, 1972.

Kelly, G. A. *The psychology of the personal constructs.* New York: Norton, 1955.

Korner, A. F. The effect of the state, level of arousal, sex and ontogenetic stage on the caregiver. In M. Lewis & L. A. Rosenblum (Eds.), *The effect of the infant on its caregiver: The origins of behavior* (Vol. 1). New York: Wiley, 1974.

Kotelchuck, M. The infant's relationship to the father: Experimental evidence. In M. E. Lamb (Ed.), *The role of the father in child development.* New York: Wiley, 1976.

Kotelchuck, M., Zelazo, P. R., Kagan, J., & Spelke, E. Infant reaction to parental separation when left with familiar and unfamiliar adults. *Journal of Genetic Psychology*, 1975, **126**, 255–262.

Lamb, M. E. Fathers: Forgotten contributions to child development. *Human Development*, 1975, **18**, 245–266.

Lamb, M. E. Effects of stress and cohort on mother- and father-infant interaction. *Developmental Psychology*, 1976, **12**, 435–443. (a)

Lamb, M. E. Interactions between eight-month-old children and their fathers and mothers. In M. E. Lamb (Ed.), *The role of the father in child development.* New York: Wiley, 1976. (b)

Lamb, M. E. Twelve-month-olds and their parents: Interaction in a laboratory playroom. *Developmental Pscyhology*, 1976, **12**, 237–244. (c)

Lamb, M. E. The development of mother-infant and father-infant attachments in the second year of life. *Developmental Psychology*, 1977, **13**, 637–648. (a)

Lamb, M. E. The development of parental preferences in the first two years of life. *Sex Roles*, 1977, **3**, 495–497. (b)

Lamb, M. E. Father-infant and mother-infant interaction in the first year of life. *Child Development*, 1977, **48**, 167–181. (c)

Lamb, M. E. The father's role in the infant's social world. In J. H. Stevens, Jr., & M. Mathews (Eds.), *Mother/child, father/child relationships.* Washington, D.C.: National Association for the Education of Young Children, 1978. (a)

Lamb, M. E. Interactions between eighteen-month-olds and their preschool-aged siblings. *Child Development*, 1978, **49**, 51–59. (b)

Lamb, M. E. The development of parent-infant attachments in the first two years of life. In F. A. Pedersen (Ed.), *The father-infant relationship: Observational studies in the family setting.* New York: Praeger, 1980.

Laosa, L. M. Maternal teaching strategies in Chicano families of varied educational and socioeconomic levels. *Child Development*, 1978, **49**, 1129–1135.

Laosa, L. M. Maternal teaching strategies in Chicano and Anglo-American families: The significance of culture and education on maternal behavior. *Child Development*, 1980, **51**, 759–765.

Laosa, L. M. The impact of parental schooling on the parent-child relationship. In I. E. Sigel & L. M. Laosa (Eds.), *Changing families.* New York: Plenum, 1983.

Lerner, R. M., & Spanier, G. B. A dynamic interactional view of child and family development. In R. M. Lerner & G. B. Spanier (Eds.), *Child influences on marital and family interaction.* New York: Academic Press, 1978.

Levenstein, P. *Home-based programs: Nightmare or dream of the future?* Paper presented at the meeting of the Society for Research in Child Development, San Francisco, March 1979.

Lewis, M., & Feiring, C. Some American families at dinner. In L. M. Laosa & I. E. Sigel (Eds.), *Families as learning environments for children.* New York: Plenum, 1982.

Lewis, M., & Freedle, R. Mother-infant dyad: The cradle of meaning. In P. Pliner, L. Krames, & T. Alloway (Eds.), *Communication and affect: Language and thought.* New York: Acacemic Press, 1973.

Lewis, M., & Kreitzberg, V. S. Effects of birth order and spacing on mother-infant interactions. *Developmental Pscyhology*, 1979, **15**, 617–625.

Lewis, M., & Weinraub, M. Sex of parent × sex of child: Socioemotional development. In R. C. Friedman, R. M. Richart, & R. L. Vande Wiele (Eds.), *Sex differences in behavior*. New York: Wiley, 1974.

Lewis, M., & Weinraub, M. The father's role in the child's social network. In M. E. Lamb (Ed.), *The role of the father in child development*. New York: Wiley, 1976.

Longhurst, T. M., & Stepanich, L. Mothers' speech addressed to one-, two-, and three-year-old normal children. *Child Study Journal*, 1975, **5**, 3–12.

Lynn, D. B., & Cross, A. R. Parent preference of preschool children. *Journal of Marriage and the Family*, 1974, **36**, 555–559.

Maccoby, E. E. *Social development*. New York: Harcourt Brace Jovanovich, 1980.

Marjoribanks, K. *Families and their learning environments*. London: Routledge & Kagan Paul, 1979.

Markus, G. B., & Zajonc, R. B. Family configuration and intellectual development: A simulation. *Behavioral Science*, 1977, **22**, 137–142.

Martin, B. Parent-child relations. In F. D. Horowitz (Ed.), *Review of children development research* (Vol. 4). Chicago: University of Chicago Press, 1975.

Martin, J. A., Maccoby, E. E., Baran, K. W., & Jacklin, C. N. Sequential analysis of mother-child interaction at 18 months: A comparison of microanalytic methods. *Developmental Psychology*, 1981, **17**, 146–157.

Matas, L., Arend, R. A., & Sroufe, L. A. Continuity of adaptation in the second year: The relationship between quality of attachment and later competence. *Child Development*, 1978, **49**, 547–556.

McGillicuddy-DeLisi, A. V. The relationship between parents' beliefs about development and family constellation, socioeconomic status, and parents' teaching strategies. In L. M. Laosa & I. E. Sigel (Eds.), *Families as learning environments for children*. New York: Plenum, 1982. (a)

McGillicuddy-DeLisi, A. V. Parental beliefs about developmental processes. *Human Development*, 1982, **25**, 192–200. (b)

McGillicuddy-DeLisi, A. V., & Sigel, I. E. Effects of the atypical child on the family. In L. A. Bond & J. M. Joffe (Eds.), *Facilitating infant and early childhood development*. Hanover, N.H.: University Press of New England, 1982.

McLaughlin, B., Schultz, C., & White, D. Parental speech to five-year-old children in a game-playing situation. *Child Development*, 1980, **51**, 580–582.

Moerk, E. L. Verbal interactions between children and their mothers during the preschool years. *Developmental Psychology*, 1975, **11**, 788–794.

Nelson, K. Structure and strategy in learning to talk. *Monographs of the Society for Research in Child Development*, 1973, **38** (1–2, Serial No. 149).

Nelson, K. E., & Bonvillian, J. D. Early language development: Conceptual growth and related processes between 2 and 4 years of age. In K. Nelson (Ed.), *Children's language* (Vol. 1). New York: Gardner, 1978.

Osofsky, J. C. Neonatal characteristics and mother-infant interaction in two observational situations. *Child Development*, 1976, **47**, 1138–1147.

Osofsky, J. D., & Connors, K. Mother-infant interactions: An integrative view of a complex system. In J. D. Osofsky (Ed.), *Handbook of infant development*. New York: Wiley, 1979.

Parikh, B. Development of moral judgment and its relation to family environmental factors in Indian and American families. *Child Development*, 1980, **51**, 1030–1039.

Parke, R. D. Perspectives on father-infant interaction. In J. D. Osofsky (Ed.), *Handbook of infant development*. New York: Wiley, 1979.

Parke, R. D., & O'Leary, S. E. Father-mother-infant interaction in the newborn period: Some finding; some observations and some unresolved issues. In K. Riegel & J. Meachum (Eds.), *The developing individual in a changing world.* (Vol. 2): *Social and environmental issues.* The Hague: Mouton, 1975.

Parke, R. D., & Sawin, D. B. The family in early infancy: Social interactional and attitudinal analyses. In F. A. Pedersen (Ed.), *The father-infant relationship: Observational studies in the family setting.* New York: Praeger, 1980.

Patterson, G. R. Mothers: The unacknowledged victims. *Monographs of the Society for Research in Child Development,* 1980, **45** (5, Serial No. 186).

Pedersen, F. A., Anderson, B. J., & Cain, R. L. Parent-infant and husband-wife interactions observed at age five months. In F. A. Pederson (Ed.), *The father-infant relationship: Observational studies in the family setting.* New York: Praeger, 1980.

Pedersen, F. A., Yarrow, L. J., Anderson, B. J., & Cain, R. L., Jr. Conceptualization of father influences in the infancy period. In M. Lewis & L. A. Rosenblum (Eds.), *The child and its family.* New York: Plenum, 1979.

Phillips, J. R. Syntax and vocabulary of mothers' speech to young children: Age and sex comparisons. *Child Development,* 1973, **44**, 182–185.

Piaget, J. *Intelligence and affectivity: Their relationship during child development.* (T. A. Brown, C. E. Kaegi, Eds. and trans.) Palo Alto, Calif.: Annual Reviews, 1981.

Plomin, R., & DeFries, J. C. Genetics and intelligence: Recent data. *Intelligence,* 1980, **4**, 15–24.

Powell, D. R. Individual differences in participation in a parent-child support program. In I. E. Sigel & L. M. Laosa (Eds.), *Changing families.* New York: Plenum, 1983.

Ramey, C. T., Farran, D. C., & Campbell, F. A. Predicting IQ from mother-infant interactions. *Child Development,* 1979, **50**, 804–814.

Reichle, J. E., Longhurst, T. M., & Stepanich, L. Verbal interaction in mother-child dyads. *Developmental Psychology,* 1976, **12**, 273–277.

Reiss, D. *The family's construction of reality.* Cambridge, Mass.: Harvard University Press 1981.

Rheingold, H. L., Hay, D. F., & West, M. J. Sharing in the second year of life. *Child Development,* 1976, **47**, 1148–1158.

Ross, G., Kagan, J., Zelazo, P., & Kotelchuck, M. Separation protest in infants in home and laboratory. *Developmental Psychology,* 1975, **11**, 256–258.

Ross, H. S., & Goldman, B. D. Establishing new social relations in infancy. In T. Alloway, L. Krames, & P. Pliner (Eds.), *Advances in the study of communication and affect.* (Vol. 3): *Attachment behavior.* New York: Plenum Press, 1977.

Rushton, J. P. Socialization and the altruistic behavior of children. *Psychological Bulletin,* 1976, **83**, 898–913.

Rutter, M. Maternal deprivation, 1972–1978: New findings, new concepts, new approaches. *Child Development,* 1979, **50**, 283–305.

Sachs, J. The adaptive significance of linguistic input to prelinguistic infants. In C. E. Snow & C. A. Ferguson (Eds.), *Talking to children: Language input and acquisition.* Cambridge: Cambridge University Press, 1977.

Sameroff, A. J., & Feil, L. A. *Parental perspectives in development.* Paper presented at the meeting of the Society for Research in Child Development, Boston, April 1981.

Scarr, S., & Weinberg, R. A. The influence of family background on intellectual achievement. *American Sociological Review,* 1978, **43**, 674–692.

Schoggen, M., & Schoggen, P. Environment forces in the home lives of three-year-old children in three population subgroups. *Darcee Papers and Reports,* 1971, **5** (2).

Sigel, I. E. Language of the disadvantaged: The distancing hypothesis. In C. S. Lavatelli

(Ed.), *Language training in early childhood education*. Urbana: University of Illinois Press, 1971.

Sigel, I. E. The distancing hypothesis revisited: An elaboration of a neo-Piagetian view of the development of representational thought. In M. E. Meyer (Ed.), *Cognitive learning*. Bellingham, Wash.: Western Washington State College Press, 1972.

Sigel, I. E. Consciousness raising of individual competence in problem solving. In M. W. Kent & J. E. Rolf (Eds.), *Primary prevention of psychopathology*. (Vol. 3): *Social competence in children*. Hanover, N.H.: University Press of New England, 1979.

Sigel, I. E. The relationship between parental distancing strategies and the child's cognitive behavior. In L. M. Laosa & I. E. Sigel (Eds.), *Families as learning environments for children*. New York: Plenum, 1982.

Sigel, I. E., McGillicuddy-DeLisi, A. V., & Flaugher, J. *Effects of atypical child on family* (Final report prepared under Grant 1 R01 MH 32301, National Institute of Mental Health).

Sigel, I. E., McGillicuddy-DeLisi, A. V., Flaugher, J., & Rock, D. A. *Parents as teachers of their own learning disabled children* (ETS RR 83–21). Princeton, N.J.: Educational Testing Service, 1983.

Sigel, I. E., McGillicuddy-DeLisi, A. V., & Johnson, J. E. *Parental distancing, beliefs and children's representational competence within the family context* (ETS RR 80–21). Princeton, N.J.: Educational Testing Service, 1980.

Sigel, I. E., & Saunders, R. An inquiry into inquiry: Question asking as an instructional model. In L. Katz (Ed.), *Current topics in early childhood education* (Vol. 2). Norwood, N.J.: Ablex, 1979.

Sinclair-de Zwart, H. Language acquisition and cognitive development. In T. E. Moore (Ed.), *Cognitive development and the acquisition of language*. New York: Academic Press, 1973.

Skinner, B. F. *Verbal behavior*. New York: Appleton Century Crofts, 1957.

Skodak, M., & Skeels, H. M. A final follow-up study of one hundred adopted children. *Journal of Genetic Psychology*, 1949, **75**, 85–125.

Snow, C. E. Mothers' speech to children learning language. *Child Development*, 1972, **43**, 549–565.

Spelke, E., Zelazo, P., Kagan, J., & Kotelchuck, M. Father interaction and separation protest. *Developmental Psychology*, 1973, **9**, 83–90.

Sroufe, L. A. The coherence of individual development: Early care, attachment, and subsequent developmental issues. *American Psychologist*, 1979, **34**, 834–841.

Sroufe, L. A., & Waters, E. Attachment as an organizational construct. *Child Development*, 1977, **48**, 1184–1199.

Staub, E. A child in distress: The influence of nurturance and modeling on children's attempts to help. *Developmental Psychology*, 1971, **5**, 124–132.

Staub, E. *The development of prosocial behavior in children*. New York: General Learning, 1975.

Staub, E. *Positive social behavior and morality* (Vol. 2). New York: Academic Press, 1979.

Streissguth, A. P., & Bee, H. L. Mother-child interaction and cognitive development in children. In W. W. Hartup (Ed.), *The young child: Review of research* (Vol. 2). Washington, D.C.: National Association for the Education of Young Children, 1972.

Sutton-Smith, B., & Rosenberg, B. G. *The sibling*. New York: Holt, Rinehart & Winston, 1970.

Taylor, H. *The IQ game*. New Brunswick, N.J.: Rutgers University Press, 1980.

Thomas, A., & Chess, S. *Temperament and development*. New York: Brunner/Mazel, 1977.

Tinsley, B. R., & Parke, R. D. Grandparents as support and socialization agents. In M. Lewis (Ed.), *Beyond the dyad*. New York: Plenum, 1984.

Troll, L. E. The family in later life: A decade review. *Journal of Marriage and the Family*, 1971, **33**, 263–290.

Troll, L. E., & Smith, J. Attachment through the lifespan: Some questions about dyadic bonds among adults. *Human Development*, 1976, **19**, 156–170.

Tulkin, S. R., & Kagan, J. Mother-child interaction: Social class differences in the first year of life. *Proceedings of the 78th Annual Convention of the American Psychological Association*, 1970, **5**, 261–262. (Summary)

Tulkin, S. R., & Kagan, J. Mother-child interaction in the first year of life. *Child Development*, 1972, **43**, 31–41.

Waters, E., Vaughn, B. E., & Egeland, B. R. Individual differences in infant-mother attachment relationships at age one: Antecedents in neonatal behavior in an urban, economically disadvantaged sample. *Child Development*, 1980, **51**, 208–216.

Waters, E., Wippman, J., & Sroufe, L. A. Attachment, positive affect, and competence in the peer group: Two studies in construct validation. *Child Development*, 1979, **50**, 821–829.

Whitehurst, G. J. & Vasta, R. Is language acquired through imitation? *Journal of Linguistic Research*, 1975, **4**, 37–59.

Yarrow, M. R., Scott, P. M., & Waxler, C. Z. Learning concern for others. *Developmental Psychology*, 1973, **8**, 240–260.

Yarrow, M. R., & Waxler, C. Z.; with the collaboration of Barrett, D., Darby, I., King, R., Pickett, M., & Smith, J. Dimensions and correlates of prosocial behavior in young children. *Child Development*, 1976, **47**, 118–125.

Zahn-Waxler, C., Radke-Yarrow, M., & King, R. M. Child rearing and children's prosocial initiations toward victims of distress. *Child Development*, 1979, **50**, 319–330.

Zajonc, R. B. Family configuration and intelligence. *Science*, 1976, **192**, 227–236.

Zajonc, R. B., & Bargh, J. The confluence model: Parameter estimation for six divergent data sets on family factors and intelligence. *Intelligence*, 1980, **4**, 349–361.

Zajonc, R. B., & Markus, G. B. Birth order and intellectual development. *Psychological Review*, 1975, **82**, 74–88.

Zajonc, R. B., Markus, H., & Markus, G. B. The birth order puzzle. *Journal of Personality and Social Psychology*, 1979, **37**, 1325–1341.

4   Families, Kin, and the Life Course: A Sociological Perspective

GLEN H. ELDER, JR.
University of North Carolina at Chapel Hill

I. Introduction

Sociological perspectives on family and kinship have followed a cyclical pattern of dominance between macroscopic structural analysis and more behavioral studies in the twentieth century. A shift from generalized evolution to the problems of changing families in urban places occurred during the early decades of heightened concern with social disorganization. Attention to problems of social order and abstract social systems emerged from the Great Depression and Second World War. Family organization replaced disorganization as a central theme. This era came to an end in the 1960s as the social order seemed to unravel under the combined force of demographic, economic, and ideological change. Theoretical analysis shifted once again to the concrete realities of families, generations, and individuals; but in the 1960s, unlike the 1920s, the process of family reorganization gained prominence relative to social disorganization. With this perspective came sensitivity to temporal issues as families were followed across their life span and historical settings, often in response to questions concerning effective adaptation.

This chapter uses the behavioral eras in family studies to pose analytical issues and comparisons that have direct implications for contemporary research. Turning points in theory generally arise when novel questions and research tasks cannot be addressed satisfactorily by conventional approaches. So it is with the two waves of behavioral studies. Both the pre-1940 era and the years beyond 1960 are distinguished by pressing social problems involving the family that called for scientific explanation

Research for this essay was presented by grant MH–34172 from the National Institute of Mental Health and grant SES83–08350 from the National Science Foundation to Cornell University (Glen H. Elder, Jr., principal investigator). I am grateful to Andrew Cherlin, Ann Crouter, Frank Furstenberg, David Kertzer, Gunhild Hagestad, and Ross Parke for extended commentary on initial drafts.

and understanding. Rural-to-urban migration is one such problem in early twentieth-century America, and cleavages between age groups in attitudes and actions represent another for the 1960s. In drawing upon ideas from past and current challenges, each epoch of changing times gave birth to a different brand of family behaviorism, from the interactionism of the first wave to the life course perspective of the second. As Thomas Kuhn (1977, p. 234) has noted, new themes generally emerge from "old theories and within a matrix of old beliefs about the phenomena that the world does and *does not contain.*"

Two sociological perspectives bridge the behavioral epochs of family studies before 1940 and after 1960. One approach is exemplified by the analytical foci and research of W. I. Thomas (e.g., Thomas & Thomas, 1928; Thomas & Znaniecki, 1918–20), with emphasis on family dynamics in a broader setting of kinship, culture, and historical change. The other relates dyadic and individual development, especially under the influence of Ernest Burgess (see Burgess, 1926; Burgess & Cottrell, 1939; Burgess & Locke, 1945; Burgess & Wallin, 1953), a one-time colleague of Thomas in the golden age of Chicago social science (Faris, 1967). These lines of inquiry are presented in the concluding section as sources of complementary perspectives (age and kinship) on the life course in the 1980s. An age-based perspective is compatible with Burgess's problem orientation, whereas the kinship approach, with its focus on the generations, finds support in the Thomas tradition.

Age locates families in historical context with the birth year of the head and places them socially through age-graded events, such as marriage and retirement (Riley, Johnson, & Foner, 1972). The conceptual language of kinship elaborates this "life course approach" in two ways. First, through the familiar concept of family cycle in which children are born, mature, and have offspring that eventually replace the parent generation; and second, through the lineal hierarchy of generational positions from child to parent, grandparent, and great-grandparent. Age and kinship distinctions currently represent key elements in a dynamic perspective on the life course of family and individual development. Both sets of factors indicate the range of possibilities for a life course approach to the family in which time, process, and context matter.

A number of conceptual distinctions acquire and lose prominence through historical swings between a macroscopic analysis of family structure which has little to say about people and a more microscopic, behavioral view of the family as a social group of individuals or actors in structured situations. The latter approach brings greater emphasis to social dynamics or processes, but it is not, as some would claim, essentially more contextual or temporal. The difference has to do with substance or kind.

Behavioral analysis locates families in the local environments of neighborhood and community, while a general structural perspective relates family structures to the larger social system. Temporal distinctions on the behavioral level appear in the synchronization of careers, in adaptations and timetables. This fine-graded approach compares with the historical expanse of structural accounts, such as the Western trend in family specialization between the pre-industrial age and the post-1940s.

The chapter begins with changing problem foci among family studies in four periods of the twentieth century: before 1929, 1930s up to 1945, the immediate postwar era, and the decades following 1960. The first and last periods coincide with the rise of behavioral approaches and their complementary distinctions regarding family process, context, and time. Studies in both periods are linked through lines of work that reflect the influence of W. I. Thomas and Ernest Burgess. The next section examines points of similarity and contrast between these perspectives on family interaction. The concluding discussion of temporality extends each perspective to the life course of families and individuals.

II. Changing Problem Foci and Times

Family organization and change identify problem foci that have structured sociological inquiry in the twentieth century. The organizational theme includes such foci as authority and power; modes of integration; the division of labor; and exchange of resources, social roles, and socialization. Social change in the family may take the form of a breakdown of conventional arrangements or customs, as in a process of disorganization, or it may involve the reworking of old patterns in the context of new demands, options, and resources. Disorganization and reorganization can occur simultaneously, achieving a balance at various times.

During the very early stage of social science, W. I. Thomas and Florian Znaniecki (1918–20) proposed a global theory of family stability and change in which social organization is maintained and transformed through processes of disorganization and reorganization. The motivating problem centered on the transition of Polish peasants from traditional rural environments to the urban settings of Europe and the United States. The hand of rural tradition subordinated the individual to collective interests, to the larger family group or kin system and its solidarity. Speaking about this solidarity, the authors (1974, pp. 91–92) observed that a "rebellious child finds nowhere any help, not even in the younger generation, for every member of the family will side with the child's parents if he considers them right, and everyone will feel the familial will behind and will play the part of a representative of the group." Disorganization of this traditional system occurred through a diminishing isolation of peasant communities as well as through the emigration of individuals and whole families. Attitudes of "I" replaced attitudes of "we" among mobile family members.

Family disorganization is manifested by loss of the controlling force of existing family norms, rules, or customs. Generally temporary in full impact, it is coupled frequently with revitalizing activities. Over the course of family life, some norms gain influence, others lose influence, and still others are modified or transformed. A stable family pattern is simply a "dynamic equilibrium of processes of disorganization and reorganization" (Thomas & Znaniecki, 1974, p. 1130). A disequilibrium favoring disorganization accelerates the process of breakdown which is eventually countered by adaptations that reorganize family life and produce "new schemes of behavior and new institutions better adapted to the changed conditions of the group" (p. 1130). Disorganization makes organized, harmonious life more valuable, thereby prompting "conscious efforts to remedy" the deficiency.

Organization, disorganization, and reorganization refer to general structures and processes in family and household, yet they have not received equal attention over the years. Thomas and Znaniecki (1974) discuss all three concepts in their pioneering study, but disorganization receives much greater emphasis. Instead of investigating how some families manage to survive and even flourish in difficult circumstances, their research probed for answers to why families become disorganized and members succumb to a demoralized condition. The individualization of the Polish peasant in America (hedonistic satisfaction, vanity values, etc.) became de facto evidence of family breakdown with the baseline defined in terms of the traditional rural order of Poland. The very nature of urban life at the time made "family pathology" especially prominent. *The Polish Peasant* mirrors such concerns in its coverage of marital demoralization, vagabondage, and sexual promiscuity.

The problematic disjuncture between custom and personal choice in family life became a dominant research orientation among sociologists of the family in the Chicago school up to 1940. Led by Thomas and Burgess, this type of inquiry represented a sharp break from the wide expanse of time in evolutionary thinking to the concrete setting. Within this mode of sociological analysis, family studies gained rigor from more precise question formulation, sounder research design, and empirical observation. Research problems were identified and specified from observations and theoretical premises so as to permit measurement and empirical tests. The dominance of Chicago thinking extended across two distinct eras on problem foci: family problems and disorganization as themes of the early 1900s and family adaptation in hard times and war, which begins with the economic collapse of the 1930s and ends with the close of World War II.

Distinctive problem orientations emerged around the turn of the century and prompted fresh thinking that had implications for subsequent work. This late stage of industrialization and an uncontrolled economy was marked by problems of the working-class family in urban settings, especially the family's precarious state of economic uncertainty and vulnerability (Modell, 1979). Corresponding issues centered on immigrant families and their problematic accommodation to urban and rural life in a new land. Problems of dependency defined a third orientation: the problems of the young and old in their socially recognized age groups, along with matters of change and deprivation among women and blacks.

During the late nineteenth and early twentieth centuries, a series of socioeconomic studies assembled a portrait of family dynamics in which economic level and need fulfillment varied in a lawful manner from marriage to old age according to household size and composition (Rubinow, 1916). The laboring man and his family were commonly trapped in a poverty cycle. Relative well-being occurred between marriage and the first child, a time when the domestic unit had one or two earners. Hard times arrived with the birth of children as the wife stopped working and consumption needs pressed available income. Conditions improved as the children reached the age of employability and wives reentered the labor market. A sharp economic decline after the children left home with their earnings often plunged the couple back into poverty. Widowhood intensified this deprivational state in old age.[1]

Mounting social problems from migration to the cities of early twentieth-century America drew attention to a process that also applies to the poverty cycle of laborers' families—the transition of families from one state to another and the resulting crisis or problem situation. Thomas and Znaniecki proposed a way to conceptualize and understand such change in *The Polish Peasant in Europe and America* (1918–20). Looking back on the

---

[1]From Rowntree's (1901) classic study of York laborers and families to other social economic research (Zimmerman, 1936), family scholars were presented with an important observation that disappeared all too quickly from studies: that family economic well-being fluctuates across the life span of working-class families and does so primarily in relation to compositional change. The major change event is loss of the principal earner by death and divorce. Poverty applies to *different* family units from year to year. Nearly 75 years later James Morgan and his collaborators at the University of Michigan (Duncan, 1984; Lane & Morgan, 1975, p. 50) have rediscovered this temporal pattern in a nationwide panel study.

empirical record, Nisbet (1969, p. 316) refers to the project as "the greatest single study done thus far by an American sociologist." The data range from narrative life histories and letters to official records, observations, and ethnographies. The study's lasting significance resides less in these data and the problem choice than in conceptualization.

The adaptational sequence of family organization, disorganization, and reorganization is one such contribution; another concerns the disparity between family expectation and resources, a perspective uniquely suited for understanding American families in the pre-Depression decades. Migration and economic change generally expanded the gap between preferred or expected conditions and the actual situation of a family. Thomas argued that the influence of economic position on family life depended on the family's claims and on how it defined the situation: "If situations are defined as real, they are real in their consequences."

Studies through the 1920s (Wandersee, 1981) observed family discontent over economics in the midst of rising income, a trend that made sense only in terms of rising expectations concerning living standards. Soaring aspirations among families of the 1920s left earners and consumers feeling that they were barely getting along, despite a substantial rise in income. The incongruity of doing better and feeling worse was especially common in the middle class. Larger economic claims on marriage were noted as a primary factor in the rising divorce rate. Between 1890 and the 1920s, Robert and Helen Lynd (1929) found an increasing impact of economic factors in Middletown on the likelihood of marital instability, even though economic well-being had improved. Symbolizing the strain and disorder theme at the time is Ernest Mowrer's (1926) book on family disorganization and Willard Waller's (1930) case study of the causal process of marital dissolution and postdivorce adjustment.

During the pre-Depression era of family studies, few issues were more salient than matters of dependency. In addition to the economic and adaptive problems noted above, they include social pressures, change in women's status, and functional change in the family unit's relation to other institutions and to society as a whole. Noting the family's transition from production to consumption, sociologist William Ogburn (1929) brought greater public visibility to the emergence of a smaller, more specialized family unit with greater equality and mutuality in marital and parent-child relationships. At the functional core of family life were childbearing, socialization, and the nurturance of personality. Observers reported a rise in the appreciation of humanistic sentiments in the middle-class family, the development of a new companionship, a genuine partnership. Ernest Burgess and Harvey Locke (1945) combined these trends in their influential thesis on the unfinished transition "from institution to companionship,

based on mutual affection, intimate communication, and mutual acceptance of division of labor and procedures of decision-making." This pre-
sumptive change in the quality and form of marriage and family soon
became a major thrust of sociological work on the family that continued up
to the 1960s.

Problems of young and old were also troublesome aspects of dependence and independence in the 1920s. Adolescence and old age were
socially recognized by this time, and both soon became targets of widespread inquiry, as illustrated by Margaret Mead's (1928) study of the
transition to adulthood, Kingsley Davis's (1940) penetrating essays on
childhood and adolescence (see also Elder, 1980a), and investigations of
the aged, their deprivations and social significance. These investigations
were motivated in part by retirement, pension, and health concerns,
especially as publicized by proponents of social insurance. A life-span
concept of developmental processes appeared in some texts and research at
this time after years of neglect (Baltes, 1979; Pressey, Janney, & Kuhlen,
1939).

ERA II, FAMILY ADAPTATIONS IN HARD TIMES AND WAR

Family studies of the 1930s show both continuity and change relative
to problem orientations of the 1910s and 1920s. Though economic pressures swamped other issues on the family, they accentuated some conditions that had claimed attention in the twenties, especially the problems of
migrant families in the city and the risk of marital failure, the one-parent
household, and remarriage. The ingredients of successful, adaptive marriages became the focal point of innovative quantitative studies of marital
adjustment, especially Burgess and Cottrell's *Predicting Success or Failure
in Marriage* (1939). Families on the move were clearly not unique to the
1930s, but the mounting problems of urban blacks from the rural South
accentuated the economic crisis of mass unemployment.

The human and urban consequences of this northward migration
occupy a major part of the 1930s research of E. Franklin Frazier, a
University of Chicago sociologist at this time. Frazier's major work is *The
Negro Family in the United States* (1939, abridged ed., 1966), a study
which Ernest Burgess (p. ix) introduced as "the most valuable contribution
to the literature of the family since the publication, twenty years ago, of
The Polish Peasant in Europe and America." Though Frazier's work
reflects the ideas of his mentor, Robert Park, he turned to *The Polish
Peasant* for an analytic framework in which to study black families and the
great northward migration. Frazier and Thomas-Znaniecki refer to the
outside penetration of isolated rural communities as a first step in the

migratory flow toward greater opportunity. Moreover, Frazier highlighted the process of family disorganization in these northern "cities of destruction" to the exclusion of an adaptive, effective side of the process (Elder, 1984b; Gutman, 1976), a bias equally characteristic of *The Polish Peasant*. In both accounts, migration undermines family organization.

These landmark studies of the Chicago era invited criticism of their emphasis on disorganization because they slighted other processes in family change, including reorganization. Though justified in many respects, critiques of the disorganization theme often reinforced another myth, that of the "over-integrated, resilient family." As Prude (1976, p. 424) correctly notes from studies of families in the working class, this work has generally failed to comprehend that a "family could be both affected by and effective in its milieu, that it could be simultaneously unsuccessful in resisting changes in its own traditions and successful in aiding its members to cope with the world in which they found themselves." The same family could be *victor* and *victim* in different domains, just as the same event has positive and negative influences.

Collapse of the economy in the Great Depression magnified and generalized social concerns, shifting attention to an examination of families in economic crisis. Unlike an exclusive "disorganization" perspective, the Depression studies gave particular attention to factors that explained the *variable* course of families under changing circumstances. Why did some family units recover effectively from income loss without lasting harm, while others disintegrated under similar conditions? Using a small sample of middle-class families, Robert Angell (1936/1965) identified family adaptability and integration as primary determinants of family outcomes during the 1930s; Cavan and Ranck (1938) examined the case records of 100 Chicago families to find that family survival and recovery varied according to the pre-Depression state of family organization; and Komarovsky (1940) stressed both normative and emotional elements of parental authority in times of unemployment. With a case study approach to 24 New Haven families in the working class, Bakke (1940) identified a modal family trajectory from disorganization *after unemployment* to reorganization, and explored deviations from this career.

The onset of World War II put America back to work; employed behavioral scientists in one of the most influential studies of modern social science, a multivolume series on *The American Soldier* (Stouffer et al., 1949);[2] and raised important questions about American family life. War

[2]*The Polish Peasant, The Negro Family,* and *The American Soldier* are generally recognized as landmark studies in sociology and in social science generally. Thus in an essay on "the American soldier and the public," Daniel Lerner (1950, p. 236) observed that "not since

brought Americans together with a common purpose, though family problems and studies had much to do with the consequences of *separation*. This break was expressed in the family absence of mothers and fathers through long hours in war industries, in the migration of war workers (Schwarzweller, Brown, & Mangalam, 1971), and in the family separations of Japanese-Americans, servicemen, and the newly divorced.

Noteworthy studies of these separations include investigations of the mass internment of Japanese-American families during the war (Thomas & Nishimoto, 1946); Reuben Hill's (1949) pioneering study of family separation and reunion among servicemen, which became a model for subsequent work on the subject of family crises (see McCubbin, Dahl, Metres, Hunter, & Plag, 1974); and William Goode's (1956) study of the postdivorce adjustment of Detroit women during the winter of 1948 when the divorce rate had soared to a new high. This was the first major study of adjustments in the divorce process since Willard Waller's *The Old Love and the New* (1930).[3] As in the Depression studies, Goode's research focused on the process by which families and individuals worked out adaptations (even reorganizations) under the terms of a new situation. Disorganization represented primarily a stage of family change and adaptation, not a career.

ERA III, FAMILIES IN AN ORGANIZATIONAL SOCIETY

Problem orientations of the postwar era were shaped by concepts of the specialized family in an emerging organizational society; a view based on long-term social development and structural change. The evolving pattern of companionship, mutuality, and independent choice in family relations was heralded as one of "the great transformations of our time"

Thomas and Znaniecki's *Polish Peasant* has there been a socio-psychological work of such scope, imaginativeness, technical rigor, and important results. . . . Social science *is* coming of age." Each study makes an enduring contribution toward understanding social change and the family. In the case of *The American Soldier*, this contribution is both theoretical (in terms of reference group theory, etc.) and empirical; servicemen became the male heads of households in postwar America. See Burr, Hill, Nye, & Reiss (1979) for a recent overview of family studies.

[3]Strongly influenced by Waller, Goode's interest in aspects of family disorganization, especially illegitimacy and divorce, has been carried on by a former student, Frank Furstenberg (1976, 1982). The major change across these professional generations appears in a more differentiated view of family and life change. In studies launched during the post-1960s era, Furstenberg has tended to give particular attention to the process by which families and individuals manage to reorganize and improve their life chances. The research question had changed.

(Young & Willmott, 1957; see also Young & Willmott, 1973). More than before, when the family seemed bound by custom and tradition, postwar families were depicted as independent, isolated, and vulnerable. The unknowns of marital success and survival in this setting continued to attract investigation (Dizard, 1968), reflecting the influence of Ernest Burgess. Concerns were expressed about the consequences of functional specialization, using an image of the "diminished family" in the midst of expanding and competitive spheres of influence—schools and peer groups, work, and the changing economy.

Studies of children in the family gave some attention to these developments by comparing families in the middle and working class, and by distinguishing between the old and new middle classes. In a classic essay that resolved much confusion, Bronfenbrenner (1958) identified historical change in the relation between social class and parental behavior as an explanation for the confusing results obtained up to that point. Class differences had declined since the 1930s. Miller and Swanson (1958) broadened the territory by focusing on change in the organization of work, from entrepreneurial to bureaucratic, as a determinant of a new mode of parental behavior; and in the 1950s Melvin Kohn (1977) with John Clausen launched a series of studies of social class and child rearing that stressed "explanation." As Kohn (1963) has noted many times, the important question is why social class matters in children's lives. How are the imperatives of social position expressed in family life? This question had not been addressed satisfactorily up to that point.

Generalized prosperity and the surging birthrate ostensibly announced a family-centered era, and yet families were pictured as losing control over their children in a battle with the all-encompassing peer group and ever larger schools. Institutional differentiation and population growth produced greater age segregation up to the 1960s and more social distance between the world of parents and that of children. Some unapplauded features of socialization by peers were examined in David Riesman's *The Lonely Crowd* (1950), James Coleman's *The Adolescent Society* (1961), and Urie Bronfenbrenner's *Two Worlds of Childhood* (1970). From other empirical studies, oppositional notions of family and agemates in socialization were replaced by a more differentiated and conditional portrait of social influence and development. One of the largest studies ever conducted on youth and the family, Charles Bowerman's Adolescent Project in the South and Mid-West (ca. late 1950s, early 1960s [see Elder, 1980b]) identified variations in the quality of family life as the principal determinant of the socialization role of peers, as ally or as adversary.

Contrary to impressions of the family "on its own," postwar studies (Adams, 1968) assembled a rich empirical account of contacts and bonds linking nuclear families with relatives in a social network. Amidst evidence of kin as a family resource, Elizabeth Bott's (1957/1971) *Family and Social Network* identified some costs of kinship in a study of relations between a couple's social network and the marital relation. Bott argued from a small number of cases that a couple's shared experience in marriage is a function of whether husband and wife come to marriage with close-knit networks and remain a participant in them. When such relations exist, the marriage assumes peripheral status as each spouse is drawn to individual spheres of activities outside the conjugal bond and nuclear family.

Empirical support for Bott's thesis is mixed, yet the work represents a pioneering study of family networks and an important sociological study of postwar social structure when viewed in terms of the research it has generated (Gordon & Downing, 1978). Of equal note at the time, the study encouraged fresh thinking about how the external and internal environments of the family are related: the family's social ecology and history, on the one hand, and its affective quality, authority structure, and interactional pattern, on the other. The study's full implications led Max Gluckman (in Bott, 1971, p. xiv) to judge it "one of the most illuminating analyses ever to emerge from social anthropology."

ERA IV, SOCIAL CHANGE AND FAMILY REORGANIZATION, POST-1960[4]

Just as the Great Depression turned analysis toward hard times, the civil strife and mass movements of the 1960s and 1970s brought social change, its antecedents and consequences, to the forefront of empirical work on the family. This emphasis stands out against the more cross-sectional character of postwar research. Though long a prime example of ahistorical bias, generational research in the 1960s became more sensitive to social and historical context.

Student protests raised questions concerning the diverse historical worlds of young and old; the contrast between postwar affluence and Depression scarcity. The generation concept did not offer precision for investigating such experience since members of a generation do *not* occupy a specific historical location. Generation thus proved ill-suited to unraveling the sources of change, especially when compared to the meanings of

---

[4]The clearest example of the shift from disorganization to reorganization in family studies appears in the questions posed. More studies began to ask how deprived or hard-pressed families were able to cope or manage under great difficulty. The controversy involving the Moynihan report (Rainwater & Yancey, 1967) on black families illustrates this changing problem orientation and conceptualization. Moynihan presented a disorganization thesis at a time when its limitations were well known.

age. Birth year locates family members in their historical setting, and the social meanings of age specify their life stage. By the end of the 1960s, temporal distinctions of generation *and* cohort (cf. Kertzer, 1983) were informing studies of social and family change. *Children of the Great Depression* (Elder, 1974), a project initiated during the late 1960s, combined both concepts to link historical change and life patterns across the generations.

Two developments were encouraged by an emerging age-based perspective on lives and families: (1) an appreciation of age differences as a source of cleavage between young and old, instead of differences between the generations, and (2) a fundamental change in the concept and study of socialization. Studies of youth protest in the 1960s were largely informed by an intergenerational model from Kingsley Davis's (1940) essay on parent-youth conflict, though empirical findings consistently pointed to smaller differences between parents and offspring than between youth and the larger adult society. In other words, differences in belief and action had less to do with lineage membership than with cohort and age-group ties. A purely generational approach to social change in youth experience neglected the relationship of youth and options, and lacked precision concerning the historical location of parents and offspring.

The second development occurred in the midst of what might be called a "golden age of socialization studies." During the early 1960s, a committee of the Social Science Research Council was organized around the topic of "socialization and personality." The end of the decade saw the publication of a book by the SSRC committee (Clausen, 1968) and the publication of a *Handbook of Socialization Theory and Research* (Goslin, 1969), as well as many chapters. Prevailing images of family upbringing still slighted father's role, the socialization experience of older children and parents, the reciprocal nature of social interaction, and the educative dimension of family influence. Though all of these biases reflect preoccupation with the early years of human development, a broader view was underway in studies of life span and life course development (Featherman, 1982). One example is the simple notion of lifelong socialization. Hidden behind this notion is a revolutionary concept in which child socialization and development are linked to such processes in the lives of parents. Changing adult behavior and functioning over the life span represent a strategic link between a family's social position and children (Kohn, 1977). Children are better understood with knowledge of the developmental experience of parents. In this sense, matters of adult development have relevance for the study of children in families.

Related to this interdependence is a change in the meaning of socialization versus social selection (cf. Scarr & McCartney, 1983). The relation between child and environment may be due to the environment's influence and to the recruitment of particular children to the environment. Recruitment may express the child's own choice as in the selection of athletic programs, summer camps, and friends. Traditionally this selection process has been viewed as a methodological problem in socialization research; researchers felt they must disentangle the effects of environment selection and influence. By contrast, a selection effect has conceptual significance within the temporal perspective of the life course where socialization represents a lifelong and reciprocal process. The individual is both product and producer of a life course. From this vantage point, a selection effect exemplifies the potential agency of the individual or family in choosing life's niches and pathways, as well as the outcome of prior socialization which shaped current choices.

Sex and race-ethnicity joined age as problematic lines of social demarcation in the 1960s and as new foci of family research by the mid-1960s. For the first time in decades, empirical studies of the black family were launched from a sociological perspective, often in response to problems that had much in common with postwar issues, such as the stability and quality of marriage (Furstenberg, Hershberg, & Modell, 1975; Scanzoni, 1971). Other questions dealt with the presumed importance of extended kin as a resource for black families, especially for those with low income and only one parent (McAdoo, 1978; Martin & Martin, 1978; Shimkin, Shimkin, & Frate, 1978; Stack, 1974). Studies of the black kin network documented the role of extended kin on matters of child care, socialization, and emotional and material aid. Especially noteworthy contributions have come from historians with a social science orientation. One example is Herbert Gutman's (1976) *The Black Family in Slavery and Freedom.*

Four trends after 1960 placed issues of women's status and role at the forefront of new directions in sociological analysis: (1) the upswing in divorce and remarriage (Carter & Glick, 1976); (2) the rising level of employed mothers (Hoffman & Nye, 1974; see Hoffman, this volume); (3) the increasing number of teenage pregnancies; and (4) the expanding proportion of older Americans in the population, especially widows. Just as the soaring divorce rate after World War II prompted questions of cause and effect, the recent upward trend in divorce and remarriage set in motion a new wave of studies concerning the effects of divorce and resulting circumstances on parents, children, and kin ties (Hetherington, Cox, & Cox, 1981; see Hetherington & Camara, this volume); and on the process by which remarriage alters and reconstitutes the household, family bonds, and kin network (Furstenberg, 1982). With over half of American mothers in the labor force of the 1970s, the balance of research on women's work has gradually shifted from antecedents to consequences, such as intellectual growth and a sense of competence (Miller, Schooler, Kohn, & Miller, 1979), childbearing plans and actions (Waite & Stolzenberg, 1976), and the division of labor and marital power (Rallings & Nye, 1979).

More than any other single factor, demographic growth of young and old made rates of teenage pregnancy and support of the aged highly visible concerns by the 1970s. Among the numerous studies of adolescent pregnancy and parenthood, Furstenberg's (1976) longitudinal analysis of a low-income black sample is especially valuable for its emphasis on how life deprivations or setbacks can be surmounted with personal and family resources. At the other end of the life span, the increasing proportion of widows and declining family size underscored the problematic state of their social support in Lopata's (1979) *Women as Widows*.

The growing prevalence of variant events in the life course (teenage pregnancy, cohabitation, mother's employment, divorce, decisions not to marry or have children) has tended to accentuate the diversity of family experience. Indeed, attitude trends from the 1950s to the late 1970s show a very pronounced increase in tolerance for Americans who do not marry (Veroff, Douvan, & Kulka, 1981). Today men and women are more likely to view rewarding family relationships in marriage and parenting as both problematic and centrally important in their lives, an orientation coupled with rising levels of education. Sensitivity to the individual in family relationships increases with education, according to this study, and partly accounts for the high level of acknowledged problems and benefits in relationships among the better educated. Consistent with the Burgess-Locke thesis on the companionate marriage, the salience of relationship issues in marriage and parenthood constitutes one of the strongest family trends in the American population between the 1950s and late 1970s.

To conclude this survey of problem foci, we come to the economic pressures of the 1970s to 1980s and their family implications. For the first time since the Great Depression, economic pressures have generated a large number of studies of unemployment and underemployment, of work-life instability and economic loss as stressors in families (Kasl, 1979). Spawned by the War on Poverty in the 1960s, the Panel Study of Income Dynamics at the University of Michigan has been following over a decade the economic fortunes of more than 6,000 American families. Using the full resources of the panel study, Duncan and Morgan (1980) found that undesirable events (job loss, divorce, involuntary residential change) generally lowered a sense of competence or efficacy among men and women. Consistent with this finding is the accumulating evidence on economic deprivation as a principal source of emotional depression (Pearlin, Lieberman, Menaghan, & Mullan, 1981), family stress, and family violence (Straus, Gelles, & Steinmetz, 1980).

OVERVIEW

The historical record for the twentieth century shows strong recurring themes in family studies. A good many problem orientations of the early decades faded after 1940, only to surface once again in the late 1960s. Both eras, early and most recent, are distinguished by problems of social change, urban distress, and socioeconomic deprivations in family life; by the visibility of marital and family dissolution; and by research issues involving differentiation by age, gender, and race-ethnicity. The two periods share an emphasis on the contextual, temporal, and dynamic elements of family patterns. According to the prevailing concept, family units are embedded in historically defined contexts where they are subject to change over time in a process of reciprocal interaction and influence among family members (Burgess & Huston, 1979; Lerner & Spanier, 1978).

The correspondence in problems extends to perspectives as well, both waning and ascending. In the two eras, we see a more behavioral emphasis through the limitations of highly abstract formulations (evolutionism, early 1900s; structural-functionalism, 1960s) and the compelling pressures of similar realities, of change and deprivation from prosperity to scarcity. Both eras in family studies emerged from the controlling influence of single paradigms and represent transitional times of diversity and vigor in theory and research. The first era was dominated by the Chicago school of social science, and two prominent members of this school (W. I. Thomas and Ernest Burgess) established distinctive lines of research on the family that extend into the second era of behavioral studies, the post-1960s. Life course studies, one of the more active domains of the second era, draw upon aspects of research and theory that correspond with the orientations of Thomas and Burgess. These orientations share a dynamic perspective that is well suited to examining basic questions of family behavior. They represent two of three analytical traditions in family studies up to the 1980s.

III. ANALYTICAL TRADITIONS:
STRUCTURAL AND INTERACTIONIST, 1920s TO 1980s

Family studies have generally followed three analytical traditions since *The Polish Peasant*: (1) structural—mainly centered on the structural or social system properties of society, the family, and their relations (Parsons, 1951); (2) behavioral—primarily focused on the action and interaction of family members, individuals; and (3) family action in structured situations—a cross-level model linking behavior to structured options and constraints. The second and third traditions draw upon interactionism, the study of social and symbolic interaction. Functionalism as practiced by Talcott Parsons and analysts of long-term structural change belong to the first category; Ernest Burgess and some contemporary practitioners of symbolic interaction illustrate the second mode of study; and W. I. Thomas's perspective on the family, relating both structural and behavioral considerations, illustrates the third perspective.[5]

STRUCTURAL AND INTERACTION ANALYSIS

In structural-functional analysis, the family is typically represented as a system of interrelated social positions and roles that is linked by functional processes to other social institutions. This concept appears in theories of long-term change in which the family system becomes more specialized through structural differentiation (Goode, 1963; Smelser, 1959). Interactionist theories (symbolic interaction, exchange, etc.) are distinguished by their behavioral emphasis (Turner, 1970). However, the contrast between structure and behavior is not always a contrast between different levels of analysis. Principles of functional analysis can be applied to social units at all levels of research, from family groups (e.g., the composition and authority structure of households) to family systems in regions and larger institutional arrangements. A cross-level example is Talcott Parsons's (with Bales, 1955) *Family, Socialization, and Interaction Process*. This volume blends the abstract level of family systems in whole societies with functional issues on the micro level, especially sex-role differentiation in families and the social requirements of group properties.

The scope of role analysis offers another view of the relation between structural and behavioral approaches. A comparative study of parenting roles in two cultures is well suited to structural analysis. But emphasis on the *development* of parental relationships and roles requires an interactional approach. Likewise, the social networks of families can be analyzed and compared as structural forms, or they can be viewed as a changing product of the preferences, social constraints, and actions of people. With groups and people in the picture, behavioral perspectives bring a dynamic

---

[5]Structural and interactionist perspectives are joined in the work of a number of scholars, including Bernard Farber, a former student of Ernest Burgess. One of his earliest books (1964) viewed the family from the perspective of both social organization and interaction. Farber's research career (see 1968, 1971, 1981), like that of other students of Burgess (such as Reuben Hill, 1970), is most characterized by a focus on kinship, a topic to which Burgess gave little attention in his own career.

element to recurring social patterns or structures. Family structure, as a relatively enduring configuration or pattern, thus represents a social construction in terms of the setting or situation, as contrasted with a given arrangement.

Writing just after the end of the World War II, Leonard Cottrell (1948, p. 125), a collaborator of Ernest Burgess and a student of George Herbert Mead, made a persuasive case for functionalism as *the* paradigm of family studies; the family, he argued, should be viewed as a "functional mechanism." A concerted effort in family studies requires "a common frame of reference for—analysis and interpretation." A good many sociologists followed this advice, but in doing so they chose a frame of reference that was frequently inappropriate for questions of primary interest. Some of these questions concerned the behavioral world of families, parents, and children, a level far removed from macro functionalism and structural trends. Throughout the postwar era, behavioral inferences from structural theory were interpreted as statements concerning actual behavior. Three examples illustrate this practice: inferences from the high rate of postwar divorce, the postwar family's specialized role in socialization, and the structural pattern of kinship.

Across each example, family trends and institutional arrangements tell something about the options and constraints families encounter, but they do not indicate what choices families make or how they work out adaptations. Thus a rising divorce rate points to the increasing risk of a fatherless upbringing, but it does not specify the actual situation of children in divorce, such as their contacts with father and other males. Building on accounts of postwar change, analysts pictured a socialization environment in which parental authority would be undermined by large schools, peer groups, and community functions. However, studies (Elder, 1980b) from the 1950s to the present document the central role of *effective* families in the lives of children and youth. Peer dependence has much to do with parental neglect. The kinship inference is based on Parsons's (1965) concept of the "isolated nuclear family" which refers to a form of social structure in the bilateral kin system of the United States. It did not claim that family units are behaviorally isolated, though countless studies in Europe and America have ignored this point.

Two commonly cited weaknesses of functional analysis have less to do with the approach itself than with prevailing modes of thought during the postwar era: (1) the neglect of conflict, tensions, violence; and (2) a lack of sensitivity to historical facts. Both limitations were equally characteristic of interactionist studies of the family through the 1950s. Thus Lewis Coser's (1956) skillful analysis of the functions of conflict did not spur research on family conflict. By tracing out the conditions under which conflict fosters integration and social integration leads to conflict, Coser generated novel insights concerning what functionalists have called the social ambivalence of family life (Merton, 1976); the social relations that pull family members in opposite or conflicting directions (e.g., a male's relation to mother and wife, the cross-pressures of kin and marital involvement [Bott, 1957/ 1971]). From Coser's early work to the present, sociological research has tended to ignore the diverse and conflicting dimensions of family relations. Thus the widely acknowledged benefits of kin support have been divorced too often from the undesired consequences, such as a sense of indebtedness or dependence.

FAMILY INTERACTION AND THE LARGER ENVIRONMENT

One cannot explain marriage, family, or socialization patterns from the vantage point of institutional forms alone. W. I. Thomas (in Volkart, 1951, p. 147) made this point by noting that "a social institution can be fully understood only if we . . . analyze the way in which it appears in the personal experience of various members of the group and follow the influence which it has upon their lives . . ." This statement was made in the early twentieth century, a time when social custom was fast losing power in the regulation of family behavior, when couples seemed to be largely independent, bound mainly by love and companionship. Family studies up to the work of Thomas had not "even pretended to study the modern family as behavior," as a "living, growing, changing thing," to use Ernest Burgess's words (in Bogue, 1974, p. 142). Out of this recognition and study came Burgess's well-known definition of the family (1926) as a "unity of interacting persons" or personalities.

Thomas and Burgess advanced different versions of an approach to family interaction, a difference most readily understood in terms of their compelling research questions. For Thomas the central question had to do with the control people and groups exercise over their environments in the course of social change. Especially problematic in this respect is the great transition between a social order in which family members are subordinated to the family collective's will (rural Poland) and a new society in which individuals strive to achieve control over their own lives and environment. Thus Thomas and Znaniecki (1974, p. 1704) suggest that marriage "almost ceases to be a social institution" owing to the decline of the old social sanctions.

This institutional void became a fundamental concern to Ernest Burgess and a wellspring of research ideas for his students. These differing emphases are illustrated by two contemporary accounts of the instability of remarriage. In the Thomas tradition, Cherlin (1978) views remarriage behavior in terms of the lack of institutional guidelines for this relationship. The high rate of instability is partly due to the incomplete institutionalization of remarriage. Furstenberg's (1982) explanation has more in common with the views of Burgess and Waller. He argues that the risk of instability among remarriages has much to do with the past marital history and learning of each partner. They may be less willing to invest in the second marriage, owing to the price of past investments that went sour. Any sign of marital difficulty is likely to make investment less appealing. Remarriages in this account are subject to a self-fulfilling prophecy of marital failure.

Lineal units and the vertical hierarchy from child to parent and grandparent were primary foci in Thomas's research, but with emphasis on the parent-child relationship. This relationship occupied a primary role in Thomas's *The Child in America* (1928, p. xiii), an issue of great public concern in the 1920s: "It is widely felt that the demoralization of young persons, the prevalence of delinquency, crime, and profound mental disturbances are very serious problems, and that the situation is growing worse instead of better" (italics removed). For Burgess, the affinal or conjugal unit was primary, with marital quality as a core domain. He found the ideas of symbolic interaction, as proposed by Charles H. Cooley, George Herbert Mead, and John Dewey, especially congenial. Marital consensus, idealization of spouse, and affective sentiments are common variables in this tradition.

Throughout a distinguished career, Thomas kept his eye on larger social structures *and* the behavior of families and individuals. Families represented actors in structured situations, not primarily the consequences of external forces. Family options and adaptations are partly a function of what families bring to situations, of the new situation and its definition. Burgess was also keenly aware of family ecologies, especially within the urban metropolis, but he showed less inclination to relate history, social structure, and ecological factors to family interaction and especially to the marital dyad where "affection, temperamental compatibility, and social adaptability" had become the key ingredients of marital success (Burgess & Cottrell, 1939). Thematic of Burgess's framework is the interplay of individual characteristics and social interaction within the family, a perspective on the dynamic relation between individual and family development. Interacting personalities may or may not lead to a social unity of family life. As in contemporary studies of stress (Liker & Elder, 1983; Weissman & Paykel, 1974), Burgess would argue that neither mode of development can be fully understood by excluding the other. Individual stress may influence and be influenced by marital and parent-child relations.

The clearest example of Burgess's dual focus on family and individual development appears in the formative stages of family life. The task is to account for the process by which two persons "with a history" at marriage become a couple and a family with a history (Berger & Kellner, 1974; Rapaport, 1964, 1967; Reiss, 1981). In other words, how does the family emerge as a social unity of interacting persons? From this interactionist perspective, the concept of a "given" family pattern is clearly secondary to a view of the family as a social unit in process. The social unity of interacting persons is problematic. This premise underlies Burgess's central concern with marital quality or adjustment.

Whatever the cultural model of family and its structural variations, the interactionist explores what people do within such frameworks. Ralph Turner, a prominent interactionist out of the Burgess-Mead tradition, refers to *crescive* or emergent bonds as primary clues to family adaptation and survival. The development of bonds of mutual identification and shared history is ultimately (1970, p. 80) "the source of assured persistence and stability in marital relationships. Their emergence between parent and child is the basis for the continuing relationship after the dependency bond has been dissolved." This concept of family as process, stressing the symbolic dimensions of family behavior, also appears in W. I. Thomas's perspective on family action in structured situations.

Thomas's resource concept of family adaptations and change has no parallel in Burgess's work, though Waller (1938, chap. 10) applied the concept to processes of evolving family relations, to bargaining and exploitation. The resource concept brings a number of issues within the framework of an interactional perspective: for example, the study of authority and power (Blood & Wolfe, 1960; Rodman, 1967), resource deprivation and force or violence (Goode, 1971), and the allocation/generation of resources in the family economy (Elder, 1974). The concept of resource is the workhorse of exchange theory on the above topics, and on the network of exchange among members of the kin system (Anderson, 1971). According to Thomas, resources are means that enable families to fulfill or meet their claims and expectations, including specific skills, knowledge, and social support. A perceived disequilibrium between claims and resources represents a crisis or problem situation, a situation that is likely to be defined as threatening, damaging, or simply stressful.

Though Burgess did not set forth an adaptive model that matched Thomas's, he too approached the study of families by relating what people carry into situations to the subsequent course of their relationships—cultural models of family life, attachments to parents, modes of problem solving, role concepts. Neither Burgess nor Thomas advanced a detailed conceptual account of family development. However, Willard Waller made some progress along this line by drawing upon their ideas.

Instead of taking family solidarity as given and studying conflicts as deviance, Waller (1938) viewed solidarity as problematic, as a process and outcome requiring explanation. He spoke of the initial ideals of solidarity which each partner brings to marriage, the clash between these ideals and reality, and the fiction of solidarity that may arise. As in marriage, the career of parenthood involves the clash of competing interests, the ambivalence of sentiments, and tensions between individuation and social integration. Using a natural history approach, Waller identified a sequence of five stages that resemble family cycle models in contemporary research: (1) dependency in the family of origin, (2) courtship, (3) the first years of marriage, (4) parenthood, and (5) the empty nest.[6] The entire sequence represents a normative model of a life trajectory. Ironically, Waller's typology undermined his objective of relating family units to social and cultural institutions. Instead of encouraging a contextual view of the family, the typology's emphasis on the reproductive process focused attention on the *interior* of family life, including the inexorable pace of individual development and aging among members of the household. In this respect, it has more in common with the Burgess tradition than with Thomas's approach.

These observations identify some points of similarity and difference between the analytical perspectives of W. I. Thomas and Ernest Burgess. Their central problems issued from the great transition between two societies, one largely agrarian and the other urban-industrial. Thomas investigated the transition's impact on families, the generations, and individuals, while Burgess turned to problems of marriage and family stability in the new land. This difference is reflected in Thomas's distinctive view of the family as an actor in structured situations, a perspective which relates the interior and exterior of family life with emphasis on the parent-child axis. For Thomas as well as Burgess, personalities and social interaction are

---

[6]These stages in a natural history favored an imprecise concept of family development by excluding events, transitions, and their differential timing. Though Waller recognized the critical elements of family timing, his ordered stages do not tell us when they occur in relation to people's lives and times. Despite such limitations, Waller's thinking on sequential phases was a forerunner of subsequent development models of families and individuals over time, especially in the thinking of a Chicago-based working group during the late 1940s and early 1950s. The group included Bernice Neugarten, Reuben Hill, Robert Havighurst, and Evelyn Duvall. Among the research examples are William Goode's (1956) investigation of the aftermath of divorce, Reuben Hill's (1970) study of family development in three generations (Hill revised Waller's 1938 family book in 1951), and Frank Furstenberg's (1976) investigation of adolescent parenthood.

part of family chemistry. Ideas of time and process inform their shared concept of family dynamics, which relates individual and family development. These ideas are most clearly expressed in concepts and studies of family transitions.

FAMILY TRANSITIONS IN CONCEPT AND RESEARCH

The concept of transition appears in Burgess's version of the passing of tradition and the rise of marital companionship and in the study of family transitions through the work of his students and collaborators. Thomas's adaptational perspective reflects his assumption that social transitions provide a strategic opportunity to observe and to study the mechanism of change. Over 50 years ago in a presidential address to his sociological colleagues (in Volkart, 1951, pp. 59–69), Thomas discussed the explanatory understanding that could be achieved by the study of family and individual behavior in situational transitions that represent either experiments of design or nature (see also Bronfenbrenner, 1979). The contemporary relevance of this position needs little emphasis. Writing in the 1970s, Parkes (1971, p. 101) refers to "psycho-social transitions" as a potentially fruitful field of study (see also Clausen, 1972; Hareven, 1978; Spanier & Furstenberg, 1983). Transitions, such as parenthood, divorce, and death, are "turning points for better or worse psycho-social adjustment. They often constitute natural experiments of great theoretical and practical importance."

Thomas's writings make at least four contributions to the study of family transitions. First, by relating family claims, expectations, or culture to resources, he provides a simple but often ignored rationale of why drastic resource changes have such power in shaping family behavior. It is the gap between claims and resources, a type of relative deprivation (Williams, 1975), that generates problems for families and not simply the resource level. The perceived gap is expressed in definitions of the situation that portray the subjective world or environment. To a large extent, economic conditions make a difference in family life through their relation to particular subjective realities, whether positive or negative. A second contribution involves the relation between how families respond to new situations and what they bring to them. A family's line of adaptation is influenced by its life history as well as by the constraints and options of the new situation. A case in point is the long established association between the prior work status of women and their labor market entry when times are difficult (Waite, 1980).

A third contribution is seen in the conditional influence of family adaptations on the effects of events. The family and individual consequences of an event depend on the specific line of adaptation. Economic loss may lead to greater indebtedness and disorganization or to expenditure reductions and multiple earners. A similar perspective appears in one of the most ambitious studies of life transitions, the Chicago project of Pearlin and Lieberman (1979). In their account, the occurrence of life events, however deprivational, does not by itself ensure distress or life disorganization. The impact depends on the resulting life circumstance, a perception that is common to Thomas's early research on families and social change.

The fourth contribution from Thomas's work involves the relation between individual and family transitions. The occurrence and timing of events and transitions in a person's life may be controlled or regulated by family imperatives. The scheduling of a son's departure from home, for example, may be dependent on the family's state of well-being. According to recent historical work (Hogan, 1981; Modell, Furstenberg, & Hershberg, 1976) control over early life transitions has shifted from the family of the late nineteenth century to the generalized requirements of formal institutions, such as workplace and school.

The relevance of Thomas's contribution also appears in the more specialized field of research on families in crisis situations. A case in point is Reuben Hill's model in *Families under Stress* (1949), which has served as a theoretical foundation for subsequent work since its publication over 30 years ago. A distinguished former student of Ernest Burgess, Hill studied two family pressure points in World War II, the departure of men for military service and their return several years later as veterans. Different adjustment processes and resources were involved during the two transitions, though both fit a general model of adaptation, called ABC-X. Factor A refers to the event which, when combined with related hardships, interacts with family resources, factor B. Family definitions of the event (C) result from the interaction of factors A and B, thereby producing a crisis (X). The modal trajectory of family adjustment runs from initial states of disorganization to a new level of organization with partial or full recovery. From the Depression research of Robert Angell (1936/1965) and others (Cavan & Ranck, 1938), Hill borrowed concepts of family resources, such as degree of integration and adaptability. *Families under Stress* views family crises in terms of the relation between resources and the change event, not as a function of the disparity between claims and resources (Hansen & Johnson, 1979), as in Thomas's model. This disparity appears in both family and individual stress.

The interaction of individual and family development, life transitions, and adaptations plays a major conceptual role in a Johns Hopkins longitudinal study of the first birth (Entwisle & Doering, 1981), a study of 120 white women, middle and working class, who were experiencing pregnancy for the first time. Sixty husbands were also part of the study. The major points of contact include an interview with the wife at the sixth or seventh month of pregnancy, interviews with the wife and husband at the ninth month, interviews with wife at birth, postpartum interviews with the wife at 2–3 weeks, and interviews with the husband at 4–8 weeks.

Two exogenous variables are part of the general model of birth experience (measured by how the women felt both emotionally and physically at two points following birth): women's preparation level—all sources of knowledge about what to expect in labor and delivery and how to use this knowledge in coping (sources included books, movies, medical classes, and preparation classes); and husband's participation, based on reports from wives—participation in preparation, labor, and delivery. Two factors represented potential linkages to birth experience, a measure of the worst pain during the first stage of labor, and level of awareness, based on medication received and level of consciousness during actual delivery. Both preparation level and husband's participation constitute sources of a woman's control over the birth experience.

The Johns Hopkins study also reflects Thomas's approach by viewing the birth experience in historical context and by relating the developmental trajectories of family and individual members. Elements of the new model of pregnancy and birth were rare in the general population up to the 1970s. As Entwisle and Doering (1981, p. 2) point out, "In 1960 men almost never entertained the thought of witnessing the births of their own children. The few who did wish to be present, were frequently barred from the delivery suite even when they themselves were physicians." By comparison, two-thirds of the husbands in the Johns Hopkins study were present at delivery. As for women's preparation, the 1960s research of Entwisle and Doering encountered problems finding couples in childbirth classes. Ten years later, sampling problems centered on the difficulty of finding couples who were *not* attending such classes, a pattern that applied to both middle and working class. In combination these trends indicate the rapidly spreading belief (Entwisle & Doering, 1981, p. 43) "that an uncomplicated birth should be primarily under the mother's and father's control rather than being controlled by medical professionals, and that *both* parents should be active rather than passive."

The social transitions studied by Thomas, Burgess, Hill, and the Hopkins project were not studied in isolation from their context, but neither Thomas nor Burgess devised a satisfactory concept of the life course for individuals and families. They were interested in developmental questions but lacked a conceptual framework with which to guide research. How are family and individual trajectories structured? What is the process linking individual and family trajectories? Within an interactionist perspective, Burgess never systematically addressed questions of this sort. His concept of the family as a "unity of interacting personalities" depicts family dynamics at a point in time or within a short period. Left out of this picture is the interweave of personal trajectories, their timetables and evolving pattern. Very similar observations on a general level could be made concerning Thomas's concepts. Life history and life organization do not add up to a satisfactory way of conceptualizing families and individuals over time.

For many years analysts have looked to the developmental perspective for insight into the dynamics of family life. Indeed, this perspective emerged in the postwar era as a response to the atemporal or static character of prevailing theories, including interactionists. In a major statement during the early 1960s, Hill and Rodgers (1964, p. 172) presented the developmental approach as uniquely suited to "account for changes in patterns of interaction over the family's life span." Concepts of adult development (such as Havighurst's [1948] developmental tasks) and the family cycle literature were applied to the "natural history of family formation, contraction, and dissolution" (p. 186). The initial promise of the approach has not been achieved to date and the reason has much to do with how it uses elements of age and kinship that mark temporal features of family structure and process.

To explain this observation, I begin with the bond between age and time in a newly emerging life course perspective; then relate temporal features of kinship to this perspective; and conclude by returning to family development as a theoretical concern. Issues of the post-1960s brought greater concern with family contexts, a theme not adequately addressed by the developmental approach. Developmental studies did not locate families in historical context and hence according to events and processes of social change; and their family stages did not occupy a precise location within the life span. For example, the childbearing stage could extend across 30 years of a woman's life. Looking back to the 1950s and 1960s, it now seems clear that the normative sequence of family stages in the developmental approach (marriage, births, etc.) was better suited to the empirical world of the 1950s, a time of relative marital stability and high fertility, than to the diversity of contemporary family forms. The latter reality is more compatible with the life course formulation. New conceptual models often arise when empirical facts do not fit established frameworks.

IV. AGE, KINSHIP, AND TEMPORALITY

Age and kinship represent complementary sources of temporality among families and individuals. Age brings a concept of age-graded trajectories and differential timing to studies of the individual and to the emergence of family patterns. In terms of social expectations, life events may occur relatively early, late, or on time. By enabling an approach to the individual life course, an age-based perspective is particularly conducive to developmental or psychological considerations, as illustrated by the writings of Burgess, Waller, Havighurst, and Neugarten. Age in the life course suggests at least two models of the interplay between individual and family development. Families or relationships may be changed by changing the personality or behavior of individuals; and individuals may be influenced through changes in their family environments. Both models depict linkages between family dynamics and the larger social structure. Examples of each are reviewed in the following pages.

Kinship distinctions broaden the life course perspective beyond a single life span, following the assumption of intergenerational dependence. Though most life event inventories still imply independence between adjacent generations, studies are beginning to document the extent to which events in one generation directly impinge on the well-being of another generation. The divorce of a middle-aged son or daughter may be just as traumatic as a personal divorce (Hagestad & Smyer, 1982). Kinship extends the conceptual framework of life course analysis through the family cycle that Thomas once studied (the process by which an older parent generation is replaced by the younger generation); and across the sequence of generational stations (child, parent, grandparent) that people traverse in their lifetimes. This sequence represents the most novel contribution of kinship distinctions to the field of life course research and family studies.

The life course implications of age and kinship build upon and extend the analytic traditions of Thomas and Burgess. There is evidence of continuity *and* development across the behavioral traditions of the 1920s and post-1960s.

THE AGES OF FAMILIES AND INDIVIDUALS

Family change variously reflects lifetime change in family members, the cultural and structural change of the family as a social unit and institutions, and historical change in the larger environment or community. A way to incorporate such distinctions in a single framework on family studies evolved in the 1960s and 1970s through conceptual elaboration of the bond between age and time (Elder, 1975, 1983; Hagestad & Neugarten, 1983; Riley, Johnson, & Foner, 1972).[7] Age relates the life span development of individuals; their course of adaptation and change in the formation, contraction, and dissolution of family units; and the forces of social and historical change, proximal and distal. The full implications of age involve three traditions of inquiry.

1. *Lifetime*, chronological age represents an approximate estimate of stage or position in the aging process. From a developmental standpoint, age alerts the investigator to subgroups that are differentially vulnerable to particular types of social change, such as the very young and old in hard times. This observation is formalized in a life stage hypothesis: social change has differential consequences for people of unequal age (see Ryder, 1965). In this domain, the lifetime meaning of age requires specification of the variables it represents.

2. *Social time* in the life course of the individual, the age-patterned or graded sequence of events (marriage, births, residential change, retirement) and social roles. The notion of family time refers to the ordering of family events and social roles by age-linked expectations, sanctions, and options. The social meanings of age represent constructions which take the form of age norms and sanctions, social timetables for the occurrence and order of events, generalized age grades (childhood, adolescence), and age hierarchies in particular settings, such as work organizations or schools. A normative concept of family time specifies an appropriate time for leaving home, mating, and bearing children.

3. *Historical time* as location in the course of social change. Birth year or entry into the system (through marriage, graduation) serves as an index of historical location. Birth year assigns family members to a birth cohort which is exposed to a particular dimension of historical experience in the process of aging. To understand the meaning and implications of birth year and cohort membership, the analyst specifies the historical events, conditions, and trends or change at the time, as well as characteristics of the

---

[7]A number of thematic principles have emerged from preliminary work in the field of life course development (Featherman, 1982). These include: (1) the lifelong process of developmental change which is synonymous with aging; (2) the multifaceted nature of such change, involving biological, social, psychological, physical, and historical events; (3) the interaction and cumulation of these events and influences; (4) the agentic role of individuals; and (5) the assumption that persons in successive cohorts are likely to age in different ways as a result of their differing historical experience. The interdisciplinary nature of this framework is one of its distinctive features. In the words of a social demographer (Cherlin, 1980, p. 11), "the collaboration of sociologists, developmental psychologists, social historians, social gerontologists, demographers, and economists has made the 'life course' one of the liveliest interdisciplinary enterprises in the social sciences." Recent accounts of the life course as an emerging approach in family studies are available in Elder (1978a, 1981a).

cohort (size, composition) which are themselves a product of historical times.

The lifetime perspective focuses attention on the inevitable and irreversible process of aging; that of social time on age differentiation in the sequential arrangement of events and roles; and that of historical time on cohort membership. In this manner, age stratifies both people and social roles; the former by historical location in cohorts, and the latter according to the age-graded social structure. Socialization and placement processes relate people and social roles in the course of aging and cohort succession. Age and the life course thus bring actors, groups, and demographic processes into a dynamic model of the family which has applications at both the macroscopic and microscopic levels.

A lifetime view of individuals and the family network entails different questions. Instead of asking whether a family is in poverty or not, we ask whether the family was *ever* in poverty over a certain period. The timing of this status in the life course and its duration bear upon the events' implications. Using this approach to the residential history of children markedly increases estimates of their exposure to single-parent households. Cohort projections by Hofferth (1984) based on children born from 1975 to 1979 indicate that approximately four out of five black children will not be living in a first-marriage household of their parents by the time they reach the age of 17. Seven out of 10 of these children will have lived in a one-parent household for a period of time. Among white children, the percentage not living in a first-marriage household at age 17 is 40.

As in E. W. Burgess's concept of the family, a "unity of interacting personalities," individuals are the elementary units of an age-based perspective on the life course. The multiple meanings of chronological age specify properties of the individual. Thus the lifetime meaning of age refers to the status of individuals in the aging process, social time refers to the timing of events and roles in lives, and historical time locates people in historical context through membership in specific birth cohorts. In effect, all three dimensions locate people and thereby their families. Through its age-heterogeneity, the family serves as a meeting ground for diverse cohorts and their life experiences (Hagestad & Dixon, 1980); a potential melting pot for age differences in belief. Common family experience may lessen cohort differences within the household, while increasing cohort variations between households.

An individual's life course is multidimensional since adult life in complex societies spans different lines of activity, from education to marriage, parenthood, work, and leisure. The general picture is one of interdependent career lines that vary in timetables, synchronization, and resource management. Each career line represents a patterned sequence of activities or roles. In applying the life course perspective to marriage and the family unit, we begin with the interlocking career lines of individuals. Analysis of the young couple centers on the social patterns formed by the joining of life courses through mate selection and their implications for marital relations, child rearing, and kin ties. Within the context of social patterns at marriage (age, class origin, education, etc.), the trajectory of family life is shaped by subsequent developments in the career lines of each spouse. A life course perspective views the family unit in terms of mutually contingent careers, and enables study of unconventional patterns, as well as the conventional, by working with the life histories of individuals.

Problematic features of the life course arise from the interlocking career lines of family members and their pattern of reciprocity and synchrony on needs, options, and resources. Differentiated careers in the life course imply some differentiation in social worlds whose demands compete for the scarce or limited resources of a family—the time, energy, affections, material resource of each member. The demands of parenthood are frequently in conflict with those of marriage, work, and civic duty, and the pressures or disadvantages are greatest when births come early in the life course (Waite, 1980). Managerial pressures from the diverse requirements and timetables of various career lines cast family units as budget centers or economies in which scarce resources are allocated to needs within and across life stages.

This model of interlocking careers implies a dynamic interactional concept of the family economy which has long been a conceptual mainstay of life course studies (Oppenheimer, 1981), though some analysts regard it as a novel perspective of the 1980s. Thus Levinson (1980, p. 271) concludes that "sociologists have generally not investigated the individual life course in its complex patterning." He attributes this failure to the specialization of fields. "The expert in occupational careers usually has little interest in the family, religion, or other systems." The strongest refutation of this claim comes from Harold Wilensky's Labor and Leisure study, an innovative and influential research program of the late 1950s and early 1960s. Writing in 1961, Wilensky (see 1981) observed that trajectories of work, family, consumption, and community participation have implications that stem from their interlocking temporal pattern. Consistent with recent national surveys on life quality, Wilensky found that job satisfaction, participation in community life, financial well-being, and psychological well-being tended to hit bottom among married men during the early childbearing and child-rearing stages.

Strong pressures arise from the asynchrony of family income and consumption curves, especially during the childbearing years. Life course planning may reduce the "squeeze" by activating one or more strategies: (1) reduction of expenditures; (2) reallocating resources such as replacing service expenditures with family labor, as in child care; and (3) increasing the match between income and outgo through savings, loans, and additional earners. Highly paid shiftwork, overtime, moonlighting, and loans from parents are common adaptations to the economic pressures of childbearing. Women and children in the labor force are seldom studied as members of a dynamic family economy (e.g., Greenberger, Steinberg, Vaux, & McAuliffe, 1980; White & Brinkerhoff, 1981) which has imperatives of its own. A major exception is Oppenheimer's (1982) study of family and work over the life span.

When viewed over time, strategies and adaptations that structure career lines are key elements in the process by which the life course evolves or develops. Examples include particular responses, such as maternal employment and doubling up, which are employed to reduce a disparity between family income and claims—to restore control relative to preferred family outcomes. Such responses alter the family's course in ways that may have consequences that differ for the family and children (Moen, Kain, & Elder, 1983). The short-run benefits of family survival may entail severe costs for children in the long run, as in the stormy conflicts of a multigeneration household.

The collective nature of family and kinship in life course analysis prompts questions regarding process. Instead of assuming family agreements or rules, we are led to ask how they are achieved and maintained. Emerging and dissolving patterns of family interaction represent a core feature of the developmental process. In all of this, Waller's perspective on family dynamics appears in new dress. Individuals can be followed across time as they engage in family building and dissolving activities. By contrast, households frequently undergo transforming changes in membership which destroy stable household identities over time. This insight emerged from the Panel Study of Income Dynamics at the University of Michigan. Over more than a decade, a team of social scientists (Duncan & Morgan, 1980) has been following this large, nationwide sample of American families. From the very beginning, the problem of tracking ever-changing domestic units made individuals the most feasible unit of study and data collection. To study household change or residential histories, the analysts had to study the coresidential experience of individuals. For similar reasons, the networks of families (Fischer, 1982) are less amenable to temporal study than the personal networks of individuals. Robert Kahn (1979) incorporates this distinction in his temporal concept of the "convoy of social support," a person's network of significant others who give and receive support over the life span.

Most discussion on the life course to this point has centered on the concept of trajectory, a career line or pathway over the life span (Elder, 1984a). Trajectories of work and family depict a long view of life course dynamics. They are marked by events in which people move from one state to another, from married to formerly married, for example, or from employed to unemployed and back to employed. These changes in state, both exit and entry, are called life transitions. Life transitions are marked by the occurrence of particular transitions, by their timing and order relative to other events, and by the duration of time between events. Beliefs and normative expectations are said to govern whether, when, and in what order transitions occur, but the extent is unknown. These attributes of a transition also affect the impact of a particular transition. The social and personal consequences of pregnancy vary according to whether the event occurred in adolescence or later, whether it occurred before or after marriage, and whether or not it is followed shortly by another pregnancy.

Family or life transitions are particularly well suited to the dynamic, temporal emphases of life course research, and a large portion of the work to date has focused on different parts of the territory: (1) the single transition and its consequences, such as divorce or remarriage (Cherlin, 1981; Furstenberg, 1982; Hagestad & Smyer, 1982; Hetherington et al., 1981); (2) concurrent and sequential transitions, such as the transition to adult roles, marriage, work, citizen (Hogan, 1981); and (3) the interdependence of widely separated transitions—the effect of early family events on the social and economic experience of retirement and old age (Hofferth, 1983). Some transitions are normatively prescribed with regard to timing, including marriage, conception, and births, while other events are idiosyncratic (accidents, acute illness, etc.) or historical (job loss in an economic recession).

Studies of family development have generally stressed the normative timing and sequence of family events, especially in relation to childbearing, while life course theory highlights the implications of departures from this format: very early and late marriage, childbirth before or without marriage, young widowhood or a prolonged dependency on parents. Women who never marry or give birth or die before maturity follow atypical life trajectories in urban industrial societies (see Uhlenberg, 1978). Atypical lives and events have become a major object of study for their psychological and social consequences. In one study, Pearlin and associates (1981) used a two-wave panel sample to trace the effects of economic misfortune to emotional depression through life strains, self-concepts, and adaptive resources, both coping and social support. Mood states (Weissman & Paykel, 1974) have profound effects for parenting behavior, the climate of families, and their adaptive potential.

By attending to individual lives across time and their interweave through emergent family patterns, life course analysis highlights the interactive relation between individual and family development. Harsh economic conditions may undermine family relationships by accentuating the irritable and erratic behavior of a family member (Liker & Elder, 1983), and such behavior is more likely when relationships are conflicted. People are changed through change in families, and families are changed through change in people. Whether simultaneous or sequential, the two processes represent prominent models in the life course field.

The mediational role of the family relative to social change appears in *Children of the Great Depression* (Elder, 1974) and in subsequent extensions (Elder, 1979). This research traces the influence of Depression hardship on children born during the early 1920s through change in the economy, relationships, and climate of 170 families. The analysis is structured in part by the adaptational perspective of W. I. Thomas. Suggestive research on changing families through change in members includes Kohn's *Class and Conformity* (1977) and Pearlin's (1981) research on adaptations to life transitions or change. With an initial focus on the relation between social class and parental values, Kohn's program of research has systematically explored the causal relation between work and personality. Less emphasis has been given to the implications of personality effects on family relations.

A. Changing People through Families

Longitudinal studies reported in *Children of the Great Depression* were designed around the assumption that historical change influences children and their life chances by changing the nature of their family environment. The children, born in the early 1920s, were followed from childhood in Oakland, California, up to the middle years of life through a series of contacts in which interview and personality data were collected. The effects of income loss (1929–33) were assessed within the middle and working class according to a model which depicted the family and its adaptations as the primary link between economic change, on the one hand, and the life experience of the child, on the other. Three general linkages guided the research:

1. *Change in the household economy.*—Drastic loss of income required new modes of economic maintenance which altered the domestic and economic roles of members, shifting responsibility to mother and the older children. Girls played a major role in household chores and acquired through family upbringing a family-centered value system. Boys contributed to the household through earnings and became more independent from parental control as a result of their employment.

2. *Change in family relationships.*—Father's loss of earnings and

resulting adaptations in family support increased the relative power of mother, reduced the level of effectiveness of parental control, and diminished the attractiveness of father as a role model. The family-centered preferences of girls were enhanced by mothers who served as primary sources of authority and affection. This family pattern is coupled with weak ties to kin or family among males in adulthood.

3. *Social strains in the family.*—Increased social ambiguity, marital and parent-child conflict, and emotional strain. Owing to such conditions, both males and females in the Oakland study during midlife tend to view the 1930s (or their adolescence) as the worst time of their lives.

Over the long-run, economic hardship entailed some disadvantages in career beginnings, but it did not produce noteworthy disabilities in adult achievement or health. The most adverse legacy occurred among the sons and daughters of working-class parents. As a study of historical variations within a single cohort, the Oakland research inevitably raised questions concerning the generality of its findings. Indeed, the timetable of the Oakland cohort suggests a favored trajectory. The participants were past the critical dependency years during the worst times of the 1930s and they left school during a period of rising prosperity. Considerations of this sort led to the design of a comparative cohort project with the addition of members from the Berkeley Guidance Study, Institute of Human Development (Elder, 1979, 1981b). A total of 214 children with birthdates in 1928–29 were followed across the 1930s and early 1940s to middle age.

The timing of historical events and lives produced a contrasting sequence of material well-being and scarcity for the Oakland and Berkeley cohorts. Prosperous times generally coincided with childhood and scarcity with adolescence in the lives of the Oakland men and women. The Berkeley adults experienced childhood during the deprivational years of the 1930s and left this decade for the pressures of wartime adolescence and an economic boom. This comparison points to more adverse and enduring psychological outcomes of economic loss (1929–33—similar to Oakland measure) in the Berkeley cohort, but mainly among the males, owing to the connection between economic and paternal deprivation and the central role of father in the psychosocial development of boys. From early childhood to middle age, family deprivation impaired the social experience, health, and psychological development of the Berkeley males. No other group in the two cohorts even approached the disadvantage of these sons of severely deprived parents. Overall the life stage hypothesis on historical effects receives modest support from this analysis.

A more focused examination of the Berkeley males in the 1930s showed that heavy income loss markedly increased their arbitrary and punitive treatment by father, but not by mother (Elder, Liker, & Cross,

1984). Such behavior increased the risk of temper tantrums and difficult behavior (irritable, negativistic, quarrelsome) among boys and even girls up to the age of 8. Hard times were most apt to increase the arbitrariness of father (use of inconsistent discipline) when he entered the 1930s with feelings of indifference and dislike toward the particular child. The effect proved to be negligible when the child was positively regarded by father.

The Depression studies and their mediational account of families represent a less innovative perspective on the life course than investigations of adult development in family change. Indeed, the latter concept still lacks prominence in family studies (Liker & Elder, 1983). Even when socialization meant simply child rearing by adults, as during the 1950s, the child studies of developmentalists were largely uninformed by matters of adult development. There was little acknowledgement that the aging process and life course of parents were relevant to parental behavior. Hartup (1978, p. 29; see rejoinder by Hill, 1981) extends this observation to the late 1970s by concluding that "family social science has not dealt very effectively with the interaction between ontogeny and the family context. Most of the family sociological literature is not a developmental literature." This charge has much truth to it, although the situation has changed dramatically since the 1960s. The field of socialization now extends across the life span (Mortimer & Simmons, 1978), and adult studies are beginning to specify the causal chain in which family change occurs through individual development.

B. Changing Families through People

This theme is one element of Kohn's fertile program of research on the psychological effects of structured conditions (Kohn, 1977, 1980), more than 20 years of work in the Laboratory for Socioenvironmental Studies of the National Institute of Mental Health. With John Clausen (organizer and first director of the Lab), Kohn launched an interview study of class and parenting during the mid-1950s in the city of Washington, D.C. This study represents a pioneering project because it pursued a question that was largely ignored at the time: "Why does social class matter for parenting or child rearing?" (Kohn, 1963). The answer has evolved across many studies. Class matters because one's position in the social structure influences life conditions that directly affect concepts of reality, values, and orientations. Though major studies continue to ignore the causal significance of class in family patterns (Lambert, Harmers, Frasure-Smith, 1979), Kohn and his colleagues have produced a series of innovative extensions and elaborations that continue into the 1980s and implement many features of a life course model. These developments are based on three data collections: a nationwide sample of men in 1964, a subsequent survey of adults in Turin, Italy, and a partial followup of the 1964 sample in the mid-1970s.

The first major step brought greater detail to the conceptual model; the second important step placed this model within a temporal framework that highlights the dynamic interrelation of career and individual development. Beginning with a single dimension of social class, Kohn soon adopted a multidimensional model of social position (occupation, education, and income) and demonstrated through research that occupation and education mattered more for values and self orientations than income—a striking contrast to the Depression studies.

The next phase involved a more differentiated approach to occupational conditions as structural imperatives that impose adaptive demands on workers. The most powerful condition is occupational self-direction; the greater the self-direction, the more the worker deals with substantively complex, nonroutinized tasks that entail minimal supervision (Miller et al., 1979, p. 91). "No matter what the sex of the worker, job conditions that directly or indirectly encourage occupational self-direction are conducive to effective intellectual functioning and to an open and flexible orientation to others." Lack of self-direction plus various pressures (time pressure, long hours, etc.) and job uncertainties (dramatic work change, risk of joblessness, etc.) markedly increased the likelihood of unfavorable evaluations of self, ineffective thinking, and rigid, intolerant social orientations.

On the outcome side of the model, Kohn's research shifted from an initial concern with parental values and behavior to adult psychological functioning—intellectual flexibility, alienation, conservative authoritarianism, valuation of self-direction. The Washington study found that "middle-class parents' higher valuation of self-direction, and working-class parents' higher valuation of conformity to external authority, influence their disciplinary practices and also the allocation, between mother and father, of responsibility for providing support to, and imposing constraints on, their children" (Kohn, 1977, p. xxxii–xxxiii). At no point in the course of the research program do we find a theoretical account of "the processes by which parents' life conditions directly or indirectly affect the personality development of their children" (Kohn, 1977, p. xxxiii). However, a substantial advance along this line occurred when Kohn and his colleagues began to view occupational conditions and adult psychological functioning as interdependent processes in a panel design. The 1974 followup of men and their wives from the 1964 study enabled the research team to examine the actual interplay of work and personality over time.

Kohn's longitudinal research on intellectual flexibility (Kohn & Schooler, 1978) clearly shows the potential contribution of the Lab studies to adult development in linking structured conditions and family patterns.

Conceptually, intellectual flexibility functions as a key mechanism by which occupational conditions (in the household and marketplace) affect the intellectual functioning of men and women. Measures of this characteristic include problem-solving expertise on cognitive problems, the tendency to agree to agree/disagree questions, responses to perceptual tasks, and the interviewer's judgment. Though highly stable across time ($r = .93$, 1964–74) with measurement error removed, men's intellectual flexibility did vary substantially by occupational conditions, especially by substantive complexity. The principal findings show a lagged effect of substantive complexity (T1) on intellectual flexibility (T2) and a contemporaneous effect of substantive complexity on intellectual flexibility. Men become more flexible through exposure to complex work environments over time; their thinking responds quickly to features of the work environment. Such change has noteworthy implications for family communication, problem solving, and decision making.

The project's agenda calls for a thorough study of relations among intellectual flexibility, values, parental behavior, and a number of operations that bring the life course of men and women into the picture. The most important operations are (1) systematic analysis of actual career patterns between 1964 and 1974, and their relation to developmental trajectories; (2) investigation of whether the estimated effects of work and personality apply to all phases of the life course, to the young adults and the late middle aged; and (3) research that examines the impact of life events and transitions on psychological functioning. Points 1 and 3 stress the life context of adult development, while point 2 tests the notion that the effect of objective events depends on the life stage in which they occur. This premise is fundamental to the concept of a culturally patterned life course and leads to the general conclusion by Brim and Ryff (1980) that the stressfulness of a transition is inversely related to its normative character and predictability.

Kohn began his program of research over 25 years ago on the question of social class in children's lives, as expressed through parental concepts of the desirable. His productive journey has spun a complex web of processes that help to explain "class effects," now viewed more broadly within the framework of social stratification. The nature of work matters because it affects the behavior, psychological health, and developmental course of adults. The latter in turn play a role in selecting their own work environments. Change in adult behavior has direct consequences for children in the home, but does this change also explain variation in the degree to which children come to hold the same preferences or values as those embraced by their parents? Kohn and his colleagues are beginning to address questions of this sort, and to move beyond the workplace and family to schools and the world of leisure activities (Kohn & Schooler, 1983). Preliminary results suggest that the substantive complexity of children's school environment is linked to their intellectual flexibility, even apart from the influence of family and parental work.

Family patterns over the life span generally evolve within a life cycle of generational succession in which newborns are socialized to maturity, give birth to the next generation, grow old, and die. In the words of an aged villager in Miner's (1939, p. 85) study of rural Quebec, life is like a turning wheel: "the old turn over the work to the young and die, and they in turn get old and turn over the work to their children." Within the life course of each generation, unexpected and involuntary events occur through life changes in related generations. Thus a young woman of 45 becomes a grandmother when her daughter has a first baby, and parents lose their status as son and daughter when their own parents die. Like social age in some respects, the road map of kinship tells family members where they are and have been in life course and family time.

KINSHIP STATUS AND GENERATIONAL TIME

Three kinship distinctions bring temporal specifications to the life course of families: (1) collaterals (siblings, spouse) or the consociates (Plath, 1980) that are part of life networks; (2) lineal extension across the generations, from child to parent to grandparent and great-grandparent; and (3) a more detailed and focused view of "the turning wheel," the family cycle by which one generation is replaced by another. Strictly speaking, this intergenerational cycle describes a process in a population and not a course followed by all couples. Some couples have children, while others do not and thereby follow a pathway that is not structured by parenthood. The never married without children represent another population subgroup which has no relevance to a family or intergenerational cycle. A brief discussion of the family cycle at this point provides a useful context in which to consider the life course across three or more generations.

In concept, the family cycle can be traced from the mid-1850s through Frederic LePlay's European studies to Rowntree's (1901) survey of York laboring families at the turn of the century to demographic studies of the family cycle in the 1930s. Paul Glick's (1947) postwar studies came along next as well as the collaboration of Reuben Hill, Evelyn Duvall, and Bernice Neugarten on a new concept of the family cycle and development. The family cycle implies change, but family change over the life span has been partitioned by stage typologies. One of the best known is Reuben Hill's (1964) model, which uses information on change in family size, major change in the status of the eldest and youngest children, and the father's occupation. In basic design, the nine stages represent a *normative* order of phases in the reproductive cycle. Most stages convey something about the age status of children, though not about the age status of parents:

> I. *Establishment* (newly married, childless); II. *New Parents* (infant–3 yrs.); III. *Preschool Family* (child 3–6 and possibly younger siblings); IV. *School Age Family* (oldest child 6–12 years, possibly younger siblings); V. *Family with Adolescent* (oldest 13–19 years, possibly younger siblings); VI. *Family with Young Adult* (oldest 20 until first child leaves home); VII. *Family as Launching Center* (from departure of first to last child); VIII. *Postparental Family*, the Middle Years (after children have left home until father retires); IX. *Aging Family* (after retirement of father). [Hill, 1964, p. 192, italics added]

This version of the family cycle refers to the reproductive process (parent-child) from the standpoint of a couple's life trajectory. The sequence of stages describes this trajectory without reference to transitions and events in the lives of offspring, parents, and grandparents. Some couples enter the "establishment" phase with living parents and grandparents, while others may have only one set of living parents and no surviving grandparents. As seen within the context of family and kinship, the two types of couples occupy very different positions relative to self-definition and support. The same distinction can be drawn between entry into parenthood with surviving parents or with no parents to call upon. At the other end of the cycle, the postparental stage or experience will vary greatly according to the presence and life stage of children and parents. In actuality, no life stage is postparental as long as the person has surviving children. As charted in the typology, children grow up and leave home, all in relation to "timeless" parents. New parents in stage II may be in their mid-thirties or in their early twenties, a difference that makes a difference in family well-being. Overall, the static nature of stage models yields "snapshots" of family development which tell us little about the actual course of a family's history or experience. Families that march through an identical sequence of stages vary markedly in their respective life courses. Much of this variation is due to the variable timing, order, and duration of family events, as determined from age data.

The strategic use of age *and* kin data in a family cycle appears more than 30 years ago in a paper by Paul Glick (1947, p. 165): "a presentation of the ages at which American married couples usually reach the several stages of the family cycle." Ten years later Lansing and Kish (1957) established empirical support for an age graded approach to the family cycle and parent-child relations. Using a model which distinguished between younger and older parents with children, they found their classification to be more powerful than merely the age of the male household head. Presumably the classification would also be more potent than one based solely on the ages of children. At least in theory, a model of the intergenerational cycle requires age, sex, and family role information.

Most research on the intergenerational aspect of this cycle is restricted to the early dependency stage of offspring; the evolving relationship between parent and child up to the time at which the child leaves home and establishes an independent domicile. The child's development usually occupies center stage, with parent development given indirect concern at best. With increasing frequency among studies, the nature of interaction and its change over time reflects the interdependence of two life courses, parent's and child's. Steinberg and Hill (1978) document change in the assertiveness of boys relative to mother as a function of age, puberty onset, and formal thinking. Rossi's (1980) cross-sectional study highlights the interdependent trajectories of mother and teenage daughter. The mothers who felt young and accepted their age were most likely to report a long life ahead and satisfying relations with their daughter. Women who expressed a desire to be younger than they were reported more trouble in rearing their daughters, more criticism, backtalk, and so on. A sense of feeling close to one's adolescent daughter was most common among women who had not experienced an elevation of aging symptoms.

The subsequent fate of relations between aging parents and offspring is largely unknown (Bengtson & DeTerre, 1980; Bengtson & Troll, 1978), although conceptualization of this bond in recent work generally parallels an earlier approach to parent-adolescent relations. In the 1950s, Bowerman (see Elder, 1980b) conceptualized these relations in terms of three adolescent orientations: associational (frequency of interaction with mother, father, etc.), affectional (affection, sense of closeness), and value (shared values, common opinions, parent as source of advice). Similar dimensions appear in a subsequent study of Danish and American adolescents (Kandel & Lesser, 1972), *Youth in Two Worlds*. At the other end of the life course, Bengston and his research team (see above) view family solidarity in terms of the three dimensions, with emphasis on older family members. Associational solidarity refers to frequency and type of contact, as well as the exchange of assistance and support. Affectual solidarity is based on emotional ties and includes evidence of relative dependence. Consensual solidarity concerns the degree of agreement on life values and standards.

The family or *intergenerational* cycle adds a distinctive feature to the life course perspective by linking the life course of parent and child. Indeed, the cycle concept refers explicitly to this link. Accordingly, the full scope of the cyclical model requires a multidimensional concept of the life course for adult offspring; a moving set of interlocking career lines, such as work, marriage, parenting, and so on. Misfortune and opportunity across these pathways may become intergenerational as well as life problems. Failed marriages and careers frequently lead adult sons and daughters back to the parental household and have profound implications for the parents' life plans regarding the later years. Conversely, economic setbacks and divorce among the parents of adolescents may impede their transition to adulthood by postponing home leaving, higher education or employment, and marriage. Each generation is bound to fateful decisions and events in the other's life course.

Sociologists have expanded this field of influence or dependence beyond the traditional two-generation cycle, and they have done so partly in response to the lengthening span of life. With increasing frequency, grandparents survive long enough to enjoy their grandchildren and even their great-grandchildren. Four-generation families have become a notable reality in American kinship and an important fact to consider in studies of the life course. This observation is skillfully developed by Gunhild Hagestad (1981, 1982) in a series of essays that begin to fill the intergenerational void between dyads at opposite ends of the life span: the Alpha dyad of young parent and child, and the Omega dyad of late middle-aged parents and their surviving parent. The youngest member of this four-generation family can anticipate moving across four generational stations in his or her lifetime, from child to the responsibilities of child and parent in the middle stations and then to the Omega position. Depending on many factors, but especially the timing of marriage and births, the age spread from Alpha to Omega can differ markedly. In one case, a 92-year-old grandmother is paired with her college-age great-grandson, while another family shows a 70-year-old Omega with her youngest descendant, a 2-year-old. The life stage of a middle-aged father and teenage sons may be coupled with no surviving parents or with as many as two parent generations.

Timetables in the family life course acquire particular significance when they are viewed across the generations. The interweave of generational trajectories means that their temporal coordination has noteworthy implications for each life course. Consider the notion of family pressure points that occur when resources are equaled or surpassed by demands (see Oppenheimer, 1982). Within the ordinary life course of a family, the key pressure point generally occurs during the childbearing and child-rearing phase. However, even more severe pressures at a later date may arise from a conjuncture of off-time events in the lives of offspring, parents, and grandparents.

A very late age at childbirth is often coupled with child-rearing problems through the adolescent years (Rossi, 1980, p. 194) and with the dependency requirements of parents and grandparents. This pressure would increase markedly if parental dependency arrived early through unexpected health impairments. The felt burden of bringing up adolescents may reflect the mounting, caretaking pressures of aged parents. Likewise, the quality of a son's care for elderly parents may depend on the extent to which his children manage to leave home and achieve economic independence. In many respects, the middle generation represents the cornerstone of the kinship economy on resource management. In line with the new kinship approaches to the black family (Shimkin et al., 1978), Hagestad (1981, p. 4) concludes that the "vulnerabilities and strengths of three or more generations are closely interconnected. . . ." Equally important, the strengths of one generation may offset the vulnerabilities of another, whether younger or older.

AGE, KINSHIP, AND THE LIFE COURSE

The temporal distinctions of age and kinship show little correspondence in the life course of families and individuals. Age data locate people in precise historical contexts (according to birth years) and in the social structure, a precision unmatched by generational status. The sequence from child to parent and grandparent applies to all times and places. Moreover, members of a specific generation may vary in age by as much as 40 years. Such differences highlight the complementary perspectives of age and kinship on family development. The study of age brings historical considerations and insights on age grading to the life course of people and families, while intergenerational analysis highlights the "given" nature of family ties, the interlocking trajectories of each generation, and the cross-generation process by which historical experiences and influences are transmitted.

Some examples of these observations are shown in figure 1, a diagram of a cross-section of three generations. When three generation units are sampled at a point in time, a sizable percentage of parents and grandparents will have the same age. The same overlap applies to parents and children. Age similarity means a common historical location and thus a corresponding temporal relation to major historical events. Generational membership or position may be less influential on beliefs or behavior than shared historical location and related experiences, such as military service. The differing influence of generation and age status becomes especially confusing when the two sources of rank yield opposing results (see Kertzer, 1982). Thus some members of a parent generation may be actually younger than some members of the child generation.

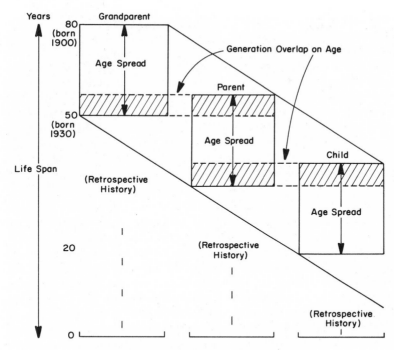

Fig. 1.—Three generations in a survey: cross-sectional

Beyond the uncertain relation between relative age and relative generational status, figure 1 illustrates two potential uses of generational location and relations. In a strictly cross-sectional slice of the generations, generational membership is merely an index of one's generational station in life, and relations between the generations are uninformed by the life trajectories of persons in each generational category. The result is a snapshot which largely ignores context and biography. The life course of each person and its relation to other trajectories are slighted. The alternative in a cross-sectional survey is to use retrospective life histories to characterize the trajectories of each person. Intergenerational ties at a point in time are thus viewed as a consequence of the developmental process in lives and relationships. Age-based notions of the life course structure this process.

An age-based view of the life course does not regard family ties over the life span as "givens." They are constructed and modified by family members, often in response to external events and the addition or loss of a member. Consistent with an interactionist account, we follow the emergence of group relations and their dissolution in separation or divorce. To paraphrase a well-known interactionist, Georg Simmel, we are led to ask how families are *possible* as social groups, structures, and cultures. Compared to the dynamic, behavioral elements of this approach, a kin-based perspective assigns more emphasis to the givens of family, to the ascribed parameters of family relationships. Kin ties are established at birth as a lifetime network of mutural rights and obligations. Law and custom may define the corporate structure of family and kin, but they do not ensure the quality or nature of these relationships, their sentiments, bonds, adaptations. By bringing a more structural vantage point to family change over time, kinship distinctions complement the behavioral orientation of age and the life course.

Family change cannot be understood without knowledge of the historical milieu of economic, demographic, and cultural forces, but this knowledge alone does not capture the dynamics of family patterns over the life span. The generational stations of people across the vertical chain of generations specify the family time of the individual, along with specific stages in the family cycle. However, this approach cannot locate people according to the life course of time and place without the social-historical facts of age. Grandmother in 1980 might be 50 or 90 years of age, with birthdates in 1930 or in 1890. The historical facts of age provide a necessary corrective to the acontextual nature of the family cycle, and the full generational sequence has much the same effect by broadening the social environment of the usual two-generation framework.

A skeletal life course for individual members of a family can be mapped in the three-dimensional space of life, family, and historical time (fig. 2). Historical time of birth and passage through the age structure define life trajectories on the grid of history and age. Persons born in 1920, 1940, and 1960 follow the same age gradient, though divergent paths may arise from the variable relation between age and events/roles. Historical events, such as war and depression, may alter the correlation between family events and age, or change their temporal arrangements—for example, full-time employment may come after first marriage in the lives of servicemen (Hogan, 1981). Another source of variation is the unstable course of family time. Though figure 2 lists four generations on the family timetable, the number and pattern of the generations can vary sharply across a single life span.

Consider a person who was born in the late 1930s and became one of several great-grandchildren of a woman in her nineties. Three higher stations in the generational series are occupied. This structure continues up to the sixth year of the child when great-grandmother dies. Only three stations remain on the generational ladder. By the time the child enters

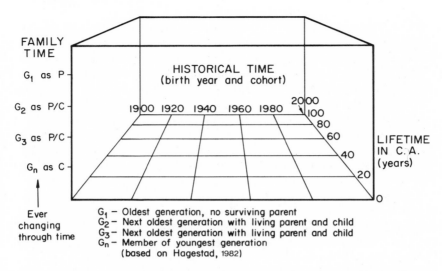

FAMILY
TIME

G_1 as P

G_2 as P/C

G_3 as P/C

G_n as C

↑

Ever
changing
through time

HISTORICAL TIME
(birth year and cohort)

1900 1920 1940 1960 1980 2000
100
80
60
40
20
0

LIFETIME
IN C.A.
(years)

G_1 – Oldest generation, no surviving parent
G_2 – Next oldest generation with living parent and child
G_3 – Next oldest generation with living parent and child
G_n – Member of youngest generation
(based on Hagestad, 1982)

FIG. 2.—Life-course trajectories in three-dimensional space: life, family, and historical time

high school, both grandparents on the maternal and paternal side have died. The structure is now based on two generations; or the family cycle of birth, maturation, reproduction, and death. In terms of figure 2, G_1 and G_n make up the generational structure until the 1930s "child" has a child. At this point, she becomes both a parent and a child.

As Hagestad (1982) argues, generational turnover in the structure of family time has implications for change in status and role, self-identity, and behavior. The parenting behavior of adults varies according to whether they have surviving parents and grandparents. Greater distance seems to occur between parents and offspring when the former move to the last position of the generational line. Identity change is perhaps the most obvious feature of generational turnover; the death of grandparents and parents entails loss of role and of well-established identities. The schedule of family time and events across the generations brings a uniquely valuable sense of the degree to which a nuclear family and its members are entwined with the fortunes and life course of kin.

Change in the nature and pattern of generational events may have profound consequences for the life course, though it offers little insight regarding the historical time or setting. A single grandparent generation may include as many as 10 3-year cohorts. The task of bringing age and generational distinctions together in a single study is illustrated by a four generation project, with data from the well-known Berkeley Guidance archive at the Institute of Human Development, Berkeley. The grandparent generation ranges in birth year from about 1850 to 1890; and the parent generation from 1888 to 1910. Members of the child generation were born shortly before the Great Depression and their own offspring began to arrive at mid-century. With the most extensive family information on the parent generation, the study centers on the full life span of this generation and its relation to family continuity and change. The analysis moves back to the social origins of the parents in the grandparental context and then forward through the lives of the parents and the births and upbringing of their children. The project ends with the parents in old age, their children in middle age, their grandchildren from adolescence to age 40, and a growing number of great-grandchildren.

Age distinctions provide greater historical accuracy for generational position and its relation to key events of social change. Members of the parent generation divide evenly into birth cohorts that encountered historical events at markedly different stages in life, before 1900 and after. Men with birthdates before 1900 were old enough for military service in World War I, and they launched both family and work careers in the generally prosperous 1920s. As a group, the nineteenth-century women were beyond childbearing when the economy collapsed. By comparison, the Depression caught the younger men and women in the midst of getting started in life, confronting them with major obstacles to family and career building during the 1930s. The women ended up with nearly one less child and their husbands generally lagged behind the career progress of older men up to the postwar era, especially within the middle class. Both effects had consequences for the evolving pattern of family life. In these results we have one example of the usefulness of the concept of *generational cohort*. By assigning family heads of the 1900 generation to generational cohorts, the impact of economic hardship on lives can be traced through intergenerational processes within and beyond the family. In David Potter's words (Fehrenbach, 1973, p. 363), such cohorts are well suited to studying how social change alters "the processes through which individuals develop their identities as persons and at the same time as members of society."

The relation of age to family roles in figure 2 offers a useful point at which to bring this examination of family temporality to a close by highlighting differences between two views of family dynamics, life course, and family development. Unlike perspectives on the life course which locate people and their family roles by age and birth year, age in the developmental framework is less a temporal index of status than one element of family roles (Hill & Rodgers, 1964). An example is the set of age-appropriate expectations that are part of the parental role. Such expectations do not tell us about the historical cohort or age status of the parent. They do not identify whether a person comes to parenting relatively late or early, or the extent to which the parental timetable of a couple meshes with the demands of work and consumption. Such questions cannot be answered when age distinctions appear only in the roles family members play. A more complete use of age differentiation in family and individual careers would increase the potential of the developmental framework for analyzing family change in specific contexts.

Another view of age in family development, as a theoretical framework, comes from its age-graded model of task sequences over the life span of individuals. Drawing from the writings of Robert Havighurst (1948) and others, the family development approach has used the notion of developmental tasks in applications that suggest a generalized cultural model on age-graded ways of successful development and aging. This life-span model is prescriptive in a normative sense as it specifies tasks that constitute appropriate accomplishments in specific life stages, and it is also proscriptive by implication. What is appropriate at one age is not necessarily appropriate at another age.

Informed by social and individual needs, the sequence of developmental tasks represents a special case of the age norms that shape decisions and events in the life course (Neugarten, More, & Lowe, 1965). However, age distinctions in family roles and a cultural model of the life span do not identify family members and their careers within the age structure. The missing elements in the developmental paradigm are the age-graded, behavioral careers of family members, their interlocking pattern and timing relative to normative expectations.

The idea of age differentiation in family development theory has less to do with developmental tasks than with the family cycle of ordered stages. As noted earlier, these stages are defined primarily by the ages of children. Families advance from one stage to another as children age and leave home. This child-oriented concept of family development differs sharply from one based on a model of developmental tasks in which stages acquire meaning or content from the interdependent, age-graded tasks of parents and child. As Havighurst (1948, p. 74) observed in the 1940s, the success of a boy or girl in meeting the tasks of adolescence is contingent on the achievements of mother and father relative to the task sequence of their middle years.

With *different* views of age and the life course, the two original strands of developmental theory, family cycle and developmental tasks, have not blended effectively. The blend has fallen short for other reasons as well, including the difference in level of analysis: the corporate and predictable nature of the reproductive cycle, as contrasted to the individual trajectory of the developmental task tradition. According to developmental theory, both individuals and families are measured against a structure of development tasks.[8] However, no conceptual or empirical efforts have been made to relate the two levels.

From a broader angle, we see the original strands of family development as part of two traditions of work (kinship and age) that are now coming together in different ways within the life course perspective. As a perspective on the family, the life course shares with developmental theory a concern with family change over the life span and with the development of family members as a major source of this change. However, it takes a different view of these foci. According to Hill and Mattessich (1979, p. 174), family development refers to "the process of progressive structural differentiation and transformation over the family's history. . . ." Research thus attends to this orderly progression, which has much to do with the birth and growth of children. The challenge for developmental analysis is to "sift invariances on the individual and family developmental levels from the peculiarities and uniqueness of cohorts on the historical level" (p. 190).

Whether unique, peculiar, or evolutionary, historical variations are prime targets for explanatory research in life course studies. Consistent with this emphasis, such studies view family change as a processual outcome of the continual interchange between the family and its members, on the one hand, and the larger environment, on the other. Change in the family life course occurs through an adaptational process in which the life-span development of family members represents only one element. By comparison, Hill and Mattessich's (1979, p. 188) account of family development considers the primary determinant "as internal, arising from the responsiveness of the family to the changing needs of its growing members." Births and deaths, individual development, impairment, and aging—these are primary sources of family change and development, not the forces of social history and ecology.

V. OVERVIEW

Sociological perspectives on family and kinship have followed a cyclical pattern of dominance over the twentieth century. The decline of fascination with questions of social origins and evolution at the turn of the century marked the beginning of a vigorous behavioral era in which studies viewed the family as an actor in situations structured by history, institutions, and

---

[8]The usual practice has been to regard the functional prerequisites of society as the task structure or sequence for families. However, the prerequisites (socialization, social control, etc.) do not follow an explicit temporal framework. Socialization, e.g., is a lifelong process; it applies to the behavioral adaptations of both young and old.

ecology. Analysis shifted from the generalized level of social structures to families and their members in specific locales. Interest in family dynamics over the life span spurred fresh thinking about conceptual models of family process or change. From the 1910s through the 1930s, the University of Chicago served as the intellectual home of this perspective, especially through the analytical influence of W. I. Thomas, Ernest Burgess, and their students.

Empirical studies in postwar America continued to reflect elements of this behavioral approach, but the conceptual design for this age of family inquiry was fashioned by structure-functionalism and Talcott Parsons's leadership. The analytical discipline of interactions between research and theory during the Chicago era largely disappeared as Parsonian theory and quantitative surveys went their separate ways. The intellectual times invited misguided efforts to draw behavioral inferences from structural theory, as in the case of the isolated nuclear family. Matters of time, place, and process received less attention from theory and research.

The behavioral thrust of family studies acquired new life in the 1960s from the convergence of problem foci and theoretical considerations that were once prominent through the 1930s. Both eras are distinguished by the pressures and dislocations of rapid change that highlight people or population issues (i.e., family and individual welfare) relative to social institutions or structures. Fertility, migration, and economic conditions became highly visible problem foci in family life before the 1940s and surfaced once again in 1960, especially in the demographic growth of young people and the elderly.

This chapter has noted the remarkable correspondence between the public issues, problem foci, and theoretical perspectives of the two eras on family and kinship. Ever since the 1950s, structural accounts have faded relative to the ascending variation of more behavioral analyses in which the family represents an actor in structured situations. These include approaches to the personal networks of family members, the process of social exchange in the kinship system, and the life course of family and individual adaptation.

Temporality has become an increasingly central feature of analytical approaches to the family, especially in a newly emerging life course perspective. Though multidisciplinary, this approach joins two major strands of sociological analysis, the study of age and the study of kinship. The bond between age and time locates family members in the age structure of society and in their historical setting. Through studies of kinship and the generations, we perceive the age-patterned life course of individuals as interwoven with the life patterns of older and younger generations. Events and transitions in one generation have consequences for members of adjacent generations. The life course of parents thus entails passage across age strata and generational stations (child to parent and grandparent) from birth to death.

The life course approach sensitizes family research to four temporal themes: (1) the interlocking life course of family members and kin; (2) the interplay between family units and members on matters of development and life chances, obligations and rights; (3) the interdependence of family, individual, and social change; and (4) causal relations between early and later events and roles over the life span. Each theme is expressed in prominent areas of life course dynamics, including family transitions, such as the birth and household departure of children, and the family economy of consumption, production, and life course management. As a concept, the family economy offers a fruitful way to examine the consequences of major family trends for the lives and developmental course of children, such as declining fertility, rising divorce and the single-parent household, and increasing levels of maternal employment. Time, process, and context are finally receiving due consideration in sociological perspectives on family and kinship.

REFERENCES

Adams, B. N. *Kinship in an urban setting.* Chicago: Markham, 1968.
Anderson, M. *Family structure in nineteenth century Lancashire.* New York: Cambridge University Press, 1971.
Angell, R. *The family encounters the Depression.* Gloucester, Mass.: Smith, 1965. (Originally published, 1936.)
Bakke, E. W. *Citizens without work.* New Haven, Conn.: Yale University Press, 1940.
Baltes, P. B. Life-span developmental psychology: Some converging observations on history and theory. In P. B. Baltes & O. G. Brim, Jr. (Eds.), *Life-span development and behavior* (Vol. 2). New York: Academic Press, 1979.
Bengtson, V., & DeTerre, E. Aging and family relations. *Marriage and Family Review,* 1980, 3, 51–76.
Bengtson, V., & Troll, L. Youth and their parents: Feedback and intergenerational influence in socialization. In R. M. Lerner & G. B. Spanier (Eds.), *Child influences on marital and family interaction.* New York: Academic Press, 1978.
Berger, P., & Kellner, H. Marriage and the construction of reality. In R. L. Coser (Ed.), *The family: Its structures and functions* (2d ed.). New York: St. Martin's, 1974.
Billingsley, A. *Black families in white America.* Englewood Cliffs, N.J.: Prentice-Hall, 1968.
Blood, R. O., & Wolfe, D. M. *Husbands and wives.* New York: Free Press, 1960.
Blumer, H. An appraisal of Thomas and Znaniecki's *The Polish peasant in Europe and America.* Bulletin 44. New York: Social Science Research Council, 1939.
Bogue, D. (Ed.). *The basic writings of Ernest W. Burgess.* Chicago: Community & Family Study Center, 1974.

Bott, E. *Family and social network: Roles, norms, and external relationships in ordinary urban families* (2d ed., preface by Max Gluckman). New York: Free Press, 1971. (Originally published, 1957.)

Brim, O. G., Jr., & Ryff, C. D. On the properties of life events. In P. B. Baltes & O. G. Brim, Jr. (Eds.), *Life-span development and behavior* (Vol. 3). New York: Academic Press, 1980.

Bronfenbrenner, U. Socialization and social class through time and space. In E. E. Maccoby, T. M. Newcomb, & E. L. Hartley (Eds.), *Readings in social psychology*. New York: Holt, 1958.

Bronfenbrenner, U. *Two worlds of childhood*. New York: Russell Sage Foundation, 1970.

Bronfenbrenner, U. *The ecology of human development*. Cambridge, Mass.: Harvard University Press, 1979.

Burgess, E. W. The family as a unity of interacting personalities. *Family*, 1926, **7**, 3–9.

Burgess, E. W., & Cottrell, L. S. *Predicting success or failure in marriage*. New York: Prentice-Hall, 1939.

Burgess, E. W., & Locke, H. J. *The family: From institution to companionship*. New York: American Book, 1945.

Burgess, E. W., & Wallin, P. *Engagement and marriage*. New York: Lippincott, 1953.

Burgess, R. L., & Huston, T. L. *Social exchange in developing relationships*. New York: Academic Press, 1979.

Burr, W. R., Hill, R., Nye, F. I., & Reiss, I. L. *Contemporary theories about the family* (Vol. 1). New York: Free Press, 1979.

Caplow, T., Bahr, H. M., Chadwick, B. A., Hill, R., & Williamson, M. H. *Middletown families: Fifty years of change and continuity*. Minneapolis: University of Minnesota Press, 1982.

Carter, H., & Glick, P. C. *Marriage and divorce: A social and economic study*. Cambridge, Mass.: Harvard University Press, 1976.

Cavan, R. S., & Ranck, K. H. *The family and the Depression*. Chicago: University of Chicago Press, 1938.

Cherlin, A. J. Remarriage as an incomplete institution. *American Journal of Sociology*, 1978, **84**, 634–50.

Cherlin, A. J. A sense of history: Recent research on aging and the family. *Leading edges: Recent developments in social and psychological aging*. Bethesda, Md.: National Institute on Aging, 1980.

Cherlin, A. J. *Marriage, divorce, remarriage: Marital formation and dissolution in the postwar United States*. Cambridge, Mass.: Harvard University Press, 1981.

Christensen, H. T. *Handbook of marriage and the family*. Chicago: Rand McNally, 1964.

Clausen, J. A. *Socialization and society*. Boston: Little, Brown, 1968.

Clausen, J. A. The life course of individuals. In M. W. Riley, M. Johnson, & A. Foner (Eds.), *Aging and society*. New York: Russell Sage, 1972.

Coleman, J. *The adolescent society*. New York: Free Press, 1961.

Coser, L. *The social functions of conflict*. New York: Free Press, 1956.

Cottrell, L. S. The present status and future orientation of research on the family. *American Sociological Review*, 1948, **13**, 123–129.

Davis, K. The sociology of parent-youth conflict. *American Sociological Review*, 1940, **5**, 523–535.

Dizard, J. *Social change in the family*. Chicago: University of Chicago and Family Study Center, 1968.

Doering, S. G., Entwisle, D. R., & Quinlan, D. Modeling the quality of women's birth experience. *Journal of Health and Social Behavior*, 1980, **21**, 12–21.

Duncan, G. J., & Morgan, J. N. *Analyses of the first eleven years of the Panel Study of Income Dynamics, five thousand American families—patterns of economic progress* (Vol. 8). Ann Arbor, Mich.: Institute for Social Research, 1980.

Duncan, G. J. *Years of poverty, years of plenty*. Ann Arbor, Mich.: Institute for Social Research, 1984.

Elder, G. H., Jr. *Children of the Great Depression*. Chicago: University of Chicago Press, 1974.

Elder, G. H., Jr. Age differentiation and the life course. In *Annual review of sociology* (Vol. 1). Palo Alto, Calif.: Annual Reviews, 1975.

Elder, G. H., Jr. Approaches to social change and the family. In J. Demos & S. Boocock (Eds.), *Turning points: Historical and sociological essays on the family*. Chicago: University of Chicago Press, 1978. (a)

Elder, G. H., Jr. Family history and the life course. In T. Hareven (Ed.), *Transitions: The family and the life course in historical perspective*. New York: Academic Press, 1978. (b)

Elder, G. H., Jr. Historical change in life patterns and personality. In P. Baltes & O. Brim (Eds.), *Life-span development and behavior*. Vol. 2. New York: Academic Press, 1979.

Elder, G. H., Jr. Adolescence in historical perspective. In J. Adelson (Ed.), *Handbook of adolescent psychology*. New York: Wiley, 1980. (a)

Elder, G. H., Jr. *Family structure and socialization*. New York: Arno Press, 1980. (b)

Elder, G. H., Jr. History and the family: The discovery of complexity. *Journal of Marriage and the Family*, 1981, **43**, 489–519 (a).

Elder, G. H., Jr. History and the life course. In D. Bertaux (Ed.), *Biography and society*. Beverly Hills, Calif.: Sage, 1981. (b)

Elder, G. H., Jr. *The course of life: Developmental and historical perspectives*. Mimeographed. Cornell University, Ithaca, N.Y., 1983.

Elder, G. H., Jr. (Ed.). *Life course dynamics: From 1968 to the 1980s*. Ithaca, N.Y.: Cornell University Press, 1984. (a)

Elder, G. H., Jr. Household, kinship, and the life course: Perspectives on black families and children. In M. Spencer, G. Brookins, & W. Allen (Eds.), *Beginnings: The social and affective development of black children*. Hillsdale, N.J.: Erlbaum, 1984. (b)

Elder, G. H., Jr., Liker, J. K., & Cross, C. E. Parent-child behavior in the Great Depression: Life course and intergenerational influences. In P. B. Baltes & O. G. Brim (Eds.), *Life-span development and behavior* (Vol. 6). New York: Academic Press, 1984.

Entwisle, D. R., & Doering, S. G. *The first birth: A family turning point*. Baltimore: Johns Hopkins Press, 1981.

Farber, B. *The family: Organization and interaction*. San Francisco: Chandler, 1964.

Farber, B. *Comparative kinship organization*. New York: Wiley, 1968.

Farber, B. *Kinship and class: A midwestern study*. New York: Basic, 1971.

Farber, B. *Family and kinship in modern society*. San Francisco: Scott, Foresman, 1973.

Farber, B. *Conceptions of kinship*. New York: Elsevier–North Holland, 1981.

Faris, R. E. L. *Chicago sociology, 1920–1932*. San Francisco: Chandler, 1967.

Featherman, D. L. The life-span perspective in social science research. In *The five-year outlook on science and technology, 1981 source materials* (Vol. 2). National Science Foundation. Washington, D.C.: Superintendent of Documents, 1982.

Fehrenbach, D. E. *History and American society: Essays of David M. Potter*. New York: Oxford University Press, 1973.

Fischer, C. S. *Networks and places: Social relations in the urban setting*. New York: Free Press, 1977.

Fischer, C. S. *To dwell among friends: Personal networks in town and city*. Chicago: University of Chicago Press, 1982.

Frazier, E. F. *The Negro family in the United States*. Chicago: University of Chicago Press, 1966. (Originally published, 1939.)

Furstenberg, F. F., Jr. *Unplanned parenthood*. New York: Free Press, 1976.

Furstenberg, F. F., Jr. Conjugal succession: Reentering marriage after divorce. In P. B. Baltes & O. G. Brim, Jr. (Eds.). *Life-span development and behavior* (Vol. 4). New York: Academic Press, 1982.

Furstenberg, F. F., Jr., Hershberg, T., & Modell, J. The origins of the female headed black family: The impact of urban experience. *Journal of Interdisciplinary History*, 1975, **5**, 211–233.

Glick, P. C. The family cycle. *American Sociological Review*, 1947, **12**, 164–174.

Glick, P. C. Updating the life cycle of the family. *Journal of Marriage and the Family*, 1977, **39**, 5–13.

Goode, W. J. *After divorce*. Glencoe, Ill.: Fress Press, 1956.

Goode, W. J. *World revolution and family patterns*. New York: Free Press, 1963.

Goode, W. J. Force and violence in the family. *Journal of Marriage and the Family*, 1971, **33**, 624–636.

Gordon, M., & Downing, H. A multivariate test of the Bott hypothesis in an urban Irish setting. *Journal of Marriage and the Family*, 1978, **40**, 585–593.

Goslin, D. A. (Ed.). *Handbook of socialization theory and research*. New York: Rand, 1969.

Greenberger, E., Steinberg, L., Vaux, A. & McAuliffe, S. Adolescents who work: Effects of part-time employment on family and peer relations. *Journal of Youth and Adolescence*, 1980, **9**, 189–202.

Grossman, F. K., Eichler, L. S., & Winickoff, S. A. *Pregnancy, birth, and parenthood*. San Francisco: Jossey-Bass, 1980.

Gutman, H. C. *The black family in slavery and freedom, 1750–1925*. New York: Pantheon, 1976.

Hagestad, G. O. Problems and promises in the social psychology of intergenerational relations. In R. Fogel, E. Hatfield, S. Kiesler, & J. March (Eds.), *Stability and change in the family*. New York: Academic Press, 1981.

Hagestad, G. O. Parent and child: Generations in the family. In T. M. Field, H. C. Huston, L. T. Quay, & G. E. Finley (Eds.), *Review of human development*. New York: Wiley, 1982.

Hagestad, G. O., & Dixon, R. A. *Lineages as units of analysis: New avenues for the study of individual and family careers*. Paper presented at the NCFR Theory Construction and Research Methodology Workshop, Portland, Oregon, October 1980.

Hagestad, G. O., & Neugarten, B. L. Age and the life course. In E. Shanas & R. Binstock (Eds.), *The handbook of aging and the social sciences* (2d ed.). New York: Van Nostrand Reinhold, 1983.

Hagestad, G. O., & Smyer, M. A. Dissolving long-term relationships: Patterns of divorcing in middle age. In S. Duck (Ed.), *Personal relationships 4: Dissolving personal relationships*. New York: Academic Press, 1982.

Hansen, D. A. & Johnson, V. A. Rethinking family stress theory: Definitional aspects. In W. R. Burr & R. Hill (Eds.), Contemporary theories about the family. New York: Free Press, 1979.

Hareven, T. K. *Transitions: The family and the life course in historical perspective*. New York: Academic Press, 1978.

Hareven, T. K. *Family time and industrial time*. New York: Cambridge University Press, 1981.

Hartup, W. Perspectives on child and family interaction; Past, present and future. In R. Lerner & G. Spanier (Eds.), *Child influences on family and marital interaction: A life span perspective*. New York: Academic Press, 1978.

Havighurst, R. J. *Developmental tasks and education*. Chicago: University of Chicago Press, 1948.

Hetherington, E. M., Cox, M., & Cox, R. Effects of divorce on parents and children. In M. Lamb (Ed.), *Nontraditional families*. Hillsdale, N.J.: Erlbaum, 1981.

Hill, R. *Families under stress*. New York: Harper & Row, 1949.

Hill, R. Methodological issues in family development research. *Family Process*, 1964, **3**, 186–206.

Hill, R. *Family development in three generations*. Cambridge, Mass.: Schenkman, 1970.

Hill, R. Theories and research designs linking family behavior and child development: A critical overview. *Journal of Comparative Family Studies*, 1981, **12**, 1–18.

Hill, R., & Mattessich, P. Family development theory and life-span development. In P. B. Baltes & O. G. Brim, Jr. (Eds.), *Life-span development and behavior* (Vol. **2**.) New York: Academic Press, 1979.

Hill, R., & Rodgers, R. H. The developmental approach. In H. T. Christensen (Ed.), *Handbook of marriage and the family*. Chicago: Rand McNally, 1964.

Hofferth, S. L. *Some long-term economic consequences of delayed childbearing and family size*. Paper presented at the annual meeting of the Population Association of America, April 1983.

Hofferth, S. L. Children's life course: Family structures and living arrangements in cohort perspective. In G. H. Elder, Jr. (Ed.), *Life course dynamics: From 1968 to the 1980s*. Ithaca, N.Y.: Cornell University Press, 1984.

Hoffman, L. W., & Nye, F. I. *Working mothers*. San Francisco: Jossey-Bass, 1974.

Hogan, D. P. *Transitions and social change*. New York: Academic Press, 1981.

Kahn, R. L. Aging and social support. In M. W. Riley (Ed.), *Aging from birth to death: Interdisciplinary perspectives* Boulder, Colo.: Westview, 1979.

Kandel, D. B., & Lesser, G. S. *Youth in two worlds*. San Francisco: Jossey-Bass, 1972.

Kasl, S. V. Changes in mental health status associated with job loss and retirement. In J. E. Barrett (Ed.), *Stress and mental disorders*. New York: Raven, 1979.

Kertzer, D. I. Generation and age in cross-cultural perspective. In M. W. Riley, R. P. Abeles, & M.S. Teitelbaum (Eds.), *Aging from birth to death* (Vol. 1): *Sociotemporal perspectives*. Boulder, Colo.: Westview, 1982

Kertzer, D. I. Generation as a sociological problem. In *Annual review of sociology* (Vol. **8**). Palo Alto, Calif.: Annual Reviews, 1983.

Kohn, M. J. Social class and parent-child relationships: An interpretation. *American Journal of Sociology*, 1963, **68**, 471–480.

Kohn, M. L. *Class and conformity: A study in values* (rev. ed.). Chicago: University of Chicago Press, 1977.

Kohn, M. L. Job complexity and adult personality. In N. J. Smelser & E. H. Erikson (Eds.). *Themes of work and love in adulthood*. Cambridge, Mass.: Harvard University Press, 1980.

Kohn, M. L., & Schooler, C. The reciprocal effects of the substantive complexity of work and intellectual flexibility: A longitudinal assessment. *American Journal of Sociology*, 1978, **84**, 24–52.

Kohn, M. L., & Schooler, C. *Work and personality: An inquiry into social stratification*. Norwood, N.J.: Ablex, 1983.

Komarovsky, M. *The unemployed man and his family*. New York: Columbia University Press, 1940.

Kuhn, T. S. *The essential tension: Selected studies in scientific tradition and change*. Chicago: University of Chicago Press, 1977.

Lambert, W. E., Harmers, J. F., & Frasure-Smith, N. *Child rearing values.* New York: Praeger, 1979.

Lane, J. P., & Morgan, J. N. Patterns of change in economic status and family structure. In G. J. Duncan & J. N. Morgan (Eds.), *Five thousand American families: Patterns of economic progress* (Vol. 2). Ann Arbor, Mich.: Instutute for Social Research, 1975.

Lansing, J. B., & Kish, L. Family life cycle as an independent variable. *American Sociological Review,* 1957, **22,** 512–519.

Lerner, D. The American soldier and the public. In R. K. Merton & P. F. Lazarsfeld (Eds.), *Continuities in social research.* Glencoe, Ill.: Free Press, 1950.

Lerner, R. M., & Spanier, G. P. *Child influences on marital and family interactions.* New York: Academic Press, 1978.

Levinson, D. J. Toward a conception of the adult life course. In N. J. Smelser & E. H. Erikson (Eds.), *Themes of work and love in adulthood.* Cambridge, Mass.: Harvard University Press, 1980.

Liker, J. K., & Elder, G. H., Jr. Economic hardship and marital relations in the 1930s. *American Sociological Review,* 1983, **48,** 343–359.

Lopata, H. Z. *Women as widows: Support systems.* New York: Elsevier, 1979.

Lynd, R. S., & Lynd, H. M. *Middletown: A study in American culture.* New York: Harcourt, Brace & World, 1929.

Martin, E. P., & Martin, J. *The black extended family.* Chicago: University of Chicago Press, 1978.

McAdoo, H. P. Factors related to stability in upwardly mobile black families. *Journal of Marriage and the Family,* 1978, **40,** 61–69.

McAdoo, H. P. (Ed.). *Black families.* Beverly Hills, Calif.: Sage, 1981.

McCubbin, H., Dahl, B., Metres, P., Hunter, E., & Plag, J. *Family separation and reunion.* Washington, D.C.: Government Printing Office, 1974.

McCubbin, H., Dahl, B., Metres, P., Hunter, E., & Plag, J. Family stress and coping: A decade review. *Journal of Marriage and the Family,* 1980, **42,** 855–871.

Mead, M. *Coming of age in Samoa.* Ann Arbor, Mich.: Morrow, 1928.

Merton, R. K. *Sociological ambivalence and other essays.* New York: Free Press, 1976.

Miller, D., & Swanson, G. E. *The changing American parent.* New York: Wiley, 1958.

Miller, J., Schooler, C., Kohn, M. L., & Miller, K. A. Women and work: The psychological effects of occupational conditions. *American Journal of Sociology,* 1979, **85,** 66–91.

Miner, H. *St. Denis: A French-Canadian parish.* Chicago: University of Chicago Press, 1939.

Modell, J. Changing risks, changing adaptations: American families in the nineteenth and twentieth centuries. In A. J. Lichtman & J. R. Challinor (Eds.), *Kin and communities: Families in America.* Washington, D.C.: Smithsonian Press, 1979.

Modell, J., Furstenberg, F. F., Jr., & Hershberg, T. Social change and the transition of adulthood in historical perspective. *Journal of Family History,* 1976, **1,** 7–32.

Moen, P., Kain, E., & Elder, G. H., Jr. Economic conditions and family life: Contemporary and historical perspectives. In R. R. Nelson & F. Skidmore (Eds.), *American families and the economy: The high cost of living.* Washington, D.C.: National Academy Press, 1983.

Mortimer, J. T., & Simmons, R. G. Adult socialization. In *Annual review of sociology* (Vol. 4). Palo Alto, Calif.: Annual Reviews, 1978.

Mowrer, E. *Family disorganization.* Chicago: University of Chicago Press, 1926.

Mueller, C. W., & Parcel, T. L. Measures of socioeconomic status: Alternatives and recommendations. *Child Development,* 1981, **52,** 13–30.

Neugarten, B. L., More, J. W., & Lowe, J. C. Age norms, age constraints and adult socialization. *American Journal of Sociology,* 1965, **70,** 710–717.

Nisbet, R. A. *Social change and history*. New York: Oxford University Press, 1969.

Ogburn, W. F. The changing family. *Publications of the American Sociological Society*, 1929, **23**, 124–133.

Oppenheimer, V. K. The changing nature of life-cycle squeezes: Implications for the socioeconomic position of the elderly. In R. W. Fogel et al. (Eds.), *Aging: Stability and change in the family*. New York: Academic Press, 1981.

Oppenheimer, V. K. *Work and the family: A study in social demography*. New York: Academic Press, 1982.

Parkes, C. M. Psychosocial transitions: A field for study. *Social Science and Medicine*, 1971, **5**, 101–115.

Parsons, T. *The social system*. Glencoe, Ill.: Free Press, 1951.

Parsons, T. The normal American family. In S. Farber, P. Mustacchi, & R. H. Wilson (Eds.). *Man and civilization*. New York: McGraw-Hill, 1965.

Parsons, T., & Bales, R. F. *Family, socialization and interaction process*. Glencoe, Ill.: Free Press, 1955.

Pearlin, L. I., & Lieberman, M. A. Social sources of emotional distress. In R. Simmons (Ed.), *Research in community and mental health* (Vol. 1). Greenwich, Conn.: JAI, 1979.

Pearlin, L. I., Lieberman, M. A., Menaghan, E. G., & Mullan, J. T. The stress process. *Journal of Health and Social Behavior*, 1981, **22**, 337–356.

Plath, D. Contours of consociation: Lessons from a Japanese narrative. In P. Baltes & O. G. Brim, Jr. (Eds.), *Life-span development and behavior* (Vol. 3). New York: Academic Press, 1980.

Pressey, S. L., Janney, J. E., & Kuhlen, R. G. *Life: A psychological survey*. New York: Harper, 1939.

Prude, J. The family in context. *Labor History*, 1976, **17**, 422–435.

Rainwater, L., & Yancey, W. L. *The Moynihan Report and the politics of controversy*. Cambridge, Mass.: M.I.T. Press, 1967.

Rallings, E. M., & Nye, F. I. Wife-mother employment, family, and society. In W. R. Burr, R. Hill, F. I. Nye, & I. L. Reiss (Eds.), *Contemporary theories about the family*. New York: Free Press, 1979.

Rapaport, R. The transition from engagement to marriage. *Acta Sociologica*, 1964, **8**, 36–55.

Rapaport, R. The study of marriage as a critical transition for personality and family development. In P. Lomas (Ed.), *The predicament of the family*. London: Hogarth, 1967.

Rapaport, R., Rapoport, R. N., & Strelitz, Z. *Fathers, mothers and society: Towards new alliances*. New York: Basic, 1977.

Reiss, D. *The family's construction of reality*. Cambridge, Mass.: Harvard University Press, 1981.

Riesman, D. *The lonely crowd*. New Haven, Conn.: Yale University Press, 1950.

Riley, M. W., Johnson, M., & Foner, A. *Aging and society*. New York: Russell Sage, 1972.

Rodman, H. Marital power in France, Greece, Yugoslavia, and the United States: A cross national discussion. *Journal of Marriage and the Family*, 1967, **29**, 320–324.

Rossi, A. S. Aging and parenthood in the middle years. In P. B. Baltes & O. G. Brim, Jr. (Eds.), *Life-span development and behavior*. New York: Academic Press, 1980.

Rowntree, B. S. *Poverty: A study of town life*. London: MacMillan, 1901.

Rubinow, I. M. *Social insurance, with special reference to American conditions*. New York: Holt, 1916.

Ryder, N. B. The cohort as a concept in the study of social change. *American Sociological Review*, 1965, **30**, 843–861.

Scanzoni, J. H. *The black family in modern society*. Chicago: University of Chicago Press, 1971.

Scarr, S., & McCartney, K. How people make their own environments: A theory of geno-type-environment effects. *Child Development*, 1983, **54**, 424–435.

Schwarzweller, H. K., Brown, J. S., & Mangalam, J. J. *Mountain families in transition*. University Park: Penn State University Press, 1971.

Shimkin, D. B., Shimkin, E. M., & Frate, D. A. *The extended family in black societies*. The Hague: Mouton, 1978.

Smelser, N. J. *Social change in the industrial revolution*. Chicago: University of Chicago Press, 1959.

Spanier, G. B., & Furstenberg, F. F., Jr. Remarriage and reconstituted families. In M. B. Sussman & S. K. Steinmetz (Eds.), *Handbook of marriage and the family*. New York: Plenum, 1983.

Stack, C. B. *All our kin: Strategies for survival in a black community*. New York: Harper & Row, 1974.

Steinberg, L. D., & Hill, J. P. Patterns of family interaction as a function of age, the onset of puberty, and formal thinking. *Developmental Psychology*, 1978, **14**, 683–684.

Stouffer, S. A., et al. *The American soldier* (Vols. **1**, **2**, and **4**). Princeton, N.J.: Princeton University Press, 1949.

Straus, M. A., Gelles, R. J., & Steinmetz, S. K. *Behind closed doors: Violence in the American family*. New York: Anchor, 1980.

Thomas, D. S., & Nishimoto, R. S. *The spoilage*. Berkeley: University of California Press, 1946.

Thomas, W. I., & Thomas, D. S. *The child in America*. New York: Knopf, 1928.

Thomas, W. I., & Znaniecki, F. *The Polish peasant in Europe and America*. New York: Octagon, 1974. (Originally published, 1918–20.)

Turner, R. H. *Family interaction*. New York: Wiley, 1970.

Uhlenberg, P. Changing configurations of the life course. In T. K. Hareven (Ed.), *Transitions: The family and life course in historical perspective*. New York: Academic Press, 1978.

Veroff, J., Douvan, E., & Kulka, R. A. *The inner American: A self-portrait from 1957 to 1976*. New York: Basic, 1981.

Volkart, E. H. *Social behavior and personality: Contributions of W. I. Thomas to theory and research*. New York: Social Science Research Council, 1951.

Waite, L. J., & Stolzenberg, R. M. Intended childbearing and labor force participation of young women: Insights from nonrecursive models. *American Sociological Review*, 1976, **41**, 235–252.

Waite, L. J., & Stolzenberg, R. M. Working wives and the family life cycle. *American Journal of Sociology*, 1980, **86**, 272–294.

Waller, W. *The old love and the new: Divorce and readjustment*. New York: Horace Liveright, 1930.

Waller, W. *The family: A dynamic interpretation* (rev. by R. Hill). New York: Dryden, 1951. (Originally published, 1938.)

Wandersee, W. D. *Women's work and family values, 1920–1940*. Cambridge, Mass.: Harvard University Press, 1981.

Weissman, M. M., & Paykel, E. W. *The depressed woman: A study of social relationships*. Chicago: University of Chicago Press, 1974.

White, L. K., & Brinkerhoff, D. B. Children's work in the family: Its significance and meaning. *Journal of Marriage and the Family*, 1981, **43**, 789–798.

Wilensky, H. L. Family life cycle, work, and the quality of life: Reflections on the roots of happiness, despair, and indifference in modern society. In B. Gardell & G. Johannson (Eds.), *Working life*. New York: Wiley, 1981.

Williams, R. M., Jr. Relative deprivation. In L. A. Coser (Ed.), *The idea of social structure: Papers in Honor of Robert K. Merton*. New York: Harcourt Brace Jovanovich, 1975.

Young, M., & Willmott, P. *Family and kinship in East London*. London: Routledge & Kegan Paul, 1957.

Young, M., & Willmott, P. *The symmetrical family*. New York: Pantheon, 1973.

Zimmerman, C. C. *Consumption and standards of living*. New York: Van Nostrand, 1936.

5 Themes in the Historical Development of the Family

TAMARA K. HAREVEN
Clark University and Center for Population Studies,
Harvard University

INTRODUCTION

The history of the family is a relatively new field that has provided a time perspective on contemporary issues as well as an understanding of behavior in the past. Some of the questions asked by family historians are similar to those asked by psychologists, anthropologists, sociologists, and economists (Elder, 1978a, 1978b; Hareven, 1971, 1974, 1976; Stone, 1981; Tilly & Cohen, 1982). Historical research on the family is unique, however, in providing a perspective on change over time as well as examining family behavior within specific social and cultural contexts. Historians thus have contributed not just examinations of diachronic changes but investigations of synchronic patterns within discrete time periods as well. The cumulative impact of studies in the history of the family has been to revise a simplistic view of social change and family behavior over time. These revisions have also generated a host of new questions, which have yet to be answered (Elder 1981; Hareven, 1977).

The most important impetus for the historical study of the family came from the "new social history" in the 1960s. Historical studies of the family share with the new social history an interest in reconstructing the life patterns of ordinary people rather than elites or celebrated individuals, a commitment to link individual and group behavior to larger social processes and to social structures, and a view of people in the past as actors confronting historical forces rather than as passive victims. Much of this research represented an effort to reconstruct patterns of people's behavior

This essay was written while I was a 1981–82 fellow at the Center for Advanced Study in the Behavioral Sciences. I am indebted to the Center and to the McArthur Foundation for support. I am also indebted to the National Institute on Aging from whom I held a Research Career Development Grant (5-KO4-AG-00026) and a research grant (AG 02468).

and perceptions from their own experience and point of view. The field, however, owes its major development to the theoretical and methodological influences of demography, psychology, sociology, and anthropology. As the field developed, new findings in the history of the family have led to the revision of generalizations about family behavior, individual development, and social change in these disciplines as well.

To reconstruct the family patterns of large numbers of ordinary people, historians of the family have delved into census records; birth, marriage, and death registers; occupational files; family letters; and diaries. The history of the family has thus provided a time perspective on the contemporary family and generated a realistic view of the complexities in the relationship between the family and other institutions confronting historical change. Beyond the specific topic of family, an understanding of how individuals and families have responded to historical change and how they in turn affect such change has considerably broadened our understanding of the process of change itself. As the field developed over the past decade and a half, historians expanded their inquiry from household and family structure to a broad range of subjects including marriage and sexual behavior, child rearing, relations with extended kin, and generational relations.

Research in the history of the family has moved from a view of the family as a household unit at one point in time to a consideration of it as a process over the entire lives of its members; from a study of discrete domestic family (or household) structure to one of the nuclear family's interaction with the wider kinship group; and from a study of the family as a separate domestic unit to an examination of its interaction with the worlds of work, education, correctional and welfare institutions, and such processes as migration. More recently, efforts to explore decision-making processes within the family have led to an investigation of strategies and choices that individual family members and family groups make (Elder, 1978b, 1981; Modell, 1978). In trying to understand the role of the family and its internal dynamics, historical research has gradually moved from a concentration on the family as an isolated unit to an exploration of its interaction with other social processes and institutions, with considerable emphasis on the role of the family in the processes of industrialization and urbanization (Anderson, 1971; Hareven, 1975, 1977, 1978a, 1982; Smelser, 1959). Finally, the life-course approach, which has greatly influenced historical research on the family in recent years, has added an important developmental dimension to the history of the family by focusing on age and cohort comparisons in ways that link individual and family development to historical events (Elder, 1978a, 1978b; Hareven, 1978b; Vinovskis, 1977).

ORIGINS OF THE FIELD

Historical studies of the family have come into vogue only within the past decade and a half, specifically since the publication in 1962 of Philippe Ariès's *Centuries of Childhood*, but not exclusively as a result of that book's impact. Ariès's book opened up a new direction for historians by focusing attention both on the concept of childhood and on the changing experience of childen in preindustrial French and English society. His conclusion that childhood as a distinct experience and stage of life was discovered only in the eighteenth century and that its discovery was closely linked to the emergence of the "modern family" has provided a model for subsequent historical studies of the origins of the modern family, most notably those by Demos, Shorter, and Stone (Demos, 1970; Shorter, 1976; Stone, 1977). In linking child development to family structure, social class, and economic and demographic changes, Ariès provided a model for a study of childhood in relation to the changing conditions of the family in society. Ariès's methods, approach, and basic conclusions have since drawn criticism. Historians have challenged his thesis that the family as an emotional entity resting on sentimental ties between husband and wife and parents and children did not exist before the eighteenth century and that Western Europe had been characterized by indifference to children prior to that time. Ariès himself has acknowledged since that, had he examined medieval sources, his conclusions might have been different. Ariès's seminal work has been used nevertheless as the major reference point for the study of the historical transition to the modern family by historians who focus on cultural rather than socioeconomic and demographic factors.

French demographers, particularly Louis Henry (1968) and Pierre Goubert (1960), provided historians with techniques of family reconstitution that were essential for reconstructing patterns of migration, fertility, mortality, and nuptiality. Their family reconstitution techniques, using individual data from parish registers, made it possible to reconstruct the family patterns of vast numbers of individuals and to link them generationally. Family reconstitution made it possible to link demographic patterns of fertility, nuptiality, mortality, and migration with family and household structure in preindustrial populations (Goubert, 1970; Henry, 1968; Vann, 1969; Wrigley, 1959, 1972). The French demographers focused primarily on demographic patterns, but members of the Cambridge Group for the History of Population and Social Structure in England, who utilized and improved on the French family reconstitution techniques, and subsequently historians of colonial American society went beyond demographic analysis to reconstruct household and inheritance patterns (Demos, 1970; Greven, 1970; Lockridge, 1966).

Family reconstitution in other Western European countries as well as in the United States and Canada facilitated a major reinterpretation of population and family behavior in the preindustrial period. The initial conclusions that emerged from this research were that geographic mobility in preindustrial society was more pervasive than had been generally assumed, that the predominant form of family (household) structure in preindustrial society was nuclear rather than extended, and that some forms of birth control were being practiced by the eighteenth century (Laslett & Wall, 1972; Wrigley, 1966a, 1966b, 1977).

Using the family reconstitution technique, Philip Greven analyzed the demographic patterns of the population in Andover, Massachusetts, from 1650 to 1800 and reconstructed the patterns of family organization over four generations. Greven's study linked demographic data to land-holding patterns in the family and concluded that the family unit thus emerged as a crucial focus of all economic transactions and as the basis of stability in an agrarian society (Greven, 1970). Demos, in contrast, used demography as the backbone for a psychosocial reconstruction of family experience in Plymouth colony. Demos related the demographic data—marriage age, birthrates, longevity, and occupation to "themes of individual development" in various stages of the life cycle, and in turn linked these to basic concepts of Puritan culture (Demos, 1970).

The application of psychological theory to the study of individual and family development within a specific historical context has been limited almost entirely to Erik Erikson's developmental model, which is a composite of psychoanalytic theory, anthropological concepts of culture and personality, and a historical perspective (Erikson, 1950). Demos chose Erikson's model because of the "need to discover the dynamic interconnections between experience at an earlier stage and a later stage, to appreciate that a child is always *developing* according to influences that proceed from within as well as from the wider environment" (Demos, 1970).

Unfortunately, Demos's psychological reconstruction of the lives of ordinary people, which places individual development in a social and demographic context, has not yet been followed by similar psychohistorical studies of the family. Most of the subsequent historical studies of childhood were reductionist in approach, establishing linkages between childhood conditions and specific historical circumstances, without adequate recognition of the complexity of family patterns (de Mause, 1975). As will be detailed below, the life-course approach and the sociology of age stratification have provided an alternative to the mechanistic use of stages with an emphasis on process and transitions. The study of the later years of life, on the other hand, has progressed in a direction which combines both behavioral and attitudinal patterns. But its emphasis has been cultural, social, and economic, rather than psychological (Achenbaum, 1978; Chudacoff & Hareven, 1979; Fischer, 1977; Hareven, 1976). As will be suggested below, the life-course approach has integrated the study of stages of individual and collective family development into a more comparative framework, but one which at the moment is primarily structural.

Sociology has had a far-reaching influence on historical research on the family, particularly on the analysis of family and household structure and kinship. It has shaped the way we study the relationships between the family and work, changing family functions, and social change, especially urbanization and industrialization. The basic theoretical framework underlying recent work in the history of the family, including the analyses of household structure and kinship patterns, and the fundamental concepts of family development, the family cycle, and the life-course approach, are all derived from sociology.

Talcott Parsons's structural-functional model of the family served as the dominant framework in the first stage of the emergence of family history. Even though historians and sociologists have now revised Parsons's generalizations about the impact of industrialization on the family, the Parsonian model still shapes historical research to some extent (Parsons, 1951; Parsons & Bales, 1955; Smelser, 1959). While following a basic structure-function approach, historians have been successful in revising several key characteristics of the Parsonian approach. Recent historical research has thus questioned the assumptions that there is a harmonious "fit" between the family and the larger social system and that it is the family's major task to serve that system; that the family is a static unit rather than a conglomerate of interacting personalities. In this respect, the most promising direction in the development of the field has come from the life-course approach. Although the life-course framework has not provided an alternative to the structural-functional perspective, it has nevertheless provided a dynamic model for the study of family development internally and over historical time (Elder, 1978a).

FAMILY AND HOUSEHOLD STRUCTURE

Before systematic historical study of the family began, other social science disciplines had generated their own myths and grand theories about continuities and changes in family behavior in the past. These prevailing assumptions claimed that "modern" family and population behavior—earlier age at marriage, family size limitation, and population mobility—were innovations introduced with industrialization and that in preindustrial society the dominant household form had been the extended family, in many cases involving three coresident generations. Industrialization was thus considered a major watershed between preindustrial and postindustrial modes of family organization and demographic behavior. Most important, the prevailing assumption was that industrialization destroyed a three-generation *coresident* family structure and led to the emergence of the isolated nuclear family—a type functionally more compatible with the demands of the "modern" industrial system than was the "traditional" extended family. Associated with these generalizations by social scientists were also popular myths that in the preindustrial period family life (along with community life) was more harmonious and that industrialization had eroded a traditional three-generational family pattern.

Research in the history of the family in the 1960s demolished some of these myths and led to the revision of a simplistic linear view of historical change. Laslett and his group firmly established the predominance of a nuclear family structure in preindustrial Western Europe and its persistence over at least the past three centuries (Laslett & Wall, 1972). (The definition of "nuclear family," following Laslett's, is a family unit consisting of parents and their children, or of a childless couple, or of one parent and children. It is necessary, however, to distinguish between "family" and "household." The most important distinguishing feature of a nuclear family is the absence of extended kin. A nuclear *family* is not, however, identical with a nuclear *household*, since the domestic group may have included nonrelatives as well.)

These findings that a nuclear household structure has persisted for at least three centuries in Western Europe, combined with similar findings for colonial American communities, have shown the three-generation household in preindustrial society—what William Goode calls "The Great Family of Western Nostalgia"—to be a myth with little basis in historical fact (Demos, 1970; Goode, 1963; Greven, 1970). Similarly, studies of household structure in nineteenth-century American communities have laid to rest the assumption that the dominant preindustrial household structure was extended and three-generational. In most early American communities the typical form of household structure was nuclear. Members of the nuclear family were, however, enmeshed in close ties with extended kin and, as Greven found in Andover, aging parents did not reside in the same household with their adult son but lived in the vicinity, on the same land, in what would be labeled a "modified extended" family structure (Demos, 1970; Greven, 1970; Smith, 1973).

In American urban communities in the nineteenth century, the dominant household structure once again was nuclear. Only about 9%–12% of these households were extended, and only about 1%–3% contained solitary residents. The remaining households were nuclear (Blumin, 1977;

Hareven, 1977; Sennett, 1970). The most important conclusion emerging from this first stage of historical research was that industrialization did not break down a great extended family—did not lead to the emergence of an isolated nuclear family. In fact, some studies have shown that industrialization and urbanization may have led to an increase in household extension (Anderson, 1971; Hareven, 1982).

Historians who emphasized the persistence of a nuclear family structure over time have drawn their major evidence from the household rather than the family. In emphasizing this continuity, they have unwittingly implied that it was the nuclear *family* rather than the household that persisted over time. In most of these studies, however, the major unit of analysis was the household, not the family. In reality, it was the household that was nuclear. Nuclear households were not always limited, however, to family members. They often included nonrelatives in addition to the nuclear family. Nor was the nuclear residential family unit itself isolated; rather, it was extended through kinship ties outside the household (Anderson, 1971; Greven, 1970; Hareven, 1978a, 1982; Yans-McLaughlin, 1977). The mistaking of household for family arose in part because the measurable entity in most studies of the family, particularly for the nineteenth century, was the residential unit. Historians used the census manuscript schedules as their major data source, which tended to reinforce this concentration on the domestic unit as if it were the entire family unit. Only in the next stage in the development of the field was more serious attention given to the pervasive kinship ties outside the individual household. Another limitation of the studies emphasizing the continuity in a nuclear household structure was that they were limited to one point in time. They did not view the household as a process that changes over the family's cycle and in relation to the organization of production and inheritance (Berkner, 1972; Goody, 1972; Hammel, 1972).

Unlike anthropologists and economists, who have made important progress in this direction, historians have not yet developed a theory of the household that differentiates its functions from those of the family unit and the wider kin group. Thoughtful attention to this question would suggest several characteristics that distinguish the household as somewhat separate from the nuclear family unit within it and from the wider kin group outside its confines. Some of these are worth noting here for methodological as well as theoretical reasons.

The household was the basic organizational unit of the family in Western society. Households formed the cells that together made up the fiber of neighborhoods and entire communities. In American cities in the late nineteenth century, only about 3% of the population lived alone. Almost all men and women expected to live out their lives in family or surrogate family settings. The household was also the basic unit of economic activity in preindustrial society and the locus of vocational training and welfare. With industrialization, and the concomitant transfer of these activities to industrial enterprises and to vocational and welfare institutions, the household ceased to be the major locus of production and welfare, but it continued to fulfill a central economic role. Household production, although limited in scale, persisted in rural areas and even in urban areas where food processing was still done at home. Through the family's control of housing space, its members were engaged in economic exchange relations with nonrelatives, servants, apprentices, and boarders and lodgers, and at times with extended kin as well. In many respects, the household continued to function as an economic unit, beyond consumption, even after it had been stripped of its status as the primary site of production. As a flexible unit, the household expanded and contracted in accordance to the family's needs and over the life course. The very changes in the organization of the household over the life course of its members suggest its responsiveness to the family's development, to economic need or opportunities, and to changing historical conditions.

Inherent in the dynamic processes of the household, however, was a contradiction in its functions. The household served as a source of order, stability, and continuity while at the same time encouraging population movement. It was in the households that new families were formed and children were reared. It was to the household that young people returned in times of need, and it was there that migrants and older people without families found a familial setting. The household was also a source of continuity in the lives of older people. At the same time, the household dislodged family members from its midst, thus generating instability in the population. Households launched children into the world when they reached adulthood, sent out members they were unable to support, or dissolved if their heads or crucial members were stricken by illness or death or became too old to maintain their independence (Hareven, 1982).

Households engaged in indirect exchanges of members across neighborhoods and wide geographic regions. As some members went out into the world, newcomers moved in. Those whose lives were disrupted by migration or death were absorbed into other families. Young people migrating to new communities expected to reside in other people's households rather than in anomic hostels. Similarly, working mothers placed young children in the homes of relatives or strangers, and dependent older people moved into other people's households. Such uses of the households of relatives, neighbors, or complete strangers permeated the entire society (Anderson, 1971; Hareven, 1982; Katz, 1975).

The emphasis on the continuity of a nuclear household structure over time should not lead us to assume that the households of the preindustrial period or of the nineteenth century were identical with the nuclear households of our time. The "nuclear" household in earlier times was far more complex; it often included nonrelatives along with the nuclear family. The presence of young people as servants and apprentices or of older people as dependent members of the household was part of the multiplicity of functions that the domestic family performed in the preindustrial period. Their presence added a significant dimension to the membership of the household which is rarely experienced in contemporary families (Laslett, 1965). Since the household functioned as a workshop, a vocational training ground, and a welfare institution, its boundaries expanded to include nonrelatives who were engaged in various degrees of economic and social relationships with the members of the nuclear family. In the preindustrial period, these nonrelatives were usually apprentices or servants; at times they were dependent individuals who were placed with families by town authorities. For young people, leaving home and living with another family was a common pattern of transition to adult roles. In the nineteenth century, following the decline of apprenticeship and particularly of the practice of live-in apprentices, nonrelatives residing in the household were predominantly servants, boarders, and lodgers (Demos, 1970; Modell & Hareven, 1973).

The presence of boarders and lodgers in nineteenth-century American and West European families suggests that the distinguishing historical variant in the organization of the household was not its extension through the presence of other kin but rather its augmentation by nonrelatives who joined in the household in an exchange relationship. In nineteenth-century American communities, only 12%–15% of urban households contained relatives other than the nuclear family, but 20%–30% of all households included boarders and lodgers. Clearly, the majority of urban households were much more likely to include nonrelatives than extended family. Boarders and lodgers were as common in the nineteenth- and early twentieth-century household as servants and apprentices had been in preindustrial families. Boarding and lodging was a life-course phenomenon, and was therefore part of the regular process of individual and family development, but it was also part of a migration process (Modell & Hareven, 1973).

For men and women in the transitional stage between departure from their parents' households and marriage, boarding offered housing they could afford in a family setting. It provided some surrogate family arrangements without the accompanying obligations and parental controls. For migrants and immigrants, boarding represented a creative use of other people's households as a means for access to jobs and social supports, through the connections of the head of the household with whom they were boarding. It was no coincidence, therefore, that migrant boarders clustered in the households of members of the same ethnic group, often former townsmen (Modell & Hareven, 1973).

For heads of households, taking in boarders augmented the family budget and provided surrogate children after their own sons and daughters had left home. Boarding thus fulfilled the function of the "social equalization of the family" (Taeuber, 1969). In working-class families in Massachusetts during the late nineteenth century, the contribution of boarders and lodgers to family income was most significant as a substitute (or, depending on family need, as a supplement) for the work of women or children, especially after the children had left home. Taking in boarders thus enabled wives to stay out of the labor force and old people to retain the headship of their household after their children had left home (Hareven, 1982; Modell & Hareven, 1973). While the economic and social role of boarders and lodgers in the family awaits further exploration, it is clear that in nineteenth-century American society the presence of nonrelatives in the household was much more widespread and significant than that of the presence of extended kin. Ongoing and future research will have to delineate, however, those aspects of family behavior where strangers were more central and those aspects that were more commonly dependent on kin in the household.

KINSHIP

Historians' transcendence of the boundaries of the household as a research unit and their examination of kinship patterns outside the household has been slow and spotty. Until fairly recently, historians have not asked meaningful questions about kinship. This could be the result of an excessive concern with the nuclearity of the household and of reliance on the household record in the census as the major unit of analysis. The difficulty of determining and reconstructing familial relationships outside the household further discourages investigations of kinship ties. Historians' confusion of "household" with "family" and the evidence of only a small proportion of extended kin present in the household, tended to reinforce historians' assumption that nineteenth-century American urban families were isolated from extended kin. Thus historical reinforcement was provided for Parsons's assertion of the "isolated nuclear family" as the dominant form of family organization in Western society.

The most marked oversight of extended kinship ties was in Richard Sennett's (1970) analysis of family patterns in a late nineteenth-century Chicago suburb. Sennett based his conclusion that the nuclear family was isolated, and, therefore ill-adapted to urban life, on a small proportion of households with extended kin present within them (Sennett, 1970). It was ironic that historians of nineteenth-century family structure tended to accept this Parsonian view, when sociologists, especially Marvin Sussman, Lee Burchinal, and Eugene Litwak, pointed to the pervasiveness of extended kinship ties and assistance in contemporary American society, thus challenging the thesis of an "isolated nuclear family" (Litwak, 1960; Sussman & Burchinal, 1962). Extended kinship ties were even more widespread in the nineteenth and early twentieth centuries; prior to the emergence of the welfare state, kin formed the very base of social security and assistance in times of crisis.

Under the influence of some of these sociological studies for contemporary society, and particularly Anderson's (1971) study of kinship in nineteenth-century Lancashire, historians began to document the continuity of kinship ties in the process of migration and the important role of kin as sources of resilience and assistance in settlement in the new environments. The prevailing historical pattern in England and the United States was one of nuclear households embedded in extended kinship ties outside the household. The overall tendency and inferred preference in the population was to include nonrelatives in the household rather than kin, while at the same time engaging in mutual assistance with kin outside the household. Whenever individuals had kin available nearby, they turned to them for assistance rather than to strangers (Anderson, 1971; Hareven, 1978a, 1982). Thus, nuclear units must be viewed as parts of a larger network of households linked through extended kinship ties. Especially in a regime of economic insecurity with hardly any other available institutional supports, the very autonomy of the nuclear family depended on reciprocity with extended kin.

Kin fulfilled a central role in mediating between the nuclear family and other institutions. They were central in organizing migration, in facilitating settlement, in finding employment, and in cushioning the shock of adaptation to new conditions. The movement of individuals or family clusters to urban areas followed a pattern of chain migration; it was directed, organized, and supported by kin.

A study of working-class life in Manchester, New Hampshire, documents the carry-over of kinship ties from rural to industrial settings. Kinship networks effectively interacted with the modern, industrial system in the late nineteenth and early twentieth century (Hareven, 1978a,

1982). Kin fulfilled a major role in labor recruitment, the organization and support of migration to the industrial community, and the placement of workers in the factory. Relatives acted as major brokers between the workers and the industrial corporations. Kinship networks also facilitated the movement of job seekers from one industrial town to another. Within the textile factory, kin also offered their relatives basic protection on the job, initiated the young and new immigrants into the work process, and manipulated the machinery and work procedures in order to effect slowdowns during periods of speedup and pressure (Hareven, 1975, 1978a, 1982).

This analysis of the internal work relations inside a major industrial corporation shows the extent to which the relationship between the workers' families and the corporation was reciprocal. Both the corporation and the workers recognized and utilized kin as key agents in their relationship. The family trained its members for industrial work and cushioned them from potential shocks and disruptions in the workplace. In this process the family developed its own defenses and brought its cultural traditions to bear on work processes and relations between workers, and between workers and management.

While kin initiated young workers or newly arrived immigrants into industrial work procedures and technology and into work disciplines and social relations among workers, they also socialized newly arrived immigrant workers to collective working-class behavior. The active role performed by family and kin group in these circumstances suggests that the family type most "fit" to interact with the factory system was not the isolated nuclear one, as has frequently been argued, but rather a family with extended kinship ties that called on the resources of a network. At the same time, in cushioning the adaptation of young workers and of newly arrived immigrants without excessively restricting their mobility, kin were instrumental in serving the industrial employer as well as advancing the interest of their own members and trying to protect them (Hareven, 1982). These important functions that kin fulfilled in their interaction with the workplace in a modern corporation exemplify both the continuity in the functions of kin as mediators between nuclear family and public institutions and their taking on new functions in response to the requirements of the industrial system.

Among immigrant populations, the vital functions of kin were not restricted to the local community. The salient role of kin extended beyond the immediate community to encompass long-distance functions as well. To be sure, kinship ties were most effective in interaction with local institutions and in meeting immediate crises. Yet kinship networks typically stretched over several communities and were most useful when conditions failed in the local community. The strength of locally based kin networks lay in stability; the strength of extended networks lay in their fluidity and continuous reorganization. The strengths of long-distance kinship networks were more instrumental during times of crisis in the local community and during migration (Hareven, 1978a, 1982).

In Manchester, New Hampshire, as in mid-nineteenth-century Lancashire and twentieth-century East London, kinship networks were embedded in the industrial town (Anderson, 1971; Bott, 1957; Young & Willmott, 1957). By contrast, the social space of French-Canadian kin extended from Quebec to Manchester and spread over other New England industrial towns. Besides serving as important backup systems, long-distance kinship networks enabled workers to experiment with different kinds of jobs, to send their sons to scout out better jobs, or to marry off their daughters. During periods of failure in the factory, kin continued to act as effective migration agents. Under these conditions, the route of migration was reversed. Earlier, workers brought their kin into the factory; now other kin enabled them to find temporary or more permanent work in other towns or to migrate back to Canada. The existence of fluid kinship networks throughout New England ensured that the needs of unemployed workers for temporary jobs and housing would continue to be met (Hareven, 1982).

Kinship networks were salient in both one's immediate neighborhood and one's workplace, as was the persistence of long-distance kinship ties in larger communities. Long-distance kin performed significant functions for migrant populations and were particularly helpful to temporary migrants, at least at the initial stages of their migration. Geographic distance did not disrupt basic modes of kin cooperation but rather led to the diversification of priorities and modes of kin interaction. Under certain conditions, migration strengthened kinship ties and imposed new functions on them. Kin affiliations in the new setting not only facilitated migration to and settlement there but also served as reminder and reinforcer of obligations and ties to premigration communities.

Appalachian mountain migrants to Ohio industrial communities in the post–World War II period followed similar patterns. In their study of migration from Appalachia to Ohio, Schwarzweller and his colleagues concluded that the kinship structure "provides a highly persuasive line of communication between kinsfolk in the home and in the urban communities. It channels information about available job opportunities and living standards directly, and therefore, it tends to orient migrants to those areas where kin groups are already established." They define a "migration system" thus: "Two subsystems (the community of origin and community of settlement) together form the interactional system in which we wish to consider the adjustment of a given group of migrants, individually and collectively. We have then, *one migration system* to consider, namely, the Beech Creek–Ohio migration" (Schwarzweller, Brown, & Mangalam, 1971, pp. 94–95).

Kinship is a process; kinship ties may be latent for a time and revived when circumstances change. The functions of kin are best examined by looking from the nuclear family outward—not just as it relates to extended kin but also in its relationship to larger social institutions.

Patterns of family integration with the workplace and the active role of kin as labor brokers between individual workers and corporations were more intensive in the textile industry. Were they as important in industries that employed males predominantly or totally? At present we lack the studies of kin involvement in other industries that would permit precise comparison. Existing studies of steel towns, such as Pittsburgh, where the labor force was mostly male suggest different patterns in the family's relationship to the workplace (Byington, 1910; Kleinberg, 1977). Families did not work as units, but male relatives often tended to work together and to assist one another in ways similar to those common in the textile industry. Even in male-dominated industries kin were active both in the workplace and in family life, but forms of assistance tended to be sexually segregated. Whereas male kin influenced the workplace, female kin assisted each other in handling personal and family crises and in securing employment wherever it was available for women in the community. A fuller understanding of the family's interaction with the industrial process depends, however, on future systematic comparisons of the role of kin in different types of industry—a question that is also relevant to developing countries today.

Underlying family relations both in the nuclear family and in the wider kin group during the nineteenth century and the first two decades of this century was a corporate view of family relations, which required an almost total commitment of individual preferences to collective family needs. Work careers of individual members were integrated into a collective family economy. Family and household structure as well as the timing of life transitions were to some extent determined by collective family needs (Chudacoff & Hareven, 1978, 1979; Hareven, 1978a; Modell, Furstenberg, & Hershberg, 1976; Modell & Hareven, 1978). This commitment to goals was also a major determinant of the participation of children, teenagers, and married women in the labor force. The view of the family as a collective economic unit and the expectation that family members would forgo or modify their own career choices in the service of their families were carryovers from rural society that served as a major form of adaptation in working-class life.

While historians are now recognizing that the overall pattern of historical change over the past century has been one of an increasing shift from a commitment to family collectivity to individual goals and aspirations, the central question is, What was the basis of interdependence among family members? What made possible the strong commitment of individuals to the family and to mutual assistance between kin that led individuals to sacrifice personal preferences?

Anderson sees reciprocity and economic exchange as the key explanation for interdependence between kin in nineteenth-century Preston, Lancashire. He defines relations among kin as "instrumental," and sees a calculating motive underlying reciprocity (Anderson, 1971). While calculation may have been the central motive in the lower strata of working-class communities, which consisted of a high proportion of immigrants, this motive does not fully explain the sacrifices that relatives made for each other when there were no direct benefits to be anticipated. Short-term, daily routine exchanges may have offered visible returns, but long-range investments were more demanding and the rewards were less certain. While benefits in short-term exchanges were more clearly tangible, it would be difficult to conceive of long-range exchanges as resting exclusively on calculation. For example, when young men and women sacrificed their opportunity for marriage or gave up opportunities for careers because of the need to support their parents, they hardly did so expecting immediate or long-range rewards. Young women who postponed marriage or never married did so because they were socialized to have a sense of responsibility for their parents or siblings, but affection and loyalty were also important components of their attitude. When they acted as surrogate parents to their siblings rather than sending them to orphanages, they did so because they placed a higher value on the preservation of family autonomy, self-respect, and good standing in the neighborhood and ethnic community than on personal happiness.

Loyalty and a commitment to "family culture" dictated such priorities in the lives of individuals, even if they were trapped into sacrifices they resented. Within the economic constraints and insecurities which the majority of the population experienced in the nineteenth century, personal preferences clearly had to give way to collective family strategies. In addition to exchange there were thus other reasons that individuals sacrificed their own preferences to collective family needs. Future work in the history of the family will have to address these questions of reciprocity and mutuality between kin and locate the historical transition from a kin-oriented to an individualized value system.

FAMILY DEVELOPMENT

THE FAMILY CYCLE

With several exceptions for the colonial period, the majority of studies in the earlier stage of research in family history were limited in their concentration on family and household at one point in time, or at best at several points in time, thus conveying the impression that family and household structures were constant over the entire life of their members. This static view of family organization was a result of historians' excessive reliance on snapshots of family organization as recorded in the census rather than from an examination of changes in the membership configuration and structure of the family and the household over its life. This limitation has been overcome gradually, first by applying the family-cycle construct and then by following a life-course approach, which offers a more comprehensive way to examine family development in a historical context. A profile of the household limited to one point in time obscured the constant movement of family members in and out of different forms of household organization over their lives.

In vigorously criticizing the "snapshot" approach to the historical study of the family, Berkner drew historians' attention to the importance of the changes that households and families undergo over their cycle, particularly in relation to the transmission of property and inheritance (Berkner, 1972). The application of the family-cycle approach to nineteenth-century patterns of household structure revealed that the household and family structure was fluid and variable over the family's life from marriage to dissolution and that individuals went through several forms of household organization over their lives. The very label of "nuclear" or "extended" household types was meaningless, therefore, unless one accounted for various changes in household organization over the life of its members. In reality, households were like a revolving stage onto which individual members would enter and from which they would exit, either under their own momentum or under the impact of external conditions (Hareven, 1974).

Historians initially found in the family cycle a flexible framework for the developmental analysis of changes in household and family structure. Its major value was in leading historians to shift the analysis of family behavior in the past from one point in time to a developmental sequence, even when using cross-sectional data. The family cycle, as formulated by Duval and Hill, measures role and structural changes in the family unit as it moves from stage to stage over the life of its members, from its formation with marriage, to its dissolution with the death of its head (Duval, 1957;

Hill, 1964, 1970). Essentially, as Elder has pointed out, the family cycle is organized around stages of parenthood (Elder, 1978a).

The family-cycle construct has enabled historians to identify the variability of patterns that appeared constant at one point in time over the lives of the household's head and of different family members. Changes in the structure of the household and in the age configurations of its members were affected to a large extent by the movement of family members through their prescribed roles over their lives. The life transitions of young family members, particularly their leaving home, getting married, and setting up independent households, all affect the structure of the family of orientation as well as the family of procreation (Glasco, 1977; Hareven, 1974). Individuals who lived in nuclear households at one point in their lives were likely to live in extended or augmented households at other points. The age configurations and memberships of individuals living in nineteenth-century households thus varied over the family cycle in accordance with patterns of migration, the availability of housing, and changing economic needs (Chudacoff & Hareven, 1978; Modell & Hareven, 1973).

Studying the family cycle also offers an effective way to examine the family as a collective unit, engaged in various activities and decisions which changed in relation to the roles and social characteristics of its members and in response to external conditions. In the area of economic behavior, for instance, the extent to which inheritance practices, the availability of housing, or migration patterns caused variation in family and household configurations may be best understood by studying family behavior along its cycle rather than at one point in time.

The family cycle has proved especially valuable for studying the conditions under which the family unit was economically vulnerable. In his study of poverty in England at the turn of the century, E. S. Rowntree identified two stages at which the family was most likely to slip into poverty; first, when the children were too young to work, and second, when the grown children had left home and the parents were too old to work (Rowntree, 1901). This approach, leading from Frederick LePlay through E. S. Rowntree into American sociological and economic studies of the family, has also influenced historical analysis. John Modell, for example, followed the family cycle in analyzing changing patterns of labor force participation and expenditure of United States workers in the late nineteenth century. He was able to identify both the family's economic strategies and rhythms of insecurity over the family's cycle (Modell, 1978).

Systematic efforts to apply the family cycle to historical data have revealed, however, some inherent limitations in this approach. Elder sees one of its major failings in its measurement of stages: "We may know where the children are in terms of age-patterned roles, but not where the parents are. Timing enters the family cycle model in relation to the children. Its full meaning requires, however, knowledge of event timing among the parents as well. From this perspective, the family cycle fails to do justice to its primary target, the temporal features of stages of parenthood" (Elder, 1978a).

Within a historical context, additional limitations of the family-cycle concept become apparent. The a priori stages in the family cycle, as defined by sociologists studying contemporary populations, cannot be consistently applied to the diverse patterns of the late nineteenth century. Paul Glick's model, followed by demographers and more recently by historians, measures mean patterns of change in stages of the family cycle from the late nineteenth century on, but it does not examine variance from the norm or differentials by sex, ethnicity, or occupation within specific time periods. Largely because of higher levels of mortality, nineteenth-century families were less likely to experience an orderly progression than are contemporary families, except when the latter are disrupted by divorce.

As Peter Uhlenberg has shown, voluntary and involuntary demographic factors affected age configurations within the family, causing considerable differences between nineteenth-century families and modal twentieth-century patterns. From his examination of the family-cycle patterns of white American women from 1870 to 1930, he concluded that the sequence of marriage, family formation, child rearing and launching, and survival until age 50 with the first marriage still intact unless broken by divorce, although always modal, was by no means prevalent for most of the population before the twentieth century (Glick, 1947, 1955, 1977; Glick & Parke, 1965; Uhlenberg, 1974, 1978).

Prior to the late nineteenth-century decline in mortality and fertility, discontinuities between different stages of the family cycle were less clearly demarcated. Children were spread along a broader age range within the family; frequently, the youngest child was starting school when the oldest was preparing for marriage. Parenthood, by contrast, often encompassed the entire adult life span. The combination of a later age at marriage and earlier mortality meant that the "empty nest" was a rare phenomenon. Fathers who survived the child-rearing years rarely lived beyond the marriage of their second child. Since the boundary between family of orientation and family of procreation was less clearly demarcated than it is today, and transitions from one stage of the family cycle to the next were less rigidly timed, nineteenth-century families did not go through clearly marked stages. For example, leaving home did not so uniformly precede marriage, and the launching of children did not necessarily leave the nest empty. Frequently a married child would return to his parents' home, or the parents would take in boarders or lodgers. Developments in the 1970s have begun to revive some of the "historical" patterns, thus blurring the contrast between past and present. Among these, most notably, are late marriages and late commencement of childbearing among professionals, the return of young adults to the parental home, or their delayed leaving.

For all these reasons, the application of a priori stages borrowed from contemporary sociology to past conditions did not always fit the historical reality. It was important, therefore, to identify the transitions at which individuals and families moved through different family configurations and roles over their lives. Rather than merely calculating median differences between stages, historians began to measure the pace at which a cohort completed its transition from one stage to the next (Modell et al., 1976).

While the family cycle continues to be a valuable construct, developmental analysis of the family in the past has been amplified through the use of the life-course approach in several directions: first by utilizing a framework which captures with greater sensitivity the erratic and complex trajectories of families and careers in nineteenth-century population groups (Elder, 1978a; Hareven, 1978b, c; Vinovskis, 1977); second, where stages do exist, by analyzing transitions from stage to stage and the accompanying roles within each stage; third, by focusing on the synchronization of individual transitions with changes in the family as a collective unit. The life course offers an approach which can address the complexities of family development in the past more effectively.

THE LIFE COURSE

The life course has provided a theoretical orientation for our understanding of the linkage between individual and family development in the context of changing historical conditions. Originating from the sociology of aging, the concept of cohorts as defined by demographers, and the life history traditions in sociology and social psychology, the life course is historical by its very nature (Baltes, 1979; Elder, 1978a; Riley, Johnson, & Foner, 1972; Neugarten & Hagestadt, 1976; Riley, 1978). Its influence on family history has been most powerful in three areas: the synchronization of individual life transitions and collective family changes; the interaction of both individual and collective family transitions with historical conditions; and the impact of earlier life transitions on later ones. ("Timing" takes into account the historical context defining the social circumstances and cultural conditions which affect the scheduling of life events, on both an individual and a familial level [Hareven, 1978b].)

Following a life-course approach, historians have begun to study how people plan and organize their roles over their lives and how they time their life transitions on the nonfamilial and familial levels in such behaviors as entering and leaving school, joining and quitting the labor force, migrating, leaving and returning home, marrying, and setting up an independent household, or how in later life individuals and couples move out of active parental roles into the "empty nest" or retire from work careers. Historians have discovered that in the past many decisions on timing which would be considered "individual" today were closely articulated to collective family timing in the past and were contingent on familial strategies rather than on individual choices.

Especially during periods when most educational, economic, and welfare functions were concentrated within the family, decisions on the timing of transitions were family based and regulated according to family priorities within the constraints of external economic and institutional factors. For example, institutional and legislative change, such as compulsory school attendance, child labor laws, and mandatory retirement, have affected the transitions of different age groups into and out of the labor force. At the same time, however, the ways in which people responded to these opportunities or constraints were also shaped by their cultural traditions.

Over their life course, people group and regroup themselves in various family units. Their individual roles and their functions vis-à-vis the family in these different clusters also vary significantly over their lives. Most individuals are involved simultaneously in several family configurations, fulfilling different roles in each. A married person, for example, is part of both a family of origin and a family of procreation and occupies a different position and fulfills a different role in each. Such an individual also figures in his or her spouse's family of origin and in the spouse's kin network. Because of the integration of individuals with the collective goals of the family, in the past life transitions such as leaving home, which appeared to be individual, were in reality integrated with the family collectivity.

Similarly marriage, which today would be considered the act of an individual or a couple, affected at least three families: the family of origin of each partner and the newly founded family. In situations where remarriage follows a spouse's death or divorce, the new spouse's family enters the orbit of relationships, while the former spouse's family does not necessarily disappear. Thus, the multiplicity of familial relationships in which individuals are engaged changes over the life course, and along with them an individual's transitions into various roles are also timed differently. Though age is an important variable defining life transitions, it is not an exclusive one. Changes in family status and in accompanying roles may be as important, if not more so.

THE TIMING OF LIFE TRANSITIONS

Central to the understanding of any life-course pattern is the impact of historical processes on the timing of individual or family transitions. Such timing is influenced by the interaction of demographic, social, and economic factors, as well as by familial preferences shaped by the family members' cultural background. Thus, for example, in the nineteenth century the timing of marriage was not strictly related to age but rather to a complex interaction among social and economic factors, cultural preferences, and institutional constraints.

Changes since the late nineteenth century in the timing of life transitions and in the synchronization of individual timetables with the collective timetable of the family are related to demographic and institutional changes as well as to cultural factors guiding internal family choices. On the one hand, as Uhlenberg (1978) suggests, over the past century, demographic developments have tended to effect greater uniformity in the life course of American families and have made it considerably more likely that the family unit will survive intact over the lifetime of its members. The decline in mortality, especially in the earlier years, has enabled a growing proportion of the population to enter prescribed family roles and, except in cases of divorce, to live out their lives in family units (Uhlenberg, 1974). The decline in mortality has meant that the chances of children's surviving into adulthood and growing up with their siblings and both parents alive have increased considerably. Similarly, the chances of women's surviving to marry, raise children jointly with a husband, and survive with a husband through the launching stage increased steadily between the late nineteenth and early twentieth centuries (Uhlenberg, 1974). For women, these changes, combined with earlier marriages and earlier completion of maternal roles, have meant a more extended period of life without children in their middle years. At the same time, women's tendency to live longer than men has resulted in a protracted period of widowhood in later life. Men, on the other hand, because of lower life expectancy and a greater tendency to remarry in old age, normally remain married until death (Glick, 1977; Glick & Parke, 1965).

The most marked discontinuity in the life course which has emerged since the nineteenth century has occurred in the middle and later years of life, namely, the emergence of the empty nest in a couple's middle age. The combination of earlier marriage and fewer children with childbearing occurring in the early stages of the family cycle and children's leaving home at an earlier point in their parents' lives has resulted in a greater prevalence of the empty nest as a characteristic of middle and old age (Glick, 1977).

In the nineteenth century, later marriage, higher fertility, and shorter life expectancy rendered different family configurations from those characterizing contemporary society. For large families, the parental stage with children remaining in the household extended over a longer period of time, sometimes over the parents' entire lives. Since children were spread in families along a broad age spectrum, younger children could observe their older siblings and near relatives moving through adolescence and into adulthood. Older siblings in turn trained for adult roles by acting as surrogate parents for younger siblings (Hareven, 1977). Most important, the nest was rarely empty, since under conditions of economic insecurity, usually one adult child remained at home throughout the parents' lives (Chudacoff & Hareven, 1979; Hareven, 1982).

Demographic factors account only in part for the occurrence or nonoccurrence of the empty nest. Children did not remain in their aging parents' household only because they were too young to move out. Even where sons and daughters were in their late teens and early twenties, and therefore old enough to leave home, at least one child remained at home to care for aging parents if no other assistance was available. Familial obligations, dictated by the insecurity of the times and by cultural norms of familial assistance, took precedence over strict age norms (Chudacoff & Hareven, 1979; Hareven, 1982). Even though the nest is now being refilled through the return of young adult children to the parental home, the flow of assistance reverses the historical pattern: children now return home because of their need for parental support, while earlier in the century at least one child was expected to remain at home in order to provide support for aging parents.

The important historical change in the timing of life transitions since the beginning of this century has been the emergence of a greater uniformity in the pace at which a cohort accomplishes a given transition. This is particularly evident in the transitions to adulthood (leaving home, marriage, and establishment of a separate household). As Modell et al. have shown (1976), over the past century transitions have become more clearly marked, more rapidly timed, and more compressed.

In contrast to our times, in the late nineteenth century transitions from the parental home, to marriage, to household headship were more gradual and less rigid in their timing. The time range necessary for a cohort to accomplish such transitions was wider, and the sequence in which transitions followed one another was flexible. In the twentieth century, transitions to adulthood have become more uniform for the age cohort undergoing them, more orderly in sequence, and more rigidly defined. The consciousness of embarking on a new stage of life and the implications of movement from one stage to the next have become more firmly established.

The historical changes over the past century, particularly the increasing rapidity in the timing of transitions and the introduction of publicly regulated and institutionalized transitions, have converged to isolate and segregate age groups in the larger society and at the same time have generated new pressures on timing within the family as well as outside its confines. The timing of life transitions has become more regulated according to specific age norms rather than in relation to the family's collective needs (Modell et al., 1976). The major historical change over the past century has been from a timing of transitions that is more closely articulated to collective family needs to a more individualized timing.

This pattern is even more visible in the timing of later life transitions in the late nineteenth century, where transitions to the empty nest, to widowhood, and out of household headship followed no ordered sequence, were not closely synchronized, and extended over a relatively long period of time. For most men who survived to old age, labor force participation and family roles generally resembled those of their earlier adult years. Only at very advanced ages did a substantial number experience definite changes in their household status. These men, however, represented only a small proportion of their age group. On the other hand, because widowhood was such a common experience, older women went through more marked transitions than did older men, although the continuing presence of adult children and others in the household meant that widowhood did not necessarily represent a dramatic transition to the empty nest (Chudacoff & Hareven, 1979; Hareven, 1982; Smith, 1979). The timing of earlier life transitions was tied to the timing of later ones through the common bond of interdependence within the family. Aging parents' need for support from their children affected the latter's transitions into independent adulthood.

The broad changes in the timing of family transitions sketched here do not take into account detailed cohort comparisons. As historical research in this area becomes more refined, it will be possible to discern differences in the timing of life transitions within as well as between cohorts. Ryder (1965) has suggested that social change occurs when there is a distinct discontinuity between the experiences of one cohort and those of its predecessors. Important historical discontinuities, however, may also occur within a cohort as a result of earlier life experiences that members of a cohort may have encountered. For example, the cohort that reached adulthood during the Great Depression experienced major discontinuities in family and work life that not only were part of an overall process of social change but that may have catalyzed further social change. Such an approach views a cohort as an age group moving through history whose social experience is influenced not only by contemporary conditions but also by experiences of earlier life events, which in turn were affected by specific historical circumstances. Variations in people's earlier life histories and in exposure to historical events by class, ethnic background, and community type would generate important differences within the same cohort.

As Elder's *Children of the Great Depression* has shown, experiences in childhood and early adulthood encountered during the Great Depression had a major impact on adjustment in later life (Elder, 1974). Within the same cohort of unemployed adults, coping with economic stress differed not only according to differences in personality, family background, and the availability of other resources, but also in terms of earlier transitions experienced—for example, how long the individual had been working and whether his or her career had been continuous and stable or had been disrupted before the Depression.

To date, historians have not had many opportunities to examine the cumulative effect of life transitions. They have not had the kind of longitudinal data which Elder used in his study of the Berkeley and Oakland cohorts who experienced the Great Depression in their childhood (Elder, 1974).

The continuous cumulative and spiral impact of earlier life transitions, as affected by historical conditions, on later ones is important both in individual lives and in the collective experience of the family as a unit. Thus, history affects people's lives both directly, at any moment of their interaction with historical forces, and indirectly, through the cumulative effect of earlier historical circumstance on their lives.

STAGES OF LIFE

Historical changes in the timing of life transitions are best understood in the context of segmentation of the life course into specific developmental stages. This process has involved the gradual societal recognition of new stages of life and their integration into the experience of everyday life. Such recognition is manifest in recently enacted legislation and the establishment of public institutions and agencies for the realization of the potential of people at a specific stage of life and for their protection within those stages. To the extent that it is possible to reconstruct a historical model, it appears that the "discovery" of a new stage of life is itself a complex process. First, individuals become aware of new characteristics in their private experience. The articulation of such a stage and of the conditions unique to it is then formulated by the professionals and eventually recognized in the popular culture. Finally, if the conditions peculiar to this stage seem to be associated with a major social problem, it attracts the attention of public agencies and its needs and problems are dealt with in legislation and in the establishment of institutions. Those public activities in turn affect the experience of individuals going through the stage and clearly influence the timing of transitions in and out of stage.

In American society, childhood was "discovered" first in the private lives of middle-class urban families in the early part of the nineteenth century. The discovery itself was related to the retreat of the family into domesticity, the segregation of the workplace from the home, the redefinition of the mother's role as the major custodian of the domestic sphere, and the emergence of sentiment as the basis of familial relationships. The new child-centeredness of urban domestic families in the early nineteenth century was also a response to two major demographic changes: a decline in infant and child mortality and an increase in the conscious practice of family limitation. After it emerged in the lives of middle-class families, childhood as a distinct stage of development became the subject of the voluminous body of child-rearing and family advice literature. This literature popularized the concept of childhood and the needs of children, prescribed the means to allow them to develop as children, and called for the regulation of child labor.

The discovery of adolescence followed a similar pattern. While puberty in itself is a universal, biological process, the psychosocial phenomena of adolescence were only gradually defined, most notably by Stanley G. Hall (1904) in the latter part of the nineteenth century. The experience of adolescence itself, particularly some of the problems and tensions associated with it, was apparent in the private lives of people reaching puberty during the second half of the nineteenth century. The congregation of young people into peer groups, and the symptoms of what might be characterized as a "culture of adolescence," were also observed by educators and urban reformers from the middle of the nineteenth century on. Anxiety over such behavior increased especially where it was connected with new immigrants. Adolescence as a new stage of life was articulated in the work of psychologists, particularly by Hall and his circle, and was also widely popularized in the literature. The extension of school age through high school in the second part of the nineteenth century, the further extension of the age limits for child labor, and the establishment of juvenile reformatories and vocational schools were all part of the public recognition of the needs and problems of adolescence.

The boundaries between childhood and adolescence, on the one hand, and between adolescence and adulthood, on the other, become more clearly demarcated during the twentieth century. In fact, as Keniston (1971) has suggested, the extension of a moratorium from adult responsibilities beyond adolescence has resulted in the emergence of another stage, youth. However, despite the growing awareness of these preadult stages, no clear boundaries on adulthood in America emerged until "old age" became prominent as a new stage of life, and with it the need to differentiate the social and psychological problems of "middle" from "old" age. The overall boundaries of adulthood and the transitions into middle age are not yet sharply defined. "Old age," though, is now recognized as a specific period of adulthood. On the public level it has a formal beginning—age 65, at least where an individual's working life is concerned—and it is institutionalized by a rite of passage, retirement and eligibility for social security (Fischer, 1977; Hareven, 1976).

The important connection between historical development and the emergence of such new stages has not been fully documented. The general contours of the pattern are beginning to emerge with some clarity, however. Whether childhood, adolescence, youth, middle, or old age were first experienced on the private, individual level, their very appearance and increasing societal recognition have affected the timing of family transitions in the past. Thus, not only has the very experience of these stages of life changed over time, but also the timing of people's entry into such stages and exit from them, and the accompanying roles involved in such timing, have changed as well.

The existential and institutional changes which have buttressed the extension of a moratorium from adult responsibilities have also affected the timing of both individual and familial transitions. Thus, the postponement of the assumption of adult responsibilities would have meant longer residence of children in the household without contributing to the family's economic effort and a resulting increase in the state of "dependency" or "semidependency" as a typical experience of adolescence. On the other end, the recognition of old age as a distinct stage, and especially its impositions of discontinuity in the form of mandatory retirement, has had a serious impact on the timing of transitions in the family economy, leading to the emergence of dependency or semidependency in old age and imposing severe tensions and demands on family obligations.

In summary, historical research in the family has undergone an important transition from the study of the family and the household at one point of time to a developmental approach, as expressed in the life-course framework. The significant historical changes in the life course have been an increasing uniformity in the timing of life transitions and a segmentation of the life course into culturally and socially recognized stages. These changes are connected with a gradual shift in the factors affecting the timing of life transitions from collective family strategies to individual preferences.

FAMILY STRATEGIES

The prevailing historical and sociological literature has concentrated on the effect of institutions on the family, but the most important development in historical research has been to redirect attention to the family and its members as actors in this process. The emphasis has shifted to the ways in which families take charge of their lives and allocate their resources and the strategies they follow in the contexts of external constraints.

Once one begins to view the family as an active agent of social change, the crucial questions focus on the internal dynamics of family strategies: How did families plan their lives, particularly under conditions of adversity and rapid social change? What kinds of strategies did they follow in their adaptation to changing conditions over their life course and over historical time? How did family members juggle multiple roles and obligations as children, parents, members of a kinship network, and workers? How were individual careers synchronized with collective family ones? How were decisions made within the family? The most important implication of this perspective is an emphasis on dynamic processes within the family and on a constantly changing interaction of personalities within it, rather than on the family as a static unit. This view is strongly linked to a life-course perspective because it assumes change and redefinition of familial strategies over the life course and in relation to external historical conditions (Elder, 1981).

Historical research on the family has begun to address these issues, particularly in relation to the family's interaction with the industrial system, family labor force strategies, and internal family economic strategies such as the allocation of resources. Economists may have exaggerated the degree to which families plot strategies rationally and calculate the respective economic values of members' services to one another (Becker, 1981). Historians have identified purposeful planning and weighing of options as the base of families' interaction with the economy. This does not necessarily mean that conscious calculation is attributed to such decisions. In the context of recent historical studies, the term "strategies" does not always imply deliberation and planning. It does assume that individuals and families made choices and established priorities when responding to external pressures or internal needs.

The internal dynamics of such a collective decision-making process in a historical context need to be explored more precisely. Family collectivity did not necessarily imply mutual deliberation among members and "democratic" participation in the process. It is possible that such decisions were imposed by the male head of the family on its members, although there is evidence that there was consultation and bargaining between husbands and wives and between parents and children. The historical pattern of change has been one of transition from authoritarian parental (especially paternal) control over the life transitions of young adult children to greater independence, and from husband-dominated decisions to a companionate relationship between husbands and wives (Degler, 1980; Hareven, 1982; D. B. Smith, 1980; D. S. Smith, 1973). The most important contribution of recent research has been to emphasize the role of the actors' cultural heritage as well as economic considerations in shaping the kinds of choices that family members made within given economic limits.

Family strategies covered various aspects of family life—ranging from inheritance to the decision to migrate and the organization of migration; from decisions on the membership of one's household to family limitation and child rearing. Some such choices involved trade-offs made in order to achieve solvency, to buy a house, to facilitate occupational advancement for one's children, to save for the future, and to provide for old age. The underlying assumption is that the family made decisions as a collective, corporate unit rather than as the sum of its individual members. For that very reason, family strategies determined the timing of life transitions, particularly leaving home, marrying, and forming a household. Examples of consciously articulated strategies are the use of kin not only to organize migration to new industrial communities but also to provide backup in the community of origin, the selection of relatives or godparents to act as custodians of children in times of crisis, living near one's kin, and prudential planning for the future such as education savings and insurance (Hareven, 1982).

The areas of family decision making that have received the closest attention from historians are the labor force participation of women and children and family (household) income and expenditure patterns. The gainful employment of children and married women outside the home posed a critical dilemma for working-class families. Economic constraints and aspirations for mobility required contributions from women's and children's labor. The participation of women and children in a collective family effort was sanctioned by the cultural values that immigrant workers brought with them from rural society. But gainful employment of mothers outside the home was not always consistent with premigration views of wives' work and conflicted with middle-class norms. In this area family

strategies had to accommodate economic constraints and cultural traditions, as well as the values of the dominant culture. The conflict between
family needs and the values of the native middle class, which censored the
employment of married women and of mothers in particular, necessitated
major adjustments by immigrant and working-class families.

Throughout the nineteenth and early twentieth centuries, women's
labor force participation followed a life-cycle pattern. Working-class
women commenced work in their teens and dropped out after marriage or
after the birth of their first child. Unlike in the 1950s and 1960s, they rarely
returned into the labor force after the completion of childrearing. Those
mothers who worked did so intermittently throughout their childbearing
years. For the most part, wives, espcially mothers, were kept out of the
labor force, except in textile communities, with their female—and family—
intensive employment patterns (Hareven, 1978c; Mason, Vinovskis, &
Hareven, 1978).

The recurring pattern in the late nineteenth and the early twentieth
centuries reflects a response to economic conditions which was shaped by
the dictates of one's own culture. Families relied first on the labor of their
children to supplement their head's income or substitute for a missing,
unemployed, or sick father. If one infers strategies from these labor force
participation patterns, a ranking of priorities would become apparent: the
widespread preference was to send one's children to work, take in boarders, or both, before sending one's wife to work. But families on the margin
of subsistence followed all three routes. The economic contribution from
children's work, especially from older children, was the most steady crucial
supplement or substitute for the head's earnings (Goldin, 1981; Hareven,
1978a, 1982; Mason et al., 1978). Children's labor was considered even
more crucial in the later years of life, as the head's earning power was
declining, or in the case of widows, where child labor was the only source of
support because widows rarely reentered the labor force. The stage in the
life course in which the family found itself was one of the most crucial
determinants of the labor force participation of children. The older the
head of household, the greater was the family's reliance on the earnings of
children (Haines, 1981).

Child labor in itself was not a uniform practice. As Goldin found in
Philadelphia in the late nineteenth century, family strategies caused differentials within child labor patterns. Whether a child worked depended
on family income; sex, age, and labor force participation of other siblings;
and the presence or absence of a parent. Whether older siblings worked or
not determined whether a younger child would seek employment. Daughters were less likely to work if they had older brothers working—a clear

expression of cultural preferences. Such preferences were evident in the fact that native-born families were less likely to send their children or wives to work than ethnic families (Goldin, 1981).

The differences in employment patterns between white and black women and children in Philadelphia confirm the impact of both cultural considerations and economic constraints. The fact that both married and widowed black women were more likely to be gainfully employed than white women could be interpreted as an expression of the poverty of black families. But black children were less likely to be employed than white children, which may reflect a trade-off within black families—a strategy of keeping children in school longer as well as a greater acceptance of married women's working. Or does it reflect the absence of employment opportunities for black children, which increased the family's dependence on the work of wives (Goldin, 1981)?

To the extent to which it is possible to reconstruct these patterns for the nineteenth century, it appears that though children's work was viewed as a basic source of income, wives' work outside the home was viewed as a supplement to the family's budget. Despite the reluctance to send wives to work, women's labor force participation was much more widespread than one would be led to believe from a "snapshot" gleaned from the census. Women tended to move in and out of the labor force, in accordance with childbearing, familial needs, and the availability of employment (Hareven, 1982). The propensity of married women to work in such industries as textiles and food processing reflected both the greater availability of opportunities for women in female-intensive occupations and a cultural preference for sending wives and daughters to jobs related to what had been traditional home industries (Yans-McLaughlin, 1977). When alternatives were available, wives and daughters tended to work in industries where several other members of their family were employed. The opportunity for several family members to work together provided a continuity between the family and the workplace and supervision and protection of young people, especially females, by their older relatives. But even when married women pursued regular and continuous careers, they considered their work supplementary to the family economy rather than primary (Hareven, 1982; Scott & Tilly, 1975).

Most of the recent examinations of family strategies have drawn on cross-sectional data which prohibit the analysis of changing family strategies over the life course, except through cohort comparison of families at different points in their life (using age or family status as a proxy). Nor has it been possible to reconstruct perceptions and priorities from census and family budget schedules except by inference from behavior. Historians have been unable, therefore, to reconstruct the decision-making process within the family as articulated by the actors themselves. The very focus on the *family* as a decision maker tends to obscure the dynamics within the family: Who made the major decisions? How did various family members respond to collective decisions imposed on them?

Interviews used to supplement quantitative, behavioral data have suggested areas of tension surrounding the trade-offs and sacrifices individuals were expected to make for the collective good of their families. Strain and conflict revolved around such issues of family timing as when to leave home, when to marry, how to allocate responsibilities for parental support among different siblings, and how to divide resources (Hareven, 1982). Most individuals and families living under conditions of economic insecurity found themselves in a double bind: on the one hand, the family's collective requirements imposed enormous pressures and burdens on individuals; on the other hand, the individual was dependent on the family for assistance in time of need (Anderson, 1971). Thus a rebellion against familial requirements, however onerous, would deprive the individual of access to the only source of support.

HISTORY OF THE FAMILY AND SOCIAL CHANGE

Recent work in the history of the family has profoundly altered our understanding of the family's response to changing social and economic conditions; it has also contributed to an understanding of the broader question how people react to social change and what change means in their lives. Since the family served as mediator between individuals and the social forces and institutions affecting them, it has both facilitated individuals' adaptation to social change and initiated change itself.

THE FAMILY'S ROLE IN THE PROCESS OF INDUSTRIALIZATION

This dual role of the family has been most explicitly documented in its relationship to industrialization. Until recently, standard sociological theory argued that the family broke down under the impact of industrialization. Adherents of the Chicago school of sociology maintained that throughout the history of industrial development, migration from rural to urban centers uprooted people from their traditional kinship networks and the pressures of industrial work and urban life caused a disintegration of the family unit. (Linton, 1959; Thomas & Znaniecki, 1918–20; Wirth, 1938).

Even sociologists who questioned the theory of social breakdown agreed with Parsons (Parsons & Bales, 1955) that the family changed from extended to nuclear to fit the requirements of the new industrial system. That is, the nuclear family was the unit most compatible with that system. These analysts have argued that detachment from the obligations and controls of extended kinship networks renders individuals more mobile and therefore more adaptable to the labor demands of industrial society. William J. Goode, a major exponent of this view, sees the conjugal family as an entity that serves industry while placing workers at the mercy of the factory: "The lower-class family pattern is indeed most 'integrated' with the industrial system," writes Goode, "but mainly in the sense that the individual is forced to enter its labor market with far less family support—his family *does not prevent industry from using him for its goals.* He may move where the system needs him, hopefully where his best opportunity lies, but he *must* also fit the demands of the system, since no extended kin network will interest itself greatly in his fate" (Goode, 1963, pp. 12–13).

During the past decade, several historical studies have convincingly refuted the claim that industrialization destroyed a three-generational family structure and have challenged the assumption that families and kin groups break down under the impact of migration to urban industrial centers and under the pressures of industrial work. There is considerable evidence that industrial life actually strengthened family ties and may have increased cohesion. Housing shortages in industrial areas necessitated at least temporary coresidence with extended kin. Hence, there was a higher degree of household extension in industrial communities than in preindustrial ones (Anderson, 1971). Rather than "forcing" sons and daughters to leave sooner, the availability of employment in industrial areas enabled young adults to work in the community, live at home, and contribute to the support of their family.

Industrial work itself did not break up the family unit. As Smelser has shown in his study of the early stages of the Industrial Revolution in Britain, textile factories recruited entire family groups as work units. Fathers contracted for their children, collected their wages, and often disciplined them in the factory. Entire families relied on the factory as their employer; the factories, in turn, depended on the recruitment of family groups to maintain a continuous labor supply (Smelser, 1959). Smelser argued, however, that by the early 1830s, the development of new machinery had introduced specialization.

Smelser argues that by the early 1830s the development of new machinery had introduced specialization, which meant that families no longer worked together in the factory. Anderson (1971) has shown, however, that in Lancashire, recruitment of workers in family groups continued in the textile industry after that time. Most important, Anderson stresses the survival of kinship ties and the continuing importance of kin in migration and adaptation to industrial conditions, even when relatives were not working in the same place. The family survived as a work unit in different forms throughout the nineteenth century. In the United States, particularly in the textile industry, the family continued to function as a work unit, and kin continued to fulfill a vital role, even under more complex industrial conditions in the late nineteenth and early twentieth centuries (Hareven, 1982).

Two conclusions which considerably revise the prevailing interpretations emerge from these historical studies. First, industrial capitalism in itself did not cause a breakdown of the family. Second, the family type most "fit" to interact with the modern factory was not the isolated nuclear type but rather a nuclear family embedded in an extended kinship network. As the experience of textile workers in Manchester, New Hampshire, shows, the role of the family and kin group went beyond assistance to its members to an interaction with the industrial employer on several levels: influencing the placement and transfer of workers to desirable jobs, socializing novices, and manipulating work schedules and procedures. Rather than simply carrying over premigration traditions, the family actually addressed the factory system on its own terms (Hareven, 1982).

The family was a broker between its members and the institutions of industrial capitalism and a facilitator of their adaptation. This does not mean that the family was in full control of its destiny, nor does it mean that workers and their relatives succeeded in changing the structure of industrial capitalism. It means, rather, that families were facilitating change as well as responding to it. In doing so, families and individuals charted their own strategies and drew on their own culture and traditions.

As recent work has begun to suggest, the crucial historical question is not merely whether the family was an active or passive agent. Rather the question is, Under what circumstances was the family able to control its environment and under what circumstances did this control diminish? How did the family reorder its priorities to respond to new conditions, and how did this reordering affect internal family relations?

To answer these questions one needs to consider not only ways industrial work affected family organization and work roles but also the ways family affected conditions in the workplace. Thus, an understanding of the family's relation to the factory requires examining the family's internal economic strategies and labor force configurations as well as its interaction with larger economic processes and institutions outside its confines. The internal structure of the family, its economic conditions, and the changes it experienced over the life course of its members affected its response to industrial time and historical time. Externally, the family's ability to retain some control over employment and work processes depended on business cycles, changes in management and in the organization of work in the factory, and the social, economic, and cultural forces in the larger society. For example, because of its central role in the recruitment of workers, it becomes clear from the Manchester, New Hampshire, study that the family was more in control of its destiny during periods of labor shortage and began to lose control under conditions of labor surplus. Thus, supply and demand was an important factor in the family's ability to control its environment (Hareven, 1982). The family's active role did not cease, however, once its influence diminished or collapsed in the workplace, as the textile industry began to decline. The family devised new responses to cope with the insecurities resulting from unemployment strikes and the final collapse of the industry.

Future work addressing these questions will have to expand the inquiry into the family's interaction with the industrial process, by further identifying and defining the circumstances under which the family was able to influence its environment or the conditions under which it had to succumb to external pressures.

THE EMERGENCE OF THE "MODERN" FAMILY

Now that historians have rejected grand theories of linear change in family behavior, a new set of questions emerges. If, as the new consensus now maintains, industrialization did not cause the first major decline in fertility, did not generate simple, nuclear households, and did not effect a drastic reorganization of family structure, did industrialization cause any significant changes in family behavior at all? If for centuries in Western Europe the prevailing form of household organization has been the nuclear family, then the historical search for the origins of the nuclear family must press further into the past; and if some of the important characteristics of "modern" family behavior preceded the Industrial Revolution, what did cause the change in family structure and behavior over the past three centuries?

While they have rejected the assumption that industrialization generated a new type of family structure, historians have agreed that industrialization has affected family functions, family values, and the timing of family transitions. Many of these changes were not necessarily linked directly to industrialization but emerged as consequences of the restructuring of the economy and of increased urbanization following industrialization. Historians agree that the most crucial change wrought by industrialization was the transfer of functions from the family to other social institutions. In Parsonian terms, what occurred here was a process of differentiation: "When one social organization becomes archaic under changing historical circumstances, it differentiates . . . into two or more roles or organizations which function more effectively in the new historical circumstances" (Smelser, 1959). The preindustrial family served as a workshop, church, reformatory, school, and asylum (Demos, 1970). Over the past century and a half, these functions have become in large part the responsibility of other institutions. The household has been transformed from a place of production to a place of consumption and for nurturing children. The family has withdrawn from the world of work, extolling privacy and intimacy as its major sources of strength, and the workplace has generally become nonfamilial and bureaucratic.

The home is viewed increasingly as a retreat from the outside world. The family has turned inward, assuming domesticity, intimacy, and privacy as its major characteristics as well as ideals. The privacy of the home and its separation from the workplace have been guarded jealously as an essential feature of family life (Cott, 1977; Degler, 1980; Welter, 1966). The commitment to the domesticity of the family is itself the outcome of a long historical process, which commenced in the early modern period in Western Europe, a process characterized by Philippe Ariès: "The modern family . . . cuts itself off from the world and opposes to society the isolated groups of parents and children. All the energy of the group is expended in helping the children to rise in the world, individually and without any collective ambition, the children rather than the family" (Ariès, 1965, p. 404).

By contrast, writes Ariès, the "premodern family was distinguished by the enormous mass of sociability which it retained. Both family and the household were the foundation of the community." Under the impact of economic growth and industrialization, the family became a specialized unit, its tasks limited primarily to consumption, procreation, and child rearing. The question is still open, however, what impact the loss of many of its former functions, combined with shrinking household membership, has had on the internal dynamics amd the quality of family relationships. According to Ariès, the contracting of family functions and the resulting privatization of family life marked the emergence of the modern family— nuclear, intensive, inward turning, and child centered—at the expense of sociability and greater integration with the community. Ariès concludes that these developments weakened the family's adaptability and deprived children of the opportunity to grow up in a flexible environment with a variety of role models to follow. To date, however, historians have done little to document and to explore closely the effect of these changes on relations within the family (Ariès, 1965).

Since change in the family is slower than in other social institutions, and since, as has been shown, the family does not merely react to change but also generates it, it has been difficult for historians to develop a typology of change in the family over time. Historians attempt to date the emergence of "the modern family," in the West, place it somewhere between 1680 and 1850. Ariès and Stone have singled out the late seventeenth and early eighteenth centuries, while Shorter dates its emergence in the late eighteenth and early nineteenth centuries. Stone identifies the emergence of the "closed domestic nuclear family" between 1640 and 1800. American historians generally date its emergence in the late eighteenth and early nineteenth centuries (Ariès, 1965; Degler, 1980; Shorter, 1976; Stone, 1977).

Stone, Ariès, and Shorter have focused on the rise of affective individualism as the major criterion of the modern family. They generally agree that the "modern" family is privatized, nuclear, domestic, and child centered and that its crucial base is the sentimental bond between husband and wife and parents and children. They have all pointed to the weakening influence of extended kin, friends, and neighbors on family ties, and to an isolation of the family from interaction with the community as the consequence of privacy and child centeredness. Marriages are based on "emotional bonding" between husband and wife and are a result of personal and sexual attraction rather than alliances between sets of parents or lineages. Stone, and to some extent Degler, see the weakening of bonds with kin as an inevitable consequence of this type of family.

While historians have generally agreed on these characteristics of modern family life, there is some disagreement over which class first initiated these changes. The scholars discussed above follow basically a "trickle-down" theory. Ariès, Stone, and, more implicitly, Degler viewed the bourgeoisie and the gentry as the vanguard, while Shorter has assigned a crucial role to peasants and workers. For American society, Degler places the origins of the "modern" family in the middle class, although he generalizes from the experience of the middle class to the entire society. The most important aspect still absent from the historical studies of long-term changes in the family over time are more systematic distinctions between social classes and a more detailed understanding of the historical process by which modes of family behavior were adopted by other classes, if indeed that was the case, and conversely what class differences have survived. (Ariès, 1965; Degler, 1980; Shorter, 1976; Stone, 1977). These studies of broad change over time also hold in common their acceptance of ideological and cultural factors as the major explanations of change in family behavior rather than social and economic ones. Shorter is the only one among them to cite "market capitalism" as the major cause for the emergence of family sentiment, but, as his critics have pointed out, he does not provide an explicit connection between these economic forces and the transformation of family relations (Tilly & Cohen, 1982).

Stone offers a "multi-causal" explanation, rather than one single factor, but like Degler he tends to favor the predominance of cultural and ideological explanations over social and economic ones (Degler, 1980; Stone, 1980). This is precisely where the most fundamental disagreements about social change and the family are likely to emerge among historians. Not only is there a lack of consensus among historians over the relative importance of ideological or socioeconomic causes in long-term changes in the family, there is also a greater need to know how the changes took place and what the nature of the interaction among these different factors was. The "grand" explanations of change are vulnerable particularly in some of these studies' claim for linear change over time. This is precisely the area where the critique which social historians have waged against modernization theory also applies to the history of the family.

The broad pattern of historical change, which was based primarily on the experience of the upper and middle classes, has tended to obscure the persistence of earlier forms of behavior among other classes. Among working-class and ethnic families, some preindustrial family characteristics have persisted, although in modified form (Hareven, 1982; Scott & Tilly, 1975).

Nor should one take for granted that the characteristics of the "modern" family, which were typical of the middle class, also held true for other classes. In the United States, for example, there has not been sufficient research over time to identify specific differences between middle-class, working-class, black, and immigrant families. There is, however, sufficient evidence to suggest that privatism, child centeredness, affective individualism, and isolation from kin—which emerged as characteristic traits of urban middle-class families, carriers of the "modern" family type—were not necessarily typical of the other classes and ethnic and racial groups. Over the nineteenth century, historians have been able to identify major differences between native-born, urban, middle-class families and immigrant, working-class, and black families. We still lack adequate systematic studies for comparisons within and among these groups. Nevertheless, there have been fundamental differences between these different family types. These differences converge around what could be considered the most central dividing line between the native middle-class family and black, immigrant, and working-class families, namely, a commitment to a collective family economy. While the central ideal and practice of middle-class family life was the separation of the spheres between the world of the home and the world of work, in working-class and immigrant families life revolved around economic responsibilities in which the work of each member was considered an integral part of the family's economy, and where instrumental relations may have taken precedence over sentiment.

Unquestionably, the overall pattern of historical change has moved in the direction of an adoption by other classes and ethnic groups of the middle-class, companionate, private, child-centered family patterns. As Modell shows (1978), even consumption patterns and tastes of immigrant families began to conform to those of native born. But the adoption of native-born, middle-class family styles by other classes and ethnic groups was by no means linear and uniform (Modell & Hareven, 1973). How the process of adaptation took place, and at what pace, is still a major subject for future research. It is clear from several studies that the adoption of "modal" patterns of behavior by different ethnic groups and various classes was selective and unevenly paced.

The realization that historical changes in the family have not taken place uniformly throughout society has led historians to react against a simplistic, linear interpretation of change and to focus instead on research which is carried out on a synchronic level, examining family interaction with societal processes and institutions within specific community contexts. While such work has already contributed to revision of earlier generalizations, one still has to face the challenge of welding ongoing research into a more systematic pattern ranging over a longer historical period.

CONCLUSION

At the moment, the contribution of historical knowledge to the overall understanding of social change and the family lies in three major areas. First, it has emphasized that in the process of change, families are *active* agents in their contacts with social, economic, and cultural forces. Second, it has shown that changes in family behavior do not conform perfectly to the traditional periodization of Western history. Third, it has demonstrated that, contrary to modernization theory, changes in family behavior (as in many other aspects of society) do not follow any simple linear trend.

The family's encounter with the modern industrial and urban system did not automatically lead to "modern" family behavior. Although the family underwent significant changes in its adaptation, especially to industrial work roles and urban living, it did not modernize in its behavior at the same pace as workers' in the factory. Indeed, workers were likely to accept and to a degree control changes in work, in part by clinging to much more gradual and less drastic transformation in family life.

People could be "modern" at work and "traditional" at home; the family preserved the initiative and choice in accepting new ways of life. Family behavior was paced differently among different social groups. Even in modern industrial society, traditional patterns persist powerfully among families of different cultural and ethnic groups because the family was a custodian of tradition as well as an agent of change. As a guardian of traditional culture, the family provided its members with continuity, a resource to draw upon in confronting industrial conditions. As the historical study of the family progresses in new directions, historians will have a greater opportunity to specify both the internal dynamics and the external processes by which families both adapted to change and initiated it.

REFERENCES

Achenbaum, A. *Old age in a new land.* Baltimore: Johns Hopkins University Press, 1978.

Anderson, M. *Family structure in nineteenth-century Lancashire.* Cambridge: Cambridge University Press, 1971.

Ariès, P. *Centuries of childhood* (R. Baldick, trans.). New York: Knopf, 1965. (Originally published, 1962.)

Baltes, P. Life-span developmental psychology: Some converging observations on history and theory. In P. B. Baltes & O. G. Brim (Eds.), *Life-span development and behavior* (Vol. 2). New York: Academic Press, 1979.

Becker, G. *A treatise on the family.* Cambridge, Mass.: Harvard University Press, 1981.

Berkner, L. The stem family and the developmental cycle of the peasant household: An eighteenth century Austrian example. *American Historical Review*, 1972, **77**, 398–418.

Blumin, S. Rip Van Winkle's grandchildren: Family and household in the Hudson Valley, 1800–1860. In T. Hareven (Ed.), *Family and kin in urban communities.* New York: Franklin Watts, 1977.

Bott, E. *Family and social network: Roles, norms and external relationships in ordinary urban families.* London: Tavistock, 1957.

Byington, M. *Homestead: The households of a mill town.* (Vol. 5): *The Pittsburgh survey.* New York: Russell Sage Foundation, Charities Publication Committee, 1910.

Chudacoff, H. & Hareven, T. Family transitions and household structure in the later years of life. In T. Hareven (Ed.), *Transitions: The family life and the life course in historical perspective.* New York: Academic Press, 1978.

Chudacoff, H. & Hareven, T. From the empty nest to family dissolution. *Journal of Family History*, 1979, **4**, 59–63.

Cott, N. *The bonds of womanhood: Woman's sphere in New England, 1780–1835.* New Haven, Conn.: Yale University Press, 1977.

Degler, C. *At odds: Women and the family in America from the Revolution to the present.* New York: Oxford University Press, 1980.

de Mause, L. (Ed.). *The history of childhood.* New York: Harper & Row, 1975.

Demos, J. *A little commonwealth: Family life in Plymouth Colony.* New York: Oxford University Press, 1970.

Duval, E. *Family development.* Philadelphia: Lippincott, 1957.

Elder, G. *Children of the Great Depression: Social change in life experience.* Chicago: University of Chicago Press, 1974.

Elder, G. Family history and the life course. In T. Hareven (Ed.), *Transitions: The family and the life course in historical perspective.* New York: Academic Press, 1978. (a)

Elder, G. Approaches to social change and the family. In J. Demos & S. Boocock (Eds.), *Turning points: Historical and sociological essays on the family.* Chicago: University of Chicago Press, 1978. (b)

Elder, G. History and the family: The discovery of complexity. *Journal of Marriage and the Family,* 1981, **43**, 489–519.

Erikson, E. *Childhood and society.* New York: Norton, 1950.

Fischer, D. *Growing old in America.* New York: Oxford University Press, 1977.

Glasco, L. The life cycles and household structure of American ethnic groups: Irish, Germans and native-born whites in Buffalo, New York, 1885. In T. Hareven (Ed.), *Family and kin in American urban communities, 1700–1930.* New York: Franklin Watts, 1977.

Glick, P. The family cycle. *American Sociological Review,* 1947, **12**, 164–174.

Glick, P. The life cycle of the family. *Marriage and Family Living,* 1955, **17**, 3–9.

Glick, P. Updating the life cycle of the family. *Journal of Marriage and the Family,* 1977, **39**, 5–13.

Glick, P., & Parke, R. New approaches in studying the life cycle of the family. *Demography,* 1965, **2**, 187–212.

Goldin, C. Family strategies and the family economy in the late nineteenth century: The role of secondary workers. In T. Hershberg (Ed.), *Philadelphia.* New York: Oxford University Press, 1981.

Goode, W. *World revolution and family patterns.* New York: Oxford University Press, 1963.

Goody, J. The evolution of the family. In P. Laslett & R. Wall (Eds.), *Household and family in past time.* Cambridge: Cambridge University Press, 1972.

Goubert, P. *Beauvais et les Beauvaisis de 1600 à 1730.* Paris: SEVPEV, 1960.

Goubert, P. Historical demography and the reinterpretation of early modern French history: A research review. *Journal of Interdisciplinary History,* 1970, **1**, 37–48.

Greven, P. *Four generations: Population, land, and family in colonial Andover, Massachusetts.* Ithaca, N.Y.: Cornell University Press, 1970.

Haines, M. Poverty, economic stress, and the family in a late nineteenth-century American city: Whites in Philadelphia, 1880. In T. Hershberg (Ed.), *Philadelphia.* New York: Oxford University Press, 1979.

Haines, M. Industrial work and the family cycle, 1889–1890. In P. Uselding (Ed.), *Research in economic history* (Vol. 4). Greenwich, Conn.: JAI, 1981.

Hall, S. *Adolescence: Its psychology and its relations to physiology, anthropology, sociology, sex, crime, religion, and education.* New York: Appleton, 1904.

Hammel, E. The Zadruga as process. In P. Laslett & R. Wall (Eds.), *Household and family in past time.* Cambridge: Cambridge University Press, 1972.

Hareven, T. The history of the family as an interdisciplinary field. *Journal of Interdisciplinary History,* 1971, **2**, 399–414.

Hareven, T. The family as process: The historical study of the family cycle. *Journal of Social History,* 1974, **7**, 322–329.

Hareven, T. Family time and industrial time: Family and work in a planned corporation town, 1900–1924. *Journal of Urban History,* 1975, **1**, 365–389.

Hareven, T. Modernization and family history: Perspectives on social change. *Signs,* 1976, **2**, 190–207.

Hareven, T. Family time and historical time. *Daedalus,* 1977, **106**, 57–70.

Hareven, T. The dynamics of kin in an industrial community. In J. Demos & S. Boocock

(Eds.), *Turning points: Historical and sociological essays on the family*. Chicago: University of Chicago Press, 1978. (a)

Hareven, T. Cycles, courses, and cohorts: Reflections on the theoretical and methodological approaches to the historical study of family development. *Journal of Social History*, 1978, **12**, 97–109. (b)

Hareven, T. *Transitions: The family and the life course in historical perspective*. New York: Academic Press, 1978. (c)

Hareven, T. *Family time and industrial time*. New York: Cambridge University Press, 1982.

Henry, L. Historical demography. *Daedalus*, 1968, **97**, 385–396.

Hill, R. Methodological issues in family development research. *Family Process*, 1964, **3**, 186–206.

Hill, R. *Family development in three generations*. Cambridge, Mass.: Schenkman, 1970.

Katz, M. The people of Hamilton, Canada West: Family and class in a mid-nineteenth-century city. Cambridge, Mass.: Harvard University Press, 1975.

Keniston, K. Psychological development and historical change. *Journal of Interdisciplinary History*, 1971, **2**, 329–345.

Kleinberg, S. The systematic study of urban women. In M. Canta & B. Laurie (Eds.), *Class, sex, and the woman worker*. Westport, Conn.: Greenwood, 1977.

Laslett, P. *The world we have lost*. London: Methuen, 1965.

Laslett, P. & Wall, R. (Eds.). *Household and family in past time*. Cambridge: Cambridge University Press, 1972.

Linton, R. The natural history of the family. In R. Anshen (Ed.), *The family: Its function and destiny* (Rev. ed.). New York: Harper & Row, 1959.

Litwack, E. Geographical mobility and extended family cohesion. *American Sociological Review*, 1960, **25**, 385–394.

Lockridge, K. The population of Dedham, Massachusetts, 1636–1736. *Economic History Review*, 2d ser., 1966, **19**, 318–344.

Mason, K., Vinovskis, M. & Hareven, T. Women's work and the life course in Essex County, Massachusetts, 1880. In T. Hareven (Ed.), *Transitions: The Family and the life course in historical perspective*. New York: Academic Press, 1978.

Modell, J. Patterns of consumption, acculturation, and family income strategy in late nineteenth-century America. In T. Hareven & Maris Vinovskis (Eds.), *Family and population in nineteenth-century America*. Princeton, N.J.: Princeton University Press, 1978.

Modell, J., Furstenberg, F., & Hershberg, T. Social change and transition to adulthood in historical perspective. *Journal of Family History*, 1976, **1**, 7–32.

Modell, J. & Hareven, T. Urbanization and the malleable household: An examination of boarding and lodging in American families. *Journal of Marriage and the Family*, 1973, **35**, 467–479.

Modell, J. & Hareven, T. Transitions: Patterns of timing. In T. Hareven (Ed.), *Transitions: The family and the life course in historical perspective*. New York: Academic Press, 1978.

Neugarten, B., & Hagerstad, G. O. Age and the life course. In R. H. Binstock & E. Shavas (Eds.), *Handbook of aging and the social sciences*. New York: Van Nostrand, 1976.

Parsons, T. *The social system*. Glencoe, Ill.: Free Press, 1951.

Parsons, T. & Bales, R. *Family, socialization, and interaction processes*. Glencoe, Ill.: Free Press, 1955.

Riley, M. Aging, social change and the power of ideas. *Daedalus*, 1978, **00**, 39–52.

Riley, M., Johnson, M. E., & Foner, A. (Eds.). *Aging and society, a sociology of age stratification* (3 vols.). New York: Russell Sage, 1972.

Rowntree, E. *Poverty: A study of town life*. London: Longmans, Green, 1901.

Ryder, N. The cohort as a concept in the study of social change. *American Sociological Review*, 1965, **30**, 843–861.

Schwarzweller, H., Brown, J., & Mangalam, J. *Mountain families in transition: A case study of Appalachian migration.* University Park: Pennsylvania State University Press, 1971.

Scott, J., & Tilly, L. Women's work and family in nineteenth-century Europe. *Comparative Studies in Society and History*, 1975, **17**, 36–64.

Sennett, R. *Families against the city: Middle-class homes of industrial Chicago, 1872–1890.* Cambridge, Mass.: Harvard University Press, 1970.

Shorter, E. *The making of the modern family.* New York: Basic, 1976.

Smelser, N. *Social change and the Industrial Revolution.* Chicago: University of Chicago Press, 1959.

Smith, D. B. *Inside the great house: Planter family life in eighteenth-century Chesapeake society.* Ithaca, N.Y.: Cornell University Press, 1980.

Smith, D. S. Parental power and marriage patterns: An analysis of historical trends in Hingham, Massachusetts. *Journal of Marriage and the Family*, 1973, **35**, 419–428.

Smith, D. S. Life course, norms, and the family system of older Americans in 1900. *Journal of Family History*, 1979, **4**, 285–298.

Stone, L. *The family, sex, and marriage in England, 1500–1800.* New York: Harper & Row, 1977.

Stone, L. Family history in the 1980's. *Journal of Interdisciplinary History*, 1981, **12**, 51–87.

Sussman, M., & Burchinal, L. Kin family network: Unheralded structure in current conceptualization of family functioning. *Marriage and Family Living*, 1962, **24**, 231–240.

Taeuber, I. Change and transition in family structures. In *The family in transition.* Washington, D.C.: Fogarty International Center Proceedings, 1969.

Thomas, W., & Znaniecki, F. *The Polish peasant in Europe and America* (3 vols.). Chicago: University of Chicago Press, 1918–20.

Tilly, L. & Cohen, M. Does the family have a history? *Social Science History*, 1982, **6**, 131–179.

Uhlenberg, P. Cohort variations in family life-cycle experiences of U.S. females. *Journal of Marriage and the Family*, 1974, **36**, 284–292.

Uhlenberg, P. Changing configurations of the life course. In T. Hareven (Ed.), *Transitions: The family and the life course in historical perspective.* New York: Academic Press, 1978.

Vann, R. History and demography. *History and Theory*, 1969, **9**, 64–78.

Vinovskis, M. From household size to the life course: Some observations on recent trends in family history. *American Behavioral Scientist*, 1977, **21**, 263–287.

Welter, B. The cult of true womanhood, 1820–1860. *American Quarterly*, 1966, **18**, 151–174.

Wirth, L. Urbanism as a way of life. *American Journal of Sociology*, 1938, **44**, 1–24.

Wrigley, E. *Population and history.* New York: McGraw, 1959.

Wrigley, E. Family limitation in pre-industrial England. *Economic History Review*, 1966, **19**, 82–109. (a)

Wrigley, E. Family reconstitution. In P. Laslett et al. (Eds.), *An introduction to English historical demography.* New York: Basic, 1966. (b)

Wrigley, E. The process of modernization and the Industrial Revolution in England. *Journal of Interdisciplinary History*, 1972, **3**, 225–229.

Wrigley, E. Reflections on the history of the family. *Daedalus*, 1977, **106**, 71–85.

Yans-McLaughlin, V. *Family and community: Italian immigrants in Buffalo, 1880–1930.* Ithaca, N.Y.: Cornell University Press, 1977.

Young, M., & Willmott, P. *Family and kinship in East London.* London: Routledge & Kegan Paul, 1957.

6   Family and School as Educational Institutions

ROBERT D. HESS
Stanford University

SUSAN D. HOLLOWAY
University of Maryland, College Park

I. Organization and Scope of the Chapter

In this chapter we review literature on the relationship between the family and the school as institutions jointly responsible for educating children and for socializing behavior that facilitates educational achievement. The first section deals with conceptualizations of the socializing and educational roles of the two institutions and of the role of the child in the school. The second section considers issues of continuity between the socialization experiences in the family and those encountered in the school. Questions of mismatch between the home and school and the consequences of certain types of discontinuities are discussed.

The third section deals primarily with the family's effect on academic achievement and on cognitive abilities that obviously support performance in the classroom. We do not distinguish between educational achievement defined as accomplishment within an educational setting and IQ or other measures of mental ability, although such a distinction might usefully be made. We summarize some evidence that molar family characteristics are associated with achievement and describe attempts to examine this relationship. These include studies of more differentiated measures of family interaction and the relation of family variables to major subject areas in school—especially reading and mathematics.

The following section describes ways families influence achievement indirectly by fostering cognitive behavior which underlies achievement in the classroom—communicative competence, cognitive "style," and related mental operations. The last section considers family influences on social and motivational aspects of behavior and the importance of these areas of development for accomplishment in an educational setting.

The discussion does have a theoretical bias. We organized material to be consistent with a view of the child as an active participant and the family as a group that facilitates the child's cognitive functioning. The forces that affect the family—stress from conflict, mutual support, poverty, chronic illness, and community and cultural influences—are seen as assisting or interfering with the family in this function. This view rejects the unidirectional conception of cognitive socialization but enables us to identify elements in the child's environment that affect achievement. The discussion deals with processes that mediate the influence of family experience on school-relevant performance.

This chapter covers a wide range of topics, for family experience and educational achievement are areas not easily described by a small number of variables. Since space limitations require that we be highly selective, we have attempted to choose research representing the state of knowledge about the topic described.

For lack of space or because they are discussed elsewhere in this volume, the chapter does not cover several relevant topics: the effects of maternal employment, divorce and/or father absence, structural characteristics (e.g., family size and birth order), the effects of schooling on parental behavior, attempts to identify genetic contributions to transmission of intelligence, and the effects of day care. Neither do we include studies of effects of parental interaction on mental abilities in infancy. These topics, while important, are less central to the theme of this chapter than those we have attempted to cover. Limits of space also require that we focus on research in the United States and other English-speaking countries, with only occasional references to studies in other cultures.

II. FAMILY AND SCHOOL AS EDUCATIONAL INSTITUTIONS

All cultures teach their young the skills required for the individual to survive as a functioning adult and for society to maintain itself. The singular aspect of schooling is that such education takes place outside the home in a setting established by the community for educational purposes. Public schooling is thus an extension of the socializing process that begins in the family; indeed, education is one form of socialization. The outcome of this joint effort depends considerably on the relationship between them. The effectiveness of the school or family can be eroded by conflict, confusion, lack of consensus in goals, or mismatch in motivation or cognitive skills.

A. CONCEPTUALIZATIONS OF THE ROLES OF FAMILY AND SCHOOL

Some writers see the family as a supportive, assisting group, delivering the child to the school in good health with proper equipment and motivation to learn. Other writers emphasize the political role of the family in helping regulate the school through participation in the governing process (Lightfoot, 1978). The school differs from the family as a socializing institution in several important ways: it is more impersonal; the contacts and relationships between adults and children are short term; the child has contact with a range of adults who offer views different from one another and different in some ways from those of his parents; and evaluation of performance is comparative, public, and recurring (Litwak & Meyer, 1974).

The school is thus an institution regulated by norms that differ from those encountered in the family. Experience in the school presumably helps prepare the child for life in an industrialized, bureaucratic society, serving the needs both of the individual and of the society. Characteristics regarded as particularly important include developing norms of *independence*—acting by oneself and accepting personal responsibility for one's behavior and its consequences; *achievement*—taking an active role in mastering assigned tasks; and *universalism*—interacting with others on the basis of a relatively few salient characteristics, including expectations about their role in the group rather than the full range of their behavior as whole persons and their personal circumstances at the moment (Dreeben, 1968).

B. THE CHILD'S ROLE IN THE SCHOOL

Like other social institutions, schools develop norms of behavior for participants. The norms that define the child's role come from two major aspects of classroom interaction: the academic curriculum, which includes official learning tasks, and the hidden curriculum, which refers to the mechanisms that maintain order and control (Jackson, 1968). Implementation of the academic curriculum requires the teacher to adopt an instructional, motivational, and evaluative role. The hidden curriculum requires that the teacher assume a managerial and socializing role.

Kedar-Voivodas (1983) distinguishes among three aspects of the child's role as student: pupil role, receptive learner role, and active learner role. The pupil role defines behavior encouraged by the hidden curriculum. Students are expected to be docile, passive, orderly, conforming, obedient, acquiescent to rules, respectful of authority, easily controllable, socially adept, willing to share human and material resources of the classroom with others, and able to control impulsivity and desire for immediate gratification.

The receptive learner role includes maintaining an acceptable level of academic achievement, performing on assigned tasks at set times and by set criteria, and working independently and efficiently. Homework must be done adequately and on time. Students are to be motivated, task-oriented, and responsible workers. The active learner role demands more than mastery of the curriculum; it is proactive, requiring an independent and exploring attitude, the challenge of authority, insistence on explanations, and self-imposed discipline. The active learner role requires behavior somewhat incongruent with the role of pupil and the receptive learner role (Jackson, Silberman, & Wolfson, 1969; Lee & Kedar-Voivodas, 1977).

Children's experience in school depends to a considerable degree on how easily and quickly they learn these roles. Teachers prefer students who fit the roles of pupil and receptive learner. In one study (Feshbach, 1969), student teachers rated children (for preference, grades, intelligence) described in story situations that presented two pairs of contrasting triadic personality clusters: flexible, nonconforming, and untidy versus rigid, conforming, and orderly; active, independent, and assertive versus passive, dependent, and acquiescent. When asked to indicate their personal preference, teachers rated the rigid, conforming, orderly child highest; the passive, dependent, acquiescent child next; the flexible, untidy, nonconforming child third; and the active, independent, assertive child last. When asked which students were likely to receive high grades, the conforming child was favored most and the nonconforming child least. However, when asked to rate the descriptions according to their likely level of intelligence, the dependent, passive, acquiescent child received the lowest ratings for both boys and girls but a difference emerged by sex. Girls who were described as rigid, conforming, and orderly were seen as most intelligent, but boys who were nonconforming and independent were given highest ratings for intelligence.

When the dimension of achievement was added to these clusters, in a follow-up study by Helton and Oakland (1977), teachers expressed feelings of "attachment" for bright, high-achieving students who were also obedient, cooperative, helpful, and well prepared, and who followed school rules, worked independently, and participated in academic activities. Personality variables appeared to have a greater influence on teachers' responses than did academic achievement. Teachers felt "rejection" for students who were the opposite of the "attachment" group—defiant, aggressive, belligerent, hard to discipline, restless, with poor work habits. In other studies, such children have been found to perform academically at a higher level than teachers expect (Willis & Brophy, 1974). Teachers in the Helton and Oakland study also expressed "concern" for students who were low achievers but who showed an interest in learning and made an effort and were also compliant and conforming to rules. Teachers were "indifferent" about students who were passive and unresponsive. Children's careers in the school depend on the acceptability of the behavior that they bring to the school from experience in the family.

III. DISCONTINUITIES BETWEEN FAMILY AND SCHOOL

Since the family and school are the major institutions in the child's life, it is not surprising that many studies have examined the effects of home-school discontinuity on academic achievement and on interaction between teachers and students. The stimulus for many of these studies was the growth of concern about educational opportunity for blacks and children of families from low-income sectors of the society. Much of this writing dealt with political issues, particularly the degree to which the school, rather than the child and family, should be modified in order to provide more continuity for children from culturally different backgrounds (Lightfoot, 1978). The emphasis during the 1960s shifted from a view that the child should be helped to acquire school-appropriate (middle-class) behavior to one in which the school and community were seen as different cultures of equal value and the burden of adapting was placed on the school or shared by school and family. These political issues are not central to the themes of this chapter, but they deserve mention since they stimulated a considerable body of research.

A. THE PROBLEM OF MISMATCH

One line of research sees discontinuity as a matter of interaction between children's aptitude and the environments of home and school. This view draws on the formulations and research that examine interaction between the learner's aptitude (a range of individual and personal characteristics, including ability level) and treatment (educational programs or instructional methods) (Cronbach & Snow, 1977).

Analysis of person-environment interactions represents an attempt to identify optimal conditions for learning for students with different needs or aptitudes. This concept has been applied to contrasts between family and school as learning environments—what Epstein (1983) calls interaction between person and place. Epstein's study applies this formulation to social, rather than instructional, features of the family and school environments, with particular focus on authority structures in the two institutions. Epstein describes two broad types of authority structures—those that share decision making with children and those that do not. Using longitudinal data from 960 eighth-grade students in 10 middle schools, she examined the effects of congruence and incongruence on independence, attitudes toward school, and grades. The results showed that students who came from low-participation families but went to high-participation schools gained in independence; children from low-participation families and low-participation schools lost. The most satisfied students were those who were initially high in independence, were from families high in participation, and went to high-participation schools. The low-low-low students were least satisfied. Students from low-participation families who went to high-participation schools gained in grades, compared with the low-low group. Epstein concludes that school environment seems to be particularly important for students from families that do not emphasize participation in decision making.

Another line of studies that use ethnographic/linguistic methods and conceptualizations examines congruence between family and school in the more detailed features of interpersonal interaction. Observations of interaction in the classroom describe much of teacher-student exchange as consisting of three parts: teacher poses a question, a single child responds, and the teacher then evaluates the response. The teacher sets the rules of exchange: one child, on one topic chosen by the teacher, in front of an audience of peers. Participants assume that there is a correct answer to the question posed and that the student's response will be openly evaluated (Mehan, 1979). The child who does well in this situation clearly fits the description of the student preferred by teachers in the Feshbach (1969) and Helton and Oakland (1977) studies. However, several ethnographic accounts of children's discourse at home or in play groups show that forms of exchange in the classroom may be incongruent with previously learned modes for communicating ideas. Children in Hawaii, for example, may respond as a group to a question from a teacher by spontaneously blurting out the answer. When a lone child is called on, he or she may be shy and have little to say. The dyadic situation may remind the child of scolding events with adults at home. In a collective relationship, these children feel more free (Au, 1980).

Heath (1983) describes patterns of language use and their relation to early learning in three different communities and notes the discontinuities and continuities between these experiences and the culture of the school. Mismatches between experience in the community and the school are not most importantly matters of vocabulary, syntax, and other structural aspects of language, although these may invoke negative reactions from teachers and peers. More significant discontinuities appear, for example, in the degree to which the language of adults encourages children to view referents out of context and to manipulate cognitive aspects of the environment imaginatively—an ability to distance themselves from events and objects in their environments. Discontinuities also appear in the ways that language sets and reinforces other social behavior—techniques for solving problems, group loyalties, and interpersonal interaction. Heath's volume is an excellent portrayal of the complexities involved in the transition from home to school and in the importance of interpreting data on differences between home and school in a cultural context.

The literature on discontinuities between family and school has contributed significantly to analyses of family effects. It is obvious, however, that not all types of mismatch are dysfunctional; children begin schooling with obvious disparity between their level of knowledge and that of the teacher. We need to know which discontinuities are harmful and why. Additional studies may offer even more complete perspectives on the processes involved in children's transition between experiences at home and at school.

B. PARENT PARTICIPATION IN CHILDREN'S SCHOOLING

In the mid-sixties, the concern about mismatch between the culture of the low-income minority family/community and that of the middle-class white school was paralleled by several studies that emphasized the role of families in preparing children for achievement in the classroom. These gave rise to pressures to involve parents in the activities of the school. The significant change in the 1960s was an increase in federal support for participation by parents in educational decisions, represented by legislation which mandated participation as a condition for federal funding. This involvement often included (1) participation in instruction as aides, volunteers, and tutors; (2) parent education to improve skills and knowledge; (3) supporting the school generally; and (4) school-community relations.

Studies of effects of parent participation have been undertaken in a wide range of socioethnic communities. Most evaluate studies that attempt to raise performance or alter undesirable classroom behavior of students. These assessments of parental participation can be grouped roughly into those that involve parents of a single classroom or school and those that evaluate the effects of participation in large-scale projects.

Studies that are limited to a single classroom or school typically focus on a specific form of student behavior and ask for responsive actions by parents. These studies show that contacts with parents initiated by either principal or staff are effective in increasing attendance of chronically absent students (Sheats & Dunkleberger, 1979), reducing talking in class and rate of completion of homework (Dougherty & Dougherty, 1977), raising the level of daily math assignments (Karraker, 1972), and reducing disruptive-aggressive behavior of third-grade students (Ayllon, Garber, & Pisor,

1975). In these studies, the teacher or the school initiated contact with parents and collaborated with them on a reinforcement schedule that was contingent on specific behaviors observed and recorded by the teacher.

Successful outcomes have also been reported from interventions that gave more general instructions to parents and were less specific about the students' target behavior and the reinforcement schedule (Beveridge & Jerrams, 1981; Radin, 1972). For example, children asked to read to their parents gained in reading skills, compared with controls, at all ability levels in a sample of several hundred students in the early grades of school in London (Hewison & Tizard, 1980; Tizard, Schofield, & Hewison, 1982).

C. EVALUATION OF LARGE-SCALE PROGRAMS

A number of national programs incorporated parental involvement into their program activities. These programs usually covered a range of services, extending to social competence and health as well as academic achievement. Several evaluations of these programs have been conducted; a brief summary of the results is included here.

Project Developmental Continuity.—In 1974, the United States Department of Health and Human Services initiated Project Developmental Continuity (PDC) to offer continuous developmental support through third grade for children from low-income families. Implementation began in 1976 at 13 sites distributed throughout the United States. A longitudinal evaluation was conducted by the High/Scope Educational Research Foundation. The evaluation concluded that there was little evidence that PDC programs enhanced children's social competence or academic achievement beyond those of Head Start children who had not gone through the PDC program. There was also little evidence that they affected the behavior of parents whose children were in the study (Bond, 1982).

Parent Child Development Centers.—Another comprehensive program that was designed to improve school-relevant skills was the Parent Child Development Center (PCDC) experiment begun in 1970 by the U.S. Office of Economic Opportunity (Andrews et al., 1982). The focus of this program was to help mothers become more effective in their child-rearing activities. Programs were developed in Birmingham, Houston, and New Orleans between 1970 and 1975 to include a comprehensive curriculum for mothers concerned with child development, child-rearing practices, nutrition and health, home management, and support services. A program was offered simultaneously for their children. Mother-child pairs entered the program when children were from 2 months to 12 months old. The evaluation revealed significant differences on several dimensions between program and control groups at all sites after 24 months of participation. Program children exceeded controls on the Stanford Binet at graduation and, at two sites, on several developmental measures. In early follow-up data, mothers and children in two of the centers maintained gains one year after the end of the program.

Home Start.—The National Home Start Demonstration Project was begun in 1972 to offer to low-income families Head Start–type comprehensive program services in their own homes rather than in a center (Hewett, 1977). The program was intended to involve parents directly in the educational development of their own children. An evaluation of Home Start concluded that children in the program gained on measures of school readiness and social-emotional development compared with controls. Children in Home Start showed gains in school readiness comparable to those in Head Start, but benefited less in social-emotional development (Love, Nauta, Coelen, & Roupp, 1975).

Follow Through Program.—Follow Through is an antipoverty program designed for students whose families are at or below the poverty line and who have participated in Head Start or a similar program. The 1967 amendments to the 1964 Economic Opportunity Act mandated parental involvement as part of the program. Evaluation studies report that some parents gained from participation and that students were more likely to stay in school and less likely to repeat a grade or be assigned to remedial classes (Rubin, Olmsted, Szegda, Wetherby, & Williams, 1983).

Even though the results of parental involvement in large-scale intervention programs are not conclusive, it seems likely that encouraging parental involvement has positive consequences for student achievement and may also benefit the parents who participate.

IV. FAMILY INFLUENCES ON ACHIEVEMENT

A. GLOBAL MEASURES OF BACKGROUND AND ACHIEVEMENT

Evidence of an association between family background and school achievement goes back at least to Galton's study of the careers of English men of science, published in 1874. Thirty-five years later, Decroly and Degand reported in 1910 that children from dissimilar occupational backgrounds performed at different levels on the mental ability scale that Binet had recently constructed (Binet & Simon, 1916). Since these reports appeared, the accumulation of evidence that family socioeconomic status is linked to school achievement has been overwhelming. The level of association varies somewhat with the measure of achievement used. SES (level of education and occupation of fathers) accounted for 28% of the variance in years of schooling in a sample of more than 20,000 males between the ages of 20 and 64 (Blau & Duncan, 1967). The results from Project Talent indicate that the probability of a student from the lower quartile of SES entering college within 5 years of high school graduation was .32 for males and .18 for females, while the probability for students from the highest quartile was .86 for males and .78 for females (Flanagan, Shaycroft, Richards, & Claudy, 1971). The effects of SES and gender also hold within ability levels. Males from the lowest ability level and the lowest SES quartile had a .14 probability of entering college within 5 years; those in the lowest ability level and highest SES quartile had a .42 probability of entering college. Comparable figures for females are .14 and .33. Males in the highest aptitude quartile but in the lowest SES quartile had a .81 probability of entering college; females in the highest quartile on ability and lowest in SES had only a .47 probability of entering college.

When scores on scholastic tests (rather than college entrance) are taken as the outcome measure, SES appears to account for somewhat less variance. Using a sample of 850 families of 11-year-old students from six ethnic groups in Australia, Marjoribanks (1980) reports that social background of parents (fathers' occupation and fathers' and mothers' education) accounted for 6% of the variance in scores on mathematics (Class Achievement Test in Mathematics, 1976), slightly more than 16% of variance on word knowledge, and 13% on word comprehension (Primary Reading Survey Tests, 1976). More intensive studies of small samples of parent-child pairs report that family characteristics, including measures of family environments and parent-child interaction, account for more than half of the variation in children's achievement (Jones, 1972).

Since both families and schools are cultural institutions, it is not surprising that the correlation between family background and school achievement varies from one nation to another and, within nations, among cultural and SES subgroups (Laosa, 1981). Evidence on this point comes from studies of ethnic groups within countries (Lesser, Fifer, & Clark, 1965; Marjoribanks, 1980) and from an international study of achievement conducted by the International Association for the Evaluation of Educational Achievement (IEA), a group of 22 national research centers organized in 1959 to conduct cross-national educational research (Husen, 1967; Thorndike, 1973; Torney, Oppenheim, & Farnen, 1976). The IEA project used a number of variables to represent home circumstances, and reports of the several subject areas included slightly different background variables. The results, however, clearly show variation from one country to another. For reading, the variance accounted for by family variables ranged from a high of 27 to a low of one; for mathematics, the range was from 12 to zero; for civic education, from 23% to two.

B. FAMILY VARIABLES ASSOCIATED WITH ACHIEVEMENT

Reports from studies of family effects describe a wide range of variables associated with school achievement or relevant mental abilities. It is not easy to summarize these results; variables that would appear to be similar (e.g., nurturance and warmth) may be defined in different ways. It is difficult to compare results from various studies because of differences in instruments and procedures or differences in data reduction strategies (e.g., frequencies vs. proportions or ratings vs. frequencies in observations of interactions). However, several categories of generally similar variables appear repeatedly in published reports, perhaps indicating some convergence in the field.

1. *Measures of verbal interaction between mothers and children.* Many studies report an association between some aspect of verbal communication in the home and school achievement: a communication index from interviews (Jones, 1972); referential communication scores (Dickson, Hess, Miyake, & Azuma, 1979); strong press for speaking correct English (Marjoribanks, 1980); requests for verbal versus nonverbal responses in teaching tasks (Hess, Holloway, Dickson, & Price, 1984; Hess, Shipman, Brophy, & Bear, 1969); requests for generative responses (Price, Hess, & Dickson, 1981); permitting children to participate in meal conversations (Bing, 1963); willingness to devote time to the child, primarily playing and talking (Freeberg & Payne, 1967); freedom to engage in verbal expression and direct teaching of language behavior (Hanson, 1975); asking information of the child (Radin, 1971); scales of the HOME, especially the verbal responsivity scores (Bradley & Caldwell, 1976, 1984; Sigel, 1982; Van Doorninck, Caldwell, Wright, & Frankenburg, 1981); how much mother reads to the child (Laosa, 1982); and engaging in more verbal interaction with families (Norman-Jackson, 1982). This is only a partial list; it includes studies of both mothers and fathers. The range of verbal features of the home that are associated with school-relevant measures, even though defined in different ways, indicates the strength of the link between aspects of the verbal environment of the home and achievement in school.

2. *Expectations of parents for achievement.* Again, the definition and techniques for measuring aspirations, press for achievement, and expectations vary from one study to another. Children's performance on school-related tasks is associated with the following types of variables: parents' achievement orientations about the children's schoolwork (Marjoribanks,

1980); press for achievement (Wolf, 1964); parental aspirations for child's educational and/or occupational attainment (Freeberg & Payne, 1967; Jones, 1972; Laosa, 1982; Marjoribanks, 1980; Williams, 1976); pressure for improvement on interaction tasks (Bing, 1963); emphasis on school achievement (Hanson, 1975); and a composite of measures of mothers' aspirations for the child's educational and occupational attainment and expectations for early mastery of developmental tasks (Hess et al., 1984; Hess, Kashiwagi, Azuma, Price, & Dickson, 1980). Again, this is a partial list of studies (see Seginer, 1983, for a review). Many studies did not include parental expectations in their research design.

    3. *Affective relationship between parents and child.* Variables that represent some aspect of the affective relationship or interaction between parents and the child are significantly correlated with achievement in a number of studies. Performance is associated with the following: "a close relationship with a demanding and somewhat intrusive mother . . ." (Bing, 1963, p. 647); maternal rejection (negatively) (Buck, Gregg, Stavraky, & Subrahmaniam, 1973); emotional responsivity scales of the HOME (Bradley & Caldwell, 1976); nurturance, defined to cover a range of maternal behavior, including verbal reinforcement (Radin, 1971, 1972); experimenter's ratings of maternal warmth (Hess et al., 1969); ratings of affective relationship (Estrada, Arsenio, Hess, & Holloway, in preparation); and avoidance of restriction and punishment (Sigel, 1982). Most of these results show that parental warmth facilitates performance, but the operative mechanisms are not usually described. Many studies did not include affective measures in their design.

    4. *Discipline and control strategies.* Several studies include some measures of maternal control and report correlations with children's performance. Different perspectives on control are used in different studies and found to be associated with performance. These include authoritative control (in contrast to authoritarian and permissive) (Baumrind, 1973); use of physical punishment (Buck et al., 1973); use of imperatives in disciplinary situations for both black families (Hess et al., 1969) and white (Hess & McDevitt, 1984b; Hess et al., 1984); discouragement index ("parent's response that appeared to intend to stop the [observed] activity, such as hitting, ignoring, physical restraint . . . 'go away,' 'shut up' " (Norman-Jackson, 1982, p. 352); and the degree of fit between authority structures at home and those at school (Epstein, 1983).

    Research on the effect of directiveness and control is hampered by the lack of common definitions of variables. There is some overlap between this category and both affect (rejection is a form of disciplining by withholding love) and feedback to performance (praise may express affection and also inform the child about the quality of performance on a task). Studies which define family variables as environmental "press" (Marjoribanks, 1980) include by assumption some degree of parental attempts to control the child's behavior. The consistent finding of an association between measures of parental control and children's achievement is impressive. This area of parental behavior deserves more careful theoretical analysis, particularly of the cognitive processes involved (Dix & Grusec, 1983; Hess & McDevitt, 1984b).

5. *Parental beliefs and attributions.* The analysis of the effect of parents' beliefs on their child-rearing behavior and on their children's school achievement is a rapidly growing but still limited field. Early work in this field includes descriptions of parental beliefs about development, including cognitive processes (Goodnow, 1984) and the relationship between beliefs or perceptions of children's ability and parental behavior with children (Sigel, McGillicuddy-DeLisi, Flaugher, & Rock, 1983).

The extent of parents' knowledge about developmental norms of infants is associated with parents' competence in child care (LeResche, Strobino, Parks, Fischer, & Smeriglio, 1983). Beliefs appear to have a greater influence on children's self-concept and expectancies about performance in mathematics than does the children's actual performance (Parsons, Adler, & Kaczala, 1982). Parental attributions about children's performance in mathematics are associated with children's actual performance and presumably govern to some degree the behavior of parents toward signs of high or low achievement (Hess, Holloway, Azuma, & Kashiwagi, in preparation).

In their extensive and detailed studies, Sigel and his associates have described the link between parental beliefs and behavior in problem-solving sessions with their children (McGillicuddy-DeLisi, 1982). Data were gathered from 120 families on parents' beliefs about development and on their teaching behavior in two types of tasks—paper folding and story-telling. To assess beliefs, parents were given 12 vignettes that involved a parent and a 4-year-old. Following presentation of the vignette, 22 probes focused on parents' views of how children attain concepts and abilities. Parental responses were coded according to 47 constructs of developmental states—for example, impulsivity, dependency, and rigidity—and processes—for example, empathy, self-regulation, and drawing inferences. For both fathers and mothers, beliefs were significant predictors of teaching behavior on both tasks, after the effects of social class and family constellation factors were taken into account. Beliefs predictive of teaching behavior depended on the nature of the task and differed between mothers and fathers.

C. EMERGING AREAS OF STUDY

The recent literature suggests that some areas of investigation are emerging which may greatly enrich the analysis of family effects. These include the concept of "distancing" (Sigel, 1982): parental behavior offering experiences that require the child to anticipate future actions or outcomes; to reconstruct past events; to employ imagination in dealing with objects, people, and events; and to draw inferences and consider alternatives. "Distancing" may have something in common with the concept of decontextualizing used to describe some features of language communities (Heath, 1983).

Another line of analysis describes parental behavior that facilitates the use of executive functions in problem-solving situations. For example, Wertsch, McNamee, McLane, and Budwig (1980) conceptualize parental influence, in part, as internalization of elements of social interaction and describe the role of parents in helping children identify essential parts of a problem (by directing gaze at elements of the task). Wood (1980) describes facilitative behavior in which parents structure tasks to match their children's capability and assist them with hints when a problem is encountered.

The work of Price and his colleagues (1981) and Price (1984) also belongs in this new wave of theoretical analysis. Building on a finding that maternal requests for verbal (i.e., "Tell me where this block should go") rather than nonverbal ("Put this block where it should go") feedback were correlated with children's performance on tests of school readiness, Price proposed that the cognitive function of maternal requests for "generative verbal responses" is to help the child rehearse or keep elements longer in short-term memory and thus facilitate storage and later retrieval. Another example of an analysis of the influence of parental actions on cognitive processing is recent work by Hess and McDevitt (1984b). In an attempt to explain the negative correlation between maternal directiveness or use of authority-based tactics in teaching and disciplinary situations and children's performance in school, they propose that the association between directiveness in both teaching behavior and disciplinary events and children's school-relevant performance comes from (1) the overload that directiveness or imperatives place on the child's attentional capacity, (2) the restraint that directiveness places on the child's initiatory behavior, thus foreclosing opportunities to generate solutions that are compatible with existing cognitive structures, and (3) attributional processes which affect self-appraisal by leading the child to infer that competence to solve problems comes from external sources.

D. WHICH FAMILY VARIABLES ARE THE MOST EFFECTIVE?

It is not possible to answer this question with results available at the present time. Not only is family research faced with problems of measurement error, experimenter effects, and generalizability, but variables with similar labels are defined in quite different ways, intensive studies use populations that differ from one another in socioeconomic and cultural properties, and statistical procedures of different studies often are not comparable.

A major question that arises in this field is the degree to which the correlations reported between family variables and child performance reflect genetic sources; few studies attempt to adjust for such effects. Some studies suggest that the association between family variables and children's IQ can be accounted for by maternal IQ (Longstreth, Davis, Carter, Flint, Owen, Rickert, & Taylor, 1981), but other analyses show family variables to be significantly associated with school-relevant skills after maternal IQ or child IQ measured at an earlier point in a longitudinal study is taken into account (Dickson et al., 1979; Hess et al., 1984).

Some researchers attempt to assess the relative impact of different family variables by statistical procedures, particularly regression analysis. Such attempts face at least three barriers. First, different measures vary in their reliability and in the validity with which they reflect everyday experience in the family. These statistical properties affect their potency in a regression analysis where they compete with other measures. Second, many family measures simultaneously represent several different psychological processes. A disciplinary event may be, at the same time, modeling of verbal behavior, negative reinforcement, an attempt to shame or create guilt, rejection, an interruption in the child's problem-solving activity, and an accusation of incompetence. These are each distinct psychological aspects of the event; it is impossible to estimate in a precise way which affects the child's cognitive operations.

Third, many family variables are intercorrelated; those that are crowded out in a regression analysis may nonetheless be psychologically important variables but lose out because of their commonality with other variables. More precise studies would be useful in clarifying the relationship between specific aspects of the family environment and acquisition of specific academic skills. However, the various features of family interaction are inextricably interlaced; they cannot be disentangled in studies of natural family interaction. Laboratory studies may help clarify whether or not a given event has an effect, but they cannot easily assess the influence of combinations of experiences or the effect of any given event in

the normal life of the family. The attempt to achieve more precise information will probably involve both theoretically based controlled studies and
attempts to test models developed in these studies through analysis of
family interaction.

E. MODELS, METHODS, AND THEORY IN FAMILY STUDIES

Although there is general agreement among social scientists that
educational achievement is associated with socioeconomic and cultural
background, there is much less agreement about the transmission processes involved and the degree to which other factors contribute to various
measures of educational attainment. A number of models have been proposed to identify the major elements of the influence process. Perhaps the
most traditional and general form of these models is the unidirectional
form: SES influences family environments and both have an impact on the
child's ability and attainment, a model called "the standard deprivation
model of social class and intelligence" (Eckland, 1971). A more complete
unidirectional model includes a more complex view of forces which create
the family environment: the parents' ability determines to some degree the
socioeconomic status of the family and helps create family environments.

A reciprocal model recognizes the effect of child ability on family
environment (Williams, 1976). Williams describes this model as indicating
a triple advantage (disadvantage) for children: (1) intellectually advantaged
parents transmit ability to children through genetic channels, (2) intelligent parents create a favorable family environment, and (3) the heightened
ability that children gain from these two sources enables them to exert
their own influence on the family environment to their cognitive benefit
(p. 82).

The current view in developmental and cognitive psychology might
be called a facilitating model. It emphasizes the active role that the young
child plays in organizing the raw data of the environment to develop
educationally useful skills. The central part of the model is the child's direct
experience with his or her environment: normal cognitive processes organize, store, and retrieve elements of the environment in problem-solving
situations. Parents facilitate these processes, providing the raw material of
experience that is needed for cognitive growth and helping the child
acquire executive cognitive strategies for solving problems (Hess & Mc-
Devitt, 1984a; Price, 1984; Sigel, 1982; Wertsch et al., 1980; Wood, 1980).
Models thus vary along a dimension of unidirectional influence of socializing agents on the child to those in which the child is the initiating actor in
constructing his or her own cognitive world.

The variables used in the analysis of family effects range from molar and diffuse to specific and transactional measures. Molar variables have general social meaning but are nonspecific with respect to the interaction between the parents/family and the child—SES, ethnicity, family size and other structural characteristics, divorce, father absence, and maternal employment. These variables are especially appropriate for unidirectional models that emphasize the impact of external events upon the child's cognitive development and achievement.

During the mid-sixties and since, many studies of family impact on achievement have tried to identify the features of the family environment through which these broad social events and conditions affected children's achievement and mental development. These studies took two general forms. The "process" studies used interviews, sometimes in combination with sessions of interaction between parents and children, to identify dimensions of the family environment that are associated with children's achievement. Variables that were central to these inquiries included nurturance (Bradley & Caldwell, 1976; Radin, 1971); achievement orientation, press for linguistic competence, aspirations, and press for independence (Dave, 1963; Marjoribanks, 1980); parental belief about children's achievement (Holloway & Hess, 1984; Sigel et al., 1983); emphasis on verbal interaction (Bing, 1963; Bradley & Caldwell, 1976); affective tone of the parent-child relationship (Bradley & Caldwell, 1976; Estrada et al., in preparation); and disciplinary and control strategies (Baumrind, 1973; Conroy, Hess, Azuma, & Kashiwagi, 1980; Jones, 1972; Marjoribanks, 1980).

A second form consists of transactional studies that used detailed analysis of interaction (usually staged) between parents and children to identify more specific parental behavior (Azuma, Kashiwagi, & Hess, 1981; Hess et al., 1969; Sigel, 1982; Wertsch et al., 1980; Wood, 1980).

The progression from molar and unidirectional to specific and reciprocal approaches to studies of parent-child transactions suggests a gradual movement toward greater specificity. Along with the attempts to identify specific elements of family-child exchanges, however, there was a surge of interest in analysis of more global variables that might be found to regulate the more specific elements of parent-child exchanges. Studies of the effects of beliefs, affective relationships, divorce, and day care are emerging as lively areas of study. Perhaps the prominent trend in the past decade is an increasing emphasis on theory. The most promising reports are those which draw from cognitive psychology to explain why certain types of interaction (discipline/control or affective interaction, for example) should be expected to have cognitive consequences.

These three dimensions—directionality, specificity, and use of theory—form a heuristic matrix against which to views the numerous studies of family effects on school achievement.

V. Effects on Different Types of Academic Abilities

Although the above summary lumps together several types of school-relevant achievement, there is evidence that family environments have differential influences on different outcomes. Studies of the effects of early intervention report that compensatory programs affect achievement in school, indicated by measures such as achievement tests, retention in grade, and assignment to classes in special education, more than they affect IQ (Lazar, Darlington, Murray, Royce, & Snipper, 1982; Miller & Bizzell, 1983; Weikart, Deloria, Lawser, & Wiegerink, 1970). Studies of family effects on adopted children indicate that family environment is more closely related to school achievement than to measures of IQ (Scarr & Yee, 1980). There is also some evidence that family variables are more closely linked to measures of verbal ability, including reading, than to measures of quantitative skills or pattern recognition (Marjoribanks, 1980; see reports of IEA study, p. 19).

A. FAMILY EFFECTS ON READING

The role of the family in fostering children's interest and skill in reading has been one of the most widely studied topics in the area of cognitive socialization. A number of research approaches have been utilized: (1) identifying early readers and studying their home environments; (2) comparing the home environments of disabled readers with those of children with no reading difficulties; (3) correlating family variables with reading scores; and (4) describing the effects of programs designed to change parents' behavior or other aspects of the home environment. The major trend in research on learning to read has been toward greater specificity in defining component skills, which include decoding the text, applying knowledge of word meaning, and interpreting the individual word meaning within the overall context of the sentence and paragraph (Calfee, 1975; Calfee, Spector, & Piontkowski, 1979). While controversy continues over the particular way in which bottom-up (i.e., decoding) and top-down (comprehension) processing are coordinated, researchers have moved toward understanding the reading process in terms of carefully defined components.

Research on the family's impact on these component skills has not yet attained comparable precision. Almost no one has attempted to link particular features of the home environment to component skills of reading (Hess, Holloway, Price, & Dickson, 1982). However, successful interventions depend on achieving a more precise understanding of exactly what it is about such family experiences that fosters competence in particular component skills of reading.

Analysis of family experience that contributes to successful reading performance has focused on five general areas: the value parents place on literacy, parents' press for achievement in reading, availability of materials for reading, amount of time spent reading with children, and children's opportunities for verbal interaction with family members. Each of these areas will be discussed in turn.

1. *Value placed on literacy.* Parents demonstrate the value they place on literacy by the amount of reading they do, the quality of their reading material, and the interest and involvement in reading they express in conversation. All of these factors have been found to relate to children's reading performance (see Hess et al., 1982, for a review). For example, parents of early readers tend to read more than those of nonearly readers (Durkin, 1966) and to characterize themselves as enjoying a variety of books (Clark, 1976). Moon and Wells (1979) found parental interest in literacy, as expressed through spontaneous comments to children in naturalistic interaction and in structured interviews, to be significantly related to knowledge of letters at preschool age and to reading accuracy, reading comprehension, and word recognition at age 7.

2. *Press for achievement.* One indicator of press for achievement is the expectations parents hold for their children's school achievement. Entwisle and Hayduk (1978) asked parents of children entering first grade to predict the children's reading grades. A second prediction was made at the end of the year. Evidence of parental influence was found in the significant movement in marks over the first year in the direction required to reduce discrepancy between parents' expectation and children's performance. In the second grade, the effect of this discrepancy seemed to decline in importance.

Another indication of press is whether parents attempt to teach their children to read. Research on early readers uncovers only occasional systematic attempts by their parents to teach reading (Clark, 1976; Durkin, 1966). More common was a responsiveness to children's interest in literacy, indicated by responding to questions about written words in everyday contexts and by willingness to read and reread children's favorite books to them (Teal, 1978). An ethnographic study of family influences on literacy

(Taylor, 1983) and an investigation of antecedents of successful reading by black second graders (Norman-Jackson, 1982) also highlight the potential role that older siblings can play in encouraging child-initiated verbal interactions related to later reading ability.

One study has attempted to separate the influence of press to achieve exerted by mothers from that of availability of literacy-related experiences such as watching "Sesame Street," owning books and records, and being read to by a parent (Hess et al., 1982). Press to achieve (including mothers' expectations for children's mastery of developmental skills, future occupation, and educational achievement) was found to be a stronger influence on letter recognition than was availability of literacy-related experiences. In homes where press was high, children performed well regardless of the resources available. However, few homes in the study were at poverty levels, and it is reasonable to assume that all had some access to school-relevant resources. The effectiveness of press to achieve may operate where adequate exposure to relevant materials or experience is available.

3. *Availability of reading and writing material.* The opportunity to use reading and writing materials at home has often been shown to correlate with reading competence. Preschool children who are exposed to these materials tend to become more proficient readers than children lacking such opportunity (Callaway, 1968; Flood, 1975; Hansen, 1969; Milner, 1951; Morrow, 1983). Parents of early readers were more likely than parents of nonearly readers to buy picture dictionaries, alphabet books, and basal readers, as well as to provide paper, pencils, and blackboards (Briggs & Elkind, 1977; Clark, 1976; Durkin, 1966). Early readers are frequently taken to the library by their parents (Berry, Fischer, Parker, & Zwier, 1971; Briggs & Elkind, 1977; Clark, 1976; King & Friesen, 1972).

While access to printed material seems logically related to growth of children's reading proficiency, the effect may be due to the more positive attitude toward schoolwork held by parents who provide these materials. However, Hess et al. (1982) found that exposure to reading materials does influence reading skills, above and beyond the influence of general orientation toward literacy.

4. *Reading with children.* The self-reported tendency of parents to read to their children is related to children's interest in reading and performance on measures of reading proficiency (Briggs & Elkind, 1977; Clark, 1976; Durkin, 1966; King & Friesen, 1972; Morrow, 1983). Detailed analyses of reading aloud episodes (Flood, 1977) reveal that the total number of words spoken, the number of questions asked by the child, the number of questions answered by the child, the number of pre- and postsession questions asked by the parent, and the amount of positive reinforcement given by the parent all correlate with reading performance.

Reading aloud to children contributes to reading skills in several ways. First, apparently it helps to clarify for children the relationship between spoken and written language. Several studies (see Stubbs, 1980, for a review) indicate that many 5-year-old children think they can read when they cannot, do not know what reading consists of, and are confused about the relationship between pictures, words, letters, and numbers. A second benefit of reading is that children are given practice in initiation-reply-evaluation sequences frequently used by teachers to elicit classroom conversations. Parents often ask children to label objects in books, then provide feedback about the correctness of the children's answer (Heath, 1980). Children also learn to "take from" books: words are seen as symbols of objects, as having labeling functions, and as having specific attributes that can be discussed and manipulated (Scollon & Scollon, 1979). Third, studies of book-reading sessions suggest that both parent and child commit all or part of the text to memory. When children recite parts of the story by heart, they may be using language more advanced than that they could produce spontaneously. This experience stretches their vocabulary and syntactic knowledge beyond its current level (Snow, Dubber, & DeBlauw, 1980).

As mentioned earlier, research on 7- and 8-year-old British children (Hewison & Tizard, 1980) indicates that children's reading skills also benefit from reading aloud to their parents. Reading to parents was associated with reading attainment after children's IQ and maternal language behavior (willingness to talk with child and responsiveness to questions) were statistically removed. These findings were confirmed by a subsequent study (Tizard, Schofield, & Hewison, 1982) in which parents of 6-year-old children were encouraged to have their children read aloud to them. For children of all ability levels, children who received extra practice at home improved over control groups and over children receiving extra help at school.

These findings are particularly noteworthy in that parents were not instructed how to respond to their children, some of the parents did not speak English, and no attempt was made to prevent the parents in the control and school-tutored groups from having their children read aloud to them at home. It is thus likely that home-tutored children's superior performance was not due to instruction but rather to the motivational aspect of having parents' involvement and interest.

5. *Opportunities for verbal interaction.*   Given their common basis in a symbolic code, it is not surprising that similar parent behaviors would influence both language development and attainment of literacy skills. Snow (1983) describes four characteristics of parent-child interaction that have been shown to support development in both areas: (1) semantic

contingency (expanding or clarifying the child's utterance); (2) scaffolding (structuring the task so that there are fewer difficult features and providing help at key points of difficulty); (3) accountability (insistence that a task be completed, such as pronouncing a word correctly); and (4) routines (word games, nursery rhymes, and rereading stories).

Snow contends that because much verbal language use is embedded within a context, it is therefore attainable by most children regardless of the home environment. However, verbal language in school (e.g., narratives and descriptions) and written language are decontextualized and mastering them depends on the parent-child interactions described above.

B. FAMILY VARIABLES AND PERFORMANCE IN MATHEMATICS

As indicated earlier, some evidence suggests that family variables are less closely related to performance in mathematics than to performance on reading and other indications of verbal competence. This evidence is not conclusive; the studies that have reported results usually do not differentiate among different aspects of competence in mathematics (e.g., concepts vs. computation; spatial ability vs. pattern recognition). It is possible that aspects of mathematics that are heavily verbal in nature—for example, word problems—may be more closely associated with family variables than spatial or computational operations. The results summarized here are thus not as precise as one might like.

There is some contradictory evidence about the relationship between gross measures of family background and performance in mathematics. Studies by Ginsburg and Russell (1981) of mathematical thinking of white and black preschoolers from middle and low SES levels found no social class or racial differences in performance on unschooled nonnumerical skills (e.g., perception of more, conservation of number, addition operations) and unschooled numerical procedures (e.g., counting words, enumeration, cardinality). They conclude that family status and characteristics have little influence on mathematical thought before formal schooling begins. This suggests that the family's influence on mathematical ability may be primarily through teaching specific school-relevant skills and through instilling a motivation to achieve. However, the work of Lesser, Fifer, and Clark (1965) is difficult to reconcile with the Ginsburg and Russell findings. In the Lesser et al. study, performance on tests of number ability and spatial ability showed both social class and ethnic differences in 320 first-grade children from four different ethnic groups each divided into high and low SES subgroups. Also Hatano, Miyake, and Tajima (1980) reported an association between maternal variables and Japanese preschool children's performance on tests of number conservation.

It is clear, however, that measures of family background are correlated with performance in school on tests of ability in arithmetic and more advanced mathematical abilities. Data from Project Talent on four high school classes (1960–63) show that correlations between family socioeconomic status and several measures of arithmetic reasoning and performance in intermediate in high school mathematics vary around .30 for both males and females (Flanagan et al., 1971). Scores on tests of computational skill for these high school classes, however, show lower correlation with family background—around .14. Unlike the data from the International Association for the Evaluation of Educational Achievement, results from Project Talent indicate that family variables do not affect reading grades more than grades in arithmetic. The results from Project Talent are supported by data from the "High School and Beyond" study conducted by the National Opinion Research Center of 58,000 sophomores and seniors in 1981. In a reanalysis of data from more than 24,000 seniors of the original sample, Walberg and Shanahan (1983) report that SES correlated at about the same level with performance on multiple choice tests of reading (.33) and two multiple choice tests of mathematics (.37 and .30). These figures are close to those reported by Project Talent and the correlation of .32 given for the United States in the IEA study.

Dave's (1963) study of family environments, using interviews to assess "press for achievement," "press for language," and "provision for general learning," found that family variables were correlated with achievement in arithmetic problem solving (Metropolitan Achievement Battery) and reading at roughly similar levels (multiple correlations of .71 and .73, respectively) but the multiple correlation with arithmetic computation was somewhat lower (.56). Marjoribanks (1972) reported similar findings for SRA Primary Mental Abilities Test (1962, rev. ed.) scores on verbal and number tests but with much lower correlations (.26) for the spatial subtest.

Longitudinal studies that included observations of interaction and maternal teaching report roughly comparable correlations between maternal variables and teachers' grades on reading and arithmetic. Using a group of 163 black mothers and their children, Hess et al. (1969) report that maternal variables assessed during preschool years correlated significantly (ranging between .20 and .35) with teacher's grades in arithmetic in the first two years of school. Relevant maternal variables included requests for verbal rather than nonverbal responses in a teaching situation, orienting the child to the teaching task, authoritarian styles in disciplinary situations (negatively), specificity of feedback in the teaching task, and general ratings of maternal warmth. These correlations were slightly but not significantly lower than correlations between these same maternal measures and grades in reading across the first two years of school.

Similar findings were reported for a group of 47 Caucasian families, when maternal variables measured at preschool were correlated with children's scores at grade 6 on the math concepts subtest of the Iowa Tests of Basic Skills (Hess et al., 1984). The maternal variables associated with performance in mathematics were expectations for achievement, authoritarian behavior (directiveness) in teaching tasks and disciplinary situations (negatively), scores on a referential communication task, requests for verbal rather than nonverbal responses in a teaching task, belief in luck as a reason for successful achievement in school (negatively), and a rating of the quality of the affective relationship between mothers and children during the preschool period. Comparable data are available from a study of 44 Japanese families (Kashiwagi, Azuma, & Miyake, 1982) which examined the relationship between maternal variables assessed during preschool years and achievement in grade 5 using both teacher ratings of performance and math scores on the WISC. In the Japanese group, the maternal behavior at preschool that was associated significantly with performance in mathematics at grade 5 included maternal expectations for achievement, use of appeals to guilt or shame in disciplinary situations (negatively), efficiency in a referential communication game, and responsiveness to the child in an interaction task.

These results indicate that family variables are associated with achievement in mathematics and that variables somewhat similar to those found in studies of reading outcomes are involved. The analyses are not precise enough to give evidence whether different elements of the family environment are instrumental in influencing achievement in mathematics and reading. The results reported here may be picking up the effects of general features of the environment; more specific elements may be involved.

VI. INFLUENCES ON SCHOOL-RELEVANT COGNITIVE BEHAVIOR

Achievement in school is not merely a matter of possessing specific relevant skills; performance in the classroom and on tests is affected by a range of supportive behavior. Family experience contributes to the acquisition of these related skills, and some studies examine this aspect of the family's role in promoting achievement in school. The areas of concern in this chapter include communicative competence, cognitive style, and memory and attention.

A. COMMUNICATIVE COMPETENCE

Perhaps the most obvious effect of language on school performance is in reading and writing, where knowledge of vocabulary and grammar are put to extensive use (Calfee, 1975; Hess et al., 1982). Language may also influence other aspects of cognitive processing underlying school performance, such as causality and logical relations (Bernstein, 1975), memory (Santa & Rankin, 1972), problem solving (Glucksberg & Weisberg, 1966), and internal regulation of behavior (Luria, 1961).

In the last decade, increasing attention has been placed on the role of parents in facilitating children's language acquisition. While initial work focused on mastery of syntactic rules, later studies have examined parents' roles in fostering communication accuracy and in teaching children the pragmatics, or appropriate social usage of language. A number of studies have also examined discontinuities in the linguistic environments of home and school.

1. *Knowledge of Syntax and Vocabulary*

The modifications parents make in their speech to toddlers are related to the children's vocabulary and syntactic ability (see Hoff-Ginsberg & Shatz, 1982, for a review). Vocabulary may be enhanced by parents' tendency to place certain words in perceptually salient positions, such as at the end of an utterance. The range of semantic relations expressed in parents' speech, as well as the intelligibility and fluency with which these linguistic features are communicated, may also have an effect on children's use of words (Nelson, Carskaddon, & Bonvillian, 1973; Newport, Gleitman, & Gleitman, 1977). Acquisition of grammar may be aided by parents' tendency to use simple sentence structures and to expand and elaborate the structure used by children (Cross, 1977). There is also some evidence that general intellectual stimulation, as measured by the HOME scale, is related to the language development of 3-year-olds (Siegel, 1982).

2. *Referential Communication*

Referential communication concerns the ability to formulate a verbal message that uniquely identifies a referent for the listener. Studies of the development of referential communication indicate that young children are likely to formulate ambiguous messages that may index more than one referent (for reviews see Asher, 1978; Robinson & Robinson, 1980).

The accuracy of mother-child communication in a referential com-

munication task was associated with school readiness at age 5, defined as
letter and number recognition, counting, and vocabulary, and at age 6,
defined as performance on alphabet and number subscales of the Metropolitan Readiness Test (Dickson et al., 1979). This relationship remained
significant even when mothers' IQ, the families' social status, and children's ability at age 4 (Palmer's Concept Familiarity Index plus Peabody
Picture Vocabulary Test) were partialed out.

Additional evidence indicates how parents may actually promote the
development of accurate referential communication. Working from samples of naturally occurring mother-child speech from the children's preschool years, Robinson and Robinson (1980) found that children with more
sophisticated knowledge about referential communication came from
homes where children's failures to communicate clearly were explicitly
noted by parents.

Further evidence of the importance of adults' role in calling attention
to ambiguity in communication is provided by a training study (Robinson &
Robinson, 1982) in which 4- and 5-year-olds given "metacognitive guidance" (i.e., information about when and why listeners understood or
failed to understand messages in referential communication tasks) improved in both performance and understanding on immediate and delayed
posttests.

3. Comprehension Monitoring

The work of Robinson and Robinson (1980, 1982) also deals indirectly
with comprehension monitoring. In their studies, adults model active
monitoring of their understanding and convey strategies for obtaining
clearer information. Markman (1977, 1979, 1981) has focused directly on
how children monitor their own comprehension and finds that comprehension monitoring is not fully active even in college students. The influence of
parents on comprehension monitoring has not been studied. It is clearly an
important issue to explore, particularly since comprehension monitoring of
spoken and written messages is such an important academic skill (Collins &
Smith, 1982).

4. Knowledge of Pragmatics

Numerous types of parent-child dialogues have been noted that may
contribute to children's knowledge about the pragmatic aspect of language.
Many middle-class parents begin teaching their children conventions
about question-answer sequences and turn taking in conversation well
before the children are able to utter their first words (Snow, 1977).

Mothers of infants give turn-taking "lessons" by initially accepting any sound as a turn. As children's language skills develop, mothers become increasingly demanding about the quality of utterance.

Another form of dialogue is the games or rituals that involve repetition of certain patterns of language (Ninio, 1980, 1983; Ninio & Bruner, 1978; Snow et al., 1980). These routines range from simple games played with infants to complex interactions with preschool and elementary school children, such as reading stories together. Such forms of communication provide an interaction opportunity that is predictable and practiced enough that both parent and child can take turns successfully. Also, in most routines there are openings in the dialogue that children can fill with responses that would exceed their linguistic capacities if it were not for the cognitive support provided by the known linguistic context.

Several studies suggest that this informal training varies considerably depending on the social class and ethnic background of the family (Au, 1980; Heath, 1983; Philips, 1972). Heath (1980), for example, found that parents in one lower-middle-class black community did not engage in the sorts of dialogue described by Snow (1977). Children were asked questions only when real information was desired, not when the adult already knew the answer. These children could not answer questions posed by the teacher that involved labeling an object, listing attributes, or giving other information that the teacher already knew. Children from a neighboring community, who had been exposed to this sort of questioning at home, had no trouble responding in the classroom.

B. COGNITIVE STYLE

Children's style in solving problems is likely to exert an important, though indirect, influence on their school achievement. For instance, children who adopt a reflective rather than impulsive problem-solving style tend to be higher achievers in school (Hess et al., 1969; Kagan, 1965). Studies of family influences on reflectivity indicate that compared to mothers of impulsive children, mothers of reflective children adopt a more positive, tactful, and indirect approach during structured interaction tasks but maintain a high level of involvement (Campbell, 1973; Hess et al., 1969). The direction of causality in this relationship is not always from parent to child. Evidence from studies of hyperactive and impulsive children indicates that mothers' negative, controlling behavior is often instituted in response to actions by their children (Halverson & Waldrop, 1970; Mash & Johnson, 1982).

Another feature of cognitive style—field independence—has been linked with high performance on tasks requiring spatial visualization,

conservation skills, and visual perspective taking (see Goodenough &
Witkin, 1977, for a review). On the other hand, field dependence is
associated with popularity and smooth interpersonal relations. Therefore,
while field independence may contribute to intellectual skills underlying
achievement, positive teacher evaluations may result from the interpersonal sensitivity characteristic of a field-dependent style. Familial antecedents of field independence include child-rearing practices that encourage
autonomous functioning and avoid dominating control, conformity, strict
authority, and punishment (Goodenough & Witkin, 1977) as well as a
teaching style based on inquiry and praise rather than negative physical
control and modeling (Laosa, 1978).

In recent years, less emphasis has been placed on traitlike notions like
field independence; instead, the goal of much research has been a more
careful specification of the process by which parent beliefs and behavior
affect children. In the latter approach, specific linkages are sought between
parent and child variables defined at a more micro level than the molar
constructs typical of the cognitive style literature.

C. BASIC COGNITIVE SKILLS: MEMORY AND ATTENTION

In past research, little notice has been taken of the ways in which
parents may shape the development of fundamental cognitive skills like
attention and memory. Recently, catalyzed partly by Soviet psychologists'
perceptions of the importance of adults in facilitating children's cognitive
processing (Vygotsky, 1962) and partly by increasing sophistication in the
information-processing conceptualizations of how these skills operate, researchers have turned to this unexplored area.

Price and his colleagues (Price, 1984; Price et al., 1981) have examined the effect of maternal communicative style on the stimulation of
mental rehearsal by preschool children. In one paper, the focus was on
mothers' tendency to ask children questions that require the generation of
original verbal responses (as opposed to responses that are nonverbal or
that allow the child to restate a phrase generated by the parent). The use of
questioning requiring verbal generation was associated with children's
performance on tasks dependent on parent-taught information, such as
knowledge of letters and numbers, and not on general measures of intelligence. Price interpreted this differential relationship as evidence that such
questioning stimulates mental rehearsal of known information rather than
generally stimulating cognitive-linguistic processes. Thus, some parents
may be providing external support of their children's mnemonic activity at
a time when children's metamemory skills are not developed enough to
detect the need for rehearsal.

Investigations of direct attempts by parents to encourage their children's use of memory strategies have met with little success. One study of mothers' style of teaching their preschool children to play a memory game found that only 13% of maternal instructions related to memory and that no category of maternal instructions was related to children's behavior in the game or to recall in a subsequent memory task (Justice & Coley, 1983).

While parents do not appear to spend much time teaching their children memory strategies directly, it is possible that in the context of everyday life they may have expectations of their children's memory that increase as the children grow older. By making increasingly stringent demands on the children to remember everyday routines, chores, the location of personal possessions, the time for certain activities, and so on, parents may be calling attention to memory processes and providing opportunity for children to acquire skills that facilitate memory. This idea is consistent with the emphasis that Soviet psychologists place on the role of adults in initial forms of cognition (Vygotsky, 1962).

In a study by Ratner (1980), the memory demands created by parents within the home setting were identified and correlated with performance by 2- and 3-year-olds on two memory tasks. Ratner found that mothers of 3-year-olds did not require more memory processing than mothers of 2-year-olds, nor did mothers of older children provide more explicit information about memory. Therefore, age-related increases in children's memory skills could not be attributed solely to their parents' increasing memory demands. However, for 3-year-olds, there were relationships between several maternal characteristics and the quality of children's memory skills. Mothers who asked more questions about past events had children who performed better on recall of past events. Children whose mothers asked many questions about present events which required memory retrieval (e.g., remembering object labels) but not for information about events removed from the immediate context were least able to retrieve information from long-term memory. Mothers' use of the word *remember* was positively related to children's memory, while other direct types of metamemory instruction were infrequent and did not correlate with memory performance.

When children enter school, the demands placed on their memory skills increase dramatically. Furthermore, memory tasks become increasingly decontextualized, moving from the "here-and-now" quality of conversations with parents (Ratner, 1980) to the abstract nature of tasks encountered in formal schooling. Brown (1978) has speculated that formal schooling is largely responsible for the development of metamemory skills, a hypothesis that accords with Flavell's notion (1981) that metamemory skills are more likely to develop when the load on memory is heavy.

Children who have an opportunity at home to develop memory strategies and a metacognitive awareness of memory will find it easier to take on the memory tasks embedded in the curriculum of formal schooling.

A second basic cognitive area that may be influenced by adults is the deployment of attention skills, including careful scanning and attending selectively to important information. In the study cited earlier by Justice and Coley (1983), parents spent a considerable amount of time orienting their children's attention to specific aspects of the environment. Wertsch and his associates (Wertsch et al., 1980) analyzed videotapes of 18 mother-child pairs, examining the verbal and nonverbal devices used by mothers to regulate children's attention to a model puzzle the children were trying to copy. Using the children's eye gaze to the model as the measure of following an effective strategy, they found that mothers' tendency to direct the children's gaze decreased with age as the children attended on their own, thereby assuming more independent task-oriented strategies.

Such studies of parental influence on children's attention strategies are just beginning, but the approach may prove to be a powerful technique for understanding the role of parent-child interaction in school-relevant tasks. Parents' attempts to orient children's attention to a task have been recorded as part of an assessment of maternal teaching styles and found to correlate with school-relevant outcomes (Hess et al., 1969). Future studies can build on this finding by specifying more precisely the currently tentative links between parent behavior, attention strategies, and performance on academic skills.

VII. FAMILY ORIGINS OF STRIVING TO SUCCEED IN SCHOOL

In this section, the focus is not on cognition or achievement per se, but on the motivational processes leading to attempting challenging tasks and working persistently and with intensity. In early work, achievement motivation was conceptualized in terms of personality characteristics such as need achievement (McClelland, Atkinson, Clark, & Lowell, 1953), self-esteem (Coopersmith, 1967), and locus of control (Rotter, 1966). Studies of antecedents of these constructs identified constellations of parent behaviors associated with each. These studies have been summarized in other publications and will not be reviewed here (Harter, 1983; Henderson, 1982; Lefcourt, 1976; Phares, 1976; Wylie, 1979).

Numerous criticisms have been brought against these constructs. Self-esteem research has been faulted for lacking adequate methods of assessment and a conceptual model that could guide investigations of family influence (Harter, 1983; Wylie, 1979). The construct of locus of control, although included in some contemporary studies, has been super-seded by research on causal attributions. In attribution theory, the cognitive processing of factors in a particular situation is recognized and the antecedents and sequelae of the attribution-making process are clearly delineated. Because of the theoretical richness of this area, it has been heavily researched. The studies that focus on family antecedents of children's attributions will be covered in somewhat more detail in this section.

Theories of the role of causal appraisal in achievement behavior, first advanced by Heider (1958) and elaborated by Kelley (1967), were expanded into studies of achievement in school by Weiner and his colleagues (Weiner, 1979, 1980). In brief, the theory states that the beliefs individuals have about the causes of a given level of performance will influence the expectation of success on subsequent tasks and their affective response to the event. The categories of explanation most often used are ability, effort, task difficulty, and luck, with training occasionally included as an explanatory possibility. These attributions represent three underlying dimensions: (*a*) locus of causation (Is the reason for success internal or external to the individual?); (*b*) stability (Does the reason fluctuate over time?); and (*c*) controllability (Can the reason for success be controlled by the individual?).

Only scanty evidence is available supporting a relationship between an individual's attributions for school performance and either motivated behavior or school achievement. While laboratory studies have shown that certain attributional patterns lower motivation (e.g., Dweck, 1975), studies conducted in naturalistic settings fail to find a relationship (Bernstein, Stephan, & Davis, 1979; Covington & Omelich, 1979). In laboratory tasks, individuals have had little opportunity to develop any concept of their own ability about the criterion task, so attributions for a given performance are more likely to be related to subsequent performance (Parsons, in press). Weiner (1983) also cautions against the use of dependent measures that are determined by many factors.

A number of studies suggest that attributions may be transmitted to children as interpretations that adults make about the children's behavior. Miller, Brickman, and Bolen (1975) found that children labeled "neat" by their teachers were neater than children who were urged to be neat over the same period of time. In a second study, these authors found that children labeled as skilled or highly motivated in mathematics increased in their mathematics performance over a group simply reinforced for correct responses. These findings have been supported in other studies where children were labeled as cooperative and charitable (Grusec, Kuczynski, Rushton, & Simutis, 1978).

Very little research exists on actual parent behavior that might influence children's attributions. Apparently, the only study in this area is an investigation of the effects of various parent socialization techniques on children's attributions for prosocial behavior (Dix & Grusec, 1983). Children ages 5–6, 8–9, and 11–13 made attributions about the helping behavior of characters in hypothetical stories, who helped under various conditions of parental influence—power assertion, modeling, and reasoning. Power assertion produced external attributions while modeled and spontaneous helping produced internal attributions, indicating that parents' socialization practices are associated with children's causal reasoning.

A number of studies have examined similarities between parents and children in their attributions about school performance. While the sample characteristics and methods for eliciting attributions in these studies vary greatly, most find that parents and children tend to hold differing beliefs.

The main technique for eliciting attributions has been to ask parents and their children for their explanations about the children's school performance, or the performance of children in general. Parents in Australia (Cashmore, 1980) and the United States (Hess et al., in preparation; Holloway & Hess, 1982) tend to put more weight than their children on ability as a key factor in explaining success, while children more often cite effort. For relatively low performance ("Why does [child] not do better?"), both American (Hess et al., in preparation; Holloway & Hess, 1982) and Japanese (Hess et al., in preparation) mothers focus more than their children on lack of effort; children tend to put more emphasis on lack of ability. However, in a study of the reasons given by Israeli parents and their fourth- and fifth-grade children for the children's performance in mathematics (Bar-Tal & Guttmann, 1981), post hoc pairwise comparisons revealed significant differences between parents and children for only 2 out of 10 attributions: quality of teaching and luck.

In addition to examining mean differences in parents' and children's attributions, some researchers have measured the similarity between a parent and child within individual families. Consistent findings have not yet emerged. In one study, involving mothers, fathers, and their fifth-through eleventh-grade children (Parsons et al., 1982), children's expectations and self-appraisals about performance in mathematics tended to match those of their parents. Little evidence of similarity between mothers and their sixth-grade children emerged in the study by Hess et al. (in preparation). There was no more similarity between parents and their own children than between parents and children unrelated to them. Furthermore, Pearson product-moment correlations between mothers and children were not significant for any of the five attribution options.

While it might be expected that parents would transmit to children their own attributions, there are several counterarguments (Holloway &

Hess, 1982). First, according to the actor-observer hypothesis (see, e.g., Jones & Nisbett, 1971), children (actors) would tend to make external attributions because of a tendency to focus on the surrounding circumstances; mothers (observers) would see their children as the salient figures, rather than the context, and would make attributions internal to the children. Another counterargument stems from the self-serving hypothesis (Greenwald, 1980), which suggests that mothers would seek to enhance their public and/or self-image by making attributions that credit themselves for high performance and blame external factors for low performance. If the children also make defensive attributions, there will be little accordance within a family.

While the attribution framework has proven fruitful for research on motivation, it is still not clear which beliefs are the most adaptive for the school setting. In the literature where certain attributions are thought to be dispositional (Metalsky & Abramson, 1981), "ideal" belief patterns have often been identified. In general, beliefs in internal and controllable factors are considered positive. However, a separate literature has been developing that focuses more closely on how contextual factors, such as whether the situation calls for cooperative or competitive behavior, might influence attributions (Ames, 1981; Ames & Felker, 1979; Holloway & Fuller, 1983). This literature suggests that the optimal attribution pattern may depend on the nature of the setting. In the classroom, for instance, students operating under the assumption that their behavior is guided by factors that they alone control may fail to accord teachers the attention and compliance they expect. More successful students may be able to sense the requirements of a given structure and adapt beliefs and behavior accordingly. These students would be able to recognize the influence of external factors when the situation called for cooperative action, while in individualistic situations internal beliefs would become salient. If the skill of adaptability is indeed important, one role of parents might be to facilitate children's skill in understanding the requirements of various situations rather than to inculcate a particular attribution pattern.

VIII. Summary and Comments

We suspect that all authors review research literature with implicit theories and biases about the processes discussed and that these theories guide selection of articles, the emphasis on different features of the results, and organization of the material. We would like to make our implicit views more apparent.

We view accomplishment in school as susceptible to socialization processes—that is, it is shaped by the interaction between the developing cognitive processes of the child and the influence of socializing agents. In many ways, the family and school cannot control cognitive activities: children remember, perceive, form categories, make associations, derive generalizations, and develop strategies for dealing with stimuli in ways that are linked to biological characteristics of our species. In many other ways, however, socializing agents affect the outcome of these basic mental operations: to some degree, they control the content—the raw material of experience—that children use in developing their mental worlds by restricting, enlarging, or selecting the material that is to be learned. They also give cultural and personal meaning to knowledge the child acquires, making some knowledge salient and valued and other information irrelevant. Socializing agents can assist the child in developing specific cognitive strategies (e.g., decontextualizing) and thus can affect performance on measures of ability. However, we see that role as facilitating normal developmental processes rather than affecting them directly.

If parents and other agents help control the acquisition of knowledge and cognitive strategies, they also affect social processes that govern ways the child will use these resources in school. The familiar motivational forces—efficacy, self-esteem, attributions about the causes of success and failure, striving to achieve and/or compete, monitoring the quality of one's work, internalizing adult standards—are to some degree affected by the socializing authorities in the child's life.

The outcomes of these processes depend to a great degree on three features of the social world in which the child lives: the consistency (consensus) among socializing agents about the goals of education, the degree to which these goals are taken seriously, and the ability of the socializing agents to counter knowledge, values, and goals that come from competing sources—for example, television and peers. If multiple sources of information and reward are diffuse or contradictory, they erode the effectiveness of family and school; discontinuities between family and school can compromise the effectiveness of both.

In a society where there is great variation in social climates among schools, the effect of family experiences will probably vary with the nature of the school. A school that values scholarship and intellectual effort expects and rewards different responses from the child from one that values other types of achievement, such as social competence and athletics. The correlation between family variables and achievement will vary, we suggest, between such schools. In the first, family experiences that facilitate problem-solving strategies may be effective; in the second, experiences that encourage motivation to achieve in academic areas may be particularly useful. The fit between the experiences at home and school deserves more detailed analysis.

A review of this sort leaves us with distinct impressions of the field. Although these are filtered through our own biases, we offer them for whatever interest they may have. The field is moving from investigations of relationships between molar family variables to attempts to describe these relationships in more precise detail. Indeed, this theme goes back at least a quarter of a century; each generation of researchers criticizes the variables of earlier studies as excessively molar in character and calls for more specific investigations. A reading of material from the past 20 years clearly indicates that we are making progress, although not as rapidly as we hoped. This push for specificity is paralleled by a push for theory and the combination suggests that work in this field over the next few years will be exciting and illuminating.

In the past, a familiar research approach has been to study global features of families and show the correlations of family variables to relatively global outcomes—IQ, grades, achievement test scores. Such studies cannot, by their nature, provide the precision that the field is now demanding; they may have served their usefulness. Family interaction is too diffuse; too many distinct activities take place in a time span of a few minutes. Furthermore, the meaning of these exchanges is tied to the family's personal history, requiring a historical perspective for adequate interpretation.

There is a need to distinguish more carefully among the impact of different features of the family environment. Too few studies, in our view, attempt to control for the contribution of parental intelligence to the family environment and to the child's ability. Conclusions will change drastically, we suspect, as some of the effects of different sources are accounted for.

A more differentiated view of the influence process will make it easier to analyze another crucial component of the process: the effect of various social events and conditions on parental behavior and beliefs. Parental resources for facilitating cognitive growth and educational achievement are affected by divorce, poverty, illness, employment, number of children, marital harmony, and support systems available in the community. They also may have a direct impact on the child. The role of such circumstances needs to be more completely understood.

One of the most productive approaches may be the comparison of family influences in different cultures. We do not suggest that one should search for universals. Indeed, such an approach would probably not be productive. If we are right in suggesting that the effects of any given element of the home environment may depend on the nature of discontinuities and continuities between home and school and the social/motivational climate of the school, one should find that different family variables are effective in different cultures. However, such research will be productive to the extent that such cultural differences are tuned to more basic theories about cognitive development, motivation, and social aspects of socialization. The prospects for future research in this field do, indeed, seem rewarding.

REFERENCES

Ames, C. Competitive versus cooperative reward structures: The influence of individual and group performance factors on achievement attributions and affect. *American Educational Research Journal*, 1981, **18**, 273–287.

Ames, C., & Felker, D. An examination of children's attributions and achievement-related evaluations in competitive, cooperative, and individualistic reward structures. *Journal of Educational Psychology*, 1979, **71**, 413–420.

Andrews, S. R., Blumenthal, J. B., Johnson, D. L., Kahn, A. J., Ferguson, C. J., Lasater, T. M., Malone, P. E., & Wallace, D. B. The skills of mothering: A study of Parent Child Development Centers. *Monographs of the Society for Research in Child Development*, 1982, **47** (6, Serial No. 198).

Asher, S. R. Referential communication. In G. J. Whitehurst & B. J. Zimmerman (Eds.), *The functions of language and cognition*. New York: Academic Press, 1978.

Au, K. H. Participation structures in a reading lesson with Hawaiian children: Analysis of a culturally appropriate instructional event. *Anthropology and Education Quarterly*. 1980, **11**, 91–115.

Ayllon, T., Garber, S., & Pisor, K. The elimination of discipline problems through a combined school-home motivational system. *Behavior Therapy*, 1975, **6**, 616–626.

Azuma, H., Kashiwagi, K., & Hess, R. D. [*Maternal attitudes, behaviors and childrens' cognitive development—Cross-national survey between Japan and the U.S.*] Tokyo: University of Tokyo Press, 1981. (In Japanese.)

Bar-Tal, D., & Guttman, J. A comparison of teachers', pupils' and parents' attributions regarding pupils' academic achievements. *British Journal of Educational Psychology*, 1981, **51**, 301–311.

Baumrind, D. The development of instrumental competence through socialization. In A. D. Pick (Ed.), *Minnesota symposium on child psychology*. Vol. 7. Minneapolis: University of Minnesota Press, 1973.

Bernstein, B. *Class, codes and control*. Vol. 1: *Theoretical studies toward a sociology of language*. New York: Schocken Books, 1975.

Bernstein, W. M., Stephan, W. G., & Davis, M. H. Explaining attributions for achievement: A path analytic approach. *Journal of Personality and Social Psychology*, 1979, **37**, 1810–1821.

Berry, M. T., Fischer, S. L. Parker, F. S., & Zwier, M. D. Average and superior readers in lab school. *Reading Teacher*, 1971, **25**, 271–275.

Beveridge, M., & Jerrams, A. Parental involvement in language development: An evaluation of a school-based parental assistance plan. *British Journal of Educational Psychology*, 1981, **51**, 259–269.

Binet, A., & Simon, T. *The development of intelligence in children*. Translated by Elizabeth S. Kite. Baltimore: Williams & Wilkins, 1916.

Bing, E. Effects of child-rearing practices on development of differential cognitive abilities. *Child Development*, 1963, **34**, 631–648.

Blau, P. M., & Duncan, O. D. *The American occupational structure*. New York: Wiley, 1967.

Bond, J. T. *Outcome of the PDC intervention, Vol. 1 and Appendices*. Ypsilanti, Mich.: High/Scope Educational Research Foundation, 1982.

Bradley, R. H., & Caldwell, B. M. The relation of infants' home environments to mental test performance at fifty-four months: A follow-up study. *Child Development*, 1976, **47**, 1172–1174.

Bradley, R. H., & Caldwell, B. M. The relation of infants' home environments to achievement test performance in first grade: A follow-up study. *Child Development*, 1984, in press.

Briggs, C., & Elkind, D. Characteristics of early readers. *Perceptual and Motor Skills*, 1977, **44**, 1231–1237.

Brown, A. L. Knowing when, where, and how to remember: A problem of metacognition. In R. Glaser (Ed.), *Advances in Instructional Psychology*. Vol. 1. Hillsdale, N.J.: Erlbaum, 1978.

Buck, C., Gregg, R., Stavraky, K., & Subrahmaniam, K. Variables associated with social class differences in the intelligence of young children. *Multivariate Behaviorial Research*, 1973, **8**, 213–226.

Calfee, R. C. Memory and cognitive skills in reading acquisition. In D. D. Duane & M. B. Rawson (Eds.), *Reading, perception and language*. Baltimore: York Press, 1975.

Calfee, R. C., Spector, H. J., & Piontkowski, C. An interactive system for assessing reading and language skills. *Bulletin*. Towson, Md.: Orton Society, 1979.

Callaway, B. Relationship of specific factors to reading. *Proceedings of the Thirteenth Annual Convention of the International Reading Association, Part I*. Vol. 13. Newark, Del.: International Reading Association, 1968.

Campbell, S. Mother-child interaction in reflective, impulsive, and hyperactive children. *Developmental Psychology*, 1973, **8**, 341–347.

Cashmore, J. *Models of intelligence and development: A child's-eye view*. Paper presented at the Jubilee Congress of ANZAAS, Adelaide, Australia, 1980.

Clark, M. M. *Young fluent readers: What can they teach us?* London: Heinemann Educational Books, 1976.

Collins, A., & Smith, E. E. Teaching the process of reading comprehension. In D. K. Detterman & R. J. Sternberg (Eds.), *How and how much can intelligence be increased?* Norwood, N.J.: Ablex, 1982.

Conroy, M., Hess, R. D., Azuma, H., & Kashiwagi, K. Maternal strategies for regulating children's behavior: Japanese and American families. *Journal of Cross-cultural Psychology*, 1980, **11**, 153–172.

Coopersmith, S. *The antecedents of self-esteem*. San Francisco: W. H. Freeman, 1967.

Covington, M. V., & Omelich, C. L. Are causal attributions causal? A path analysis of the cognitive model of achievement motivation. *Journal of Personality and Social Psychology*, 1979, **37**, 1487–1504.

Cronbach, L. J., & Snow, R. E. *Aptitudes and instructional methods*. New York: Irvington, 1977.

Cross, T. G. Mothers' speech adjustments: The contributions of selected child listener variables. In C. E. Snow & C. A. Ferguson (Eds.), *Talking to children: Language input and acquisition*. Cambridge: Cambridge University Press, 1977.

Dave, R. The identification and measurement of environmental process variables that are related to educational achievement. Unpublished doctoral dissertation, University of Chicago, 1963.

Dickson, W. P., Hess, R. D., Miyake, N., & Azuma, H. Referential communication accuracy between mother and child as a predictor of cognitive development in the United States and Japan. *Child Development*, 1979, **50**, 53–59.

Dix, T., & Grusec, J. E. Parental influence techniques: An attributional analysis. *Child Development*, 1983, **54**, 645–652.

Dougherty, E. H., & Dougherty, A. The daily report card: A simplified and flexible package for classroom behavior management. *Psychology in the Schools*, 1977, **14**(2), 191–195.

Dreeben, R. The contribution of schooling to the learning of norms. *Harvard Educational Review*, 1968, **37**(2). (Reprint Series no. 1)

Durkin, D. *Children who read early.* New York: Teachers College Press, 1966.

Dweck, C. S. The role of expectations and attributions in the alleviation of learned helplessness. *Journal of Personality and Social Psychology*, 1975, **31**, 674–685.

Eckland, B. K. Social class structure and the genetic basis of intelligence. In R. Cancro (Ed.), *Intelligence: Genetic and environmental influences.* New York: Grune & Stratton, 1971.

Entwisle, D. R., & Hayduk, L. A. *Too great expectations: The academic outlook of young children.* Baltimore: Johns Hopkins University Press, 1978.

Epstein, J. L. Longitudinal effects of family-school-person interactions on students outcomes. *Research in Sociology of Education and Socialization*, 1983, **4**, 101–127.

Estrada, P., Arsenio, W., Hess, R. D., & Holloway, S. D. *Affective quality of the mother-child relationship: Consequences for children's cognitive development.* 1984, in preparation.

Feshbach, N. D. Student teacher preferences for elementary school pupils varying in personality characteristics. *Journal of Educational Psychology*, 1969, **60**, 126–132.

Flanagan, J. C., Shaycroft, M. F., Richards, J. M., & Claudy, G. J. *Five years after high school.* Palo Alto, Calif.: American Institutes for Research, 1971.

Flavell, J. H. Cognitive monitoring. In W. P. Dickson (Ed.), *Children's oral communication skills.* New York: Academic Press, 1981.

Flood, J. E. Predictors of reading achievement. An investigation of selected antecedents to reading. Unpublished doctoral dissertation, Stanford University, 1975.

Flood, J. E. Parental styles in reading episodes with young children. *Reading Teacher*, 1977, **30**, 864–867.

Freeberg, N. E., & Payne, D. T. Dimensions of parental practice concerned with cognitive development in the preschool child. *Journal of Genetic Psychology*, 1967, **111**, 245–261.

Galton, F. *English men of science: Their nature and nurture.* London: MacMillan, 1874.

Ginsburg, H. P., & Russell, R. L. Social class and racial influences on early mathematical thinking. *Monographs of the Society for Research in Child Development*, 1981, **46** (6, Serial No. 193).

Glucksberg, S., & Weisberg, R. W. Verbal behavior and problem solving: Some effects of labeling in a functional fixedness problem. *Journal of Experimental Psychology*, 1966, **71**, 659–664.

Goodenough, D. R., & Witkin, H. A. *Origins of the field-dependent and field-independent cognitive styles.* Princeton, N.J.: Educational Testing Service, 1977.

Goodnow, J. J. Change and variation in ideas about childhood and parenting. In I. E. Sigel (Ed.), *Parental belief systems: Psychological consequences for children.* Hillsdale, N.J.: Erlbaum, 1984.

Greenwald, A. G. The totalitarian ego: Fabrication and revision of personal history. *American Psychologist*, 1980, **35**, 603–618.

Grusec, J. E., Kuczynski, L., Rushton, J. P., & Simutis, Z. M. Modeling, direct instruction, and attributions: Effects on altruism. *Developmental Psychology*, 1978, **14**, 51–57.

Halverson, C. F., & Waldrop, M. F. Maternal behavior toward own and other preschool children: The problem of "ownness." *Child Development*, 1970, **41**, 839–845.

Hansen, H. S. The impact of the home literacy environment on reading attitude. *Elementary English*, 1969, **46**, 17–24.

Hanson, R. A. Consistency and stability of home environmental measures related to IQ. *Child Development*, 1975, **46**, 470–480.

Harter, S. Developmental perspectives on the self system. In P. H. Mussen (Ed.), *Handbook of child psychology*. Vol. **4**. New York: Wiley, 1983.

Hatano, G., Miyake, K., & Tajima, N. Mother behavior in an unstructured situation and child's acquisition of number conservation. *Child Development*, **51**, 377–385.

Heath, S. B. Questioning at home and at school: A comparative study. In G. Spindler (Ed.), *Doing the ethnography of schooling: Educational anthropology in action*. New York: Holt, Rinehart, & Winston, 1980.

Heath, S. B. *Ways with words: Language, life, and work in communities and classrooms*. Cambridge: Cambridge University Press, 1983.

Heider, F. *The psychology of interpersonal relations*. New York: Wiley, 1958.

Helton, G. B., & Oakland, T. D. Teachers' attitudinal responses to differing characteristics of elementary school students. *Journal of Educational Psychology*, 1977, **69**, 261–266.

Henderson, R. W. Personal and social causation in the school context. In J. Worell (Ed.), *Psychological development in the elementary years*. New York: Academic Press, 1982.

Hess, R. D., Holloway, S. D., Azuma, H., & Kashiwagi, K. *Causal attributions by Japanese and American mothers and children about performance in mathematics*. (1984, in preparation).

Hess, R. D., Holloway, S. D., Dickson, W. P., & Price, G. G. Maternal variables as predictors of children's school readiness and later achievement in vocabulary and mathematics in sixth grade. *Child Development*, 1984, in press.

Hess, R. D., Holloway, S. D., Price, G. G., & Dickson, W. P. Family environments and the acquisition of reading skills: Toward a more precise analysis. In L. M. Laosa & I. E. Sigel (Eds.), *Families as learning environments for children*. New York: Plenum, 1982.

Hess, R. D., Kashiwagi, K., Azuma, H., Price, G. G., & Dickson, W. P. Maternal expectations for mastery of developmental tasks in Japan and the United States. *International Journal of Psychology*, 1980, **15**, 259–271.

Hess, R. D., Shipman, V. C., Brophy, J. E., & Bear, R. M. *The cognitive environments of urban preschool children: Follow-up phase*. Graduate School of Education, University of Chicago, 1969.

Hess, R. D., & McDevitt, T. M. Some antecedents of maternal attributions about children's performance in mathematics. In R. Ashmore & D. Brodzinsky (Eds.), *Perspectives on the family*. Hillsdale, N.J.: Erlbaum, 1984. (a)

Hess, R. D., & McDevitt, T. M. Some cognitive consequences of maternal intervention techniques: A longitudinal study. *Child Development*, 1984, in press. (b)

Hewett, K. D. *Partners with parents: The Home Start experience with preschoolers and their families*. Washington, D.C.: U.S. Department of Health, Education and Welfare, Office of Human Development Services, 1977.

Hewison, J., & Tizard, J. Parental involvement and reading attainment. *British Journal of Educational Psychology*, 1980, **50**, 209–215.

Hoff-Ginsberg, E., & Shatz, M. Linguistic input and the child's acquisition of language. *Psychological Bulletin*, 1982, **92**, 3–26.

Holloway, S. D., & Fuller, B. Situational determinants of causal attributions: The case of working mothers. *Social Psychology Quarterly*, 1983, **46**, 131–140.

Holloway, S. D., & Hess, R. D. Causal explanations for school performance: Contrasts between mothers and children. *Journal of Applied Developmental Psychology*, 1982, 3, 319–327.

Holloway, S. D., & Hess, R. D. Mothers' and teachers' attributions about children's mathematics performance. In I. Sigel (Ed.), *Parental belief systems: The psychological consequences for children*. Hillsdale, N.J.: Erlbaum, 1984.

Husen, T. (Ed.). *International study of achievement in mathematics: A comparison of twelve countries*. Vols. 1–2. New York: Wiley, 1967.

Jackson, P. *Life in classrooms*. New York: Holt, Rinehart & Winston, 1968.

Jackson, P., Silberman, M., & Wolfson, B. Signs of personal involvement in teachers' descriptions of their students. *Journal of Educational Psychology*, 1969, **60**, 22–27.

Jones, P. A. Home environment and the development of verbal ability. *Child Development*, 1972, **43**, 1081–1086.

Jones, E. E., & Nisbett, R. E. *The actor and the observer: Divergent perceptions of the causes of behavior*. New York: General Learning Press, 1971.

Justice, E. M., & Coley, D. D. *Parental behaviors in a memory relevant setting: How parents "teach" children to remember*. Paper presented at the biennial meeting of the Society for Research in Child Development, Detroit, 1983.

Kagan, J. Reflection-impulsivity and reading ability in primary grade children. *Child Development*, 1965, **36**, 609–628.

Karraker, R. J. Increasing academic performance through home-managed contingency programs. *Journal of School Psychology*, 1972, **10**, 173–179.

Kashiwagi, K., Azuma, H., & Miyake, K. Early maternal influences upon later cognitive development among Japanese children: A follow-up study. *Japanese Psychological Research*, 1982, **24**, 90–100.

Kedar-Voivodas, G. The impact of elementary children's roles and sex roles on teacher attitudes: An interactional analysis. *Review of Educational Research*, 1983, **53**, 414–437.

Kelley, H. H. Attribution theory in social psychology. In D. Levine (Ed.), *Nebraska Symposium on Motivation*, Vol. 15. Lincoln: University of Nebraska, 1967.

King, E. M., & Friesen, D. T. Children who read in kindergarten. *Alberta Journal of Educational Research*, 1972, **18**, 147–161.

Laosa, L. M. *Maternal teaching strategies and field dependent-independent cognitive styles in Chicano families*. Princeton, N.J.: Educational Testing Service, 1978.

Laosa, L. M. Maternal behavior: Sociocultural diversity in modes of family interaction. In R. W. Henderson (Ed.), *Parent-child interaction: Theory, research, and prospects*. New York: Academic Press, 1981.

Laosa, L. M. Families as facilitators of children's intellectual development at 3 years of age: A causal analysis. In L. M. Laosa & I. E. Sigel (Eds.), *Families as learning environments for children*. New York: Plenum, 1982.

Lazar, I., Darlington, R. B., Murray, H., Royce, J., & Snipper, A. Lasting effects of early education: A report from the Consortium for Longitudinal Studies. *Monographs of the Society for Research in Child Development*, 1982, **47**(2–3, Serial No. 195).

Lee, P. C., & Kedar-Voivodas, G. Sex role and pupil role in early childhood education. In L. G. Katz (Ed.), *Current topics in early childhood education* (Vol. 1). Norwood, N.J.: Ablex, 1977.

Lefcourt, H. M. *Locus of control: Current trends in theory and research*. Hillsdale, N.J.: Erlbaum, 1976.

LeResche, L., Strobino, D., Parks, P., Fischer, P., & Smeriglio, V. The relationship of observed maternal behavior to questionnaire measures of parenting knowledge, attitudes, and emotional state in adolescent mothers. *Journal of Youth and Adolescence*, 1983, **12**, 19–31.

Lesser, G. S., Fifer, G., & Clark, D. H. Mental abilities of children from different social class and cultural groups. *Monographs of the Society for Research in Child Development*, 1965, **30**(4, Serial No. 102).

Lightfoot, S. L. *Worlds apart: Relationships between families and schools*. New York: Basic, 1978.

Litwak, E., & Meyer, H. J. *Schools, family, and neighborhood: The theory and practice of school-community relations*. New York: Columbia University Press, 1974.

Longstreth, L. E., Davis, B., Carter, L., Flint, D., Owen, J., Rickert, M., & Taylor, E. Separation of home intellectual environment and maternal IQ as determinants of child's IQ. *Developmental Psychology*, 1981, **17**, 532–541.

Love, J. M., Nauta, M. J., Coelen, C. G., & Roupp, R. R. *National Home Start evaluation*: Interim report VI, Executive Summary: Findings and recommendations. Ypsilanti, Mich.: High/Scope Educational Research Foundation; Cambridge, Mass.: Abt, 1975.

Luria, A. R. *The role of speech in the regulation of normal and abnormal behavior*. New York: Pergamon, 1961.

McClelland, D. C., Atkinson, J. W., Clark, R. A., & Lowell, E. L. *The achievement motive*. New York: Appleton-Century-Crofts, 1953.

McGillicuddy-DeLisi, A. V. The relationship between parents' beliefs about development and family constellation, socioeconomic status, and parents' teaching. In L. M. Laosa & I. E. Sigel (Eds.), *Families as learning environments for children*. New York: Plenum, 1982.

Marjoribanks, K. Environment, social class and mental abilities. *Journal of Educational Psychology*, 1972, **63**, 103–109.

Marjoribanks, K. Cognitive performance: A model for analysis. *The Australian Journal of Education*, 1975, **19**, 156–166.

Marjoribanks, K. Family environments. In H. J. Walberg (Ed.), *Educational environments and effects*. Berkeley, Calif.: McCutchan, 1979.

Marjoribanks, K. *Ethnic families and children's achievements*. Sydney: Allen & Unwin, 1980.

Markman, E. M. Realizing that you don't understand: A preliminary investigation. *Child Development*, 1977, **48**, 986–992.

Markman, E. M. Realizing that you don't understand: Elementary school children's awareness of inconsistencies. *Child Development*, 1979, **50**, 643–655.

Markman, E. M. Comprehension monitoring. In W. P. Dickson (Ed.), *Children's oral communication skills*. New York: Academic Press, 1981.

Mash, E. J., & Johnston, C. A comparison of the mother-child interactions of younger and older hyperactive and normal children. *Child Development*, 1982, **53**, 1371–1381.

Mehan, H. *Learning lessons*. Cambridge, Mass.: Harvard University Press, 1979.

Metalsky, G. I., & Abramson, L. Y. Attributional styles: Toward a framework for conceptualization and assessment. In S. D. Hollon & P. C. Kendall (Eds.), *Assessment strategies for cognitive-behavioral interventions*. New York: Academic Press, 1981.

Miller, L. B., & Bizzell, R. P. Long-term effects of four preschool programs: Sixth, seventh, and eighth grades. *Child Development*, 1983, **54**, 727–741.

Miller, R. L., Brickman, P., & Bolen, D. Attribution versus persuasion as a means for modifying behavior. *Journal of Personality and Social Psychology*, 1975, **31**, 430–441.

Milner, E. A study of the relationship between reading readiness in grade one school children and patterns of parent-child interaction. *Child Development*, 1951, **22**, 95–112.

Moon, C., & Wells, G. The influence of home on learning to read. *Journal of Research in Reading*, 1979, **2**(1), 53–62.

Morrow, L. M. Home and school correlates of early interest in literature. *Journal of Educational Research*, 1983, **76**, 221–230.

Nelson, K. E., Carskaddon, G., & Bonvillian, J. D. Syntax acquisition: Impact of environmental assistance in adult verbal interaction with the child. *Child Development*, 1973, **44**, 497–504.

Newport, E. L., Gleitman, L. R., & Gleitman, H. A study of mothers' speech and child language acquisition. *Papers and Reports on Child Language Development*. (No. 10.) Stanford, Calif.: Stanford University Press, 1977.

Ninio, A. Picture book reading in mother-infant dyads belonging to two subgroups in Israel. *Child Development*, 1980, **51**, 587–590.

Ninio, A. Joint book reading as a multiple vocabulary acquisition device. *Developmental Psychology*, 1983, **19**, 445–451.

Ninio, A., & Bruner, J. S. The achievements and antecedents of labelling. *Journal of Child Language*, 1978, **5**, 1–15.

Norman-Jackson, J. Family interactions, language development, and primary reading achievement of black children in families of low income. *Child Development*, 1982, **53**, 349–358.

Parsons, J. E. Attributions, learned helplessness, and sex differences in achievement. In S. R. Yussen (Ed.), *The growth of reflection*. New York: Academic Press, in press.

Parsons, J. E., Adler, T. F., & Kaczala, C. M. Socialization of achievement attitudes and beliefs: Parental influences. *Child Development*, 1982, **53**, 310–321.

Phares, E. J. *Locus of control in personality*. Morristown, N.J.: General Learning Press, 1976.

Philips, S. V. Participant structures and communicative competence: Warm Springs children in community and classroom. In C. B. Cazden, V. P. John, & D. Hymes (Eds.), *Functions of language in the classroom*. New York: Teachers College Press, 1972.

Price, G. G. Mnemonic support and curriculum selection in teaching by mothers: A conjoint effort. *Child Development*, 1984, **55**, 659–668.

Price, G. G., Hess, R. D., & Dickson, W. P. Processes by which verbal-educational abilities are affected when mothers encourage preschool children to verbalize. *Developmental Psychology*, 1981, **17**, 554–564.

Radin, N. Maternal warmth, achievement motivation, and cognitive functioning in lower-class preschool children. *Child Development*, 1971, **42**, 1560–1565.

Radin, N. Three degrees of maternal involvement in a preschool program: Impact on mothers and children. *Child Development*, 1972, **43**, 1355–1364.

Ratner, H. H. The role of social context in memory development. In M. Perlmutter (Ed.), *New directions for child development: Children's memory*. San Francisco: Jossey-Bass, 1980.

Robinson, E. J., & Robinson, W. P. Egocentrism in verbal referential communication. In M. Cox (Ed.), *Are young children egocentric?* New York: St. Martin's, 1980.

Robinson, E. J., & Robinson, W. P. The advancement of children's verbal referential communication skills: The role of metacognitive guidance. *International Journal of Behavioral Development*, 1982, **5**, 329–355.

Rotter, J. B. Generalized expectancies for internal versus external control of reinforcement. *Psychological Monographs*, 1966, **80**(1, Whole No. 609).

Rubin, R. I., Olmsted, P. P., Szegda, M. J., Wetherby, M. J., & Williams, D. S. Long term effects of parent education Follow Through Program participation. Paper presented at the annual meeting of the American Educational Research Association, Montreal, April 1983.

Santa, J. L., & Rankin, H. B. Effects of verbal coding on recognition memory. *Journal of Experimental Psychology*, 1972, **93**, 268–278.

Scarr, S., & Yee, D. Heritability and educational policy: Genetic and environmental effects on IQ, aptitude and achievement. *Educational Psychologist*, 1980, **1**, 1–22.

Scollon, R., & Scollon, S. The literate two-year-old: The fictionalization of self. *Working Papers in Sociolinguistics*. Austin, Tex.: Southeast Regional Laboratory, 1979.

Seginer, R. Parents' educational expectations and children's academic achievements: A literature review. *Merrill-Palmer Quarterly*, 1983, **29**, 1–23.

Sheats, D. W., & Dunkleberger, G. E. A determination of the principal's effect in school-initiated home contacts concerning attendance of elementary school students. *Journal of Educational Research*, 1979, **72**(6), 310–312.

Siegel, L. S. Early cognitive and environmental correlates of language development at 4 years. *International Journal of Behavioral Development*, 1982, **5**, 433–444.

Sigel, I. E. The relationship between parental distancing strategies and the child's cognitive behavior. In L. M. Laosa & I. E. Sigel (Eds.), *Families as learning environments for children*. New York: Plenum, 1982.

Sigel, I. E., McGillicuddy-DeLisi, A. V., Flaugher, J., & Rock, D. A. *Parents as teachers of their own learning disabled children*. (ETS RR-83-21). Princeton, N.J.: Educational Testing Service, 1983.

Snow, C. E. The development of conversation between mothers and babies. *Journal of Child Language*, 1977, **4**, 1–22.

Snow, C. E. Literacy and language: Relationships during the preschool years. *Harvard Educational Review*, 1983, **53**, 165–189.

Snow, C. E., Dubber, C., & DeBlauw, A. *Routines in mother-child interaction*. Paper presented at the annual meeting of the American Educational Research Association, Boston, 1980.

Stubbs, M. *Language and literacy: The sociolinguistics of reading and writing*. London: Routledge & Kegan Paul, 1980.

Taylor, D. *Family literacy*. Exeter, N.H.: Heinemann Educational Press, 1983.

Teal, W. H. Positive environments in learning to read: What studies of early readers tell us. *Language Arts*, 1978, **55**, 922–932.

Thorndike, R. L. *Reading comprehension education in fifteen countries: International studies in evaluation*. Vol. 3. New York: Wiley, 1973.

Tizard, J., Schofield, W. N., & Hewison, J. Collaboration between teachers and parents in assisting children's reading. *British Journal of Educational Psychology*, 1982, **52**, 1–15.

Torney, J. V., Oppenheim, A. N., & Farnen, R. F. *Civic education in ten countries: An empirical study. International studies in evaluation*. Vol. 4. New York: Wiley, 1976.

Van Doorninck, W. J., Caldwell, B. M., Wright, C., & Frankenburg, W. K. The relationship between 12-month home stimulation and school achievement. *Child Development*, 1981, **52**, 1080–1083.

Vygotsky, L. B. *Thought and language*. Cambridge, Mass.: M.I.T. Press, 1962.

Walberg, H. J., & Shanahan, T. High school effects on individual students. *Educational Researcher*, 1983, **12**, 4–9.

Weikart, D. P., Deloria, D. J., Lawser, S. A., & Wiegerink, R. Longitudinal results of the Perry Preschool Project. *Monographs of the High/Scope Educational Research Foundation*. Vol. 1. Ypsilanti, Mich.: High/Scope Foundation, 1970.

Weiner, B. A theory of motivation for some classroom experiences. *Journal of Educational Psychology*, 1979, **71**, 3–25.

Weiner, B. *Human motivation*. New York: Holt, Rinehart & Winston, 1980.

Weiner, B. Some methodological pitfalls in attributional research. *Journal of Educational Psychology*, 1983, **75**, 530–543.

Wertsch, J. V., McNamee, G. D., McLane, J. B., & Budwig, N. A. The adult-child dyad as a problem-solving system. *Child Development*, 1980, **51**, 1215–1221.

Williams, T. Abilities and environments. In W. H. Sewell, R. M. Hauser, & D. L. Featherman (Eds.), *Schooling and achievement in American society*. New York: Academic Press, 1976.

Willis, S., & Brophy, J. Origins of teachers' attitudes toward young children. *Journal of Educational Psychology*, 1974, **66**, 520–529.

Wolf, R. *The identification and measurement of environmental process variables related to intelligence*. Unpublished doctoral dissertation, University of Chicago, 1964.

Wolf, R. Achievement in the United States. In H. J. Walberg (Ed.), *Educational environments and effects*. Berkeley, Calif.: McCutchan, 1979.

Wood, D. J. Teaching the young child: Some relationships between social interaction, language and thought. In D. R. Olson (Ed.), *The social foundation of language and thought*. New York: Norton, 1980.

Wylie, R. *The self-concept*. (Vol. 2): *Theory and research on selected topics*. Lincoln: University of Nebraska Press, 1979.

7   Work, Family, and the Socialization of the Child

LOIS WLADIS HOFFMAN

University of Michigan

How does work affect the family and, in turn, the child? Whether we mean by work the employment status of the parents and their particular jobs, or work in the sense of the economic organization of the society generally, the influence is pervasive and profound. Family size, kinship structure, authority relations, the division of household tasks, marital stability, material resources, the amount of time members spend together, interaction patterns, attitudes and ideology, child-rearing goals, intra- and interpersonal tensions—there are data to show that all of these are affected by work.

And yet we know very little about the psychological linkage between these two major spheres of life—work and family. There are anthropology studies showing how kinship structures and women's roles are tied to the predominant economic activity of the society (Blumberg, 1974); there are historical studies showing how the change from agriculture to industrialized manufacturing changed the nature of family life (Anderson, 1971; Smelser, 1959); and wonderful micro-analytic studies, such as Tilly's (1980) study of the turn-of-the-century weaving families in northern France, showing how work life and family life were almost indistinguishable in certain occupational settings. Demographers have demonstrated the link between economics and family size—showing, for example, how the quick harvesting of the rice crop, when it is threatened by heavy rains, as in the Philippines, requires the assistance of many children, thus making the utility of a large family greater than the cost (Hoffman & Hoffman, 1973; Mueller, 1976). But psychologists have only rarely focused on the relationship between these two major institutions of society.

There were a few ground-breaking studies, like Kohn's work (1959a, 1959b, 1963) on how social class affects child-rearing styles and Miller and Swanson's study (1958) of how the larger economic setting, entrepreneurial or bureaucratic, influences the link between social class and child rearing, but little was built on the broken ground. Some studies in the fifties

(Hoffman & Lippitt, 1960; McKinley, 1964; Oeser & Hammond, 1954) considered the relationship between the power potential of the man's job and his power expression in the family, but they operated from a simple two-variable hypothesis. Since in some cases there is compensation (the man who is power frustrated on his job expressing his power needs in the family) and in other cases there is carryover (the man who is accustomed to expressing power carrying that pattern into his home), the two-variable approach yielded little. But, by and large, few psychologists even tackled the topic. The major reason, as Bronfenbrenner and Crouter (1982) have suggested, is not that the questions are unimportant, but rather that they are very complex. It cannot be done with two variables. As has been pointed out before (Bronfenbrenner & Crouter, 1982; Hoffman, 1974c; Hoffman & Lippitt, 1960; Lewin, 1935), the many links in the chain of causality need to be spelled out and attention needs to be paid to the conditioning variables. Only by attending to the complexity—in the theories constructed and the empirical designs executed—can progress be made.

Because the data are limited, this review will focus more on conceptualization than on research results. Four major independent variables will be considered: (a) the general economic conditions, (b) socioeconomic class, (c) the father's job, and (d) the mother's job. Empirical work will be brought in illustratively, but the major focus will be on explicating how these variables might affect the family and the child. At this point in our knowledge, it seems that there is more value both for future research and for practical application in spelling out these conceptual links than in an exhaustive research review.[1]

It is difficult to select any aspect of family life that does not affect the child, but the child will be the focus here. For this reason, the chapter will deal with the effects of work on the family, rather than the reverse, though the influence is clearly two directional (Kahn, 1980; Rossi, 1971). Finally, although this is a topic where cross-cultural and historical analysis is relevant, the chapter will concentrate on the United States today.

GENERAL ECONOMIC CONDITIONS

The primary unit of analysis in this chapter will be the individual family, and the main focus will be on the occupations of the parents; nevertheless,

---

[1]Bronfenbrenner and Crouter (1982) provide an excellent review of work and the family and the impact on the child from a historical perspective, and Kanter (1977) has a very thorough review of work and the family from a sociological vantage. There are also several recent reviews of the effects of maternal employment on the child (Hoffman, 1979, 1980b, 1981).

it is important to keep in mind that the general prevailing economic-occupational setting also affects the child through his family. These general economic conditions may include a broad range of factors, such as the degree of technology; the dominant economic activity; the nature of economic organization; the economic cycles, such as depression and prosperity; labor force participation rates of men, women, and children; and other economic and occupational patterns that more or less describe the society as a whole or a meaningful social unit or community within the society. In considering the impact of economic factors at this broad level, three kinds of influence will be noted: (*a*) general economic conditions may be important determinants of the family and child-rearing patterns throughout the society, affecting even families outside their immediate wake; (*b*) general economic conditions may affect family life through intervening variables (i.e., they may increase the likelihood of an event taking place that will, in turn, affect the child and the family); (*c*) general conditions may provide a setting which influences the relationship between other variables that are closer to the family on the causal chain. The distinction among these different kinds of influence could be applied to any of the four classes of independent variables to be discussed in this chapter—general economic conditions, social class, father's job, or mother's job. It seems more important to consider these distinctions here, however, because the general economic condition represents a level that is rarely operationalized or even considered in psychology. It is more remote from the behavior to be explained. The more formal explication of the different patterns of influence exerted, then, seems particularly useful here.

AS INDEPENDENT VARIABLE

Conceptualizing the prevailing economic conditions as the independent variable is not the métier of the child psychologist, who, in America at least, seeks to explain individual differences more than commonalities. For the historian interested in social change, effects of general social conditions are crucial, and changes in family life over time are often seen as the result of changed economic conditions. For the sociologist or anthropologist interested in examining the conditions that shape one social group and distinguish it from another, the prevailing economic context is a natural independent variable. Thus, historians and sociologists have spelled out repeatedly the significance of industrialization for the family form (Ogburn & Nimkoff, 1955; Parsons, 1955; Schneider, 1957; Smelser, 1959). With increased and advanced industrialization, the amount of economic activity that can be effectively carried out inside the family has diminished. Not only does the father now earn his living outside the home, but increasingly the mother's economic contribution has shifted there. Education requirements for children increase, and children move from being an economic asset to being an economic liability. The modern conjugal family as we know it is seen as primarily a product of economics and the organization of work.

An important theme in the relationship between the economic setting and the family's socialization of the child, one that comes from anthropology and sociology but has been picked up and developed by psychologists, builds on the idea that the family socializes the child for the adult roles he or she will occupy (Barry, Bacon, & Child, 1957). Since the economic activities and organization shape and almost define the adult roles, the socialization pattern will be heavily affected. In a hunting society, for example, those traits likely to be valued and encouraged in sons are the traits that are functional to effective hunting—courage, strength, dexterity, timing. It is not that parents planfully encourage these traits in order to make their sons good hunters, but rather that in such a society these traits have been associated with the most successful men and have acquired a desirability that seems intrinsic. The toys and games of children also reflect their eventual adult roles. In the hunting society the male child's toys are miniature tools of the hunter and the games incorporate hunting forms.

This general idea that the occupational roles of the parents affect their socialization patterns so that children are shaped for similar adult roles has been invoked in several psychological investigations and theories. Hoffman (1977), for example, has suggested that sex differences in socialization patterns reflect the traditional expectation that girls will grow up to be mothers and boys will grow up to be breadwinners. Accordingly, little girls have been encouraged to develop those traits that are consistent with mothering, and their toys and games are miniature versions of the mother role. Boys, on the other hand, have been encouraged to develop traits consistent with the occupational roles of the society, and their toys and games are miniature versions of occupational roles. With increased female employment across the life span, however, and with the decrease in family size and the percentage of the adult years devoted to active mothering, corresponding changes in socialization practices are occurring. As the adult occupational roles of men and women converge, a corresponding decrease in sex-differentiated child-rearing patterns is predicted.

The work of Miller and Swanson (1958) might be similarly conceptualized. These investigators hypothesized that the child-rearing patterns of parents would reflect those values and goals that were consistent with the traits a man experienced as valuable in his work. They suggested that American society had been moving from an entrepreneurial style of occupational organization to a bureaucratic style. The former pattern, characterized by smaller business organizations, simple division of labor, and mobility through competition and risk taking, was seen as consistent with child-rearing patterns that encouraged independent achievement, individual responsibility, and self-control. Bureaucratic occupational structure, on the other hand, characterized by large organizations, with several levels of authority, greater job security through seniority, and mobility through interpersonal skills and the ability to have smooth relations within the organization, was seen as consistent with child-rearing patterns less interested in self-control than accommodation and stressing interpersonal interaction more than independence. The theory was consistent with the idea that child-rearing patterns in the country were being *generally* affected as the society moved toward the bureaucratic occupational structure, although the empirical investigation compared families with fathers employed in the entrepreneurial setting and families with fathers in the bureaucratic. On the whole, these findings supported the hypothesis; setting differences were more pronounced than the more conventional class differences. Despite the importance of this theory, subsequent research has been meager (Caudill & Weinstein, 1969; Gold & Slater, 1958).

The study has been criticized (Kanter, 1977) for not sufficiently spelling out the linkages between the occupational setting and child-rearing patterns, particularly those of the wife, but the implication of this work is that occupational pursuits shape the parents' values and affect their notions of what qualities will be valuable for children, thus influencing their child-rearing patterns.

The prevailing economic-occupational structure in these various examples is seen as affecting the family life and socialization patterns in the society generally, even for those families whose economic pursuits do not conform to the majority. Thus, even the nonhunting families in the hunting society will not be immune from the social milieu. While they may be different in important respects from their neighbors, even they are likely to value the hunting-relevant traits more than comparable members of a nonhunting society. At the same time, while the occupational structure of a society may exert an influence on families generally, the impact may be more immediate on the families that conform to the general type. Thus, in Hoffman's work, diminished sex differentiation in child-rearing was expected to occur in both the families with employed and nonemployed mothers because even though the nonemployed mothers may not directly participate in the new occupational form, they experience it through their observations and the new social milieu. The change, however, occurs most rapidly in the employed-mother homes, where the impact is direct and salient, and the new child-rearing pattern is functionally more appropriate for the family needs. Similarly, in the Miller and Swanson work it was expected that where the father was engaged in a bureaucratic occupation the family socialization pattern would be different from where he was engaged in an entrepreneurial occupation, yet the former pattern was seen as becoming the dominant one and the more pervasive, affecting eventually even the entrepreneurial family.[2]

Both of these analyses, it should be noted, involved not only an effort to show how occupational structure can affect child-rearing patterns via the family, but also a hypothesis about social change: Changes in the occupational structure of a society will bring about changes in the child-rearing patterns of a society. The hypothesis suggests a sort of self-adjusting mechanism. Through this process persons are socialized to fit the new economic roles. Erikson (1963) has proposed that there is a match between the socialization effects of the culture-specific child-rearing practices employed to meet the child's needs at each developmental stage and the personalities appropriate for the society's functioning. This process would suggest a mechanism by which such a match is achieved in a changing society.

EFFECT THROUGH AN INTERVENING VARIABLE

In the above examples, the effects of the economic-occupational structure pervade the entire society. Though the timing and intensity of their impact on various families may differ, effects are carried through various cultural forms, the media, and even—in modern America—through the advice of child-rearing experts. A different type of approach to the study of how general economic conditions affect the child and the family is taken by Elder (1974, 1978) in some of his work on the effects of the Great Depression. Although some of Elder's analysis and discussion suggests general effects of the economic cycle, his major work focuses on distinguishing families whose incomes declined sharply from those who were relatively nondeprived. In this interesting longitudinal research, Elder notes that the families that suffered substantial financial loss experienced (a) shifts in the economic roles of family members, with increased economic activities by mothers and teenagers; (b) changes in family relationships and authority patterns; and (c) emotional strain. The children who were in early adolescence at the time were studied up into middle age. By and large, the children in the financially affected families, particularly those who were

---

[2]As a somewhat different example, in a cross-cultural study of parents' perceptions of the benefits and costs of having children (Hoffman, 1980c), it was found that parents involved in agriculture were most likely to cite the economic advantage of children and to value large families. But also, in the countries that were predominantly agricultural, even the urban families involved in manufacturing were more likely to subscribe to these values than their counterparts in nonagricultural countries.

middle class before the Depression, showed positive effects from this stress. Compared to youths in the families that were not affected, their subsequent development showed better success educationally, maritally, and in terms of personal satisfaction. The positive effect seemed to be the result of the greater responsibility and family cooperation that was imposed upon them as the family coped with the financial loss.

In this particular analysis, the general economic state, the Depression, affects the family in that it increases the chances that a family will undergo severe economic hardship. It operates, in this case, through an intervening variable, the family's financial loss. The effects are not observed in the contemporaneous families that were less affected by the prevailing economic conditions.

THE ECONOMIC SETTING AS A CONDITIONING VARIABLE

Although it is rarely studied empirically, one way in which the general economic environment influences the family and the child is through its effect on the relationships among other variables. Thus it is reasonable to suppose that some of the stigma of the father's job loss during the Depression was mitigated by the widespread nature of such occurrences.[3] It is a stress to be jobless in a jobless world; it is a different stress, and perhaps a greater one, to be jobless in a period of prosperity. Thus the relationships among the variables under investigation may be different in one economic setting than in another.

Perhaps the clearest example of the possible impact of the economic setting as a conditioning variable can be made by considering the effects of maternal employment on the child. The relationship between the mother's employment status and a family or child outcome variable might be different in studies carried out during the early fifties than in studies carried out in the mid eighties. The prevailing economic situation in the United States was quite different in these two times. In the early fifties, maternal employment was uncommon and even rare if the mother had preschool children; in the eighties, maternal employment is the mode. The mothers who worked during the fifties were a "select" group; compared to other women they were either particularly motivated or particularly able. From that fact alone the effects on their families would be different from the effects on families when most mothers work simply as a matter of course or social expectation. In addition, the world frowned on employed mothers in

---

[3]That the father's job was a stigma leading to loss of status in the family even during the Depression, however, is documented in several studies of that period (Angell, 1936; Komorovsky, 1940; Cavan & Ranck, 1938).

the fifties; they were under pressure from others and from themselves to prove their employment was not having the adverse effects expected. It is possible that their excellent record of avoiding such effects, as well as some of their failures, such as the occasionally noted guilt response that led to overcompensation (Hoffman, 1961), were a function of that internal and external censure that is much diminished today. The children of employed mothers in the eighties no longer need think of themselves as special either. It is reasonable then to assume that the increased labor force participation of mothers, a marked economic change in the United States, is not only a factor in itself that affects the American family, as discussed above, but it also impacts on the relationship between the mother's employment status and the family or child outcomes. In a period of high maternal employment, the correlates of mother's employment status might be quite different from when employment rates are low.

SUMMARY

Thus, at a macro-analytic level, the economic organization and conditions of society affect the family and the child in a variety of ways. They may operate as independent variables affecting, for example, the prevailing child-rearing goals of the society. Or they may operate through an intervening variable: The example cited was based on Elder's study of the 1930s Depression. This economic condition increased the likelihood of financial loss for families, and some of the effects were quite specific to whether or not the particular family experienced severe loss. Finally, this broad level of economic influence can also operate as a conditioning variable, affecting the interaction among other more micro-analytic variables. In some ways, for example, the father's unemployment may be different when paternal unemployment is general than when it is less common. Similarly, maternal employment may have a different significance for the family and the child when it is a prevalent pattern than when it is unusual. As indicated above, however, economic variables, considered at this broad level, are not often examined in developmental psychology. More attention has been given to the other major independent variables to be considered here—social class, the father's job, and the mother's job.

SOCIAL CLASS

Through his family, a child is assigned to a particular social class, an assignment based largely on the father's occupation. It represents the child's socioeconomic position in society and much of his development is shaped by this status. The child's access to health facilities, nutrition, and education; his physical environment, neighborhood, and peers; the kind of child-rearing patterns he experiences; the size of his family, its authority structure, and its stability—all are related to social class. So pervasive is the influence of social class that it is a standard procedure to control on class in any child development study designed to examine the relationship between other variables. That is, so many independent and dependent variables in developmental research relate to social class that one must pull out its effects in order to examine other relationships.

There is not total consensus among social scientists about how social class should be defined, though there is considerable agreement about the components that distinguish the social classes—the occupation of the father, family income, education, social status, power, and a style of life. The father's occupation as the major determinant of the family's social class position has been defended by a number of social scientists (Aldous, Osmond, & Hicks, 1979; Blau & Duncan, 1967a; Caplow, 1853; Hall, 1975), but social class is such a global concept that some experts have suggested that the term be abandoned entirely and only the more specific components be used in analysis. In addition, researchers have differed as to how many levels need to be distinguished in considering social class. Although the seminal work by Warner, Meeker, and Eells (1949) distinguished six groups, most of the child development research has contrasted only two, distinguishing only between a "middle class" (sometimes called "white collar") and a "lower class" (sometimes called "blue collar"). Furthermore, the lower class selected for study has sometimes included semiskilled workers with fairly steady employment and sometimes focused only on the families of unskilled workers with frequently reoccurring periods of unemployment. In addition, few studies have explored the dynamics of racial or ethnic components of social class behavior, though several have controlled these variables statistically, while others have explored social class differences within groups homogeneous with respect to race (Davis & Havighurst, 1946; Hess & Shipman, 1965).

These issues of conceptualization and measurement have been discussed in a number of previous publications and thus need not be repeated here (Aldous et al., 1979; Bendix & Lipset, 1953, 1956; Hess, 1970). In trying to integrate the results of the various social class studies, however, it is important to keep in mind the differences among studies in how social class has been operationalized. This problem is paramount where research findings from different investigations are inconsistent; apparent inconsistencies in research results often occur because different operational definitions have been used (Block, 1976). The problem is less severe, however, when research findings converge. In the potpourri of data on the relationship between social class and the child's family experience, there is enough cross-study consistency to pull out some common observations and to speculate about the process that is involved.

Another source of differences among studies in their findings is a quite different one: different results may reflect historical change. In previous reviews of the literature on social class differences in child-rearing patterns, which cover investigations conducted since 1928 (Bronfenbrenner, 1958; Deutsch, 1973; Hess, 1970), there are revealed both constancies over the years and changes. Bronfenbrenner has noted, for example, the shift from before World War II, when middle-class mothers were less likely to breast-feed, earlier to wean, and less likely to feed on demand, to the more recent pattern where the social class differences on these behaviors are reversed. On the other hand, the difference noted by Duvall (1946) in the forties that lower-class parents valued obedience and respect for authority more than middle-class parents has been consistent over the years. A hypothesis to explain these shifts and constancies might be that, as Bronfenbrenner suggests, the middle class is more responsive to the advice of experts, and so for those parental behaviors that are subject to expert opinion, social class differences may shift, with the middle class being quicker to adopt the newly touted way and the lower class shifting only after a delay. In contrast, however, when the child-rearing pattern reflects values that characterize the way the parents relate to other institutions— their occupational roles per se or their occupationally derived status and power in the society generally—the stability of the child-rearing differences may prevail as long as the class differences in relationships to other institutions prevail.

The precesses by which the child is shaped by social class membership are manifold, and only a few will be considered here. The discussion will concentrate on these more stable social class differences in child-rearing patterns. For a more thorough coverage of the vast literature on social class influences on the child's socialization in the family, the reader is referred to previous reviews by Aldous et al. (1979), Bronfenbrenner (1958), Deutsch (1973), Gecas (1979), and Hess (1970).

POWER IN SOCIETY AND PARENTAL INFLUENCE TECHNIQUES

Though work demands and job characteristics may vary from occupation to occupation within a social class, as will be discussed later in this chapter, the members of a socioeconomic class generally share a common power position and similar opportunity structures. The view that lower-class parents have less power in society than middle-class parents has often been cited as one of the factors behind social class differences in child-rearing patterns.

A repeated finding over the years is that lower-class parents in their attempts to influence their children rely on ascribed power more than middle- or upper-class parents. Thus, they are more likely to say "Do it" "Because I say so," or "That's the rule." They are more likely to use what M. L. Hoffman (1960) calls "power assertive techniques." They are less likely, on the other hand, to give reasons for the requirement, try to induce the child to become intrinsically motivated to comply, or attend to extenuating circumstances that the child might bring out, all of which are more characteristic of middle- and upper-class parents (Bernstein, 1961, 1964; Bronfenbrenner, 1958; Cohen & Hodges, 1963; Hess & Shipman, 1965. 1967; M. L. Hoffman, 1960, Kohn, 1959a, 1959b, 1963, 1980; Waters & Crandall, 1964).

This style of parent-child interaction reflects the parent's own experience in the social system. The lower-class parent's supervisor on the job is not likely to explain the basis for rules and requirements and, since the lower-class person is not likely to participate in the setting up of the rules or to be involved in the overall operation, it is quite likely that he is not familiar with the substantive rationale of his workplace and its functioning. Its rules may thus often seem arbitrary and absolute. The lower-class person's experiences with the other institutions of society are similar. He is not likely to take part in setting their policies but is subject to their rules. He is not in a good position for special consideration; he lacks the influence and the know-how to circumvent their impact. From the vantage of the lower-class adult, a "rule is a rule"; understanding it is difficult and useless; it applies without regard to extenuating circumstances. Since the lower-class adult is more likely to have authoritarian, rule-governed experiences himself, his views of the social order are affected, and so are his asymmetric power interactions in his family. He is less involved in the making, changing, and bending of rules in society, so the existence of rules and authority structures seems more compelling than their rationale. As a parent, the mother may know the hygienic basis for the requirement that her child brush his teeth, but the real answer to "why?" is "because you are supposed to" or "because I said so."

In addition, unqualified power-assertive influence techniques are much more efficient. Because of larger families, less adequate housing, and fewer resources, the lower-class mother may not be in a position to afford the luxury of the more time-consuming reason-based patterns.

The effects of discipline based on the assertion of power and rules rather than on explanation, reasoning, and induction have been documented in a number of different research projects. Hess, Shipman, Brophy, and Baer (1968) have not only shown that lower-class mothers use this type of control more than middle class, but have also demonstrated that the use of such control is negatively related to performance on cognitive tasks, reading readiness, and verbal development as measured by laboratory performance and standard tests. Bernstein (1958, 1960, 1964) has suggested that this distinction between the social classes in parent-child interaction leads to two different styles of linguistic codes—restricted and elaborated, with greater linguistic versatility by the middle-class child the result. M. L. Hoffman (1960; Hoffman & Saltzstein, 1967) has provided data to show that the use of these different types of influence techniques affects the child's moral development. The heavy use of unqualified power assertion is associated with aggressiveness in the child and an externalized morality, that is, moral conformity to avoid punishment. Inductive discipline, on the other hand, is associated with a more flexible and humanistically based conscience in the child. The specific theories differ, but among the processes seen as connecting the lower-class style of parental influence techniques to these outcomes are: (*a*) they engender in the child a sense of inefficacy, (*b*) they fail to communicate rationality in life, and (*c*) they do not provide verbal enrichment.

The lower-class style of parent-child interaction reflects the parent's own sense of inefficacy in the larger society, and it engenders that same sense in the child (Battle & Rotter, 1963; Hess, 1970). The child is controlled by the greater power of his parents and inescapable absolute rules, just as the parent is controlled in relationships outside the family. This is in contrast with the middle-class child, who is more often given the basis for the required behavior so that it feels less coercive, is capable of being changed, and can sometimes be affected by him. A sense of efficacy is seen as an important prerequisite for academic achievement, political action, and efforts to affect a wide variety of outcomes (Crandall, Katkovsky, & Crandall, 1965; Kar, 1971; Lefcourt, 1966).

Particularly important, the middle-class child is learning that there is rationality in the world. He is being given training in reasoning, the concept that order and events have a rational base, and reward for his own reasoning because a well-thought-out response can sometimes elicit a reprieve. Much of cognitive development takes place because the child seeks order and rationality in his experiences. New experiences and the accumulation of cognitive discrepancies will lead to a higher level of understanding most effectively when the child expects to find a rational order. The parent who bolsters his discipline with reasons communicates to the child that there is order and rationality to life, an important element in cognitive development.

Finally, the middle-class style requires more verbal interaction. The explanations that accompany the parental influence techniques are not only training in reasoning for the child but also training in language use. The sentences are longer and more complex. A verbal response by the child is frequently called for, or at least appropriate and acceptable.

Thus there are several theories that suggest that because lower-class parents have a low power position in which they are subject to rules and authorities both on the job (Kohn, 1959a, 1959b, 1963, 1980) and in relation to the other institutions of society (Hess & Shipman, 1965, 1967), their parent-child interaction replicates their experience but with them in the authority roles. This kind of interaction in turn is seen as affecting the child, leading to his own feelings of inefficacy (Battle & Rotter, 1963; Strodtbeck, 1958), providing a less enriching cognitive environment (Bernstein, 1958, 1960, 1964; Hess et al., 1968), and leading to a less flexible and less altruistic morality (M. L. Hoffman, 1960; Hoffman & Saltzstein, 1967).

SIMILARITY OF SOCIAL CLASS IN FAMILY AND SCHOOL

A related process by which the child is molded by his social class membership focuses not on the child-rearing patterns within the home but on the compatibility between the family's socioeconomic class and the class patterns prevailing in other relevant institutions of society. Particular attention has been given to the schools. Schools have been described as middle class. The teachers, curriculum, goals, and expected behavior have all been seen as based on middle-class values (Charters, 1963; McGuire, 1950; Warner, Havighurst, & Loeb, 1944). The transition from home to school is thus seen as easier for the middle-class child. For him there is consistency between the values of his family and the school. He enters having had experience in the kind of behavior required. His speech, manners, and dress conform to the expectations of teachers, thus increasing the rapport between them. He is accustomed to the symbolic reward system used by the school, unlike the lower-class child who is more motivated by tangible rewards (Terrel, Durkin, & Wiesley, 1959; Zigler & DeLabry, 1962). Since education is more likely to be relevant to the occupations of his parents and his own occupational goal, it is more meaningful in his life. Middle-class parents are also more comfortable in the school setting and are more likely than lower-class parents to attend school functions and communicate with teachers. Thus, the major institution in the child's life besides the family is experienced very differently by children growing up in a lower-class family environment and in a middle-class one. The stress between the lower-class family and the school is expressed in the often-reported orientation toward school given by lower-class mothers—"Keep out of trouble" (Hess & Shipman, 1968). It suggests a hostile environment and sets the child up for one.

RESOURCES AVAILABLE

Another group of factors by which social class affects the family and the child has to do with differences in the resources available. Health care, food, appropriate equipment, and space are all differentially distributed to families along social class lines (Kovar, 1981). Deutsch (1963) has focused on the high noise level in the lower-class home in its dysfunction for language development and for developing effective attention sets. Some researchers have been particularly concerned with the divergencies in educational opportunities, for even when the effects of ability are controlled there are social class differences in access to higher education (Aldous et al., 1979).

An additional resource that seems to be differentially available is parental time: the amount of attention each child receives from parents varies with social class. Lower-class parents engage in less personally directed speech and less reciprocal interaction even with infants (Kagan, 1978), both of which are important for cognitive development (Levenstein, 1970). Data also show that lower-class parents spend less time in child-care activities generally (Hill & Stafford, 1978). Furthermore, they have more children to care for (Campbell, 1968; Orshansky, 1965). Particular significance is attached to this last pattern by the extensive documentation by Zajonc and Markus (1975) of a negative association between family size and IQ. Furthermore, the adverse effect of increased family size is augmented by lower-class status. In lower-class families statistically significant IQ differences are noted between children in families with two and three children; in upper-middle-class families, comparable differences occur between four and five children (Clausen & Clausen, 1973).

SOCIAL CLASS AND FAMILY STRESS

One final aspect of social class, and particularly lower-class status, should be mentioned. Because of larger families and limited resources, there is likely to be a higher level of stress in the lower-class family and a greater vulnerability to crisis. This higher stress can affect the child in a number of ways. First, it can have a direct impact, for the child is affected by being reared in a stressful environment. In addition, it has already been noted that some of the child-rearing patterns of the lower class could be a reaction to the stress of day-to-day life rather than (or in addition to) reflecting the values and patterns of their work and general social situation. Thus, the lower class has consistently over the years shown a greater demand for obedience by children and used more power-assertive and physical discipline. Some theories (e.g., Kohn, 1963) have explained this as a pattern that reflects the nature of lower-class jobs, and some theories (e.g., Hess & Shipman, 1967) see this as reflecting the nature of lower-class interactions with the various institutions of society. It is also possible that it is a response to stress. The harassed parent does not have the time and patience to explain to the child or to negotiate. Power-assertive techniques and the demand for obedience have an efficiency. Such techniques, and particularly the use of physical punishment, are often resorted to even in middle-class families when the parent feels hassled or upset. It is possible that these patterns then come out of the more stressful life conditions and that they become legitimized as a form of dissonance reduction; that is, the parent rationalizes as acceptable the behavior he or she engages in out of stress.

Furthermore, the high level of stress in the lower class makes it more difficult for the family to cope with new problems or a crisis situation. Thus death, divorce, and illness may have a more debilitating effect on the family and the child when even noncrisis functioning involves strain. Herzog and Sudia (1973) have suggested that the negative effects of father absence occur because of the income loss, and this is more traumatic in the lower class because it is often a push into extreme poverty. These effects may also be exacerbated in the lower class because there is less emotional resiliency.

High stress and coping difficulties are often seen as the link between lower-class status and higher rates of certain social pathologies, such as juvenile delinquency, teenage pregnancy, and child abuse. The correlation between social class and social problems is often confused by class-related differences in detection and reporting, but there are studies suggesting that the high levels of family stress often associated with poverty increase the likelihood of these outcomes (Gil, 1970; Parke & Collmer, 1975). Thus the high level of strain in the lower-class family has a direct impact on the child and also an indirect impact through its effects on family interaciton patterns and reactions to crisis.

* * *

Clearly, social class, like the economic system generally, affects the family and the child directly, through certain intervening variables that may not always occur, and by providing a setting that influences the interaction of other variables. The processes of influence discussed here have only lightly touched on a vast and important topic that has been extensively analyzed and researched. Yet, despite an enormous volume of data (not all of good quality) indicating the existence of social class differences, there is still a great deal that is not yet known about how these differences operate to bring about effects on the family and the child.

Perhaps because the task seems so great, the influence of social class so pervasive, and the results of previous efforts so frustrating and inadequate, some researchers have turned instead to a more focused question: How does the parent's particular job affect the family? This question is not concerned with the money the job brings or its impact on the family's position in the social status system, but rather on the job as it is experienced by the worker. It is a more limited question, but it, too, is not an easily answered one.

The Father's Job

Almost all of the research that has focused on the nature of the parent's job as affecting the family has considered only the father's employment. The maternal employment studies, which will be discussed in the next section, have concentrated mainly on whether or not there is a job, sometimes on whether it is part or full time, but rarely on the kind of job it is. The father's job, however, has been considered from a number of standpoints. One group of studies follows the general line of the hypothesis already discussed—that the parent comes to value the traits that are required for success in his work and to encourage these qualities in his children. A second group of studies views the link between occupation and family in terms of the father's psychological state. Certain needs, habits, or satisfactions are created on the job and these affect the father's behavior in the family. A third group of studies to be considered here defines the work in terms of time demands and explores how the father's availability affects the family. The fourth group focuses on the situations where job performance requires the participation or cooperation of other family members. Finally, there is a limited body of research that has investigated the impact on the family of the father's job loss—of unemployment—and this topic will also be discussed.

OCCUPATION AS SHAPER OF VALUES

Kohn's work (1963, 1980) is meant to be a study of social class more than specific job effects, but his hypothesis is that the structure and content of activities in the father's job affect his value orientations and his child-rearing practices. According to Kohn, middle-class or white-collar occupations involve manipulating ideas, symbols, and interpersonal relations and require flexibility, thought, and judgment. Lower-class or blue-collar occupations require manipulating physical objects and are more standardized, less complex, and more supervised. Because of these differences, middle-class fathers would be expected to value self-direction and independence in their children—qualities demanded by their own occupations—while lower-class fathers would value obedience and conformity. Kohn's data supported this prediction, and more-or-or less corresponding differences in reported child-rearing practices were also found: lower-class parents used more physical punishment and judged the child's misbehavior in terms of the consequences, while middle-class parents used more "psychological" discipline, such as "love withdrawal," and judged misbehavior in terms of the child's intent. Further, when the father's job involved autonomy and working with people, the parents were more likely to stress achievement, independence, and self-reliance to their children (Pearlin & Kohn, 1966). Many of the differences predicted by Kohn's theory have been found in other studies (Gecas & Nye, 1974; Pearlin, 1970), but whether or not these differences are a function of the nature of the father's job is not clear. Even in Kohn's work, education seemed to have an effect independent of the job per se, while the work of Lueptow, McClendon, and McKeon (1979) suggests education is the more potent variable and, further, that the data supporting Kohn's hypothesis have not adequately controlled on the related extrinsic aspects of the father's occupation. The real test of this specific hypothesis requires examining differences among occupations within the same general socioeconomic class and education category, but it is very difficult to untangle the independent effects of these highly interrelated variables.

Very little research of this sort.has been carried out. The idea that specific occupations can become shapers of values that extend into the family was developed by the sociologist Everett Hughes (1958), but the accompanying research focused on the community of workers in specific occupations, not on family effects. A few small studies have tried to relate specific within-class occupations to parental discipline techniques (Steinmetz, 1974) and at-home leisure patterns (Gerstl, 1961) and these show certain consistencies between job patterns and family behavior, but it is difficult to unravel the causal connection. If, for example, a college professor values education for his children more than a businessman does, is it because he is a professor? Or is he a professor because he values education?

In a study of college students, Mortimer (1974, 1976) demonstrated that sons did tend to choose their fathers' occupations, or, if not the same, to pick jobs involving similar occupational experiences and rewards, a pattern which has been seen as reflecting the communication of values from father to son. The findings also indicated that the most effective transmission of vocational values from father to son occurred when there was a close father-son relationship with a prestigious father—the combination that in several previous studies has been associated with sons' identification and modeling (Hetherington, 1967; Hoffman, 1961).

It is important to note that there are such conditioning factors—that is, that other aspects of the situation may influence whether or not parent-child similarity in occupational outlook is likely to develop. In fact, under some conditions, effects can be reversed. The parent's work can be experienced negatively by the parents, or perceived negatively by the child, and thus affect the child's occupational choice in a different direction. Immigrant parents, for example, have sometimes been described as pushing their children toward education in order to escape their parents' occupational roles (Howe, 1976; Sarasan, 1973). And, though the general pattern shows mother-daughter similarity in employment status, daughters of nonemployed mothers will sometimes choose a career to avoid their mothers' fate (Bram, 1974), while, in at least one study (Baruch, 1972a), daughters of employed mothers who saw the dual role as a hardship were likely to choose nonemployment for themselves.

THE FATHER'S PSYCHOLOGICAL STATE

A psychological process commonly assumed to link the father's occupation with his family role is a frustration-aggression model: the job creates frustrations that the father takes out in the family. A man may be on the bottom of the power hierarchy at work, but he is on the top at home; aggression engendered on the job that cannot be expressed there for fear of negative sanctions is displaced to the safer target, the family. The idea of parental authority over children as a compensation for power frustration at work comes up in the work of Blau and Duncan (1967b) and Hoffman and Manis (1979), and some empirical support comes from research by McKinley (1964). Particularly at the higher socioeconomic levels, McKinley found that fathers low in autonomy in their work were more likely to be hostile and severe with their sons. Rainwater (1965), in a study of the lower-income family, presents data suggesting that the occupationally frustrated father may take out his frustrations on his wife, while Hoffman's data (M. L. Hoffman, 1960) suggest that power assertiveness by the father over the wife leads to assertiveness by the mother over the child in what is interpreted as a pecking order.

The idea of the family as fulfilling complementary needs, needs unsatisfied or aroused at work, does not have to imply a negative effect on the family, as in the frustration-aggression hypotheses. In Hoffman's work on the value of children to parents (Hoffman & Hoffman, 1973; Hoffman &

Manis, 1979; Hoffman, Thorton, & Manis, 1978), children are seen as satisfying those psychological needs that are not met by other aspects of life. While these may be power needs, they may also be needs for morality or self-esteem, needs for a sense of accomplishment, needs for affiliative satisfaction, needs for fun and stimulation. An implication of this work is that to the extent that these needs are not satisfied on the job, the man may seek to satisfy them in the family. Energy, effort, warm interaction, high performance standards, enthusiasm, and joy may thus go into parenting because the job is not an alternative source of gratification.

To see the family as a place to express the frustrations of the job, or as an alternative source of gratifying needs not satisfied on the job, or as providing compensation of any sort is to expect a difference in the man's behavior in these two worlds. A very different hypothesis is that there will be carry-over of style. Although there are data consistent with this view (Gerstl, 1961; Steinmetz, 1974), it is very difficult to know whether the similarity of behavior is sheer habit carry-over, or a reflection of values formed on the job as discussed above, or correlation without causality, a function of self-selection. Several studies have tried to show that certain personalities are attracted to certain occupations (Roe, 1956), and thus it is possible that some of the similarity in behavior in the two settings reflects the qualities of the person and not the effects of one setting on the other. The idea of the preacher who preaches to his family, the salesman who "sells" the behaviors he wants his children to follow, or the professor who answers his children's questions with a lecture is popularly believed but rarely researched. The two hypotheses—one of compensation between the two roles and one of carry-over—are not really incompatible. It is quite possible that gratifying behaviors are replicated, while needs generated or left unsatisfied on the job lead to compensatory gratification seeking in the family.

Another theory of carry-over—mood carry-over—has been seen as the link between occupation and family (Dyer, 1964; Hammond, 1954; Sennett & Cobb, 1972). This is recently represented by the work of Piotrkowski (1979). Piotrkowski has conducted a small-scale clinical style investigation of the interface between occupations and family life among young blue-collar families. She sees the linkage more in terms of morale than in terms of specific mechanisms. Three interface patterns are identified: positive carry-over, negative carry-over, and energy deficit. According to Piotrkowski, positive carry-over, in which a kind of good feeling for work carries over into the home, can come from the positive qualities of the job, or simply because a job is not stressful or totally absorbing. This investigator finds little evidence for the family as providing compensatory gratification for unsatisfying employment, but rather that a job that leaves the man feeling assaulted and depleted leads to a kind of depression and low involvement in the family. She is aware that a very satisfying and absorbing job can also lead to decreased involvement in the family, just as a job that is unsatisfactory and draining, but, perhaps because of her lower-class sample, this is not prominent in her discussion. The implicit focus in this investigation, which is a kind of participant-observation study, is on the mood and energy level of the man as he comes into the house from his work. The link between work and family is a carry-over of morale.

Certain occupations have been singled out as particular sources of strain with negative carry-over for family life. For example, a number of problems associated with family disorganization and personal stress—divorce, family violence, and alcoholism—are particularly frequent in the families of urban policemen. Although it is not impossible that there are selective factors involved, the source of these problems seems to lie to a considerable extent in the tension-producing conditions of work. The exposure to the seamier side of life, intimacy with violence, temptations of bribery, the presence of personal danger, and the hostility of the neighborhoods in which one works all combine to make urban police work particularly stressful. The high rate of personal and family difficulties among the police seems to reflect this situation (Kroes & Hurrell, 1975; Lewis, 1973; Nordlicht, 1979; Symonds, 1970). Military families have also been studied because of their high rate of wife and child abuse (Myers, 1979).

On the other hand, some occupations have been singled out because they lure and involve the worker, pulling him toward his work and away from his family. Although two national sample investigations have reported that most Americans see their family roles as more satisfying than their occupational roles (Hoffman & Manis, 1978; Veroff, Douvan, & Kulka, 1981), and although Piotrkowski did not encounter the seductive job pattern in her lower-class sample, there are investigations of executive and professional occupations that have noted that the man may focus his involvements and satisfaction on his occupation to the diminishment of his family roles. This pattern may develop because the work is more attractive and satisfying, because it is particularly relevant to the person's dominant needs, or as a compensation for family difficulties. It might also develop because adequate performance in a particular occupation is objectively very demanding. However, the theme of the father who invests so much of himself in his work that his family life is diminished is a common one in the mass media and in studies of men and women in the higher-status occupations (Elliott, 1978; Heath, 1977; Kanter, 1977; Rapaport & Rapoport, 1965; Whyte, 1956). In a recent national sample study (Veroff et al., 1981) over half of the college-educated men reported that work interfered with their family life, while only 21% of the grade-school-educated men did.

Four different routes by which the father's job-engendered psychological state affects his family have been noted here. Two assume that the behavior at home is different from at work—the father expressing needs aroused at work that could not be expressed there or the father seeking satisfactions from his family that his work does not provide. Two assume that behavior at home is similar to that at work—accustomed or satisfying behaviors on the job are replicated at home, or the mood and morale of the job carry over into the family situation. In most of the work, in this area, the investigator has put all of his chips on one of these patterns, found an instance of it, and pulled out of the game. It seems reasonable to assume that all four patterns exist, and a more valuable investigation into how the father's state provides a link between the job and the family would be to try to discover when one pattern operates and when another. Furthermore, a fuller understanding of these processes might require considering not only the occupational situation but also the family situation, because the effects on the family would probably involve a more complex interaction than implied by the unidimensional models discussed here.

WORK TIME

The man's availability to his family is affected by the hours he works—both the number of hours plus commuting time and the particular schedule. In general, men in higher occupational groups, especially executives and independent professionals, work longer hours on the job (Riesman, 1958; Wilensky, 1961), but blue-collar workers are more likely to hold down more than one job. It has been suggested, in fact, that the shorter work week in the United States may have diminished the working hours only for white-collar occupations such as clerical and low-level administration (Kanter, 1977; Willmott, 1971). Most data indicate that a father is less likely to have two jobs when his wife is employed. However, Pleck and Rustad (1980) report an opposite trend for parents of preschool children: fathers of preschool children whose wives are employed spend about 2½ more hours per week in paid employment than comparable fathers whose wives are not employed.

Perhaps because the range of working hours for men is limited, there have been few studies of this variable. The fact that the father is out of the house at work while the mother is more likely to be at home is important in a number of child development theories (e.g., Lynn, 1974), but the number of hours the father works has rarely been considered. When this variable has been studied, it has been more often in relation to the marital than the parental relationship. Clark, Nye, and Gecas (1978), for example, investigated but found no relationship between husband's job time and marital satisfaction. Clark and Gecas (1977) also report, however, no relationship between the number of hours the father works and his parental role as reported by his wife. There are studies that indicate that fathers who spend long hours at work do report more work-family conflict and, interestingly, their hours of work also predict their wives' work-family conflict. Wives' work hours, on the other hand, predict only their own role strain, not their husbands' (Greenhaus & Kopelman, 1981; Keith & Schafer, 1980).

On the other hand, there are data on the seasonal work schedules of men—specifically, on the effects of the long months of father absence required among Norwegian fishermen—and some recent investigations of shift work times and of flexible work schedules. The studies of the Norwegian fishing village families revealed a pattern much like the pattern of the families of war-absent fathers and fatherless families. The most often noted effect on children of the permanent, temporary, or repeated absence of the father has been "dependency" in sons. Because of the absence of the male model, because of the absence of the father's influence, or because of the effects of the father's absence on the mother-son relationship, the sons have often been seen as dependent, nonassertive, or less masculine in some way (Herzog & Sudia, 1973; Lynn & Sawrey, 1959; Tiller, 1958). As Herzog and Sudia (1973) have noted, however, it is not at all clear that this effect is a negative one, for to some extent it is based on questionable indices of masculinity. The question of how much occupation-engendered father absence would have comparable effects to those observed in the fishing families has not been investigated, but to the extent that an occupation takes the father away from the family so that the primary family unit consists of the mother and children, similar dynamics might be set in motion.

Several exploratory studies have considered the effects of shift work on the family (Aldous, 1969; Landy, Rosenberg, & Sutton-Smith, 1969; Lein et al., 1974; Mott et al., 1965). Night-shift work tends to increase the amount of father-child contact if there are preschoolers, but to diminish it if there are school-aged children. In fact, one study found that daughters whose fathers worked night shifts when they were between 5 and 9 years of age had lower quantitative scores on college entrance tests than a group whose fathers had similar occupations but did not work night shifts (Landy et al., 1969). The researchers suggest that night-shift work be considered as a point on a father-absence continuum. There is evidence that afternoon shifts are even more of an interference with the paternal role than night shifts (Mott et al., 1965).

Effects of shift work have also been noted on the marital relationship, much of which is mediated by the atypicality of the pattern. The couple's social life is diminished, and the wives sometimes resent the husband's obtrusive presence during the day. In fact, while it has sometimes been suggested that the ideal way of working out child-care arrangements when the mother is employed involves having the parents work different shifts, Lein and her colleagues (1974) note that some of the wives in their research sought shifts at the same time as their husbands because, although it made child-care arrangements more difficult, it was less of a strain on the marital relationship. A similar pattern has been observed in the flexitime studies: though the assumption is that dual-wage couples will use the opportunity to extend the hours of parental supervision, it is often used instead to extend the precious couple-alone time.

Flexitime refers to the opportunity for employees to pick their hours of employment within certain limits. Sometimes it involves the opportunity to start the work day earlier or later and sometimes to work extra hours 4 days a week to eliminate 1 whole day. A number of studies have been undertaken to examine the effects of such flexibility on family life (Bohen & Viveros-Long, 1981; Stein, Cohen, & Gadon, 1976; Winett & Neale, 1981). The advantages of flexitime for alleviating specific stress situations in the family are obvious and have been anecdotally demonstrated. Furthermore, it is possible to do studies that examine the cost-efficiency effects for the company instituting the policy. So far, however, the research on effects of flexitime on family life is too fraught with problems of self-selection (e.g., Do families with most stress choose flexitime?), heterogeneity of sample, and limited atheoretical goals to make a substantive contribution. The perceived need for flexitime is clear, however: in a nationwide study of work attitudes, Quinn and Staines (1979) found that the two most common problems mentioned by American workers both pertained to scheduling, first with respect to the days and second with respect to the hours. Thus, it may be an answer to a number of social problems, such as the balancing of child-rearing functions and employment hours, whether or not it is a rich area for research.

INVOLVEMENT OF OTHER FAMILY MEMBERS

In Kanter's (1977) thorough review of the literature on the occupational-family interface, she distinguishes occupations in terms of how "absorptive" they are. "Absorptiveness" has two sides to it—the commitment of the worker, already discussed, and the extent to which there are obligations for other family members. There are clear task requirements for the nonpaid wives among executives (Kanter, 1977; Whyte, 1951, 1956), politicians, the military (Goldman, 1973), clergy (Douglas, 1965; Scanzoni, 1965; Taylor & Hartley, 1975), small business owners, farmers, and others. So demanding can these requirements be that in some cases the wife as well as the husband is evaluated by the organization before a job offer is made (Whyte, 1951), and the wife's unpaid responsibilities may make it impossible for her to obtain employment herself (Mortimer, Hall, & Hill, 1976). In some occupations, such as farming and the clergy, there may also be work or life-style requirements for the children.

The entire family is also affected quite directly when geographical moves are required by the job. Family moves have been independently studied in terms of their impact on family stress (Nieva & Rieck, 1980), pregnancy patterns (Hoffman & Wyatt, 1960; Renshaw, 1976), depression in wives (Weissman & Paykel, 1972), and patterns of adjustment in male and female children.

UNEMPLOYMENT

It seems very likely that in the next few years the aspect of the father's work that will be the most examined for its effects on the family and the child is its absence, but the present data base on unemployment is very sparse. The outstanding research in this area is the work of Elder already mentioned (1974, 1978), and this is conceptualized broadly enough to have theoretical significance for the new investigations, but this research and most of the other work on unemployment effects were carried out during the 1930s, and thus have a limited application to the new situation. The research done during the Depression of the 1930s (Angell, 1936; Cavan & Ranck, 1938; Komorovsky, 1940) will be useful as a guide to the conceptualization of the new research and as a basis for comparison, but it cannot be automatically generalized to unemployment in the 1980s.

The research of the 1930s revealed family difficulties around the loss of income, the father's loss of self-esteem, and the frequent loss of respect for the father by the mother and children. Several studies (Angell, 1936; Elder, 1974) also found that family integration and support, with continued respect for the father and the maintenance of his own self-esteem, alleviated many of the negative outcomes and, as evidenced by Elder's longitudinal research, even facilitated ego development in the adolescent children.

This research should be helpful in predicting modern family responses to unemployment, but there are a number of complexities introduced if some of the intervening social changes are considered. Take, for example, just two of the many differences between the present and the former situations: (a) a program of unemployment insurance and federal aid has come into operation in the intervening years providing a cushion for the immediate impact of unemployment but also a higher level of expectation about federal support; and (*b*) there is increased sex-role equalitarianism and greater acceptance of maternal employment. How these changes will mediate the effects of unemployment is not clear, but they are likely to represent important differences. Should one expect that the impact of unemployment in the 1980s will strain the family less because of federal programs, or will these supports raise expectations and thus increase the anger at their inadequacy? Is the increased acceptability of maternal employment sufficient to lessen the ego threat of job loss to the husband, or is the male's role as the *major* breadwinner still very salient in the United States, as several studies suggest (Garland, 1972; Hoffman, 1977; Lein et al., 1974; Veroff et al., 1981)? And how are the family dynamics affected when both parents in a dual-wage family lose their jobs? The point is that there have been changes over the years that will influence the way in which unemployment affects the family, and it has been 50 years since the phenomenon has been investigated to any extent. While the new research can be enriched by the old, it is unlikely that previous results will be replicated in the new social situation.

One thing is certain, however, and that is that unemployment is a family tension. Cobb and Kasl (1977) have reported a longitudinal study of workers unemployed when two Michigan plants were closed. The study followed the workers from before the plant closed, during the rumor stage, and after its closing, comparing them to workers in similar communities who did not lose their jobs. Negative effects peaked at various stages and included depression, anxiety, sleep loss, reduced activity level, physiological symptoms, and reduced interaction with others. As in the family studies carried out during the Depression of the 1930s, social support was important in lessening some of the trauma of the job loss. While Cobb and Kasl did not focus on the effects on the family and the children, it seems clear that such emotional and interpersonal responses would strain family relations. In fact, a number of studies suggest that the economic change engendered by unemployment may have a more severe impact on the family and the child than a stable but low economic status (Margolis & Farran, in press; Moen, Kain, & Elder, 1981).

There is also a considerable body of research showing an association between paternal job loss and intrafamily violence—wife beating and child abuse (Justice & Duncan, 1977; O'Brien, 1971; Parke & Collmer, 1975; Steinmetz & Straus, 1974). Parke and Collmer have summarized possible connections between the father's unemployment and family violence: (*a*) the greater amount of time the father spends at home, which increases the probability of conflict; (*b*) a possible increase in the father's discipline role; (*c*) a reaffirmation of the father's power in the face of status loss; and (*d*) tension from the diminished resources and its accompanying strains. These authors also present the Steinmetz and Straus (1974) argument that the father's unemployment might increase his own violence in the family, and his wife's violence through the frustrations she experiences when her husband is unemployed, but that the wife's unemployment would not be a comparable stimulus because her status is "less likely to be job-defined" (Parke & Collmer, 1975, p. 529). Although it may be true that the woman's status is not as intensely job defined (Hoffman, 1972), these authors may be underestimating the strains of the mother's own unemployment. The four processes cited above might be seen as operating for unemployed mothers also, and there could even be additional pressures such as the greater possibility that the mother has the exclusive care of the children—that she is with them all day under these frustrating conditions without the relief of a partner. While the association between parental unemployment and family violence seems solid, its dynamics and its relationship to maternal unemployment are still not understood.

Before turning to questions about the mother's employment, however, note should also be made of the fact that there is very little research on the effects of unemployment among middle-class families. In recent years, because of shifts in population patterns, technological developments, and changed government policy, the United States has experienced unemployment among professional workers such as engineers and teachers. Such highly trained professionals have found themselves unemployed totally or forced to take jobs inappropriate for their skills. The family dynamics accompanying this kind of unemployment have not yet been investigated.

THE MOTHER'S JOB

As Bronfenbrenner and Crouter (1982) pointed out, while it is the unemployment of the father that has been considered disrupting of the family and damaging to the child, it is the employment of the mother that has been presumed to have this effect. The former assumption has not been totally accurate, as Elder's work suggests, but the latter assumption has been almost totally inaccurate, as 50 years of research attest (Hoffman, 1963, 1974c; Maccoby, 1958; Mathews, 1934; Stolz, 1960). One major reason why the myth of the negative effects of maternal employment has persisted, while the research has failed to substantiate the belief, is that the myth is based on the assumption that the employed-mother family is just like the "typical" traditional family of 20 or more years ago; in fact, however, the employed mother has never fit that image. The stereotype of the traditional family may have been apt for some families in past generations, but it did not fit the employed-mother family even then. The employed mother had fewer children, older children, outside relatives living in the household, more education or greater economic need, and probably more energy and better health (Nye & Hoffman, 1963). And the image of the traditional family of past generations does not fit the modern family at all. Family size is smaller, modern technology has enormously diminished the amount of necessary housework and food preparation, women are more educated, marriages are less stable, life expectancy is increased and youthfulness has been extended, expectations for personal fulfillment have expanded, and traditional sex-role attitudes are no longer fully accepted (Hoffman, 1977). These two points—(a) that employed mothers are different from nonemployed in many ways besides employment status, and (b) that new social conditions require a reconsideration of maternal employment effects—are basic to understanding the role of maternal employment in the socialization process. Accordingly, these two issues will be taken up before moving into the more substantive discussion.

GENERAL ISSUES IN MATERNAL EMPLOYMENT STUDIES

Selective Factors

The fact that employed mothers are different from nonemployed with respect to motivational factors and facilitating conditions, and that these differences need to be controlled in studying the effects of maternal employment, has been so often repeated and is so thoroughly documented that it seems unnecessary to mention the point again. Unfortunately, there is ample evidence that the point needs repeating. Most researchers have learned that employed mothers are more likely to be poor and husbandless, and so social class and family intactness are usually controlled. On the other hand, studies often fail to control on the number of children or their ages, even when such controls are obviously essential. The time-use studies, in which subjects are asked to keep daily records of how they spend their time, provide a good example. Since employed-mother families include fewer children in general, and fewer preschoolers and infants in particular, there are fewer child-care tasks to perform. Researchers using time-use data based on heterogeneous samples have often reported that there are no differences between husbands of employed women and husbands of nonemployed in participation in household tasks but failed to control on family size and the ages of the children, thus obscuring the higher participation of fathers in employed-mother families that shows up in comparisons where the number and ages of the children are matched (Hoffman, 1977, 1983; Pleck & Rustad, 1980; Robinson, 1978; Walker & Woods, 1976).

While failure to control on these variables may seem to be obvious errors, there are comparable problems that are more subtle. For example, researchers often study effects of maternal employment on preschoolers by obtaining a sample of children in full-time day care and exploring differences between the children of the employed and the nonemployed mothers. Typically, these studies find that, if there are differences, they favor the children of the employed mothers, showing higher scores on various measures of adjustment or cognitive development. However, even when the two groups are matched on variables such as family size and ordinal position, the design cannot escape the fact that there are different reasons for sending each group to a day-care center. The children of employed mothers are typically there because of a need for child-care during the mother's working hours, but the nonemployed mother's children may be there because of some disturbance in the home or because of some attitude of the mother toward the child. Thus the selective factors operating are different for the two groups, and this might introduce a bias that affects the other differences in adjustment or development. What are assumed to be differences resulting from maternal employment status may be differences resulting from different sets of selective factors.

Here is another example—also not obvious. As society moves from a situation of maternal employment as the atypical pattern to maternal employment as the mode, there may be new selective factors to consider that explain why some mothers resist employment. Thus, in a previous publication it was suggested (Hoffman, 1980b) that the repeated finding in studies of poverty groups of higher social and cognitive development scores for the children of employed women may represent an effect of maternal employment, or it may represent selective factors. Specifically it was suggested that in circumstances where maternal employment seems particularly appropriate, the employment resisters may represent a more troubled or less competent group, and it may be these problems rather than employment status that the differences reflect.

New Social Conditions

Perhaps the most eloquent testimony to the point that the effects of maternal employment cannot be considered as though this pattern had been laid on the traditional family of the past is presented in Table 1. These data indicate first that maternal employment has gone from a rare pattern to the modal pattern. This shift alone means that the selective factors will

TABLE 1
LABOR FORCE PARTICIPATION RATES OF MOTHERS
WITH CHILDREN UNDER 18, 1940–1980

Year	Mothers (%)
1980	56.6
1978	53.0
1976	48.8
1974	45.7
1972	42.9
1970	42.0
1968	39.4
1966	35.8
1964	34.5
1962	32.9
1960	30.4
1958	29.5
1956	27.5
1954	25.6
1952	23.8
1950	21.6
1948	20.2
1946	18.2
1940	8.6

SOURCES.—U.S. Department of Commerce, Bureau of the Census, 1980a; U.S. Department of Labor, Bureau of Labor Statistics, 1981a; U.S. Department of Labor, Women's Bureau, 1977.

be different, as already indicated. It is not "going to work" that selects "special" mothers but rather "not going." It also means, as discussed earlier, that the significance of maternal employment for the family will be different; for example, mothers are less likely to feel guilty or unusual, fathers are less likely to feel it is a mark of their failure, children are less likely to feel special, neighboring families will be having similar experiences, and the employed-mother family is more likely to be similar to the families the children will form when they are adults. And, on the other side, nonemployed mothers are more likely to feel pressure to justify their own nonemployment.

Another important implication of the data in Table 1 is that since the magnitude of the change is so great, the trend so steady, there must be other accompanying social changes. Such a change does not happen in a vacuum. The increased maternal employment rates are a response to some new events, accompanied by several other responses to these events, and the cause of still other changes. Such is the nature of social systems: a change in one part involves a change in others. It is important to understand these social changes to see how maternal employment fits into the picture.

The events that contributed to the high maternal employment rates depicted in Table 1 can be classified into four general categories. One set of changes describes the more macro-economic level. Thus, a very general change that has its origins well before the 1940 date in the table is the development of industrialization to the point where outside-the-home production is economically advantageous, where it is more economically efficient to earn wages and buy a loaf of bread than to stay home and bake it. This describes a historical trend, precise predictions depending on some of the more micro-level changes. There are other changes at a broad social level that might also be considered here that describe the increased demand for female labor. These include the changed nature of the jobs themselves such that they are seen as appropriate for women as well as men, the general economic expansion, and demographic factors such as the low birthrate in the 1930s, which created a labor scarcity in the 1950s (Hoffman & Nye, 1974; Oppenheimer, 1973).

A second group of changes altered the housewife-mother role. These changes, like those in the first set, were largely in response to technological and scientific advance, and while the first group operated more to pull women into the labor force, these made it more feasible for mothers to work. Modern household appliances; advanced food processing, storage, and delivery systems; and time-saving products, such as the no-iron fabrics, have enormously diminished the amount of work required for operating a household. Smaller family size, facilitated by improved contraceptive techniques, has meant fewer children to care for and a shorter period with preschoolers.

It is important to emphasize that it was necessary housework that had diminished, because, as one study indicated, a common report of mothers was that when not employed they spent a great ideal of time on housework that was unnecessary (Hoffman, 1974b); and up until recently, time-use studies indicated that nonemployed wives put in as many hours on domestic tasks as in the 1920s (Hall & Schroeder, 1970; University of Michigan, 1973; Walker, 1969). The more recent time-use data, however, show substantial reductions in household task hours. Robinson (1977, 1980) found a considerable decrease in housework time for all women between 1965 and 1975, and Pleck and Rustad (1980) reported that the same period showed a shift from a heavy work overload among employed wives to a pattern in which employed wives looked very much like the husbands in total number of work hours—at home and on the job—while nonemployed wives stood out as "uniquely low."

Third, these same changes in the household, along with other related

events, have made the role of full-time housewife and mother less psychologically satisfying. Women's satisfaction in the traditional housewife role
decreased markedly between the mid-fifties and the mid-seventies, evidenced in the replication of the national survey, Americans View Their
Mental Health (Veroff et al., 1981). The new feminist ideology may have
augmented this discontent, but much of it is also a response to the changed
nature of the role itself. The decrease in required homemaking time and in
the number of children may make the role of full-time homemaker seem an
insufficient contribution and an inadequate use of the woman's ability,
particularly when she knows that she could use her time to earn money for
the family. An additional factor is the upswing in women's educational
levels that began in the sixties (Hoffman, 1974a), which may have increased
the housewife's discontent as well as her ability to obtain more satisfying
employment. If the first group of changes provided a pull into the labor
force, and the second group operated as facilitators, this group might be
seen as a push out of the full-time housewife role.

Finally, a fourth group of changes has to do with economic insecurity:
Mothers' motivations for employment and for establishing occupational
competence have increased because of rising divorce rates, the increased
number of female-headed households, and economic circumstances that
make it necessary for wives to be employed in order to maintain an
acceptable (objectively or subjectively) standard of living.

Simply focusing on these changes that have led to the increase in
maternal employment reveals how family life has changed and indicates
the fallacy of analyzing the effects of maternal employment as though it
were occurring in the traditional family of generations ago. The present-
day nonemployed mother is not like the nonemployed mother of that time.
In view of the social changes that have occurred over the years, the role of
the present-day nonemployed mothers may be as new as the role of the
majority of the present-day mothers, who are employed. In considering
now how the mother's employment affects the child's socialization in the
family, it is important to keep this new social situation in mind.

MATERNAL EMPLOYMENT STATUS AS A SHAPER OF VALUES

In the preceding discussion of the effects of the father's job, one group
of studies explored the idea that the father's occupation affects the child
because the traits required for success in that occupation are valued and
passed on to the child. Some support for this hypothesis as applied to the
mother's job is provided in a recent study of lower-class employed mothers
of preadolescent children (Piotrkowski & Katz, 1982). The extent to which

the mother's job allowed for autonomy and the utilization of skill predicted to the child's performance in an academic summer program—high autonomy going with the child's more frequent absence from classes and high skill utilization going with the child's higher academic performance. For the most part, however, studies that view the mother's work as shaping the child's values are different from the studies of the father's work in a number of respects. First, by and large, it is not the mother's particular occupation that has been considered but her employment status per se. Second, it is not so much the activities of the job that are seen as important as the roles and activities in the family that mediate employment effects. To describe the research on the mother's employment as shaping values, then, it is necessary to first consider effects on family roles and activities.

Research findings indicate that when the mother is employed the division of labor between the husband and wife is less traditional. Though the woman maintains the larger share, the husband of an employed woman participates more in housework and childcare (Bahr, 1974; Baruch & Barnett, 1981; Gold & Andres, 1978c; Hill & Stafford, 1978; Hoffman, 1974b, 1977, 1983; Pleck, Lang, & Rustad, 1978; Robinson, 1978). Recent data, as well as a reanalysis of the 1950s data from the Blood and Wolfe study (1960), do not support the idea that employed wives have more decision-making power generally in the household but, rather, that working increases the wife's say in money matters and the husband's say in household routines following their respective participation patterns (Hoffman & Manis, 1978; Quarm, 1977). School-aged children are more likely to have household responsibilities and to participate in tasks. The data suggest that the employed mother, except when guilt intervenes, is more likely to encourage independence in her children. Studies of lower socioeconomic populations and one-parent families have found that employed mothers are more likely to have structured rules for their children and consistency between theory and practice (Hoffman, 1974c, 1977). All of these differences between the families of employed and nonemployed women can be seen as functional adaptations. The greater participation of the father and children in household tasks helps to compensate for the wife's outside employment. The independence training of the children and the rule-governed household also diminish the need for steady maternal surveillance.

One effect of the mother's employment on the family, then, is that the traditional sex-based division of labor is diminished. To a greater extent than in the family of the nonemployed woman, the two parents share the breadwinner, housekeeping, and child-care functions. This difference is reflected in the child's conception of what adult men and women are like, what roles are appropriate, and, for the girl, what her own life will be like as an adult. Both sons and daughters of employed mothers are less stereotyped in their views of men and women, and this has been demonstrated even among preschool children (Gold & Andres, 1978c; Hartley, 1960; Miller, 1975). They do not see the sharp distinctions that the children of nonemployed women see, and, specifically, they are not as likely to see competence as a peculiarly male trait nor warmth as a peculiarly female trait. Both sons and daughters of employed mothers are more likely to approve of maternal employment, and the daughters are more likely to expect to be employed themselves when they are mothers. Further, the adolescent daughters of employed mothers are more likely to be already employed (Hoffman, 1974c; Marantz & Mansfield, 1977; Romer & Cherry, 1978; Vogel, Broverman, Broverman, Clarkson & Rosenkrantz, 1970).

As pointed out in previous reviews (Hoffman, 1974c, 1979, 1980b), there is a great deal in the employed-mother family to increase the academic-occupational competence of daughters and to contribute to positive adjustment generally. Reflecting the mother's own occupational role, academic-occupational competence in women is respected in the working-mother family. Further, the mothers provide models for their daughters that are more consistent with occupational roles and achievement orientations, and the daughters of employed mothers are more likely to indicate that they want to be like their mothers (Baruch, 1972b; Douvan, 1963). Diminished sex-role stereotyping, according to Bem's work (1975), is associated with a better socio-psychological adjustment generally.

Furthermore, the two child-rearing patterns most often associated with employed-mother families, which can be seen both as functionally adapative and as reflecting the values implicit in the maternal employment situation, also contribute positively to the daughter's development. In the traditional family, dependency is encouraged in daughters. This pattern has been seen as a source of excessive affiliative concerns and a block to top achievement and the development of independent coping skills (Block, 1979; Hoffman, 1972, 1977). Thus, the encouragement of independence in the employed-mother family is a boon to daughters. It is not clear whether it is an advantage or disadvantage to sons, however. Sons generally receive more independence training than daughters, and while this seems to have provided them with an advantage in the nonemployed-mother family, it may be excessive in the employed-mother family (Bronfenbrenner & Crouter, 1982; Hoffman, 1980b). The other child-rearing pattern commonly associated with maternal employment is the higher level of household responsibilities required of children. Though it can obviously be overdone, the relationship of this pattern to ego development and self-esteem for both sons and daughters has already been noted (Elder, 1978; Medrick, 1981; Smokler, 1975).

THE MOTHER'S PSYCHOLOGICAL STATE

In discussing the effects of the father's occupation on the family and the child, it was noted that some hypotheses suggested a reciprocality or complementarity between job and family such that the needs created or left unsatisfied in one sphere would seek expression in the other, while others suggested a commonality of behavior, either because rewarding or habitual patterns would be repeated in the home or because the mood or morale would carry over. These same patterns could be applied to the mother's work.

Complementary Need Satisfaction

The theory developed by Hoffman and her colleagues (Hoffman & Hoffman, 1973; Hoffman & Manis, 1978; Hoffman, et al., 1978), already discussed, has been applied to mothers as well as fathers: this theory states that the needs expressed in parenting will be affected by whether or not they are satisfied through other routes. This research focuses on nine basic needs, later reduced to eight: the needs for love, fun and stimulation, adult status and social identity, achievement, a sense of morality or feeling good about oneself, having power or influence, economic security, and "expansion of self," that is, a sense of significance or perception of meaning in life. Parenting is seen as one of several ways of satisfying these needs. If the need is strong and there is no alternative way of obtaining satisfaction, parenting may become the major means, and both fertility behavior and parenting style will be affected. The data supported the hypothesis that women who were employed would be less likely to cite as a major advantage of having children that it gave them a sense of identity or feeling of attaining adulthood. They were also less likely to indicate that a major advantage was that children were a source of stimulation. These particular needs are capable, at least in part, of being satisfied by employment. The employed women were *not* less likely to indicate that children were a major source of love or any of the other less work-relevant needs, nor did they indicate any less enthusiasm for motherhood.

This research, as well as other studies, however, found a link between mothering attitudes and the extent to which employment provides achievement satisfaction. The data indicated that women who had held high-status occupations before motherhood but were currently not employed were the most likely to see children as a source of achievement satisfaction (Hoffman & Manis, 1978). Whether they expressed this through excessive achievement demands on their children, wanting to mother a great many children, or through excellence in mothering was not explored in that study, but the first two patterns have been demonstrated in other research. Birnbaum (1975) found that women who had shown high achievement in college but did not work after marriage were excessively involved in their children's achievement, more so than a comparable group who were professionally employed. Livson and Day (1977) analyzed longitudinal data from the Berkeley Growth Study and found that women who showed high academic achievement before marriage but did not pursue careers were the ones particularly likely to have larger families during the Baby Boom years of the 1950s, expressing achievement needs as mothers through number.[4] Thus there is evidence from several quarters that high achievement needs that are not satisfied through employment may affect mothering attitudes and behavior.

The complexities of this connection are further illustrated by a longitudinal study of women who were college students in 1965. Women who showed a pattern of high achievement in college but who also had anxiety about too much academic-occupational success, the pattern known as "fear of success," later became pregnant when they were on the verge of a success, particularly one that threatened to surpass their husbands'. The data supported the hypothesis that for women with fear of success, occupational-academic success vis-à-vis the important man in their lives would be seen as threatening to the relationship or to their sense of femininity. The pregnancy, though unconsciously motivated, was a means of strengthening the relationship and reaffirming femininity (Hoffman, 1977).

Morale

The link between the mother's occupation and the family-based socialization patterns has often been considered in terms of morale. While some writers expect employed women to have higher morale because of the satisfactions of outside employment, and others expect them to be stressed because of work overload, there is agreement that satisfaction with one's employment status—whether that status is employee or full-time homemaker—will have a positive effect on family relations, mothering behavior, and child outcomes. A number of studies support this prediction (Birnbaum, 1975; Farel, 1980; Kappel & Lambert, 1972; Woods, 1972; Yarrow, Scott, De Leeuw, & Heinig, 1962). As has often been pointed out, however, the causal direction involved in these studies is not clear, for satisfaction could be the consequence of the happy outcome as well as the antecedent. There have been some attempts to deal with this problem but

---

[4]There is a complicated trade-off between women's employment and fertility that is discussed more fully in a previous publication (Hoffman, 1974b).

none was entirely successful. Hoffman (1961), in a study that linked job satisfaction to child-rearing patterns, tried to show that her measure of satisfaction was closely related to the woman's occupation and thus a consequence of the particular job, not the family variables.

The measures of satisfaction vary a great deal from study to study. For example, Hoffman's measure was an attitude toward the job, while the measure used by Yarrow and her colleagues, as in most of this research, was an attitude toward the combined mother-worker role. The outcomes predicted in these two studies were accordingly different. Yarrow, like most of the investigators, was operating from a morale hypothesis, with morale seen not as job engendered, but based on dual-role satisfaction. The prediction, borne out by the data, was that satisfied mothers, whether employed or not, would be more "adequate" as mothers. The Hoffman study was not one of general morale. Focusing on work attitude, the prediction was that employed mothers who enjoyed work were more likely to feel guilty, to try to compensate for their employment but also to overcompensate, while a different pattern was predicted for the employed mothers who saw their jobs as more functional than pleasant.

Two other studies that also compared the mother's intrinsic job satisfaction to a functional orientation found positive effects of the former. In an early study by Kliger (1954), women who worked because of interest in the job were more likely than those who worked for financial reasons to feel that there was improvement in the child's behavior as a result of employment. Kappel and Lambert (1972), in a study which, like the Hoffman study, obtained independent measures from parents and children, found that the 9- to 16-year-old daughters of full-time employed mothers who were working for self-oriented reasons had higher self-esteem and evaluated both parents more highly than did either the daughters of full-time employed mothers who were working for family-oriented reasons or the daughters of nonemployed mothers.

However, the simple hypothesis that for men a generally satisfying occupation leads to positive family interaction has not been applied much to women. It is an oversimplification for men, and more obviously so for women because of traditional ideology and the prevailing dual-role pattern. Employed women still maintain the major responsibility for housework and child-care, and this influences the occupation-family relationship. Nevertheless, there is increasing attention to the idea that employment, in the absence of dual-role *stress*, may provide a valuable morale boost to mothers. Although complaints about the dual-role problems are common in surveys, complaints about the full-time housewife-mother role are at least as common (Veroff et al., 1981). Employed mothers, most notably in recent studies, are more likely to indicate overall satisfaction with their lives than the nonemployed (Gold & Andres, 1978a, 1978b, 1978c). In studies using mental health indices, employed women generally indicate more positive adjustment although for mothers this effect is more apparent when their husbands also provide some child-care assistance (Kessler & McRae, 1981, 1982). Furthermore, both national sample data and class-specific studies show that the psychological satisfaction that employment provides is not peculiar to the middle class (Kessler & McRae, 1982). To the blue-collar working women as well, employment provides evidence of self-worth, an opportunity for adult companionship, challenge, stimulation, and a sense of achievement that they do not experience as full-time homemakers, as indicated specifically in the data reported by Walshok (1978) and also by Ferree (1976) and Rubin (1977). National sample data indicate also that women's work commitment is increasing. A larger percentage of employed women in the United States say that they would continue working even if there were no monetary need—76% in 1976; more nonemployed mothers say they would like to work and plan to soon; and, as already indicated, housework has diminished over the years as a source of satisfaction (Veroff et al., 1981).

Thus, while it obviously depends on many aspects of the situation, there is increasing evidence of a growing morale problem among nonemployed mothers (Birnbaum, 1975; Gold & Andres, 1978a, 1978b, 1978c). In Birnbaum's study of educated women this was particularly salient. The nonemployed mothers, in comparison with the professionally employed, had lower self-esteem and less sense of competence, felt less attractive, expressed greater concern over identity issues, and more often indicated feelings of loneliness. They described parenthood more in terms of the sacrifices it entailed and less in terms of enrichment and self-fulfillment. They voiced more anxiety about the children, and they expressed ambivalence and regret about their children's movement toward independence as they matured. It was noted earlier that employed mothers generally stress independence more than nonemployed and that this pattern was consistent with the functional needs of their situation. The *psychological* needs of the nonemployed mother may also operate to extend and encourage dependency. In view of the changes in the housewife-mother role already discussed, the full-time homemaker may be unintentionally nurturing dependency in her children as she seeks to enhance, prolong, and justify her role.

On the other hand, there is also evidence that when maternal employment involves excessive strain from the hassle of juggling two roles, effects may be disruptive for the family and the child. For example, studies of black families in poverty circumstances have generally found that the children of employed mothers have higher scores on cognitive, social, and personal adjustment tests, except where there is particular strain, as when substitute supervision is not adequate or the family includes six or more children (Cherry & Eaton, 1977; Woods, 1972). The fact that several studies across social class have shown more positive child outcomes associated with part-time than full-time employment has also been interpreted in terms of differences in role strain (Hoffman, 1974c; Kappel & Lambert, 1972). Further, the perception by college-age daughters that their mothers were under stress from employment affects their own aspirations. Under these conditions, the tendency, indicated earlier, for daughters of employed women to seek dual roles themselves is reversed (Baruch, 1972a).

Interest in the mother's morale as the linkage between her employment status and the child's socialization in the family has been given a new boost by the recent rapid increase in employment rates for mothers of preschoolers. In 1980, 45% of the mothers of preschool children in families with the father present were employed, and 59% of the mothers of preschoolers in father-absent households. For families with children under 3, the comparable figures were 41% and 47% (U.S. Department of Labor, 1981b). While the prevalent maternal employment pattern can be seen as adaptive and functional to the school-aged child's development for many reasons, the only nonmonetary advantage that maternal employment is seen as offering the very young child is the mother's improved morale. It has already been shown that maternal employment offers a number of advantages for school-aged daughters. Even for sons, the roles represented by the parents are more likely to be consistent with their own adult roles. The less rigid stereotyping that goes along with the family patterns in the employed-mother family has been shown as advantageous for both sexes (Bem, 1975). Furthermore, the needs of the growing child require the mother to loosen her hold, and this task may be easier for the employed woman whose job is an additional source of identity and self-esteem. For the mother of preschool children, however, the major route by which maternal employment might have a positive effect is that some mothers are happier when employed and thus more effective as mothers. Accordingly, studies of maternal employment during the early years have been particularly interested in this issue, and much of the recent research showing positive morale among employed mothers with carry-over for the child looked at employment during the child's early years (Farel, 1980; Gold & Andres, 1978c; Gold, Andres, & Glorieux, 1979; Hock, 1980).

WORK TIME

Like the man, the woman's availability to her family is affected by the hours she is employed—both the number of hours plus commuting time and the particular schedule. Unlike with men, there is a wide variation in these hours for women. Forty-three percent of the mothers in America were not employed at all in 1980, and of the 57% who were, 29% were employed less than 35 hours per week (U.S. Department of Labor, 1981a). Furthermore, women more than men are employed for less than 12 months a year and their employment is often discontinuous; that is, they enter and leave the labor force more often. There is such variation in the hours of employment for women that Goldberg (personal communication) has suggested that it be operationalized as a continuous variable. There are three recent studies of married women that considered the number of hours of work as a continuous variable in relation to family adjustment and time patterns. Staines and Pleck (1983) found a negative relationship between the time women spend in employment and the time they spend in family roles, but Robinson (1977) did not. Piotrkowski and Crits-Christoph (1981) found no relationship to self-reported measures of family adjustment. None of these studies, however, was focused on the child, and not all subjects were parents. The studies of *maternal* employment usually measure work status as a dichotomous variable, with all women who are employed more than a certain number of hours called employed and all others called nonemployed. Sometimes there is a distinction between full-time and part-time employment; sometimes the middle group is excluded from the study. Despite these imprecisions, however, researchers have at least been more interested in studying how the family is affected by the mother's than the father's time out of the home and on the job.

Nevertheless, there is inadequate information on how the mother's employment affects her family availability, and particularly her availability to her children. The time-use studies in which subjects are asked to keep daily records of how they spend their time should have such information, but these data have generally been obtained for other purposes, and thus the results reported are not well suited for providing the answers needed here. One problem already noted is that inadequate attention is given to selective factors that differentiate employed from nonemployed women, and thus one cannot tell if differences in time use reflect employment effects or other aspects of their lives. A second problem is that the descriptions of household activity have been too crude. For example, until recently, child-care time might include laundering diapers or close personal interaction between parent and child; they were not differentiated. Recent research, however, has attempted to remedy this situation, and a distinction has been made between "primary childcare" and "child contact" (Robinson, 1978), or among "direct," "indirect," and "available" child contact (Goldberg, 1977, 1978).

In general, the data indicate that the employed mother does spend less time with each child, but this differs by social class and by the definition of child contact. Hill and Stafford (1978), for example, include as child care physical care, teaching, reading, talking, playing, and providing medical care. They report that women employed more than 20 hours a week spend less time in per child care whether the child is a baby, preschooler, grade schooler, or high schooler. They also note that the differences vary with the education of the mother, and the employed-nonemployed difference is considerably less for college-educated women. Employed college-educated women reduce mainly "personal care time," which is primarily sleep, and "passive leisure," which is primarily television watching. These authors still report, however, a 25% deficit in child-care time for employed college-educated mothers of preschoolers. On the other hand, Goldberg (1978), in a study of middle-class preschool children enrolled in a nursery school, found no difference in the amount of direct one-to-one interaction between the mother and the child, although the full-time employed mothers did have less "available" time with the child (when the mother was within calling distance) and less "indirect" time (when the two were in the same room engaged in separate activities).

At best, these data leave a number of questions unanswered. One that is probably unanswerable is, How do children today compare to yesterday's children with respect to maternal contact time? It is possible that employment fills in time previously consumed by greater household burdens and more children. If so, differences between employed- and nonemployed-mother families may reflect an unprecedented amount of mother-child interaction in the nonemployed-mother family. As noted in previous publications, the amount of maternal attention a child receives is not infinitely valuable. There is an optimum level that varies with the child's age. Whether maternal employment today facilitates or hinders achieving this level is a complicated and interesting issue (Hoffman, 1979, 1980b).

Nature of the Mother-Child Interaction

In addition to the question of how the mother's time on the job affects the quantity of the interaction between mother and child, there is the question of whether or not it affects the nature of this interaction, that is, its quality. There are a number of ways in which the quality might be affected. The time spent at work might improve the mother's morale or contribute to a feeling of work overload, both of which have been discussed in the previous section. Employment might also lead to a conscious decision on the part of the mother to compensate for her absence by increasing the intensity of the interaction or its quality by setting up special times for nondiverted interaction and special activities. Employed women report this pattern in several studies (Hoffman, 1980b). Furthermore, recent research has obtained behavioral observations of mother-infant interaction that revealed a more intense interaction for the employed mothers (Pederson, Cain, Zaslow, & Anderson, 1981; Schubert, Bradley-Johnson, & Nuttal, 1980). Employed mothers were highly interactive—higher, specifically, in social play and verbal interaction. The data reported by Pederson and his colleagues were collected in the evening of a workday and may reflect the mother's efforts to compensate for her absence during the day or enthusiasm for the interaction that was less intense in the mother who had been with the infant all day. These researchers note that the employed mother's interaction style was one that has typically been found to characterize fathers, including social play and a physically robust way of handling the infant, and they suggest that the often-noted differences in parenting style between fathers and mothers might be a function of work roles, that it might represent a form of greeting and renewing contact after absence.

The Pederson data are also interesting in their implications for the effects of the mother's employment on the father's family behavior. Though typically maternal employment is seen as increasing father-child interaction, these data showed fathers as less interactive when their wives were employed than when they were not. It may be that the after-work hours in the dual-wage family are devoted to mother-infant interaction, whereas in the single-wage family this is the father's special time. The possibility that maternal employment during the child's infancy squeezes the father out while the mother makes up for her absence is consistent with the fact that the studies of maternal employment and infant attachment in the middle class found no employment-status differences for mother-infant attachment (Chase-Lansdale, 1981; Hock, 1980), but the one study that looked at *father*-infant attachment found more insecurity in the dual career families, though only for sons, not daughters (Chase-Lansdale, 1981).

Care in the Mother's Absence

As important as the questions of how the mother's time at work affects the quantity and quality of her interaction with the child are the questions of how the child is being cared for in her absence. While the mother's employment may sometimes coincide with the child's public school hours, this is not possible with the preschool child and usually imperfectly achieved with the school-aged child.

A widespread concern is that many of these children go unsupervised. Data on this issue are grossly inadequate. What data do exist suggest that the children of employed mothers have more unsupervised hours per day than the children of nonemployed (Glueck & Glueck, 1957; Gold & Andres, 1978b), but no study has investigated whether the unsupervised time is excessive, extensive, inappropriate for the child's age, or monitored by telephone contact. Further, there are no adequate data on how this unsupervised time is used by the child. Bronfenbrenner and Crouter (1982) suggest that lack of supervision may increase the socialization impact of the peer group, diminishing that of the family—a pattern that might provide a link between maternal employment in the middle class and the sometimes-observed lower academic performance of sons. Hoffman (1980a), in discussing a related theory, has raised questions about sex differences, that is, whether there are differences between sons and daughters in both the amount of unsupervised time and its significance for development. This is a rich area for study. Depending on the age of the child and the circumstances, it cannot be assumed without investigation that periods without supervision have a negative impact on the child.

For the most part, however, substitute care is provided by other members of the family, relatives, friends, baby-sitters, home-based day care, day-care centers, and after-school programs. All of these affect the family and the child. If the extra care comes from sources outside the family, it may be that the exposure to these outside socialization agents diminishes the intensity and relative exclusiveness of family influence. If the extra help comes from within the family, a change in the family structure and organization may result. The differences between family structure in dual- and single-wage families have already been described. As indicated, many of these differences can be seen as functional shifts to accommodate to the mother's absence, with considerable impact on the child. The increase in the father's participation in household tasks and child care and the diminishment of the sex-based division of labor in the family are particularly important links between the mother's employment and the child's socialization (Hoffman, 1979).

Part-Time Employment

A few studies have differentiated part-time maternal employment from full-time. The results were summarized a decade ago by Hoffman and Nye (1974, p. 228) as follows: "[these studies] found part-time employment an unusually successful adaptation to the conflict between the difficulties of being a full-time housewife and the strain of combining this role with full-time employment. These mothers seem to be physically and psychologically healthy, positive toward their maternal roles, and active in recreational and community activities. Their children compare favorably to the other groups with respect to self-esteem, social adjustment, and attitudes toward their parents; scattered findings suggest that their marital satisfaction is the highest of the three groups." As Hoffman and Nye also noted, part-time employment is difficult to find, pays less, often excludes employee benefits, and may be inappropriate for career advancement. Perhaps because of these difficulties, and perhaps because it has been accepted that part-time employment does not disrupt family life, little subsequent research on this pattern had been conducted until recently. The new interest in maternal employment and the preschool child has brought with it renewed attention to part-time employment. The "part-time" pattern is more common for employed mothers with preschool children than for mothers with only school-aged children: About one-third of the former were employed part-time. Recent studies of these younger families are consistent with the pattern noted earlier. In a particularly interesting study of 3-year-olds, Bronfenbrenner and his colleagues found that mothers employed part-time had the most positive attitudes toward their children (Bronfenbrenner & Crouter, 1982). This study also found interesting sex-of-child differences: sons were viewed most positively by mothers who worked part-time while mothers who worked full-time were least positive. Both employed-mother groups expressed more positive attitudes toward daughters than did the full-time homemakers. These results may have significance for the previously noted differences in the apparent effects of maternal employment for sons and daughters. It is possible that the higher activity level of boys than girls (Hoffman, 1977) makes part-time employment a particularly satisfying compromise for the mothers of boys, at least when the children are young.

Duration, Timing, and Long-Term Effects

In this section, time has been conceptualized as it has in most research—contemporaneously. No attention has been given to the duration of employment or to the timing of changes in employment status in relation to the state of the family, the child's age, or other specific events such as divorce, although these are important ways to consider the "time" aspect of the woman's employment. Furthermore, studies that look only at the correlations with maternal employment at one point in time can even be misleading.

Ahistorical research can be misleading in at least three ways: (*a*) employment at one age in the child's life may have an effect that only shows up later, (*b*) data may indicate a contemporaneous effect that actually disappears with time, and (*c*) the traits that seem maladaptive at one age may develop into strengths as the child matures, or the converse pattern may emerge. As an example of the first, the studies that show no differences between infants of full-time employed mothers and nonemployed mothers (e.g., Hock, 1980) do not necessarily mean there are no effects. There could be effects that are not manifest until a later age. The second possibility, that of an observed effect that disappears with time, can be seen in the parallel studies by Gold and Andres (1978a, 1978b) carried out with different-aged children. None of the negative symptoms correlated with maternal employment in the 10-year-old sample was found with the adolescent sample. This could indicate that maternal employment effects are different for 10-year-olds than for adolescents, but since most of the employed mothers of adolescents in their sample had also been employed when the children were 10, it may also mean that the effects observed at 10 wash away by adolescence. The third possibility, that a trait changes its manifestation as the child matures, has been demonstrated generally in the longitudinal work of Kagan and Moss (1962). In the case of maternal employment research, it has been suggested elsewhere (Hoffman, 1980b) that the pattern of better school performance by the middle-class sons of nonemployed mothers may reflect cognitive ability or simply conformity to adult standards, a distinction that would affect the prognosis for later development. If the better school performance is based on conformity, the manifestation at older ages and higher academic levels might be considerably less positive.

Duration, timing, and long-term effects of maternal employment have not been totally ignored by researchers, however. Burchinal (1963), in a study of adolescents, used retrospective reports of the mother's employment history to see how employment at different periods in the child's development affected the child in adolescence. Romer and Cherry (1978) used a similar technique with subjects at several different ages to see if sex-role attitudes were more affected by the child's age at the time of the mother's employment or the child's age at the time of measurement. Gold and Andres (1978b, 1978c) examined duration of maternal employment as a variable as well as current status (and in all of their research, it should be noted, even "current status" was defined as requiring continuous employment for a specified number of years). The retrospective studies, however, have turned out to be more complicated than might be anticipated. A common problem has to do with the ever-intrusive selective factors. Researchers who carefully match their samples with respect to current maternal employment status ignore this issue when introducing previous employment history (Hoffman, 1981).

Both short-term and long-term longitudinal designs have also been employed to investigate some of the issues raised here (Cherry & Eaton, 1977; Hetherington, 1979; Moore, 1975). The Moore study is particularly interesting. Begun in the 1950s in England, children who received full-time mothering during their preschool years were compared to a group whose mothers were out of the home for regular periods, in most but not all cases because of maternal employment. The development of these children was followed through adolescence and is in fact currently being reassessed (Moore, personal communication). The pattern revealed at adolescence would not have been easily foreseen earlier. One of the particularly interesting outcomes was that boys who received full-time mothering during their preschool years were good students but also were more conforming, fearful, and inhibited as adolescents. This combination of qualities is consistent with the suggestion above that the academic performance of the sons of nonemployed mothers may reflect conformity with adult standards rather than cognitive ability per se, that is, that it may reflect a pattern of oversocialization. If so, the performance advantage might be lost at higher intellectual tasks where comformity is less advantageous than in the public schools. The common response to the finding that one group shows better school performance is that such a group must have had superior socialization. In fact, however, higher school performance might be obtained at a cost in mental health and self-fulfillment and might not predict intellectual development in the college years and beyond. It is probably not irrelevant to these results that Moore's data were collected in England where family size was smaller than in America during the 1950s. One of the difficulties with long-term longitudinal research is that one often learns a great deal about a pattern that no longer exists. Moore's English data may be more relevant to the situation in the United States today, at least with respect to family size, than if the same study had been carried out in America.

The Hetherington study, a short-term longitudinal one, is the only study that looked at the timing of employment status with respect to other significant events in the family in evaluating its impact on the child. In a study of the effects of divorce on 4-year-olds, Hetherington found that adverse effects were diminished when the mother had been employed before the divorce. The mother's job helped her to cope more effectively, both psychologically and economically. A particularly difficult situation, on the other hand, occurred when the mother started work at the time of the divorce. The new job helped the mother in some ways, such as providing self-esteem and new social contact, but it was difficult for the child because it increased the disruption in routines and thus added to the child's losses.

RESOURCES

An important way in which the mother's job affects the family and the child's socialization is through the money it brings. In low-income groups, the mother's wages make a considerable difference. According to 1979 statistics compiled by the Women's Bureau, 14.8% of the two-parent families were categorized "poor" when the mother did not work, and 3.8% when she was in the labor force (U.S. Department of Labor, 1980). In father-absent homes the significance of the mother's wages for escape from poverty was even greater. In Cherry and Eaton's (1977) longitudinal study of lower-class black families, the highest per capita income was found in the dual-wage families and the lowest in the mother-headed, nonemployed families; and families headed by single employed women were financially better off than couples with nonemployed wives.

The study by Cherry and Eaton examined the relationship between maternal employment during the first 3 years of the child's life and various indices of cognitive and physical development at ages 4, 7, and 8. The generally positive associations between maternal employment and scores on the Illinois Test of Psycholinguistic Ability and the Wechsler Preschool and Primary Scale of Intelligence, as well as positive relationships with physical development, were in part mediated by the higher per capita income. Maternal employment related to higher per capita income; higher per capita income related to higher cognitive and physical development scores at least for this sample of low-income families. Earlier in this chapter the stress of poverty was discussed; the mother's wages are also important ameliorators of this stress.

The effect of the mother's wages on the middle-class family is not as clearly documented. Interview data indicate that it may be a means of maintaining the family's accustomed standard of living in periods of inflation or when there is no other income, of taking pressure off the father, or simply enabling the family to spend more on necessities or luxuries (Lein et al., 1974). Several studies examined the relationship between the mother's employment status and children's college plans, but no clear pattern emerged (Hoffman, 1974c). Where the range of income is wider, as in the "middle class," it is difficult to demonstrate the effects of an increment.

A popular theory in sociology is that the woman's occupation and the wages she contributes to the family provide a resource that increases her family power (Blood & Wolfe, 1960; Goode, 1964). As noted earlier, maternal employment does seem to increase the woman's say in economic decisions. As such this may increase her status in the family and contribute to the children's greater respect for female competence.

Finally, data indicate a higher divorce rate for families with employed wives (Sawhill, Peabody, Jones, & Caldwell, 1975). At least part of the explanation for the relationship seems to be that the monetary resource and the woman's wage-earning ability enable the divorce to take place. In some cases, in fact, the employment was undertaken to make a divorce possible. Data do not indicate less marital happiness in employed-mother families, but rather that the woman's greater economic independence enables a wanted divorce to take place.

THE FATHER'S AND THE MOTHER'S JOBS

There have been both parallels and divergencies in considering the effects on the family of the mother's and the father's employment. The four general processes examined—employment as something that shapes the family values, influences the worker's psychological state, imposes time and schedule demands, and provides resources—have served to organize both discussions. The independent variable in the discussion of the mother's occupation, however, has typically been employment versus nonemployment. Some research has considered the effects of preferring to work while nonemployed, but unemployment per se has not been studied. Furthermore, studies that considered the mother's particular job in its effects on the family have been rare. There has been research on women in selected occupations, such as engineering (Perrucci, 1970), medicine (Cartwright, 1972; Walsh, 1977), and management (Hennig & Jardim, 1977), but the focus of these investigations has not been on family effects. The father's occupation, on the other hand, has been considered in its more specific aspects—its capacity for expressing authority, for example—and there has been some research on the family impact of the father's involuntary unemployment. These differences are not, of course, capricious. Fathers are not voluntarily "nonemployed." The mother is more likely to have child-care and household responsibilities with which work time competes. There are a wider variety of male occupations for specification. Studies of unemployment were most often conducted in the 1930s when maternal employment was uncommon.

Furthermore, and for similar reasons, the dependent variables have been different. The studies of the father's occupation, since they look at a more specific independent variable, have also looked for more specific effects, and these studies have not been burdened by the "social problem" label. The dependent variables in the maternal employment studies, on the other hand, have often been too broad and evaluative to be meaningful. It seems likely that both maternal employment and nonemployment carry certain strengths and vulnerabilities for the child, as well as influences not capable of evaluation, and the social as well as scientific value of these studies will be enhanced when this is more widely appreciated. Previous reviews of maternal employment effects (Hoffman, 1963, 1974c, 1980a, 1980b) have already argued for the need to specify employment, consider the various conditioning variables, and spell out the intervening processes, all of which are points that could also be made about studies of paternal employment. But the maternal employment studies are also particularly in need of more sharply defined dependent variables.

In view of these divergencies between the studies of maternal and paternal employment, it is not surprising that few research endeavors have examined the effects of both simultaneously. There are some qualitative investigations of dual-wage couples that have considered the mutual accommodations and adjustments that are involved when both parents work (Garland, 1972; Holmstrom, 1972; Lein et al., 1974; Poloma, 1972; Rapaport & Rapoport, 1971). And several studies have reconsidered the Parsonian hypothesis that the division of functions between spouses, and particularly the unilateral occupational commitment that circumvents competition between spouses, is functional to marriage. The possibility that a women's superior occupational status is disturbing to the marital relationship has been investigated in several studies. Both Garland (1972) and Safilios-Rothschild (1976) suggest that there is a problem, but it can be tolerated if the husband's income is higher. Hoffman (1977) found, as already indicated, that there is a problem for some women, and a pregnancy may result. But Richardson (1979) found no marital difficulty associated with the woman's greater occupational prestige, and several studies suggest that when the husband's occupation leads to new experiences and growth, the marital relationship does better if the wife has a comparable kind of occupation (Dizard, 1968; Levinson, 1964; Seidenberg, 1973).

None of the studies dealing with the possible threat of occupational competition examined effects on the child's socialization experiences, though effects might be expected. It has been suggested elsewhere (Hoffman, 1979), for example, that the strained relationship sometimes observed between fathers and sons when mothers are employed in the blue-collar class is a function of the perception that maternal employment undermines the father's prestige. This perception does not typically prevail in the middle class but might under conditions of occupational competition. Social scientists have not yet dared, however, to tackle the complex task of analyzing the interactions among the occupations of each parent, family patterns, and the child's socialization.

SUMMARY AND CONCLUSIONS

In an effort to explore the effects of work on the family and the child's socialization, four independent variables were considered: (*a*) general economic conditions, or the organization of work at the broad social level; (*b*) social class, which is determined to a considerable extent by the father's occupation; (*c*) the father's job; and (*d*) the mother's job. The general economic conditions were seen as affecting the family form, its structure, and its values. A society socializes its children to fill the adult roles; these roles are largely determined by economic factors at this broad social level, and child-rearing patterns reflect these adult role expectations. There are differences within the society, but also general influences that can be seen as characterizing all of its members, distinguishing them as a group. Thus, general economic conditions were described as having their own impact on the family and the child's socialization, though they also were seen as operating through intervening variables and as a setting that affects the impact of the more specific influences on the family.

Social class was discussed as affecting the family and the child through its significance for the parent's power position in society, which is replicated in child-rearing practices. Because lower-class parents are subject to unexplained rules and authority on the job and in relation to other institutions in society, they reflect this in their authority relations with their children; this perpetuates in the child the parents' own social-class-derived sense of ineffectiveness and provides a less stimulating cognitive environment. In addition, the social class of the child's family affects the degree of similarity he experiences with the school, which is middle class, the resources that are available to him, and the levels of stress and vulnerability to crisis that prevail in the family.

Both the father's and the mother's jobs were seen as influencing the values perpetuated in the family, as affecting the parent's needs and emotions that are expressed in the family, and as making demands on time that might otherwise be spent with the family. For the father, the focus was on the particular job; for the mother, it was employment status per se. Up until the present, unemployment has been viewed as a problem only for men, while employment has been viewed as a problem for women; for both economic and psychological reasons, however, unemployment may now be a problem for both, and social change has made the role of the nonemployed housewife increasingly difficult and increasingly rare.

Social change was viewed as particularly important in analyzing the effects of maternal employment on the family. While there are data that make possible comparisons between the current families of employed women and full-time housewives, there are no data to indicate which represents more continuity with mothers of the past. Decreases in the amount of required housework time and family size, as well as shifts in social norms and the prevalent maternal employment patterns, can lead one to see the current employed mother as like the nonemployed mother of the past, while the current nonemployed mother represents a new pattern.

In analyzing the jobs of each parent, the effect on the other was noted—that is, how the husband's job sometimes pulled the wife into activities connected with his career and the wife's job pulled the husband into activities in the household—yet research has rarely considered the jobs of both simultaneously. As Bronfenbrenner and Crouter (1982) have also suggested, there is need for parallel analysis, in which similar questions are asked about the jobs of each, and interactive analysis, in which the jobs of both are simultaneously considered.

REFERENCES

Aldous, J. Wives' employment status and lower-class men as husband-fathers: Support for the Moynihan thesis. *Journal of Marriage and the Family,* 1969, **31**, 469–476.

Aldous, J., Osmond, M., & Hicks, M. Men's work and men's families. In W. Burr, R. Hill, I. Reiss, & F. I. Nye (Eds.), *Contemporary theories about the family.* New York: Free Press, 1979.

Anderson, M. *Family structure in nineteenth century Lancashire.* Cambridge: Cambridge University Press, 1971.

Angell, R. E. *The family encounters the Depression.* New York: Scribner's, 1936.

Bahr, S. J. Effects on power and division of labor in the family. In L. W. Hoffman & F. I. Nye (Eds.), *Working mothers.* San Francisco: Jossey-Bass, 1974.

Barry, H. A., Bacon, M. K., & Child, I. L. A cross cultural survey of some sex differences in socialization. *Journal of Abnormal Social Psychology,* 1957, **55**, 8.

Baruch, G. K. Maternal influences upon college women's attitudes toward women and work. *Developmental Psychology,* 1972, **6**, 32–37. (a)

Baruch, G. K. *Maternal role pattern as related to self-esteem and parental identification in college women.* Paper presented at meeting of the Eastern Psychological Association, Boston, April 1972. (b)

Baruch, G. K., & Barnett, R. C. Fathers' participation in the care of their preschool children. *Sex Roles,* 1981, **7**, 1043–1055.

Battle, E. S., & Rotter, J. B. Children's feeling of personal control as related to social class and ethnic groups. *Journal of Personality,* 1963, **31**, 482–490.

Bem, S. I. Sex-role adaptability: One consequence of psychological androgyny. *Journal of Personality and Social Psychology,* 1975, **31**, 534–643.

Bendix, R., & Lipset, S. M. (Eds.). *Class, status and power: A reader in social stratification.* Glencoe, Ill.: Free Press, 1953.

Bendix, R., & Lipset, S. M. (Eds.). *Class, status, and power: Social stratification in comparative perspective* (2d ed.). New York: Free Press, 1966.

Bernstein, B. Some sociological determinants of perception. *British Journal of Sociology,* 1958, **9**, 159–174.

Bernstein, B. Language and social class. *British Journal of Sociology,* 1960, **11**, 271–276.

Bernstein, B. Social class and linguistic development: A theory of social learning. In A. H.

Halsey, J. Floud, & C. A. Anderson (Eds.), *Economy, education and society.* New York: Free Press, 1961.

Bernstein, B. Elaborated and restricted codes: Their social origins and some consequences. In J. Gumperz & D. Hymes (Eds.), The ethnography of communication. *American Anthropologist Special Publication*, 1964, 66, 55–69.

Birnbaum, J. A. Life patterns and self-esteem in gifted family oriented and career committed women. In M. S. Mednick, S. S. Tangri, & L. W. Hoffman (Eds.), *Women and achievement.* Washington, D.C.: Hemisphere, 1975.

Blau, P. M., & Duncan, O. D. *The American occupational structure.* New York: Wiley, 1967. (a)

Blau, P. M., & Duncan, O. D. Men's work and men's families. In *The American occupational structure.* New York: Wiley, 1967. (b)

Block, J. H. Issues, problems, and pitfalls in assessing sex differences. *Merrill-Palmer Quarterly*, 1976, 22, 283–308.

Block, J. H. *Personality development in males and females: The influence of differential socialization.* Master Series Lecture, annual meeting of the American Psychological Association, New York, 1979.

Blood, R. O., Jr., & Wolfe, D. M. *Husbands and wives.* Glencoe, Ill.: Free Press, 1960.

Blumberg, R. L. *Structural factors affecting women's status: A cross-cultural paradigm.* Paper presented at the meeting of the International Sociological Association, Toronto, 1974.

Bohen, H., & Viveros-Long, A. *Balancing jobs and family life: Do flexible work schedules help?* Philadelphia: Temple University Press, 1981.

Bram, S. *To have or have not: A social psychological study of voluntarily childless couples, parents-to-be, and parents.* Unpublished doctoral dissertation, University of Michigan, 1974.

Bronfenbrenner, U. Socialization and social class through time and space. In E. Maccoby, T. Newcomb, & R. Hartley (Eds.), *Readings in social psychology.* New York: Holt, 1958.

Bronfenbrenner, U., & Crouter, A. *Work and family through time and space.* In S. B. Kamerman & C. D. Hayes (Eds.), *Families that work: Children in a changing world.* Washington, D.C.: National Academy Press, 1982.

Burchinal, L. G. Personality characteristics of children. In F. I. Nye & L. W. Hoffman (Eds.), *The employed mother in America.* Chicago: Rand McNally, 1963.

Campbell, A. The role of family planning in the reduction of poverty. *Journal of Marriage and the Family*, 1968, 30, 236–245.

Caplow, T. *The sociology of work.* Minneapolis: University of Minnesota Press, 1953.

Cartright, L. K. Conscious factors entering into decisions of women to study medicine. *Journal of Social Issues*, 1972, 28, 201–216.

Caudill, W., & Weinstein, H. Maternal care and infant behavior in Japan and America. *Psychiatry*, 1969, 32, 12–43.

Cavan, R. S., & Ranck, K. *The family and the Depression.* Chicago: University of Chicago Press, 1938.

Charters, W. W., Jr. The social background of teaching. In N. L. Gage (Ed.), *Handbook of research on teaching.* Chicago: Rand McNally, 1963.

Chase-Lansdale, P. L. *Effects of maternal employment on mother-infant and father-infant attachment.* Unpublished doctoral dissertation, University of Michigan, 1981.

Cherry, R. R., & Eaton, E. L. Physical and cognitive development in children of low-income mothers working in the child's early years. *Child Development*, 1977, 48, 158–166.

Clark, R. A., & Gecas, V. *The employed father in America: A role competition analysis.* Paper presented at the Annual Meeting of the Pacific Sociological Association, 1977.

Clark, R. A., Nye, F. I., & Gecas, V. Work involvement and marital role performance. *Journal of Marriage and the Family*, 1978, **40**, 9–22.

Clausen, J. A., & Clausen, S. R. The effects of family size on parents and children. In J. T. Fawcett (Ed.), *Psychological perspectives on population*. New York: Basic, 1973.

Cobb, S., & Kasl, S. *Termination: The consequences of job loss* (Publication No. 77–224). Washington, D.C.: DHEW (NIOSH), 1977.

Cohen, A., & Hodges, H. Characteristics of the low-blue-collar class. *Social Problems*, 1963, **10**, 4.

Crandall, V. C., Katkovsky, W., & Crandall, V. J. Children's beliefs in their own control of reinforcements in intellectual-academic achievement situations. *Child Development*, 1965, **36**, 91–109.

Davis, A., & Havighurst, R. J. Social class and color differences in child rearing. *American Sociological Review*, 1946, **11**, 698–710.

Deutsch, C. P. Social class and child development. In B. M. Caldwell & H. N. Ricciuti (Eds.), *Review of child development research* (Vol. 3). Chicago: University of Chicago Press, 1973.

Deutsch, M. The disadvantaged child and the learning process. In A. H. Passow (Ed.), *Education in depressed areas*. New York: Columbia University, 1963.

Dizard, J. *Social change in the family*. Chicago: Community and Family Study Center, University of Chicago, 1968.

Douglas, W. *Ministers' wives*. New York: Harper & Row, 1965.

Douvan, E. Employment and the adolescent. In F. I Nye & L. W. Hoffman (Eds.), *The employed mother in America*. Chicago: Rand McNally, 1963.

Duvall, E. M. Conceptions of parenthood. *American Journal of Sociology*, 1946, **57**, 193–203.

Dyer, W. G. Family reactions to the father's job. In A. Shostak & W. Gomberg (Eds.), *Blue-collar world: Studies of the American worker*. Englewood Cliffs, N.J.: Prentice-Hall, 1964.

Elder, G. H., Jr. *Children of the Great Depression: Social change in life experience*. Chicago: University of Chicago Press, 1974.

Elder, G. H., Jr. Approaches to social change and the family. *American Journal of Sociology*, 1978, **84**, 1–38.

Elliot, F. R. Occupational commitments and paternal deprivation. *Child Care, Health, and Development*, 1978, **4**, 305–315.

Erikson, E. H. *Childhood and society* (2d ed.). New York: Norton, 1963.

Farel, A. N. Effects of preferred maternal roles, maternal employment, and sociographic status on school adjustment and competence. *Child Development*, 1980, **50**, 1179–1186.

Ferree, M. Working class jobs: Housework and paid work as sources of satisfaction. *Social Problems*, 1976, **23**, 431–441.

Garland, T. N. The better half? The male in the dual professional family. In C. Safilios-Rothschild (Ed.), *Toward a sociology of women*. Lexington, Mass.: Xerox College Publishing, 1972.

Gecas, V. The influence of social class in socialization. In W. Burr, R. Hill, I. Reiss, & F. I. Nye (Eds.), *Contemporary theories about the family*. New York: Free Press, 1979.

Gecas, V., & Nye, F. I. Sex and class differences in parent-child interaction: A test of Kohn's hypothesis. *Journal of Marriage and the Family*, 1974, **36**, 742–749.

Gerstl, J. E. Leisure, taste, and occupational milieu. *Social Problems*, 1961, **9**, 56–68.

Gil, D. G. *Violence against children: Physical child abuse in the United States*. Cambridge, Mass.: Harvard University Press, 1970.

Glueck, S., & Gleuck, E. Working mothers and delinquency. *Mental Hygiene*, 1957, **41**, 327–352.

Gold, D., & Andres, D. Developmental comparisons between adolescent children with employed and nonemployed mothers. *Merrill-Palmer Quarterly*, 1978, **24**, 243–254. (a)

Gold, D., & Andres, D. Developmental comparisons between 10-year-old children with employed and nonemployed mothers. *Child Development*, 1978, **49**, 75–84. (b)

Gold, D., & Andres, D. Relations between maternal employment and development of nursery school children. *Canadian Journal of Behavioral Science*, 1978, **10**, 116–129. (c)

Gold, D., Andres, D., & Glorieux, J. The development of Francophone nursery school children with employed and nonemployed mothers. *Canadian Journal of Behavioral Science*, 1979, **11**, 169–173.

Gold, M., & Slater, C. Office, factory, store, and family: A study of integration setting. *American Sociological Review*, 1958, **23**, 64–74.

Goldberg, R. J. *Maternal time use and preschool performance.* Paper presented at the meeting of the Society for Research in Child Development, New Orleans, March 1977.

Goldberg, R. J. *Development in the family and school context: Who is responsible for the education of young children in America?* Paper presented at the National Association for the Education of Young Children Annual Conference, New York, August 1978.

Goldman, N. The changing role of women in the armed forces. *American Journal of Sociology*, 1973, **78**, 892–911.

Goode, W. J. *The family*, Englewood Cliffs, N.J.: Prentice-Hall, 1964.

Greenhaus, J. H., & Kopelman, R. E. Conflict between work and nonwork roles: Implications for the career planning process. *Human Resources Planning*, 1981, 4, 1–10.

Hall, F. T., & Schroeder, M. P. Time spent on household tasks. *Journal of Home Economics*, 1970, **62**, 34–46.

Hall, R. H. *Occupations and the social structure* (2d ed.). Englewood Cliffs, N.J.: Prentice-Hall, 1975.

Hammond, S. B. Class and family. In O. A. Oeser & S. B. Hammond (Eds.), *Social structure and personality in a city.* London: Routledge & Kegan Paul, 1954.

Hartley, R. E. Children's concepts of male and female roles. *Merrill-Palmer Quarterly*, 1960, **6**, 83–91.

Heath, D. B. Some possible effects of occupation on the maturing of professional men. *Journal of Vocational Behavior*, 1977, **11**, 263–281.

Hennig, M., & Jardim, A. *The managerial woman.* Garden City, N.Y.: Anchor Press/Doubleday, 1977.

Herzog, E., & Sudia, C. Children in fatherless families. In B. M. Caldwell & H. N. Ricciuti (Eds.), *Review of child development research* (Vol. 3). Chicago: University of Chicago Press, 1973.

Hess, R. D. Social class and ethnic influences on socialization. In P. Mussen (Ed.), *Carmichael's manual of child psychology* (Vol. 2). New York: Wiley, 1970.

Hess, R. D., & Shipman, V.C. Early experience and the socialization of cognitive modes in children. *Child Development*, 1965, **34**, 869–886.

Hess, R. D., & Shipman, V. C. Cognitive elements in maternal behavior. In J. P. Hill (Ed.). *Minnesota symposia on child psychology* (Vol. 1). Minneapolis: University of Minnesota Press, 1967.

Hess, R. D., Shipman, V. C., Brophy, J., & Baer, D. *The cognitive environment of urban preschool children.* Chicago: Graduate School of Education, University of Chicago, 1968.

Hetherington, E. M. The effects of familial variables on sex typing, on parent-child similarity, and on imitation in children. In J. P. Hill (Ed.), *Minnesota symposia on child psychology* (Vol. 1). Minneapolis: University of Minnesota Press, 1967.

Hetherington, E. M. Divorce: A child's perspective. *American Psychologist*, 1979, **34**, 851–858.

Hill, C. R., & Stafford, F. P. *Parental care of children: Time diary estimates of quantity, predictability, and variety*. Working paper series, Institute for Social Research, University of Michigan, Ann Arbor, 1978.

Hock, E. Working and nonworking mothers and their infants: A comparative study of maternal care-giving characteristics and infant social behavior. *Merrill-Palmer Quarterly*, 1980, **26**, 79–101.

Hoffman, L. W. Effects of maternal employment on the child. *Child Development*, 1961, **32**, 187–197.

Hoffman, L. W. Effects on children: Summary and discussion. In F. I. Nye & L. W. Hoffman (Eds.), *The employed mother in America*. Chicago: Rand McNally, 1963.

Hoffman, L. W. Early childhood experiences and women's achievement motives. *Journal of Social Issues*, 1972, **28**, 129–156.

Hoffman, L. W. The employment of women and fertility. *Merrill-Palmer Quarterly*, 1974, **20**, 99–119. (a)

Hoffman, L. W. Psychological factors. In L. W. Hoffman & F. I. Nye (Eds.), *Working mothers*. San Francisco: Jossey Bass, 1974. (b)

Hoffman, L. W. Effects of maternal employment on the child—a review of the research. *Developmental Psychology*, 1974, **10**, 204–228. (c)

Hoffman, L. W. Changes in family roles, socialization, and sex differences. *American Psychologist*, 1977, **32**, 644–657.

Hoffman, L. W. Maternal employment: 1979. *American Psychologist*, 1979, **34**, 859–865.

Hoffman, L. W. *The effects of maternal employment on the academic attitudes and performance of school-aged children*. Unpublished report prepared for the National Institute for Education, Washington, D.C., 1980. (a)

Hoffman, L. W. The effects of maternal employment on the academic attitudes and performance of school-aged children. *School Psychology Review*, 1980, **9**, 319–336. (b)

Hoffman, L. W. *Assessment of the adequacy of measurement and theory in a cross-cultural investigation of the value of children to parents*. Paper presented at the International Congress of Psychology, Leipzig, July 1980.(c)

Hoffman, L. W. *Dual-wage family and the preschool child*. Talk delivered at Yale University, Bush Center in Child Development, April 6, 1981.

Hoffman, L. W. Increased fathering: Effects on the mother. In M. Lamb & A. Sagi (Eds.), *Social policies and legal issues pertaining to fatherhood*. Hillsdale, N.J.: Erlbaum, 1983.

Hoffman, L. W., & Hoffman, M. L. The value of children to parents. In J. T. Fawcett (Ed.), *Psychological perspectives on fertility*. New York: Basic, 1973.

Hoffman, L. W., & Lippitt, R. O. The measurement of family life variables. In D. Goslin (Ed.), *Handbook of research methods in child development*. New York: Wiley, 1960.

Hoffman, L. W., & Manis, J. D. Influences of children on marital interaction and parental satisfactions and dissatisfactions. In R. Lerner & G. Spanier (Eds.), *Child influences on marital and family interaction: A life-span perspective*. New York: Academic Press, 1978.

Hoffman, L. W., & Manis, J. D. The value of children in the United States: A new approach to the study of fertility. *Marriage and the Family*, 1979, **42**, 583–596.

Hoffman, L. W., & Nye, F. I. *Working mothers*. San Francisco: Jossey-Bass, 1974.

Hoffman, L. W., Thornton, A., & Manis, J. D. The value of children to parents in the United States. *Population: Behavioral, Social, and Environmental Issues*, 1978, **1**, 91–131.

Hoffman, L. W., & Wyatt, F. Social change and motivation for having larger families: Some theoretical considerations. *Merrill-Palmer Quarterly*, 1960, **6**, 235–244.

Hoffman, M. L. Power assertion by the parent and its impact on the child. *Child Development,* 1960, **31**, 129–143.

Hoffman, M. L. Childrearing practices and moral development: Generalizations from empirical research. *Child Development,* 1963, **34**, 295–318.

Hoffman, M. L., & Saltzstein, H. D. Parent discipline and the child's moral development. *Journal of Personality and Social Psychology,* 1967, **5**, 45–57.

Holmstrom, L. *The two-career family.* Cambridge, Mass.: Schenkman, 1972.

Howe, I. *World of our fathers.* New York: Harcourt Brace Jovanovich, 1976.

Hughes, E. C. *Men and their work.* Glencoe, Ill.: Free Press, 1958.

Justice, B., & Duncan, D. F. Child abuse as a work-related problem. *Journal of Behavior Technology, Methods and Therapy,* 1977, **23**, 53–55.

Kagan, J. The child in the family. In A. S. Rossi, J. Kagan, & T. K. Hareven (Eds.), *The family.* New York: Norton, 1978.

Kagan, J., & Moss, H. A. *Birth to maturity.* New York: Wiley, 1962.

Kahn, R. L. Work, stress and social support. In D. G. McGuigan (Ed.), *Changing family, changing workplace.* Ann Arbor: University of Michigan, 1980.

Kanter, R. M. *Work and family in the United States: A critical review of research and policy.* New York: Russell Sage, 1977.

Kappel, B. E., & Lambert, R. D. *Self-worth among the children of working mothers.* Unpublished manuscript, University of Waterloo, Ontario, Canada, 1972.

Kar, S. B. Individual aspirations as related to early and late acceptance of contraception. *Journal of Social Psychology,* 1971, **83**, 235–245.

Keith, P. M., & Schafer, R. B. Role strain and depression in two-job families. *Family Relations,* 1980, **29** 483–488.

Kessler, R. C., & McRae, J. A., Jr. Trends in the relationship between sex and psychological distress: 1957–1976. *American Sociological Review,* 1981, **46**, 443–452.

Kessler, R. C., & McRae, J. A., Jr. The effects of wives' employment on the mental health of married men and women. *American Sociological Review,* 1982, **47**, 216–227.

Kliger, D. *The effects of employment of married women on husband and wife roles: A study in cultural change.* Unpublished doctoral dissertation, Yale University, 1954.

Kohn, M. L. Social class and the exercise of parental authority. *American Sociological Review,* 1959, **24**, 352–366. (a)

Kohn, M. L. Social class and parental values. *American Journal of Sociology,* 1959, **64**, 337–351. (b)

Kohn, M. L. Social class and parent-child relationships: An interpretation. *American Journal of Sociology,* 1963, **68**, 471–480.

Kohn, M. L. *Personlichkeit, beruf und soziale schichtung: Ein Bezugsrahmen.* Heidelberg: Klett-Cotta, 1980.

Komorovsky, M. *The unemployed man and his family.* New York: Dryden, 1940.

Kovar, M. G. *Better health for our children: A national strategy.* (Vol. 3): *A statistical profile.* Washington, D.C.: Public Health Service, Office of the Assistant Secretary for Health and Surgeon General, 1981.

Kroes, W. H. & Hurrell, J. J. *Job stress and the police officer: Identifying stress reduction techniques.* Washington, D.C.: Department of Health, Education and Welfare, Public Health Service, December 1975.

Landy, F., Rosenberg, B. G., & Sutton-Smith, B. The effects of limited father absence on cognitive development. *Child Development,* 1969, **40**, 941–944.

Lefcourt, H. M. Internal versus external control of reinforcement: A review. *Psychological Bulletin,* 1966, **65**, 206–220.

Lein, L., et al. *Work and family life* (Final report to the National Institute of Education, 1974). Cambridge, Mass.: Center for the Study of Public Policy, 1974.

Levenstein, P. Cognitive growth in preschoolers through verbal interaction with mothers. *American Journal of Orthopsychiatry*, 1970, **40**, 426–432.

Levinson,ʼ H. *Emotional problems in the world of work*. New York: Harper & Row, 1964.

Lewin, K. *A dynamic theory of personality*. New York: McGraw-Hill, 1935.

Lewis, R. Toward an understanding of police anomie. *Journal of Police Science and Administration*, 1973, **1**, 484–490.

Livson, N., & Day, D. Adolescent personality antecedents of completed family size: A longitudinal study. *Journal of Youth and Adolescence*, 1977, **6**, 311–324.

Lueptow, L., McClendon, M., & McKeon, J. Father's occupation and son's personality: Findings and questions for the emerging linkage hypothesis. *Sociological Quarterly*, 1979, **20**, 463–475.

Lynn, D. *The father: His role in child development*. Monterey, Calif.: Brooks/Cole, 1974.

Lynn, D., & Sawrey, W. L. The effects of father-absence on Norwegian boys and girls. *Journal of Abnormal and Social Psychology*, 1959, **59**, 258–262.

Maccoby, E. E. Children and working mothers. *Children*, 1958, **5**, 83–89.

Marantz, S. A., & Mansfield, A. F. Maternal employment and the development of sex-role stereotyping in five- to eleven-year-old girls. *Child Development*, 1977, **48**, 668–673.

Margolis, L., & Farran, D. Unemployment: The health consequences for children. *North Carolina Medical Journal*, in press.

Mathews, S. M. The effects of the mothers' out-of-home employment upon children's ideas and attitudes. *Journal of Applied Psychology*, 1934, **18**, 116–136.

McGuire, C. Social stratification and mobility patterns. *American Sociological Review*, 1950, **15**, 195–204.

McKinley, D. G. *Social class and family life*. New York: Free Press, 1964.

Medrich, E. *The serious business of growing up: A study of children's lives outside of school*. Berkeley: University of California Press, 1981.

Miller, D. R., & Swanson, G. E. *The changing American parent*. New York: Wiley, 1958.

Miller, S. M. Effects of maternal employment on sex-role perception, interests, and self-esteem in kindergarten girls. *Developmental Psychology*, 1975, **11**, 405–406.

Moen, P., Kain, E. L., & Elder, G. H. *Economic conditions and family life: Contemporary and historical perspectives, 1981*. Washington, D.C.: National Academy of Sciences, Assembly of Behavioral and Social Sciences, Committee on Child Development and Public Policy, 1981.

Moore, T. W. Exclusive early mothering and its alternatives. *Scandinavian Journal of Psychology*, 1975, **16**, 256–272.

Mortimer, J. T. Patterns of intergenerational occupational movements: A smallest-space analysis. *American Journal of Sociology*, 1974, **79**, 1278–1299.

Mortimer, J. T. Social class, work, and the family: Some implications of the father's occupation for familial relationships and sons's career decisions. *Journal of Marriage and the Family*, 1976, **38**, 241–256.

Mortimer, J. T., Hall, R., & Hill, R. *Husbands' occupational attributes as constraints on wives' employment*. Paper presented at the annual meeting of the American Sociological Association, New York, August 1976.

Mott, P. E., et al. *Shift work: The social psychology, and physical consequences*. Ann Arbor: University of Michigan Press, 1965.

Mueller, E. The economic value of children in peasant agriculture. In R. G. Ridker (Ed.), *Population and development*. Baltimore: Johns Hopkins University Press, 1976.

Myers, S. S. Child abuse and the military community. *Military Medicine*, 1979, **144**, 23–25.

Nieva, V. F., & Rieck, A. *Job related moves: Effects on whole-family conflicts, stresses and satisfactions*. Paper presented at the American Psychological Association, Montreal, September 1980.

Nordlicht, S. Effects of stress on the police officer and family. *New York State Journal of Medicine*, 1979, **79**, 400–401.

Nye, F. I., & Hoffman, L. W. *The employed mother in American*, Chicago: Rand McNally, 1963.

O'Brien, T. E. Violence in divorce-prone families. *Journal of Marriage and the Family*, 1971, **33**, 292–298.

Oeser, O. A., & Hammond, S. B. *Social structure and personality in a city*. New York: Macmillan, 1954.

Ogburn, W. F., & Nimkoff, M. F. *Technology and the changing family*. New York: Houghton Mifflin, 1955.

Oppenheimer, V. K. Demographic influence on female employment and the status of women. *American Journal of Sociology*, 1973, **78**, 946–961.

Orshansky, M. Who's who among the poor: A demographic view of poverty. *Social Security Bulletin*, 1965, **28**, 3–32.

Parke, R. D., & Collmer, C. W. Child abuse: An interdisciplinary analysis. In E. M. Hetherington (Ed.), *Review of child development research* (Vol. 5). Chicago: University of Chicago Press, 1975.

Parsons, T. The American family: Its relation to personality and the social structure. In T. Parsons & R. F. Bales (Eds.), *Family, socialization and interaction process*. Glencoe, Ill.: Free Press, 1955.

Pearlin, L. I. *Class context and family relations: A cross-national study*. Boston: Little, Brown, 1970.

Pearlin, L. I., & Kohn, M. L. Social class, occupation, and parental values: A cross-national study. *American Sociological Review*, 1966, **31**, 466–479.

Pederson, F. A., Cain, R., Zaslow, M., & Anderson, B. Variation in infant experience associated with alternative family role organization. In L. Laesa & I. Sigel (Eds.), *Families as learning environment for children*. New York: Plenum, 1981.

Perrucci, C. C. Minority status and the pursuit of professional careers: Women in sciences and engineering. *Social Forces*, 1970, **49**, 245–258.

Piotrkowski, C. S. *Work and the family system: A naturalistic study of working-class and lower-middle-class families*. New York: Free Press, 1979.

Piotrkowski, C. S., & Crits-Christoph, P. Occupational life and women's family adjustment. *Journal of Family Issues*, 1981, **2**, 126–147.

Piotrkowski, C. S., & Katz, M. H. Indirect socialization of children: The effects of mothers' jobs on academic behaviors. *Child Development*, 1982, **53**, 1520–1529.

Pleck, J., Lang, L., & Rustad, M. *Men's family work, involvement, and satisfaction*. Unpublished manuscript, Wellesley College Center for Research on Women, 1978.

Pleck, J., & Rustad, M. *Husbands' and wives' time in family work and paid work in the 1975–1976 study of time use*. Unpublished manuscript, Wellesley College Center for Research on Women, 1980.

Poloma, M. M. Role conflict and the married professional woman. In C. Safilios-Rothschild (Ed.), *Toward a sociology of women*. Lexington, Mass.: Xerox College Publishing, 1972.

Quarm, D. E. A. *The measurement of marital powers*. Unpublished doctoral dissertation, University of Michigan, 1977.

Quinn, R. P., & Staines, G. L. *The 1977 quality of employment survey*. Ann Arbor: Institute for Social Research, Survey Research Center, University of Michigan, 1979.

Rainwater, L. *Family design: Marital sexuality, family size, and contraception*. Chicago: Aldine, 1965.

Rapaport, R., & Rapoport, R. N. Work and family in contemporary society. *American Sociological Review*, 1965, **30**, 381–94.

Rapaport, R., & Rapoport, R. N. *Dual career families*, Baltimore: Penguin, 1971.

Renshaw, J. R. An exploration of the dynamics of the overlapping worlds of work and family life. *Family Process*, 1976, **15**, 143–165.

Richardson, J. G. Wife occupational superiority and marital troubles: An examination of the hypothesis. *Journal of Marriage and the Family*, 1979, **41**, 63–72.

Riesman, D. Work and leisure in post-industrial society. In E. Larrabee & R. Meyersohn (Eds.), *Mass leisure*. Glencoe, Ill.: Free Press, 1958.

Robinson, J. P. *Change in Americans' use of time: 1965–1975*. Cleveland: Cleveland Communications Research Center, Cleveland State University, 1977.

Robinson, J. P. *How Americans use time: A sociological perspective*. New York: Praeger, 1978.

Robinson, J. P. Housework technology and household work. In S. F. Bern (Ed.), *Women and household labor*. Beverly Hills, Calif.: Sage, 1980.

Roe, A. *The psychology of occupations*. New York: Wiley, 1956.

Romer, N., & Cherry, D. *Developmental effects of preschool and school age maternal employment in children's sex role concepts*. Unpublished manuscript, Brooklyn College of the City University of New York, 1978.

Rossi, A. *Assessing women's history: Our feminist predecessors*. Paper presented at the Center for Continuing Education of Women, University of Michigan, Ann Arbor, October 19, 1971.

Rubin, L. *Worlds of pain*. New York: Basic, 1977.

Safilios-Rothschild, C. Dual linkages between the occupational and family systems: A macrosociological analysis. *Signs*, 1976, **1**, 51–60.

Sarason, S. B. Jewishness, blackishness, and the nature-nurture controversy. *American Psychologist*, 1973, **28**, 962–971.

Sawhill, I. V., Peabody, G. E., Jones, C. A., & Caldwell, S. B. *Income transfers and family structure* (Urban Institute Working Paper No. 979–03). Washington, D.C.: Urban Institute, 1975.

Scanzoni, J. H. Resolution of occupational-conjugal role conflict in clergy marriages. *Journal of Marriage and and the Family*, 1965, **27**, 396–402.

Schneider, E. V. *Industrial society*. New York: McGraw-Hill, 1957.

Schubert, J. B., Bradley-Johnson, S., & Nuttal, J. Mother-infant communication and maternal employment. *Child Development*, 1980, **51**, 246–249.

Seidenberg, R. *Corporate wives—corporate casualties?* New York: AMACOM, 1973.

Sennett, R., & Cobb, J. *The hidden injuries of class*. New York: Knopf, 1972.

Smelser, N. J. *Social change in the industrial revolution: An application of theory to the British cotton industry*. Chicago: University of Chicago Press, 1959.

Smokler, C. S. Self-esteem in pre-adolescent and adolescent females (Doctoral dissertation, University of Michigan, 1975). *Dissertation Abstracts International*, 1975, **35**, 3599B. (University Microfilms No. TS2 75–00,813)

Staines, G. L., & Pleck, J. H. *The impact of work schedules on the family*. Ann Arbor, Mich.: Institute for Social Research, 1983.

Stein, B. A., Cohen, A., & Gadon, H. Flextime: Work when you want to. *Psychology Today*, 1976, **10**, 40–43.

Steinmetz, S. K. Occupational environment in relation to physical punishment and dogmatism. In S. Steinmetz & M. Strauss (Eds.), *Violence in the family*. New York: Dodd, Mead, 1974.

Steinmetz, S. K., & Straus, M. A. (Eds.). *Violence in the family*. New York: Dodd, Mead, 1974.

Stolz, L. M. Effects of maternal employment on children: Evidence from research. *Child Development*, 1960, **31**, 749–783.

Strodtbeck, F. L. Family interaction, values, and achievement. In D. McClelland, A. Baldwin, U. Bronfenbrenner, & F. Strodtbeck (Eds.), *Talent and society*. New York: Van Nostrand, 1958.

Symonds, M. Emotional hazards of police work. *American Journal of Psychoanalysis*, 1970, **2**, 155–160.

Taylor, M., & Hartley, S. The two person career. *Sociology of Work and Occupations*, 1975, **24**, 354–372.

Terrel, G., Jr., Durkin, K., & Wiesley, M. Social class and the nature of the incentive in discrimination learning. *Journal of Abnormal Social Psychology*, 1959, **59**, 270–272.

Tiller, P. O. *Father absence and personality development in children of sailor families*. (Nordisk Psykologi's Monographs, Series No. 9.) Oslo: Bokhjrnet, 1958.

Tilly, L. Women, work and family. In D. G. McGuigan (Ed.), *Changing family, changing workplace*. Ann Arbor: University of Michigan, 1980.

U.S. Department of Commerce, Bureau of the Census. *Population profile of the United States, 1978, population characteristics* (Current Population Reports, Series P-20, No. 336). Washington, D.C.: Government Printing Office, April 1979.

U.S. Department of Commerce, Bureau of the Census. *Population profile of the United States, 1979, population characteristics* (Current Population Reports, Series P-20, No. 350). Washington, D.C.: Government Printing Office, May 1980. (a)

U.S. Department of Commerce, Bureau of the Census. *Americans and living arrangements*. Paper prepared for the White House Conference on Families, 1980. (b)

U.S. Department of Labor, Bureau of Labor Statistics. *Marital and family characteristics of workers, March, 1980* (ASI 6748-58, news release on microfiche). Washington, D.C. Department of Labor, 1981. (a)

U.S. Department of Labor, Bureau of Labor Statistics. *Marital and family characteristics of labor force* (Special Labor Force Report No. 237). Washington, D.C.: Department of Labor, 1981. (b)

U.S. Department of Labor, Women's Bureau. *Working mothers and their children*. Washington, D.C.: Government Printing Office, 1977.

U.S. Department of Labor, Women's Bureau. *The employment of women: General diagnosis of developments and issues*. Washington, D.C.: Government Pringing Office, 1980.

University of Michigan, Office of Research Administration. Household work, 1926–1965. *Research News*, 1973, **22**, 6–7.

Veroff, J., Douvan, E., & Kulka, R. *The inner American: A self-portrait from 1957 to 1976*. New York: Basic, 1981.

Vogel, S. R., Broverman, I. K., Broverman, D. M., Clarkson, F., & Rosenkrantz, P. Maternal employment and perception of sex roles among college students. *Developmental Psychology*, 1970, **3**, 384–391.

Walker, K. E. Homemaking still takes time. *Journal of Home Economics*, 1969, **61**, 621–624.

Walker, K. E., & Woods, M. *Time use: A measure of household production of family goods and services*. Washington, D.C.: American Home Economics Association, 1976.

Walsh, M. R. *Doctors wanted: No women need apply*. New Haven, Conn.: Yale University Press, 1977.

Walshok, M. L. Occupational values and family roles: A descriptive study of women working in blue-collar and service occupations. *Urban and Social Change Review*, 1978, **11**, 12–20.

Warner, W. L., Havighurst, R. J., & Loeb, M. B. *Who shall be educated?* New York: Harper, 1944.

Warner, W. L., Meeker, M., & Eells, K. *Social class in America*. Chicago: Science Research Associates, 1949.

Waters, E., & Crandall, V. J. Social class and observed maternal behavior from 1940–1960. *Child Development*, 1964, **35**, 1021–1032.

Weissman, M. M., & Paykel, E. S. Moving and depression in women. *Society*, 1972, **9**, 24–28.

Whyte, W., Jr. *The organization man.* New York: Doubleday, 1956.

Whyte, W., Jr. The wives of management. *Fortune*, October 1951, pp. 86–88, 204–213; November 1951, pp. 109–111, 150–158.

Wilensky, H. L. The uneven distribution of leisure: The impact of economic growth on "free time." *Social Problems*, 1961, **9**, 107–45.

Willmott, P. Family, work, and leisure conflicts among male employees: Some preliminary findings. *Human Relations*, 1971, **24**, 575–84.

Winett, R. A., & Neale, M. S. Flexitime and family time allocation: An analysis of a system change on individual data. *Journal of Applied Behavior*, 1981, **14**, 39–46.

Woods, M. B. The unsupervised child of the working mother. *Developmental Psychology*, 1972, **6**, 14–25.

Yarrow, M. R., Scott, P., De Leeuw, L., & Heinig, C. Childrearing in families of working and non-working mothers. *Sociometry*, 1962, **25**, 122–140.

Zajonc, R., & Markus, G. Birth order and intellectual development. *Psychological Review*, 1975, **82**, 74–88.

Zigler, E., & DeLabry, J. Concept-switching in middle-class, lower-class and retarded children. *Journal of Abnormal Social Psychology*, 1962, **65**, 267–273.

8   Child, Family, and Community

URIE BRONFENBRENNER
PHYLLIS MOEN
Cornell University

JAMES GARBARINO
Pennsylvania State University

Our goal for this chapter is to review existing research dealing with community influences on family functioning and child development and to offer a set of conceptual guidelines for future investigations on this topic. In spite of the recent resurgence of interest in the ecological embeddedness of families in a wider network of social systems (Brim, 1975; Bronfenbrenner, 1979), the amount of empirical work in this area is still meager. Part of the difficulty in approaching this task stems from the fact that such terms as "community" or "neighborhood" have not as yet been perceived as important referents by the gatekeepers of the field of child development. This is evident by the scattered references to this topic in major handbooks of research on child development, annual reviews, and other bibliographic sources such as *Child Development Abstracts*.

With these caveats in mind, the chapter turns to a clarification of some theoretical and methodological issues and to the identification of some major research questions. The studies are of two major kinds: (1) those that deal with effects of the community as a whole; (2) those that examine the influence of specific aspects of community life. The latter may be further subdivided into three categories: (*a*) formal community organizations and institutions (e.g., health and welfare services, schools, day-care services, and religious institutions); (*b*) informal community structures (e.g., social

We wish to express our appreciation to two anonymous reviewers for useful criticisms and suggestions and, especially, to the editor of this volume, Ross Parke, for his concern lest families and children get lost in the metropolis and the macrosystem. We trust this final revision has found its proper focus; may our science and our society do likewise. We would also like to express appreciation to our colleague Phil Schoggen for his generosity in sharing his knowledge of and contributions to psychological ecology, and to Gerri Jones for her invaluable assistance in bibliographical work and in the preparation of innumerable revisions of the manuscript.

networks of kin, friends, or neighbors; community behavior settings); and
(c) sources of family-community disequilibrium (e.g., residential mobility,
changing family forms and functions). Taking these distinctions into
account, the outcome of our labors is conveniently organized under six
headings as follows: (1) The Nature of Community and Community Effects;
(2) General Community Effects; (3) Effects of Formal Community Structures; (4) Effects of Informal Community Structures; (5) Sources of Family-
Community Disequilibrium; and (6) Future Perspectives.

I. THE NATURE OF COMMUNITY AND COMMUNITY EFFECTS

As we might expect, formal definitions of the concept of community have
been almost exclusively the province of the discipline of sociology. In this
context, community has been defined primarily in structural and functional
terms, but with some recognition, often reluctant, of psychological elements as well. The following formulation from the *International Encyclopedia of Social Sciences* (1968) is representative: "A community . . . , is a
territorially bounded social system or set of interlocking or integrated
functional subsystems (economic, political, religious, ethical, educational,
legal, socializing, reproductive, etc.) serving a resident population, plus
the material culture or physical plant through which the subsystems operate. The community concept does not include such characteristics as
harmony, love, we-feeling, or intimacy, which are sometimes nostalgically
imputed to idealized pre-industrial communities . . . , but it does include
a minimum of consensus" (3: 163).

Other definitions (e.g., Gans, 1968; Hillary, 1955; Hoult, 1969;
Mitchell, 1979; Warren, 1973) are less comprehensive, but always include
one or more of the three key elements in the above formulation: (1)
residence within a delimited area; (2) a set of interlocking economic and
social systems serving the needs of the resident populations; and (3) some
feeling of common identity and fate. Appropriately enough, these same
elements reappear in operational form in empirical studies on the relation
of community to the lives of families and children. As we shall see,
however, the elements are incorporated differentially both in sequence
and degree, with the first—area of residence—receiving the earliest and
the greatest attention.

The reason for this de facto priority derives primarily from methodological rather than substantive considerations. But before turning to this
issue, we must first take cognizance of a construct closely related to that of
community both in theory and in practice, the notion of neighborhood.
Neighborhood is typically defined as a smaller version of the community

(e.g., Hoult, 1969; Mitchell, 1979). A comparison of the terms ordinarily used in the two definitions suggests a qualitative difference as well. Specifically, with respect to the three elements of community, neighborhood exhibits a somewhat different profile, with emphasis placed on informal rather than formal systems, and on feelings of shared identity and common fate.

For the purposes of this review, we have included research relating to either context, provided some empirical link was or could be established to the characteristics of families or children. More precisely, we were interested in scientific studies showing, or purporting to show, that the development of specified characteristics of families or individuals can be attributed to influences emanating from the community as a whole or from one or more of its constituent subsystems. In the interest of brevity, we shall refer to this phenomenon in subsequent discussion as a "community effect."

The demonstration of community effects turns out to be no simple matter. The complexity derives from the various forms that a community effect can take, the intricacy of the structures and processes involved, and the difficulty of demonstrating the existence and direction of causal connections in the presence of a multitude of possibly confounding factors. The nature of the problem is perhaps best conveyed with the aid of a concrete example. One of the principal areas of research on community effects relates to rural-urban differences in family characteristics and individual development. The early studies in this sphere employed a seemingly straightforward design, still often used today, involving the direct comparison of samples drawn from city and country areas. In general, the findings from investigations of this sort reveal that, in comparison to their urban counterparts, rural familes exhibit more traditional values and child-rearing practices, while the children themselves show lower levels of ability and achievement. Yet even a beginning student in the social sciences can point to a serious methodological flaw in this type of design: the observed differences cannot be ascribed primarily to the influence of a rural versus urban environment without first taking into account possible differences by social class that might explain the obtained results.

But the usual strategy of dealing with such problems by controlling for possibly confounding variables, while providing important information, may also introduce some new complications that are both methodological and substantive in nature. To begin with, as structures involving "a set of interlocking or integrated functional subsystems," communities of contrasting types are likely to differ along many dimensions simultaneously. Moreover, among these dimensions are some that, like social class, have been shown to affect family functioning and development. These include such factors as age, sex, family size, ethnicity, and religion, as well as what Bronfenbrenner and Crouter (1983) have called the "new demography": single- versus two-parent families, the employment status of both mother and father, the use of day care, and—perhaps soon—the extent of father's participation in household activities. To return to our specific example, it is highly likely that rural and urban communities differ along most, if not all, of these dimensions, and that these differences in turn contribute to the observed contrasts in the psychological characteristics of rural versus urban populations. Does this mean that all of these factors must be controlled before any claims can be made for the existence of community effects? If so, any truly informative research on the topic would require enormous samples beyond the reach of most investigators, including those who, we shall argue below, have demonstrated the influence of community factors on family functioning and human development.

Beyond the issue of logistical feasibility, there is a more compelling reason to question the scientific validity, let alone the necessity, of regarding all such variables solely as sources of confounding. This statement would appear to contradict the basic methodological argument adduced earlier for the importance of introducing statistical controls. How can the two assertions be reconciled? The resolution of this paradox requires consideration of both theoretical and methodological issues. Specifically, it entails recognition of the substantive nature of the "interlocking or integrated functional subsystems" that make up the community. Such subsystems include the economic base of the community; its demographic composition and class structure; patterns of geographic and social mobility; its political, economic, educational, and religious institutions; community social networks; the ideologies associated with each of these structures; and, especially, the ways in which they are "interlocked."

The last phrase is crucial for an understanding of the nature of community and of community effect. As an integrated system, the community is more than the sum of its parts. Community effects are therefore multiplicative rather than additive. The effects derive from the coexistence and joint impact of particular subsystems and the nature of the linkages between them. Hence, the influence of the community on families and the individuals who reside within it cannot be validly measured solely by assessing and aggregating the contributions of each of its constituent subsystems. Correspondingly, if statistical controls are introduced for the influence of particular parameters, this is likely to fragment and distort community effects rather than to isolate them in purer form. For example, in research on the impact of the neighborhood on juvenile delinquency in large American cities, it is conceivable that controlling for race can wash out any neighborhood effect. It would be a mistake, however, to conclude from such a finding that neighborhood characteristics have no effect on delinquency, for the neighborhoods in which the conditions are most conducive to delinquent behavior may also be those in which a particular racial group is forced to live. Under these circumstances, race becomes a proxy variable for a complex of community subsystems that is especially likely to evoke criminal acts.

The above example illustrates a major problem in research on community. For most investigators in this sphere, the question of primary interest is how families and individuals are affected as a result of living under particular community conditions. But communities are not closed systems; some people stay, others move in or out. These migration patterns are hardly random, since they can be influenced by such community conditions as the availability of jobs, quality of schools, presence or absence of particular ethnic groups, and so on. Hence, a community or neighborhood difference in the psychological characteristics of individuals or of family behavior can reflect the influence of two somewhat different kinds of process. The first, which is of primary concern in the present chapter, is the effect on human beings of living under particular kinds of community conditions; the second, which for present purposes becomes a source of confounding, is a product of community forces that affect which groups move into the community, which move out, and which remain. Community life involves both of these processes. For purposes of reference, we may refer to the first mechanism as "community socialization" and to the second as "community selection." The task of the developmental researcher is to distinguish between them in order to establish the existence and nature of the first.

We are now in a position to set forth the analytic steps involved in establishing the existence of a community effect on family functioning or child development. Five such steps are usefully distinguished. Although two or more of them are often combined in the same investigation, we present them separately to illuminate the specific scientific task involved. Each is followed by one or more concrete examples.

1. *Demonstrating variation in community structures.* As a point of departure, it is necessary to specify particular community features presumed to influence family or individual development and then to show that communities in fact differ with respect to the features in question. In some instances, as in the urban-rural contrast, such variation is almost self-evident. In relation to other parameters, however, one has first to determine the extent of diversity. For instance, in the pages that follow we shall encounter studies documenting community differences with respect to a range of factors, including economic resources, job opportunities, health and social services, day-care facilities, schools, volunteer organizations,

and informal social networks. Many, but not all, of these factors have been shown in prior investigations to be capable of influencing the behavior of families and the development of individuals.

2. *Demonstrating psychological variations across communities.* This step entails showing that the psychological characteristics of families and individuals differ systematically as a function of particular features of communities. For example, Steinberg, Catalano, and Dooley (1981) found that as the number of jobs in the community decreases, the rate of child maltreatment rises.

3. *Establishing effects at a community level.* We have stated that a community is more than the sum of its parts. Hence, it is not sufficient to show that persons living in different kinds of communities exhibit different psychological characteristics. One must also demonstrate that the observed result is not simply an aggregate of relationships occurring at lower levels of social structure, but represents a manifestation of processes taking place at the higher-order level of the community as a whole. To return to the previous example, the fact that child abuse rises as the number of jobs in the community declines may have nothing to do with communities but simply reflect an effect of unemployment on child mal-treatment, irrespective of where the family lives. To implicate the com-munity, it would be necessary to demonstrate that the observed rela-tionship is a function of forces lying outside both family and workplace, and characterizing the community as a larger system. For example, one might show that high unemployment rates in a community are associated with a higher incidence of child abuse even among families in which the bread-winner was not unemployed.

4. *Distinguishing community processes of socialization versus selec-tion.* But if the foregoing finding were obtained, it would still be open to alternative explanations. On the one hand, it might reflect a genuine community effect—an expression in parental behavior of feelings of frustra-tion generally shared by residents in an area of high unemployment irrespective of their own job status. On the other hand, both aspects of the phenomenon may be the products of a selective process—for example, families disorganized by conflict and violence may be less likely to leave an economically deprived community in order to seek employment else-where.

Perhaps the most common source of selection effect is variation in social class composition either between communities or within the same community over time. Since many psychological characteristics are sys-tematically related to a family's socioeconomic status, community varia-tions in the distribution of families by social class constitute a major source of potential confounding in the study of community effects on family life and child development. For this reason, possible differences by social class composition must be taken into account before any conclusion can be drawn about a community effect.

It should be noted that community differences resulting from selective processes, even though they cannot be taken as evidence of a community effect, may have considerable importance both for social science and for public policy and practice. Thus, for an understanding of social processes at the macro level, it is essential to describe and analyze how persons of similar family backgrounds and psychological characteristics end up living in the same geographic area under similar social and economic conditions. On the practical side, knowledge that persons with particular family backgrounds and psychological characteristics are concentrated in certain communities or neighborhoods is highly relevant for agencies engaged in community planning or administration, or for families facing decisions about where to live.

5. *Identifying sources and mechanisms of community effects.* Demonstrating that psychological differences between people living in different communities cannot be explained by selective processes argues strongly for the existence of a community effect. But such a demonstration, taken by itself, does not reveal either the nature of the effect or its origins. Let us suppose, for example, that the relation between unemployment and child abuse turns out to be much higher in some communities than in others. Let us suppose further that this finding cannot be accounted for by differential migration patterns, differences in social class composition, or other selective factors. We now have persuasive evidence for a community effect. But we still do not know what it is about a community that can increase or reduce the destructive effect of unemployment on parents' treatment of their children. We need to identify some feature of community life that serves as a mediating mechanism. One such possible mechanism is the existence and extent of a supportive network between families in the community that could buffer the impact of economic stress on family functioning (Cochran & Brassard, 1979). Evidence bearing on this hypothesis will be considered in a later section of this chapter. For the moment, we wish only to show the importance, as the last step in establishing a community effect, of identifying the particular properties of the community that can ultimately affect families and children and of specifying the process through which these properties achieve their impact.

Of the five analytic steps required for demonstrating a community effect, the first two are far more easily achieved than the remaining three. Indeed, it is the necessity of the last three requirements that sets severe limits on present-day knowledge in this domain, for, as we shall see, only a handful of researchers have recognized and met the need to rule out effects resulting from mere aggregation or the operation of selective processes, and fewer still have demonstrated how specific features of community life have functioned to produce differences in the characteristics of families and children living in different communities. The overwhelming majority of investigations conducted to date have been confined to the first two stages in the analytic process: documenting variation in community structures presumed to affect the well-being of families and children, or reporting statistical associations between the demographic or structural characteristics of a community and the psychological characteristics of families and individuals residing within the community. Both types of studies point to the possibility, but not to the fact, of community influence on psychological processes and outcomes.

With these clarifications of theory and method, we are now in a position to review the existing research literature as it bears on the following substantive questions: (1) What aspects of community structure and community life represent actual or potential influences on family functioning and human development? (2) What are the processes and causal pathways through which these influences operate? (3) What are the implications of existing knowledge for future research and, where the inference is warranted, for public policy and practice?

II. GENERAL COMMUNITY EFFECTS

URBAN-RURAL DIFFERENCES IN INTELLECTUAL DEVELOPMENT

Probably the earliest, and certainly the most numerous, investigations in this sphere have been concerned with urban-rural differences in mental development. The overwhelming majority of these studies have focused on intellectual ability as measured by mental tests and have documented the consistent finding that city children obtain higher scores than their country counterparts. However, most of these studies have failed to control for the families' socioeconomic status and other sources of confounding at lower levels of social structure, which—through aggregation—could account for the observed differences. A second major problem characterizing almost all of these investigations is substantive rather than methodological: the absence of any theoretical framework that might account for the contrasting intellectual performance of rural and urban subjects.

It has been difficult to find studies that are not seriously limited by one or both of these shortcomings. An outstanding exception is a two-stage investigation carried out in rural and urban areas in Switzerland. The first study (Meili & Steiner, 1965) was conducted when the pupils were 11 years old. The researchers found that performance in both intelligence and achievement tests increased as a function of the amount of industry and traffic present in the area. The relationship was still significant after controlling for social class, but the influence of the latter variable was more powerful than that of locality. In both cases, measures of academic achievement were more affected than those of intelligence.

The fact that significant differences remained after controlling for socioeconomic status raises the question of what other factors within each type of community operate to produce the observed variation in intellectual performance. It is difficult to see how the presence of industry and traffic could have a direct effect in this regard; some other, more proximal aspects of the community must be involved. Four years later, in a followup study, Vatter (1981) undertook to investigate the nature of these more immediate influences. As a framework for this phase of the inquiry, he drew on earlier work by Klineberg (1935, 1938) and Wheeler (1942) to formulate what he called the "stimulus hypothesis": the superior cognitive functioning observed in city children is presumed to be a product of exposure to the richer and more differentiated cultural environment typifying the urban scene. Vatter also added a second, longitudinal hypothesis, positing a cumulative effect: as a result of the children's continued exposure to contrasting community environments, group differences at age 15 were expected to be even greater than those observed previously at age 11.

At the most general level, the findings with the 15-year-olds revealed much the same pattern that had been detected 4 years earlier. But, contrary to expectations, the observed differences were not more pronounced. Indeed, in the case of achievement test scores, the gap had decreased, particularly in the most remote rural areas, a finding that Vatter attributes primarily to the leveling effect of schooling. In line with this interpretation, differences on measures of intelligence remained significant, with rural children still obtaining lower scores. Information bearing directly on the stimulation hypothesis was obtained from questionnaires filled out by the students about their daily activities within the community, and about the nature of existing community facilities (e.g., availability and use of libraries, attendance at lectures and other public presentations, learning opportunities outside the home, etc.). As a basis for comparison, information was also obtained on activities at home, such as parental assistance with schoolwork, mealtime conversations, helping around the house, and the use of radio and television. The two sets of measures were then related to test results, at both the individual and the community level. In support of the Vatter's stimulus hypothesis, the richness of environmental opportunities and activities increased markedly along the continuum from remote rural areas to urban centers. More critically, there was a significant positive relation between indices of the community environment and mental test scores. Finally, community factors appeared to exert a stronger influence than intrafamilial variables (median r of .41 vs. .26). (The only exception was "helping around the house," which showed a substantial negative correlation with test scores.)[1] Vatter is quick to point out, however, that, notwithstanding the evidence in support of the stimulation hypothesis, there is another possible explanation. The observed psychological outcomes could be a product of the differential power of urban versus rural communities to attract, expel, or retain residents on the basis of their abilities, motivation, or other differentiating characteristics. To control for the confounding influence of such selective processes, it would be necessary to demonstrate that psychological changes had occurred over time in the *same* persons or groups as a function of exposure to contrasting community conditions (in this instance, rural vs. urban). By keeping the research subjects constant, differences attributable to change in sample would be ruled out. Unfortunately, in the present instance, the children in the followup study were not identical to those included in the initial investigation, since they constituted a subsample reduced in size both for logistical reasons and as the result of attrition.

The power of an appropriately designed longitudinal study is illustrated in the classical investigations by Klineberg (1935, 1938) of intellectual changes among children in black families who were migrating from rural to urban areas. In his first study, Klineberg (1935) found that mental test scores in a sample of 12-year-old migrant boys increased as a function of length of urban residence. The second study (1938) was even more conclusive, since intelligence measures had been administered to the same children before and after migration. Fortunately for the purposes of the inquiry, in the baseline assessment the migrant youngsters averaged somewhat below nonmigrants in the same rural schools. After moving into the urban environment, however, they gradually improved, exhibiting progressively higher levels of mental ability. Here is clear evidence of a community effect, but in this early study, the specific features of city life accounting for the gains, and the processes involved, were not examined.

Despite scientific shortcomings in even the best-designed studies, the weight of the available evidence points to the conclusion that, in general, urban settings are more conducive to children's intellectual development than are rural settings. A plausible explanation for this phenomenon, and

[1] Vatter's findings and interpretation are consistent with those of an earlier study by Lehman & Witty (1927). These investigators found a greater variety of children's activities in urban settings as a function of richer environmental opportunities and cultural resources. This research, however, did not include any data on the children's intellectual development.

one that is supported by research evidence, is Vatter's (1981) stimulation hypothesis.

URBANIZATION AND PSYCHOPATHOLOGY

But if city environments foster cognitive growth, they appear to have the opposite effect in another key domain of human functioning, that of social and emotional development. To quote one of the leading investigators working in this area, "Psychosocial problems are much more common in the inner cities than in areas of small towns. This is a *real* difference in the prevalence of disorder and not just an artifact of recognition or of differential migration" (Rutter, 1981, p. 623).

The thesis that community factors play a significant role in the genesis of mental illness and behavior disorders has a long history. First conceived and crudely implemented 150 years ago in France by Guerry (1883) and Quetelet (1835), the idea was revived and put on a firmer scientific footing in the 1920s and 1930s by the Chicago sociologists Shaw (Shaw, Zorbaugh, McKay, & Cottrell, 1929) and Faris and Dunham (1939). Shaw, using an ethnographic approach, introduced the term "delinquency area" as an ecological concept. Faris and Dunham argued on the basis of correlational evidence that residence in deteriorated urban areas was a contributing factor in the etiology of psychiatric illness. Their conclusion was quickly challenged by the counterargument that patients tended to drift into such areas as a result of their disorder (Myerson, 1940). It is not until relatively recently that well-designed studies have demonstrated that processes of selective migration, and other potential sources of confounding, cannot adequately account for the observed differences between urban and rural settings in the prevalence of socioemotional disturbance. For example, in a comparison of rates of mental disorder in inner London and the Isle of Wight, Rutter and his colleagues (Rutter, Cox, Tupling, Berger, & Youle, 1975; Rutter & Quinton, 1977) confined their samples to children and parents born and bred only in the given area. With migration effects thus controlled, rates of psychiatric disorder were still much more frequent in the metropolis. Nor could the observed effects be explained by any community differences with respect to ethnicity, social class, or other demographic factors (Quinton, 1980; Rutter & Madge, 1976). Indeed, the same social class position appeared to have a different significance in urban versus rural environments, with low socioeconomic status being a much stronger predictor of mental illness in the city than in the country.[2] In the

[2]Similar findings were reported in an earlier study by Clausen & Kohn (1959). The correlations between neighborhood characteristics and the development of psychiatric disorders were greater in large cities than in smaller ones.

light of this series of findings, Rutter concluded, "It seemed that there must be something about living in the city which predisposed to mental disorder" (1981, p. 612).

What is this "something"? Rutter's own efforts to answer this question have yielded results of particular relevance for child development. For example, taking advantage of the longitudinal design of the London–Isle of Wight study, Rutter (1980) analyzed community differences as a joint function of age of onset and type of disorder. "The results were striking in showing that the biggest difference between London and the Isle of Wight applied to *chronic* disorders of *early* onset. . . . The least difference was found with psychiatric conditions beginning in adolescence for the first time. Moreover, the difference also mainly applied to disorders associated with serious family difficulties. In short, the problems most characteristic of city children were those beginning early, lasting a long time, and accompanied by many other problems in the family" (Rutter, 1981, p. 613). These findings raise the possibility that the observed community differences may simply reflect the aggregation of vulnerable families. To clarify this issue, Rutter and Quinton (1977) compared rates of psychiatric disorder in different neighborhoods controlling for such factors as the proportion of low-status, low-income families and single-parent households. They found that families were affected irrespective of their background characteristics, so that in general persons living in a vulnerable area shared a higher risk of psychiatric disorder. In short, to use Rutter's words, the effect was to some extent ecological as well as individual.

Such an effect can operate in two ways. It can impinge on children directly, or indirectly through the child's family. To investigate these possibilities, Rutter and his colleagues (1975, 1977) developed an index of "family adversity" including such factors as marital discord and dissolution, mental disorder or criminality in the parents, large family size, and other conditions known to be associated with higher levels of psychiatric disturbance and social deviance. Again the results were striking, but this time in the opposite direction. With the degree of family adversity controlled for, the difference between London and the Isle of Wight in rates of child psychiatric illness all but disappeared. The authors interpret this result as indicating that the main adverse effects of city life on children are indirect, resulting from the disruption of the families in which they live. As we shall see, this two-stage sequence from community to family to child emerges as one of the principal causal pathways for the operation of community influences on human development.

But whether the pathways are direct or indirect, the key question remains, What is it about large cities that contributes to family and individual disorganization? As Rutter points out, community size per se does not appear to be the critical factor for at least two reasons. First, within large cities there is considerable variation in rates of psychiatric disorder from one area to another (Quinton, 1980; Rutter & Madge, 1976). Second, the population density within an area is not a significant predictor of psychiatric or social pathology (Rutter & Madge, 1976). What is?

Several studies offer positive answers to that question, but the investigations are limited by now familiar shortcomings in research design. To begin with, all of the relevant investigations we have been able to find employ an additive model in which the community is defined operationally as the sum of its parts. Nevertheless, the results can be instructive in terms of the elements that make up the total. For example, in a comprehensive field study of a Nova Scotia county, Leighton and his co-workers (Hughes, Tremblay, Rapoport, & Leighton, 1960; Leighton, 1959; Leighton, Harding, Macklin, Macmillan, & Leighton, 1963) examined the relation between rates of psychiatric disorder in local communities and their level of "sociocultural disintegration" as measured by a series of indicators such as "high frequency of broken homes, few and weak leaders, few patterns of recreation, high frequency of crime and delinquency, and weak and fragmented network of communications" (Hughes et al., 1960, p. 87). As hypothesized, communities characterized by higher levels of disintegration exhibited higher rates of psychiatric disturbance. In this comparatively early study, no attempt was made to determine which components of the integration index were contributing most to the observed relationship or whether the effect extended to individual families who did not themselves exhibit characteristics included in the integration index.

Similar findings, with similar methodological shortcomings, appear in other community studies of psychiatric illness (e.g., Srole et al., 1962, 1975). Nevertheless, over the years such investigations have achieved some notable scientific gains, primarily in the form of greater specificity on both sides of the basic equation. For example, Clausen and Kohn (1959), in a study of the relation of rates of schizophrenia to community structure, showed that these rates were determined in part by differences in institutional patterns for labeling and serving mental patients. In a finding that may be related, Rabkin and Struening (1976) reported systematic variations in psychiatric disorder as a function of the relative prominence of a particular ethnic group within the community: "[When] a given ethnic group constitutes a smaller proportion of the total population in an area, diagnosed rates of mental illness increase in comparison both to the rates for other ethnic groups in that area and to the rates of the same ethnic group in neighborhoods where its members constitute a significant proportion of majority" (1976, p. 1019).

Another dimension of community structure is tapped in an investigation by Kogan, Smith, and Jenkins (1977). These investigators constructed a multivariate index of community stress (similar to Leighton's levels of sociocultural disintegration) measuring the extent of health and socioeconomic deprivation. Among the components entering into the index were the proportion of families receiving Aid to Dependent Children, rates of premature and out-of-wedlock birth, and the prevalence of venereal disease. The dependent variables were reports of psychological difficulties manifested by children and of disturbances in the parent-child relationship. The innovative element in the research was the analysis of effects at successively smaller social units, ranging from counties, through neighborhoods and census tracts, to individual families. Predictions became increasingly better as the level of analysis moved from the more distal to the more proximal structures. The finding is consistent with a previously stated general principle emerging from this body of research, namely, community influences affect the child primarily indirectly through their impact on the family. At the same time, the design of the research does not permit distinguishing purely aggregate phenomena from genuine community effects.

Evidence for the operation of processes at the higher-order community level comes from studies of the dramatic differences in rates of infant mortality among health districts within the same city and the factors contributing to this variation. For example, in a recent report on the "State of the Child" in the city of New York, the authors (Lash, Sigal, & Dudzinski, 1980) cite mortality rates ranging from a low of 6.6 per 1,000 in some districts to as high as 43.5 in others, representing a one to seven ratio. A study conducted under the auspices of the National Institute of Medicine (Kessner, Singer, Kalk, & Schlesinger, 1973) indicated that a substantial percentage of such variation could be accounted for by the availability and quality of prenatal care services existing in each district. The investigators concluded that the city's infant mortality rate could be reduced by as much as one-third by providing adequate care to all pregnant women.

Evidence that such an effort could be successful is documented in another report published by the National Academy of Sciences (*Toward a National Policy for Children and Families*, 1976): "The ability to operate a targeted program effectively is demonstrated by the record of the Maternal and Infant Care Project of the U.S. Department of Health, Education, and Welfare. In Denver, Birmingham (Alabama), and Omaha the infant mortality rate fell off dramatically, from 34.2 in 1964 to 21.5 in 1969 . . . in Birmingham, from 25.4 in 1965 to 14.3 in 1969; and in Omaha, from 33.4 in 1964 to 13.4 in 1969. These programs also significantly reduce the incidence of prematurity, repeated teenage pregnancy, the number who conceive after 35, and the number of families with more than four children" (p. 58).

More recently, efforts to enhance support systems for young, high-risk mothers during the prenatal and perinatal period have apparently resulted in decreased infant morbidity (O'Connor, Vietze, Hopkins, & Altemeir, 1977; Olds, 1980, 1981). Such results are appropriately considered community effects because the changes in policies, practices, and priorities they represent reflect decisions by community policymakers and shifts in the role of community institutions (Garbarino, 1980a).

Evidence for the operation of community influences also appears in relation to another source of stress for children and their development: child abuse. For example, a series of investigations by Garbarino and his colleagues traces the causal chain from community ecology to parent-child interaction. The first study documented correlations at the county level relating socioeconomic and demographic sources of maternal stress to rates of child maltreatment (Garbarino, 1976). In a second study of neighborhoods within a single metropolitan county, Garbarino and Crouter (1978) used multiple regression techniques to relate socioeconomic, demographic, and attitudinal data to rates of child maltreatment. With regard to 20 subareas and the 93 census tracts, 81% and 52% of the variance, respectively, were accounted for by five variables—two measures of average family income, an index of geographic mobility, the percentage of single-parent households, and the proportion of employed mothers with young children. The research validated and extended the earlier findings, and formed the basis for a more detailed investigation of relevant factors in the neighborhood ecology (Garbarino & Sherman, 1980).

For the latter purpose, multiple regression techniques were employed to identify two neighborhoods matched for socioeconomic level and demographic composition but differing markedly in the rate of child maltreatment (130 per 1,000 families vs. 16). Interviews with key informants, ranging from elementary school principals to mail carriers, were used to develop profiles for the two neighborhoods. Samples of families were drawn from each neighborhood, and interviews were conducted to identify perceived stresses and supports, with special emphasis on sources of health care, social networks, evaluation of the neighborhood, and the use of family support systems. The findings are interpreted as supporting the concept of differential neighborhood risk for child abuse. Although the two neighborhoods were similar in socioeconomic status (in both, 72% of the population was classified in the low-income category), families in the high-risk area reported a lower evaluation of the neighborhood as a place to live. In general, in comparison with its control, the high-risk neighborhood exhibited an overall pattern of social impoverishment.

The reader will have observed that most of the studies reviewed in this section, including the series just described, are based on aggregate statistics. Hence, they fail to satisfy the requirements of the third and fourth analytic steps set forth at the beginning of this chapter. As a result, such studies are open to alternative interpretations in terms of selective processes that attract, expel, or retain particular kinds of families in a given community or neighborhood. It is equally true, however, that the very same findings could reflect a genuine community effect. Given this possibility, such studies and their results represent a significant scientific contribution, since they identify those particular aspects of community life that are most likely to influence family functioning and human development.

Such investigations, however, do not exhaust the scientific information available about community characteristics potentially important for the well-being of children and families. There are other researches that contain additional evidence, albeit on a weaker empirical base. The differential in scientific power derives from the fact that all of the studies cited thus far have satisfied the requirements of at least the second of the five requisite analytic steps outlined earlier in this chapter. The remaining investigations we shall discuss, however, fall short of this criterion at one of two levels. They either fail to go beyond the first step or do not fully satisfy the requirements of the second. Thus, there are a great many researches that simply document variation in some aspect of community life that might plausibly affect children and families but do not report any data on actual outcomes. A second group do provide such data but relate them only to substructures within the community without introducing either communities or neighborhoods as units of analysis. This is a common characteristic, for example, of most studies investigating the influence of social networks on family processes. The existence of functional relationships between these two domains is clearly demonstrated, but no evidence is presented for variation at the level of the community with respect to either set of variables, or the relationship between them. Nevertheless, both types of studies illuminate the *possible* impact of specific community factors on family functioning and child development. For this reason, they merit our attention. We consider first the significance of formal community organizations and institutions.

III. Effect of Formal Community Structures

Families come into contact with a host of community agencies concerned, at least tangentially, with family well-being. In this section we will look at five facets of the community environment directly affecting family life, ranging from health, welfare, and social services to schools, day-care facilities, and religious institutions. In examining data on geographic distribution, we have found that services of all types are block-booked by neighborhood and community; access and availability depend on where one lives. This means that the quality and quantity of services to families are stratified in the same way that communities are stratified, by income. We have also found that services are commonly provided to individuals rather than to the family as a system, with resulting inefficiencies and inequities. A case in point is the provision of health services.

HEALTH SERVICES

The significance of health services in this analysis of the community as a context for development is revealed in the following documentation of discrepancies in access to services, their availability and quality, and the orientations of service providers to their clients. Health is the sine qua non of adult and child development, and yet access to the health care system, even health itself, is contingent on the community in which one lives and correspondingly on one's socioeconomic status. Families living in poverty areas have a 30% higher infant mortality rate than families in nonpoor areas. Similarly, they are 30% more likely to have infants with low birth weights (Sanger, 1979).

A major factor affecting the utilization of health services is their accessibility. For example, one determinant of the use of private physicians is the number of such professionals in a given community. Sanger (1979) points out that several areas in New York City have less than 13 private general practioners per 100,000 residents. There are also major shortages of physicians and dentists in small towns and rural areas and other thinly populated areas outside standard metropolitan statistical areas (U.S. Department of Commerce, 1980).

Transportation problems also make certain health delivery systems inaccessible to poor families. Davis and Reynolds (1977) found that the poor spend 50% more time traveling to and waiting to see a physician than do the nonpoor. Logistics are especially problematic for poor women, particularly single parents. Moreover, services are often situated in different locations: "Obstetric care is likely to be available at one site, family planning at another, and pediatric care at still another. Often women, with small children in tow, attempt to negotiate the multiplicity of locations, wasting hours in transit and in uncomfortable clinic waiting areas. This disorganization is usually accompanied by lack of coordination and results in inefficient, if not inappropriate, care" (Neale, 1979, p. 47).

Recognition of inequity in the distribution of health services has led to a number of efforts involving reorganization of such services along neighborhood lines. For example, in 1965, in response to strong criticisms of the existing health care system, a new model of comprehensive care, in the form of Neighborhood Health Centers, was initiated by the Office of Economic Opportunity. Though originally designed to serve all residents of a community, the Neighborhood Centers were eventually limited to low-income families so as not to compete with the existing private health care system supported by the organized medical profession (Sardell, 1980). Insofar as we have been able to discover, however, neither in this or in any other instance has there been any systematic investigation of whether the introduction of neighborhood delivery systems leads to greater utilization, especially by the more disadvantaged segments in the population, with corresponding improvement of family health and well-being.

WELFARE AND SOCIAL SERVICES

As in the case of health care, we are concerned here primarily with services provided to poor families. Such services, whatever their source of funding or policy formation, are implemented by community agencies at the local level. Again, as with health care, there has been a concern about the distribution of services within and across communities. Prior to the late 1950s there was a trend toward centralization; since then, in part as an effort to reach "hard-core families," there has been a move toward neighborhood provision of services and an increased concern with the community (Kahn, 1976). Local services were to be both accessible and comprehensive. As a result, by 1970 there were 2,000 neighborhood service centers across the nation. Perlman's (1975) study of the Roxbury Multi-Service Center in Boston's black community provides insight into the structure, goals, and functioning of these decentralized service delivery systems. The Roxbury Center was governed by a community-based board of directors and had three principal service units: employment services, legal aid, and general social services. The center was located at the intersection of four census tracts. In one of the tracts, over one-fifth of the population (15 and older) used the agency, compared with 10%–15% for the other tracts. The value of service delivery where people live was borne out by data concerning use of the center; utilization varied directly with the distance from home (as did frequency of contact). Over 40% of the people using its services lived within half a mile of the center.

Because the neighborhood centers were designed to connect people with other social services, the clients were often referred to other agencies in Roxbury and Boston. An ongoing concern in the service delivery system field is the process of information and referral. Access can be hampered as easily by lack of knowledge as by transportation difficulties. In the Roxbury center, nearly half the clients reported informal sources of referral; only 10% had heard of the agency's services through the media, while 43% had been referred from other social agencies (Perlman, 1975). Kamerman and Kahn's study of social services in the United States found that while some people learn about and obtain services through directories issued by volunteer and public agencies and by telephone hotlines and outreach services, many find services through "word of mouth of friends and relatives" (1981, pp. 465–469). The authors point out that many people who may need services are not using them.

The availability of information about social services, and their geographic and socioeconomic accessibility, clearly affects the well-being of families and children. It is therefore both curious and regrettable that there is little research about the actual impact of these aspects of formal community structure on family functioning and on the behavior and development of children.

In addition to issues of information and accessibility, welfare and social services in the United States confront yet another problem: concern about encouraging and perpetuating dependency. Families receiving welfare benefits are often viewed as lacking motivation and self-reliance, and are treated accordingly by the agencies that serve them and by the general public. Robert Lynd's words, written in 1946, ring true today: ". . . the American code attaches special shame to recourse to social agencies for aid. Not until one reaches the wealthy who can pay—and pay handsomely enough to be impersonal about it—for the services of child psychologists, psychoanalysts, lawyers, divorce courts, and so on does seeking help become a relatively matter-of-fact affair—our type of society augments the fact of human trouble with an extra loading of social shame" (1946, p. ix).

An early study of the urban poor (Koos, 1946) sought to determine why families were not aware of agencies intended for their use as well as why families that knew of the existence of services did not utilize them. Those refusing assistance from social agencies did so because they felt a degradation in acceptance, both in terms of the stigma attached to "charity" and because of the interventionist nature of social work. Whether institutional aids today are less distasteful to needy families is a question deserving of research.

Street, Martin, and Gordon (1979) voice a contemporary view: "The poor need not only the ability to deal with the bureaucracy, but also great amounts of patience (as when welfare officials refuse to make appointments and keep recipients waiting interminably), high tolerance for rudeness and insult (as when indigent users of hospital emergency rooms find that no one even notices they are trying to ask questions), and a rare readiness to make their private lives public (as when one is questioned about one's sex life by a stranger in an open cubicle of a welfare office)" (p. 69).

Such attitudes and behaviors represent manifestations of what Bronfenbrenner and Weiss (1983) refer to as the "deficit model," which they regard as especially characteristic of welfare programs in the United States. The following passage describes the nature and dynamics of the model:

> Our policies and practice, past and present, are based on what can be called a "deficit model." The model pervades all types of social services, but its distinctive properties are revealed in highest relief in our welfare system. To qualify for help, potential recipients must first prove that they and their families are inadequate—they must do so in writing, a dozen times over, with corroborating documentation, so that there can be little doubt that they, and their children, are in fact the inadequate persons they claim to be. Moreover, our mode of service is categorical: to obtain needed help, potential recipients must first be classified into the types of problems they represent. The only way in which they become whole human beings again is to have enough things wrong. Then they can be defined, and dealt with, as "problem children," or better still for bureaucratic purposes, as "multiproblem families." [P. 395]

The stigmatizing power of the deficit model presumably derives from the attitudes toward welfare recipients conveyed by the agencies that serve them and by the general public. It is this circumstance that makes the phenomenon relevant to any discussion of community effects. It seems likely that the presence and strength of a deficit model orientation, and its expression in everyday life, would vary not only across agencies within a community but also from neighborhood to neighborhood and from one community to the next. Support for this expectation comes from a unique study of the community effects of Project Head Start (Kirschner Associates, 1970). The study involved surveys conducted in 58 communities scattered across the United States in order "to determine whether or not relevant changes in school systems and health services had occurred since the inception of local Head Start programs" (p. 40). The results of the investigation are summarized in the following passage: "Education and health have traditionally been provinces of professionals, who somewhat aloof from public contact and control, have protected, taught and disseminated middle-class values for the benefit of middle-class families. In the brief period of less than half a decade, concurrent with the life of Head Start, these institutions have changed remarkably. They have become concerned with the needs and the problems of the poor and of the minorities and have manifested this concern by revising curricula, schedules, approaches, services, etc. They have increasingly involved the public, including the poor, in positions of influence, and they have changed employment critieria so that neighborhood people without professional credentials occupy important paraprofessional positions" (p. 19).

The findings of the Kirschner report are noteworthy in two respects: (1) they document the existence of community-shared attitudes and practices regarding the needs of poor families and their children; and (2) they demonstrate the possibility of changing such attitudes and practices, again on a community-wide basis, through the introduction of new programs that involve the active participation of different segments of the community, including the program beneficiaries themselves. The specific strategies employed in such programs, and assessments of their effects on children and families, are documented in a number of recent studies (for summaries see Bronfenbrenner, 1974; Bronfenbrenner & Weiss, 1983; Darlington, Royce, Snipper, Murray, & Lazar, 1980; Kotelchuck, Schwartz, Anderka, & Finison, 1983).

At the same time, there remains one important missing link in the chain of empirical evidence. To our knowledge, the alleged destructive effects of the deficit model on human development, plausible as they may seem, have never been documented in systematic research. The issue is not only whether the effects exist but, if they do, what structures in the community are the principal vehicles for their transmission. Is the image of incompetence communicated to children directly through their experience in community settings, such as day-care programs, preschools, and schools; or does the process operate indirectly through the demeaning ways in which the children's parents are treated by personnel in public agencies, by employers and co-workers, and by the general public? These are researchable questions that have thus far remained conspicuously unresearched.

SCHOOL-COMMUNITY RELATIONS

Our concern here is not with how schools per se can affect human development, an immense topic in its own right, but how the relation of the school to the rest of the community can influence what happens in the immediate settings in which development takes place, such as the family, the classroom, the peer group, and—for adolescents and youth—the workplace. Unfortunately, even to a greater extent than in the other areas considered previously, our discussion in this sphere is limited by the paucity of relevant research evidence. If we limit ourselves to well-designed, systematic studies, findings bear on the topic only indirectly.

For example, working in poor residential areas in Mexico City, Almeida (1976, 1978) offered an 8-week training course in child development, in one case for teachers alone, in another for teachers and parents together. In each of six neighborhoods, one sixth-grade classroom was randomly assigned to the experimental treatment (parents plus teacher) and another to the control group (teachers only). The weekly 2-hour training sessions were conducted by persons who lived and worked in the immediate neighborhood. The investigator hypothesized that parental participation would result in enhanced motivation and learning on the part of pupils as a function of increased mutual understanding and convergent value commitments on the part of parents, teachers, and children. The analysis revealed a significant interaction effect, with the teacher-parent combination being quite effective in some neighborhoods and not at all in others. Indeed, in certain neighborhoods, control groups also showed significant gains, although not as large as those achieved in the experimental classrooms.

Since each pair of classrooms was located in two schools in the same neighborhood, it occurred to Almeida that some feature of the neighborhood (such as school-community relations or ethnic tensions) might account for the differential effects. He therefore returned to each neighborhood to interview parents, teachers, and school personnel. In the course of this inquiry, Almeida discovered that the schools exhibiting greatest gains were located in neighborhoods having the most highly developed social networks, with the result that some experimental and control families were actually in communication with each other. Under these circumstances, not only the experimental classrooms but those of the control groups showed improvement, presumably as a function of horizontal diffusion. Indeed, by the time Almeida returned to Mexico City for the followup interviews, he found that one or two parents from experimental neighborhoods were serving as leaders in a repetition of the parent participation program at the request of, and for the benefit of, former control group families. Several other studies have demonstrated the beneficial effects on children's school performance and behavior of strengthening ties between home and school, especially in urban environments (Böttcher, 1968; Collins, Moles, & Cross, 1982; Conner, 1950; Holley, 1916; Lightfoot, 1978; Rodick & Henggeler, 1980; Smith, 1968; Tangri & Leitch, 1982). Only Almeida's work, however, explicitly examines the role of the neighborhood and the community in the establishment and maintenance of home-school relationships.

Regrettably, even less is known about the implications for school effectiveness of other aspects of community life. For example, the relationship between community characteristics and level of school achievement appears to differ from one community to the next; in general, the more deprived the community, the greater the variance attributable to school effects (Coleman, 1966; Garbarino, 1981). In another domain, a number of studies have documented a relation between school size and antisocial behavior (Barker & Gump, 1964; McPartland & McDill, 1970; Turner & Thrasher, 1970; Wicker, 1969). It seems likely that school size is confounded with school location, with larger schools serving larger catchment areas and smaller schools being neighborhood-based. Yet, to our knowledge, no investigation has been designed to unravel the separate and joint contribution of these correlated but distinguishable factors. A third source of community effect is indicated by the results of a national survey conducted by the Children's Defense Fund (1974) on children out of school. The survey revealed marked variations from community to community, and neighborhood to neighborhood, in the percentages of children enrolled in school. Neither the causes nor the consequences of such variation have been systematically examined.

DAY CARE AND COMMUNITY

One indicator of the quality and quantity of community support for families is the provision of day care. Indeed, evaluations of community development often use provision of child care as a social indicator. Garbarino's studies of child maltreatment reinforce this view. In the comparison both of counties (Garbarino, 1976) and of neighborhoods (Garbarino & Sherman, 1980), community support for child care emerged as a significant correlate of a lower incidence of child abuse and neglect.

We know that there is a substantial need for day care, given the dramatic shift in the proportion of mothers with young children working outside the home. We also know that the predominant providers of day care are the informal rather than the formal support systems of the community. The 1975 National Child-Care Consumer Study (U.S. Department of Commerce, 1976) indicated that for children under 6 years of age, in-home ("babysitter") care is most common (26%), followed by care in someone else's home (16%), followed by nursery school (8%), with center-based day care trailing far behind (3%). With these figures in mind, it should come as no surprise that the richness of the informal support systems surrounding home-based day care is regarded as one of the most important dimensions of the community-family interface (Collins & Watson, 1976; Unger & Powell, 1980). In addition, the formal support systems represented by the "day-care council" may also be an important aspect of this interface, since this agency typically provides key services to home-based day-care providers.

Although it is reasonable to suppose that the existence of day-care services in a community would have positive consequences for both families and children, the fact remains that adequately designed studies of this phenomenon are almost nonexistent. To be sure, there are a great many

investigations of the effects of day care per se. The general conclusion
reached by reviewers of this body of research is that day care makes little
difference for development, except for children from severely disadvantaged backgrounds (e.g., Belsky, Steinberg, & Walker, 1982). From the
perspective of our present concern, however, existing studies have two
serious limitations. First, as Belsky et al. point out, these researches deal
almost exclusively with direct effects of day care on the child, while
overlooking what may be more potent influences on family functioning.
Second, and more critical for our purpose, the largest units of analysis in
these studies are individual children and families rather than neighborhoods or communities. The findings at the two different levels need not
necessarily be the same. For example, the availability of day care in a
community may be more consequential for parents and their children than
its actual use, so that families are affected whether or not a particular child
happens to be enrolled.

Similar considerations apply to yet another, more recent aspect of
family-community concerns: the provision of after-school care for children
in the 6–13-year age range (Levine, 1977). A report by the Census Bureau
(U.S. Department of Commerce, 1976) indicates that roughly 13% of the
children aged 7–13 whose mothers work outside the home cared for
themselves (and 4% of the 3–6-year-olds did so). Close to 2 million children
fit into this category and they are twice as likely to come from single- rather
than two-parent families. Levine's review (1977) documents the importance of community commitment in providing for after-school care, yet few
communities are currently doing very much to meet the needs of these
"latchkey" children (Garbarino, 1980b). Nor are there any data on the
effects of such care when it is made available.

RELIGIOUS INSTITUTIONS

Religious organizations are particularly salient in communities when
viewed from the perspective of families. Most institutions, such as schools
and hospitals, deal directly with individuals, not families, even though part
of their mission may be to serve families. As Caplan (1976, p. 23) points out,
only religious institutions are involved with the entire family over each
stage of its life cycle.

Historically, religious activities have functioned in an organizing
capacity within communities, but their role in terms of formal worship
services may be waning. National surveys reveal a drop in formal religious
participation through the 1970s; in 1978, 38% of the people interviewed
said they never attended religious services, compared to only 29% in 1972

(U.S. Department of Commerce, 1980). Still, more Americans belong to church-related groups than to any other type of voluntary association, Moreover, a growing number believe that religion is increasing its influence (U.S. Department of Commerce, 1980).

Apart from the theological aspects of organized religion, religious associations constitute a major source of social support for a wide spectrum of individuals and their families. Caplan (1974, 1976) has pointed to the value of churches and synagogues as organized support systems, but no research data exist to verify the significance of religious institutions to family life. Berger and Neuhaus (1977) remind us that on any given Sunday "there are probably more people in churches than the total number of people who attend professional sports events in a whole year" and that "there are close to 500,000 local churches and synagogues voluntarily supported by the American people" (p. 27). But there has been no systematic study of the role of institutions of religion in tending to the economic and social welfare of families within a community, across a broad socioeconomic spectrum.

We hypothesize that, for many families, religious institutions are extremely salient both as sources of support and as child-rearing systems in their own right. Their utility extends beyond the socialization function of transmitting a common core of values to the next generation. Religious associations promote ethnic as well as theological identity, provide a range of support services for families and children, and become a focal point for community activities. Perhaps most noteworthy of all, they are one of the few social institutions according major importance and status to parenthood and to child rearing. Researchers concerned with the well-being of families and children would do well to attend to the part played by religious institutions within the community, but at present this area remains a scientific terra incognita.

The reader will have noted, in our discussion of community institutions, that the capacity of such formal structures to function effectively often depends on the existence and operation of informal systems of social support existing within the community. We turn next to an examination of such informal structures.

IV. INFORMAL COMMUNITY STRUCTURES

Two types of informal structures found in all communities are of special importance to families and children. The first are *social networks*, of interconnections between community members (Bott, 1957; Mitchell,

1969); the second are what Barker and Wright (1955) have called *behavior settings*, places in the community in which people engage in particular kinds of activities.

SOCIAL NETWORKS

Community can be conceptualized as a network of relationships related to place. Social networks have been defined by Elizabeth Bott as "all or some of the social units (individuals or groups) with whom a particular individual or group is in contact" (1957, p. 320). In this section, our concern is more specific: the informal relations of family members, relatives, friends, neighbors, and co-workers, and the significance of these primary ties for family well-being and child development. Mitchell (1969) proposes a procedure for evaluating social networks in terms of their structure (such as size, density), content (type of linkage), and function (what networks are used for). For example, networks can be large or small, between individuals of the same or different sex, age, or socioeconomic status, and maintained for a variety of purposes. The functional aspects of informal networks are particularly salient for an analysis of families and community. Accordingly, we will explore two broad and often intertwined uses of social ties: as an *interpersonal resource* (and thereby a source of emotional support as well as actual services for family members) and as a *practical resource*, providing information and access to more formal organizational aid. Networks as a social resource can also be a conduit to power, a means of exerting influence and gaining preferred treatment.

SOCIAL NETWORKS AS AN INTERPERSONAL RESOURCE

Social science research documents the importance of friends and relatives in providing exchanges of goods and services as well as psychological support for family members (see Adams, 1966; Babchuck, 1963; Bott, 1957; Hill, 1970; Litwack & Szelenyi, 1969; McAdoo, 1978; Stack, 1974). An early study of poor families facing problems in the 1940s (Koos, 1946) showed that families turned to relatives more times than to other individuals as sources of aid (p. 86). Other informal sources of advice included druggists, bartenders, and priests.

There has been an enduring sociological debate regarding the isolation of the nuclear family from the network of kin. Theorists like Wirth (1938) and Parsons (1949) maintained the reality of that isolation as a consequence of both social and geographic mobility. But research has underscored the bonds between relatives (see, e.g., Adams, 1966; Bott, 1957; Hill, 1970; Litwak, 1960; Litwak & Szelenyi, 1969; McAdoo, 1978;

Stack, 1974; Sussman, 1959; Young & Willmott, 1957). A cross-cultural study of the elderly and their families in the United States, England, Denmark, Yugoslavia, Poland, and Israel found that most older people live within 10 minutes of one of their children. Over 70% of the respondents had seen at least one of their children the previous week (Shanas, 1973).

A more recent (1978) national survey in the United States (Campbell, 1981) found that 20% of the adults interviewed saw one or more relatives every day and 40% saw one or more relatives a week. Only 30% of the population has little contact with members of their extended family, seeing their kin less than once a month. Only one in 20 adults appeared to be socially isolated, reporting having no close friend or relative nearby (p. 101).

A major study of the links between families and communities has been carried out by Fischer (1977). Using data from the 1965–66 Detroit Area Study on 985 white males, and the 1967 NORC survey on 230 men and women, Fisher showed that characteristics of people's families affect the ways and extent to which they are socially involved in their neighborhoods. One of the issues addressed by Fischer and his colleagues is the importance of proximity in the development and maintenance of social relations. Previous research (see Litwak & Szelenyi, 1969; Wellman, 1976) had shown that friends beyond the neighborhood and relatives were more important than neighbors in terms of intimacy and support. In an sample of Detroit men, Fischer found only one-third of the men had one of their closest friends living in the same neighborhood. In the corresponding sample of women, nearly two-thirds reported that most of their friends lived outside the neighborhood, and 60% stated that they had no relatives living nearby. Fischer also reports a social class difference in the level of intimacy of friendship among Detroit men. Those with low incomes viewed friends living in the neighborhood as more intimate than nonneighborhood friends. Men with high income, on the other hand, described their neighborhood friends as less intimate than nonlocal friends. The authors conclude "that money enables people to reach beyond their localities for their most intimate ties, while the lack of money makes proximity more important" (p. 171).

The presence of children in the home affects the quality and quantity of a family's social network. Fischer (1977) found that families with children were most strongly connected to the neighborhood and to kin. Families living in houses, especially those owning their own homes, were more likely to become locally involved with friends and neighbors than those living in apartments. An important correlate of the proximity of one's social network appears to be income. Families of higher social class were less likely than those of lower social class to have kin or friends living nearby.

Fischer suggests that large incomes may provide people both with a greater choice *of* neighborhood and a greater freedom *from* neighborhood (p. 152). Higher-class families are not restricted by place in their social relationships.

One group, housewives, however, are restricted, and therefore particularly vulnerable to social isolation. Feree (1978) found that 41% of the nonemployed married women (housewives) in her sample reported they did not get much chance to see people during the day. This isolation appears to be more marked for lower-class women; Williams (1958) found that housewives in working-class families had fewer social contacts than did those of the middle class.

Kasarda and Janowitz's seminal study of community attachment (1974) underscores the importance of continuity in the establishment and maintenance of social relationships. The length of residence was an important correlate of the relative number of acquaintances, the number of relatives living nearby, and the proportion of all friends and relatives in the local community. The investigators found that "neither social class nor stage in the life-cycle are so powerful or consistent in affecting local bonds as is the length of residence" (p. 344).

Informal social supports provide families with a sense of integration into the community, an integration that is the rule rather than the exception. Campbell's 1978 survey found that only 5% of adult Americans do not know a single one of their neighbors by name; only 9% have never visited with any of them (1981, p. 104).

In terms of our interest in this chapter, the key question becomes, How do social networks affect family functioning and the behavior and development of the child? Although a number of hypotheses have been proposed for guiding research in this area (Bronfenbrenner, 1979; Cochran & Brassard, 1979), empirical evidence is as yet meager and limited in scope. We have already cited Almeida's post hoc finding that his home-school intervention program was more effective in neighborhoods having the most highly developed social networks (Almeida, 1976, 1978), and the work of Garbarino pointing to the role of supportive social networks as a buffer against child abuse (Garbarino, 1976; Garbarino & Sherman, 1980). Corroborative evidence for the latter result appears in two additional studies. In an investigation of social factors influencing child maltreatment, Giovannoni and Billingsley (1970) identified two environmental factors in the lives of families that had a preventive effect: the existence of a functional kinship network, and church attendance. Similarly, in a longitudinal study carried out in Hawaii, Werner and Smith (1982) focused special attention on a subgroup of their sample whom they designated as "vulnerable but invincible." These were adolescents and youth who, over the course of their lives, had been exposed to poverty, biological risks, and family instability but who nevertheless developed into competent and autonomous young adults. A major environmental factor that distinguished this group from their socioeconomically matched "nonresilient" controls was the presence of an informal multigenerational network of kin.

Three more recent investigations have focused more sharply on the relation of social networks to family processes, with the last study raising a provocative question about the direction of causal influence. Crockenberg (1981) interviewed mothers of 3-month-old infants about their sources of social support. The mothers were asked who helped them when they needed help, and whom they talked to when they were concerned about the baby. In accord with her hypothesis, Crockenberg found that support received by the mother when the infants were 3 months old was positively related to the strength of the infant's attachment to its mother, with the effect being most pronounced in families in which the infant exhibited an irritable temperament. In constructing her index of social support, however, Crockenberg did not distinguish between persons living within or outside the household; thus the possibility remains that the observed effects were due primarily to help provided by the father or older children rather than kinfolk, friends, neighbors, or co-workers. This ambiguity was resolved in a subsequent investigation by Crnic, Greenberg, Ragozin, Robinson, and Basham (1983). Working with a sample of mothers of premature and full-term 4-month-old infants, the researchers distinguished sources of extrafamilial support from that obtained from the husband or unmarried live-in partner. Both types of support were significantly related to maternal levels of satisfaction, with respect both to life in general and to role as a parent. Relationships with observational measures of mother-infant interaction and infant state, however, were much lower, with significant effects being limited to support obtained from the husband or partner. As the authors note, this finding may be an artifact of the statistical procedure employed, since the measures of extrafamilial support were entered last in the regression equation.

With the exception of Almeida's work, none of the foregoing investigations analyzed social networks in terms of their distribution within or across neighborhoods or other spatially defined areas. As noted at the beginning of this chapter, "residence within a delimited area" is central to the definition of community. Hence, the absence of geographic linkage in almost all existing studies of the impact of social networks on families and children leaves a major scientific gap in assessing the influence of social networks as an aspect of community structure.

Methodological and substantive problems of another order are raised by the results and interpretation of a recent study based on a large sample

of school children in six German states (Schneewind, Beckmann, & Engfer, 1983). Using a structural equation model (Jöreskog, 1973, 1978;
Lohmöller, 1979a, 1979b), the investigators found that the social development of the child was a function of the extent to which parents involved
their children in their own adult social networks. The latter, in turn,
showed a direct causal connection with the level of expressive activities
within the family; *but*, in the analytic model employed, these intrafamilial
activities were viewed as a cause rather than a consequence of the parents'
extrafamilial involvements. In other words, extensive social networks were
seen as a by-product of an active and vigorous family life, rather than the
reverse.

Viewed as a whole, existing studies of the relation of community social
networks to family functioning and child development present a picture of
much promise, but considerable unclarity both in theory and research
design. In particular, it is important, in future research, to distinguish
extrafamilial from intrafamilial sources of support; to differentiate members of the social network in terms of their geographic location; and to
clarify the directions of causal influence between families and social networks. Resolution of the last issue requires information on whether the link
was initiated by persons from within or outside the household.

BEHAVIOR SETTINGS

In a series of publications spanning 3 decades, Barker, Wright, and
their colleagues (Barker, 1960, 1968; Barker & Schoggen, 1973; Barker &
Wright, 1955; Gump & Adelberg, 1978; Schoggen, 1983; Wright, 1969,
1971) have documented the fact that children and adults behave differently
in different settings within the community and have demonstrated that the
ratio of the number of residents to the number of settings is a critical factor
in determining the variety of experiences that a person growing up in a
given community will have. Based on these observations, Barker and his
colleagues have developed what they refer to as the "theory of undermanning" (Barker, 1960; Barker & Schoggen, 1973; Schoggen, 1983). "The
main thesis of this theory is that undermanned settings exert more pressure than adequately manned or overmanned settings on potential participants to enter and take part in the operation and maintenance of the
settings" (Schoggen, 1983, p. 150). A number of investigations have been
carried out to test predictions based on the theory. For example, Wright
and his associates (Wright, 1969, 1971) compared samples of children ages
6–11 living in two contrasting communities: *Largetown*, population of
33,000, and *Smalltown*, composite of three communities with populations
under 1,400. In line with predictions from the theory, the children in

Smalltown occupied more positions of responsibility and power within their behavior settings than their age-mates in Largetown. The investigators also found that the children of Smalltown knew much more about the settings and the people in their community, especially adult nonrelatives.

Similar findings are reported by Barker and Schoggen (1973) in their comparison of an English and an American town, identified by the pseudonyms of Yoredale and Midwest, respectively. Since community settings in Midwest were undermanned, the children became more deeply involved in more responsible roles and activities. As a result, "Midwest children are more important and more powerful—they are truly less expendable than Yordale children; this is the kernel of the difference in the towns' public child rearing systems" (Barker & Schoggen, 1973, p. 410).

The foregoing statement clearly carries implications for human development; that is, one would expect children growing up under community conditions of undermanning to develop a different set of abilities, motivations, and character traits from youngsters reared in communities with fewer opportunities and demands for responsible involvement. For example, in a recent statement, Schoggen has suggested that growing up in a small community "carries significant benefits for the development of both cognitive and social competence" (Schoggen, personal communication).

Although this hypothesis follows almost inevitably from the reported observations, it is curious that no researchers have yet undertaken to investigate the developmental effects of exposure to undermanned community settings. The issue takes on special significance in view of the fact that the undermanning hypothesis would appear to predict more favorable intellectual development for children growing up in small towns, a result directly contrary to the research of Vatter (1981) and other investigators cited earlier, documenting the more advanced cognitive abilities of children and adults raised in urban settings. Perhaps the contradiction is resolvable by distinguishing social cognition from more symbolic forms of intellectual functioning. The problem clearly poses an exciting challenge for future research.

A rather different perspective on community settings emerges in the work of European researchers. Whereas Barker and his associates have focused primarily on community environments for children, European investigators have been concerned with differentiating the residential ecology of families. In France, the current work takes its impetus from the classic two-volume study by Chombart de Lauwe (1959–60), *Famille et habitation* ["Family and housing"]. In German-speaking Europe, a larger body of research takes its point of departure from the pioneering study by Muchow and Muchow (1935), and, following their lead, is more diversified in character. For example, a recent compilation by Walter (1981, 1982) fills two volumes with well-designed studies by more than a score of investigators representing a variety of theoretical orientations. Thus, in one report, Bargel and his associates (1981) develop the concept of *Soziotope* for classifying types of residential areas. They then apply their taxonomy to rural and urban districts in the West German state of Nordhessen in order to demonstrate that contrasting forms of *Soziotope* are associated with different family life-styles. Other investigators have focused on variation in socialization practices found in different community areas both urban (Behnken & Zinnecker, 1981; Strohmeier & Herlth, 1981) and rural (Jaeggi, 1965). While valuable in providing concepts and methods for distinguishing community environments, these studies exhibit two shortcomings that are critical to an interest in the effect of community factors on family functioning and child development. First, little attention is paid to the confounding influence of migration and other selection processes; second, the final link from family functioning to developmental processes and outcomes is present only by implication.

V. Sources of Family-Community Disequilibrium

This section discusses three sources of dissonance in the family-community interface: residential mobility, changing family forms, and changing family functions.

RESIDENTIAL MOBILITY

One-fifth of America's population moves every year. Most families do so willingly, moving where the jobs are and seeing the move as an opportunity for social and/or economic advancement. For some, like the military family, moving is part of the job, a way of life. For others, moving is an unwelcome necessity, a factor beyond their control.

Moving almost always disrupts the family's formal and informal links with a community, though people who move voluntarily do so because they perceive real advantages from a change in location. Fischer's (1977) review of the literature underscores the costs and benefits in terms of changes in social relations and life-styles that accompany a move. Fischer (1977) and Kasarda and Janowitz (1974) stress the importance of residential stability in fostering both social and associational ties: the longer family members reside in a community, the more likely they are to be involved with neighbors and with local activities.

The obverse is also true. For instance, the transiency of military families is reflected in the shallow relationships that characterize these

most mobile of families. Lagrone (1978) labels this a kind of "gypsy phenomenon": military people are seen by the nearby community as transients
and are often targets of mistrust and hostility. Not only does this further
isolate the family and cause them to stay within the confines of the base: it
presents a difficult situation for the children attending public schools. They
have to break into peer groups repeatedly as the "new kid" and are often
the school's scapegoats.

In addition to the long-distance moves experienced by military and
other families, there are also local changes of residence. Most local moves
are made because of changes in family composition (such as marriages and
births) which make existing housing no longer adequate (Fischer, 1977).

Some types of families are more mobile than others. For example, a
study of geographic mobility during the first 3 years of life of children in
"alternative families" (single parents or cohabiting couples) in California
found that 59% of these families changed their residence during that 3-year
period, compared to only 35% of the traditional husband-wife families.
There are also differences by class. Blue-collar families and the less educated tend to move where they have kin, while white-collar families tend to
move in response to occupational opportunities. Poor or black families are
more likely to be forced out of their homes than are white or financially
better off families (Fischer, 1977).

Families who rent face a number of problems, including restrictive
rental practices. In a recent national survey, interviewing both tenants and
managers of rental units, Marans, Colten, Groves, and Thomas (1980)
found that one in four rental units excludes families with children. The
report reminds us that there exists no national legislation which prevents
discrimination against children. Yet nearly half of all the families interviewed said that they had difficulties in finding a place to live because of
restrictive rental practices. A second study (Greene & Blake, 1980) of
complaints in response to public service announcements underscored the
problems of families seeking rental housing. Some couples expecting their
first child were required to move from their apartments. Others com-
plained that rental units accepting children were either too expensive or
substandard, or both. Still others were forced to live far from their jobs,
commuting long distances to work. Minorities and women heading families
were the most likely to suffer from restrictive rental policies.

Finding adequate housing at reasonable prices is becoming increasingly problematic for American families. The high rate of geographic
mobility, rising costs of housing, rising interest rates, the "condominiumiz-
ing" of apartments, and restrictive rental practices—all contribute to the
unmet needs of families and to the dissonance between community and
family. This means that the family as a child-rearing system must often deal

with the fundamental problem of shelter before other concerns can be attended to. For many low-income families public housing becomes an unwelcome solution, unwelcome because of the absence of safety and amenities. Interviews with Chicago welfare mothers (Moen, 1980) portray lives of unsafe streets, stairways, and elevators, where children cannot venture out alone and the plumbing or heat is invariably out of order. Decent shelter may well be a prerequisite as a context for optimum development, but it is certainly not acknowledged as a right for families in the United States.

If these are the stresses of moving, what are the effects on family functioning and the development of the child? Here we confront a remarkable dearth of evidence. The only research we have been able to find that has given at least partial attention to this problem is a longitudinal study conducted in Finland (Pitkanen-Pulkinnen, 1980; Pulkinnen, 1982). The investigator used geographic mobility as one index of the instability of the family environment in childhood and preadolescence. This measure proved to be a major predictor of later aggressiveness and dependency during adolescence and early adulthood. The much-needed studies in this area should take into account both the direct and indirect effects on the child of the simultaneous disruption of established patterns of relations with the peer group, the school, and the neighborhood, as well as the subsequent processes of rebuilding such linkages in the new location. Of special significance in this regard is the experience of newly immigrant families, particularly those who come from and enter into markedly contrasting environments with respect to values, customs, and socioeconomic conditions.

CHANGING FAMILY FORMS

That the American family is changing in form and function has become a truism; the implications of these changes in terms of the formal and informal linkages between families and communities, however, have yet to be fleshed out. As Stolte-Heiskanen (1974) suggests, changes in families, whether it be the same family over time or varying family structures within a community, create new family needs which must be attended to.

Part of the alterations in needs can be attributed to variations in both requirements and resources over the life cycle. Hill has shown that families are most vulnerable to inadequate resources (such as income and housing) during the years when families are rearing school-aged children and adolescents (Aldous & Hill, 1969; Hill, 1980). Moen (1983) found that families with preschoolers have a higher probability of unemployment of the major breadwinner than do families with older children. Other studies reinforce the idea of changes in family pressures and supports over time

(Grimm, Motz & Thompson, Gove, 1976; Moen, Kain, & Elder, 1983; Wilensky, 1963). For example, Hill (1970), in looking at three generations of families—married children, their parents, and their grandparents— found that married children involved in childbearing leaned heavily on their parents for help in times of crisis. Mattessich (1978) suggests that families with preschool children have high needs for material and nonmaterial support and tend to look to kin for advice as well as help with child care and financial assistance.

A major precipitator of new needs is changes in family structure. Single parents, especially single-parent women, tend to be more isolated than married parents and therefore have few social supports as well as scarce financial resources (Schorr & Moen, 1979). A study of children in alternative family life-styles—single parents and unmarried couples— found a difference in the type of community organization that these families were likely to attend in comparison to the more traditional husband-wife couples. For example, single parents and cohabiting couples were less likely to attend formal associations (such as church groups and political organizations), and more likely to attend groups such as single women's groups and Lamaze or other "pregnancy" groups (Eiduson & Alexander, 1978). There was, however, little variation in the use of community resources such as libraries and community centers between traditional and nontraditional families.

Families formed by remarriage are another emerging and often neglected family form. As Furstenberg (1978) points out, we know little about the transitions into and out of families or the ways that formal and informal networks can facilitate these transitions. An important by-product of remarriage for families with children is a complex and larger kinship system. The relationships between biological and surrogate parents as well as between children and both new and old kin have yet to be fleshed out. In terms of community factors, the residential pattern of the multiple sets of parents and grandparents may be particularly significant for the child's emotional security and developing sense of identity. In addition, new family forms, such as families created by remarriage or single-parent families, are not always well served by the existing family-community interface. Services and programs are too often tailored for the traditional husband-wife family. Thus, alternative family forms challenge conventional views of what is required in the way of linkages within the community.

CHANGING FAMILY FUNCTIONS

There are two aspects of the alterations in the functioning of families that contribute to the disharmony between families and communities. The first is the reallocation of work roles, the sharing by both men and women of the breadwinner role. Having both spouses work has ramifications for communities as well as for the individual families. The competing claims on resources, especially time and energy, present new demands for child-care facilities, restaurants, shops, and services available at convenient hours. The ramifications of the revolution in women's roles have yet to be spelled out for society at large, even as we are beginning to trace the impacts on individual families and their children (Bronfenbrenner, Alvarez, & Henderson, 1984; Bronfenbrenner & Crouter, 1982; Moen, 1982).

The second change is a more general one, less visible and yet in many ways more pervasive. It involves the redistribution of responsibilities between the private and public sectors, specifically, the division of responsibility between the family and society. The charge (which is by no means documented by data) is that a coalition of social scientists and helping professionals have invaded the home, that these intrusions into family life have resulted in a loss of self-sufficiency, and that the public sector is taking on what are rightfully the family's responsibilities (Lasch, 1977). The argument is in many ways a traditional one, based on individualistic assumptions: that "families can and should be left to take care of themselves" (Koos, 1946, p. 122) and that those who can take care of themselves should be given minimum assistance. The issue is the degree to which family functions are being usurped by community institutions. As Moroney (1976) puts the question, Do policies primarily substitute for the family, or attempt to support it? He suggests that various programs may be located on a continuum ranging from substitution to support. The relative responsibility of society and the family for the care of family members remains ambiguous; that ambiguity contributes to gaps in the provision of community services as well as discrepancies between what is expected or desired and what is provided. The consequences of such dissonances for family functioning and child development, however, have yet to be addressed in systematic research.

VI. FUTURE PERSPECTIVES

We have now completed our review of investigations dealing with community influences on family functioning and individual development. It remains for us to consider the implications of these studies for future activity both in science and in public policy. To provide a basis for such consideration, it is useful to summarize the principal conclusions emerging from our analysis of existing research results. In view of the paucity of evidence bearing directly on the topic, the conclusions are necessarily tentative.

In the light of the scientific findings taken as a whole, influences on psychological processes and outcomes appear to operate in a dialectical fashion. Thus, the evidence points to two kinds of processes that, depending on the balance between them, can either reinforce or counteract each other. On the one hand, as revealed in studies of urban and rural differences, the community can facilitate development by providing a diversity of resources and challenging experiences that offer both stimulus and scope for psychological growth. On the other hand, results from an increasing number of studies, especially in recent years, highlight the importance, both for family functioning and for individual development, of community structures—informal as well as formal—that can serve as sources of stability and support.

We are reminded in this connection of one of the most dramatic and successful (but, alas, nonscientific) experiments ever carried out involving the creation of communities designed to realize unfulfilled human potential. We refer to the so-called colonies conceived and conducted by the Soviet educator-psychologist, A. S. Makarenko (1955), for the rehabilitation of the thousands of homeless children and youth who were roaming the Soviet Union after the civil wars. Among them were youngsters with extensive court records of housebreaking, armed robbery, and manslaughter. The goals and patterns of community life that Makarenko introduced were remarkably effective in changing motivation and behavior. The youthful residents were ultimately able to reenter society as useful citizens, and a substantial number rose to positions of considerable responsibility in Soviet life. To describe what he regarded as the core community conditions essential for facilitating psychological growth, Makarenko offered the following formulation: "The maximum of support with the maximum of demand." In Makarenko's view, community conditions which resulted in the primacy of one over the other—in either direction—would undermine the course of constructive human development. The absence in one's surroundings of challenge, responsibility, and the expectation of competence could, he argued, be as destructive as material want or social rejection.

Makarenko's thought-provoking conclusions were not based on systematic research. In the scientific studies we have examined, however, the same two dialectical forces of challenge versus support emerge as features of a community environment conducive to human development. But scientific investigation still has far to go before it can shed light on the validity of Makarenko's dialectical principle. Any progress in this direction must take into account the present state of our knowledge and the prevailing focus of research activity in the field. A useful framework for this assessment is provided by the outline, presented earlier in this chapter, of the scientific steps necessary to establish the existence of a community effect on psychological processes and outcomes. For example, if we project the research conducted to date against this frame of reference, we can readily see what has been accomplished and what remains to be done. An overwhelming proportion of investigations carried out to date fall in the first two domains (1) demonstrating variation in community features presumed to influence the psychological characteristics of families and children; and (2) documenting an association between psychological characteristics and various aspects of community structure. Far fewer in number are studies in the remaining three spheres. All three are concerned with discovering the functional connections or processes underlying the statistical associations established in the two preceding phases. Despite their small number, the investigations that have been carried out in these three "process" areas demonstrate both the methodological feasibility and the substantive and theoretical importance of conducting research of this sort. The question then becomes, What specific studies should be done? Stating the issue more precisely, what particular aspects of community systems on the one hand, or their psychological consequences on the other, should constitute the major foci of future investigation?

Some answers to this question are suggested by an examination of the knowledge gleaned in the first two domains of inquiry. Specifically, it would appear important to give priority to those community features that have been shown both to vary systematically from one community context to another and to be associated with contrasting psychological characteristics. Among the community systems that meet both of these criteria are local health programs, social services, and financial aids available from public and private agencies. The issue is not only the existence of such resources, but their accessibility to the community residents who need them most. To judge from the research we have reviewed, a key factor determining such accessibility is the existence of social networks that connect families and individuals with the main sources of material and social assistance.

It is here that we encounter a major gap in studies of community influences on family functioning and individual development. As we have seen, there are a substantial number of researches that document the differential distribution, across communities and neighborhoods, of various types of human support systems, both material and social. In other words, Step 1 is well represented. There is an equally impressive body of evidence demonstrating a statistical association between differences by type of community and the psychological characteristics of community residents. These studies fall under Step 2. What is missing is knowledge about the causal linkages between these two domains, that is, information about the particular intervening structures and mechanisms through which variations in the nature and availability of community support systems produce differences in family functioning and individual development. These are the issues addressed in Steps 3–5 of the analytic sequence we proposed as essential for identifying a community effect on family processes and developmental outcomes.

But the missing links in the causal chain are not the only substantial scientific gap in studies of community effects on families and children. Even more conspicuous by its absence is a developmental perspective— the recognition that community has different meanings for children of different ages and for their families. It is a reflection of the present state of knowledge (or, perhaps better said, state of ignorance) that we have not been able to find a single study that compared the community experience of children of different ages or of families at different stages of the life cycle. The only evidence we have of the importance of such developmental distinctions is indirect. For example, it is probably no coincidence that the age group most susceptible to the disruptive impact of urban environments on psychosocial development were very young children and their families, whereas the beneficial effects of the city on intellectual growth were observed in youngsters of school age. Nor is it accidental that studies of family social networks have concentrated on mothers of infants, while older children are the primary focus of research on community behavior settings. Each of these research choices implies a research question by omission. Do urban settings also enhance cognitive development in children of preschool age? Do rural environments reduce psychopathology in adolescence? Do parental support networks become irrelevant for the development of school-age children? At the most general level, what aspects of community life are the most significant for the well-being of families, and the development of children, at successive stages of the life cycle? These questions define a challenging research agenda that, if implemented, will make much more rewarding the experience of future authors, and readers, of the second review chapter on this same topic, when it is written some years hence. May the progress of our science soon merit such a second coming. In the meantime, there is much work to be done.

References

Adams, B. *Kinship in an urban setting.* Chicago: Markham, 1966.

Aldous, J., & Hill, R. Breaking the poverty cycle: Strategic points for intervention. *Social Work*, 1969, **14**, 3–12.

Almeida, E. *An experimental intervention for the development of competence in Mexican sixth grade children.* Unpublished doctoral dissertation, Cornell University, Ithaca, N.Y., 1976.

Almeida, E. Effects of parental involvement in teacher training. *International Journal of Psychology*, 1978, **13**, 221–236.

Babchuck, N. Primary friends and kin: A study of the associations of middle class couples. *Social Forces*, 1963, **43**: 483–493.

Bargel, T., et al. Sozial und raumliche Bedingungen der Sozialisation von Kindern in Verschiedenen Soziotopen. Ergebnisse einer Befragung von Eltern in Landgemeinden und Stadvierteln Nordhessens. In A. H. Walter (Ed.), *Region und Sozialisation* (Vol. 1). Stuttgart: Frommann-Holzboog, 1981.

Barker, R. G. Ecology and motivation. In M. R. Jones (Ed.), *Nebraska Symposium on Motivation*. Lincoln: University of Nebraska Press, 1960.

Barker, R. G. *Ecological psychology: Concepts and methods for studying the environment of human behavior*. Stanford, Calif.: Stanford University Press, 1968.

Barker, R. G., & Gump, P. V. *Big school, small school*. Stanford, Calif.: Stanford University Press, 1964.

Barker, R. G., & Schoggen, P. *Qualities of community life: Methods of measuring environment and behavior applied to an American and an English town*. San Francisco, Calif.: Jossey-Bass, 1973.

Barker, R. G., & Wright, H. F. *Midwest and its children: The psychological ecology of an American town*. New York: Harper & Row, 1955. (Reprinted by Archor Books, Hamden, Conn., 1971)

Behnken, I., & Zinnecker, J. Grundschule im Wohnquartier: Erkundungen zu einer regional versteckten Klassenschule. In A. H. Walter (Ed.), *Region und Sozialisation*. Stuttgart: Frommann-Holzboog, 1981.

Belsky, J., Steinberg, L. D., & Walker, A. The ecology of day care. In M. E. Lamb (Ed.), *Child rearing in nontraditional families*. Hillsdale, N.J.: Erlbaum, 1982.

Berger, P. L., & Neuhaus, R. J. *To empower people: The role of mediating structures in public policy*. Washington, D.C.: American Enterprise Institute for Public Policy Research, 1977.

Bott, E. *Family and social network: Roles, norms and external relationships in ordinary urban families* (2d ed.). London: Tavistock, 1957.

Böttcher, H. R. Schuleinstellung der Eltern und Schulerfolg der Kinder. *Schule und Psychologie*, 1968, **7**, 193–202.

Brim, O. G. Macro-structural influences on child development and the need for childhood social indicators. *American Journal of Orthopsychiatry*, 1975, **45**, 516–524.

Bronfenbrenner, U. The origins of alienation. *Scientific American*, 1974, **231**, 53–61.

Bronfenbrenner, U. *The ecology of human development: Experiments by nature and design*. Cambridge, Mass. Harvard University Press, 1979.

Bronfenbrenner, U., Alvarez, W. F., & Henderson, C. R., Jr. Working and watching: Maternal employment status and parents' perceptions of their three-year-old children. *Child Development*, 1984, **55**, in press.

Bronfenbrenner, U., & Crouter, A. C. Work and family through time and space. In S. B. Kamerman & C. D. Hayes (Eds.), *Families that work: Children in a changing world*. Washington, D.C.: National Academy Press, 1982.

Bronfenbrenner, U., & Crouter, A. C. The evolution of environmental models in developmental research. In W. Kessen (Ed.), *History, theories, and methods*. Vol. 1 of P. H. Mussen (Ed.), *Handbook of child psychology* (4th ed.). New York: Wiley, 1983.

Bronfenbrenner, U., & Weiss, H. B. Beyond policies without people: An ecological perspective on child and family policy. In E. Zigler, S. L. Kagan, & E. Klugman (Eds.), *Social policy for children and their families: A primer*. Cambridge: Cambridge University Press, 1983.

Campbell, A. *The sense of well-being in America: Recent patterns and trends.* New York: McGraw-Hill, 1981.

Caplan, G. *Support systems and community mental health: Lectures on concept development.* New York: Behavioral Publications, 1974.

Caplan, G. The family as a support system. In G. Caplan & M. Killilea (Eds.), *Support systems and mutual help.* New York: Grune & Stratton, 1976.

Children's Defense Fund. *Children out of school in America.* Cambridge, Mass.: Children's Defense Fund, 1974.

Chombart de Lauwe, P. H. *Famille et habitation* (2 vols.). Paris: Centre National de la Rechérche Scientifique, 1959–60.

Clausen, J. A., & Kohn, M. Relation of schizophrenia to the social structure of a small city. In B. Pasamanick (Ed.), *Epidemiology of mental disorder.* Washington, D.C.: American Association for the Advancement of Science, 1959.

Cochran, M. M., & Brassard, J. Child development and personal social networks. *Child Development,* 1979, **50,** 601–616.

Coleman, J. S. *Equality of educational opportunity.* Washington, D.C.: Government Printing Office, 1966.

Collins, A., & Watson, E. *Family day care.* Boston, Mass.: Beacon, 1976.

Collins, C., Moles, O., & Cross, M. *The home-school connection: Selected partnership programs in large cities.* Boston, Mass.: Institute for Responsive Education, 1982.

Conner, J. D. Parent participation pays dividends. *California Journal of Elementary Education,* 1950, **19**(1), 136–146.

Cooper, B., & Gath, D. Psychiatric illness, maladjustment, and juvenile delinquency: An ecological study in a London borough. *Psychological Medicine,* 1977, **7,** 465–474.

Crnic, K. A., Greenberg, M. C., Ragozin, A. A., Robinson, N. M., & Basham, R. Effects of stress and social supports on mothers in premature and full-term infants. *Child Development,* 1983, **54**(1), 209–217.

Crockenberg, S. B. Infant irritability, other responsiveness, and social support influences on the security of infant-mother attachment. *Child Development,* 1981, **52,** 857–865.

Darlington, R., Royce, J. M., Snipper, A. S., Murray, H. W., & Lazar, I. Preschool programs and later school comparisons of children from low-income families. *Science,* 1980, **208,** 202–204.

Davis, K., & Reynolds, R. *The impact of medicare and medicaid on access to medical care* (Tech. Ser. Reprint T-0130). Washington, D.C.: Brookings, 1977.

Eiduson, B. T., & Alexander, M. W. The role of children in alternative family styles. *Journal of Social Issues,* 1978, **34**(2), 149–160.

Faris, R. E. L, & Dunham, H. W. *Mental disorders in urban areas.* Chicago: University of Chicago Press, 1939.

Feree, M. M. Working-class jobs: Housework and paid work as sources of satisfaction. *Social Problems,* 1976, **23,** 431–441.

Fischer, C. S. *Networks and places: Social relations in the urban setting.* New York: Free Press, 1977.

Furstenberg, F. F., Jr. *Recycling the family: Perspectives for researching a neglected family form.* Paper presented at the meeting of the American Sociological Association, San Francisco, 1978.

Gans, H. J. *People and plans: Essays on urban problems and solutions.* New York: Basic, 1968.

Garbarino, J. A preliminary study of some ecological correlates of child abuse: The impact of socioeconomic stress on mothers. *Child Development,* 1976, **47,** 178–185.

Garbarino, J. Changing hospital childbirth practices: A developmental perspective on prevention of child maltreatment. *American Journal of Orthopsychiatry*, 1980, **50**, 588–597. (a)

Garbarino, J. Latchkey children: Getting the short end of the stick? *Vital Issues*, 1980, **30**(3), 1–4. (b)

Garbarino, J. *Successful schools and competent students*. Lexington, Mass.: Lexington, 1981.

Garbarino, J., & Crouter, A. Defining the community context of parent-child relations. *Child Development*, 1978, **49**, 604–616.

Garbarino, J., & Sherman, D. High-risk neighborhoods and high-risk families: The human ecology of child maltreatment. *Child Development*, 1980, **51**, 188–198.

Giovannoni, J., & Billingsley, A. Child neglect among the poor: A study of parental adequacy in families of their ethnic groups. *Child Welfare*, 1970, **49**, 196–204.

Gove, W. R., Grimm, J. W., Motz, S. C., & Thompson, J. D. The family life cycle: Internal dynamics and social consequences. *Sociology and Social Research*, 1976, **57**, 182–195.

Greene, J. G., & Blake, G. P. *How restrictive rental practices affect families with children*. Washington, D.C.: Department of Housing and Urban Development, 1980.

Guerry, A. M. *Essai sur la statistique morale de la France*. Paris: Crochard, 1883.

Gump, P. V., & Adelberg, B. Urbanism from the perspective of ecological psychologists. *Environment and Behavior*, 1978, **10**(2), 171–191.

Hill, R. *Family development in three generations*. Cambridge, Mass.: Schenkman, 1970.

Hill, R. Status of research on families. In U.S. Department of Health and Human Services, *The status of children, youth and families, 1979*. Washington, D.C.: Government Printing Office, 1980.

Hillary, G. A., Jr. Definitions of community: Areas of agreement. *Rural Sociology*, 1955, **20**, 111–123.

Holley, C. E. *The relationship between persistence in school and home conditions*. Unpublished doctoral dissertation, University of Illinois, 1916.

Hollingshead, A. D. *Elmstown's youth: The impact of social class on youth*. New York: Wiley, 1949.

Hoult, T. F. *Dictionary of modern sociology*. Totowa, N.J.: Littlefield Adams, 1969.

Hughes, C. C., Tremblay, M-A., Rapoport, R. N., & Leighton, A. H. *People of cove and woodlot*. New York: Basic, 1960.

International encyclopedia of the social sciences (Vol. 3). New York: Macmillan, 1968.

Jaeggi, U. *Berggemeinden im Wandel*. Bern: Paul Haupt, 1965.

Jöreskog, K. G. A general method for estimating a linear structural equation system. In A. S. Boldberg & O. D. Duncan (Eds.), *Structural equation models in social sciences*. New York: Academic Press, 1973.

Jöreskog, K. G. Structural analysis of covariance and correlation matrices. *Psychometrika*, 1978, **43**, 443–477.

Kahn, A. J. Service delivery at the neighborhood level: Experience, theory, and fads. *Social Science Review*, 1976, **50**, 13–14.

Kamerman, S. B., & Kahn, A. J. *Child care, family benefits, and working parents: A study in comparative policy*. New York: Columbia University Press, 1981.

Kasarda, J. D., & Janowitz, M. Community attachment in mass society. *American Sociological Review*, 1974, **39**, 328–339.

Kessner, D. M., Singer, K., Kalk, C. E., & Schlesinger, E. R. *Infant death: An analysis by maternal risk and health care*. Washington, D.C.: Institute of Medicine, 1973.

Kirschner Associates, Inc. *A national survey of the impacts of Head Start centers on community institutions*. Albuquerque, N.M.: Kirschner Associates, 1970.

Klineberg, O. *Negro intelligence in selective migration*. New York: Columbia University Press, 1935.

Klineberg, O. The intelligence of migrants. *American Sociological Review*, 3, 218–224, 1938.

Kogan, L., Smith, J., & Jenkins, S. Ecological validity of indicator data as predictors of survey findings. *Journal of Social Service Research*, 1977, 1, 117–132.

Koos, E. L. *Families in trouble*. Morningside Heights, N.Y.: King's Crown, 1946.

Kotelchuck, M., Schwartz, J. B., Anderka, N. T., & Finison, K. F. *WIC participation and pregnancy outcomes*. Unpublished manuscript, Massachusetts Statewide Evaluation Project, 1983.

Lagrone, D. M. The military family syndrome. *American Journal of Psychiatry*, 1978, 135, 1040–1043.

Lasch, C. *Haven in the heartless world: The family besieged*. New York: Basic, 1977.

Lash, T. W., Sigal, H., & Dudzinski, D. *State of the child: New York City* (Vol. 2). New York: Foundation for Child Development, 1980.

Lehman, H. C., & Witty, P. A. *The psychology of play activities*. New York: Barnes, 1927.

Leighton, A. H. *My name is legion*. New York: Basic, 1959.

Leighton, D. C., Harding, J. S., Macklin, D. B.; Macmillan, A. M., & Leighton, A. H. *The character of danger*. New York: Basic, 1963.

Levine, J. *Day care and the public schools*. Newton, Mass.: Educational Development Center, 1977.

Lightfoot, S. L. *Worlds apart: Relationships between families and school*. New York: Basic, 1978.

Litwak, E. Geographic mobility and extended family cohesion. *American Sociological Review*, 1960, 25, 385–394.

Litwak, E., & Szelenyi, I. Primary group structures nad their function: Kin, neighborhoods and friends. *American Sociological Review*, 1969, 34, 465–481.

Lohmöller, J. B. *Estimating parameters of linear structural relation models under partial least-squares criteria*. Munich: Forschungsbericht 79.01 aus dem Fachbereich Pädagogik der Hochschule der Bundeswehr München, 1979. (a)

Lohmöller, J. B. *Residuals in PLS modeling*. Paper presented at the Workshop on Soft Modeling Applications, Department of Political Sciences, University of Geneva, October 22–23, 1979. (b)

Lynd, R. Foreword. In E. C. Koos, *Families in trouble*. Morningside Heights, N.Y.: King's Crown, 1946.

McAdoo, H. R. Factors related to upwardly mobile black families. *Journal of Marriage and the Family*, 1978, 40, 61–69.

McPartland, J., & McDill, E. *The unique role of school in the causes of youthful crime*. Baltimore: Johns Hopkins Press, 1970.

McKinlay, J. B. Social networks, lay consultation, and help-seeking behavior. *Social Forces*, 1973, 52, 275–292.

Makarenko, A. A. *The road to life*. Moscow: Foreign Languages Publishing House, 1955.

Marans, R. W., Colten, M. E., Groves, R. M., & Thomas, B. *Measuring restrictive rental practices affecting families with children: A national survey*. Ann Arbor, Mich.: Institute for Social Research, 1980.

Mattessich, P. *The family life cycle and three forms of social participation*. Unpublished manuscript, University of Minnesota, 1978.

Meili, R., & Steiner, H. Eine Untersuchung zum Intelligenzniveau elfjahriger der deutschen Schweitz. *Schweizerisch Zeitschrift fur Psychologie und ihre Anwendungen*, 1965, 24, 23–32.

Mitchell, G. D. *Dictionary of sociology*. London: Routledge & Kegan Paul, 1979.

Mitchell, J. C. (Ed.). *The concept and use of social networks in urban situations*. Manchester: Manchester University Press, 1969.

Moen, P. Family impacts of the 1975 recession: Duration of unemployment. *Journal of Marriage and the Family*, 1979, **41**, 561–572.

Moen, P. Unpublished data. Ithaca, N.Y.: Cornell University, Department of Human Development and Family Studies, 1980.

Moen, P. The two-provider family: Problems and potentials. In M. E. Lamb (Ed.), *Nontraditional families: Parenting and child development*. Hillsdale, N.J.: Erlbaum, 1982.

Moen, P. Unemployment, public policy and families: Forecasts for the 1980's. *Journal of Marriage and the Family*, 1983 **45**, 751–760.

Moen, P., Kain, E. L., & Elder, G. H., Jr. Economic conditions and family life: Contemporary and historical perspectives. In R. R. Nelson & F. Skidmore (Eds.), *American families and the economy: The high costs of living*. Washington, D.C.: National Academy Press, 1983.

Moroney, R. M. *The family and the state: Considerations for social policy*. New York: Longman, 1976.

Muchow, M., & Muchow, H. H. *Der Lebenstraum des Grosstadtkindes*. Hamburg: Riegel, 1935.

Myerson, A. Mental disorders in urban areas. *American Journal of Psychiatry*, 1940, **96**, 995–997.

National Academy of Sciences, Committee on Child Development Research and Public Policy. (1981). *Toward a national policy for children and families*. Washington, D.C.: Government Printing Office.

Neale, A. The health care system vs. women and the poor. *Hospital Progress*, 1979, **60**, 40–50.

O'Connor, S., Vietze, P., Hopkins, J., & Altemeir, W. Postpartum extended maternal-infant contact: Subsequent mothering and child health. *Sociological Pediatric Research* (Abstract), 1977.

Olds, D. Improving formal services for mothers and children. In J. Garbarino, S. H. Stocking, & Associates, *Protecting children from abuse and neglect*. San Francisco, Calif.: Jossey, Bass, 1980.

Olds, D. *The Prenatal/Early Infancy Project*. Progress report to the Bureau of Maternal and Child Health Research Grants Division, Bureau of Community Health Services (HHS MCR-360403-05), 1981.

Parsons, T. (Ed.). *Essays in sociological theory*. New York: Free Press, 1949.

Perlman, R. *Consumers and social services*. New York: Wiley, 1975.

Pitkanen-Pulkkinen, L. The child in the family. *Nirdisk Psykologi*, 1980, **32**, 147–157.

Pulkkinen, L. Self control and continuity in childhood-delayed adolescence. In P. Baltes & O. Brim (Eds.), *Life span development and behavior* (Vol. 4). New York: Academic Press, 1982.

Quetelet, A. *Physique sociale: Un essai sur le developpement de facultés de l'homme*. Paris: Bachelier, 1835.

Quinton, D. Family life in the inner city: Myth and reality. In M. Marland (Ed.), *Education for the inner city*. London: Heinemann, 1980.

Rabkin, J. G., & Struening, E. L. Life events, stress and illness. *Science*, 1976, **194**, 1013–1020.

Rodick, J. D. & Henggeler, S. W. The short-term and long-term amelioration of academic and motivational deficiencies among low-achieving inner-city adolescents. *Child Development*, 1980, **51**, 1126–1132.

Rutter, M. *Changing youth in a changing society*. Cambridge, Mass.: Harvard University Press, 1980.

Rutter, M. The city and the child. *American Journal of Orthopsychiatry*, 1981, **51**, 610–625.

Rutter, M., Cox, A., Tupling, C., Berger, M., & Youle, W. Attainment and adjustment in two geographical areas. I. The prevalence of psychiatric disorder. *British Journal of Psychiatry*, 1975, **126**, 493–509.

Rutter, M., & Madge, N. *Cycles of disadvantage*. London: Heinemann, 1976.

Rutter, M., & Quinton, D. Psychiatric disorder—ecological factors and concepts of causation. In H. McGurk (Ed.), *Ecological factors in human development*. Amsterdam: North-Holland, 1977.

Sanger, M. B. *Welfare of the poor*. New York: Academic Press, 1979.

Sardell, A. The mobilization of bias in primary care policy: The case of neighborhood health centers. *Policy Studies Journal*, 1980, **9**, 206–212.

Schneewind, K., Beckmann, M., & Engfer, A. *Eltern und Kinder*. Stuttgart: Kohlhammer, 1983.

Schoggen, P. Behavior settings and the quality of life. *Journal of Community Psychology*, 1983, **11**, 144–157.

Schorr, A. L., & Moen, P. Single-parent and public policy. *Social Policy*, 1979, **9**, 15–21.

Shanas, E. Family-kin networks in cross-cultural perspective. *Journal of Marriage and the Family*, 1973, **35**, 505–511.

Shaw, C. R., Zorbaugh, F. M., McKay, H. D., Cottrell, L. S., Jr. *Delinquency areas*. Chicago: University of Chicago Press, 1929.

Smith, M. B. School and home: Focus on achievement. In A. H. Passow (Ed.), *Developing programs for the educationally disadvantaged*. New York: Teachers College Press, 1968.

Srole, L., & Associates. *Mental health in the metropolis: The midtown Manhattan study*. New York: Harper & Row, 1962.

Srole, L., & Associates *Mental health in the metropolis: The midtown Manhattan study*. New York: Harper & Row, 1975.

Stack, C. *All our kin*. New York: Harper & Row, 1974.

Steinberg, L., Catalano, R., & Dooley, D. Economic antecedents of child abuse and neglect. *Child Development*, 1981, **52**, 975–985.

Stolte-Heiskanen, V. Social indicators for analysis of family needs related to the life cycle. *Journal of Marriage and the Family*, 1974, **36**, 592–600.

Strauss, M. A., Steinmel, S. K., & Gelles, R. J. *Behind closed doors*. New York: Doubleday, 1981.

Street, D., Martin, G. T., Jr., & Gordon, L. K. *The welfare industry: Functionaries and recipients in public aid*. Beverly Hills, Calif.: Sage, 1979.

Strohmeier, K. P. & Herlth, A. Sozialraumliche Bedingungen familialer Sozialisation. Eine vergleichende Untersuchung von Wohnquartieren in Bielefeld, Felsenkirchen und Munster. In H. Walter (Ed.), *Region und Sozialisation*. Stuttgart: Fromman Verlag, 1981.

Sussman, M. B. The isolated nuclear family: Fact or fiction: In M. B. Sussman (Ed.), *Sourcebook in marriage and the family*. Boston: Houghton Mifflin, 1959.

Tangri, S. S., & Leitch, M. L. *Barriers to home and school collaboration: Two case studies in junior high schools*. A final report submitted to the National Institute of Education. Washington, D.C.: Urban Institute, 1982.

Turner, C., & Thrasher, M. *Handbook of developmental psychology*. Englewood Cliffs, N.J.: Prentice-Hall, 1970.

Unger, D., & Powell, D. Supporting families under stress: The role of social networks. *Family Relations: Journal of Applied Child and Family Studies*, 1980, **29**, 566–574.

U.S. Department of Commerce, Bureau of the Census. *Daytime care of children*. Current Population Reports, Population Characteristics Series P-20, No. 298, 1976.

U. S. Department of Commerce, Bureau of the Census. *Social indicators III*. Washington, D.C.: Government Printing Office, 1980.

Vatter, M. Intelligenz und regionale Herkunft. Eine Langsschnittstudie im Kanton Bern. In A. H. Walter (Ed.), *Region und Sozialisation* (Vol. 1). Stuttgart: Frommann-Holzboog, 1981.

Walter, H. *Region und Sozialisation* (Vol. 1). Stuttgart: Fromman-Holzboog, 1981.

Walter, H. *Region und Sozialisation* (Vol. 2). Stuttgart: Fromman-Holzboog, 1982.

Warren, R. L. *The community in America* (2d ed). Chicago: Rand-McNally, 1973.

Wellman, B. *Urban connections* (Research Paper no. 84). Toronto: University of Toronto, Centre for Urban and Community Studies, 1976.

Werner, E. E., & Smith, R. S. *Vulnerable but invincible.* New York: McGraw-Hill, 1982.

Wheeler, L. R. A comparative study of the intelligence of East Tennessee mountain children. *Journal of Educational Psychology,* 1942, **33**, 321–334.

Wicker, A. School size and students' experiences in extracurricular activities: Some possible implications for school planning. *Educational Technology,* 1969, **9**, 44-47.

Wilensky, H. L. The political economy of income distribution: Issues in the analysis of government approaches to the reduction of inequality. In: J. M. Yinger & S. J. Cutler (Eds.), *Major social issues: A multidisciplinary view.* New York: Free Press, 1978.

Williams, J. H. Close friendship relations of housewives residing in an urban community. *Social Forces,* 1958, **4**, 358–362.

Wirth, L. Urbanism as a way of life. *American Journal of Sociology,* 1938, **44**, 3–24.

Wright, H. F. *Children's behavior in communities differing in size, 1,2,3, & supplement.* (Report on NIMH project grant H01G98). Mimeographed. Lawrence: University of Kansas, Department of Psychology, 1969.

Wright, H. F. Urban space as seen by the child. *Courrier du Centre International de L'Enfance,* 1971, **21**, 485–495.

Young, M., & Willmott, P. *Family and kinship in East London.* Baltimore: Penguin, 1957.

9 Ethnic Families of Color

ALGEA HARRISON
Oakland University

FELICISIMA SERAFICA
Ohio State University

HARRIETTE McADOO
Howard University

What does it mean to be a member of an ethnic family within American society? Is it merely an economic definition, or does it pertain wholly to the physical differences that separate groups? How does this family membership affect the lives of parents and children, and what do social and behavioral scientists know about these families? These are some of the questions that will be explored in this review chapter. Ethnic families in the United States are composed of adults and children who are commonly classified as belonging to groups that reflect national, racial, and cultural backgrounds that differ, in varying degrees, from the majority of American families of European descent. Ethnic families share unique social and cultural heritages that are passed on from generation to generation (Mindel & Habenstein, 1976). The physical characteristics associated with membership in racial groups of color have been used inconsistently to identify these groups of ethnic families. Some family groups are defined biologically and some by national origin, religion, or language. Many authors have used race to identify those of African or Asian descent, but ethnicity to identify those of European descent. There has often been confusion in classifying those of Hispanic origin because of the long-existing racial mixtures within this group, or Native Americans because of their diversity of cultures and their failure to fall easily within a single racial category.

The term "minority families" is also commonly used in developmental literature but is considered by writers in the area of ethnic families as undesirable. "Minority families" has been identified as an unsuitable category name because it connotes the subordination of groups that in some environments may not be minorities, but in fact numerical majorities

(Peterson, 1980). Ethnics of color are family groups which have had an unequal access to power and which are stigmatized in terms of assumed inferior traits or characteristics (Mindel & Habenstein, 1976). In this review we will use the identifying term "ethnics" or "ethnic families of color."[1] The ethnic families of color included are Asian Americans, Afro-Americans, Hispanic Americans, and Native Americans.

This review of ethnic families of color will be focused on several themes: (1) conceptual and methodological research issues; (2) demographic and family trends; (3) ethnic family groups, and (4) socialization goals and patterns. Further, the review is limited to empirical investigations that have examined traditionally relevant psychological variables in child development research, family literature that examines families as units, and relevant works of sociologists and anthropologists. These themes will be applied to the various ethnic groups where appropriate and the major ethnic groups will be highlighted.

Conceptual and Methodological Research Issues about Ethnic Families of Color

CONCEPTUAL ISSUES

The lack of a well-defined conceptual orientation directing the scientific investigation of ethnic families and their children has been a source of concern to many writers. We have identified several major conceptual issues in our review of the scientific literature on ethnic families of color. These are (*a*) dual orientation, (*b*) assimilation orientation, (*c*) comparative studies, (*d*) social problem perspective, and (*e*) lack of ethnic perspective.

Dual Orientations

The accumulated body of knowledge about families and children has been described as having a dual orientation. The researcher uses an objective empirical orientation for collecting normative and generic data on nonethnic middle-class subjects, while an applied comparative orientation for identifying deviancy or deficits may be used for ethnic subjects (Myers, 1982). This dual conceptual orientation has been criticized for the following implicit assumptions: (1) the acceptance as scientific fact of the notion that European behavior is preferred and normative; (2) the assump-

---

[1]The term "ethnic" as used in this chapter refers to ethnic families of color only. Nonethnic refers to the majority population.

tion of equivalence of culture, color, and class; (3) the assumption of homogeneity of ethnic communities; (4) the assumption of a Western philosophical bias in examining family structures and functioning; and (5) philosophical orientations that function as barriers to objective truths (Baratz & Baratz, 1970; Deloria, 1981; Guthrie, 1980; Laosa, 1978; Myers, 1982; Nobles, 1980; Staples & Mirandé, 1980). Indeed, some consider the majority of the research on ethnic families to be atheoretical (Staples & Mirandé, 1980).

The dual orientation is also reflected in the perception that nonethnic middle-class families function mainly in isolated nuclear units (Hareven, 1971; Uzoka, 1979), as contrasted with ethnic extended families' kin-help systems (Keefe, Padilla, & Carlos, 1979), and has led to an allusive hierarchical evaluation of family functions. The emphasis has been placed on the structure of the nuclear family per se, rather than on the functional patterns that can be found within the various structural or cultural arrangements of parents and their involvement in wider family groupings.

Assimilation Orientation

A number of the studies in this review were conceptualized, implicitly or explicitly, within assimilation theory (Gordon, 1964). Asian Americans have been characterized as the model minority—an assimilation and acculturation success story (Huang, 1976; Kitano, 1969, 1981; Sue & Kitano, 1973; Suzuki, 1980). The major determinants of their success were considered to be the unity, stability, and strength of Asian families and the congruence between family values and American ideals.

"Assimilation," here, is defined as the gradual absorption of a minority by a dominant group, resulting in the loss of the minority group's identity in an enlarged and homogeneous society. Four major steps in the assimilation process have been postulated: acculturation (cultural or behavioral assimilation); absence of prejudice (structural, marital, identificational, attitude receptional); absence of discrimination (behavioral receptional); and absence of value and power conflicts (civic assimilation) (Gordon, 1964). Using this framework, investigators have examined the changes in family structure and socialization among generations of Asian-Americans, or have compared Asian Americans to Anglo-Americans, in order to assess the degree of acculturation or to study the consequence of value conflicts.

Recently Asian-American social and behavioral scientists have questioned the usefulness of the assimilation theory (Liu, 1980; Sue, 1980). From a developmental perspective, the assimilation theory is limited by its one-sided and unidirectional view of individual or group interaction with the environment. It emphasizes the ethnic group's progress in approximating the nonethnic group's socialization practices, without examining the factors that determine why some practices are changed while others are not, and without looking at the potential positive contributions of ethnic socialization patterns to the problems facing parents in both nonethnic and ethnic groups. From another perspective, Glenn (1983) has argued forcefully for an institutional rather than an assimilation framework. An institutional framework that takes into consideration political and economic conditions might be more useful for understanding Asian-American families.

Comparative Studies

Ethnic children have most often been included in ongoing research for comparative purposes rather than from an interest in ethnicity per se. Two theories, psychoanalytic and behavioristic, have provided the conceptual framework for majority of the research on child-rearing practices and outcomes (Yarrow, Campbell, & Burton, 1968). These theories focus on the parent-child relationship as an important determinant of behavior in children. The usual child behaviors investigated—dependency, aggression, and conscience—emerge from conceptualizing parental behavior broadly as acceptance and rejection of the child and reward and punishment of behaviors and their expected effect in major areas of socialization (Yarrow et al., 1968). These areas of development have been of concern both for theoretical and practical reasons. Related concepts (e.g., independence training, competitiveness, self-esteem, etc.) have been the focus of studies on relationships between patterns of child rearing and child behaviors. The performance of ethnic subjects on instruments assessing these concepts have been used to show how variations in family structure, ethnicity, socialization practices, and socioeconomic status influence deviations from the norm defined in studies of nonethnic middle-class subjects. Research on child behavioral outcome variables includes occasional studies of the performance of ethnic children on cognitive and personality variables identified as keys to understanding processes defined by nonethnic middle-class ecology. Examples of such studies are the relations of Anglo- and Mexican-American children's locus-of-control beliefs to parents' and teachers' socialization practices (Buriel, 1981); social and familial correlates of self-esteem among American Indian children (Lefley, 1974); cognitive abilities of Afro-American children (Harrison, 1979a, 1979b); and Chinese-American child-rearing practices and juvenile delinquency (Sollenberger, 1968).

A generous portion of the literature on ethnic families and children has accumulated from the comparative approach. This literature has been criticized for several weaknesses: (*a*) unidirectionality, (*b*) assuming causality from correlational data, (c) subjective measures of quality of home environment, (d) emphasis on problem populations, (e) exclusion of Afro-American fathers, (f) Western cultural bias, and (g) confounding of variables (Allen, 1978; Billingsley, 1968, 1971; Guthrie, 1980; Mathis, 1978; McAdoo, 1981; Myers, 1982; Nobles, 1980; Peters, 1981; Slaughter, 1979; Trimble, 1977). For a historical perspective see Billingsley (1971), Myers (1982), and Staples (1971). If the criticisms are valid, very few of the findings from these earlier studies can be considered definitive and instructive. As a result, information on ethnic families and children is limited and narrow. Segments of the literature have some merit, however, if reviewed from the perspectives of appropriate research strategies and the ethnic culture's values and goals.

Social Problem Perspective

Another conceptual approach to the study of ethnic families has been to view them as social problems (Billingsley, 1971; Trimble, Goddard, & Dinges, 1977). The most controversial example is the Moynihan (1965) report on Afro-American families, to which others responded with valid criticisms (Carper, 1971; Ryan, 1971; Staples, 1971b). Nonetheless, this view continued to dominate the type of questions asked in studying Afro-American families.

The social problem approach is somewhat less prevalent in current research, as a result of the valid criticisms and as the female single head of household have become an issue. With rising divorce rates, and increased numbers of women entering the labor market and becoming heads of households, the mother-child dyad in the family system is being reexamined. Hoffman's (1974) writings on working mothers and Hetherington, Cox, and Cox's (1979) writings on the impact of divorce on children were influential in changing the perspective on these issues. It is interesting that very few of these studies have included ethnics as subjects (Hoffman, 1974).

Nevertheless, the early intervention projects generated by the theories of Bloom (1964), Deutsch (1964), Hunt (1964), and others had the effect of studying ethnic family life as a social problem. They postulated that a significant proportion of cognitive development occurred between conception and the age of 4. "Infants and young children who did not have adequate experiences and stimulation of the semi-autonomous central processes demanded for acquiring skill in the use of linguistic and mathematical symbols and for the analysis of causal relationships" (Hunt, 1964, p. 236) were defined as culturally deprived. Rebuttals of this position were advanced and generated additional explorations into the experiential factors that shape cognitive and socio-emotional development (e.g., Barnes, 1980; Farnham-Diggory, 1970; Ginsburg & Russell, 1981).

Concurrently, intervention programs for ethnic low-SES children were initiated (e.g., Bereiter & Engelman, 1966; Slaughter, 1983; Weikart, Kamii, & Radin 1966; etc.). The conceptual orientation of the intervention programs varied, and Slaughter (1979) cogently clarified the difference between assumptions of therapeutic intervention and developmentally based educational intervention programs. The former assume that "parents *lack* the necessary behavioral repertoires to affect their children's development, whereas, the latter assume that the repertoires *are* available, but that parental deployment of available personal resources often requires external support and heightened awareness of the linkage between their children's behavior and their own" (p. 2). Generally, social scientists accept the premise that these early intervention studies were valuable in addressing some of the concerns regarding low SES and its effects on family life and the developing child (Zigler, Lamb, & Child, 1982). Issues and findings of the early intervention movement were reviewed and summarized by Gray and Wandersman (1980), Horowitz and Paden (1973), and Lazar and Darlington (1982).

Lack of Ethnic Perspective

The variables considered relevant to the socialization process have been derived from studies of nonethnics and have limited value in illustrating the experiences of ethnic families. Generally the concerns and perspectives of ethnic families have not been reflected in these variables. For example, among Native American families the tribe is a primary socializing unit, and an attempt to understand the socialization process must do more than examine the dyadic parent-child interactions. In the future, it is to be hoped that social scientists who are aware of the diverse ethnic cultures and historical experiences of families will conduct their investigations in the context of the ethnic culture.

The bicultural perspective is a useful one in studying ethnic families. Parents want their children to function both in the dominant culture and in the ethnic milieu. Laosa (1977) defines biculturalism as "an individual's ability to function optimally in more than one cultural context and to switch repertoires of behavior appropriately and adaptively as called for by the situation" (p. 29). Studies focusing on parental socialization strategies that permit children to function effectively in two cultures would be worthwhile. Normative-descriptive studies of different groups from a bicultural perspective would provide much needed baselines against which to assess secular changes in socialization practices across age and time.

METHODOLOGICAL ISSUES

The body of literature on ethnic families and children includes several critiques of the methodologies and research designs of studies using ethnic subjects. The validity of the accumulated findings on ethnic family life and developmental trends in the behavior of ethnic children have been questioned. Some of the major reasons are sampling-criteria difficulties in identifying populations, equating SES of groups being compared, and ethnicity of the examiner.

Difficulties in Identifying Populations

One problem of methodology has been the inability to identify accurately the prevalence of many of the components of ethnic classification. Only recently have there been attempts to make accurate Hispanic identifications, in spite of the large increases in this population. When Hispanics are coded in the data collected by states, each group tends to use a different system (Gillespie, Greeley, Houts, & Sullivan, 1983, pp. 27–28). In an effort to standardize such coding, "self-identification" was used on the 1980 census and data collection forms. However, this has not answered all the needs for accurate identification of those in ethnic groups and does not allow for longitudinal studies across these groups.

Socioeconomic Status and Comparative Groups

The findings in the pool of research on ethnic subjects are beset by the problem of comparative research designs that failed to match subjects on criteria that were known to affect the dependent variables. The most common error in comparative studies has been the confounding of ethnicity and class. Subjects from poverty or low-SES ethnic families in Head Start or other intervention programs have often been contrasted in their performance with nonethnic middle-class subjects (Deutsch, 1964; Gary, 1976; Myers, 1982). The generations and migration waves of Asian-American families, in addition to ethnicity and social class, have sometimes been confounded. Findings from comparative studies become functionally independent from the authors' cautions, and have been used in an explanatory manner without question.

The practice of using the standard measures of socioeconomic status developed for middle-class nonethnic families to assess the status of ethnic families has been questioned. Sociologists have used the term social stratification "to describe a social system in which individuals, families, or groups are ranked on certain hierarchies or dimensions according to their access to or control over valued commodities such as wealth, power, and status" (Mueller & Parcel, 1981, p. 14). One's relative position (and associated score) on a particular hierarchy (or combination of hierarchies) may be referred to as one's SES. Socioeconomic status categories do not have the same meaning across ethnic and nonethnic cultures (Alvirez & Bean, 1977). Moreover, ethnic families, by definition, differ from nonethnic families in their access to or control over valued commodities. For example, groups of Chicano low-SES subjects would differ in their economic status as well as their ethnicity from groups of Anglo-American low-SES subjects.

In sample selection, investigators have been attentive to the need to control socioeconomic status, generational status, or geographical location. However, they did not always control for all three factors in the same studies. In addition, the SES in the country of origin of the immigrant subject, the migration wave, and the circumstances in which the immigrants found themselves on arrival were often ignored, although these factors were relevant to socialization goals and techniques.

Ethnicity of Examiner

One of the methodological flaws in the body of literature on ethnic children has been the frequent use of examiners who were not of the same ethnic origins as the examinee. There are a series of studies of the significant interaction between ethnicity of examiner and examinee on performance scores of Afro-American subjects on tasks assessing cognitive abilities and personality traits (Brand, Ruiz, & Padillo, 1974). The findings are inconsistent, and most of the controversy has centered on the effect of the examiner's ethnicity on IQ test scores of Afro-American subjects (Sattler, 1970). Moore and Retish (1974) found that the main effect of the examiner's ethnicity was significant for verbal performance, and full-scale IQ scores among a sample of Afro-American preschool children enrolled in a Head Start program. Subjects earned higher mean scores when tested by an Afro-American examiner rather than an Anglo-American examiner.[2] This study was especially significant because it illustrated a problem in the evaluation of early intervention projects. A large percentage of the subjects

---

[2]The term "Anglo-American" refers to any English-speaking, nonethnic, nonblack member of the majority population.

in those studies were Afro Americans and the ethnicity of the examiner was not always noted or controlled, although it is a safe assumption that most were nonethnic.

Coates (1972), in keeping with the bidirectional model of research on adult-child dyads (Bell, 1968), investigated the effect of children's ethnicity on the behavior of adults toward children. It was found that Anglo-American male adults make more negative statements to an Afro-American male child than to an Anglo-American male child during training on a discrimination problem. Anglo-American female adults did not differentiate between the ethnic groups on this task. Both Anglo-American male and female adults, however, judged Afro-American children more negatively than Anglo-American children in ratings of personality traits.

Similar studies have been conducted on the effect of ethnicity of child on behavior, expectations, and attitudes of teachers. Findings have been inconclusive about the reciprocal effect of ethnicity in the examiner-examinee dyad, and this warrants continued exploration in future research on children in ethnic families. Furthermore, empirical studies bearing on this issue have yet to be conducted with Asian-American and other ethnic groups of color. Therefore, caution should be exercised in accepting the validity of research reports where the examiner and examinee were not of the same ethnic origins (Brand, Ruiz, & Padillo, 1974).

SUMMARY

The lack of a credible conceptual framework to organize the study of ethnic families and children has hampered the collecting of data that could increase our knowledge about the diversity and complexity of the coping and responsive behaviors of human beings. The variables that have been considered relevant to the socialization process come from conceptualizations of nonethnic middle-class ecology. A dual comparative orientation has guided the inclusion of ethnic subjects into the mainstream of scientific investigations of family life. The limited approach of assimilation theory has been the framework for investigations of Asian-American family life. The predominance of a social problem perspective has circumvented scientific inquiry into the dynamics of ethnic family life. The accumulated literature suffers from shortcomings in identification of ethnic populations, inappropriate comparison groups, and failure to control for ethnicity of the examiner.

Focused, insightful information about the relationship between ethnicity and larger social systems, and about how ethnicity is transmitted intergenerationally through socialization, has been scarce. Very seldom have data on child behavioral outcomes reflected the ethnic populations' goals, values, and techniques in the socialization process. The research that has been done thus far on Asian-American families tends to be descriptive rather than explanatory. Not a single experiment was found on Asian-American families. However, many writings suggest that ethnic parents socialize their children to function in both the dominant culture and the ethnic culture. Explorations from this predictive approach should assist in identifying contextual sources of variability among ethnic families. Clearly future research from this perspective is needed for a more valid assessment and understanding of how ethnic families socialize their children.

DEMOGRAPHIC AND FAMILY TRENDS

DEMOGRAPHIC STATUS

The latest demographic census data on ethnic status come from the 1980 census runs and more frequent estimations from samples of the Current Population Survey (CPS). Ethnic groups of color in 1983 constitute 20% of the U.S. population. The remaining 80% of the population are grouped under white, regardless of ethnic origin. The Hispanics are divided among Mexicans (59%), Puerto Ricans (15%), Central and South Americans (7%), Cubans (6%), and "other Spanish" (13%). The percentages of ethnic groups in the total population of the United States are presented in Table 1.

The number of Afro-Americans and Hispanics has increased significantly because of the younger age and higher fertility rate of these groups. To this number must be added recent increases in legal and illegal immigration. From 1970 to 1978, the population of Hispanics increased by 33%, an increase that was three times greater than that of Afro-Americans (12%) and almost six times greater than that of Anglo-Americans (6%). It

TABLE 1
DISTRIBUTION OF ETHNIC GROUPS IN THE UNITED STATES

ETHNIC GROUP	NUMBER IN POPULATION	PERCENTAGE OF POPULATION
Afro-American	26,495,025	11.6
Hispanics	14,605, 883	6.4
Asian, Pacific Islanders	,726,440	1.4
Native Americans, Eskimos, Aleut	1,418,195	.6
Whites, all groups	181,236,644	80.0
Total	226,545,805	100.0

SOURCE.—Dorothy Bailey, Bureau of the Census, personal communication via Library of Congress, Congressional Research Service, December 16, 1983.

has been predicted that persons in groups of color will constitute an even larger proportion of the population in 1990 and may outnumber Anglo-Americans by the end of the century (McAdoo, 1982).

FAMILY TRENDS

Several trends are beginning to occur in all American families. Among them are (*a*) increased participation in the labor market by mothers of young children (mothers of 59% of all children and of 47% of children under 6 years); (*b*) small increases in participation of fathers in child-rearing activities, partially due to maternal employment; (*c*) increased egalitarian decision making by parents; (*d*) increased childbearing outside of marriage, (*e*) increased refusal of fathers to support their children after separation or divorce; (*f*) increased feminization of family poverty; and (*g*) increased residential compounding, due to economic stresses.

One of the reasons these trends are being adopted by both nonethnic and ethnic families is economic stress. Periods of stress cause deviations from the traditional models and encourage families to form distinctive adaptive strategies (Hareven & Modell, 1980). These family changes have occurred because of financial strains that make the family wage earned by the father no longer sufficient to support the entire family. Other changes have occurred because of modifications of values in all families concerning the position of women. Ethnic women have traditionally played strong roles in the financial aspects of the family. This egalitarian pattern had earlier been misinterpreted as female dominance in Afro-American homes.

Ethnic Family Groups

AFRO-AMERICAN FAMILIES

Afro-American families represent a fusion of many cultures, races, and ethnic groups. The majority are descendants of the enslaved Africans, but there is a large Caribbean, Native American, Hispanic, and European blend within the groups. The typical family presented in the literature comes from the urban, economically depressed section of the group population. Repeatedly, social and behavioral scientists underestimate the diversity within this ethnic group.

Extended family interactions and mutual help patterns are strong because of cultural patterns and economic necessity. Religion has a very important role in the lives of majority of the families. Mothers and fathers are in the labor market and are usually equally involved in the family

decision making. There are class and regional differences in family values
and life-styles, which have resulted in variations of basic cultural patterns.
Among upwardly mobile families, many of the strong patterns of interaction and support have continued (McAdoo, 1978a).

Afro-American families tend to be nuclear, but a higher proportion of
these families are attenuated. Income levels dictate education, medical
care, access to contraceptives, and aspirations for future achievements. All
these variables tend to modify fertility levels (Harrison, 1981). The imbal-
ance in sex ratio (Guttentag & Secord, 1983) and the lack of job training and
career options within the communities have had an impact on young
families.

ASIAN-AMERICAN/PACIFIC ISLANDER FAMILIES

The category Asian-American/Pacific Islander encompasses over 20
nationality groups (Kitano, 1981). Among the former, the most numerous
are the Japanese, Chinese, Filipinos, and Koreans. The latter are many
fewer in number and include the Samoans and Guamanians, among others.
Among these groups are diverse nationalities and cultures. They also differ
in the timing of their mass migrations to the United States and in the factors
that prompted them to migrate, the areas where they settled, their reception by the host culture, their size, and other demographic factors such as
the ratio of single individuals to families or males to females. In the past,
some writers have assumed a commonality between Asian-American families due to Confucianism, a pervasive factor in Japan and China, but Suzuki
(1980) questions whether this influence still prevails among current Asian-
American immigrants who represent diverse geographical, political, economic, cultural, and social structures. In addition to these group differences, there are within-group differences (age, generation, social class,
education, personality) which might qualify any generalizations made
about Asian-American/Pacific Islander families.

The earlier immigrants were men; the women remained at home,
earlier by custom but later because of discriminatory laws. These laws
inhibited the development of families for many years, and at the same time
antimiscegenation laws prohibited intermarriage in 15 states. Despite a
heavy influx of "picture brides" from Japan and Korea between 1907 and
1924 (Kim, 1983), a disproportionate ratio of men to women among
Chinese, Koreans, and Filipinos continued until 1970. Thus, in addition to
Asian-American extended and nuclear families, there were long-distance
families (Lott, 1978) of which the nominal head lived and worked in the
United States while his wife and children resided in his native country.
Also, there were households composed of nonrelated individuals, often

from the same town or region. Such communal arrangements were the only family life that many Asian-American men knew. These different structures reflected the Asian concept of family as a structure which extended across time and space, including not only immediate household kin but also one's ancestors, one's descendants, and one's relatives in other households, whether they were one or ten thousand miles away (Lott, 1978).

World War II brought many changes to these families. Over 120,000 West Coast Japanese were incarcerated. This dislocation of families meant the loss of the parents' control over their children and brought grief to the more traditional fathers. This experience accelerated the assimilation of many youth into American society, for some were released to attend college in the Midwest and East or to join the military.

The political alliances with China and the Philippines during this same time resulted in the formation of more Chinese and Filipino families. Six thousand Chinese women came to the United States under the War Brides Act (Kim, 1983). Many of the marriages took place between individuals whose ages were not very far apart, but others resulted in "late families" (Lott, 1978, p. 14), which were simple nuclear families characterized by a large age difference, sometimes as much as one generation, between husband and wife. Existing data suggest that a significant number of late and war-bride families are now single-parent families, headed by a woman who is usually a widow in the former case and a divorcee in the latter (Lott, 1978). In sum, political, economic, and social conditions gave rise to differences in family formations that resulted in the great diversity among Asian-American families today.

Currently, information collected on Asian-American families consists mainly of essays on economic, political, and sociological issues rather than research articles. The scientific literature varies; there is very little documentation of smaller groups such as the Koreans and Filipinos, but more information exists about such populous groups as the Japanese and Chinese. Hence, the descriptions of family structure presented below deal only with Japanese- and Chinese-American families.

JAPANESE-AMERICAN FAMILIES

The typical Japanese-American family today is nuclear in its residential pattern, but it has been called a modified extended family (Johnson, 1972) because of the extent and closeness of its ties to relatives. Although family ties remain strong, relationships among its members seem to have become modified; the traditional patriarchal pattern, with the father at the top of the hierarchy, followed by sons, then daughters, and last by the

mother (Kitano, 1969), appears less frequently in the second generation
(nisei) and third generation (sansei), according to Suzuki (1980). Furthermore, husband-wife relationships tend to be more complementary
(Fujitomi & Wong, 1973; Johnson, 1972). Unlike traditional Japanese-
American families where the dominant relationship was between father
and son, the strongest relationships today are said to be those between
husband and wife and between wife and children. The father in today's
Japanese-American family may play with his children, but unlike his
Anglo-American counterpart he does not attempt to become a close com-
panion: he still thinks that a certain distance between parent and child is
necessary in order to engender respect and obedience (Suzuki, 1980).
Empirical studies are needed to confirm these impressions that husband-
wife and parent-child relationships have changed in contemporary
Japanese-American families.

CHINESE-AMERICAN FAMILIES

The typical Chinese-American household today often consists solely of
parents and children. However, Huang (1976) states that it would be
appropriate to think of Chinese-American families as having a semi-
extended rather than nuclear structure. Grandparents live apart yet close
to their married children, and these families often include, for long periods
of time, visiting relatives from Taiwan, Hong Kong, or mainland China.
Traditionally, the Chinese kinship system was based on the patrilineal line.
Daughters who married and went to live in their husbands' households
assumed subordinate roles therein and ceased to be members of their
biological families (Huang, 1976; Suzuki, 1980). Nowadays, depending on
various factors, the role of women in the Chinese-American family may
deviate from the traditional. For example, the more educated and Amer-
icanized the woman, the higher is her status within the family. Nevertheless, there remains a tendency for the wife to assume the role of helper
rather than truly equal partner to her husband (Huang, 1976). In a sample
of 69 Chinese-American women interviewed by Sollenberger (1968), only
47% reported that responsibility for making decisions about all aspects of
their lives was mutually shared between husband and wife.

HISPANIC FAMILIES

Among the Hispanic ethnic subgroups, there is great variety in
academic achievement and background characteristics. Hispanics have
lower incomes than Anglo-Americans, but Cubans and other Latin American have higher incomes than Mexican, Puerto Rican, or non-Hispanic

blacks. Differences of background and economic and educational opportunity have resulted in differential academic achievement. Cubans had the highest level of educational aspirations, followed by Mexican Americans and Puerto Ricans.

The use of Spanish within the families varies among the subgroups. Cubans (70%) were found to use Spanish more often than Puerto Ricans (48%), Mexican Americans (32%), or other Latin Americans (17%). However, all of the groups were similar in their self-assessed English-proficiency measure (Peng, 1982). The use of Spanish in the home was not found to relate to achievement scores. But proficiency in English *and* Spanish and SES level of the family were the best predictors of achievement.

In the Hispanic groups with separate census tabulations, 48% of the women worked. Mexican-American women have higher labor force participation (57%) than the other groups: Puerto Rican (11%), Cuban descent (9%) (U.S. Department of Labor, 1980). Women of Mexican origin have more children in their families than Puerto Rican families and other Hispanic women, but still had the most workers. Puerto Rican mothers tended to be younger than others, a reflection of the continuing movement of youth to the mainland.

CHICANO FAMILIES

The literature has presented Chicano families, who tend to live in the Southwest, in Catholic communities, as traditionally male dominated, with the father making the key decisions and not involved in family maintenance tasks. Recent work has challenged the old assumptions as simplistic and ethnocentric (Alvirez & Bean, 1976; Bacca-Zinn, 1980; Mirandé, 1977; Montiel, 1970; Murillo, 1971; Romano & Arce, 1968; Staples & Mirandé, 1980; Yando, Seitz, & Zigler, 1979). Chicano family processes have been found to be more complex and varied than can be understood by any single theory.

Hawkes and Taylor (1975) found that the most common approach to decision-making tasks by Chicano parents was egalitarian. Ybarra (1982) found a wide range of conjugal roles from partriarchal to egalitarian patterns of interaction. Values of acculturation, involvement, and assimilation in their own group or in Anglo society were not found to be related to the father's involvement in family household tasks. The extent to which parents held Mexican values predominately was also not related to dominance and child-rearing activity within the family. The strongest influence on conjugal roles was the participation of the mothers in the labor forces. When mothers worked outside the home, fathers helped more. However, whether the mothers worked or not did not influence decision making or other areas of their family relationships. Bacca-Zinn (1980) also found shared decision making in most families, with the strongest trends where mothers work.

PUERTO RICAN FAMILIES

Although migration from their agrarian culture began in the early 1900s, Puerto Ricans did not solidify as an ethnic group until the 1980s; therefore the family patterns are more fluid than in other groups (Garcia-Preto, 1982). Although almost all of the Puerto Rican families in the United States lived in New York at the 1970 census, now only one-half live there (Roger, 1982).

Racial and cultural mixtures of white, black, Spanish, African, Corsican, and Taino Indian are common within families. These combinations are influenced by other circumstances in Puerto Rico and the American mainland.

Puerto Rican families also have an active and intense involvement with their extended families. They prefer to handle their problems within the family rather than by social service professionals (Badill-Ghali, 1977). The elastic kinship boundaries incorporate friends of the family, who become like parents, often as sponsors at baptism. When crises occur, children may easily be transferred from one family group to another for temporary care.

NATIVE AMERICANS

Native Americans are the only ethnic group of color without allegiance to another country of origin, for they had been in America for thousands of years before they were discovered by the Europeans. The overall characteristic of families from this group is diversity of culture and languages. Despite the ethnocentric tendency to group them together, the tribal and nation differences are as great as those found between nation-states in Europe. Native American marriage and family patterns were adapted to the geographic and economic demands of their environment (McAdoo, 1978b; Spencer & Jennings, 1965). They practiced almost every known type of marriage: some in the Northeast were monogamous; other groups in the Northwest practiced polygamy. Some families were patrilocal and the men predominated in the production of food, while agricultural groups in the East and Southwest were matrilocal (Eggan, 1966). Early European settlers were often confused by this diversity, judging it by their more limited marriage and family practices. Each group's practices were consistent with its religious beliefs and compatible with its environment. However, the laws established by Europeans legitimized only the newer set-tlers' practices.

The strategies that survived from their earliest cultures have enabled Native Americans to maintain their families. These include a strong sense of tribalism and pride in their heritage. Tribal values continue to be stressed in many areas and are often taught to the children by their elders. Families are reported to be less child-centered than the society at large and children are encouraged to become self-reliant at early ages. Discipline can be a tribal concern with shame as a tool (Price, 1977; Sample & Smith, 1973).

There has been a reawakening of tribalism and nationalism within many Native American groups, fueled by the similar awakening of other ethnic groups. Tribes have been more active in the education of their children. The Native American–controlled community college systems have contributed to this progress. They are still relatively new; therefore research will be needed in the future to assess the effect of the tribal control over the schools. In reaction to past and present abuses Native American groups have made 20 policy-related requests, proposals for historic changes in the relationship between the native peoples and the United States of America (Trail of broken treaties, 1974).

RECENT IMMIGRANTS

Empirical research on the families of the new immigrants from the Caribbean and Asia has also been very limited. The family structures and economic statuses these immigrants are able to maintain depend on the acceptance shown to them on their arrival. Families from Haiti have had great difficulty gaining entry, legal status, and therefore legitimate jobs. Immigration itself places strains on the traditional extended family arrangements. However, families have actively followed the chain migra-tion patterns set by earlier groups.

Another recent example are the Vietnamese, who arrived after the change of regimes in Vietnam and the American withdrawal. Early waves of Vietnamese have made impressive economic gains through hard work and family cooperation. Nevertheless, problems frequently appear from the pressures of surviving economically in an alien society. Changes in the traditional family structure and values have contributed to stress.

FUTURE TRENDS IN ETHNIC FAMILIES OF COLOR

Projections of the future organization of these families are difficult if not impossible to make. Any attempt to predict the trends of ethnic families must take into account the group's cultural background, sociohistorical experiences, and the context in which the group must exist, as well as the interactions between these factors. Lott (1978) has noted that, with the exception of immigration policies, institutional factors do not play as significant a role in family organization as they did earlier in the history of Asian Americans. Native American, Hispanic, and Afro-American families continue to find that institutions play important roles. At most, we can say the following about future trends:

1. Families that have lived in the United States for more than a generation will exhibit a nuclear family structure in residential patterns, but will continue to maintain close ties and frequent interactions with relatives.

2. Husband and wife relationships will become more egalitarian, as will relations between siblings, while parents may become less authoritarian toward their children.

3. The continuing influx of new immigrants ensures the continued existence of extended families, until the latest arrivals (e.g., elderly parents, adult siblings) set up their own households.

4. The inclusion of refugees among the new immigrants suggests that there will also be augmented families, where nonrelatives live within households as members of the family.

Additional trends have been predicted earlier (Peters & McAdoo, 1983):

5. There will be a convergence of the life-styles of ethnic and nonethnic families, because of mutual life experiences in changing family structures and roles within families.

6. There will be increased involvement in family ethnicity and interest in traditions of earlier generations.

7. There will be an increased need for the extended family mutual support patterns and residential compounding among ethnic families of color who continue to face economic discrimination in a shrinking economy.

8. Economic and family life-style differences will continue to enhance diversity within ethnic groups due to differences in SES and immigration experiences.

SOCIALIZATION GOALS AND PATTERNS

The psychological processes and determinants of influence on socialization are the same for all family systems. Nevertheless, it is postulated that the content of the socialization message differs for ethnic families as a reflection of ethnic values and goals, and of the social status of the family system within the larger system.

Given the state of research in this area, and the need to achieve some degree of coherence, we will limit this review to a discussion of the socialization goals and patterns of two main groups, namely, Afro-American and Asian-American families. Contemporary psychological studies will be reported and directions for future research will be suggested. For a historical background, the reader is referred to Billingsley (1971), Huang (1976), Kikumura and Kitano (1980), Lott (1978), Myers (1982), Peters (1981), Staples (1971b), and Suzuki (1980).

AFRO-AMERICAN FAMILIES

The Afro-American family's socialization goals and patterns have been described in a few studies by writers investigating the life-style of urban, economically limited families. For the purpose of our review, these studies offer limited information about Afro-American families. We will focus here on the literature that is relevant to the specific socialization goal, bicultural adaptation, that is pervasive among Afro-American families.

We also reviewed investigations of mother-infant interaction patterns among low-SES urban Afro-Americans. These studies illustrate how investigations with ethnic subjects can contribute to knowledge of conceptual and developmental issues without resorting to a social problem perspective.

Major Socialization Goals and Techniques

Generally, the most encompassing parental goal of Afro-American families has been identified as preparing the child to function in both the ethnic and nonethnic cultures (Peters, 1981; Slaughter, 1979; Staples, 1971b; Valentine, 1971). The relationship between this socialization goal and maternal child-rearing patterns was explored by Young (1974) in a selected sample. Other writers have described parenting techniques of Afro-American families. However, Young's writings were selected for review because of their relevance to the socialization goal of bicultural adaptation consistently identified by Afro-American family researchers.

Young examined, and found similarities between, the socialization process in samples of low-SES Afro-Americans in both a rural southern community (1970) and an urban northern setting (1974). After analyzing the observations, she postulated a behavioral interactional pattern in the mother-child relationship. This she termed the goal persistence–cue perception interpersonal pattern. Young (1974) further postulated that the pattern was related to another observed pattern, rapid shifting of attention, inherently a prerequisite for success in the previous pattern. The goal persistence–cue perception interpersonal pattern fosters bicultural adaptation because its essence was "the training of techniques of adaptation to persons and situations, while at the same time maintaining a strong sense of independent self" (Young, 1974, p. 405). The dynamics of the pattern were observable within the framework of a contest between mother and child. The mother established an authority position to set limits and give content to the socialization message (e.g., independence training, etc.). Concurrently, the behavioral sequence incorporated reciprocity, the sequential behaviors involved both persons taking opposite positions and reversing themselves. The messages conveyed to the child in the pattern were aspects of interpersonal interaction: (*a*) that authority figures have power, (*b*) persistence and manipulativeness in pursuing goals, (*c*) that it is alright to pursue goals, (*d*) independence; (*e*) the ability to judge the disposition of others towards self, and (*f*) adaptiveness to others.

This series of studies suggests a speculative interpretation of the effect of the goal persistence–cue perception interpersonal pattern of Afro-American children. Afro-American children are taught that authority figures set limits; that there are culture differences in limits; that cues for these differences are interpersonal and come from authority and social figures; and that differences dictated the methods of pursuing one's goals. Further, the fostering of reciprocity instills the idea that the environment is negotiable. Simultaneously, Afro-American children learn cultural differences, namely, that nonethnic culture differs from ethnic culture in how much importance is placed on pursuing one's goal, and how sensitively tuned the culture is to facilitating that process. Thus, the goals persistence–cue perception interpersonal pattern facilitated interpersonal sensitivity and bicultural adaptation. Without question this speculative interpretation requires rigorous scientific inquiry.

In addition, Young's (1970, 1974) findings could be used as a framework for understanding some of the socialization practices among low-SES Afro-Americans reported by researchers, for example individualistic and independent orientation, controlling the child by role expectancy, applying strict arbitrary rules, and demanding mature independent behavior (Bartz & Levine, 1978; Hess & Shipman, 1965; Slaughter, 1979). Also, this framework is useful in interpreting the differences in self-esteem across contexts (school, peer group, home) among Afro-American children (Hare, 1977); differences in ability to distinguish between society's view of their racial group and their view of themselves

(McAdoo, 1977); and the tendency of Afro-American mothers to choose the most intense punishment regardless of type (e.g., love oriented or power assertive) (Alston, 1979). These findings are more parsimonious if they are interpreted within the context of a descriptive socializing pattern that fosters bicultural adaptation. To understand the subliminal interplay and messages in a socialization process aimed at bicultural adaptation requires more than superficial observations and completion by parents of question-naires developed for parents who socialize toward unicultural adaptation. The latter approach poses the danger of excluding possible variables that could offer insights into the socialization process. The latter procedure also has the inherent fault of collecting data in a framework conceptualized and normalized with respect to families for whom there is continuity between home and the wider culture. Inevitably, the possibility exists of discon-tinuity between the wider cultural systems and Afro-American family systems.

Mother-Infant Interaction Patterns

For the past decade researchers have focused on the mother-infant relationship, since there are theoretical postulations, documented by empirical evidence, that early life experiences are important to the child's cognitive and socioemotional development. The majority of investigations have observed mother-child interactions in nonethnic middle class fami-lies. Findings from a limited number of studies of Afro-American, urban, low-SES mother-infant dyads were insightful concerning the issue of dif-ferential effects of mother and infant characteristics and temperament (Thomas, Chess, & Birch, 1970) in caregiver-infant interactions. Data from Field, Widmayer, Stringer, and Ignatoff's (1980) home stimulation pro-gram indicated that age of mother and birth status of infant influenced the caregivers' perception of infant temperament. Teenage mothers of pre-term infants perceived their infants' temperaments as difficult. In another sample with full-term infant, mothers' perceptions of infants' temperament significantly related to mothers' behavior. Among Milliones's (1978) sam-ple of mothers, the more difficult in temperament the mother perceived the infant, the less responsive was the mother. Similarly, observation by Brown et al. (1975) suggested that the mothers' behavior was also in-fluenced by the infants' behavior. Infants who were active, vocalized frequently, and kept their eyes open had mothers who looked at them and spent more time in care giving activities. Mothers who received more drugs during delivery and whose infants were generally passive spent more time holding, feeding, and stimulating their newborns. Moreover, the sex and size of the infant influenced the behavior of mothers. Mothers were more affectionate toward (e.g., rubbed, patted, touched, kissed, rocked, and talked) their male infants than their female infants. It was also reported that mothers vocalized more to heavy male infants, and the authors concluded "that in this population large male infants are most valued" (Brown et al., 1975, p. 685).

Also important in the socialization process is the observed motor precocity among Afro-American infants younger than 24 months (Bayley, 1965; King & Seegmiller, 1973; Knobloch & Pasamanick, 1953; Williams & Scott, 1953). King and Seegmiller (1973), as part of a larger study, indicated that Afro-American male infants' mean Bayley Psychomotor scores were significantly greater than the standardization sample at 14, 18, and 22 months. The researchers attributed the finding to environmental etiology. Interestingly, Field et al. (1980) reported that the mothers in their sample rated their infants more optimally on motor items than the Brazelton examiners. These findings suggest a fruitful area for future study of the reciprocal nature of mother-infant interactions and its impact on the physical development of the child.

Studies of mother-infant interactions among Afro-American, urban, low-SES families also address the issue of differential performance on IQ tests at 3 years of age in selected populations. The mother-child interaction has been used as an explanatory variable for differential achievement scores between Afro-American and Anglo-American children at 3 years. Scientific evidence suggests that mother-infant interactions during the first 24 months are meaningful for subsequent cognitive and social development (Bradley, Caldwell, & Elardo, 1979; White & Watts, 1973). Yet infant test data from a series of comparative studies of Afro-American infant and standardization samples document the lack of difference between them (Bayley, 1965; King & Seegmiller, 1973). Further, Bakeman and Brown (1980), in their longitudinal study of mother-infant interactions, found that although early interaction varied across kinds of infants (e.g., preterm to full-term), different interactive experiences were not associated with different outcomes. The inconclusiveness of the findings suggest the need for future research.

In sum, researchers generally agree that the overriding socialization goal of Afro-American families is bicultural adaptation. After extensive observations of caregiver-child interactions among low-SES Afro-American families, Young (1970, 1974) postulated a goal persistence—cue perception interpersonal socializing pattern in these families. Previous research findings were interpreted from this pattern, since it was described as pertinent to the socialization goal of bicultural adaptation. The need for future scientific inquiry was underscored.

Observers of mother-infant interactions have noted that birth status, sex, size, perceived temperament, and activity level influenced the perceptions of mothers and their behavior toward their infants. Researchers have noted a generalized motor precocity among Afro-American infants and a tendency among Afro-American mothers to rate their infants highly on test items describing motor behaviors. These findings suggest future scientific explorations in these areas. Finally, evidence from studies of mother-infant interaction among urban, low-SES families questioned the contention that mother-infant interactions could explain the differential performance and IQ test scores at 3 years of age among selected populations of Afro-American children.

ASIAN-AMERICAN FAMILIES

Theoretical and empirical work on Asian-American families has been strongly influenced by what might be called, for lack of a better phrase, the social science perspective. The distinguishing characteristic of this approach, employed by sociologists and anthropologists, is an interest in the linkages among social structure, social values, and socialization. Briefly, the underlying assumptions are that social values are closely linked to the aims and structure of a particular society. In turn, these values determine socialization goals and techniques. The available literature is written from this perspective, and the review that follows is organized along these lines. Sociological and anthropological descriptions are included in order to provide a baseline for future psychological studies of Asian-American family structures, socialization goals, and techniques.

Japanese-American Families

Major Socialization Goals and Techniques

Socialization goals and techniques might be better understood and appreciated if they were examined from the perspective of the societal values and norms that reflect the means of survival. In regard to Japanese Americans, for example, consider a proposal by Nakane (1970) that traditional Japanese society has a "frame" structure, in which identification is situational, or with respect to a particular institution, rather than general or cutting across institutional lines. Each frame is a relatively autonomous organization, distinguishable from other frames.

The maintenance of such a structure requires a high degree of in-group unity and cohesion; careful attention to organizational structure through rank and status; and heavy dependence on the organization for economic, social, emotional, and psychological support that, in turn, assures loyalty to one frame. In other words, group consciousness, deference to authority, dependence, and commitment expressed through mutual responsibility and reciprocity are highly valued. These values, translated into major socialization goals, are inculcated in the young through the *ie* (family, household, house), which is the primary unit of organization and is considered the most important frame for early socialization and upbringing. Today, the *ie* remains the primary context of the Japanese American's socialization and its scope has been broadened to include the entire Japanese-American community in a particular setting.

Those writing about contemporary Japanese-American families maintain that the major socialization goals are still those derived from traditional values (Kitano & Kikumura, 1976; Suzuki, 1980). These are to instill in the child a sense of collectivity rather than individuality, filial piety, dependence on the *ie*, obedience to authority, and a sense of responsibility and obligation to the *ie*. To achieve these goals, a variety of techniques are employed. It should be noted here that while the use of certain techniques has been empirically investigated, adherence to the above-mentioned values and goals has not. The closest thing to a study of values we found was a comparative investigation reporting that Japanese-American parents gave significantly higher ratings of importance than did Anglo Americans to seven descriptors of social competence in children: considerate, cooperative, well behaved, gets along, happy, persistent, and self-controlled (O'Reilly, Ebata, Tokuno, & Bryant, 1980). More direct assessments of the cultural values and socialization goals of Japanese-American families are needed.

Collectivity and group identification.—The development of the Japanese-American child's awareness that he or she is a member of a group whose interests take precedence over his or her own individual interest, and the socialization practices associated with the acquisition and maintenance of group identification, have not yet been examined empirically by developmental psychologists. However, the work of several social scientists suggests some concepts and techniques that might be involved. The development of group awareness probably entails the child's acquiring a concept of the *ie* or primary socialization unit, which in the United States consists of the family and the local Japanese community. A probable corollary of this development is the emergence of the opposite concept, the other or out-group, which is typically the *haku-jin* or Anglo American. In addition, it has been proposed that the concepts of "face" and "shame" play important roles in maintaining group identification and conformity. Early in life, the Japanese-American child learns that one must be concerned about presenting "a good face," particularly to the *haku-jin* (Anglo American). This constant reference to the out-group not only helps the child to differentiate between his group and the out-group, it also teaches that what an individual does (good or bad) casts a reflection on himself and his family, as well as the entire community. The concept of shame is critical for the successful application of social control statements such as "What will other people think?" Finally, group slogans, mottoes, and traditions are also used to enhance the sense of ethnic solidarity. For example, Yanagisako (1977) found that among modern Japanese, pairs of female kin (mother-daughter, sister-sister) play active roles in promoting family ties and kin solidarity, particularly through arranging family events and holiday gatherings.

Dependence upon the ie.—Another important socialization goal is instilling dependence on the *ie*. The concept of *amae*, meaning to depend on and to presume the other's benevolence, is an important socialization construct, even among the current generation of Japanese Americans. Dependence on the family, particularly the parents, is fostered. Caudill (1952) reported that parental dependence was characteristic of the nisei (second generation) as well as the issei (first generation). A study (Connor, 1974) of three generations of Japanese-Americans provides further evidence that despite the acculturation of each successive generation, the importance of family and the inculcation of dependency behaviors persist.

How is the early dependence of the infant upon the primary caregiver maintained and generalized to other members of the family? It has been suggested by Caudill and Frost (1974) that co-sleeping arrangements, bathing together, and eating are familial activities that foster mutual dependence in a Japanese family. Such co-sleeping arrangements and communal bathing are no longer practiced by contemporary Japanese-American families, but many nisei recalled such family activities. Furthermore, some of the old ways still persist. Caudill and Frost (1974) found that the sansei or third-generation Japanese-American mother, like her Japanese counterpart, carries and cuddles her infant a great deal and spends a large amount of time playing with him. However, she engages in more vocalization to her infant, and does more positioning and less rocking, than the Japanese mother. The result is that the yonsei (fourth generation) infant engages in greater amounts of happy socialization and physical activity, with lesser amounts of unhappy vocalization.

Such parental indulgence might be expected to result in spoiled, pampered, dependent children and adults. But one can hardly say these things of the Japanese. What are the socialization practices that check these possible adverse consequences? To begin with, there is a definite period when the child is indulged, but past a certain age the child is expected to act in a more mature manner and reversals to immature behavior are swiftly, and sometimes severely, punished, usually by the father. Initially indulgent, with a high degree of tolerance for any behavior, especially in his sons, the father establishes certain limits, which if overstepped elicit immediate and severe discipline.

There is some evidence that the degree of restrictiveness exercised by the modern Japanese-American woman may have eased. Kitano (1961) administered the Parental Attitude Research Instrument (PARI) to a group of 43 nisei and 26 issei and found statistically significant intergenerational differences. These results were confirmed in a subsequent study (Kitano, 1964) of two age groups (30–40 years and 50–75 years) of Japanese-American women and Japanese women matched on age, social class, and marital status. The older group of Japanese-American women held the most restrictive attitudes toward child rearing; the next most restrictive group was the older group of women in Japan, and the least restrictive were the younger Japanese-American women. It is interesting to note that although significant differences between generations emerged for both cultures, like generations in the two cultures did not differ in their child-rearing attitudes.

Filial piety and obedience.—Among the Japanese, respect, obedience, and filial piety are highly emphasized, along with observance of rank order within the family structure. There is more information available about how deference to authority as a socialization goal is attained. Principally, it is accomplished through the child's acquisition, via spontaneous discrimination or differentiation, didactic instruction, and observational learning, of rank and status cues that determine the style of interaction and the prescribed linguistic forms for addressing those above or below the child in status. This is best illustrated by the set of norms regulating the *oyabun-kobun* or parent-child relationship, wherein appropriate reciprocal behavior is expected from each party (Kitano & Kikumura, 1976). Children are expected to respect and obey their parents, and to display a deferential manner in communication and behavior, which involves *enryo* or reserve and constraint. The rules related to the norm of *enryo* learned early in the Japanese family include those governing interaction with peers. A child quickly learns the importance of sensitivity to the reactions of others, reticence, modesty, indirection, and humility and is punished for boastful, aggressive, loud, and self-centered behavior. In the ideal social interaction with one's peers, neither person dominates the other; by "bad mouthing" ones-self and complimenting others, modesty is preserved and self-validation is achieved by both partners (Kikumura & Kitano, 1980). The social interactional rules related to the norm of *enryo* are not as explicitly defined as in the preceding generations, but one can still observe this pattern in a Japanese-American setting. DeVos (1955) and Spiro (1955) claim that parental authority has been eroded over the years.

Responsibility and obligation to the ie.—The socialization goal of developing a sense of obligation also acts as an effective counterforce to the possible negative effects of excessive unilateral dependence on the family. The Japanese-American child learns that he or she may count on the family but they, too, rely on him or her.

Instilling a sense of obligation and responsibility to the family arose out of the need for perpetuation of the *ie* as the primary unit of social organization. Such continuity depends on an intricately balanced system of reciprocal responsibilities and obligations. The moral and legal duty for continuing the *ie* was vested originally in the house head (*kacho*) who, as eldest son and heir to the property rights, had the obligation of securing a stable environment for its members and of providing arrangements for marriage, occupation, food, and living comforts. However, each member also had an obligation to dedicate his or her life for the advancement and good reputation of the *ie*. This obligation continues with some modification today. Johnson (1977) found that among nisei parents and their sansei offspring, duties and obligations had become less burdensome and easier to fulfill because the responsibility of aged parents was shared by the entire sibling group rather than borne solely by the eldest son. The rule of primogeniture has changed to equal inheritance, introducing more symmetry into sibling relationships. This structural change and the sharing of filial responsibility have actually increased kin solidarity (Yanagisako, 1977).

To summarize, the four major socialization goals of the Japanese-American family are interrelated. These goals arise out of traditional Japanese values, which reflect Confucian concepts of collectivity, order and hierarchy, and obligation.

Chinese-American Families

Major Socialization Goals and Techniques

Traditional Chinese society has been described as situation centered, oriented toward the clan rather than the broader society or the central government. The clan consists of persons with the same surname, all of whom are considered to be descended through the patrilineal line from a common ancestor. As with the Japanese *ie*, the preservation of the Chinese clan rests on group cohesion, dependence on the clan, adherence to organizational structure, and a deep sense of loyalty. These, therefore, are

the values underlying socialization toward collectivity and group identification, dependence, filial piety and obedience, and a sense of obligation and
responsibility to the clan. Parenthetically, it should be noted that although
the above-mentioned values are assumed still to be held by contemporary
Chinese Americans, to date there have been no psychological studies on
this topic.

Collectivity and group identification.—The Chinese individual has
been described by Sung (1979) as someone who subordinates his own
wishes for the common goal. Such self-sacrifice is predicated on an orientation toward collectivity instead of individualism. The acquisition of such an
orientation involves the development of a group or ethnic awareness, as
well as identification with and preference for the group.

Three studies provide some empirical evidence regarding ethnic
awareness, identification, and preference of Chinese-American children.
The early studies suggested that perhaps the socialization to a group
orientation might be weakening in contemporary Chinese-American families. Springer (1950) reported that when 3–6-year-old Chinese children
living in Hawaii were asked to identify themselves, they pointed to pictures of Japanese instead of Chinese children. Similarly, Fox and Jordan
(1973) found that urban Chinese-American children between the ages of 5
and 7 showed significantly less preference for identification with their own
race than did same-age black or white children. In contrast, Ou and
McAdoo (1980) found no support for what has sometimes been referred to
as the "self-hatred hypothesis." These investigators examined ethnic
awareness, identification, and preference in two age groups (Grades 1–2
and 5–6) of 192 Chinese-American children from urban and suburban
middle-class families, using a modification of the original Clark's doll test.
They found that by age 7, almost all the children showed awareness of racial
differences based on physical characteristics and were able to make correct
self-identifications, that is, to point to the child "who is like you." Analyses
of variance did not reveal any grade or sex differences on mean ethnic
preference scores. However, a χ^2 analysis of responses to individual items
showed that (1) significantly higher proportions of the older children
preferred to play with a Chinese playmate and thought that their own skin
color was nice, and (2) first- and second-grade girls preferred Chinese
playmates whereas their male counterparts expressed a preference for
white playmates. Ou and McAdoo (1980) suggest that the low preference
for their own race expressed by the children in the Fox and Jordan (1973)
study might be due to the dominant society's attitudes toward ethnics at
that time, or to these children's low SES, which may have made them less
inclined to choose ethnic peers with harsher living conditions. Research is
needed to clarify further the separate and interactive effects of SES and the

dominant society's attitudes toward ethnic groups on the developmental ethnic identification and preference in Chinese-American children.

With the exception of a finding reported by Ou and McAdoo (1980) that positive parental attitudes toward the Chinese culture are significantly and positively related to their children's ethnic identity, there is almost no scientifically derived information on the specific techniques employed by Chinese-American parents to promote the initial acquisition of group identification. Empirical studies are required, too, to test the hypothesis that group identification, once it has been acquired, is maintained by the extensive informal and formal social networks that exist in Chinese-American communities, through such mechanisms as shame and conflict with the majority group (Hsu, 1948; Suzuki, 1980).

Dependence on the clan.—Available literature on contemporary Chinese-American families continues to emphasize a sense of dependency on the family as a major socialization goal (Huang, 1976; Suzuki, 1980). Dependence is functionally adaptive because it maintains close affective ties within the family and heightens the individual's feeling of security. It is brought about primarily through a permissive, indulgent approach during the early years of a child's life (Bunzel, 1950; Hsu, 1948). Empirical support for this hypothesis was reported by Sollenberger (1968). Chinese-American mothers, asked to respond to the interview used earlier by Sears, Maccoby, and Levin (1957) in their classic study of child-rearing patterns, gave answers that when compared with those of the original sample were significantly more lenient about late weaning, toilet training, and regular bedtime.

Total dependence is not, however, the objective. Young (1972) found that immigrant Chinese children in Hawaii were expected to do things for themselves at an early age, although they received constant, strict supervision, their would-be friends were carefully screened by their mothers, and they were discouraged from socializing with people outside the family until they were much older. Similar practices were observed in a more recent study of immigrant Chinese children in New York (Sung, 1979). All of the above-mentioned practices might indeed bring about dependency, but one must be careful about assuming that they are employed for that purpose. Perhaps they are reactions to beng transplanted to a different culture, with a different language, and to an ethnic-group status. More acculturated Chinese-American women favor independence for their children at an earlier age than do immigrant Chinese mothers, or for that matter, Jewish, Protestant, Black, Greek, French-Canadian, and Italian mothers in Hawaii (Young, 1972). So, out of necessity, do recent immigrant Chinese mothers in New York City, who, because of prevailing employment conditions, have to work away from their homes (Sung, 1979).

Filial piety and obedience.—According to Huang (1976), filial piety is one of the values that has united the Chinese family for centuries. Even today, both the Chinese in Chinatown and those (often professionals) who live elsewhere still show respect to the older members of the family. Socialization, therefore, places great emphasis on the goal of inculcating respect and obedience toward the elders of the family. One way in which the young are socialized to show respect is through modeling or didactic instruction about the appropriate kin terms of address between individuals in different age groups. However, the major approach to socialization for compliance appears to be a combination of nurturance and strict discipline, used in sequence.

Using the PARI, Kriger and Kroes (1972) found that Chinese-American mothers were significantly more restrictive or controlling, although not more hostile and rejecting, than Jewish and Protestant mothers. The controlling attitude noted by Kriger and Kroes (1972) might be related to the Chinese-American mother's belief that formal instruction of her children is integral to the maternal role (Steward & Steward, 1973). This more didactic approach was evidenced in the relatively more statements and fewer questions made by Chinese-American mothers, compared with Anglo-American mothers, while teaching their 3-year-old sons a sorting and motor skill game (Steward & Steward, 1973). It should be noted that this formal, didactic approach was combined with contingent positive feedback. The latter is consistent with positive responsiveness, permissiveness, and indulgence toward the young child (Suzuki, 1980).

Guided by an implicit notion of developmental readiness (Bunzel, 1950), the Chinese divide childhood into two periods. Prior to school age, children are indulged and treated gently by both parents. Upon reaching school age, they are no longer indulged. They are expected to assume duties and responsibilities in the household, subjected to stricter discipline, and taught in various ways that their actions will reflect not only on themselves but on the entire family, so that they must behave well (Suzuki, 1980). It has been suggested that the earlier indulgence and gentle treatment instills feelings of security and confidence in the child which counteracts or reduces the frustrations imposed by the later more rigid discipline (Sollenberger, 1968). Also, the mother's earlier permissiveness may enable her, when the child is older, to control the latter's behavior effectively through appeals to his or her sense of obligation, shame, and guilt, in combination with limited amounts of punishment (Suzuki, 1980).

How compliant are Chinese offspring? There is actually very limited scientific evidence bearing on this issue. Steward and Steward (1973) found that Chinese-American (and Mexican-American) children exhibited a higher proportion of accepting responses than did Anglo-American children while being taught a game by their mothers. They interpreted this finding as an indication that deference to elders, culturally required of the Chinese-American child, generalized to the learning setting. The only other source of empirical support for the hypothesized compliance of Chinese Americans is a study by Sue and Sue (1971). This revealed that Chinese-American college students, compared with their Anglo-American peers, are less autonomous, less independent from parental controls and authority figures, more obedient, conservative, conforming, inhibited, socially introverted, and more likely to withdraw from social contacts.

The findings above concerning college students raise questions about the possible effects of socialization for compliance on the self-concept and anxiety levels of American children and youth. The available data on these topics are reassuring. In the study by Ou and McAdoo (1980), Chinese-American children in two age groups attained relatively high scores on three self-concept measures: Piers-Harris Children's Self-Concept Scale, Engle Self-Concept Test, and Porter's Self-Portrait Drawing. Also, their mean scores on the State-Trait Anxiety Inventory for Children (Spielberger, 1973) ranked below the fortieth percentile. The generalizability of these findings may be limited, though, by the fact that these children came from intact middle- and upper-class professional families.

Concern that the strong emphasis on filial piety and strict obedience to parents in the Chinese-American family could lead to value conflicts between Chinese-born parents and their American-born children has been expressed by Huang (1977). Again, there is a paucity of empirical data bearing on this topic.

Obligation and responsibility to the clan.—Even as the Chinese-American mother caters to the needs of her child, she is also engaged in the socialization task of imbuing her child with a sense of obligation, which she continues to maintain as the child grows older (Suzuki, 1980). Precisely how she does this is not clear. One may infer from the writings of social scientists that it is accomplished through precept and example, with occasional appeals to the child's feelings of attachment and group identification. Commitment to a reciprocal system of obligations and responsibilities is an important developmental outcome that deserves more attention from investigators of socialization patterns. What are the steps in its emergence? What parental practices are related to its acquisition and maintenance? Empirically derived answers to these questions are needed.

Subordinate Goals and Techniques

Thus far in this review of research there has been no reference to the socialization of affection, aggression, assertion, and achievement. This omission was deliberate. In our view, these constructs are more appropriately considered as subordinate rather than superordinate goals. We contend here that restrained affection, nonaggression, nonassertion, and achievement are valued by Chinese (and Japanese) families not so much for their own sake as for their respective contributions toward the attainment of such societal goals as group solidarity and the system of mutual obligations that insures group prosperity. Restraint in the overt expression of affection, aggression and assertion is emphasized. We hypothesized that such restraint is necessary to maintain group organization and cohesion. Group stability is maintained through careful attention to an elaborate organizational structure based on rank and status. The open display of affection, particularly between members who differ in rank and status, might cause a disruption of ordered relationships. Similarly, in order to preserve harmony within the group, it is essential to inhibit direct aggression. Outspokenness and conspicuous behavior are likewise discouraged because they make an individual stand out, a violation of the norm that the whole rather than the part is important.

As for achievement, it is valued because it will bring honor to the clan, and when, as sometimes happens, it is accompanied by wealth, the benefits are shared. These perspectives on affection, aggression, assertion, and achievement are said to have been derived from Confucianism. One can only speculate how Confucius himself might have been influenced by the social context in which he lived and formulated his philosophy.

Chinese-American and Japanese-American families are stereotyped as socializing their children to show restraint in affection, aggression, or assertion, and to be hardworking and achievement oriented. But empirical studies of the relevant socialization techniques are rare and are available only for aggression and achievement orientation. Sollenberger's (1968) sample of Chinese Americans differed significantly from Sears et al.'s (1957) sample in each of three categories for degree of permissiveness concerning aggression among siblings. In contrast to Anglo-American mothers, significantly more of the Chinese Americans said that they were not at all permissive or that they were only moderately permissive. Furthermore, none said that they were entirely permissive. Significant group differences also emerged in regard to the mother's propensity to demand that a child be aggressive in appropriate situations. Compared with the Anglo-American sample, the Chinese-American mothers were significantly more likely to say that they made no demands whatsoever on the child to be aggressive in appropriate situations (74%), that they make moderate demands (10%), or that they made slight demands (7%) for appropriate aggressive behavior. Finally, when asked to what extent they have pressured their child to fight back, 74% said that they would never do it under any circumstances; others said that they might sometimes offer slight (18%) or moderate (8%) encouragement. None said that they would ever strongly urge the child to defend himself or punish the child if he should come home for help.

Thus, from an early age, the Chinese child is given no encouragement to engage in aggressive behavior. Furthermore, prosocial behaviors such as sharing, cooperation, and peaceful resolution of conflict are presented to him via models. An early study (Columbia Research in Contemporary Cultures, 1950, cited in Sollenberger, 1968) suggests that siblings play a role in this particular socialization process. According to some participants in this study, older children are encouraged to set an example for their siblings in gentleness, manners, and willingness to acquiesce. They are constantly reminded to *jang* their younger siblings, that is, to give up pleasure or comfort in favor of someone else, to give in during a quarrel, and to render a polite refusal in favor of someone else.

Data concerning the socialization of achievement are available from the study by Young (1972) that was cited earlier. Chinese immigrants and Chinese-American children living in Hawaii did not differ significantly on measures of achievement, achievement motivation, and achievement orientation. This finding suggests that the authoritarian and restrictive practices of Chinese immigrants do not necessarily lead to lower need achievement and actual underachievement, a concern raised by Kriger and Kroes (1972), perhaps, because achievement is highly valued. However, whereas the Westerner might value achievement as a form of self-actualization, Chinese Americans prize it because it enhances the status of the clan and helps to assure its well-being and survival.

The results of two studies support the hypothesized value of achievement in contemporary Chinese-American families. Young's (1972) study showed that although the two groups of Chinese mothers expected their boys to achieve in social situations (e.g., interactions with their peers) at a later age, in areas of academic achievement and caretaking, they expected their sons to achieve at an earlier age than did Anglo-American mothers (a comparison based on previous data). Similarly, Sollenberger (1968) reported that significantly more Chinese-American mothers (41%) than their Anglo-American counterparts (11%) expressed a belief that it was very important for the child to do well in school. About 70% of them, in contrast to only 30% of the Anglo-American mothers, expected their children to go to college. However, they were less optimistic about their offspring's graduation; only 16% of them expected the child to finish college whereas 37% of the comparison group did, a difference that was statistically significant.

Clearly, the socialization aims of Asian Americans include the development of self-control in matters of emotional expression, aggression, and self-assertion while fostering achievement. What we need are more data on the specific techniques used. It has been hypothesized (Huang, 1976; Kitano & Kikumura, 1976; Suzuki, 1980) that a variety of techniques ranging from praise or recognition, indirect techniques such as deprivation of special privileges or withdrawal from the family's social activities, and even physical punishment are used, but the effects of each of these and conditions under which it is employed still must be studied scientifically.

SUMMARY

Given the state of research in this area, and the need to achieve some degree of coherence, we limited this review to a discussion of the socialization goals and patterns of Afro-American and Asian-American families.

The major socialization goal of Afro-American families is bicultural adaptation. The postulated socialization pattern of goal persistence–cue perception interpersonal pattern has been identified as one of the parenting techniques used to fulfill a prescribed socialization goal. This pattern facilitates bicultural adaptation because it teaches techniques for assessing the culture and using environmental cues to make adaptive responses, and at the same time fosters a consistent sense of self. Findings from studies of mother-infant interaction patterns of urban, low-SES Afro-American dyads were insightful on issues pertaining to the socialization process. Age of mother and sex and birth status of infants were found to have a differential effect on mother-infant interaction patterns. A generalized motoric precocity among Afro-American infants has been documented. This finding and the lack of difference between Afro-American infants and standardization sample on infant tests suggest areas for future research activity.

The major socialization goals of Japanese-American families are collectivity and group identification, dependence upon the *ie*, filial piety and obedience, and responsibility and obligation to the *ie*. Although the major socialization goals of these families have been postulated, proposed parenting techniques to foster the goals have rarely been empirically examined. It has been proposed that the concepts of "face" or "shame," high levels of vocalization and cuddling, age-level parental expectations, and social interactional rules are techniques used by Japanese-American families to achieve their socialization goals.

The socialization goals of Chinese-American families are very similar to those of Japanese-American families. The development of group identification in the child is important to the goals of both groups. Empirical investigations regarding ethnic awareness, identification and preference of Chinese-American children are inconclusive. Nurturance and strict discipline used in sequence, positive responsiveness, permissiveness, and appeals to obligation to the clan are suggested parenting techniques of Chinese-American parents.

Clearly, more empirical investigations into the socialization goals and techniques of all ethnic families of color are needed. Especially desirable would be empirical investigation of truly representative samples of ethnic families. The majority of research on Afro-Americans has been conducted with urban, northern, low-SES families, which has lead to distorted perceptions of this ethnic group in the social science literature. It is important that the research methodology improve and consideration be given to multiple and interactive sources in the family and the larger system. Descriptive studies should be supplemented with correlational and experimental investigation.

Conclusions

Personalities of individuals and family systems are shaped by the characteristics of the social ecologies in which they live. Ethnic family membership affects the lives of parents and children. Social and behavioral scientists know very little about these families because of conceptual and methodological shortcomings in the accumulated body of literature and because they lack a well defined conceptual framework that would generate empirical investigations. Although there are a limited number of experimental studies of ethnic families of color, descriptive and sociological writings have provided most of the insights. There is great diversity within and between ethnic family groups, though they share a limited number of common features. Finally, the content of socialization within ethnic families differs from the socialization message commonly described in social science literature.

Outworn conceptualizations have limited the scientific inquiry into the dynamics of family life among ethnic families of color. Rather than increase our knowledge of family adaptability and flexibility, comparative and assimilation frameworks have often fostered harmful labels and stymied more fruitful inquiries. The social problem perspective on ethnic families of color has dulled appreciation for the richness of cultural pluralism. Indeed, the methodological flaws in the accumulated body of knowledge suggest the need to reexamine many assumptions about ethnic families of color.

The latest census data point up the need for social and behavioral scientists to increase their knowledge of ethnic families. Ethnic groups of color in 1983 constituted 20% of the U.S. population, and the percentage is expected to increase in the future. Studies of ethnic groups can increase our understanding of human behavior generally, but even more important, failure to make such studies will leave us, as scientists, in the position of knowing very little about a large segment of the American people.

Descriptive and sociological writings suggest a rich diversity within and between ethnic groups. In reviewing studies of any one or more ethnic families, one becomes keenly aware of variations in life-styles, values, family structures, religious practices, and beliefs. One must be cautious in representing any particular group, because there will be as much diversity found within as between groups. Yet there are elements that ethnic groups may share to varying degrees. Some of these have been found to be (*a*) frequent interactions and involvement with members of family support networks, (*b*) extended family help exchange patterns that may include friends who become "fictive" relatives, (*c*) economic vulnerability due to exclusion from participation in the economic systems of the broader community, and (*d*) religious institutions with strong influence upon family life and beliefs.

These common elements are seen to influence the manner in which ethnic families and children adapt to the culture in which they live. Importantly, the values of countries of origins and racism in America have affected the socialization goals of ethnic families. The Afro-American family socialization goal of bicultural adaption is an accommodation to the realities of American social systems that continue to exclude free participation by persons of Afro-American heritage. Similarly, Japanese-American socialization techniques are a reflection of the experiences of these families in America, including internment during World War II. Yet their major socialization goals arise out of traditional Japanese values, which reflect Confucian concepts of collectivity, order and hierarchy, and obligation. Confucian concepts have shaped also the socialization goals of Chinese-American families.

The review has repeatedly referred to instances where more scientific studies are needed to clarify findings and illuminate issues. Regrettably, there has been a limited number of rigorous scientific investigations of ethnics in family and developmental literature. Foremost, in our view, is the need for a more careful assessment of the changing roles of family members and how these changes affect relationships within the family and the functions served by the contemporary ethnic family. We need baseline data on a national level, and these might be achieved through a collaborative network of research projects, each dealing with a particular Afro-American, Asian, or Hispanic group. Second, empirically derived information about social values and socialization goals of the different groups is needed. For each of the major goals identified, and perhaps for their respective subgoals, theoretically based, methodologically rigorous studies delineating the sequence of goal attainment and the child-rearing practices employed could be conducted. Third, more scientific information is required about the relationship of specific child-rearing practices to particular developmental outcomes. And fourth, at a conceptual level, research on ethnic families needs to be more appropriately linked to contemporary family and developmental theories.

It is vital that ethnic families should be studied from the perspective of their individual cultures. Social and behavioral scientists should be careful not to perpetuate myths and stereotypes regarding ethnic families of color. Finally, research activities in the area of ethnic families and children should be emphasized as a means of increasing our knowledge regarding the universality and adaptiveness of human beings.

References

Allen, W. R. The search for applicable theories in black family life. *Journal of Marriage and the Family*, 1978, **40**, 117–129.

Alston, L. *A comparison of maternal discipline response by type and intensity.* Paper presented at the biennial meeting of the Society for Research in Child Development, San Francisco, March 1979.

Alvirez, D., & Bean, F. O. The Mexican American family. In C. H. Mindel & R. W. Habenstein (Eds.), *Ethnic families in America*. New York: Elsevier, 1976.

Bacca-Zinn, M. Employment and education of Mexican American women: The interplay of modernity and ethnicity in eight families. *Harvard Educational Review*, February 1980, 47–62.

Badill-Ghali, J. Culture sensitivity and the Puerto Rican client. *Social Casework*, 1977, **55**, 100–110.

Bakeman R., & Brown, J. V. Early interaction: Consequences for social and mental development at three years. *Child Development*, 1980, **51**, 437–447.

Baratz, S., & Baratz, J. Early childhood intervention: A social science-based institutional racism. *Harvard Educational Review*, 1970, **1**, 29–36.

Barnes, E. J. The black community as the source of positive self-concept for black children: A theoretical perspective. In R. Jones (Ed.), *Black psychology*. New York: Harper & Row, 1980.

Bartz, K., & Levine, E. Childrearing by black parents: A description and comparison to Anglo and Chicano parents. *Journal of Marriage and the Family*, 1978, **40**, 709–719.

Bayley, N. Comparisons of mental and motor test scores for ages 1–15 months by sex, birth order, race, geographical location, and education of parents. *Child Development*, 1965, **36**, 379–411.

Bell, R. A reinterpretation of the direction of effects in studies of socialization. *Psychological Review*, 1968, **75**, 81–95.

Bereiter, C., & Engelmann, S. *Teaching disadvantaged children in the preschool*. Englewood Cliffs, N.J.: Prentice-Hall, 1966.

Billingsley, A. *Black families in white America*. Englewood Cliffs, N.J.: Prentice-Hall, 1968.

Billingsley, A. The treatment of Negro families in American scholarship. In R. Staples (Ed.), *The black family*. Belmont, Calif.: Wadsworth, 1971.

Bloom, B. *Stability and change in human characteristics*. New York: Wiley, 1964.

Bradley, R. H., Caldwell, B. M., & Elardo, R. Home environment and cognitive development in the first 2 years: A cross-lagged panel analysis. *Developmental Psychology*, 1979, **15**, 246–250.

Brand, E., Ruiz, R., & Padillo, A. Ethnic identification and preferences: A review. *Psychological Bulletin*, 1974, **81**, 860–890.

Brown, J. V., Bakeman, R., Snyder, P. A., Fredrickson, W. T., Morgan, S. T., & Helper, R. Interactions of black inner-city mothers with their newborn infants. *Child Development*, 1975, **46**, 677–686.

Bunzel, R. *Explorations in Chinese culture*. Unpublished manuscript, New York, 1950.

Buriel, R. The relation of Anglo- and Mexican-American children's locus of control beliefs to parents' and teachers' socialization practices. *Child Development*, 1981, **52**, 104–113.

Carper, L. The Negro family and the Moynihan report. In R. Staples (Ed.), *The black family*. Belmont, Calif.: Wadsworth, 1971.

Caudill, W. Japanese-American personality and acculturation. *Genetic Psychology Monographs*, 1952, **45**, 3–102.

Caudill, W., & Frost, L. A comparison of maternal care and infant behavior in Japanese-American, American, and Japanese families. In W. P. Lebra (Ed.), *Youth, socialization, and mental health*. Honolulu: University Press of Hawaii, 1974.

Coates, B. White adult behavior toward black and white children. *Child Development*, 1972, **43**, 143–154.

Connor, J. W. Acculturation and family continuities in three generations of Japanese Americans. *Journal of Marriage and the Family*, 1974, **36**, 159–165.

Deloria, V. Native Americans: The American Indian today. *Annals of the American Academy of Political and Social Sciences*, 1981, **454**, 139–149.

DeVos, G. *Acculturation and personality structure: A Rorschach study of Japanese Americans*. Unpublished doctoral dissertation, University of Chicago, 1955.

Deutsch, M. Facilitating development in the pre-school child: Social and psychological perspectives. *Merrill-Palmer Quarterly*, 1964, **10**, 249–264.

Eggan, R. *The American Indian: Perspectives for the study of social change*. Chicago: Aldine, 1966.

Farnham-Diggory, S. Cognitive synthesis in Negro and white children. *Monographs of the Society for Research in Child Development*, 1970, **35**(2, Serial No. 135).

Field, T. M., Widmayer, S. M., Stringer, S., & Ignatoff, E. Teenage, lower-class, black mothers and their preterm infants: An intervention and developmental follow-up. *Child Development*, 1980, **51**, 426–436.

Fox, D., & Jordan, V. Racial preference and identification of black, American, Chinese, and white children. *Genetic Psychology Monographs*, 1973, **88**, 229–286.

Fujitomi, I., & Wong, D. The new Asian-American woman. In S. Sue & N. H. Wagner (Eds.), *Asian-Americans: Psychological perspectives* (Vol. 1). Palo Alto, Calif.: Science & Behavior Books, 1973.

Garcia-Preto, N. Puerto Rican families. In M. McGoldrick, J. Pearce, & J. Giordana (Eds.), *Ethnicity and family therapy*. New York: Guilford, 1982.

Gary, L. E. A mental health research agenda for the black community. *Journal of Afro-American Issues*, 1976, **4**(1), 50–60.

Gillespie, F., Greeley, A., Houts, M., & Sullivan, L. Public policy, ethnic codes and hispanic vital statistics. *La Red/The Net*, 1983, **70**, 9–13.

Ginsburg, H. P., & Russell, R. L. Social class and racial influences on early mathematical thinking. *Monographs of the Society for Research in Child Development*, 1981, **46**(6, Serial No. 193).

Glazer, N. Beyond the melting pot twenty years after. *Journal of American Ethnic History*, 1981, **1**, 43–55.

Glazer, N., & Moynihan, D. *Beyond the melting pot*. Cambridge, Mass.: MIT Press, 1970.

Glenn, E. N. Split household, small producer and dual wage earner: An analysis of Chinese-American family strategies. *Journal of Marriage and the Family*, 1983, **45**, 35–46.

Gordon, M. *Assimilation in American life*. New York: Oxford University Press, 1964.

Gray, S. W., & Wandersman, L. P. The methodology of home-based intervention studies: Problems and promising strategies. *Child Development*, 1980, **51**, 993–1009.

Guthrie, R. V. The psychology of black Americans: An historical perspective. In R. L. Jones (Ed.), *Black psychology*. New York: Harper & Row, 1980.

Guttentag, M., & Secord, P. *Too many women? The sex ratio question*. Beverly Hills, Calif.: Sage, 1983.

Hare, B. K. Racial and socioeconomic variations in preadolescent area-specific and general self-esteem. *International Journal of Intercultural Relations*, 1977, **1**, 31–51.

Hareven, T. K. The history of the family as an interdisciplinary field. In T. K. Robb & R. Rothery (Eds.), *The family in history: Interdisciplinary essays*. New York: Harper & Row, 1971.

Hareven, T. K., & Modell, J. Family patterns. In S. Thernstrom (Ed.), *Harvard encyclopedia of American ethnic groups*. Cambridge, Mass.: Harvard University Press, Belknap Press, 1980, 345–354.

Harrison, A. Locus of control and problem-solving abilities in young black children: An exploratory analysis. In A. Boykin, A. Franklin, & J. Yates (Eds.), *Research directions of black psychologists*. New York: Russell Sage, 1979. (a)

Harrison, A. Relationship between cognitive style and selective attention in black children. In A. Boykin, A. Franklin, & J. Yates (Eds.), *Research directions of black psychologists*. New York: Russell Sage, 1979. (b)

Harrison, A. Attitude toward procreation among black adults. In H. McAdoo (Ed.), *Black families*. Beverly Hills, Calif.: Sage, 1981.

Horowitz, F., & Paden, L. The effectiveness of environmental intervention programs. In B. M. Caldwell & H. N. Ricciuti (Eds.), *Review of child development research* (Vol. 3). Chicago: University of Chicago Press, 1973.

Hawkes, G. R., & Taylor, M. Power structure in Mexican and Mexican American farm labor families. *Journal of Marriage and the Family*, 1975, **37**, 807–811.

Hess, R. S., & Shipman, V. C. Early experiences and the socialization of cognitive development in children. *Child Development*, 1965, **36**, 869–886.

Hetherington, E. M., Cox, M., & Cox, R. Family interactions and the social, emotional, and cognitive development of children following divorce. In V. C. Vaughn & T. B. Brazelton (Eds.), *The family: Setting priorities*. New York: Science & Medicine Publishers, 1979.

Hoffman, L. W. Effects of maternal employment on the child: A review of the research. *Developmental Psychology*, 1974, **10**, 204–228.

Hsu, F. L. K. *Under the ancestors' shadow*. New York: Columbia University Press, 1948.

Huang, L. J. The Chinese American family. In C. H. Mindel & R. W. Habenstein (Eds.), *Ethnic families in America*. New York: Elsevier, 1976.

Hunt, J. M. The psychological basis for using pre-school enrichment as an antidote for cultural deprivation. *Merrill-Palmer Quarterly*, 1964, **10**, 209–248.

Johnson, C. L. *The Japanese-American family and community in Honolulu: Generational continuities in ethnic affiliation*. Unpublished doctoral dissertation, Syracuse University, 1972.

Johnson, C. L. Indebtedness: An analysis of Japanese American kinship relations. *Journal of Marriage and the Family*, 1977, **39**, 351–363.

Keefe, S. E., Padilla, A. M., & Carlos, M. L. The Mexican-American extended family as an emotional support system. *Human Organization*, 1979, **38**, 144–152.

Kikumura, A., & Kitano, H. H. L. The Japanese American family. In R. Endo, S. Sue, & N. N. Wagner (Eds.), *Asian-Americans social and psychological perspectives* (Vol. 2). Palo Alto, Calif.: Science & Behavior Books, 1980.

Kim. E. Asian women in America. In *With silk wings: Asian American women at work*. San Francisco: Asian Women United of California, 1983.

King, W., & Seegmiller, D. Performance of 14-to-22-month-old black, first-born male infants on two tests of cognitive development. *Developmental Psychology*, 1973, **8**, 317–326.

Kitano, H. H. L. Differential child-rearing attitudes between first and second generation Japanese in the United States. *Journal of Social Psychology*, 1961, **53**, 13–19.

Kitano, H. H. L. Inter- and intra-generational differences in maternal attitudes toward child rearing. *Journal of Social Psychology*, 1964, **63**, 215–220.

Kitano, H. H. L. *Japanese Americans: The evolution of a subculture*. Englewood Cliffs, N.J.: Prentice-Hall, 1969.

Kitano, H. H. L. Asian-Americans: The Chinese, Japanese, Koreans, Filipinos, and Southeast Asians. *Annals of the American Academy of Political and Social Science*, 1981, **454**, 125–138.

Kitano, H. H. L., & Kikumura, A. The Japanese American family. In C. H. Mindel & R. W. Habenstein (Eds.), *Ethnic families in America*. New York: Elsevier, 1976.

Knobloch, H., & Pasamanick, B. Further observations on the behavioral development of Negro children. *Journal of Genetic Psychology*, 1953, **83**, 137–157.

Kriger, S. F., & Kroes, W. H. Child-rearing attitudes of Chinese, Jewish, and Protestant mothers. *Journal of Social Psychology*, 1972, **86**, 205–210.

Laosa, L. M. Cognitive styles and learning strategies research: Some of the areas in which psychology can contribute to personalized instruction in multi-cultural education. *Journal of Teacher Education*, 1977, **28**, 26–30.

Laosa, L. M. Maternal teaching strategies in Chicano families of varied educational and socioeconomic levels. *Child Development*, 1978, **49**, 1129–1135.

Lazar, I., & Darlington, R. Lasting effects of early education: A report from the consortium for longitudinal studies. *Monographs of the Society for Research in Child Development*, 1982, **47**(2–3, Serial No. 195).

Lefley, H. P. Social and familial correlates of self-esteem among American Indian children. *Child Development*, 1974, **45**, 829–833.

Liu, W. T. Asian American research: Views of a sociologist. In R. Endo, S. Sue, & N. N. Wagner (Eds.), *Asian-Americans: Social and psychological perspectives* (Vol. 2). Palo Alto, Calif.: Science & Behavior Books, 1980.

Lott, J. T. Institutional and social factors shaping the growth of Asian American families. In *Conference on Pacific and Asian American Families and HEW-related issues: Summary and recommendations*. Washington, D.C.: U.S. Government Printing Office, 1978.

Mathis, A. Contrasting approaches to the study of black families. *Journal of Marriage and the Family*, 1978, **40**, 667–676.

McAdoo, H. P. The development of self-concept and race attitudes of young black children over time. In W. E. Cross, Jr. (Ed.), *Third Conference on Empirical Research in Black Psychology*. Washington, D.C.: National Institute of Education, 1977.

McAdoo, H. P. Factors related to stability in upwardly mobile black families. *Journal of Marriage and the Family*, 1978, **40**, 761–776. (a)

McAdoo, H. P. Minority families. In J. Stevens & M. Mathews (Eds.), Mother/child, father/child: Relationships. Washington, D.C.: National Association for Education of Young Children, 1978. (b)

McAdoo, H. P. Demographic trends for people of color. *Social Work*, 1982, **27**, 15–23.

McAdoo, H. P., & Terborg-Penn, R. Historical trends and perspectives of Afro-American families. *Trends in History* (in press).

McAdoo, J. L. Involvement of fathers in the socialization of black children. In H. McAdoo (Ed.), *Black families*. Beverly Hills, Calif.: Sage, 1981.

Milliones, J. Relationships between perceived child temperament and maternal behaviors. *Child Development*, 1978, **49**, 1255–1257.

Mindel, C. H., & Habenstein, H. W. (Eds.), *Ethnic families in America*. New York: Elsevier, 1976.

Mirandé, A. The Chicano family: A reanalysis of conflicting views. *Journal of Marriage and the Family*, 1977, **11**, 747–756.

Montiel, M. The social science myth of the Mexican American Family. *El Grito: A Journal of Contemporary Mexican American Thought*, 1970, 3, 56–63.

Moore, C. L., & Retish, P. M. Effect of the examiner's race on black children's Wechsler preschool and primary scale of intelligence I.Q. *Developmental Psychology*, 1974, **10**, 672–676.

Moynihan, D. P. *The Negro family: The case for national action* (For U.S. Department of Labor, Office of Policy Planning and Research). Washington, D.C.: Government Printing Office, 1965.

Mueller, C. W., & Parcel, T. L. Measures of socioeconomic status: Alternatives and recommendations. *Child Development*, 1981, **52**, 13–30.

Murillo, N. The Mexican American family. In N. Wagner & M. Haug (Eds.), *Chicanos: Social and psychological perspectives*. St. Louis: Mosby, 1971.

Myers, H. F. Research on the Afro-American family: A critical review. In B. Bass, G. Wyatt, & G. Powell (Eds.), *The Afro-American family: Assessment, treatment and research issues*. New York: Grune & Stratton, 1982.

Nakane, C. *Japanese society*. Berkeley: University of California Press, 1970.

Nobles, W. African philosophy: Foundations for black psychology. In R. L. Jones (Ed.), *Black psychology*. New York: Harper & Row, 1980.

Nobles, W. African-America's family life: An instrument of culture. In H. McAdoo (Ed.), *Black families*. Beverly Hills, Calif.: Sage, 1981.

O'Reilly, J. P., Ebata, A. T., Tokuno, K. A., & Bryant, B. K. *Sex and ethnic differences in parental attitudes toward social competence for their children*. Unpublished manuscript, University of Hawaii, 1980.

Ou, Y., & McAdoo, H. *Ethnic identity and self-esteem in Chinese children*. Washington, D.C.: National Institute of Mental Health, December 1980.

Peng, S. *National Center for Educational Statistics Bulletin*. (NCES 82-2286). Washington, D.C.: U.S. Department of Education, July 1982.

Peters, M. F. Parenting in black families with young children: A historical perspective. In H. McAdoo (Ed.), *Black families*. Beverly Hills, Calif.: Sage, 1981.

Peters, M., & McAdoo, H. The present and future of alternative lifestyles in ethnic American cultures. In E. Macklin & R. Rubin (Eds.), *Contemporary families and alternative lifestyles*. Beverly Hills, Calif.: Sage, 1983.

Peterson, W. Concepts of ethnicity. In S. Thernstrom (Ed.), *Harvard encyclopedia of American ethnic groups*. Cambridge, Mass.: Harvard University Press, Belknap Press, 1980.

Price, J. A. North American Indian families. In C. H. Mindel & H. W. Haberstein (Eds.), *Ethnic families in America*. New York: Elsevier, 1976.

Roger, L. *Migrant in the city: The life of an action group.* New York: Basic, 1982.

Romano, O., & Arce, C. H. The anthropology and sociology of Mexican Americans: The distortion of Mexican American history. *El Grito,* 1968, **2**(Fall), 13–26.

Ryan, W. Savage discovery: The Moynihan report. In R. Staples (Ed.), *The black family.* Belmont, Calif.: Wadsworth, 1971.

Sample, W., & Smith, R. *Class differences and sex roles in American kinship and family structure.* Englewood Cliffs, N.J.: Prentice-Hall, 1973.

Sattler, J. M. Racial "experimenter effects" in experimentation, testing, interviewing, and psychotherapy. *Psychological Bulletin,* 1970, **73,** 137–160.

Sears, R. R., Maccoby, E. E., & Levin, H. *Patterns of child rearing.* Evanston, Ill.: Row, Peterson, 1957.

Slaughter, D. *A dimension of the family as educator: Mother as teacher.* Paper presented at the biennial meeting of the Society for Research in Child Development, San Francisco, 1979.

Slaughter, D. Early intervention and its effects on maternal and child development. *Monographs of the Society for Research in Child Development,* 1983, **48**(4, Serial No. 202).

Sollenberger, R. T. Chinese-American child rearing practices and juvenile delinquency. *Journal of Social Psychology,* 1968, **74,** 13–23.

Spencer, R., & Jennings, J. *The Native Americans.* New York: Harper & Row, 1965.

Spielberger, C. *STAIC preliminary manual.* Palo Alto, Calif.: Consulting Psychologists Press, 1973.

Spiro, M. E. The acculturation of American ethnic groups. *American Anthropologist,* 1955, **57,** 1240–1252.

Springer, D. Awareness of racial differences of preschool children in Hawaii. *Genetic Psychology Monographs,* 1950, **41,** 214–270.

Staples, R. The myth of the black matriarchy. In R. Staples (Ed.), *The black family.* Belmont, Calif.: Wadsworth, 1971. (a)

Staples, R. Towards a sociology of the black family: A theoretical and methodological assessment. *Journal of Marriage and the Family,* 1971, **33,** 119–138. (b)

Staples, R., & Mirandé, A. Racial and cultural variations among American families: A decennial review of the literature on minority families. *Journal of Marriage and the Family,* 1980, **42,** 157–173.

Steward, M., & Steward, D. The observation of Anglo-, Mexican-, and Chinese-American mothers teaching their children. *Child Development,* 1973, **44,** 329–337.

Sue, S. Psychology theory and implications for Asian Americans. In R. Endo, S. Sue, & N. N. Wagner (Eds.), *Asian-Americans: Social and psychological perspectives* (Vol. 2). Palo Alto, Calif.: Science & Behavior Books, 1980.

Sue, S., & Kitano, H. H. L. Asian American stereotypes. *Journal of Social Issues,* 1973, **29,** 83–98.

Sue, S., & Sue, D. W. Chinese-American personality and mental health. *Amerasia-Journal,* 1971, **1,** 36–49.

Sung, B. L. *Transplanted Chinese children* (Report to the Administration for Children, Youth, and Family, U.S. Department of Health, Education, and Welfare). New York: City University of New York, Department of Asian Studies, 1979.

Suzuki, H. H. The Asian-American family. In M. D. Fantine & R. Cardenas (Eds.), *Parenting in a multicultural society.* New York: Longman, 1980.

Thomas, A., Chess, S., & Birch, H. G. The origin of personality. *Scientific American,* 1970, **223,** 102–109.

Trail of broken treaties: B.I.A., I'm not your Indian anymore. *Akwesasne Notes,* 1974, **6,** 1–93.

Trimble, J. E. The sojourner in the American Indian community: Methodological issues and concerns. *Journals of Social Issues*, 1977, **33**, 159–174.

Trimble, J. E., Goddard, A., & Dinges, N. *Review of the literature on educational needs and problems of American Indians: 1971 to 1976.* Seattle: Battell Human Affairs Research Centers, 1977.

U.S. Department of Labor, Women's Bureau. *Employment goals of the world plan of action: Developments and issues in the United States.* Washington, D.C.: Government Printing Office, July 1980.

Uzoka, A. F. The myth of the nuclear family. *American Psychologist*, 1979, **34**, 1095–1106.

Valentine, C. Defiiciency, difference and bicultural model of Afro-American Behavior. *Harvard Educational Review*, 1971, **41**, 135–157.

Weikart, D. P., Kamii, C. K., & Radin, N. *Perry preschool project: Program report.* Ypsilanti, Mich.: Ypsilanti Public Schools, 1966.

White, B., & Watts, J. *Experience and environment.* Englewood Cliffs, N.J.: Prentice-Hall, 1973.

Williams, J., & Scott, R. Growth and development of Negro infants: 4. Motor development and its relationship to child rearing practices in two groups of Negro infants. *Child Development*, 1953, **24**, 103–121.

Yanagisako, S. J. Women-centered kin networks in urban bilateral kinship. *American Ethnologist*, 1977, **4**, 207–226.

Yando, R., Seitz, V., & Zigler, E. *Intellectual and personality characteristics of children: Social-class and ethnic-group differences.* Hillsdale, N.J.: Erlbaum, 1979.

Yarrow, M. R., Campbell, J. D., & Burton, R. V. *Child rearing.* San Francisco: Jossey-Bass, 1968.

Ybarra, L. When wives work: The impact on the Chicano family. *Journal of Marriage and the Family*, 1982, **44**, 169–178.

Young, N. F. Independence training from a cross-cultural perspective. *American Anthropologist*, 1972, **74**, 629–638.

Young, V. H. Family and childhood in a southern Negro community. *American Anthropologist*, 1970, **72**, 269–288.

Young, V. H. A black American socialization pattern. *American Ethnologist*, 1974, **1**, 405–413.

Zigler, E. F., Lamb, M. E., & Child, I. L. *Socialization and personality development.* New York: Oxford University Press, 1982.

10 Psychological and Developmental Perspectives on Expectant and New Parenthood

JOY D. OSOFSKY AND HOWARD J. OSOFSKY
Menninger Foundation

Most perspectives on expectant and new parenthood have focused on psychological upheavals or psychopathology rather than considering this time as one of developmental progression. However, this period can be conceptualized as a major developmental phase for the mother and father as individuals and as a couple. While the responsibilities of pregnancy and new parenthood may contribute to marital and family dysfunction, they may also lead to growth. As will be apparent in this review, most studies in this area have been designed within a clinical-descriptive tradition, frequently utilizing a psychodynamic approach, rather than within a research tradition with careful specification of variables and methods. While the pathological perspective has received more focus, the developmental approach is compelling. Recent work in this area reflects a shift from the predominance of clinically oriented retrospective studies to both a prospective approach and one that explores the concurrent interaction of variables that exert mutual influences in complex ways. There has been a corresponding shift from focus on the individual, usually the mother, to the interactive process with more emphasis on the father and infant. The parenting couple and the reciprocal influences within the family have been other important areas receiving recent attention.

Pregnancy and new parenthood have at times been described as a "crisis," especially for the mother, but also for the father and the couple in their relationship. Perhaps the concept is of value in emphasizing the normative struggles and upheavals that couples experience in adapting to parenthood, especially with a first pregnancy. It has also been used historically within a psychodynamic framework in attempting to understand and explain severe stress due to medical, intrapsychic, family, or socioeconomic difficulties and the more unfavorble outcomes that characterize a limited number of individuals' and couples' responses to impending and new parenthood. However, for most couples, with some support a favorable adjustment can be achieved. Further, although important, conceptualizing pregnancy and new parenthood as a crisis does not appear to convey adequately the developmental adjustments and potential growth that may characterize this period.

While the developmental model will require more study and understanding, this approach appears to reflect the recent direction of research in this area. Many of the older data oriented to clinical practice and problem situations have been compounded by methodological difficulties. At the same time, the material frequently has provided rich and relevant information. Although there are discrepancies in design and inconsistencies in theoretical orientation, the research findings coming out of these studies are useful in providing information and perspectives that may be of help in future formulations and planning. In this review, we will focus first on expectant motherhood, then expectant fatherhood, followed by the experiences of the couple; finally, we will consider the interactive relationship with the infant, reflecting some of the perhaps more promising current developments in this area.

EXPECTANT MOTHERHOOD

A number of investigators have studied patterns of psychological adjustment during pregnancy. In general, strategies have incorporated the use of psychological tests, repeat interviews during and following pregnancy, and evaluations by clinic staff. Unfortunately, the samples studied, the independent variables utilized, and the research strategies designed have varied widely with little attempt at replication or validation of findings—a problem noted repeatedly in this area. However, it would seem worthwhile to note a small number of particularly pertinent studies.

Entwisle and Doering (1981) have carried out one of the most extensive recent investigations. With an anthropological perspective they attempted to describe and chronicle the family life cycle of 120 women having a first child and 60 of their husbands from the sixth month of pregnancy to 6 months after birth. The data, based on 10–12 hours of interviews with these couples, provide information about family formation, pregnancy and birth, prior socialization, self-concepts, attitudes toward each other, sex-role attitutdes, and sexual behavior. These investigators also attempted to determine causal linkages between circumstances and events during pregnancy and their effects on later psychological and social functioning. They found that prior preparation helps couples to cope better with pregnancy, labor, and delivery and to have more realistic expectations about the process of child rearing. Social support from family, friends, and community also seems to help the couples adjust more easily to pregnancy, labor and delivery, and the new baby. Their approach to gaining an understanding of issues involved in family formation, while useful, is primarily descriptive.

Based on our studies utilizing a case-study approach (Osofsky & Osofsky, 1980), we have found that women undergo considerable stresses and upheavals during the course of pregnancy and following the birth of the baby, especially a first child. Many women experience fears and concerns about themselves and the unborn baby. They commonly worry whether the baby will be normal. They also worry about the physical changes in their bodies, how they will be able to give birth, and how this process will change them. Women are also aware of alterations in their relationships with their husbands, particularly the changes that are anticipated following the birth of the baby. They are concerned about changes in their work and home patterns and how their adult relationships will be affected after they become parents. We have found that being able to share these concerns with their husbands and other interested persons is particularly helpful to women in facilitating their adjustment and promoting growth.

Shereshefsky and Yarrow (1973) summarized the findings of their study involving 62 predominantly middle-class families during pregnancy and early parenthood. The women underwent psychological testing and repeat psychiatric interviews beginning at 3–4 months of pregnancy and continuing until 6 months following delivery. Home visits and interviews with the husbands were carried out, but primary emphasis was on data obtained from the wife—a limitation of the study. Further, because of the global nature of the design, specific conclusions were difficult to obtain. In general, personality factors were related to maternal adaptation. In particular, women's perceptions of their mothers were related to their reactions to and ability to cope with their own pregnancies. Fewer relationships were noted between the couple's patterns of mutual support and pregnancy outcome. However, serious marital disharmony was found in 21% of the families initially, and considerable individual disruptions, including occasional episodes of infidelity during the pregnancy, were noted. Families burdened with more stresses initially and those already involved in serious marital disharmony at the time of pregnancy tended to experience more stress than others in the sample. Adaptive problems could be identified early in the pregnancy, and the degree of maternal acceptance was significantly related to several aspects of the infant's adaptation.

Leifer (1977) studied 19 white, middle-class primigravidas using extensive interviews and personality measures. Within this framework she found that the degree of personality stability achieved by early pregnancy was predictive of psychological growth experienced throughout pregnancy and early parenthood. For most women, the early phases of parenthood were also experienced as a period of crisis, frequently exceeding that of pregnancy. While most women experienced pregnancy and early parenthood as a period of psychological stress, only part of the sample concomitantly experienced a growing sense of adulthood and personality integration suggestive of a new developmental stage; this finding is consistent with that of Rossi (1968), suggesting that the emotional upheaval accompanying pregnancy should not necessarily be viewed as a step toward maturation. At the same time, and consistent with Bibring, Dwyer, Huntington, and Valenstein (1961), Leifer found that the development of maternal feelings throughout pregnancy resulting in attachment to the fetus is usually indicative of future ability to adequately nurture the infant. It should be emphasized that the findings coming out of this study are based on interviews from which the assumptions and conclusions about anticipated behaviors are drawn.

Weigert, Wenner, Cohen, Fearing, Kvarnes, and Ohaneson (1968) have studied 52 predominantly middle-class, well-educated, white, Protestant women, usually from the beginning of the second trimester of pregnancy until 3 months postpartum. The women all underwent psychological testing and had repeat psychiatric and social work interviews. In addition, their husbands were interviewed once during the pregnancy and once following the delivery. On the basis of the interview data, they reported that during the pregnancy 28 of the subjects developed a significant increase in emotional difficulties that were not specifically elaborated. All women experienced an increase in their dependency needs. Two principal areas of marital conflict emerged related to patterns of dominance-submission and methods of meeting each other's needs. Especially important were struggles revolving around the woman's sense of femininity and her relationship with her mother. Women who were unable to use their mothers as models more frequently experienced emotionally difficult pregnancies.

While recognizing the limitations of those and other similar studies, including methodological problems based on subjective methods of data collection and nonreplication of findings (Coleman, 1969; Davids & Rosengren, 1962; Hollender & McGehee, 1974), the pattern that seems to emerge suggests that the woman's adjustment to pregnancy depends to a considerable extent on her circumstances and her earlier relationship with her own mother, the effects of the pregnancy on her life and work patterns and her ability to adjust to them, and the support that is available to her from her husband, family, and the community.

RELATIONSHIPS BETWEEN PSYCHOLOGICAL ADJUSTMENT
AND PREGNANCY OUTCOME

In considering the available data concerning the relationships between psychological adjustment and pregnancy outcome, a useful perspective is provided by McDonald's (1968) review article. In considering
pertinent articles that appeared during the prior 15 years, he noted that
while the data supported the notion of a positive relationship between
psychological and physiological functioning during pregnancy, no causal
relationships between emotional factors and obstetric complications had
been established. Consistent with his conclusions, there continues to be a
need for carefully designed methodological studies and a better integration
among theoretical, methodological, clinical, and research issues.

Some investigators have suggested that there is a need to study
women before they become pregnant to determine the psychological
impact of prior and subsequent events on the physical course of pregnancy.
For example, Heinstein (1967), in studying the relationship between expressed attitudes and feelings of pregnant women and physical complications of pregnancy in 156 low-income women, found that during pregnancy
somatic complaints increased significantly when compared via recall with
similar somatic problems that occurred before the women were pregnant.
The data suggested that the stress of pregnancy per se was accompanied by
few physical complaints and fears. Rather, a cluster of attitudes and feelings indicative of general moodiness, depression, and overdependency was
significantly associated with physical complaints.

Chertok (1969) studied 200 married, primiparous French women with
semistructured interviews and psychological tests administered intermittently during the course of pregnancy and while the women were in the
hospital giving birth. Special emphasis was placed on negative experiences
and difficulties encountered during development and pregnancy such as
traumatic early experience and illness, unfavorable environmental circumstances, social and medical, or difficulties during pregnancy. Women
with many negative experiences based on the interview and psychological
data appeared particularly likely to have difficulties during labor and
delivery, when they were immature, dependent, and quite anxious. Those
with fewer negative experiences in the presence of these traits had fewer
difficulties with labor and delivery.

Several investigators (Gorsuch & Key, 1974; Jones, 1978; Lubin,
Gardener, & Roth, 1975) studied the effects of personality and anxiety
states on the pregnancy and labor and delivery experience. Although there
are ambiguities and methodological inconsistencies, there appears to be

some consistency in the findings across the studies, with a relationship between anxiety and life stresses and symptoms experienced during pregnancy and subsequent complications during labor and delivery.

In several studies, the effectiveness of classroom instruction concerning the social and psychological changes associated with new motherhood has been investigated as a way to reduce postpartum emotional difficulties, including anxiety and conflict. Gordon and Gordon (1960) randomly selected an experimental group from expectant parents' classes to participate in two systematic 40-min instruction periods on the social and psychological adjustments to parenthood. The control group was selected from the same parents' classes and matched to the experimental group by background history questionnaires. Both groups were administered questionnaires before and after an additional instruction period for the experimental group on social and psychological adjustment to a baby. The emotional reactions of both groups were judged by their obstetricians at 6 weeks and 6 months on a four-point scale, the dimensions or reliability of which were not specified. Based on the follow-up questionnaires and obstetricians ratings, women in the psychologically instructed classes coped more easily with labor and delivery and reported fewer problems handling their infants than did the controls.

According to Entwisle and Doering (1981), a major source of stress comes from the parents' inexperience in caring for young infants, as most couples are overly optimistic about infant care prior to childbirth. The better prepared mothers overall who then sought out preparatory classes tended to cope better with childbirth and the subsequent adjustment to the child. Our studies (Osofsky & Osofsky, 1980) have indicated the importance of a realistic understanding of the adjustments to the new baby that may be necessary in order that the mother not be too surprised or overwhelmed by the necessary tasks and changes in her life.

From a research standpoint, it is crucial to develop reliable and valid outcome measures that will be meaningful and applicable across studies. As has been shown in the studies that have been reviewed, such measures are not yet available. As was evident in the Chertok (1969), Entwisle and Doering (1981), and Osofsky and Osofsky (1980) studies, conflict with the motherhood role as well as personal insecurity related to past experience is important in determining the development and duration of emotional disorders of pregnancy and childbearing. Despite the methodological problems, Gordon and Gordon (1960) demonstrated that simple instructions directed toward reducing conflict appear to have significant and lasting beneficial effects on the social adjustment and mental and physical health of mother and child.

EXPECTANT FATHERHOOD

In comparison to the literature on expectant motherhood, considerably less work has been carried out on the psychological aspects of expectant fatherhood. Some authors have described from a psychoanalytic perspective the male's developmental progression toward fatherhood (Brunswick, 1940; Erikson, 1950; Jacobson, 1950; Kestenberg, 1975 [and as cited by Parens, 1975]; Ross, 1975, 1977, 1979). However, the clinical studies that are available concerning adjustment to expectant and new fatherhood have in general focused on emotional difficulties that men experience during their wives' pregnancies or new parenthood rather than on the process itself as a developmental phase. Since 1970 there has been some increase in the number of studies done, although they have dealt primarily with somewhat related areas such as the role of the father during labor and delivery and a reconsideration of the role of the father in child development (See Lamb, 1981; Parke, 1979). Fundamental developmental considerations of mechanisms of the coping process have continued to receive relatively little emphasis, and there has been a tendency to continue to minimize the adjustments that normal males make in response to pregnancy and new parenthood.

In addition to her interest in the pregnant woman, Benedek (1959, 1970) discussed the adaptational situation of fatherhood, which she conceptualized as a normal maturational and developmental process, influenced by early parent-child and sibling relationships. Just as the father can influence his wife's attitudes, his attitude toward the child may be influenced by his relationship with his wife, and the emotional course of pregnancy may stabilize or disrupt the marriage.

In a recent study, Herzog (1979) followed 103 men whose wives gave birth to an apparently premature infant at 25–39 weeks of gestation. He utilized retrospective analytically oriented interviews for up to 24 months following the delivery. While reporting marked individual differences in the men's experiences, he noted that 35 of the men were in touch with feelings and fantasies pertaining to the pregnancy. Herzog has found considerable shifts in the men's sexual fantasies, a reworking of feelings about their fathers, and in some a preoccupation with gastrointestinal symptoms. Especially after quickening he observed the appearance of aggressive fantasies, concerns about hurting the baby, and a sense of magic and mystery about the process of creation. Although the numbers of men reporting feelings may have been diminished because of the retrospective nature of the study, and the feelings described may have been influenced by the stress of the baby's being born prematurely, there are suggestions of common themes and an orderly reworking of earlier issues—at least for some of the men.

In our interviews of 20 well-educated, middle-class couples carried out during the wife's pregnancy (Osofsky & Osofsky, 1980), we have found that men undergo stresses, upheavals, and adjustments during their wives' pregnancies and following the birth of the baby. In addition to their sense of excitement and pride, they worry about the current and anticipated changes in their lives and in their relationships with their wives. Sometimes feelings of neediness and rivalry toward the coming baby may emerge. Most men have described a greater sense of responsibility, which at times feels overwhelming. Some men also experience feelings of envy of their wives' ability to reproduce. They may feel like bystanders, unable to experience the changes directly. Some embark on creative projects of their own. Some withdraw from their wives and the coming baby. If the conflictual feelings are not discussed or dealt with, at least in some cases, marital disruption and disharmony may result. In men without overt psychiatric symptoms preceding the pregnancy, considerable lability and unsettled feelings have emerged during the pregnancy and following the birth of the baby. Consistent with Erikson's (1950, 1973) descriptions of the disequilibrium that can herald the beginning of a new growth phase, these normal men experience conflicts during their wives' pregnancies that tend to be more easily resolved than those of the more disturbed men. Life circumstances, including degree of economic stability, religious background and patterns, family and community supports, and the strength of the marital relationship, play important roles in the individuals' ability to grow with the experience.

Several studies have investigated the impact of childbirth education and increased training for parenthood on fathers' adjustment. In a study of 46 men from heterogeneous backgrounds, some of whom received Lamaze training and some of whom did not (the numbers in each group were not specified), Wente and Crockenberg (1976), utilizing retrospective interviews and questionnaires, found that while the training did not result in an easier adjustment to fatherhood, lack of knowledge about parenting was predictive of high adjustment difficulty. Their findings suggested that the most effective interventions deal with the husband-wife relationship as well as the parent-child relationship in easing the transition to parenthood. From a different perspective, Fein (1976) interviewed 30 men who attended childbirth preparation classes with their wives before and after the birth of a first child. He found that the development of some kind of coherent role was important to the men's adjustments to postpartum family life. He suggested that there is a need for more research on men's preparations for parenting, involvement in the birth process, and participation in family life. Despite the methodological weaknesses, the findings from these studies appear to be consistent with those concerning female adjustment.

On the basis of the available literature, it is clear that general psychological adjustment of fathers during pregnancy has been a much neglected area, as has been the father's relationship to his infant until very recently. The father's role is a very significant one during pregnancy in terms of his own adjustment and his relationship to his pregnant wife. It is important to gain a better understanding of the husband's ability to change with and support his wife during the pregnancy and to understand his contribution to family function or dysfunction.

A limited number of studies have focused on the male's development of emotional symptoms in response to his wife's pregnancy or the birth of their baby. Most of these focus on clinical studies and reports from which the male's emotional adjustment is assumed (Ginath, 1974; Jarvis, 1962; Wainwright, 1966). Consistent with the work of others, in our own studies (Osofsky, 1982), we have observed men with gross psychiatric disturbance apparently precipitated by expectant or new fatherhood. The "couvade syndrome," including abdominal pain for which no physical cause could be found, has long been described as affecting some men during their wives' pregnancies (Cavenar & Weddington, 1978). Because of the subjective nature of the existing work in this area, there is a need for serious and careful study. Defining and identifying the significant changes that occur and the necessary adjustments that are required as well as strategies for intervention and support would be valuable and helpful.

Expectant Parenthood: Concerns of the Couple

Since significant changes in the marital relationship often begin during pregnancy and go on to affect the early and later parent-infant and parent-child relationships, and since a growing number of marriages are terminating, frequently in the early years after the birth of children, it is crucial to look more carefully at the adjustments that occur both within the individuals and in the marital relationship during pregnancy and following childbirth. In this way it may be possible to learn how the period can be used as a maturational phase leading to positive developmental growth for the couple and the family.

A small number of studies have focused sociologically on the general effects of the coming of the first child on the marital relationship and the family. From this perspective, pregnancy is generally conceptualized as precipitating a crisis in a more negative sense than the normative developmental growth phase concept proposed earlier. Dyer (1963) and LeMasters (1964) indicated that the birth of a first child may be experienced as a crisis or time of upheaval by both parents requiring significant shifts in the marital relationship to incorporate the baby into the marriage. The crisis reaction observed by LeMasters (1964) in his study of 46 couples did not appear to be the result of unwanted children, bad marriages, neuroses, or other psychiatric disabilities. Rather, the birth of the first child forced reorganization of the family as a social system with marked shifts for both the woman and the man to achieve a successful adjustment to parenthood.

Dyer (1963) studied the level of family organization up to the time of the pregnancy, the impact of the pregnancy on the family, and the recovery and subsequent level of family reorganization. In his study of middle-class couples, he found that the addition of the first child forced them to reorganize many of their roles and relationships. A majority of couples experienced the birth as bringing about very significant changes in their lives. The degree to which the advent of parenthood represented a crisis event in the negative sense appeared related to (a) the state of the marriage and family organization at the birth of the child, (b) the couple's preparation for marriage and parenthood, (c) the couple's marital adjustment after the birth of the child, and (d) social background and situational variables such as the number of years married, the degree to which the pregnancy was planned, and the time that had passed since the birth of the child. Hobbs (1965) found, in contrast to the LeMasters and Dyer studies, that the degree of difficulty reported seemed to be mainly related to income. However, the lack of objective measurement tools to study the extent to which the birth of the first child may be disruptive for the family contributes to the unclarity and inconsistencies in this area of research.

More recently, Feldman (1971), who followed couples in upstate New York, found that contrary to usual expectations, children have a negative effect on their parents' relationship from the time of pregnancy through the children's own adulthood. Initially the women felt concerns about their identity and personal aspirations. Husbands tended to feel left out and neglected, with symptoms sometimes worsening when their wives found parenthood satisfying. Even when parenthood was planned, many couples felt trapped. Following the birth of the baby, Feldman noted a persistence of personal problems, some sexual problems, and marital conflicts. He found that stated discrepancies in childrearing styles during pregnancy related to marital difficulty following the birth of the child.

Cowan, Cowan, Coie, and Coie (1978) noted that changes that occur when having a child call for the ability to negotiate and solve problems. Partners may have to seek alternative means to provide each other with gratification. They have found that successful couples are probably able to reserve some time for one another rather than letting the baby pervade all aspects of their marital life.

From a behavioral systems theory framework, Vincent, Harris, Cook, and Brady (1979) have attempted to understand the advent of children as they may influence the marriage. They have found that the extent of marital disruption is related to existing levels of marital discord, parental expectations, temperament of the infant, change in husband-wife roles, cost-benefit shifts in marital exchange and couple change skills. Their goal is to teach parenting and relationship skills to couples in order to promote a more positive adjustment to parenthood.

SOCIOLOGICAL CONTRIBUTORS TO FAMILY FUNCTION

When one considers the adjustments that couples must make in the process of becoming parents and the resultant impact on their marital relationship and function as parents, several sociological factors have to be taken into consideration. One concerns the age of the couple.

While the stresses and disequilibrium that women and men experience in the process of becoming parents are difficult in general, the tasks for adolescent couples appear even harder. The females may have to deal with difficult psychological and realistic situations. They need to cope with the adjustments of marriage and the responsibilities of parenthood at a time when they may not have resolved developmental tasks and issues of consolidation and identity that in our society need to occur during adolescence (McArnarney, 1983; Moore, Waite, Hofferth, & Caldwell, 1978; Osofsky & Osofsky, 1978). At least in part related to their changing roles and responsibilities, they are less likely to complete as many years of schooling as their classmates, and they are more likely as the years pass to have less satisfying and prestigious and lower-paying jobs than their peers (Card & Wise, 1978). Because adolescent marriages are frequently preceded by conception (Hetzel & Cuppetta, 1973; Zelnik & Kantner, 1980), the couple may also have to struggle with consolidating their marriage with a limited courtship and with the burdens accompanying the care of a child (Furstenberg, 1976; Osofsky & Osofsky, 1970; Osofsky, Osofsky, Kendall, & Rajan, 1973; Pohlman, 1969). When pregnancy precedes marriage, couples tend to fare less well financially than their peers (Freedman & Thornton, 1979), and a combination of factors—youthful age, economic instability, family pressures, individual problems, and inadequate social supports—contribute to a much higher incidence of divorce in these couples than in the population at large (Card & Wise, 1978; Furstenberg,

1976; McCarthy & Menken, 1979; Moore et al., 1978; Stack, 1974). In recent issues of the *Journal of Social Issues* (1980) and the *American Journal of Orthopsychiatry* (1980) many important issues regarding teenage parenting were explored, including an attempt to understand both the positive and negative consequences for the teenage mother and those involved with her when she bears a child and undertakes the role of teenage parent.

Another sociological factor concerns the changes in support systems that have occurred in recent decades. Available support, particularly on a long-term basis, from family, professionals, society, and religion groups, is in general more limited than it was at a time when there was less geographic mobility and different values prevailed. Couples may receive little help from their parents, who may indeed perceive of the marriage as pulling them away from the family network (Stack, 1974). Community services are often fragmentary and crisis oriented and do not fill the void created by the decline in traditional supports. In our evaluation of a community-based intervention program, those women and couples at highest social risk appear to have the least consistent and adequate support systems (Osofsky & Osofsky, 1981). Other forms of support, such as welfare programs, have results that are complex and difficult to interpret. For example, while there are obvious benefits from welfare programs, there have been discrepant findings concerning whether there is an association between payment level and marital breakup (Cherlin, 1977; Cutright, 1971; Moles, 1976). Sawhill, Peabody, Jones, and Caldwell (1975) have found a lower frequency of remarriage among divorced women who were welfare recipients, an association that may have multiple explanations.

Another important consideration that has received more emphasis in recent years is the influence both of economics on choices concerning when and whether to have children and of pregnancy on the economic structure and the resultant stability of the family. Low-income couples in general, and black couples in specific, may find themselves facing considerable financial difficulty following the birth of an infant. Job opportunities are limited for the men, and deprivation may result if the wife does not work. The black couple may find themselves in a particularly difficult situation. The husband's current and future opportunities are frequently limited. The wife may be able to earn more money than he, but at menial jobs that both find degrading. Stated and unstated resentments of both spouses about the husband's economic difficulties, the wife's working following childbirth, and the quality of each of their jobs may contribute to family dysfunction (Furstenberg, 1976; Rainwater, 1970). Although questioning the reasons, a number of studies have indicated that economic resources and satisfaction—and perceptions that the male is economically successful—contribute strongly to marital stability (Cherlin, 1977; Cutright, 1971; Furstenberg, 1976). Even when the couple do not separate until the children are in school, significant marital instability may be present at a much earlier point (Campbell, Converse, & Rodgers, 1976; Cherlin, 1977).

DEVELOPMENTAL PROCESSES AND STRESSES FOR THE COUPLE

A limited number of authors have considered the major adjustments that the couple as a unit undergo during the process of pregnancy and early parenthood (Benedek, 1970; Bibring et al., 1961; Shereshefsky & Yarrow, 1973; Wenner, Cohen, Weigert, Kvarnes, Ohaneson, & Fearing, 1969). However, in spite of clinical recognition that couples undergo significant stresses, which has been confirmed in our own experience and preliminary research (Osofsky & Osofsky, 1980), the subject has not been studied in depth. Recently, preliminary attempts have been made to develop measures to predict couples strengths and vulnerability and to develop techniques of appropriate intervention (Belsky, 1984; Cowan & Cowan, 1983).

Jessner (1964) has discussed pregnancy as a period of stress within the marriage, focusing on the transition from romantic to marital love occurring during this period of time. Some of the potential areas of stress that concern a pregnant woman include loss of or desertion by her husband, changes in body image, changes in her personality during pregnancy, hopes that having a child will improve a frustrating marriage, conflict between having a career and the demands of motherhood, resentments of the changes that do not have to be made by the father, feelings of self-centered estrangement and exclusion, and overall fears and anxieties of pregnancy, labor, and delivery. All of these factors can put stress on even the most well-balanced individuals and marital relationships.

In our work (Osofsky & Osofsky, 1980) we have found that for some couples expectant and new parenthood can be disorganizing, while for others it represents a developmental opportunity for maturation and new growth. Their lives will change in meaningful and irreversible ways, and as with other major growth steps, they may experience significant discomfort as well as pleasure. Prior to the birth of the baby, the wife and husband, although close, are relatively autonomous. With the pregnancy they experience important shifts in themselves and in their relationship with one another; few, if any, individuals are the same afterward as they were before the pregnancy.

PRENATAL, PARENT, AND INFANT FACTORS AS
INFLUENCES ON THE DEVELOPING RELATIONSHIP

Utilizing a psychodynamic framework, Benedek (1949) explored in some depth the implications that the prenatal experience has on the formation of the early mother-child relationship. She proposed that a woman's identification with her own mother motivates her attitude toward motherhood and determines her behavior toward her children. According to Benedek, after delivery, while preparing for lactation, mothers, particularly primiparous mothers, may experience an "emotional lag." For the 9 months of pregnancy a woman is preparing to love the baby. After delivery she may be surprised by a lack of feeling for the child. If mothers are disappointed in themselves by a lack of love for or acceptance of the child they may become anxious, and the insecurity toward the child may begin to affect their early relationship. She felt that the early postpartum emotional lag is a critical time during which the husband's relationship to his wife and his readiness for gratifying his wife's dependency needs may be very important. Further, and suggesting the importance of other components of changing prenatal and perinatal care, recent research (Entwisle & Doering, 1981) has shown that the overall adjustment of the couple to the birth of the first baby is influenced to a great extent by their preparation for childbearing and child rearing.

Harmon and Emde (1980), in their recent investigation, did not find the "emotional lag" described by Benedek. They suggested that this emotional reaction may have been related to: (1) the birthing hospital experience, wherein mothers and their infants were kept apart for most of the first 3 postpartum days, and (2) the obstetric sedation, which dampened the responsiveness of both mother and infant. With changes in hospital practices involving less sedation and less separation, this "maternal emotional lag" phenomenon may occur less frequently. The more recent research in this area reflects a concern with family influences during pregnancy rather than just the care of the pregnant woman.

The couple's ability to deal with the stresses of pregnancy and cope with the demands of new parenthood as well as the specific characteristics of their child significantly influence both their marital stability and the optimal development of their child. Ainsworth, Blehar, Waters, and Wall (1978), Bowlby (1973), Brazelton and Als (1979), Klaus and Kennell (1976), Sroufe (1979), and Winnicott (1965), among others, have tried to describe and delineate the factors that contribute to the mother's attachment to her infant and the infant's attachment to his or her mother. According to these authors' works, attachment has both constitutional and experiential components consisting of behaviors, feeling states, and affectional bonds. The mother's devotion and her willingness to sacrifice her own interests for the sake of her child appear to be influenced by her internal capacities, hormonal and physiological factors occurring at certain critical times, and the behaviors and appearance of the infant. The reciprocal infant's attachment to his or her mother is also influenced by constitutional components and maternal behaviors.

Richards (1971) noted the importance of distinguishing social interaction from other systems of interaction such as attachment. In contrast with the care-giving system, social interaction involves mutual, reciprocal exchanges. In the parent-infant system, both behave so as to produce or maintain the behavior of the other, thus fostering an optimal range of arousal.

In recent years, we have become more aware of the many often unpredictable factors that can influence the developing parent-infant relationship. For example, Sander (1964, 1965, 1970) has pointed out that timing, intensity, and modality of mothers' and infants' behavior must become organized together in order to achieve and maintain the coordination and relative stability of interaction patterns. During the first day of life, some infant behaviors (i.e., increased irritability, crying, wakefulness, and so on) are vulnerable to what might seem to be minor variations in the environment (i.e., change in temperature, tenseness of mother, change in physical local, and others). This vulnerability can in turn affect interaction with the mother. Sander observed that the first 10 days of life was the optimal period in which to establish initial regulatory coordinations of the cyclic functioning of neonates with their caretaking environments. For example, neonates who were rooming with their mothers achieved a "synchronous" sleep-wake cycle with their mothers. In comparison with infants who stayed in the nursery, these infants were active during the day and spent most of their evening hours asleep. The nursery infants were more "asynchronous" and unpredictable in their schedule. Kaye and Brazelton (1973) noted that dyssynchronous interaction resulted from a lack of maternal sensitivity to the infant's needs during feeding. Maternal effectiveness in that situation was found to be related to behaviors during the infant's suck-pause sequence. For example, auditory stimulation too early in the pause period was most likely to prolong the pause and to delay feeding. The appropriateness of a mother's response to her infant's cessation in sucking either facilitated or impeded the feeding process.

Kopp and Parmelee (1979) recently reviewed some of the factors that may affect this early developing interactive relationship. They concluded that (1) events linked to early prenatal life have more serious effects for a greater number of individuals than those that occur in later prenatal or perinatal life; (2) there is much individual variation in outcome that is not always possible to explain; (3) supportive child-rearing conditions are associated with higher intellectual scores among children with Down's syndrome, preterm birth, and intrauterine growth retardation; (4) infant developmental status, particularly in the first year of life, does not show high levels of prediction to early childhood intellectual status; and (5) severe physical impairment is not always asssociated with intellectual impairment. It would seem useful to review some of the specific factors that may affect the patterns of development within the individual and for the parent-infant interaction process.

The effects of medication administered during the perinatal period have been studied extensively in relation to infant development and, to a lesser extent, the development of the parent-infant relationship. Brackbill (1979) reviewed the available literature and her own work concerning obstetrical medication and infant behavior and concluded that drugs given to mothers during labor and delivery have subsequent effects on infant behavior that may last for some period of time. The strongest effects can be seen in selected areas of cognitive function and gross motor abilities.

In a recent study, Murray, Dolby, Nation, & Thomas (1981) investigated the effects of epidural anesthesia on newborns and mother-infant interaction, and found that the effects of drugs were strongest on the first day. At 1 month, they observed few differences between groups, but unmedicated mothers reported their babies to be more sociable, rewarding, and easy to care for; these mothers were also more responsive to their babies' cries. Thus, although the specific effects of the medication appeared to abate considerably, consistent with Brazelton's (1971) hypothesis, early encounters with a medicated and disorganized baby may have built up a false picture that interferred with the development of a reciprocal relationship.

Before turning to a discussion of "at risk" infants and effects on parents, it may be useful to consider factors that can place parents themselves at "higher risk" for parenting disorders. There is a consistency in the available literature (Hall, Pawlby, & Wolkind, 1979; Richards, 1979) indicating that many women who have been subjected to one or a series of separations in childhood, especially when these occurred in a psychosocially disadvantaged environment, have difficulty as adults in mothering their own children. This issue is particularly important for mothers who are separated from their infants. Parents who have themselves experienced a depriving psychosocial environment as children may be more vulnerable to separations that even under more optimal conditions can stress the parent-infant system. These findings are consistent with the earlier cited psychodynamic theoretical understanding of the adjustments to pregnancy and new parenthood.

Infants and parents who are "at risk" for a variety of reasons may have a more difficult time developing reciprocal patterns of interaction (Ricciuti, 1983). Historically, much of the research in this area has dealt with the effects of premature birth on the family, with particular focus on the mother. Prugh, as noted by Harmon and Culp (1981), mentioned that the mother often feels anxious and guilty, the guilt coming from her concerns that because she has a premature infant, she did something wrong during her pregnancy. Women may feel inadequate in caring for the infant in comparison with the doctors and nurses at the hospital (Emde, 1981). A topic that has received considerable focus and controversy over the years has been the effects of separation of the infant from the mother as a problem leading to later difficulties in parenting. Leiderman and colleagues (Barnett, Leiderman, Grobstein, & Klaus, 1970; Leiderman & Seashore, 1975; Leifer, Leiderman, Barnett, & Williams, 1972) compared mothers who were separated from their infants during the intensive-care period with mothers who were allowed to enter the intensive-care unit while the infant was hospitalized. They found more family disruption for mothers who were separated from their infants in terms of subsequent divorce or giving up of the infant. These studies are particularly interesting in light of the work of Klaus, Kennell, and co-workers (Kennell, Voos, & Klaus, 1979; Klaus & Kennell, 1976), indicating that being deprived of contacting and caring for their newborn child may make some mothers vulnerable. While the Klaus and Kennell studies have been criticized of late based on methodological weaknesses and overgeneralizations from samples of disadvantaged populations, the ideas coming out of the studies have been helpful in stimulating further work in this important area (see Svejda , Pannabecker, & Emde, 1981). Emde and Brown (1978) and Klaus and Kennell (1976) described the effects of vulnerable infants on parents, including the mourning process that follows the birth of an infant who does not meet parental expectations. Herzog (1979) pointed out the subsequent problems that can develop for the family when the father becomes engaged with an infant who is transported to an intensive-care regional center with mothers being left out. In order to promote mother-infant attachment, it is very important for fathers to nurture the mothers so that they will be able to overcome the problems of separation, and it is important for professionals to help the parents understand the developmental course.

Detailed studies have shown behavioral differences between premature and full-term infants and the effects on the caregivers. Beckwith and Cohen (1978), Brown and Bakeman (1980), Field (1980), and Goldberg

(1979) have all found that premature infants solicit different caretaking interactions than those elicited by full-term infants. They found that care-givers were more active with preterm infants and more likely to initiate behavioral exchanges than were caregivers of full-term infants, perhaps related to the passivity of the premature infant and the mother's feeling that she has to take more responsibility to establish an interaction. It has been well established that premature infants are represented in a dispro-portionate number among abused and neglected infants, possibly due to their being more difficult to manage or care for and exhibiting extreme irritability as well as marked passivity. Frodi, Lamb, Leavitt, Donovan, Neff, and Sherry (1978) found that the cry and facial movements of prema-ture infants were more aversive than the cries and facial movements of full-term infants. However, Beckwith and Cohen (1978), Goldberg (1979), and Harmon and Culp (1981) all found that mothers may have a closer relationship with their preterm than their full-term infants, including more parental activity and a tendency toward overprotectiveness. Harmon and Culp (1981), in their study of 30 premature infants and their families, did not find the degree of family disruption that had been reported previously (Leiderman & Seashore, 1975; Leifer et al., 1972). They suggest that the differences in their findings may be due to the parents making more effort in their individual and family adjustment and to hospital environments offering more support to parents of premature infants. Other specified factors, including improved medical care and better outreach efforts, may also have played a role. Futher, a quarter of the families that they at-tempted to follow could not be contacted, and this may have influenced their findings.

In spite of its weaknesses, the work of Klaus and Kennell (1976), concluding that early separation of infants and mothers immediately after birth may contribute to a vulnerable mother's difficulty in caring for her infant, has influenced clinical care. Their work and that of others (Barnett et al., 1970; Minde, 1980) has resulted in changes in hospital practices that have fostered more interaction between mothers and their infants. Barnett et al. (1970) found that in spite of long-held fears, when mothers were allowed to visit and touch their premature infants as early as the second day after birth, there was a decrease rather than an increase of infection. They found that mothers who were given the opportunity for early contact felt more confident in their ability to care for their infants, although there were no differences in caretaking behavior.

Field (1980) studied full-term, postmature, and high-risk premature infants, observing patterns of mother-infant interaction. She found that both preterm and postterm infants showed significantly more gaze aversion than full-term infants during observations carried out while feeding and in

face-to-face play. Because both the post and premature infants had received low scores on subtests of the Brazelton Neonatal Behavioral Assessment Scale measuring an infant's interactive abilities, Field concluded that
the interactive difficulties shown by both high-risk groups were not due to
initial mother-infant separation but to poorer CNS organization. Field
confirmed her early results in a later study showing that mothers of
premature infants showed a greater amount of activity than did the full-
term mothers. A conclusion that can be drawn based on the studies of early
contact and patterns of development is that initial contact between mothers
and premature infants does not seem to make a crucial difference for the
mother's later caretaking skills and the development of the neonate. Campbell and Taylor (1980) suggest that there does not seem to be a sensitive
period of bonding between mothers and premature infants but rather a
period of education and getting used to one's infant over time.

Minde, Trehub, Corter, Boukydis, Celhoffer, and Marton (1978)
attempted to isolate some of the characteristics of parents who have difficulty dealing with small infants, rather than basing assumptions on generalizations about low-income or disadvantaged parents being poor parents
for prematures. They found that the high-, low-, and medium-interactive
mothers remained that way for at least the first 3 months following their
infant's discharge from the hospital, and that the low-interacting mothers
consistently reported poor relationships with their own mothers and with
the father of the infant, while the high-interactive mothers reported more
satisfactory previous interpersonal relationships. The high-activity
mothers tended to respond more contingently to their infant's social and
gross motor behaviors, while lower-activity mothers seemed to interact
more randomly.

Because stress as well as support is an important issue for new parents,
we need to consider the stress of prematurity on the parent-infant interactive system. The initiation of patterns considered normal for full-term pairs
is delayed in preterm pairs, which can result in delay or depression of some
interactive patterns with less reward or reciprocity in the relationship;
thus, establishing an effective interaction pattern may be a more difficult
process for the parents. While the majority of preterm pairs make relatively successful adaptations due to the enormous capacity for compensation, early interactive stress is one of the features of this parent-infant
interaction system. Parke and Tinsley (1982) point out that in addition to
the disequilibrium created by the birth of any infant requiring additional
caretaking and life-adjustment tasks, the birth of a high-risk infant either
premature, ill, or handicapped further increases the pressure within a
family in a number of ways. In addition to arriving earlier than expected,
the infants deviate from the usual norms in terms of appearance, cry,

feeding behavior, developmental progress, and interactive demands, which may place the parents under greater stress. In Frodi et al.'s (1978) follow-up comparing parental reactions to the cry and appearance of both a full-term and a premature infant, it was found that the cry of the premature infant resulted in greater autonomic arousal than the full-term cry, as well as a parental rating of greater disturbance, irritability, and annoyance. These reactions occurred if the cry was associated with a picture of a full-term or a preterm infant, and the arousal effects were particularly pronounced when the parents were exposed to both the sight and cry of a premature infant.

Parents of preterm infants may have unrealistic expectations concerning the developmental timetable that these infants are likely to follow in that they usually progress slower in motor, social, and cognitive areas than their full-term peers, at least during the first 2 years (Field, 1979). This observation is particularly interesting in relation to two sets of data. Egeland and Brunnquell (1979) found that lack of accurate knowledge of developmental timetables may be a factor in child abuse. In addition, de Lissovoy (1973), in a study of 48 couples, 46 of whom were expecting a child at the time of their marriage, with the women ranging in age from 15 to 18 and the men between the ages of 14½ and 19, found that there was a much greater incidence of restrictive and sometimes punitive behavior. He attributed this behavior not only to ignorance or lack of experience but also to the parents' personal, social, and economic frustrations, which contributed to the disenchantment in their marital relationships, as well as their behavior toward their children. In light of the greater incidence of abused babies among prematures, it can be concluded that high-risk babies of young mothers may be particularly vulnerable.

Discussion and Conclusion

In this review, we have considered the impact of expectant and new parenthood on the woman and man as individuals, on their marital relationship, and on their styles of parenting. The literature has reflected the confusion in conceptualizing pregnancy as either a time of normative developmental growth or a period precipitating a crisis understood in terms of psychological difficulties. The work on expectant fatherhood has clearly been weighted toward this latter perspective. While the pathological perspective has permeated studies in this area, with much of the research being from a retrospective, clinical-descriptive tradition, a research perspective with careful specification of variables often prospective in nature studied within a developmental framework appears to be emerging. Further, more focus is being placed on the success of the individual and couple in accomplishing necessary tasks during the period of expectant and new parenthood that may have an important impact on their parenting ability and the developing parent-infant relationship (Belsky, 1984; Cowan & Cowan, 1983; Osofsky, 1980). There appears to be a concurrent movement toward a systems approach (see Vincent et al., 1979) with concern for the causal sequences and interactive patterns over time. Systems approaches require new structural and time-series methods in order to conceptualize increasing organization over time and mutual interactions among systems (see Porges, 1979; Sackett, 1979). These approaches will exert a profound influence on research in this area.

Several important research directions appear fruitful based on past empirical research and theoretical formulations. A perspective utilizing a developmental approach may provide a broader overall framework for understanding pregnancy and new parenthood. Important components of this perspective include recognition of past experiences, individual differences, and consistent patterns of behavior and coping capacities as predictors both of current adjustment and of interventions that may be most useful. As a theoretical base is better formulated, careful studies involving clear specification of variables and methodologies can be developed utilizing both clinical and research settings. It will be important to develop more objective methods that are reliable and valid, and that take into account the depth of psychological experience that influences the process and its outcome. These measures should be designed to be useful to investigators from different disciplines who are pursuing similar approaches to the problem. Prospective studies initiated during the prenatal period that have a theoretical basis and that employ consistent and replicable assessments may provide the means for gaining a better understanding of the process, achieving more adequate prediction and indentification of difficulties, and developing more effective interventions. If a developmental perspective can be conceptualized with carefully specified variables and methods, we may be able to gain a better understanding of the pregnancy and parenting process for the individuals and couples and provide important information that will aid in facilitating optimal parent-infant interaction.

REFERENCES

Ainsworth, M. D., Blehar, M., Waters, E., & Wall, S. *Patterns of attachment.* Hillsdale, N.J.: Erlbaum, 1978.
Barnett, C., Leiderman, P. H., Grobstein, R., & Klaus, M. Neonatal separation: The maternal side of interactional deprivation. *Pediatrics*, 1970, **45**, 197–205.

Beckwith, L., & Cohen, S. E. Preterm birth: Hazardous obstetrical and postnatal events as related to caregiver-infant behavior. *Infant Behavior and Development*, 1978, **1**, 403–411.

Belsky, J. The determinants of parenting: A process model. *Child Development*, 1984, **55**, 83–96.

Benedek, T. The psychosomatic implications of the primary unit: Mother-child. *American Journal of Orthopsychiatry*, 1949, **19**, 642–654.

Benedek, T. Parenthood as a developmental phase: A contribution to the libido theory. *Journal of the American Psychoanalytic Association*, 1959, **7**, 389–417.

Benedek, T. The psychobiology of pregnancy. In E. J. Anthony & T. Benedek (Eds.), *Parenthood: Its psychology and psychopathology*. Boston: Little, Brown, 1970.

Bibring, G. L., Dwyer, T. F., Huntington, D. S., & Valenstein, A. F. A study of the psychological processes in pregnancy and of the earliest mother-child relationship, I: Some propositions and comments. *Psychoanalytic Study of the Child*, 1961, **16**, 9–24.

Bowlby, J. *Attachment and loss* (Vol. 2). New York: Basic, 1973.

Brazelton, T. B. Influence of perinatal drugs on the behavior of the neonate. In J. Hellmuth (Ed.), *The exceptional infant.* (Vol. 2): *Studies in abnormalities.* New York: Brunner/Mazel, 1971.

Brazelton, T. B., & Als, H. Four early stages in the development of mother-infant interaction. *Psychoanalytic Study of the Child*, 1979, **34**, 349–371.

Brown J. V., & Bakeman, R. Relationships of human mothers with their infants during the first year of life: Effects of prematurity. In R. W. Bell & W. P. Smotherman (Eds.), *Maternal influences and early behavior*. New York: Spectrum, 1980.

Brunswick, R. M. The preoedipal phase of libido development. *Psychoanalytic Quarterly*, 1940, **9**, 293–319.

Campbell, A., Converse, P., & Rodgers, W. *The quality of American life*. New York: Russell Sage, 1976.

Campbell, S. B. G., & Taylor, P. M. Bonding and attachment: Theoretical issues. In P. M. Taylor (Ed.), *Parent-infant relationships*. New York: Grune & Stratton, 1980.

Card, J., & Wise, J. Teenage mothers and teenage fathers: The impact of early child-bearing on the parents' personal and professional lives. *Family Planning Perspectives*, 1978, **10**, 199–205.

Cavenar, J. O., & Weddington, W. W. Abdominal pain in expectant fathers. *Psychosomatics*, 1978, **19**, 761–768.

Cherlin, A. The effect of children on marital dissolution. *Demography*, 1977, **14**, 264–272.

Chertok, L., with Bonnaud, M., Borelli, M., Donnet, J. J., & D'Allones, C. R. *Motherhood and personality*. London: Tavistock, 1969.

Coleman, A. D. Psychological state during first pregnancy. *American Journal of Orthopsychiatry*, 1969, **37**, 788–797.

Cowan, C. P., Cowan, P. A., Coie, L., & Coie, J. D. Becoming a family: The impact of a first child's birth on the couple's relationship. In W. Miller & L. Newman (Eds.), *The first child and family formation*. Chapel Hill: University of North Carolina Press, 1978.

Cowan, P. A., & Cowan, C. P. Quality of couple relationships and parenting stress in beginning families. Paper presented at the biennial meeting of the Society for Research in Child Development, Detroit, 1983.

Cutright, P. Income and family events: Marital stability. *Journal of Marriage and the Family*, 1971, **33**, 291–306.

Davids, A., & Rosengren, W. R. Social stability and psychological adjustment during pregnancy. *Psychosomatic Medicine*, 1962, **24**, 579–583.

de Lissovoy, F. Child care by adolescent parents. *Children Today*, 1973, **2**, 22–25.

Dyer, E., Parenthood as crisis: A re-study. *Marriage and Family Living*, 1963, **25**, 196–201.

Egeland, B., & Brunnquell, D. An at-risk approach to the study of child abuse: Some preliminary findings. *Journal of the American Academy of Child Psychiatry*, 1979, **18**, 219–235.

Emde, R. N. Personal communication, 1981.

Emde, R. N., & Brown, C. Adaptation to the birth of a Down's syndrome infant. *Journal of the American Academy of Child Psychiatry*, 1978, **17**, 299–323.

Entwisle, D. R., & Doering, S. G. *The first birth*. Baltimore: John Hopkins Press, 1981.

Erikson, E. *Childhood and society*. New York: Norton, 1950.

Erikson, E. Growth and crisis of the "healthy personality." In C. Kluckholm, H. Murray, & D. Schneider (Eds.), *Personality in nature, society and culture*. New York: Knopf, 1973.

Fein, R. Men's entrance to parenthood. *Family Coordinator*, 1976, **25**, 341–350.

Feldman, H. The effects of children on the family. In Andree Michel (Ed.), *Family issues of employed women in Europe and America*. Lieden: Brill, 1971.

Field, T. M. Interaction patterns of high-risk and normal infants. In T. M. Field, A. Sostek, S. Goldberg, & H. H. Shuman (Eds.), *Infants born at risk*. New York: Spectrum, 1979.

Field, T. M. Interactions of preterm and term infants with their lower- and middle-class teenage and adult mothers. In T. M. Field, S. Goldberg, D. Stern, & A. M. Sostek (Eds.), *High-risk infants and children*. New York: Academic Press, 1980.

Freedman, D., & Thornton, A. The long-term impact of pregnancy at marriage on the family's economic circumstances. *Family Planning Perspectives*, 1979, **11**, 6–21.

Frodi, A., Lamb, M., Leavitt, L., Donovan, W., Neff, C., & Sherry, D. Father's and mothers' responses to the faces and cries of normal and premature infants. *Developmental Psychology*, 1978, **14**, 490–498.

Furstenberg, F. *Unplanned parenthood*. New York: Free Press, 1976.

Ginath, Y. Psychoses in males in relation to their wives' pregnancy and childbirth. *Israel Annals of Psychiatry*, 1974, **12**, 227–237.

Goldberg, S. Premature birth: Consequences for the parent-infant relationship. *American Scientist*, 1979, **67**, 214–220.

Gordon, R. E., & Gordon, K. Social factors in the prevention of emotional difficulties in pregnancy. *Journal of Obstetrics and Gynecology*, 1960, **15**, 433–438.

Gorsuch, R. L., & Key, M. K. Abnormalities of pregnancy as a function of anxiety and life stress. *Psychosomatic Medicine*, 1974, **36**, 352–362.

Hall, F., Pawlby, S. J., & Wolkind, S. Early life experiences and later mothering behavior: A study of mothers and their 20-week old babies. In D. Shaffer & J. Dunn (Eds.), *The first year of life*. New York: Wiley, 1979.

Harmon, R. J., & Culp, A. A. The effects of premature birth on family functioning and infant development. In I. Berlin (Ed.), *Children and our future*. Albuquerque: University of New Mexico Press, 1981.

Harmon, R. J., & Emde, R. N. Unpublished manuscript, 1980.

Heinstein, M. I. Expressed attitudes and feelings of pregnant women and their relations to physical complications of pregnancy. *Merrill-Palmer Quarterly*, 1967, **13**, 217–238.

Herzog, J. M. Disturbances in parenting high-risk infants: Clinical impressions and hypotheses. In T. F. Field (Ed.), *Infants born at risk*. New York: Spectrum, 1979.

Hetzel, A., & Cuppetta, M. Teenagers: Marriages, divorces, parenthood, and mortality. Vital and Health Statistics, United States Department of Health, Education, and Welfare, Series 21, No. 23, 1973.

Hobbs, D. F. Parenthood as crisis: A third study. *Journal of Marriage and the Family*, 1965, **27**, 367–372.

Hollender, M. H., & McGehee, J. B. The wish to be held during pregnancy. *Journal of Psychosomatic Research*, 1974, **18**, 193–197.

Jacobson, E. Development of the wish for a child in boys. *Psychoanalytic Study of the Child,* 1950, **5**, 139–152.

Jarvis, W. Some effects of pregnancy and childbirth on men. *Journal of the American Psychoanalytic Association,* 1962, **10**, 689–700.

Jessner, L. Pregnancy as a stress in marriage. In E. M. Nash, L. Jessner, & D. W. Abse (Eds.), *Marriage counseling in medical practice.* Chapel Hill: University of North Carolina Press, 1964.

Jones, A. C. Life change and pyschological distress as predictors of pregnancy outcome. *Psychosomatic Medicine,* 1978, **40**, 402–412.

Kaye, K., & Brazelton, T. B. Unpublished manuscript, 1973.

Kennell, J. H., Voos, D. K., & Klaus, M. N. Parent-infant bonding. In J. D. Osofsky (Ed.), *Handbook of infant development.* New York: Wiley, 1979.

Kestenberg, J. S. *Children and parents: Psychoanalytic studies in development.* New York: Aronson, 1975.

Klaus, M. H., & Kennell, J. H. *Maternal-infant bonding.* St. Louis: Mosby, 1976.

Kopp, C. B., & Parmelee, A. H. Prenatal and perinatal influences on infant behavior. In J. D. Osofsky (Ed.), *Handbook of infant development.* New York: Wiley, 1979.

Lamb, M. *The role of the father in child development* (2d ed.). New York: Wiley, 1981.

Leiderman, P. H., & Seashore, M. J. Mother-infant neonatal separation: Some delayed consequences. In *Parent-infant interaction.* Amsterdam: Associated Publishers, 1975.

Leifer, A., Leiderman, P. H., Barnett, C. R., & Williams, J. Effects of mother-infant separation on maternal attachment behavior. *Child Development,* 1972, **43**, 1203–1218.

Leifer, M. Psychological changes accompanying pregnancy and motherhood. *Genetic Psychology Monographs,* 1977, **95**, 55–96.

LeMasters, E. E. Parenthood as crisis. In R. Susman (Ed.), *Handbook on the family.* Glencoe, Ill.: Free Press, 1964.

Lubin, B., Gardener, S. H., & Roth, A. Mood and somatic symptoms during pregnancy. *Psychosomatic Medicine,* 1975, **37**, 136–146.

McArnarney, E. R. The vulnerable dyad—adolescent mothers and their infants. In V. J. Sasserath (Ed.), *Minimizing high-risk parenting.* Skillman, N.J.: Johnson & Johnson, 1983.

McCarthy, J., & Menken, J. Marriage, remarriage, marital disruption and age at first birth. *Family Planning Perspectives,* 1979, **11**, 21–30.

McDonald, R. L. The role of emotional factors in obstetric complications: A review. *Psychosomatic Medicine,* 1968, **30**, 222–237.

Minde, K. Bonding of parents to premature infants: Theory and practice. In P. M. Taylor (Ed.), *Parent-infant relationships.* New York: Grune & Stratton, 1980.

Minde, K., Trehub, S., Corter, C., Boukydis, C., Celhoffer, L., & Marton, P. Mother-child relationships on the premature nursery: An observational study. *Pediatrics,* 1978, **61**, 373–379.

Moles, O. Marital dissolution and public assistance payments: Variations among American states. *Journal of Social Issues,* 1976, **34**, 87–101.

Moore, K., Waite, L., Hofferth, S., & Caldwell, S. *The consequences of age at first childbirth: Marriage, separation, and divorce.* Washington, D.C.: Urban Institute, 1978.

Murray, A. D., Dolby, R. M., Nation, R. L., & Thomas, D. B. Effects of epidural anesthesia on newborns and their mothers. *Child Development,* 1981, **52**, 71–82.

Osofsky, H. J. Expectant and new fatherhood as a developmental crisis. *Bulletin of the Menninger Clinic,* 1982, **46**, 209–230.

Osofsky, H. J., & Osofsky, J. D. Adolescents as mothers: Results of a program for low income pregnant teenagers with some emphasis upon infants' development. *American Journal of Orthopsychiatry,* 1970, **40**, 825–834.

Osofsky, H. J., & Osofsky, J. D. Normal adaptation to pregnancy and new parenthood. In P. M. Taylor (Ed.), *Parent-infant relationships*. New York: Grune & Stratton, 1980.

Osofsky, H. J., Osofsky, J. D., Kendall, N., & Rajan, R. Adolescents as mothers: An interdisciplinary approach to a complex problem. *Journal of Youth and Adolescence*, 1973, **2**, 233–249.

Osofsky, J. D., & Osofsky, H. J. Teenage pregnancy: Psychosocial considerations. *Clinical Obstetrics and Gynecology*, 1978, **21**, 1161–1174.

Osofsky, J. D., & Osofsky, H. J. *Final report on Healthy Start Program*. Prepared by Department of Social and Rehabilitation Services, State of Kansas, October 1981.

Parens, H. Parenthood as a developmental phase. *Journal of American Psychoanalytic Association*, 1975, **23**, 154–165.

Parke, R. D Perspectives on father-infant interaction. In J. D. Osofsky (Ed.), *Handbook of infant development*. New York: Wiley, 1979.

Parke, R. D., & Tinsley, B. R. The early environment of the high-risk infant: Expanding the social context. In D. Bricker (Ed.), *Application of research findings to intervention with at-risk and handicapped infants*. Baltimore: University Park Press, 1982.

Pohlman, E. *Psychology of birth planning*. Cambridge, Mass.: Schenkman, 1969.

Porges, S. W. Developmental designs for infancy research. In J. D. Osofsky (Ed.), *Handbook of infant development*. New York: Wiley, 1979.

Rainwater, L. *Behind ghetto walls*. Chicago: Aldine, 1970.

Ricciuti, H. N. Interaction of multiple factors contributing to high-risk parenting. In V. J. Sasserath (Ed.), *Minimizing high-risk parenting*. Skillman, N.J.: Johnson & Johnson, 1983.

Richards, M. P. Social interaction in the first weeks of human life. *Psychiatria Neurologia Nuerochirurgia*, 1971, **74**, 35–42.

Richards, M. P. Effects on development of medical interventions and the separation of newborns from parents. In D. Shaffer & S. Dunn (Eds.), *The first year of life*. New York: Wiley, 1979.

Ross, J. M. The development of paternal identity: A critical review of the literature of nurturance and generativity in boys and men. *Journal of the American Psychoanalytic Association*, 1975, **23**, 783–817.

Ross, J. M. Towards fatherhood: The epigeneses of paternal identity during a boy's first decade. *International Review of Psychoanalysis*, 1977, **4**, 327–349.

Ross, J. M. Fathering: A review of some psychoanalytic contributions on paternity. *International Journal of Psychoanalysis*, 1979, **60**, 317–327.

Rossi, A. S. Transition to parenthood. *Journal of Marriage and the Family*, 1968, **30**, 26–39.

Sackett, G. P. The lag sequential analysis of contingency and cyclicity in behavioral interaction research. In J. D. Osofsky (Ed.), *Handbook of infant development*. New York: Wiley, 1979.

Sander, L. W. Adaptive relationships in early mother-child interaction. *Journal of American Academy of Child Psychiatry*, 1964, **3**, 231–264.

Sander, L. W. The longitudinal course of early mother-child interaction. In B. M. Foss (Ed.), *Determinants of infant behavior* (Vol. 3). London: Methuen, 1965.

Sander, L. W. Regulation and organization in the early infant-caretaker system. In R. Robinson (Ed.), *The brain and early behavior*. London: Academic Press, 1970.

Sawhill, I., Peabody, G., Jones, C., & Caldwell, S. *Income transfers and family structure*. Washington, D.C.: Urban Institute, 1975.

Shereshefsky, P. M., & Yarrow, L. J. *Psychological aspects of a first pregnancy and early postnatal adaptation*. New York: Raven Press, 1973.

Sroufe, L. A. Socioemotional development. In J. D. Osofsky (Ed.), *Handbook of infant development*. New York: Wiley, 1979.

Stack, C. *All our kin*. Chicago: Aldine, 1974.

Svedja, M. J., Pannabecker, B. J., & Emde, R. N. *Parent-to-infant attachment*. Unpublished manuscript, 1981.

Vincent, J. P., Harris, G. E., Cook, N. I., & Brady, C. P. *Couples become parents: A behavioral systems analysis of family development*. Paper presented at the biennial meeting of the Society for Research in Child Development, San Francisco, 1979.

Wainwright, W. H. Fatherhood as a precipitant of mental illness. *American Journal of Psychiatry*, 1966, **123**, 40–44.

Weigert, E. V., Wenner, N. K., Cohen, M. B., Fearing, J. M., Kvarnes, R. G., & Ohaneson, E. M. *Emotional aspects of pregnancy*. Final Report of Washington School of Psychiatry Project: Clinical Study of the Emotional Challenge of Pregnancy, 1968.

Wenner, N. K., Cohen, M. B., Weigert, E. V., Kvarnes, R. G., Ohaneson, E. M., & Fearing, J. M. Emotional problems in pregnancy. *Psychiatry*, 1969, **32**, 389–410.

Wente, A. S., & Crockenberg, S. Transition to fatherhood: Lamaze preparation, adjustment difficulty and the husband-wife relationship. *Family Coordinator*, 1976, **25**, 351–358.

Winnicott, D. W. *The maturational processes and the facilitating environment*. New York: International Universities Press, 1965.

Zelnik, M., & Kantner, J. Sexual activity, contraceptive use and pregnancy among metropolitan-area teenagers: 1971–1979. *Family Planning Perspectives*, 1980, **12**, 230–231, 233–237.

11   Families in Transition:
The Processes of Dissolution
and Reconstitution

E. MAVIS HETHERINGTON
University of Virginia

KATHLEEN A. CAMARA
Tufts University

INTRODUCTION

Divorce, life in a one-parent family, and remarriage are becoming increasingly common experiences in the lives of parents and children. Past psychological and sociological research on divorce has focused on the effects of changes within family structure on the intellectual, social, and psychological functioning of children and adults. A sizable body of literature now exists on the outcomes of divorce for family members. However, until recent years, little attention has been paid to the process of transition represented by separation, divorce, life in a one-parent family, and remarriage or to the factors that may lead to reduced or increased risk of disturbance for children and adults. Families experiencing divorce are faced with a number of changes including the diminution of financial resources, changes in residence, assumption of new roles and responsibilities, establishment of new patterns of intrafamilial interaction, reorganization of routines and schedules, and eventually the introduction of new relationships into the existing family. The nature of these changes demands resources that generally extend beyond those possessed by individual family members. It is our intent in this chapter to examine the nature of divorce and subsequent transitions in family life that accompany the structural changes in the family.

Due to the large body of literature on the subject of divorce, we have been selective in our coverage of the topic. Our discussion is restricted to issues related to the process of divorce and remarriage and to the types of resources available to assist families in transition. The reader may refer to several available comprehensive reviews of the literature on the effects of divorce (see Bloom, Asher, & White, 1978; Camara, Baker, & Dayton, 1980; Hetherington, 1981; Hetherington, Camara, & Featherman, 1982a; Kitson & Raschke, 1981; Shinn, 1978).

Demographic Patterns of Divorce and Remarriage in the United States

Statistics contained in population reports from the vital statistics data published by the National Center for Health Statistics, from survey data from the U.S. Bureau of the Census (1980, 1981, 1983) and from the recent Report of the Select Committee on Children, Family, and Youth (1983) challenge the facade of stability in American family life. The increase in the number of young adults who are postponing marriage, the overall rise in marital dissolution through divorce, and the substantial increase in the number of one-parent households represent major departures from the traditional nuclear family form.

Between 1970 and 1982, the ratio of all divorced persons per 1,000 to husbands and wives in intact marriages rose by 114%, from 47 per 1,000 to 109 per 1,000. Demographers estimate that if current rates hold for the next 10–20 years, approximately half of the marriages begun in the mid-1970s will end in divorce (Cherlin, 1981). The rising incidence of divorce appears to be a major factor in the growth of single-parent households. The number of divorced men and divorced women maintaining families doubled between 1970 and 1982 (Report of Select Committee on Children, Youth, and Families, 1983). Consequently, more adults are now single parents who live with their children or who live apart from their children in some form of household other than the conventional married two-parent family.

Changes in the family lives of children in the past 12 years have been dramatic. In 1970, 85% of children under the age of 18 lived in two-parent families; by 1982 that figure had dropped to 75%. In the same period, the percentage of children living in a one-parent household had almost doubled, going from 12% to 22%. Thus one in every five children in the United States under the age of 18 years lives with only one parent. Although this increase to some extent is attributable to the rise in births to unwed mothers, the main cause is separation and divorce. In 1970 9% of children lived with separated or divorced mothers and 1% with fathers only; by 1982, the equivalent figures were about 14% with mothers and 2% with fathers. Although the change in births to never-married mothers has been great, shifting from 0.8% in 1970 to 4.4% in 1982, this still represents a small proportion of the children living in one-parent households. It is estimated that 1.2 million children each year experience the divorce or separation of parents.

An increase in the rate of separation and divorce, as well as the delay of marriage, occurred during the 1970s among both black and white adults. In 1982, one-half of the black families with children present were one-parent families. At the same time, 17% of white families with children were one-parent households. Although a larger proportion of black children live in one-parent families compared to the proportion of all children living in one-parent families, the rate of increase in this proportion has been less rapid since 1970 among black children than children of other races (Glick, 1980). It should be noted that the majority (two-thirds) of all one-parent households in the United States are maintained by white mothers or fathers. Black children under 18 years constitute 35% of all children living with one parent.

Although the incidence of divorce among black couples has increased over the past 10 years, there are some dissimilarities in the marital status of black and white adults that deserve mention. Cherlin (1981) notes that black married couples have a greater probability of separating than do white couples, and blacks who are separated remain separated for longer periods of time than do whites before obtaining a divorce. Consequently, the proportion of separated but not divorced persons is greater for blacks than for other races (Cherlin, 1981). This difference may be the result of the many "never married" black mothers reporting themselves as "separated" (Cherlin, 1981; Glick, 1980).

The most recent information from census bureau surveys indicates an increase in the rate of remarriage among divorced adults. Approximately five out of every six men and three out of every four women remarry after a divorce. About half of those who remarry generally do so within 3 years of their divorce (Cherlin, 1981). A slight decline in the remarriage rate during the late 1970s may be explained by the tendency for divorced adults to enter into living-together arrangements (Glick & Spanier, 1980). The proportion of divorced persons who remarry appears to be higher among whites than among blacks, and blacks who do remarry tend to delay remarriage longer than their white counterparts (Glick, 1980; Spanier & Glick, 1980b).

The increases in the percentage of divorces that involve children have resulted in an increase in the number of remarriages among adults with children. In 1978, 6.5 million children under 18 were living with a biological parent and a stepparent. By 1990, it is estimated that approximately 7 million children, or 11% of all children under 18 years, will experience the remarriage of at least one parent (Glick, 1980). Such remarriages represent the reorganization of families into what is commonly called a reconstituted family with children of one or both parents merged into the new family structure. Many of these children will experience a third major change in their family lives following parental divorce and remarriage, the termination of their parents' second marriage. According to estimates by the National Center for Health Statistics, about 40% of remarriages can be expected to end in divorce within a 10-year period (Cherlin, 1981).

The rise in marital dissolution and remarriage means that a large proportion of American's children will spend part of their childhood living with a single parent or with a biological parent and a stepparent. The profiles of the American family are changing because of the increased incidence of divorce and remarriage. Although these emergent family forms may eventually be normative, they are nonetheless problematic and present intricate interplays between the dynamics of marriage and parenthood.

METHODOLOGICAL PROBLEMS IN THE STUDY OF FAMILY TRANSITIONS

Efforts to develop a base of empirical knowledge of family transitions and reorganizations have been limited severely by the lack of sophisticated methods to describe the complex processes of family life. Much of the research on family life after divorce has focused on "outcomes" derived from comparisons of diverse structural forms of the family with the conventional two-parent households. Little attention has been paid to the variations in life experiences, individual, or cultural factors, or to the dynamic process of change that divorce entails.

Methodological problems of research in this area have been identified in previous reviews of the parental separation literature (Camara, Baker, & Dayton, 1980; Herzog & Sudia, 1973; Hetherington et al., 1982a; Shinn, 1978). Primary among the problems are the lack of appropriate comparison groups and the failure to identify whether one-parent status is due to death, divorce, or separation. Factors such as the age, sex, and developmental status of the child and the parents at the onset of separation, as well as the length of separation or presence of other significant adults, are not specified in many studies of the effects of parental separation. Although socioeconomic status, race, and parental education are known correlates of parental behaviors and styles of family interaction, much of the research on divorce fails to control or account for the variance associated with social and cultural factors. Frequently, the effects of parental separation are confounded with lower-income status of the family, so that it is difficult to determine whether adverse effects are due to divorce, living in a household with one adult, or the diminution of financial resources. In addition, the sex of parent is almost invariably confounded with custodial status of the parent since most studies are run on mother-custody families, which are the ones most readily available for research.

Sampling procedures used in research designs pose additional problems in interpreting and generalizing results from studies. Survey researchers have shown great concern with obtaining large representative samples but little with establishing the validity or reliability of their measures. There seems to be an assumption in much of the survey and interview work on divorce that people do what they say they do. In contrast, many psychologists tend to devote great effort to developing reliable and valid techniques but use small, often highly selected samples of convenience. Samples drawn from unrepresentative populations such as clinical populations, or from different historical periods, or on the basis of duration of living in a one-parent household are subject to tendencies to distort and misrepresent the social demographic character of divorce. Cohort problems must be considered as attitudes toward divorce, reasons for living in a one-parent home, the characteristics of adults and children who encounter this form of family life, and the supports available to them have changed.

Much confusion and inconsistency in empirical reports of the effects of divorce on children and parents have come from a view of divorce as a single event rather than as a transition that involves a range of experiences in the lives of family members that extend over time. There is great variability in the responses of adults and children to divorce and to the new forms of family life they encounter. These variations need to be examined in relation to other conditions within the family, for example, changes in economic status, alterations in the relationships between parents and children, and availability of familial and extrafamilial support services for parents and children.

The major shortcoming of recent research on divorce and postdivorce family life is the absence of an interpretive framework for the large body of data that has accumulated. The use of a phenomenological approach in gathering life experience information from participants in the research process has provided valuable descriptive data on family life during and after divorce, but this approach remains basically atheoretical in its view of families and divorce.

THEORIES OF FAMILY FUNCTIONING

The diverse and complex family forms which have emerged in this country in the last decade render previous theories and research inadequate to describe contemporary American family life. In situations where parents live apart from their children, where marital bonds are severed but parental bonds remain linked through the shared children of previous marriages, and where the responsibilities for rearing children are left primarily to one parent, there are few, if any, guidelines for family functioning.

Such theories of family life as those of Talcott Parsons and other sociologists of the 1940s and 1950s described a set of "universals" or common goals for the family based on philosophical views about human nature and society. Parsons and Bales's (1955) structural-functional model of family functioning required a division of sex-linked parental roles with the father as instrumental leader and the mother as the expressive caregiver. These perspectives on family structure, roles, and the processes of socialization no longer adequately undergird current conditions of family life where one adult has the responsibility for the daily care of children. Hence, in the past 30 years, there has been a shift in theoretical perspectives on the study of families. Grand-scale theories that attempted to explain the interrelations among family and society and individual family members have been replaced by empirically based approaches that describe smaller sets of phenomena within families, such as the loss of a parent through death or divorce. Researchers using this line of inquiry have sought to describe the family as it actually functions in everyday life and to derive theory inductively from empirical data.

Where existing psychological theories are incorporated into explanations of the phenomenon of divorce, they frequently lack a comprehensive or consolidated view of the complex family system or may be inappropriately applied to the problems of divorce and one-parent child rearing. For example, research on "father absence," based on a psychoanalytic perspective, was directed primarily toward the study of influence of not having a father present on an individual's personality development. This perspective failed to note the modifying effects of a mother or significant others and the important role of changes in family process associated with divorce. Attachment theorists have been similarly narrow in viewing divorce as a loss of the primary attachment figure—father or mother, husband or wife—and have been less concerned with the emergence of new attachment bonds or with the increased salience of remaining attachment figures or with changes in family process that preceded or accompanied divorce.

Socialization theories, when applied to postdivorce family life, have focused on the effective management of children through the establishment of appropriate discipline practices, role models, and expectations for children's behaviors. This theoretical framework places little emphasis on the emotional context for family functioning and on ecological factors that may affect the family in transition. Kurdek (1981) made a significant advance beyond these earlier conceptualizations of divorce when he proposed an ecological model of divorce that viewed the divorced family in its relation to larger social and cultural contexts in which it is embedded.

While each of these theoretical perspectives may be useful in describing important elements of the divorce and family transition process, they do not adequately describe the interrelationship of these components and the dynamic conditions of family life that are specific to separation and divorce. Theories of parental loss through death and the stages of the grieving process when applied to the experiences of those undergoing separation and divorce are similarly flawed in their failure to differentiate between the conditions of permanent loss of a parent or spouse and the temporary loss or change in the form of a relationship, in the voluntary nature of divorce, in the high level of conflict that usually precedes and accompanies a divorce but not a death in the family, and in the greater availability of support following the death of a spouse.

The need for a dynamic theory of family life that describes the complexity and variation existing in responses to divorce has led to the application of family systems theories derived from clinical models of family functioning. Interactionist and structuralist approaches, such as those described by Burgess (1926), Minuchin (1974), Stryker (1972), and Turner (1970), focus on the interactional behaviors and communication processes of families. The developmental or family-life-cycle approach, such as that proposed by Aldous (1978), Duvall (1977), and Hill and Rogers (1964), focuses on the various stages of family life and the processes of transition accompanying entry and exit from each stage. Behavioral approaches, developed by Liberman (1970), Patterson, Reid, Jones, and Conger (1975), and Weiss (1978), emphasize interactional behavior and the adaptiveness of families in achieving functional relationships. The emphasis of these models on the complexity and dynamic nature of family interaction is useful in describing the phenomena of separation, divorce, or remarriage.

The most influential framework for theory construction stemming from interactional systems and developmental orientations is the stress and coping model first formulated by Hill (1949) and later extended by a number of other investigators (Hultsch & Plemons, 1979; Lazarus, 1981; McCubbin & Patterson, 1981). This approach focuses on the process of change occurring during periods of crisis within the family life cycle. A crisis event is defined as the time when an individual or family is faced with a problem which cannot be solved quickly by means of the normal range of problem-solving mechanisms (Caplan, 1976). Hill's crisis model consists of a two-part framework for understanding a family's experience with a crisis. During the first stage, an event occurs which interacts with a family's available resources for meeting the demands of the event and with the definition the family holds of the event. This interaction produces a state of crisis. The second stage of the model describes the process of family adjustment which involves a period of disorganization, recovery, and eventual reorganization of the family system (Hetherington, Cox, & Cox, 1982b; Walsh, 1982).

The stress and coping model is used to describe the normal course of family life during which various stressors may be present. The adaptation to stress is dependent on the nature, timing, duration, and perception of stress and on the availability of appropriate personal, family, and extrafamilial resources. The application of this model to the process of family transitions has several advantages. First, it offers a dynamic framework for the study of family functioning in a society where change is constant and where traditional forms of family life are rapidly changing. Second, there is practical utility in the stress and coping model in its focus on the adaptive process. Within this approach, attempts are made to uncover the strategies, responses, and functional behaviors that lead to early and stable adjustment. Finally, the model is consistent with contemporary phenomenological approaches to research on family life in that stress is defined by individuals experiencing a crisis event. The occurrence of stressors may lead to positive or negative consequences depending on the life stage of the individual, the surrounding conditions of family life, and the family members' perceptions of the life event.

Although the consequences of stress can emerge in many areas, there are now solid empirical grounds for asserting that divorce contributes substantially to the development of numerous types of bodily, mental, and behavioral malfunctioning. However, both clinicians and researchers have commented on the great variety of responses to these stresses. Some individuals are able to adjust with relative ease to the life changes associated with marital disruption and emerge functioning competently or even enhanced following divorce. Other individuals suffer prolonged negative psychological, social, and economic sequelae from divorce from which they may never fully recover (Bloom et al., 1978; Hetherington et al., 1982b; Kitson & Raschke, 1981; Kurdek, 1981; Wallerstein & Kelly, 1980; Weiss, 1975).

A modified version of the models of family stress and systems theory may be useful in trying to explain the diversity of outcomes following divorce. The adaptation to divorce is based on an interaction between past and present life hardships and stressful life experiences, the perception of the situation, and the personal, familial, and extrafamilial resources available to deal with the stressful concomitants of divorce. These will vary with the social and cultural ecology in which the family is embedded, with the life stage of the family members, and with the historical cohort to which the family belongs. The interplay among these factors and their impact change over time and vary for different family members.

STRESS AND COPING MODEL APPLIED TO DIVORCE

Divorce is best conceptualized as a series of transitional life experiences rather than a single discrete event. Therefore, the observed or reported impact of divorce on family members will vary with the point in the transition process at which the family is studied. In the period of separation and divorce stresses associated with conflict, loss, change, uncertainty, and restructuring may be the critical stressful factors. This period is characterized by a transition from family disorganization through a period of testing a variety of coping behaviors, some successful and some unsuccessful, to a new stage of family reorganization and equilibrium. If this crisis is not compounded by multiple stresses and continued hardships, most family members adapt to the divorce and their new life situation within a few years (Hetherington et al., 1982; Weiss, 1975). The longer-term adjustment is related to more sustained or concurrent conditions associated with life in a one-parent household, usually headed by a mother. These conditions may involve altered economic resources, sustained alterations in parent-child relationships, changing personal support systems, and changed relationships in friendship networks, neighborhood, school, or workplace. It should be noted that deleterious transactional effects are often associated with divorce where divorce increases the probability of other associated stressful events occurring. For example, divorce may result in economic duress for the custodial mother which may lead not only to shifts in residence to poorer housing and less desirable neighborhoods, but also may result in forced maternal employment and unavailability of the mother. Because of such adverse transactional effects, members of divorced families are at higher risk for the development of psychological problems than those in nondivorced families (Bloom et al., 1978; Hetherington, 1981).

After coping with the stress and changes accompanying separation, divorce, and life in a one-parent family, finally for most families, a stage of remarriage occurs that leads to the need to adapt to yet another restructuring of the family and set of tasks for the family to solve. It has been suggested that the chance of appreciable sustained negative outcomes from a single stress such as divorce is minimal (Hodges, Wechsler, & Ballantine, 1971; McCubbin & Patterson, 1981; Rutter, 1979a); however, when a series of stressful life events accompanies divorce this cumulative stress is more likely to have adverse sequelae.

PERCEPTIONS AND EXPECTATIONS

The pattern of relationships among stresses associated with divorce and factors that modify their outcomes over time is not well understood. Although the interweaving of hardship and stressors may follow divorce, the effects vary with the individuals' interpretation of the events and the existence and utilization of available resources.

Since divorce usually involves intense emotion, acrimony, and change, it is not surprising that the perception of divorce and expectations about life experiences associated with marital dissolution vary across families and even among members of the same family. When husbands and wives describe their marriage or divorce, it is often difficult to recognize that the same relationship is involved (Barnard, 1972; Chiriboga & Cutler, 1977; Hetherington, et al., 1982b; Levinger, 1966; Scanzoni, 1968; Weiss, 1975). Women are more likely to express long-term dissatisfactions with their marriages. They focus on infidelity or lack of communication, affection, and common interests or shared activities as the precipitating events for the divorce. Men are most likely to name in-law or sexual problems. Weiss (1975) calls these descriptions of the marital breakdown "accounts." Variations in accounts are associated with such things as social class, sex, race, age, and personality. Accounts are modified, developed, and elaborated on over time. It has been proposed that the altered perceptions and social meanings attached to the divorce process may help the family make the experience seem more rational and suggest ways to overcome the stressful situation (Gehrhardt, 1979; Venters, 1979). However, it seems likely that if perceptions among family members are too divergent or are too far removed from reality, family problem solving will be hindered rather than facilitated (Gottman, 1979). Discrepancies in family accounts are related to ongoing conflict. There has been no study directed at elucidating the psychological processes such as attribution and dissonance reduction that might modify variations in accounts.

Just as there are variations in the perception of divorce, there are great differences in expectations about life following marital disruption. These expectations about such things as anticipated poverty, loneliness, independence, or opportunities for self-actualization may be as important as the actual changes that occur in adjusting to family stress and divorce (Boss, 1977; Howard, 1974; McCubbin & Patterson, 1981).

It may be varying appraisals of divorce that explain the finding that the response to divorce is related both to the locus of control and to the developmental status or life stage of the individual. Individuals who feel internally controlled appraise their situation differently and are more likely to use effective active problem-solving strategies than are externally controlled individuals. In addition, older adults, especially those over fifty, are more likely to perceive the future with greater pessimism, as having fewer possible positive options, and to report greater unhappiness and personal discomfort than do younger divorcing persons (Chiriboga, 1982; Lazarus & DeLongis, 1983). The perception of events as being out of phase, as occurring at an inappropriate time of life, may also contribute to the greater distress of the elderly in response to the divorce (Hultsch & Plemons, 1979).

PERSONAL, FAMILY, AND EXTRAFAMILIAL RESOURCES

Finally, the response to divorce will be modified by the resources available for stress management. These include personal resources such as financial, educational, health, and psychological resources (George, 1980); family resources such as cohesion, adaptability, communication, and problem-solving skills (Burr, 1973; McCubbin, Joy, Cauble, Comeau, Patterson, & Needle, 1980; Olson, Sprenkle, & Russell, 1979); and social supports (Hess & Camara, 1979; Hetherington et al., 1982b; Kitson & Raschke, 1981) such as neighbor, kin, and friendship networks and self-help groups. Although these resources have been examined in family stress studies they have not all been systematically studied in relation to coping with divorce.

INDIVIDUAL OR FAMILY RESPONSE TO DIVORCE

Most of the psychological and sociological literature has focused on the stress and coping of individuals in response to divorce. However, some of the family systems research has dealt with the impact of stressful life events on the total family rather than on the individuals within the family (Burr, 1973; Hansen & Johnson, 1979; Hill, 1958; McCubbin & Patterson, 1982). It seems that some combination of the two conceptual levels of stress and coping in divorce is necessary. A focus on individual adjustment or dyadic relationships may yield a different picture than is found with a view of the family system as the unit for analysis (Reiss, 1981). It is possible for intrafamily functioning to be adequate when intraindividual functioning is unsatisfying. Similarly, there can be vast discrepancies between the rates and adequacy of adjustment of individual family members. In some cases one family member's mode of coping may be destructive to the adaptation of another. Divorced parents may neglect a child in their egocentric pursuit of self-gratification. Distressed children may reject a parent and form a hostile alliance with the other parent or escape into the peer group in order to resolve their own problems.

In summary, the stress and coping model is useful in understanding the various ways in which individuals and families adapt to the changing circumstances that accompany divorce and remarriage. Next we examine some of the factors that mediate the effects of divorce.

Factors Mediating the Effects of Divorce

Although we are still at a preliminary stage in our understanding of the nature of divorce and separation, recent studies have provided empirical evidence for the identification of several elements of family interaction accompanying the divorce and postdivorce process which are related to family functioning. The amount of conflict that persists among family members, the loss or unavailability of one parent, changes in the relationship between parents and children, and changing responsibilities and roles of family members are some of the most salient changes in family relationships that influence the outcome of divorce.

CONFLICT

There are few divorces that are not preceded and accompanied by conflict and acrimony, and in many cases conflict is continued or escalated following separation and divorce (Hess & Camara, 1979; Hetherington et al., 1982b; Wallerstein & Kelly, 1980). Many parents report that contacts with the legal system tend to intensify family problems as the divorcing couple attempts to settle issues of custody, visitation, and divorce. Both conflict between spouses or ex-spouses and between parents and children can lead to the development of behavior disorders in children (Emery & O'Leary, 1982; Hess & Camara, 1979; Hetherington et al., 1982b; McDermott, 1968, 1970; Rutter, 1979a, 1979b; Wallerstein & Kelly, 1980; Westman, Cline, Swift, & Kramer, 1970). Interparental conflict to which the child has not been directly exposed does not appear to be associated with psychopathology in children (Hetherington et al., 1982b; Porter & O'Leary, 1980; Rutter, Yule, Quinton, Rowland, Yule, & Berger, 1974).

The relationship between family conflict and behavior disorders is closer and more consistently found for boys than for girls (Block, Block, & Morrison, 1981; Cadoret & Cain, 1980; Emery & O'Leary, 1982; Hess & Camara, 1979; Hetherington et al., 1979; Porter & O'Leary, 1980; Rutter, 1971; Wolkind & Rutter, 1973). When family conflict occurs, boys are more often exposed to parental battles and disagreements and get less support than girls (Hetherington et al., 1982b). Boys are more likely to respond to stressful situations with undercontrol and girls with overcontrol (Emery, 1982). There also is a suggestion that males interpret family disagreements less favorably than do females (Epstein, Finnegan, & Gythell, 1979).

Although conflict has harmful effects in both one- and two-parent households, the effects of conflict are more deleterious in divorced families than in nondivorced families. This seems to be attributable to the protective buffering effect that a very good relationship with either parent can play in attenuating the effects of disharmony in a two-parent household, whereas only an exceptionally good relationship with the custodial parent can serve this function in a divorced family. The noncustodial parent who is not available to mediate in day-to-day altercations is not an effective buffer, although highly available noncustodial parents have more impact than those who are less available (Hess & Camara, 1979; Hetherington, Cox, & Cox, 1979). It should be noted that the cluster of stressful events associated with divorce may initially result in more disrupted functioning in divorced families than in conflict-ridden nondivorced families, however, in the long run if children go into a stable one-parent household the escape from conflict is likely to enhance their adjustment (Hess & Camara, 1979; Hetherington et al., 1982b; Wallerstein & Kelly, 1980).

There is support for the position that it is in part the conflict associated with divorce rather than the loss and separation that leads to conduct disorders, since death of a parent is less likely to lead to such behavior problems (Douglas, Ross, Hammond, & Mulligan, 1966; Gibson, 1969; Gregory, 1965).

ATTACHMENT, SEPARATION, AND LOSS

Many theorists view issues of attachment and loss as being central in the divorce process (Bowlby, 1973; Goldstein, Freud, & Solnit, 1973; Weiss, 1975). These factors play an important role for both the divorcing adults and their children.

Attachment between divorced spouses.—The bonds of attachment are lingering. The period immediately following divorce often is characterized by ambivalence—anger, distrust, and animosity accompanied by preoccupation, concern, and often jealousy of the other person (Hetherington et al., 1982b; Kitson, 1982; Weiss, 1975). Even people who desired or initiated the divorce may be astonished and distressed to have such feelings continue (Hetherington et al., 1982b). Spanier and Castro (1979a, 1979b) report that only one-quarter of their respondents felt no continuing bonds of attachment following divorce. The formation of a new intimate relationship and remarriage seem to be the most powerful factors in terminating these bonds. However, the remarriage of an ex-spouse will often reactivate feelings of betrayal, violated dependency needs, remorse, and anger very similar to those experienced at the time of divorce, even in divorced partners who have remarried first (Hetherington et al., 1982b). It has been proposed that the irrational and maladaptive acrimony and controversy that accompany divorce may be a means for maintaining emotional involvement. Indifference and disengagement often are harder to accept from a previously intimate partner than anger. The provocative disagreements may be a way of keeping intense emotion, albeit negative emotion, alive as a form of continued involvement (Hetherington et al., 1982b). The emotional divorce may follow long after the legal divorce. It is difficult to separate responses to loss of attachment from apprehension about change. Partners may be dependent on each other without having positive feelings toward each other.

Widely fluctuating mood changes from ebullience to depression immediately following divorce may give way to negative affect as divorced persons replace unrealistically optimistic expectations about life after divorce with the realities of attaining those expectations. Positive affect begins to predominate later as new relations are formed and family members adapt to their new situation. Although immediately following divorce the person who initiated the divorce appears to be less disturbed, one year later this difference is not found (Hetherington et al., 1982b; Weiss, 1979a).

Continued attachment to the former spouse is associated with high levels of distress and problems in developing independence and role redefinition (Brown, Felton, Whiteman, & Manela, in press; Hynes, 1979; Kitson & Sussman, 1978; Marroni, 1977; Weiss, 1975). On the basis of the currently available research, it is impossible to determine the causal direction in this relationship.

Parent-child attachment and loss.—One of the important things to keep in mind about the decision to divorce is that it is a decision made by parents and not by children, and it is usually viewed as a solution to the problems of parents and not those of children. Children more often perceive divorce as a cause than as a resolution of their difficulties (Hetherington et al., 1982b; Wallerstein & Kelly, 1980), and most children respond negatively to the separation and loss of a parent involved in divorce. Although the specific response to divorce varies with the developmental status of the child, common immediate responses at all ages are anger, anxiety, depression, dependency, yearning for the lost parent, and fantasies of reconciliation.

Laws regarding custody have changed recently, and few states have laws that advocate the preferential status of mothers as custodial parents. However, judges still are more likely to award custody to mothers than to fathers (Lindeman, 1977; Minuchin, 1974; Pearson, Munson, & Thoennes, 1982; Weitzman & Dixon, 1979). The new sex-neutral custody laws have tended to increase custody disputes and the number of fathers requesting custody with little increase in the number of fathers gaining sole custody and very modest increases in the number of fathers gaining joint, shared, or split custody (Emery, Hetherington, & Fisher, 1984; Lindeman, 1977; Pearson, Munson, & Thoennes, 1982; Weitzman & Dixon, 1979). It has been reported that fathers with joint custody are more likely than those only with visitation rights to remain involved with their children (Greif, 1979). However, since fathers who desire or fight for joint custody may be more involved with their children before the divorce, it is difficult to interpret this finding.

The absence of a father in the household usually means less social, emotional, and financial support, and less help for the mother in decision making, child rearing, and household tasks. However, in marriages where the father has been distant, uninvolved, and nonsupportive, there may be little to lose and much to gain from opportunities for new relationships, self-sufficiency, and relief from conflict. For children, the absence of a father may mean the loss of emotional support, an effective role model, agent of socialization, trainer of skills, disciplinarian, and buffering agent. Considerable research evidence has accumulated that fathers respond differently to their children than do mothers and that fathers may play a unique role in the socialization of children. In addition, children respond in a different way to fathers than to mothers. This is particularly apparent in the area of discipline and compliance where children tend to be less disruptive and more obedient with fathers than with mothers (Hetherington et al., 1982b).

Furstenberg recently has reported that by 2 years after divorce many children see their noncustodial fathers rarely or not at all (Furstenberg, 1982). Thus for many children divorce means true loss of the noncustodial parent accompanied by increased salience of the custodial parent. Conflicts about visitation, remarriage, the birth of new children in a remarriage, and geographical distance all contribute to diminished contact between noncustodial parents and their children. An important finding is that fathers' postdivorce relationships cannot be predicted from their predivorce relationships with their children. Many previously intensely attached fathers cannot tolerate part-time parenting and become disengaged, other fathers who had little predivorce contact with their children become active, competent parents.

The experience of visitation is often stressful for both parents and children. The intense scheduled contact and the desire to entertain the child, to be what Weiss has called a "tour guide father," is an abnormal way for parents and children to interact. In addition, Wallerstein has reported that the "datelike" quality of visitation may make fathers and daughters apprehensive about their encounters. As children become older and would normally become increasingly involved with peers, they may begin to view enforced visits with their fathers as a burden and an interference with their social lives.

Fathers are more likely to maintain contact with sons than with daughters (Hess & Camara, 1979) and the visits are longer between fathers and sons than between fathers and daughters (Hess & Camara, 1979; Hetherington et al., 1982b). In addition, as sons grow older, mothers are more likely to yield them to the care of their fathers, especially if the father has remarried and the mother has not, or if the son is difficult to handle (Furstenberg, Spanier, & Rothschild, 1982; Hetherington et al., 1982b). There is some indication that continued contact with fathers may be more important in the adjustment of sons than daughters (Hetherington et al., 1982b; Santrock & Warshak, 1979). Santrock and Warshak (1979) report that elementary school-aged children adjust better in the custody of the same-sexed parent. The samples in this study are small, and the study must be replicated before great weight is put on the findings. Camara (1982), in a preliminary report of findings of a study of early elementary school-aged children, found that a positive relationship with the same-sexed parent was associated with children's social competence with same-sexed peers. Although sustained contact with the father may not be as important in the development of self-control, sex typing, and cognition in girls as in boys, there is evidence that there may be a delayed effect on girls of lack of availability of a father that may emerge in the form of precocious sexual preoccupation and disruption in heterosexual relations in adolescence (Hetherington, 1972; Wallerstein & Kelly, 1980).

CHANGES IN PARENT-CHILD RELATIONS FOLLOWING DIVORCE

Changes in parent-child relations are associated with the emotional responses and adjustment of individual family members and with the redefinition of roles and responsibilities in the restructured family.

The altered parent.—In the period immediately following separation and divorce, the emotional disturbance experienced by family members often exacerbates children's and parents' distress. Children often encounter greatly altered parents; although the parents are physically the same, their behavior seems unfamiliar and unpredictable. In this period parents show wide mood swings from soaring euphoria as they contemplate the opportunities for a more gratifying, less conflictual life-style and crashing depressions as they confront the difficulties in attaining this goal. Robert Weiss has likened this emotional lability to riding on an elevator with only two buttons—penthouse and basement.

Other symptoms in adults that often accompany divorce include the inability to work effectively, poor health, weight changes, insomnia and sleep disturbances, sexual dysfunction, lethargy, and increased drinking, smoking, and drug use (Bloom et al., 1978; Goode, 1965; Hetherington et al., 1982b). Although continued contact with the noncustodial parent can have important positive effects on children and custodial mothers, the adjustment and emotional problems of the custodial parents are particularly important in determining the coping and adaptation of children in one-parent households following divorce. The important point is that children with a custodial parent who is ill, withdrawn, depressed, anxious, or dissatisfied are at increased risk of encountering parent-child relationships associated with adverse emotional outcomes. It should be kept in mind that both the parents and children are undergoing a stressful experience. The angry, preoccupied, and depressed parent may be unable to respond to the needs of the distressed child and the demands, anxiety, and rage of the child may exacerbate the tensions of the parent.

Parenting.—In the period surrounding separation and divorce, both parents express concern about their relations with their children and their competence as parents. This is marked in divorced mothers of sons, who report themselves to have more problems in child rearing and to be more helpless, stressed, incompetent, and depressed than do divorced mothers of daughters (Colletta, 1979; Hetherington et al., 1982b). However, in general, noncustodial parents, whether they are mothers or fathers, experience fewer stresses in day-to-day child rearing but feel more dissatisfied, deficient, powerless, and shut out in their relations with their children (Furstenberg et al., 1982; Hetherington et al., 1982b).

In the period accompanying divorce there is often what has been called a diminished capacity to parent (Wallerstein & Kelly, 1980), a breakdown in parent behaviors, followed by improvement in child-rearing practices in the second year after divorce. During the first year following divorce both parents communicate less well with their children, are more erratic in enforcing discipline, are less affectionate, and make fewer maturity demands (Hetherington et al., 1982b).

Immediately following divorce, noncustodial fathers may actually spend more time with their children than they did before the divorce, but this contact rapidly diminishes (Furstenberg et al., 1982; Hetherington et al., 1982b). Fathers become more indulgent and permissive and less available following divorce (Hetherington et al., 1982b), however, divorced fathers have less difficulty controlling their children and gaining compliance than do divorced mothers.

Both divorced and remarried mothers experience more difficulty in their role as parents than do nondivorced mothers (Furstenberg et al., 1982; Hetherington et al., 1982b; Zill, 1983). Custodial mothers of young children usually tend to increase their use of power assertive, restrictive, and negative sanctions (Burgess, 1978; Colletta, 1979; Hetherington et al., 1982b; Kriesberg, 1970; Phelps, 1969). They are inconsistently and ineffectually authoritarian, particularly in their relations with sons. Custodial mothers and sons often get involved in escalating reciprocal cycles of coercive behavior. Divorced mothers in comparison to nondivorced mothers seem more often to instigate aggression and noncompliance in sons and to have more difficulty terminating their sons' coercive behavior once it has begun (Hetherington et al., 1982b; Patterson, 1982).

In both one- and two-parent families high stress accompanied by dissatisfaction with support systems is associated with more restrictive and harsher parent-child relationships (Colletta, 1979). The combination of poor control and infantilization of young children by divorced mothers may be more common for mothers of younger than older children (Wallerstein & Kelly, 1979; Weiss, 1975) and in middle than lower socioeconomic status one-parent families (Colletta, 1979).

In one-parent families older children may assume more power and responsibility in the family and participate more actively in decision-making processes (Fulton, 1979; Kurdek & Siesky, 1979; Weiss, 1979a, 1979b). Eldest children in particular are likely to find themselves assuming increased responsibility for child care (Zill, 1983). Although the household tasks and chores assigned may not differ in one- and two-parent homes, children in one-parent households tend to perceive themselves as having greater responsibilities than do their peers from two-parent households. The presence of a second adult in the home may alter the context of children's participation so that children in two-parent households perceive their chores as "helpful," while children in one-parent households perceive their assistance as "necessary" for family functioning (Camara, 1980).

Weiss (1979b) has argued that this increased power and responsibility may be associated with self-sufficiency in children and egalitarian, friendly, companionate relationships between divorced parents and their adolescent children. Children become junior partners in the family. However, the push toward the assumption of adult roles and responsibilities, toward what Weiss (1979b) has called "growing up faster," in some school-aged and adolescent children is also associated with resentment, feelings of helplessness, precocious sexuality, and withdrawal from the family (Kelly, 1978; Wallerstein, 1978; Wallerstein & Kelly, 1980).

Custodial parents, in attempting to deal with task overload, may assign too many, or too difficult, or age-inappropriate tasks to their children. In addition, parents in their distress may expect children to act as an emotional support or fill some of the roles of the divorced spouse. This may involve inappropriate self-disclosure by the parents which escalates the anxiety of the child. Role reversals where children are offering support to parents are common. Thus, relief for a disturbed or overburdened parent may result in an overburdened or emotionally enmeshed child. If the child is unwilling or unable to respond to the needs of the parent, the child may feel overwhelmed, incompetent, guilty, and resentful.

PARENT-CHILD RELATIONS AND THE ADJUSTMENT OF CHILDREN

In the period immediately following divorce children may be more aggressive, noncompliant, whining, nagging, dependent, and unaffectionate with their parents, teachers, and peers. This response is more intense and enduring in boys than in girls. If they are not exposed to additional stresses both boys and girls show markedly improved adjustment in the 2 years following divorce, although at this time boys from divorced families are still manifesting more problems than those from nondivorced families. Two recent nationwide surveys show that boys from divorced families show more problems in school and difficulties in self-control and aggression than do girls or children from nondivorced families (Guidubaldi, Perry, & Cleminshaw, 1983; Zill, 1983). However, it should be noted that the vast majority of children in divorced families function as well as those in nondivorced families.

The deleterious outcomes for children have been found to be related to changes in family functioning following divorce rather than attributable to family structure. During periods of high stress children require more structure and stability as well as more nurturance and support in their environments (Hetherington et al., 1982b). Problems in adjustment are least likely to occur if children find themselves in a warm, predictable, secure, conflict-free environment. Emotional disturbance in children is minimized if household routines are well organized, if discipline is authoritative and consistent (Hetherington et al., 1982b), if there is warmth, support, and good communication between parents and child (Hess & Camara, 1979; Hetherington et al., 1982b; Jacobson, 1978; Wallerstein & Kelly, 1980), and if the custodial parent is happy and well adjusted

(Hetherington, Cox, & Cox, 1981; Wallerstein & Kelly, 1980). In addition, the continued relation between the divorced parents plays a significant role in successful coping in children. Low conflict and absence of mutual denigration, high support and agreement on child rearing and discipline, and frequent contact with the noncustodial parent, if that parent is not extremely deviant or destructive, are associated with positive adjustment in children (Hess & Camara, 1979; Hetherington et al., 1982b; Nelson, 1981; Wallerstein & Kelly, 1980). Many effective divorced families continue to function as an integrated parenting system after divorce, although the divorced spouses are living in different households.

CHANGING RESPONSIBILITIES AND ROLES

In the transition from marriage, through separation and divorce, to life in a one-parent household, and to remarriage, roles are redefined, altered, added, and lost. The ambiguity of roles for divorced couples and their children often makes this transformation of roles difficult. The divorced parents change in their legal, social, emotional, parental, and economic provider roles.

Some of the most pervasive changes confronting members of divorcing families are those associated with finances. For men, divorce is followed by no drop or a moderate increase in income, and a decrease in assets and stocks of durables such as housing and savings (Cherlin, 1981; Espenshade, 1979; Hoffman, 1977). This contrasts with a dramatic decrease in income for most women (Weitzman, 1981). Since women usually have custody of the children and often obtain no child support, the economic situation of these mother-headed households is even more disparate if we consider the income-to-needs ratio rather than absolute income. Divorced women attempt to cope with these financial problems through economizing behavior, obtaining welfare, and entering the work force. Work is more effective than welfare in improving the financial situation of women (Espenshade, 1979), however, many divorced women have neither the training nor the experience to obtain well-paying employment and to compensate for the costs of child care. Divorced mothers are more likely to have short-term positions or low-paying part-time jobs. This may affect the child by necessitating discontinuous or inadequate provisions for child care. If the mother feels overburdened by the multiple demands placed on her, or dissatisfied with her job, she may be harassed and unavailable to her children. It has been said that divorce may lead not only to father absence but also to mother absence because of the task overload experienced by mothers in one-parent households (Weitzman, 1981). Downward economic mobility is associated with poorer quality housing, neighborhoods, and child care, and with changes in maternal employment, geographic mobility, and loss of social networks. High degrees of environmental change are related to social and psychological maladjustment in children and divorced parents (Kitson & Raschke, 1981; Kurdek & Blisk, 1982; Nelson, 1981; Stohlberg, 1981). When fathers have custody of children they undergo less economic duress, thus children in father-custody homes are less likely to encounter the high-risk factors associated with financial need.

Both custodial mothers and fathers complain of the problems in being a lone parent assuming responsibilities for raising children and running a household. However, fathers are more likely to have assistance and support in these roles (Brandwein, Brown, & Fox, 1974; Ferri, 1973; George & Wilding, 1972; Hetherington et al., 1982b; Katz, 1979; Spanier & Castro, 1979a, 1979b). Single custodial fathers and mothers report that they are more likely to depend significantly on other adults for the socialization of their children. They are more likely than parents in two-parent households to attribute children's levels of social and academic competence to the interactions children have with their teachers and other caregivers (Camara, 1982).

The changing roles of divorced couples extend beyond household and parenting. They encompass new relations with the ex-spouse and new economic, vocational, and social roles. The shift in the social role from being married to being a single person is often a difficult one. Divorced adults complain of social life being organized around married couples, of being lonely, isolated from old friends, and having difficulty in forming new relationships. When new friendships are formed it is often with other single or divorced people in similar situations. Divorced women, especially nonworking women and women with young children, may feel trapped in a child's world.

Newly divorced adults report feeling anxious, inept, and stressed in heterosexual relations. Divorced women are seen as easy sexual targets; divorced men perceive themselves as being expected to perform sexually on demand. Increased rates of sexual dysfunction are reported by divorced males (Hetherington et al., 1982b). Casual sexual relations are often unsatisfying and there is a yearning, frequently accompanied by apprehension, for a more stable, intimate relationship. This is reflected in the high rate of remarriage. Over three-quarters of divorced adults remarry, and half of those who will remarry do so within 3 years of divorce (Cherlin, 1981; Spanier & Furstenberg, 1982). The formation of a new intimate relationship is associated with increases in happiness and life satisfaction for both divorced men and women (Hetherington et al., 1982b).

REMARRIAGE

Although there have been a large number of studies of divorce and one-parent families, it is only within the last decade that social scientists have turned their attention to the remarried or reconstituted family. Cherlin (1978) has suggested that remarriage is an "incomplete institution," that is, the roles and relationships among family members in a reconstituted family are poorly defined. Cherlin proposes that the normative ambiguity of roles and expectations within remarriage result in stress and confusion in the reconstituted family.

Much that has been written about remarriage has been based on clinical reports and impressions of those working with reconstituted families in family counseling settings. The descriptions of problems faced by those entering a second marriage are included in essays and conceptual reports which offer useful frameworks for the study of remarriage. Few empirical studies of the remarriage and family reconstitution process exist. Research to date has been plagued by methodological problems similar to those found in research on divorce and parental absence. The variability in the emergent family forms following divorce and remarriage poses significant problems for the design of systematic studies of the remarriage process. Families may be reconstituted in several ways. A remarriage may involve one or two previously married adults who may or may not have children. These children may live in the same household with the remarried parent and new spouse, or they may have a "visiting" relationship with the parent and stepparent. In some instances, children are brought together into a "blended" family where two previously married adults live together with both sets of children in a shared household.

Most studies of remarriage have failed to account for the effects of the timing of remarriage or the number of years elapsed since divorce of one or both partners and subsequent remarriage. Adults entering into a remarriage situation may also differ in their experiences with marriage and parenthood. Moreover, the age and developmental status of children and the life stage of parents at the time of divorce and remarriage are seldom taken into consideration in examining the effects of remarriage.

Spanier and Furstenberg (1982) have suggested that the interpretation of the new family system emerging after remarriage is dependent on whether remarriage is viewed as part of the aftermath of a previous marriage or as a discrete event. Entry into a second marriage is unlike entry into a first marriage since adults and children carry their own previous histories of marriage and family experience. When a remarriage occurs, individuals must revise their definitions of marriage, redefine their roles, and negotiate new relationships. The lingering effects of a first marriage on a second, particularly when children are involved and where marriage partners share concerns about child rearing, present a complex set of adjustments for family members. The decision to remarry is accompanied by changes in adult roles and responsibilities, alterations in the constellation of families, residential changes, and realignment of family ties (Bohannon, 1970; Camara, Weiss, & Hess, 1981; Cherlin, 1981; Hetherington et al., 1981; Spanier & Furstenberg, 1982; Visher & Visher, 1982; Weingarten, 1980).

When a remarriage occurs, children have membership in two families: the first marriage nuclear family and the remarried family. They may also have ties with a third family if the noncustodial parent remarries. To reach successful integration within the remarried family, individuals must be able to acknowledge the affection and allegiance that exist among family members regardless of living arrangements (Ransom, Schlesinger, & Derdeyn, 1979; Walker & Messinger, 1979). The difficulty or ease in establishing new relationships among individuals in the reconstituted family is dependent on the willingness of these individuals to relinquish or alter the roles and boundaries of the former nuclear family (Walker & Messinger, 1979).

The remarriage of divorced adults presents new challenges to all family members and may have differential effects on each member depending on individual perceptions of the remarriage. Although research on remarriage and family reconstitution is still in its early stages, several patterns have emerged in the literature which deserve further investigation.

EFFECTS OF REMARRIAGE ON ADULTS

Remarriage reduces many of the stresses experienced by custodial parents following divorce. Concerns about finances, task overload, and household disorganization which are pervasive problems of divorced women diminish when women remarry (Hetherington et al., 1981). However, if divorced men remarry before their ex-spouses, their concerns about finances increase and they are apt to feel burdened by the need to support or partially support two households (Hetherington et al., 1981). There is preliminary evidence to suggest that the economic support of children and the remarried mother with custody of children is provided primarily by the new spouse, with a majority of noncustodial fathers terminating financial support for their children within a few years following the remarriage of the ex-wife (Spanier & Furstenberg, 1982).

The establishment of a satisfying heterosexual relationship following divorce has been related to a positive self-image and greater self-esteem for the divorced person (Hetherington, Cox, & Cox, 1978; Spanier & Castro, 1979a, 1979b). In a longitudinal study of divorce among parents of preschool children, Hetherington et al. (1982b) found that the establishment of new intimate relations and remarriage were powerful factors in attenuating the intensity of the divorced couple's relationship. However, remarriage of a spouse often was accompanied by feelings of depression, helplessness, anger, and anxiety. Anger expressed by the custodial mother toward the ex-husband was almost an invariable concomitant of remarriage of the ex-spouse even when the mother was the first to remarry. Sometimes this anger took the form of reopening conflicts about finances or visitation, sometimes it was directed at the children and their split loyalties, and often it focused on resentment and feelings of competition with the new wife. About half of the men whose ex-wives remarried reported that they approved of the new husband, in contrast to less than a quarter of the women whose husbands remarried. New wives seemed to exacerbate feelings of discomfort by entering into a competitive relationship with the ex-wife in which criticism of the children, of the first wife's child rearing, and of the economic burden of the previous family were the combative focus.

Drawing on data from a longitudinal study of divorce and remarriage among 200 divorced adults in central Pennsylvania, Spanier and Furstenberg (1982) also concluded that the availability of some form of supportive intimate relation was important to the well-being of adults following marital dissolution. However, most individuals reported an increased sense of well-being 3–4 years after marital separation regardless of marital status. Spanier and Furstenberg found no significant differences in measures of well-being between men and women or between individuals with children in their household and individuals without children in their household. Individuals with the greatest sense of well-being were more likely to be remarried 3–4 years after their final separation. While remarriage cannot be said to enhance the psychological well-being of all adults, it clearly does so in certain cases (Hetherington et al., 1981; Spanier & Furstenberg, 1982). Though there have been some reports that there is a higher likelihood of divorce following remarriage than first marriages, it has been argued that the main difference may be in the timing and not in the frequency of divorce. Couples in unsatisfying second marriages are less likely to prolong their indecision about divorcing. After having gone through the divorce process once, they feel less constrained to stay in a poor marriage and less apprehensive about the unknowns in marital dissolution and single life.

EFFECTS OF REMARRIAGE ON CHILDREN

The remarriage of parents has particular significance for the children involved. It is reasonable to assume that remarriage may present a child with additional adjustments which may be stressful and difficult (Duberman, 1975; Langer & Michael, 1963; Messinger, 1976; Visher & Visher, 1979; Wilson, Zucker, McAdams, & Curtis, 1975). The remarriage may signify the finality of the parents' divorce and may end children's fantasies of reconciliation. In addition, alterations in relationships with the biological parents may occur as well as the need to adapt to the stepparent and his or her kin. There is some evidence to suggest that involvement and visitation by noncustodial fathers diminish markedly after remarriage (Furstenberg, Spanier, & Rothschild, 1980; Hetherington et al., 1981). Frequently, fathers reduce their participation in their first family as they become involved in a new relationship, particularly when the former spouse remains single. When divorced men or women defer marriage, they are more likely to share parental responsibilities more equally than when one or both remarry (Camara et al., 1981; Furstenberg et al., 1980). It should be noted that continued involvement with the child by a divorced father even after remarriage leads to positive outcomes for children, especially for boys (Camara et al., 1981; Hess & Camara, 1979; Hetherington et al., 1981).

Bernard (1972) acknowledges that many variables may influence the successful integration of family members into the stepfamily unit, in particular, the timing and method of introduction of a new spouse into the family and the age, sex, and attitude of children. Adolescents, particularly those in the custody of the remarried parent, appear to have the most complex reactions (Bernard, 1972; Hetherington et al., 1981). Children in the preadolescent and adolescent period (ages 9–15) are less likely to accept even a good stepparent than are younger or older children (Hetherington et al., 1981). In addition, in blended families in which both sets of children reside in the same household, both parents are more likely to report high rates of marital conflict, disagreement about child rearing, dissatisfaction with the spouse's parental role, and differential treatment of natural children and stepchildren (Hetherington et al., 1981).

Most researchers note the great variability in responses of stepparents to stepchildren (Bossard, 1956; Camara et al., 1981; Fast & Cain, 1966; Hetherington et al., 1981). Fast and Cain (1966) conclude that no matter how much skill a stepparent possesses in adopting a parent role, he cannot succeed because social norms make it inappropriate for him to do so. Attempts to reproduce the nuclear family in the "step" situation cannot succeed since the stepfamily must be considered a structurally different type of child-rearing unit.

Stern (1978) has suggested that it may take up to 2 years for stepfathers to form a friendly relationship with their stepchildren and to achieve a partnership in a disciplinary role with their wives. Hetherington et al. (1981) reported that many stepfathers tended either to be disengaged and inattentive and to give the mother little support in child rearing, or to be extremely actively involved in child rearing and often restrictive in dealing with their stepchildren, especially stepsons. However, the most effective role for the stepfather seemed to be one where he supported the mother's discipline rather than trying either to take over or to totally relinquish responsibility. If the natural parent welcomed the involvement of the stepparent, and if the stepparent was an authoritative parent, warm, willing to set consistent limits and to communicate well with the stepchild, children in stepparent families, particularly boys, functioned better than those in unremarried families or conflict-ridden, nondivorced families (Hetherington et al., 1981). However, a recent national survey of American children suggests that these conditions may be difficult to attain. Zill (1983) found that mothers and teachers report that children in stepfather families show more problems in the home and in the school than do children from nondivorced families. Less is known about the influence of stepmothers on the behavior of children since most children reside with their biological mothers.

It seems likely that in future years more children and adults are going to experience living in a diverse array of family forms. The research to date suggests that divorce and remarriage involve a reorganization and modification of family relationships rather than the termination of family relationships. These relationships become increasingly complex with the introduction of a broader network of kin in reconstituted families. The long-term impact of these transitions in family relations on parents and children remains unknown.

THE PROCESS OF ADAPTATION

The changes in family life that accompany the experience of separation, divorce, and remarriage present a number of problems that challenge even the most adaptive and healthy of families. Changes in residence, changes in the distribution of economic resources, assumption of new roles and responsibilities by parents and children, establishment of new patterns of interaction among family members, reorganization of household routines and schedules, and the eventual integration of new family members into the existing family structure are just a few of the transitions faced by families in the midst of divorce and remarriage.

The way in which members of a divorcing family cope with the multiple stresses and role transitions is moderated by the resources available to them. These involve personal, familial, and nonfamilial resources. In considering the effectiveness of resources in easing family transitions, the fit between the needs of the family and the types of available resources must be examined.

RESOURCES FOR ADULTS

Individual attributes and psychological factors may serve as resources in coping with divorce. It is difficult to separate cause and effect in evaluating the role of psychological factors in coping with divorce, but separation and divorce are associated with a wide variety of physical and emotional disorders. Divorced adults are overrepresented in admission rates to psychiatric facilities and have greater susceptibility to motor vehicle accidents, illness, physical disability, alcoholism, suicide, and death from homicide (see Bloom et al. [1978] for a comprehensive review of this literature). Despite the fact that women are exposed to greater child-rearing and economic stress following divorce, the relationship between psychopathology and marital disruption is stronger for men than for women (Bloom et al., 1978). It is not clear whether people with emotional problems are more likely to get divorced or whether divorce induces long-lasting maladjustment in adults. Longitudinal studies indicate that following divorce there is at least a short term increase in psychological problems such as anxiety, feelings of external control, depression, substance abuse, sexual dysfunction, low self-esteem, and disturbances in sleeping and eating (Hetherington et al., 1982b; Wallerstein & Kelly, 1980). Parents with psychological or physical disorders will be less able to cope with the hardships they confront, and their children will have less stable parents to support them and be responsive to their needs. Zill (1983) found that feelings of rejection and unhappiness in children are correlated with psychological disturbance in mothers, and that divorced or unhappily married mothers are more likely to be depressed and dissatisfied.

Independence and nontraditional sex roles are related to coping in divorced women (Brown, Perry, & Harburg, 1977; Brown & Manela, 1978; Granvold, Pedler, & Schellie, 1979; Hetherington et al., 1982b). Older women also have more difficulty adjusting to divorce (Barringer, 1973;

Chiriboga, 1982; Chiriboga, Roberts, & Stein, 1978; Goode, 1956; Marroni, 1977; Pais, 1978). High self-esteem, low anxiety, feelings of internal control, open-mindedness, tolerance for change, and freedom from economic concerns are associated with low distress and ease of adjustment to marital disruption for both men and women (Chiriboga et al., 1977; Hetherington et al., 1982b; Spanier & Castro, 1979a, 1979b; Wallerstein & Kelly, 1980; Weiss, 1975).

In addition, family factors such as low conflict and mutual support between the divorced spouses or between parents and children, and family cohesiveness are related to coping with stress. Continued contact with a positively involved, supportive noncustodial father is the most effective support in child rearing that a divorced, single mother can have (Hetherington et al., 1982b).

Social isolation is related to disruptions in family functioning and to problems in the emotional well-being of family members in both one- and two-parent households (Abernathy, 1973; Brown, 1976; Colletta, 1979; Edwards & Klemmack, 1973; Goode, 1956; Hetherington et al., 1982b; Hynes, 1979; Marroni, 1977; Pearlin, 1975; Raschke, 1977; Weiss, 1975). Married couples rely less on external supports than do divorced, single, and widowed adults (Gibson, 1972). It has been proposed that single mothers make more nonreciprocated requests for aid than do married women and that this high level of unilateral demands eventually reduces the availability of resources in the support network (Brassard, 1977).

Support from friends and family usually facilitates the parenting role and is associated with life satisfaction, personal growth, and less distress for both men and women (Abernathy, 1973; Bernard, 1972; Colletta, 1979; Hetherington et al., 1982b; Goode, 1956; Raschke, 1977; Weiss, 1975). The formation of new intimate relations plays a particularly important role in life satisfaction for divorced men and women (Barringer, 1973; Goode, 1956; Hetherington et al., 1982b).

The relationship with kin following divorce is a complex one. The interaction between the divorced adult and his or her parents continues, and contacts may even increase following divorce, but contact with other relatives and with in-laws decreases (Anspach, 1976; Duffy, 1981; Spicer & Hampe, 1975). The child's relations with the kin of the noncustodial parent are mediated through contact with the noncustodial parent, which may be infrequent. Relatives, especially grandparents, frequently provide financial and emotional support and assistance in child care (Furstenberg, 1979; Hetherington et al., 1982b; Shanas, 1973), however, the extent of this support may be moderated by the relatives' approval of the decision to divorce (Kitson, Moir, & Mason, 1980).

Extended family, welfare, and community services are used as resources following divorce more often by low-income than moderate-income mothers (Colletta, 1979; Spicer & Hampe, 1975). Although low-income parents report that they receive more economic, household, and child-care help than do moderate-income mothers, they are less satisfied with the help they receive (Colletta, 1979). They may be because the level of need experienced by low-income mothers is greater.

RESOURCES FOR CHILDREN

The resources available for supporting children in coping with divorce have been studied less than those for adults. The resources available to children vary both with the developmental status and sex of the child. The limited social and cognitive competencies of the young child, the child's dependence on parents, and his or her more exclusive restriction to the home situation will be associated with different stresses, resources, and responses than those of the more mature, skillful, and independent older child. Young children are less able to understand the divorce situation, the behavior and feelings of their parents, their own contribution to the divorce, and to evaluate possible outcomes. With age, children become increasingly able to appraise the complex array of factors that led to the divorce, understand the motives of their parents, and respond constructively to the practical and economic problems in divorce (Wallerstein & Kelly, 1980). Although constructive relations with both the custodial and noncustodial parents continue to play an important role in the adjustment of adolescents, older children do have many more resources available outside of the home. Older children can find sources of support and gratification in the peer group, school, neighborhood, and workplace that can help to counter the deleterious effects of an adverse home situation (Camara, 1980; Hetherington, 1981; Hetherington et al., 1982b).

As noted earlier, boys are more adversely affected by family conflict and divorce than are girls. This may be not only because boys are exposed to conflict and stress more often than are girls, but also because boys receive less support and are viewed more negatively by parents, peers, and teachers (Hetherington et al., 1982a, 1982b; Santrock, 1975; Santrock & Tracey, 1978; Wallerstein & Kelly, 1980). Boys confront more negative sanctions, inconsistency and opposition, and lack of sensitivity and responsiveness to their needs, particularly from divorced mothers. It may be that the combination of dependence, demandingness, and aggression often found in boys following divorce is a particularly noxious one that leads to rejection by others, or that males, even young males, may be perceived as needing less support than do females in times of stress.

Grandparents offer support not only to their divorced children but also to their grandchildren. Children in homes in which there is a mother and grandmother are better adjusted than those in which the mother is alone (Kellam, Ensminger, & Turner, 1977; Kellam, Adams, Brown, & Ensminger, 1982). Grandfathers often take over skills training, educational, and recreational roles with grandsons following divorce (Hetherington et al., 1981, 1982b). A good relationship with a grandfather, an older brother, or a stepfather is associated with improved social and personal functioning in boys from divorced families (Hetherington et al., 1981; Santrock, Warshak, Lindberg, & Meadows, 1982; Wohlford, Santrock, Berger, & Liberman, 1971; Zill, 1983). The relationship between the adjustment of boys and remarriage may in part be modified by enhanced parenting of sons by divorced mothers when these mothers have the support of an involved but not domineering or intrusive stepfather (Hetherington et al., 1981).

The effects of older siblings and stepparents on girls is less clear. Recent studies have reported no differences between the adjustment of girls in homes with a divorced mother alone or with a stepfather (Hetherington et al., 1981) or adverse effects of a stepfather (Santrock et al., 1982).

There has been a pervasive pessimism about the effectiveness of schools in moderating the outcomes of adverse home environments. However, Hetherington et al. (1982b) found that over the course of the 2 years following divorce, the social and cognitive development of young children from divorced families was enhanced if children were in schools with explicitly defined schedules, rules and regulations, and with consistent, warm discipline and expectations for mature behavior. It is proposed that under stress young children gain security in a structured, safe, predictable environment. It should be noted that these are some of the same characteristics in parent behavior that are associated with self-control and intellectual development in children from divorced families. Young children under high stress may not be able to exert internal control and may require more external controls than either less stressed or more mature children.

In the same study, it was found that play and peer relations were substantially disrupted in the first year following divorce. Girls received more support from peers and teachers than did boys. Even after the behavior of the boys had begun to improve in the second year following divorce, they were viewed more negatively and were not given the same warmth, acceptance, and support as either girls from divorced families or boys from nondivorced families. This was a situation where a change was beneficial following divorce. If children were moved to a new school in the second year following divorce when their behavior was improving, their reputation did not follow them and they were more positively regarded and responded to by peers and teachers. Little is known about the role of teachers and peers as support systems for older children from divorced families.

SERVICE PROGRAMS FOR FAMILIES

Divorce and remarriage involve an ongoing process of change in family life associated with new needs, new problems, and the challenge of developing of new competencies at each phase of transition. The nature of these changes frequently demands resources that extend beyond those possessed by family, kin, or schools. Over the past 10 years, in response to the growing needs of American families for supportive services during times of family transition, many resource programs, both formal and informal, have been developed. (For a more detailed review of programs and policies for divorcing and divorced families see Emery, Hetherington, & Fisher [1984].)

In general, the goals of programs for families undergoing separation, divorce, or remarriage are to (1) resolve conflict, (2) reduce the psychological distress felt by family members in response to divorce and remarriage, (3) improve the skills of parents in managing and setting limits for their children's behavior, (4) establish new coping strategies and methods for adapting to new roles each family member may need to assume, (5) provide a network of resources available for continued support of families experiencing the stress of reorganization, (6) improve family functioning, and (7) help families cope with issues specific to divorce and remarriage (Camara et al., 1980).

Current mental health services for individuals and families are grouped according to three forms of treatment: primary, secondary, and tertiary levels. Primary intervention is a preventive approach to mental health with a focus on the dissemination of information and provision of resources to "normal" population of families before the appearance of a crisis or severe problem. Secondary treatment strategies are offered during a period of crisis or to a specific population "at risk" because of a set of circumstances or conditions in their lives. This crisis model approach is designed to facilitate adjustment under the assumption that appropriate assistance given at the time of crisis can prevent the development of more severe pathologies. Tertiary treatment approaches are focused, intensive efforts designed to assist families with already identified problems in functioning.

A large number of programs designed specifically to help parents and children adjust during the process of divorce or remarriage are primary or secondary preventive efforts. Although tertiary services are offered for persons experiencing serious psychological problems, most divorce and remarriage support services are intended to work with families undergoing stressful changes before more serious problems develop. Examples of preventive programs are "hot-lines" of information phone services for parents, single-parent and stepparent organizations designed to inform parents and children of potential problems and to provide support groups for parents and children, educational workshops sponsored by colleges, churches, or community centers, family life education classes for children, or programs offered through the media.

Divorce mediation has recently been found to be an effective means of resolving conflict between opposing parties in divorce. It has been argued that mediation permits divorcing parties to remain more involved in the decision-making process and to avoid extended contacts with the legal system which tend to escalate conflict. There are few studies of the effects of divorce mediation. However, research findings indicate that divorce mediation increases out-of-court settlements and feelings of well-being of divorcing adults, and decreases court costs and returns to court for future litigation (Bahr, 1981; Irving, Bohm, MacDonald, & Benjamin, 1979).

Services currently offered to children and families experiencing divorce and remarriage use a variety of approaches including individual therapy sessions with one family member, family counseling approaches, and group meetings with participants from similar backgrounds of experience. The services may be focused on child-centered, relationship-centered, parent-centered, adult-centered, or family-centered interventions or any combination of these. Most intervention efforts for divorced and remarried families have been time limited and crisis oriented. In other words, generally services have been restricted to a 6–8-week period following divorce or remarriage. Although recent research has suggested the need for continuing support for some families during the 2-year period following separation and during the early years of remarriage, most support services are designed to assist individuals during the early stages of transition. Even self-help groups, such as Parents Without Partners, direct much of their program time to "newcomers," the recently divorced.

Traditionally, assistance to families in crisis has been provided through mental health centers, private practice counselors, or family service agencies. More recently, community-based agencies and organizations have sponsored programs for families and have increased the opportunities and types of assistance available to parents and children. (For a review of such programs, refer to Baker, Druckman, Flagle, Camara, Dayton, Egan, & Cohen, 1980.)

Little is known about the effectiveness of any of the existing intervention programs. Few programs have included any systematic evaluation of their services. Programs that have reported "positive" results have relied primarily on client-satisfaction reports. Few programs have included any behavioral data or observations of family functioning in reports of program success, and evaluations that have been conducted are usually too flawed in method and design to permit interpretable conclusions. In addition, in most intervention studies of divorce, there is no comparison or alternative treatment group. A notable exception to this is in the Divorce Adjustment Project conducted by Stohlberg (1981) in which parents and teachers report improvement in the adjustment of children undergoing treatment.

In summary, intervention programs need to make more effective use of existing research literature in the design and implementation of their efforts. In turn, more empirical information is needed that is directly relevant to the planning and design of support services. In addition, services are offered predominantly to Caucasian, middle-income families. It is not known what kinds of services will appeal and be effective with diverse ethnic and socioeconomic groups. Research designed to develop and evaluate new services and programs could make a significant contribution in meeting the needs of the large number of families experiencing marital transitions.

Summary

The best statistical evidence suggests that in future years more adults and children are going to experience living in a diverse array of family environments. Research studies show that divorce and remarriage are experiences that involve major reorganizations and modifications of family relationships. Frequently, restructuring the family brings with it additional stresses which, depending on the available resources and the vulnerability of the family, may create a crisis situation in which adults and children may be unable to respond effectively. To date, little is known about the factors that contribute to successful and deleterious outcomes of divorce and remarriage or to the effectiveness of formal intervention efforts designed to assist families in transition.

As is the case in much of the research on family life, there is a need to examine the experience of divorce and remarriage within a life span and sociocultural perspective. It is clear that there are differences in the way children of different ages and adults at different points in the life cycle respond to divorce, yet little is known about the psychological or social factors that mediate these differences. In addition, to date, there are no methodologically sound studies of the processes of family dissolution or remarriage among black, hispanic, or other ethnic groups. Nor are there systematic studies of the phenomena of family changes among lower-income families. As we have noted in our review, there is tremendous variation in children's and parents' responses to divorce and remarriage. Given the diversity of cultural and ethnic backgrounds of those experiencing dissolution and remarriage, it is reasonable to expect that the experience of divorce for Caucasian middle-income families cannot be generalized to all other ethnic and socioeconomic groups.

There is empirical evidence to suggest that black families provide a home environment culturally different from Euro-American families in a number of ways (Abrahams, 1970; Gay, 1975; Ladner, 1971; Lewis, 1975; Nobles, 1974; Young, 1970). Recent research on black families points to the significant influence of kin in the lives of black children (McAdoo, 1978; Nobles, 1978; Stack, 1974) and the characteristic child-rearing behaviors of black parents, which are designed to enable black children to cope with everyday exigencies or crisis situations (Gutman, 1976; Hill, 1971; Stack, 1974). It has been suggested that one aspect of the socialization of black children is that it prepares them for survival in an environment that is hostile, racist, and discriminatory against blacks (Peters, 1981). These socialization patterns and extended family networks may modify the effects of divorce and separation on black families.

Finally, there is a need to reexamine some of our attitudes and assumptions about contemporary family life in the United States, with a focus on the diversity of family forms, their needs, strengths, and weaknesses. Attention should be focused on the identification of policies and practices that can strengthen family life and contribute to the well-being of parents and children in a variety of family forms. Perhaps it is time to review and revise our definitions of the purpose and function of marriage and to examine cultural values and expectations for American family life. What do we expect of the family in America? There is a need for a discussion of directions for the future, or we will, in our absence of direction, allow events to shape the family in ways that are destructive and difficult to reverse. Perhaps more than any new research direction, we need to provide opportunities for reconsideration of the nature of marriage, family life, and commitment in America.

REFERENCES

Abernathy, V. Social network and response to the maternal role. *International Journal of Sociology of the Family*, 1973, **3**, 86–92.

Abrahams, R. D. *Deep down in the jungle*. Chicago: AVC, 1970.

Aldous, J. *Family careers: Developmental change in families*. New York: Wiley, 1978.

Anspach, D. F. Kinship and divorce. *Journal of Marriage and the Family*, 1976, **38**, 343–350.

Bahr, S. J. An evaluation of court mediation for divorce cases with children. *Journal of Family Issues*, 1981, **4**, 160–176.

Baker, O. V., Druckman, J., Flagle, J., Camara, K., Dayton, C., Egan, J., & Cohen, A. *The identification and development of community-based approaches for meeting the social and emotional needs of youth and families in variant family configurations*. Final Report. Palo Alto, Calif.: American Institutes for Research, February 1980.

Barringer, K. D. *Self-perception of the quality of adjustment of single parents-without-partners organizations*. Unpublished doctoral dissertation, University of Iowa, 1973.

Barnard, J. *The future of marriage*. New York: Bantam, 1972.

Block, J. H., Block, J., & Morrison, A. Parental agreement-disagreement on child-rearing orientations and gender-related personality correlates in children. *Child Development*, 1981, **52**, 965–985.

Bloom, B. L., Asher, S. J., & White, S. W. Marital disruption as a stressor: A review and analysis. *Psychological Bulletin*, 1978, **85**, 867–894.

Bohannan, P. The six stations of divorce. In P. Bohannan (Ed.), *Divorce and after*. Garden City, N.Y.: Doubleday, 1970.

Boss, P. A clarification of the concept of psychological father presence in families experiencing ambiguity of boundary. *Journal of Marriage and the Family*, 1977, **39**, 141–151.

Bossard, J. H. S. *The large family system*. Philadelphia: University of Pennsylvania Press, 1956.

Bowlby, J. *Attachment and loss*. Vol. **2**. *Separation, anxiety, and anger*. New York: Basic, 1973.

Brandwein, R. A., Brown, C. A., & Fox, E. M. Women and children last: The social situation of divorced mothers and their families. *Journal of Marriage and the Family*, 1974, **36**, 490–514.

Brassard, J. *The nature and utilization of social networks in families facing differing life circumstances*. Unpublished manuscript, Cornell University, 1977.

Brown, P. *Psychological distress and personal growth among women coping with marital dissolution*. Unpublished doctoral dissertation, University of Michigan, 1976.

Brown, P., Felton, B. J., Whiteman, W., & Manela, R. Attachment in adults: The special case of recently separated marital partners. *Journal of Divorce*, in press.

Brown, P., & Manela, R. Changing family roles: Women and divorce. *Journal of Divorce*, 1978, **4**, 315–328.

Brown, P., Perry, L., & Harburg, E. Sex role attitudes and psychological outcomes for black and white women experiencing marital dissolution. *Journal of Marriage and the Family*, 1977, **39**, 549–561.

Burgess, E. W. The family as a unity of interacting personalities. *The Family*, 1926, **1**, 3–9.

Burgess, R. L. *Project interact: A study of patterns of interaction in abusive neglectful and control families*. Final Report. National Center on Child Abuse and Neglect, 1978.

Burr, W. F. *Theory construction and the sociology of the family*. New York: Wiley, 1973.

Cadoret, R. J., & Cain, C. Sex differences in predictors of antisocial behavior in adoptees. *Archives of General Psychiatry*, 1980, **37**, 1171–1175.

Camara, K. A. Children's construction of social knowledge: Concepts of family and the experience of parental divorce. (Doctoral dissertation, Stanford University, 1979). *Dissertation Abstracts International*, 1980, **40**, 3433B.

Camara, K. A. *Social interaction of children in divorced and intact households*. Paper presented at the Tenth International Congress of Psychiatry and Allied Prefessions, Dublin, July 1982.

Camara, K. A., Baker, O., & Dayton, C. Impact of separation and divorce on youths and families. In P. M. Insel (Ed.), *Environmental variables and the prevention of mental illness*. Lexington, Mass.: Heath, 1980.

Camara, K. A., Weiss, C. P., & Hess, R. D. *Remarried fathers and their children*. Paper presented at the biennial meeting of the Society for Research in Child Development, Boston, April 1981.

Caplan, G. The family as a support system. In G. Caplan & M. Killilea (Eds.), *Support systems and mutual help*. New York: Grune & Stratton, 1976.

Cherlin, A. J. *Marriage, divorce and remarriage*. Cambridge, Mass.: Harvard University Press, 1981.

Cherlin, A. Remarriage as an incomplete institution. *American Journal of Sociology*, 1978, **84**, 634–650.

Chiriboga, D. A. Adaptation to marital separation in later and earlier life. *Journal of Gerontology*, 1982, **37**, 109–114.

Chiriboga, D. A., & Cutler, L. Stress responses among divorcing men and women. *Journal of Divorce*, 1977, **1**, 95–105.

Chiriboga, D. A., Roberts, J., & Stein, J. A. Psychological well-being during marital separation. *Journal of Divorce*, 1978, **2**, 21–36.

Colletta, M. D. Support systems after divorce: Incidence and impact. *Journal of Marriage and the Family*, 1979, **41**, 837–846.

Douglas, J. W. B., Ross, T. M., Hammond, W. A., & Mulligan, D. G. Delinquency and social class. *British Journal of Criminology*, 1966, **6**, 294–302.

Duberman, L. *The reconstituted family: A study of remarried couples and their children*. Chicago: Nelson Hall, 1975.

Duffy, M. Divorce and the dynamics of the family kinship system. *Journal of Divorce*, 1981, **5**, 3–18.

Duvall, E. M. *Marriage and family development*. Philadelphia: Lippincott, 1977.

Edwards, J. N., Klemmack, D. L. Correlates of life satisfaction: A re-examination. *Journal of Gerontology*, 1973, **28**, 497–502.

Emery, R. E. Marital turmoil: Interparental conflict and the children of discord and divorce. *Psychological Bulletin*, 1982, **92,**, 310–330.

Emery, R. E., Hetherington, E. M., & Fisher, L. Divorce, children and social policy. In H. Stevenson & A. Siegel (Eds.), *Children and social policy*. Chicago: University of Chicago Press, 1984.

Emery, R. E., & O'Leary, K. D. Children's perceptions of marital discord and behavior problems of boys and girls. *Journal of Abnormal Child Psychology*, 1982, **10**, 11–24.

Epstein, N., Finnegan, D., & Gythell, D. Irrational beliefs and perceptions of marital conflict. *Journal of Consulting and Clinical Psychology*, 1979, **67**, 608–609.

Espenshade, T. J. The economic consequences of divorce. *Journal of Marriage and the Family*, 1979, **41**, 615–625.

Fast, I., & Cain, A. C. The stepparent role: Potential for disturbances in family functioning. *American Journal of Orthopsychiatry*, 1966, **36**, 485–491.

Ferri, E. Characteristics of motherless families. *British Journal of Social Work*, 1973, 3, 91–100.

Fulton, J. A. Parental reports of children's post-divorce adjustment. *Journal of Social Issues,* 1979, **35**, 126–139.

Furstenberg, F. F. *Remarriage and intergenerational relations.* Paper presented at a workshop on stability and change, Annapolis, Md., March 1979.

Furstenberg, F. F. *Remarriage.* 1982 Report to Planning Committee on Divorce, National Academy of Science Meeting, Stanford, Calif.

Furstenberg, F. F., Spanier, G. B., & Rothschild, N. *Patterns of parenting in the transition from divorce to remarriage.* Paper presented at the NICHD, NIMH, and NIA Conference on Women: A Developmental Perspective, Washington, D.C., 1980.

Furstenberg, F. F., Spanier, G. V., & Rothschild, N. Patterns of parenting in the transition from divorce to remarriage. In P. W. Berman & E. R. Ramey (Eds.), *Women: A developmental perspective.* NIH Publication No. 82–2298, 1982.

Gay, G. Cultural differences important in education of black children. *Momentum,* 1975, 30–33.

George, L. *Role transitions in later life.* Belmont, Calif.: Brooks/Cole, 1980.

George, V., & Wilding, P. *Motherless families.* London: Routledge & Kegan Paul, 1972.

Gerhardt, V. Coping and social action: Theoretical reconstruction of the life event approach. *Sociology of Health and Illness,* 1979, **1**, 195–225.

Gibson, H. B. Early delinquency in relation to broken homes. *Journal of Child Psychology and Psychiatry and Allied Disciplines,* 1969, **10**, 195–204.

Gibson, R. Family network: Overheralded structure in past conceptualizations of family functioning. *Journal of Marriage and the Family,* 1972, **34**, 13–23.

Glick, P. C. Remarriage: Some recent changes and variations. *Journal of Family Issues,* 1980, **1**, 455–498.

Glick, P. C., & Spanier, G. B. Married and unmarried cohabitation in the United States. *Journal of Marriage and the Family,* 1980, **42**, 19–30.

Goldstein, J., Freud, A., & Solnit, A. *Beyond the best interests of the child.* New York: Free Press, 1973.

Goode, W. J. *After divorce.* New York: Free Press, 1956.

Gottman, J. M. *Marital interaction: Experimental investigations.* New York: Academic Press, 1979.

Granvold, D. K., Pedler, L. M., & Schellie, S. G. A study of sex role expectancy and female postdivorce adjustment. *Journal of Divorce,* 1979, **2**, 383–393.

Gregory, I. Anterospective data following childhood loss of a parent. *Archives of General Psychiatry,* 1965, **13**, 110–120.

Greif, J. B. Fathers, children and joint custody. *American Journal of Orthopsychiatry,* 1979, **49**, 311–319.

Guidubaldi, J., Perry, J. D., & Cleminshaw, H. K. The legacy of parental divorce: A nationwide study of family status and selected mediating variables on children's academic and social competencies. *School Psychology Review,* 1983, **2**, 148.

Gutman, H. G. *The black family in slavery and freedom: 1750–1925.* New York: Random House, 1976.

Hansen, D., & Johnson, V. Rethinking family stress theory: Definitional aspects. In W. Burr, R. Hill, F. Nye, & D. Reiss (Eds.), *Contemporary theories about the family.* Vol. 1. New York: Free Press, 1979.

Herzog, E., & Sudia, C. E. Children in fatherless families. In B. Caldwell, Jr. & H. Ricciuti (Eds.), *Review of child development research.* Vol. 3. Chicago: University of Chicago Press, 1973.

Hess, R. D., & Camara, K. A. Post-divorce family relationships as mediating factors in the consequences of divorce for children. *Journal of Social Issues,* 1979, **35**, 79–96.

Hetherington, E. M. Effects of father absence on personality development in adolescent daughters. *Developmental Psychology*, 1972, **7**, 313–326.

Hetherington, E. M. Children and divorce. In R. Henderson (Ed.), *Parent-child interaction: Theory, research and prospect*. New York: Academic Press, 1981.

Hetherington, E. M., Camara, K. A., & Featherman, D. L. *Cognitive performance, school behavior and achievement of children from one-parent households*. Washington, D.C.: National Institute of Education, 1982. (a)

Hetherington, E. M., Cox, M., & Cox, R. The aftermath of divorce. In J. H. Stevens, Jr. & M. Matthews (Eds.), *Mother-child, father-child relations*. Washington, D.C.: National Association for the Education of Young Children, 1978.

Hetherington, E. M., Cox, M., & Cox, R. Family interaction and the social emotional and cognitive development of children following divorce. In V. Vaughan & T. B. Brazelton (Eds.), *The family: Setting priorities*. New York: Science & Medicine Publishing Co., 1979.

Hetherington, E. M., Cox, M., & Cox, R. Divorce and remarriage. Paper presented at the meeting of the Society for Research in Child Development, Boston, April 1981.

Hetherington, E. M., Cox, M., & Cox, R. Effects of divorce on parents and children. In M. Lamb (Ed.), *Nontraditional families*. Hillsdale, N.J.: Erlbaum, 1982. (b)

Hill, R. *Families under stress*. New York: Harper & Row, 1949.

Hill, R. Generic features of families under stress. *Social Casework*, 1958, **49**, 139–150.

Hill, R. *The strengths of black families*. New York: National Urban League, 1971.

Hill, R., & Rogers, R. H. The developmental approach. In H. T. Christenson (Ed.), *Handbook of marriage and the family*. Chicago: Rand McNally, 1964.

Hodges, P. H., Wechsler, R. C., & Ballantine, C. *Divorce and the preschool child: Cumulative stress*. Paper presented at the meeting of the American Psychological Association, Toronto, August 1971.

Hoffman, S. Marital instability and the economic status of women. *Demography*, 1977, **14**, 67–76.

Howard, A. *Ain't no big thing: Coping strategies in a Hawaiian-American community*. Honolulu: University of Hawaii Press, 1974.

Hultsch, D. F., & Plemons, J. K. Life events and life-span development. In P. Baltes & O. Brim (Eds.), *Life span development and behavior*. Vol. **2**. New York: Academic Press, 1979.

Hynes, W. J. *Single parent mothers and distress: Relationships between selected social and psychological factors and distress in low-income single parent mothers*. Unpublished doctoral dissertation, Catholic University of America, Washington, D.C., 1979.

Irving, H., Bohm, P., MacDonald, G., & Benjamin, M. *A comparative analysis of two family court services: An exploratory study of conciliation counseling*. Toronto: Welfare Grants Directorate, Department of Mental Health and Welfare and the Ontario Ministry of the Attorney General, 1979.

Jacobson, D. S. The impact of divorce/separation on children. III. Parent-child communication and child adjustment, and regression analysis of findings from overall study. *Journal of Divorce*, 1978, **2**, 175–194.

Katz, A. J. Lone fathers: Perspectives and implications for family policy. *Family Coordinator*, 1979, **28**, 521–528.

Kellam, S. G., Adams, R. G., Brown, C. H., & Ensminger, M. A. The long-term evolution of the family structure of teenage and older mothers. *Journal of Marriage and the Family*, 1982, **4**, 539–554.

Kellam, S. G., Ensminger, M. A., & Turner, J. T. Family structure and the mental health of children. *Archives of General Psychiatry*, 1977, **34**, 1012–1022.

Kelly, J. B. *Children and parents in the midst of divorce: Major factors contributing to differential response*. Paper presented at the National Institute of Mental Health Conference on Divorce, Washington, D.C., 1978.

Kitson, G. C. Attachment of the spouse in divorce: A scale and its application. *Journal of Marriage and the Family*, 1982, **44**, 379–393.

Kitson, G. C., Moir, R. N., & Mason, P. R. Family social support in crises: The special case of divorce. Unpublished manuscript, Case Western Reserve University, 1980.

Kitson, G. C., Raschke, H. J. Divorce research: What we know; what we need to know. *Journal of Divorce*, 1981, **4**, 1037.

Kitson, G. C., & Sussman, M. B. *The process of marital separation and divorce: Male and female similarities and differences*. Paper presented at the meetings of the American Sociological Association, New York, 1978.

Kriesberg, L. *Mothers in poverty: A study of fatherless families*. Chicago: Aldine, 1970.

Kurdek, L. A. An integrative perspective on children's divorce adjustment. *American Psychologist*, 1981, **36**, 856–866.

Kurdek, L. A., & Blisk, D. Dimensions and correlates of mothers' divorce experiences. *Journal of Divorce*, 1983, **6**, 1–24.

Kurdek, L. A., & Siesky, A. E. An interview study of parents' perceptions of their children's reactions and adjustment to divorce. *Journal of Divorce*, 1979, **3**, 5–18.

Ladner, J. A. *Tomorrow's tomorrow: The Black woman*. New York: Doubleday, 1971.

Langer, T. S., & Michael, S. T. *Life stress and mental health*. New York: Free Press, 1963.

Lazarus, R. S. The stress and coping paradigm. In C. Eisdorfer, D. Cohen, A. Kleinman, & P. Maxim (Eds.), *Models for clinical psychopathology*. Jamaica, N.Y.: Spectrum, 1981.

Lazarus. R. S., & DeLongis, A. Psychological stress and coping in aging. *American Psychologist*, 1983, **38**, 245–254.

Levinger, G. Sources of marital dissatisfaction among applicants for divorce. *American Journal of Orthopsychiatry*, 1966, **36**, 803–807.

Lewis, D. The black family: Socialization and sex roles. *Phylon*, 1975, **26**, 471–480.

Liberman, R. Behavioral approaches to family and couple therapy. *American Journal of Orthopsychiatry*, 1970, **40**, 106–118.

Lindeman, J. *Contested custody and the judicial decision-making process*. Ph.D. dissertation, Florida State University, College of Social Sciences, 1977.

McAdoo, H. P. Factors related to stability in upwardly mobile black families. *Journal of Marriage and the Family*, 1978, **40**, 761–778.

McCubbin, H. I., Joy, C. B., Cauble, E. A., Comeau, J. K., Patterson, J. M., & Needle, R. H. Family stress and coping: A decade review. *Journal of Marriage and the Family*, 1980, **42**, 855–871.

McCubbin, H. I., & Patterson, J. M. *Family stress and adaption to crises: A double ABCX model of family behavior*. Paper presented at the annual meeting of the National Council on Family Relations, Milwaukee, October 1981.

McCubbin, H. I., & Patterson, J. M. Family adaptation to crises. In: H. McCubbin, A. Cauble, & J. Patterson (Eds.), *Family stress, coping, and social support*. New York: Springer, 1982.

McDermott, J. F. Parental divorce in early childhood. *American Journal of Psychiatry*, 1968, **124**, 1424–1432.

McDermott, J. F. Divorce and its psychiatric sequelae in children. *Archives of General Psychiatry*, 1970, **23**, 421–427.

Marroni, E. L. *Factors influencing the adjustment of separated or divorced Catholics*. Unpublished master's thesis, Norfolk State College, 1977.

Messinger, L. Remarriage between divorced people with children from a previous marriage: A proposal for preparation for remarriage. *Journal of Marriage and Family Counseling,* 1976, **2,** 193–200.

Minuchin, S. *Families and family therapy.* Cambridge, Mass.: Harvard University Press, 1974.

Nelson, G. Moderators of women's and children's adjustment following parental divorce. *Journal of Divorce,* 1981, 4, 71–83.

Nobles, W. W. Africanity: Its role in black families. *Black Scholar,* 1974, 10–17.

Nobles, W. W. Toward an empirical and theoretical framework for defining black families. *Journal of Marriage and the Family,* 1978, **40,** 679–690.

Olson, D. H., Sprenkle, D. H., & Russell, C. S. Circumplex model of marital and family systems: Cohesion and adaptability dimensions, family types, and clinical application. *Family Process,* 1979, *18,* 3–27.

Pais, J. S. *Social-psychological predictions of adjustment for divorced mothers.* Unpublished doctoral dissertation, University of Tennessee, Knoxville, 1978.

Parsons, T., & Bales, R. T. *Family, socialization, and interaction process.* Glencoe, Ill.: Free Press, 1955.

Patterson, G. R. *Coercive family process.* Eugene, Ore.: Castalia, 1982.

Patterson, G. R., Reid, J. B., Jones, R. R., & Conger, R. E. *A social learning approach to family intervention.* Eugene, Ore.: Castalia, 1975.

Pearlin, L. I. Sex roles and depression. In N. Datan & L. Ginsberg (Eds.), *Life-span developmental psychology: Normative life crises.* New York: Academic Press, 1975.

Pearson, J., Munson, P., & Thoennes, N. Legal change and child custody awards. *Journal of Family Issues,* 1982, **3,** 5–24.

Peters, M. F. Parenting in black families with young children: A historical perspective. In H. P. McAdoo (Ed.), *Black families.* Beverly Hills, Calif.: Sage, 1981.

Phelps, D. W. Parental attitudes toward family life and child behavior of mothers in two-parent and one-parent families. *Journal of School Health,* 1969, **89,** 413–416.

Porter, B., & O'Leary, K. D., Marital discord and childhood behavior problems. *Journal of Abnormal Child Psychology,* 1980, **8,** 287–295.

Ransom, W., Schlesinger, S., & Derdeyn, A. P. A stepfamily in formation. *American Journal of Orthopsychiatry,* 1979, **49,** 36–43.

Raschke, H. J. The role of social participation in postseparation and postdivorce adjustment. *Journal of Divorce,* 1977, **1,** 129–139.

Reiss, D. *The family's construction of reality.* Cambridge, Mass.: Harvard University Press, 1981.

Rutter, M. Parent-child separation: Psychological effects on the children. *Journal of Child Psychology and Psychiatry and Allied Disciplines,* 1971, **12,** 233–260.

Rutter, M. Protective factors in children's responses to stress and disadvantage. In M. W. Kent & J. E. Rolf (Eds.), *Primary prevention of psychopathology.* Vol. 3. Hanover, N.H.: University Press of New England, 1979. (a)

Rutter, M. Maternal deprivation, 1972–1978: New findings, new concepts, and approaches. *Child Development,* 1979, **50,** 283–305. (b)

Rutter, M., Yule, B., Quinton, D., Rowland, O., Yule, W., & Berger, M. Attainment and adjustment in two geographical areas. III. Some factors accounting for area differences. *British Journal of Psychiatry,* 1974, **125,** 520–533.

Santrock, J. W. Father absence, perceived maternal behavior and moral development in boys. *Child Development,* 1975, **46,** 753–757.

Santrock, J. W., & Tracey, R. L. Effect of children's family structure status on the development of stereotypes by children. *Journal of Educational Psychology,* 1978, **70,** 754–757.

Santrock, J. W., & Warshak, R. A. Father custody and social development in boys and girls. *Journal of Social Issues*, 1979, **35**, 112–125.

Santrock, J. W., Warshak, R. A., Lindberg, C., & Meadows, L. Children's and parents' observed social behavior in stepfather families. *Child Development*, 1982, **53**, 472–480.

Scanzoni, J. A social system analysis of dissolved and existing marriages. *Journal of Marriage and the Family*, 1968, **30**, 452–461.

Shanas, E. Family-kin networks and aging in cross-cultural perspective. *Journal of Marriage and the Family*, 1973, **35**, 505–511.

Shinn, M. Father absence and children's cognitive development. *Psychology Bulletin*, 1978, **85**, 295–324.

Spanier, G. B., & Castro, R. F. Adjustment to separation and divorce: A qualitative analysis. In G. Levinger & O. C. Moles (Eds.), *Divorce and separation: Context, causes, and consequences*. New York: Basic, 1979. (a)

Spanier, G. B., & Castro, R. F. Adjustment to separation and divorce: An analysis of 50 case studies. *Journal of Divorce*, 1979, **2**, 241–253. (b)

Spanier, G. B., & Furstenberg, F. F. remarriage and reconstituted families. In M. B. Sussman & M. Steinmetz (Eds.), *Handbook of marriage and the family*. New York: Plenum, 1982.

Spanier, G. B., & Glick, P. C. Paths to remarriage. *Journal of Divorce*, 1980, **3**, 283–298.

Spicer, J., & Hampe, G. Kinship interaction after divorce. *Journal of Marriage and the Family*, 1975, **28**, 113–119.

Stack, C. B. *All our kin: Strategies for survival in a black community*. New York: Harper & Row, 1974.

Stern, P. N. Stepfather families: Integration around child discipline. *Issues in Mental Health Nursing*, 1978, **1**, 50–56.

Stohlberg, A. *The divorce adjustment project*. Paper presented at the meeting of the Southeastern Psychological Association, April 1981.

Stryker, S. Symbolic interaction theory: A review and some suggestions for comparative family research. *Journal of Comparative Family Studies*, 1972, **3**, 17–32.

Turner, R. *Family interaction*. New York: Wiley, 1970.

U.S. Bureau of the Census. *Population characteristics*. Current Population Reports, Series P–20, No. 349. Washington, D.C.: Government Printing Office, 1980.

U.S. Bureau of the Census. *Population profile of the United States: 1980*. Current Population Reports, Series P–20, No. 363. Washington, D.C.: Government Printing Office, 1981.

U.S. children and their families: Current conditions and recent trends. A Report of the Select Committee on Children, Youth and Families. Ninety-eighth Congress. Washington, D.C.: Government Printing Office, 1983.

Venters, M. *Chronic childhood illness, disability and familial coping: The case of cystic fibrosis*. Unpublished doctoral dissertation, University of Minnesota, 1979.

Visher, E. B., & Visher, J. S. *Stepfamilies: A guide to working with stepparents and stepchildren*. New York: Brunner/Mazel, 1979.

Visher, J. S., & Visher, E. B. Stepfamilies and stepparenting. In F. Walsh (Ed.), *Normal family processes*. New York: Guilford, 1982.

Walker, K. N., & Messinger, L. Remarriage after divorce: Dissolution and reconstruction of family boundaries. *Family Process*, 1979, **44**, 185–192.

Wallerstein, J. S. *Children and parents 18 months after parental separation: Factors related to differential outcome*. Paper presented at the National Institute of Mental Health Conference on Divorce. Washington, D.C., February 1978.

Wallerstein, J. S., & Kelly, J. B. Children and divorce: A review. *Social Work*, 1979, 468–475.

Wallerstein, J. S., & Kelly, J. B. *Surviving the breakup: How children and parents cope with divorce*. New York: Basic, 1980.

Walsh, F. Conceptualizations of normal family functioning. In F. Walsh (Ed.), *Normal family processes*. New York: Guilford, 1982.

Weingarten, H. Remarriage and well-being—national survey evidence of social and psychological effects. *Journal of Family Issues*, 1980, **1**, 533–559.

Weiss, R. *Marital separation*. New York: Basic, 1975.

Weiss, R. *Single-parent households as settings for growing up*. Paper presented at the National Institute of Mental Health Conference on Divorce, Washington, D.C., February 1978;.

Weiss, R. S. *Going it alone*. New York: Basic, 1979. (a)

Weiss, R. S. Growing up a little faster: The experience of growing up in a single-parent household. *Journal of Social Issues*, 1979, **35**, 97–111. (b)

Weitzman, L. J. The economics of divorce: Social and economic consequences of property, alimony and child custody awards. *U.C.L.A. Law Review*, 1981, **28**, 1181–1268.

Weitzman, L. J., & Dixon, R. B. Child custody awards: Legal standards and empirical patterns for child custody, support and visitation after divorce. *University of California at Davis Law Review*, 1979, **12**, 473–521.

Westman, J. D., Cline, D. W., Swift, W. J., & Kramer, D. A. The role of child psychiatry in divorce. *Archives of General Psychiatry*, 1970, **23**, 416–420.

Wilson, K. L., Zucker, L., McAdams, D. C., & Curtis, R. L. Stepfathers and stepchildren: An exploratory analysis from two national surveys. *Journal of Marriage and the Family*, 1975, **37**, 526–536.

Wohlford, P., Santrock, J. W., Berger, W. E., & Liberman, D. Older brothers' influence on sex-typed aggressive and dependent behavior in father absent children. *Developmental Psychology*, 1971, **4**, 124–134.

Wolkind, W., & Rutter, M. Children who have been "in care"—an epidemiological study. *Journal of Child Psychology and Psychiatry and Allied Disciplines*, 1973, **14**, 97–105.

Young, V. Family and childhood in a southern Negro community. *American Anthropologist*, 1970, **72**, 269–288.

Zill, N. *Happy, healthy and insecure*. New York: Doubleday, 1984.

Author Index

Subject Index